The Truth of Ups and Downs

Cosmic Inequality

Lily Chung

Eloquent Books

Eloquent Books
An imprint of Strategic Book Group
P.O. Box 333
Durham, CT 06422
www.StrategicBookGroup.com

ISBN: 978-1-60911-104-5

Printed in the United States of America

This book is a birth from the passion for the truth: the cosmic truth we cannot prove through an experiment with a test tube, but it accounts for the only reality.

It is dedicated to all readers who value the fundamental truth of their lives, are serious about what their lives can offer, and are determined to get the most value out of life. It is also especially created as a tribute to readers who supported my other two books: The Path to Good Fortune*:* The Meng *and* Succeed Naturally, the I Ching Way.

Contents

1
Introduction

Cosmic Inequality: The Need for a Solution

On the personal level, most of us have gone through ups and downs in life, some in violent swings and others in dramatic cycles. The few having a stable, quiet life all along must have also experienced some unexpected changes and surprises every now and then. We tend to take it as a way of life and pay little attention to the reasons.

Should there be some reasons for the ups and downs? Why would the person with the same endowments all along go through good and bad periods? We all agree that President Richard Nixon was smart and hard working, truly a good president. Being a successful politician for so long and a two-term vice president, why did he have to step out from Capital Hill to cool off for four years before he could return to be the president? Why did he lose the campaign? Could he have avoided the Watergate incident?

Evidently, our ability to make decisions changes periodically. Should there be some reasons for that? What influences the change? Why did Superman, Christopher Reeve, incur a fatal fall from a horse in the prime of his life while he excelled so much in so many sports? Were there reasons? If yes, wouldn't it be a blessing to do something in anticipation of such changes, to avoid the disaster?

The observant and perceptual among us must have noticed a pattern of some happenings. John Kennedy, Jr., had four key events falling in the following sequence: death of father, 1963; death of step-father, 1975; resignation from prosecutor post, 1987; death, 1999—all in the interval of a twelve-year period. Was there a reason for such regularity? They all took place in the wood year (the rabbit year in the Chinese lunar calendar), the year when his fatal element was in charge. Could he have avoided the final fatal event?

Why do people marry and divorce? Why did Jacqueline Kennedy Onassis marry twice in a metal year and was widowed twice in the wood year, the so-called rabbit year in the Chinese calendar? Why did Linda Evans (the head actress in a big hit TV series, "Dynasty") break practically all of her relationships (including divorce) in wood years? Why did Ingrid Bergman commit extramarital affairs in the given time period? While divorce is a rule among movie stars, and some divorce more than half a dozen times over their lifetimes, Gary Cooper stayed in one marriage all his life.

My book (written in Chinese) on Truth of Relationship documented the ups and downs in marriage in terms of cosmic flow cycle.

Among the population worldwide, some enjoy great entitlements without work, some easily succeed in a major way, while many toil and struggle endlessly in circles all their lives. We all agree there is an element of luck involved in the process. But how does luck work? Why does it favor a certain few individuals?

People also differ in physical look, ability, personality, and many other things; what determines such an outcome? Why can't we make the choice? We are prone to consider that hard work will bring us success. But why are so many hard workers going nowhere?

These questions have puzzled some uncompromising perceptual minds worldwide since the dawn of world history. Knowing the cause of the change would enable us to move in tune with the flows, live to our full potential, and gain a good control of our destiny. It is virtually a universal dream!

With joint efforts over a long process of about eight hundred years, a few sages in China invented a system to address such issues. If we include the time when the lunar calendar was first used, the total process would have taken a few thousand years, as the procedure is only made possible with the use of perpetual lunar calendars.

The procedure is called the *four pillars,* or Bazi. This divination system explains the various aspects of the total cosmic inequality among human beings, how cosmic flows impact our endowments, and the course of our lives.

Such cosmic flow cycles were registered in the perpetual lunar calendars that formed the fundamental building blocks for the divination system. This four pillar system, together with the conversion of the perpetual lunar calendars, was first introduced to the Western world in my book, *The Path to Good Fortune* (published in 1997 by Llewellyn in Minnesota).

The book has been very well received over the globe. Besides discussions on the procedure, it includes a set of lunar calendars extending from 1920 to 2030, registering the daily, monthly, and annual move of cosmic flows. Using these calendars, readers can map out their energy system and trace the timely energy path over their life course. Diligent and serious readers can thus work out their action table to take advantage of the good timely flows and tune down the impact of bad flows, consequently leading a more productive life!

However, due to the complexity of the procedure in the book, only a small population benefits from the system. Many need help to interpret the flow pillars. Upon feedback from readers, to make the system more accessible to busy people, I therefore wrote, *The Easy Ways to Harmony* as its supplement.

The book covers many simple formulas not discussed in the *Path to Good Fortune* and requires only finger work to match signs to read the messages; it does not require proficiency in analysis. These formulas deliver quick messages on the four pillars. The book has been a popular pamphlet worldwide among readers who are serious about their lives. But it has no lunar calendars or methodology on the procedure.

Over the last ten years, as the interest in the four pillars has been gaining momentum through global workshops of other metaphysicians over Europe, Americas, and Australia, there is an increasing demand for *The Path to Good Fortune.* Unfortunately, the book is out of print, and used ones sold on the Internet are no longer available. *Easy Ways to Harmony,* available only through the author and some students, is also running low in supply. To address the new demand, I have designed this new version.

BIRTH OF A NEW BOOK

Since the publication of the *The Path to Good Fortune,* I have applied the procedure to the lives of celebrities worldwide, in order to verify the universal validity of the system. They include a large number of Nobel Prize winners, Olympic Gold Medalists, great leaders in other fields, and the mentally retarded. The findings, besides being highly encouraging, have tremendously enriched my insight into the four pillars.

On the other hand, feedback from my readers had led me to a new front of research. To my amazement, I have discovered many challenging Bazi systems that were way beyond my wildest imagination. None could come close to the cases in current Bazi textbooks. Their complexity presents new roadblocks to interpretation. Many rules and formulas on the classic methodology have proven to be inadequate; they call for tests and verification. To compound the problem, many students have a hard time calculating the luck cycle.

The awakening new light calls for a new book. I have fine-tuned some formulas, introduced more simple rules, and, above all, I have devised a new foolproof procedure to eliminate the major roadblocks in analyzing the Bazi for beginners and advanced users.

CONTENTS OF THE BOOK

This book combines the good points of *The Path to Good Fortune* and *Easy Ways to Harmony,* and it offers much more that is unavailable in any current publications on the subject.

First, it has the complete set of lunar calendars from 1920–2030 included in the appendix, the complete procedure of mapping out our four pillars, and all the tools displayed as diagrams to interpret the system. All are found in the *The Path to Good Fortune.*

Secondly, simple formulas and special stars, which require only finger work, as shown in the *Easy ways to Harmony,* have been doubled in number in this publication; each is illustrated with more enlightening well-known life examples, enriching insight to the analysis of the four pillars.

Above all, as an innovative approach, the book introduces a foolproof procedure to determine the beneficial and damaging elements for each Bazi, the key to leading our life properly. It is a global breakthrough in the analysis of the four pillars.

All examples in the book are well-known celebrities, offering ample room for readers to verify each application. In each example, we include two contrasting groups of key life events of the person to display the impact of cosmic flows: positive events for the "ups" and negative for the "downs" in the individual's life.

Upon finding out the nature of our cosmic flows, we can use the calendars in the appendix to plan our action table accordingly. Following discussions on strategy in attuning to the flows after most illustrations, readers can learn from each example to fine-tune their own strategy on feng shui design.

These easy-to-follow examples will serve as a worksheet model, guiding readers to clearly and easily see how flows impact their lives.

2

Mapping Your Destiny

The Cosmic Order

The cosmos, as the Chinese sages perceived it, is a space composed of five components known as the five elements: wood, fire, metal, water, and earth. Each element has its own domain: wood/east, fire/south, metal/west, water/north, earth/center.

Each element takes turn ruling the universe. Wood reigns in spring, when all vegetation thrives. Fire takes its turn as summer approaches, when the heat evaporates the water. Metal power is strongest in fall; it undermines the earth and chops the wood. Water rules in winter; it weakens the earth and drains the metal.

In the ending month of each season, the dominant element wanes in power, leaving a gap for earth to fill in. Earth dominates the months of March, June, September, and December in the lunar calendar.

The domain of the five elements is summarized in Figure 2A:

Each element has two genders: yin and yang; each gender represents a different group of objects, and it subsequently carries a different energy. Altogether, there are ten different kinds of energy in the space. Our gracious sage devised ten signs (in Chinese characters) to denote their spatial distribution. They are called *stems,* meaning above ground.

Their connotations are listed in Figure 2B.

As these elements interact with one another, turn into a different element sometimes and change in strength with time, there is a need to show such a condition. Our sage(s) have invented twelve signs to show the time elements involved during the process. They are called *branches,* meaning spreading out from the stems or upon the ground. They represent the following categories: twelve months of the lunar year, the twelve days in a fixed cycle, and the twenty-four hours in a day divided in twelve pairs, i.e., each sign for a two-hour period. All these categories are indicated in Figure 2C.

Each of the stems and branches is in a Chinese character. These characters are so unique and technical that their connotations are understood only by people trained in some area of

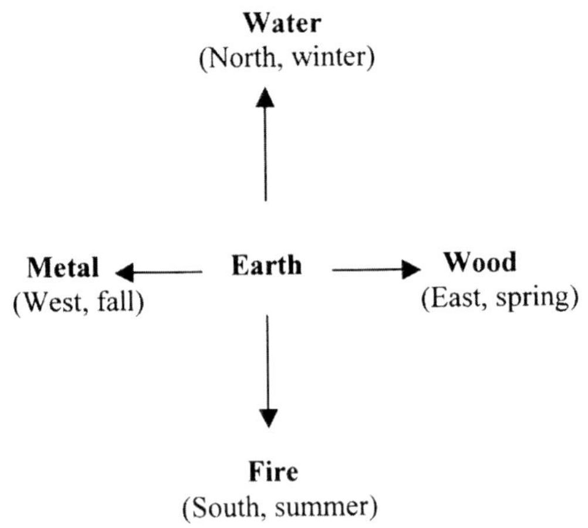

Figure 2A: Domain of Elements

T: yang wood, trees, forest, lumber; symbolizing kindness and fairness.
t: yin wood, branches of a tree, plants, shrubs, gentle and flexible, symbolizing kindness and fairness.
F: yang fire, the sun, great heat; being strong, bright and hot, symbolizing courtesy and quick wit.
f: yin fire, all man-made fire in all forms, symbolizing warmth and intelligence.
E: yang earth, massive dry earth, embankment, mountain, walls, symbolizing reliability and integrity.
e: yin earth, moist earth, mud to support vegetation; symbolizing some integrity.
M: yang metal, metal ore and heavy metal tools; symbolizing justice, decisiveness, a sharp mind.
m: yin metal, refined metal, small tool, jewelry; symbolizing shiny, sleek, elegant, polished and delicate.
R: yang water, rivers, lakes and all ground water bodies; flexible and changeable, symbolizing wisdom and creativity.
r: yin water, rain, drizzle, snow, fog, dew or mist; symbolizing elegance and creativity.

Figure 2B Connotation of Ten Stems

metaphysics. For convenience of presentation and interpretation on the system, I have converted these characters into the English alphabet.

These branches are also used by another metaphysical system. It is the popular twelve-animal system, discussed in tons of literature and practiced worldwide. Each animal is assigned a branch. These animal signs are also included in the table for your reference. As a matter of fact, this system has become part of the Bazi.

To indicate the changing strength of the elements over time, each stem is matched to a branch as shown in Figure 2D. What makes the pairing tricky is the unequal number of signs in each group. In each round of pairing, two signs in the branch group are left without a matching mate. These two signs from the first round become the first two matching signs for the second round. Thus, it takes six stems groups and five branch groups to complete a full, complete match. The grouping is clearly indicated in Figure 2D.

Each pair of one stem and one branch is called a *pillar.* The two signs can be written as vertical or horizontal; either way, the stem always comes first, i.e., on the top or the left of the two

Branches	Stem Equivalents	Lunar months	Domain	Hours	Animals
R	r, rain	November (winter)	North	11pm-1am	Rat
g	r, rain e, earth m, metal	December (winter)	Northeast	1-3am	ox
T	T, trees F, the sun E, dry earth	January (spring)	Northeast	3-5am	Tiger
t	t, plants	February (spring)	East	5-7am	Rabbit
W	E, dry earth t, plants r, rain	March (spring)	Southeast	7-9am	Dragon
f	E, dry earth M, metal ore F, the sun	April (summer)	Southeast	9-11am	Snake
F	f, fire e, mud	May (summer)	South	11am-1pm	Horse
d	e, mud f, fire t, shrubs	June (summer)	Southwest	1-3pm	Goat
M	M, metal ore R, rivers,etc	July (fall)	Southwest	3-5pm	Monkey
m	m, yin metal	August (fall)	South	5-7pm	Rooster
H	E, dry earth m,yin metal f, yin fire	September (fall)	Northwest	7-9pm	Dog
r	R, rivers, etc T, trees	October (winter)	Northwest	9-11pm	Pig

Figure 2C Branches and their Stem Equivalents

```
T t  F f  E e  M m  R r        T t  F f  E e  M m  R r
R g  T t  W f  F d  M m        H r  R g  T t  W f  F d

T t  F f  E e  M m  R r        T t  F f  E e  M m  R r
M m  H r  R g  T t  W f        F d  M m  H r  R g  T t

T t  F f  E e  M m  R r        T t  F f  E e  M m  R r
W f  F d  M m  H r  R g        T t  W f  F d  M m  H r
```

Figure 2D Stem and Branch pairing

signs. Since the pillar represents the energy of the elements at a given point, each is also called a *flow pillar,* or simply a *flow,* presenting a given cosmic energy.

A full cycle of time period takes sixty pillars. Each year, month, and day is assigned with a pillar as shown in the lunar calendars in the appendix of this book. The cycle repeats continuously in perpetual order. The identical pillar appears in the frequency of sixty, i.e., sixty years, sixty months (five years) or sixty days (approximately two months). Each pillar tells the climate or flow condition of the year, the month, or the day. For example, an "RR" year will bring plenty of rain, an "FF" day in an "ff" month is likely to be the warmest day in the month.

It takes experience, knowledge, and skill to interpret such pillars. There is elaborate discussion on reading such pillars in the *Path to Good Fortune.* We'll also discuss how to read pillars during the analysis of the individual energy system, in later chapters.

How do we define an hour? The twenty-four hours of a day are divided into twelve zones. Each two-hour zone is defined by one of the branches. These zones are listed in Figure 2E.

AM	PM
11pm-1am,R	11am-1pm, F
1-3, g	1-3, d
3-5, T	3-5, M
5-7, t	5-7, m
7-9, W	7-9, H
9-11, f	9-11, r

Figure 2E Hour Zones (all alphabet letters are branches)

By now we have completed the cosmic order. It is ready for readers to consult, test, verify, and learn more about the cosmic flows. Diligent readers could also study the *Path to Good Fortune* to gain some proficiency with the system.

Readers will gain more insight as we analyze the divination illustrations in later chapters. It is a big topic, requiring a substantial research effort on the part of the individual.

THE ORIGIN OF BAZI (FOUR PILLAR DIVINATION)

The perpetual lunar calendars of cosmic flows have become the fundamental building blocks of the Bazi system. It was the monument of the joint efforts of a few sages over a long process of about eight hundred years.

It started from the observation of a sage, C. S. Tung (179–104 BC), a great scholar in the Han dynasty. He noticed how the energy (consequently the effect of luck in achievement) of humans shifting with the timely flow in the lunar calendars. He sorted out the patterns of response and documented the changes. In other words, Tung initially documented the impact of cosmic flow on humans.

His documents were discovered by another sage, S. C. Lee (762–813 BC), several hundred years later in the Tong dynasty. Lee was able to incorporate the ideas of the yin and yang, and the cosmic flows and birth data, into a divination tool. It became the forerunner of the Bazi.

A few decades later, another sage (a monk without birth data) named Tze-Ping Hsu fine-tuned Lee's work with some corrections and enriched it with elaborate formulas. He created a monumental manuscript on Bazi, originally called the four pillars. The divination system is known as Tze-Ping Divination.

The divination system, together with the conversion of the perpetual lunar calendars, was first introduced to the Western world in *The Path to Good Fortune.* We'll briefly include the key to the procedure.

Readers can find out how the system works by the numerous live illustrations of well-known individuals in a later part of this book. The four-pillar divination procedure consists of two parts: the birth composite and the luck cycle.

Birth Composite

To begin, we need the individuals complete and accurate birth data including year, month, day, and time. To properly analyze the completed birth composite, we need the birthplace as well, as the climate of a birthplace functions as part of the cosmic flows, a crucial input. The birthplace data would not affect the charting of the birth composite in any manner.

We illustrate the procedure in Figure 2F.

The chart displays two examples, male and female. Gender, which represents the two fundamental forces in the cosmos, is the most crucial issue in metaphysics. Individuals born at the same time and same place will have the same birth composite (endowments), but different genders follow a different life course, i.e., males and females with the same birthday have different luck cycles.

Before we start, read the notes on using the lunar calendars and try to understand all the tables and charts in this chapter. It takes patience and effort to properly understand our life in order to succeed! Good value carries a great price!

As the illustration uses a simplified calendar for convenient illustration, readers are encouraged to make a copy of the calendar for 1965 from the appendix to follow the discussions.

John and Sue both were born on July 30, 1965, at 6:00 P.M. Both have the same birth composite. Here are the steps:

Locate the birth year from the appendix and make a copy of it, preferably enlarging it for easy reading. In the case of our illustration, it is 1965. It is simple to retain the key information for easy illustration.

Highlight your birthday and the climate divider of your birth month to make it convenient to count the days in between.

Locate the year, month, and day pillars from the calendar as shown in Figure 2F, and copy each pillar as shown.

To work out the hour pillar, we need an additional table. Go to Figure 2E (p. 8), check out the branch for hour 6:00 P.M., which is "m" from the 5–7 slot in the P.M. column.

Write the "m" next to the day branch. This "m" becomes the pillar branch of the hour pillar.

Locate the matching hour stem from Figure 2G. To do this, find the day stem "t" on the self row (see "t" with a star in Figure 2G, in the first row), and on the hour column, find "m" as the required hour; on the intersection of "t" and "m," locate "t" (with a star) as the hour stem.

Write "t" on the hour stem, next to the day stem.

We have completed the birth composites for John and Sue. They both have the same eight-letter alphabets, equivalent to the eight Chinese characters. The system is therefore called the "eight words," pronounced as "Ba Zi" (Ba = eight, Zi = word) in Chinese. As each birth composite has four pillars, the system is also called the *four pillars*. They are just alternative ways of referring to the same system.

As we will be using the term "birth composite" frequently for illustration in this book, we will abbreviate it as BC for convenience of discussion throughout the book, on all illustrations.

In the Bazi, and in all pillars, letter alphabets on the top are stems, and on the bottom, branches. In the calendars on the appendix, all flow pillars are, however, displayed horizontally for convenience in formatting; in such format, the first alphabet is the stem, the second is the branch.

Pay special attention to the day stem in the birth composite. It is the key of the birth composite. It is termed the "self," representing the owner of the birthday; in our illustration, it is John or Sue. It is "t," yin wood, a plant, so both John and Sue are classified as a plant by birth; the sign carries wood flow—yin wood, to be specific.

1965 **tf snake**

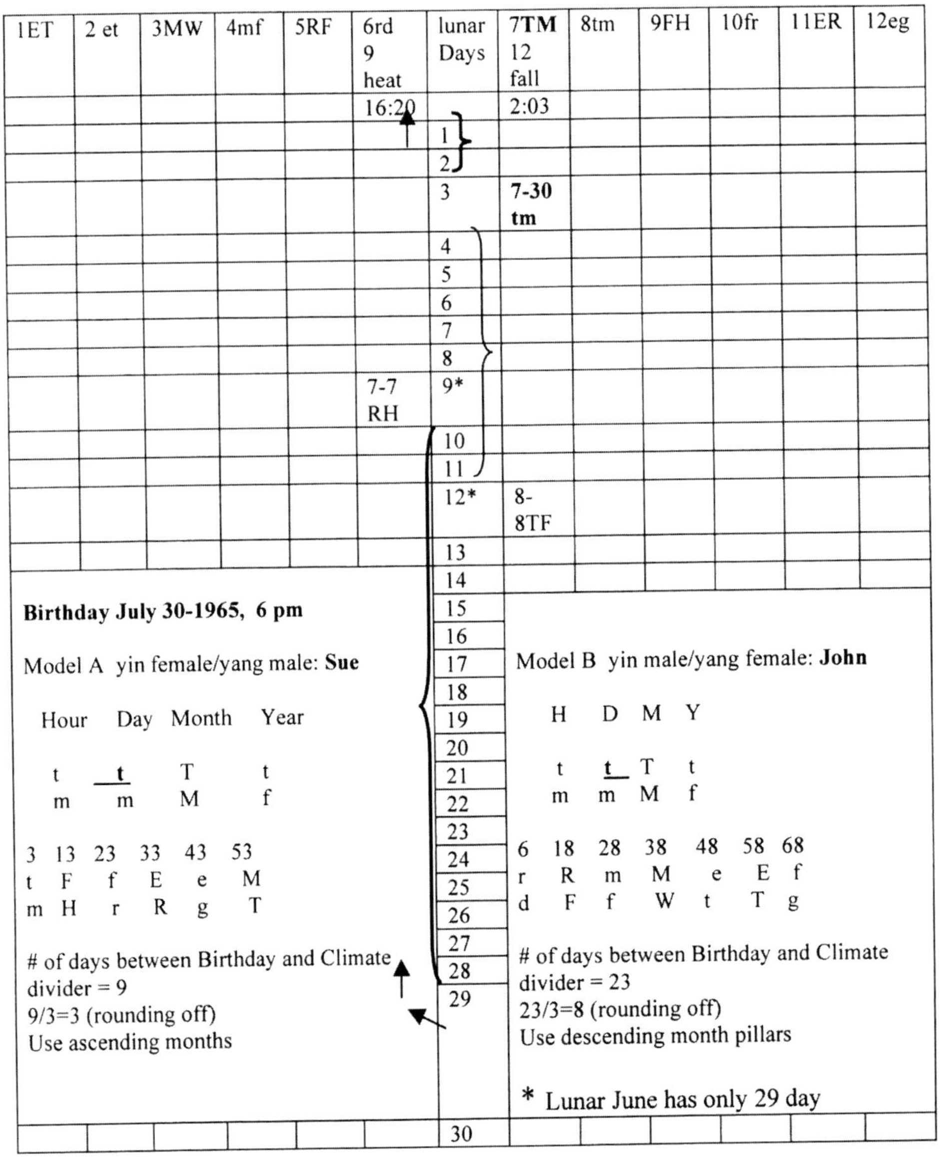
1ET
2 et
3MW
4mf
5RF
6rd 9 heat
lunar Days
7TM 12 fall
8tm
9FH
10fr
11ER
12eg
16:20
2:03
1
2
3
7-30 tm
4
5
6
7
8
7-7 RH
9*
10
11
12*
8-8TF
13
14
15
16
17
18
19
20
21
22
23
24
25
26
27
28
29
30
Birthday July 30-1965, 6 pm
Model A yin female/yang male: Sue
Hour Day Month Year
t t T t
m m M f
3 13 23 33 43 53
t F f E e M
m H r R g T
# of days between Birthday and Climate divider = 9
9/3=3 (rounding off)
Use ascending months
Model B yin male/yang female: John
H D M Y
t t T t
m m M f
6 18 28 38 48 58 68
r R m M e E f
d F f W t T g
# of days between Birthday and Climate divider = 23
23/3=8 (rounding off)
Use descending month pillars
* Lunar June has only 29 day

Figure 2F Construction of BaZi and Luck Cycle

Luck Cycle

The energy from the four pillars in our BC tells our endowments, which subsequently translate into our ability, character, and the total outlook. This fundamental energy also changes every five years following the onset of new flows from our luck cycle. It is the second part of the divination system.

The course of the luck cycle for the same BC (birthday) varies with gender. Gender is a fundamental, big issue in Chinese metaphysics, a distinction for the yang and yin forces. Figure

Self▶ Hour▼	**T**	**t☆**	**F**	**f**	**E**	**e**	**M**	**m**	**R**	**r**
R	T	F	E	M	R	T	F	E	M	R
g	t	f	e	m	r	t	f	e	m	r
t	F	E	M	R	T	F	E	M	R	T
T	f	e	m	r	t	f	e	m	r	t
W	E	M	R	T	F	E	M	R	T	F
f	e	m	r	t	f	e	m	r	t	f
F	M	R	T	F	E	M	R	T	F	E
d	m	r	t	f	e	m	r	t	f	e
M	R	T	F	E	M	R	T	F	E	M
m	r	t☆	f	e	m	r	t	f	e	m
H	T	F	E	M	R	T	F	E	M	R
r	t	f	e	m	r	t	f	e	m	r

Figure 2G Hour Stems

2F has two models to illustrate the course of luck cycle for different genders. The year pillar of your BC is the key to determining the model to use.

Basically, a female should have a yin year pillar, i.e., both alphabets in the year pillar are small letters, while a male should have yang pillar with both letters in the year pillar in capital letters. This group falls into the natural mode, following the natural order of moving forward, i.e., in ascending month order; births in this category uses "Model A."

Others in the reverse order, i.e., a female with a yang year pillar and a male with a yin year pillar follow "Model B."

Let us go to Figure 2F and start the illustration on "model A." Sue is a female with a year pillar of "tf," so she is a yin female, following Model A.

Readers are reminded to make a copy of 2F to follow our discussions. The study of metaphysics takes great patience. As the calendar is a simplified one from the actual calendar in the appendix, it is also crucial to have a copy of the complete calendar in order to properly follow the illustration. Here is the procedure:

Locate her birthday of 7/30, which is bolded; it corresponds to the day of lunar July 3.

Locate the climatic divider after her birthday, in the same month (lunar July), which is the "fall"; it falls on lunar July 12, as indicated in the first row. Mark the lunar July 12 on the lunar day that is an equivalent of the Western day, August 8.

Get a total count of the days between August 8 and July 30. As the time included covers some hours from both days, the counting as a rule includes either the birthday or the climatic divider. Thus the total count is nine days.

Divide nine by three, which is a constant number for all births, part of the formula for the procedure. This number becomes the initial year for the first luck pillar. Add ten to each following pillar as shown. You can use as many pillars as you like.

Copy the lunar monthly flow after lunar July from the calendar (on the top row as shown), i.e., tm in lunar August for the first pillar starting at age three, FH in lunar September for age thirteen, etc. You can keep going to the month pillars in the calendar for 1966 after you use up all month pillars in 1965.

John, as a yin male, uses "Model B." As a male with the yin year pillar (in the wrong gender of pillar), he does not have the proper outfit for the game of life, so to speak. He is therefore pushed backward to correct the error; his luck cycle goes by the descending month order. That is, he has to use the climate divider of the previous month, the first month of his reversal journey.

Here is the procedure:

Locate the climatic divider before his birthday. There is no climatic divider on the two days before his birthday in lunar July, so we have to locate it in the preceding month, lunar June. It falls into the 9 (7/7 in the Western calendar).

Count the days from lunar July 2 (solar July 29, the day before his birthday) all the way downward to lunar June 29 and back up to lunar June 9, the climate divider. The counting includes two days in lunar July and twenty-one days in lunar June from 29–9, with a total of twenty-three. See the days included in the bolded bracket. The counting includes either the birthday or the climate divider, depending where you start.

Divide twenty-three by three and round up the product as eight.

Use eight as the initial luck pillar number.

Copy the monthly pillar of lunar June; it is "rd," and "RF" as the second, etc.

This completes the procedure of Model B. As you can see, the last pillar of the luck cycle goes to the last lunar month of 1964.

As we will refer to the "luck cycle" frequently during our discussions in later parts of the book, we abbreviate it as LC.

As you can see, the person born on the same day in a different gender goes through a different luck cycle, i.e., life course. Gender is a big issue in cosmic order; one has to be all yin or all yang to be properly positioned.

Reading Your Bazi

Our Bazi covers a whole array of data and information. Reading the Bazi is a complicated process. It can be understood at different levels according to our proficiency of analysis. Let us start with the fundamentals.

Position of the Pillars

Our Bazi stands for a complete cycle of sixty cosmic years. Each pillar governs about fifteen years of life, starting from the number of the LC period. The year pillar represents the influence from our grandparents, ancestors, and in some cases a part of our parents. Its energy mostly affects the first quarter of our lives. The initial age of our luck pillars matters; it becomes the beginning age of the period.

As there are two letters in one pillar, the stem governs the first seven and half of the first quarter, while the branch governs the other half of the quarter. That is, in our illustration, for Sue, the stem "t" governs her life from age three to ten and a half; for John, from seven to fourteen and a half. The initial period starts from the initial LC number and extends to seven and a half more years. The influence from the branch "f," which follows the "t" stem, starts from ten and a half to eighteen for Sue, and fourteen and a half to twenty-two for John.

The month pillar represents parents and sometimes older brothers or relatives. The influence of this pillar stays with the self for life, while it becomes more significant in the early mid-life. The month branch is the key to determining the strength of the signs of the BC. That is, if the self is wood, being born in the spring months of T, t, the individual is born at the right time and will be in good mental and physical health; other wood signs in the BC are also indications of good strength.

The day pillar officially represents the third quarter of one's life. However, like the month branch, it has lasting effects over the self's life. Its branch represents the **spouse palace** of the self, determining the quality of the marriage and the benefits the spouse can offer.

The hour pillar is the weakest among all four pillars, mainly showing effects in the last quarter of one's life. It indicates the quality of our children and the help we are likely to get from friends.

Overall, the dividing lines for all signs are blurry; like the luck pillars, there is a transition zone for all periods.

Interaction of the Five Elements

To see how these seven signs relate to the self, we have to explain how the five elements relate to one another. There are numerous kinds of interactions, but there are two basic ways the five elements interact:

Inter-breeding: The five elements support or empower one another in the following manner:

In the process, water makes the wood grow, wood fuels the fire, fire firms up the earth, earth provides a home base for the metal to grow, and metal generates the water.

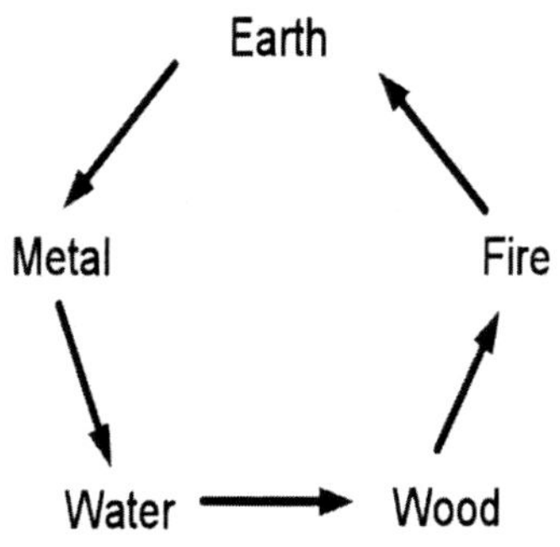

Figure 2H Inter-breeding

Inter-ruling: The five elements control one another in the following manner:

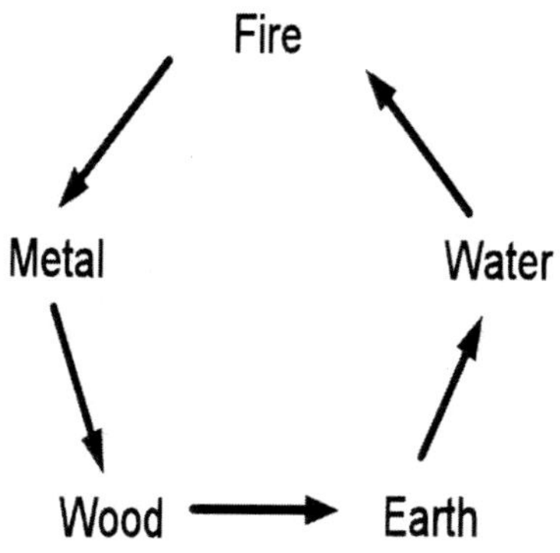

Figure 2I Inter-ruling of elements

In the process, water extinguishes fire, fire melts down the metal, metal chops down the wood, wood pokes into the earth, and earth absorb/blocks the water.

In the BC, the self is the key to determining how the five elements interact. What rules the self element becomes its ruler. For example, both Sue and John are "t" self, and all the metal signs ("M" and "m"s) are the rulers of Sue and John. What does the ruler do? It controls and disciplines, refining and making the person behave. A powerful ruler makes the person a hard worker; many scholars have strong rulers in their BC.

The ruler subsequently represents the career star for both male and female, since it controls. In the old days, as males controlled the women, it also means the spouse of the female. A woman with powerful and beneficial ruler(s) has great potential for a great supporting husband (provided the self is not too weak). For the male, a good ruler is almost the perquisite for having a good heir. These are just the simplified principles. We will touch upon other details in our illustrations later in this book.

All the signs of the same element of the self become the kin/siblings. As Sue and John have three more wood signs in the BC, in reality, both are likely to have a few siblings. What do siblings do? They either support or fight with the self, most likely doing both at separate times. A weak self benefits from siblings, while a strong/capable self hurts by siblings. Again, we will touch on the subject in our illustrations.

The element the self controls becomes its money. What "t" controls is the earth. There is hardly any earth sign for either Sue or John. We have to check the stem equivalents in the branch (Figure 2C); there is "E" in the year branch "f." Thus, they both got a hidden money sign. Since the sign is on the branch, it is grounded, meaning secure savings. However, it is more accessible to his or her siblings (the other kin, T and t); he or she might not have the money, and their siblings are more likely to be financially better off.

The money sign is very tricky; it is like money—being powerful enough to create so many blessings, it could also do many evils. Sometimes a strong money sign could be very harmful. Readers will learn more on the subject in our illustrations.

The element that empowers the self becomes its grantor, and for Sue and John, being the wood self, it is water. Again, there is only one water sign (R) hidden in branch "M," it is more accessible to "T," and it is in the mother position. Thus, his parental care/love is most likely leaning in favor of his older brother. For a weak self, a strong grantor is a wonderful thing to have.

The element that the self supports is the offspring, figuratively meaning children. It governs the ability of expression/communication skill. For the female, it governs her potential of having good pregnancy/great children.

For Sue and John, it is the fire sign. It is the "F" hidden in "f." Being hidden within the earth and metal house, it is by no means strong or helpful to the self's communication skill. For Sue, it could mean an unsuccessful pregnancy, a miscarriage, or a hard time to raise great children. For John, it is hard to succeed in art or another career requiring great expressive skill.

Depending on the nature of the self sign, the elements for each category are different. For easy reading, they are summarized in Figure 2J, Interrelation among the Five Elements.

Unraveling the truth of life is a complicated job. Thorough understanding goes to the diligent and passionate readers. However, our Bazi can be understood on different levels depending on what criteria we use and our knowledge to use such tools. Personal background, training, education, and attainment in life philosophy all play a role in the analysis. Passion for the truth in life matters a lot!

Stems → / Self ↓	T, t Wood	F, f Fire	E, e Earth	M, m Metal	R, r Water
T, t	Kin	Offspring	Money	Ruler	Grantor
F, f	Grantor	Kin	Offspring	Money	Ruler
E, e	Ruler	Grantor	Kin	Offspring	money
M, m	Money	Ruler	Grantor	Kin	Offspring
R, r	Offspring	Money	Ruler	Grantor	Kin

Figure 2J Interrelation between the Five Elements

3

Interactions of Cosmic Signs

This chapter discusses the fundamental rules on how the twenty-two signs interact among themselves to send out various messages. Depending on the nature of the signs and how they stand in our BC, we can derive a fundamental message without going into the in-depth analysis of the big picture in the BC. Below are some simple rules.

Most examples we use to explain the rules in this book do not have birth data as public record, therefore only three pillars which do not include the hour pillar. In reality, it has been very common for metaphysicians to analyze a Bazi without the hour pillar. The analysis has proven to be satisfactory for most cases.

Stem Pairings

The ten self stems listed can be divided into five pairs, each consisting of one yang sign and one yin. They are listed below:

Te tM Fm fR Er

Each represents a harmonious pair, which applies to all kinds of relationships, whether business, marital, or social. For example, any T self is likely to get along well with any e self in marriage, business, and friendship, or in the family. There might be minor conflicts between the pairs, but the two are basically compatible. The same principle applies to the other four pairs.

How does it work? First, you need to know and remember your self type (i.e., your day stem in the BC). Secondly, you need the birth data of your partner to find out his or her self-type. If the two selves match any of the five pairs, that is a harmonious pair. There is no guarantee of great fortune; they will however, live in peace.

Having a pairing self as a boss will enhance your luck in your career, as the boss is on your side. A child who pairs with a parent will have a competitive edge over his or her siblings in dealing parents. A pairing self as your child will save you headaches in parenting. Romantic partners in the fR pair make great lovers. If your child as an "f" self falls into love with an "R" self, it would be almost impossible to break the bond. Pairing selves make great friends as well. You may want to test how the idea works for you.

A "T" self is also likely to have better luck during the time when the "e" flow dominates the cosmos, and so on for other pairs. For instance, 1996 (FR) was a good year for an "m" self. Why?

"F" was the ruling boss of the year, and the "m" selves get natural protection from the cosmic King. Since the "F" is the ruler of the "m," it is like having your best friend as your boss in the company, and you are favored for rewards. Expect a promotion and/or pay increase. This analogy applies to the other four pairs.

When the pairing self sign shows up in one's luck cycle, the same idea also applies. Let us examine one interesting case to show you how it works.

Let us begin with the example of Ted Kaczynski (the Unabomber) who had mailed bombs to different people in the United States, causing some deaths and many to be injured.

Ted Kaczynski—May 22, 1942

?	t	t	R
?	r	f	F

5	15	25	35	45	55
F	f	E	e	M	m
F	d	M	m	H	r

Ted Kaczynski mailed about sixteen bombs during the period from May 1978 to 1994. Surprisingly, there were no bombing incidents during the five to six years between mid 1987 and May 1993, from age forty-five to forty-nine. Why?

This particular period fell into his "M" period in the LC. He is a "t" self, which pairs with "M." Under the caring flow of his pairing boss, M, he felt being protected and cared; he had peace, no urge to explode his frustration. The "M" as a metal sign controls the yin wood, keeping him in place and staying in order.

The other side of stem pairing would mean easy big money to the self. It is the most auspicious when it happens in the BC of the self; it is a lifetime of easy wealth. Below are two good well-known examples.

Rosalyn Carter—August 28, 1927

T	e	f
F	m	t

The "e" as a money sign to the self "T" means money voluntarily entering into the pocket of the pairing person. Can you see why Rosalyn became rich so easily? The branch "m" is her ruler, the spouse of the self, and it is empowered by the moist earth immediately on the top. She became rich as a natural course.

The next illustration gives you more idea on the pairing works. Banting became rich as a great discoverer of insulin. Money was pouring into his pocket through global sources. With "e" on the father position, it is related to his immediate family, good genes, and parental guidance, or other higher-up assistance, a prize from an authority or government, functioning like a natural father. It is in his BC, staying with him over his lifetime.

Fred Banting—November 14, 1891

<u>T</u> <u>e</u> m
W r t

Everyone can benefit from stem pairing at some point in life for something in different momentum. Try to locate your pairing stem flows from the calendar, and take notes on your luck responding to such flows. Highlight the year, month, and day of pairing stem, and focus on these special time periods to plan your action table. Stay focused and aggressive in such time periods.

Note the nature of the signs, and search for the sources for such signs. Relate your action to such sources. Stem pairings not involving the self are also good indicators of the good personal skill to connect others.

BRANCH INTERACTIONS

As indicators of relationship, branches offer more clues than stems. They interact with themselves in a more complicated fashion. Keep in mind that, at any given point, the branches in the year flows, in the luck cycle, and in the birth composite all interact with themselves, resulting in various processes. We will focus our discussion on the following three categories.

Branch Pairing

The twelve branches can also be divided into six pairs that indicate good relationship. Here are the six pairs.

Rg Tr Wm Fd Mf Ht

Figure 3A Six Branch Pairings

Like the stem pairs, branch pairs consist of one yang sign and one yin, as indicated in the chart below. You can find these pairs in either the BC alone, or between the BC and LC, or combining with the year flow, month flow, or day flow.

Pairing branches in the BC indicate good social skills—a person who relates well with others. The position where the pair occurs also indicates a specific relationship.

In the year and month position, the self relates well to parents and older relatives; in the month and spouse position, the self relates well to the spouse, and the couple works closely for a common goal; in the hour and day position, the self relates well to children and friends.

When a pairing occurs between a sign in the cosmic year and one in the BC, the self can expect some fortunate developments in that particular year, such as marriage, promotion, or success of any kind. Below are some documented examples.

Philip Anderson—December 13, 1923

M T r
M R r

Won the Nobel Prize in 1977 (ff); cosmic year branch f paired with day branch M in the BC.

Patty Hearst—February 20, 1954

f	F	T
d	T	F

Being sentenced to seven years of imprisonment in 1975, she was set free in 1979 (way ahead of schedule); President Carter commuted her sentence. Was it the work of cosmic flow? Her birth year, 1954, was TF, and the cosmic year, 1979, was ed; ruling branch d paired with her year branch F (Fd is a branch pair), making her a favorite of the ruling boss. She got lucky!

Sometimes, branch pairing results in marriage or intense romance. Although it is not always true, there is no shortage of good examples.

The marriages of Henry Kissinger precisely demonstrate this. He married twice, in 1949 (eg) and 1974 (TT), respectively. His system:

Henry Kissinger—May 27, 1923

M	f	r
R	f	r

In 1949, g paired with day branch R. In 1974, T paired with r in the year pillar.

Some extremely fortunate systems have pairs in both the stems and the branches. Such a combination creates great success. The self is likely to be extremely intelligent and successful. The BC of Peter Debye (March 24, 1884), Nobel Prize1936 in chemistry, is a typical example.

Peter Debye—March 24, 1884

<u>r</u>	<u>E</u>	T
<u>m</u>	<u>W</u>	M

In the BC, rE (stem) and Wm (branch) are the pairs. The pairing can take place anywhere in the BC as long as the pairing signs are right next to each other. Pairings involving the day pillar are the most fortunate.

Branch Trios

A trio is a powerful indicator of good relationship and good fortune in most cases. Its function and momentum of significance vary with each BC. The twelve branches are divided into four groups, each with three specific signs. There are two sets of trios. Figure 3B displays the first of the two groups.

As shown in Figure 3B, r, R, and g form a trio in the north, turning all three signs into a water team, everyone in the team losing its original nature functioning as water together. T, t, and W in the east form a wood team with every sign functioning as wood. The same principle goes with the other two groups of metal and fire.

This trio is the most powerful combination of signs; all three signs have to be present to make the team work. These trios are called *cardinal* trios.

The other trio group connects every three signs in a triangle, as indicated below the display of the cardinal trios in Figure 3B.

These triangular trios are less powerful than the cardinal trios. They are, however, more flexible. Any two of three teammates in a trio can form a partial trio, termed an *alliance.* For example, in the water trio of M, R, and W, there could be three water alliances of MR, MW,

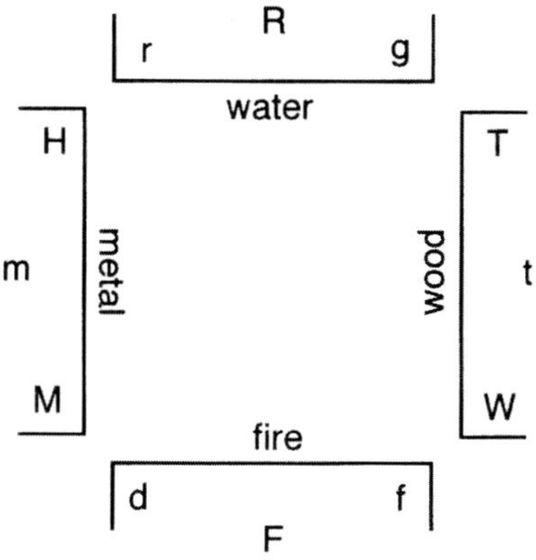

Figure 3B The Branch Trios

Triangular trios: **M R W_ water** **T F H _fire**
f m g _ metal **r t d _ wood**

and RW. An alliance, being also an indicator of good fortune, is less powerful. The same principle applies to other trio and alliance combinations.

To follow the discussion on trios, it may help if you make a copy of the chart so you can refer to it without flipping through the pages.

A trio is powerful because all the signs in a trio merge into one element and function as one element. The resulting element of each trio is indicated in the chart.

If the trio happens to be the favorite element for the self, tremendous luck can be expected. A complete good trio in the BC makes the self very well liked, well loved, and able to relate exceedingly well with everyone. Consequently, the self is most likely very successful. A trio developed jointly by branches from the LC or cosmic year at a given time will convey great fortune at that point, such as a wonderful marriage or big success of any kind.

Let us begin with Margaret Thatcher's system:

Margaret Thatcher—October 13, 1925

?	M	F	t
?	F	H	g

9	19	29	39	49
F	f	E	e	M
H	r	R	g	T

Thatcher is a yang metal, "M" self. The metal ore needs to be refined by intense fire, turning it into a sharp sword before it could conquer the world! Thatcher was fortunate enough sitting on a fire alliance, which is fueled by a wood sign. However, only a fire trio could raise her to the top slot.

The missing teammate "T" did set in to carry her to the mountaintop. At age fifty-four, when the "T" from her LC joined her "F" to form a fir trio, she became the prime minister of England.

The same idea goes with the case of Herb Caen, a great journalist from San Francisco, who passed away in February 1997.

Herb Caen—April 3, 1916

?	M	R	F
?	F	W	W

He was, like Margaret Thatcher, a piece of metal ore. Again, there was not enough fire to sharpen him. In fact, the fire was far less. His luck turned around in 1958 (EH); while the big earth absorbed the excess water in his BC, the "H" from the year flow joined the F in his BC to form a partial fire trio.

What happened? He earned a then princely salary of $38 thousand (a huge sum in 1958 when college professors made less than $10 thousand), the highest income he ever earned.

President Jimmy Carter also got lucky from a partial trio.

Jimmy Carter—October 1, 1924

r	T	T
g	H	R

2	12	22	32	42	52
t	F	f	E	e	M
r	R	g	T	t	W

President Carter is a water (rain) self, a formidable problem solver, but not ideally strong enough to be a powerful achiever. He needs a lot more water to build momentum for great success. A water trio would maximize his luck. A partial water trio occurred in 1976 (FW), when he became the President of the United States. Year flow W joined the R in his BC to form a partial water alliance, empowering the self. The water self could leap!

Finally, let us finish our discussion on the trio with the example of Pearl Buck, Nobel Prize winner in 1938 in literature.

Pearl Buck—June 26, 1892

e	f	R
g	d	W

7	17	27	37	47
F	t	T	r	R
F	f	W	t	T

She won the prize in 1938 (ET) at age forty-six, during the t period in her LC. The year flow T, and her LC flow t, teamed up with the W in her BC to form a wood trio (Figure 3B), her most powerful ruling boss, bringing a climax of luck to her life.

Branch Clashing

Although good relationship is always desirable, bad relationship seems to be very common. Branch clashing from the Meng system sheds some light on the issue. There are six clashing pairs as indicated in the figure above. Both signs of a clashing pair are in the same gender—

both yang or both yin. Clashing signs indicate unsteady relationship, unstable life, and disruptions such as divorce, illness, or financial loss. Powerful clashing signs, occurring more than twice in the BC, could lead to a turbulent life, full of events that are out of control.

The six clashing pairs are:

RF gd TM tm WH fr

Figure 3C The Six Clashing Pairs

A self with clashing signs on the year and month branches relates poorly or loosely with one's immediate family. Since these signs are in the first two quarters of the BC, it also indicates unstable family life in one's early part of life. The self is always better off staying away from the immediate family. In fact, that is the only way to prosper as the move alone absorbs the bad flow.

Clashing branches in the month and spouse position could indicate unsteady marriage, but the message is not as strong. It does not cause great concern for the marriage. Clashing branches in the day and hour positions indicate either conflicts with or separation from children. It is better for the parents to stay away from their children during their adulthood. People having clashing branches in their BC tend to have more social conflicts in their lives.

The onset of a clashing branch from the year flow or luck cycle to one's BC is a good indicator of disruptions or change at that point in life. Depending on the position where the clash occurs, and the nature of the branches, each clashing indicates a different message. The following examples will shed some light on the idea.

Ted Kaczynski was arrested in April 3, 1996, for mailing bombs. Why? Recall that he was born in 1942 (RF), and the ruling flow for 1996 was FR. The R clashed on his year branch F.

The lesson, as wise ancient Chinese perceived it, is not to take any shortcuts or commit any wrongdoings during your clashing period. The wise person identifies such difficult times ahead and takes precautions to avoid loss or disasters.

The resignation of Brian Mulroney (March 20, 1939), prime minister of Canada, also involved the clashing pairs. He was born in an "et" year and resigned in 1993, an "rm" year, when "m" clashed with his year branch "t" (check the clashing pairs).

To give some more idea on the message of branch clashing, let us go back to the system of Margaret Thatcher. Her husband died in 2003 (rd); the "d" clashed onto the "g" in her year branch.

COSMIC ANIMALS

In a popular Chinese astrology, each branch is assigned an animal. Readers knowledgeable on the astrology of the twelve animals can update their knowledge from our discussions on how the branches work. These animals actually represent the twelve branches and interact among themselves exactly like the twelve branches. These animals are shown in the clashing chart of the branches below, Figure 3D.

As indicated, the tiger and monkey are clashing with each other, as are the dragon and the dog, so on and so forth, each pair in a vertical straight line. The same animal signs apply to the natural pair in branches; that is, the ox and the rat are in good terms with each other, as are the tiger and the pig, etc., each in a horizontal straight line as shown in the branch pairing figure.

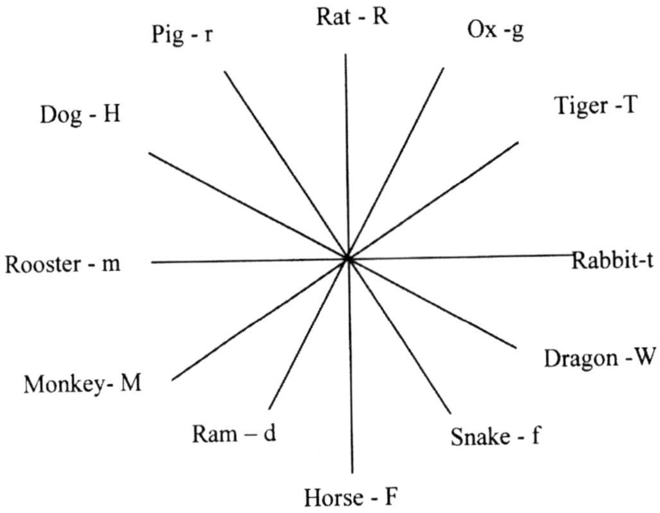

Figure 3D Cosmic Animals

We can continue the game to the chart of the trio in triangles of branches. The following are the animal groups in trio: dog, horse, and tiger; ox, snake, and rooster; rat, dragon, and monkey; pig, goat, and rabbit.

We can clearly see that each animal has one enemy (the clashing sign), one good friend (the pairing branch), and two teammates (the other two signs in the trio). For example, the rat has the horse (F) as its enemy, the ox (g) as its best friend, and the dragon (W) and monkey (M) as its teammates. You can determine the team for each animal by following this example.

Each animal has a domain of thirty degrees, taking turns ruling the cosmos for one year; one rotation takes twelve years. The order starts with the rat as the first one, followed by the ox, as shown in Figure 3D, going in a clockwise rotation. The ruling animal (ruling flow) affects our luck significantly. Let's illustrate with an example.

During year 1996 (FR), the rat (branch R) ruled. The ox (g) was the luckiest, as it is the best friend of the rat; the boss favors and rewards his best friend. Next in luck were the monkey and the dragon, as they fall in the trio of the rat, the teammates. Who fares the worst? Naturally, the horse, as it is the number one enemy of the boss, a clashing mate. Those born in horse years tended to have a difficult year. This divination system of cosmic animals gives one indication of your luck in a particular year; to find out more details, we need more charts and additional knowledge on other divination systems.

How valid is the theory? All of us can test it.

Before we do, let's remember that good or bad luck is a relative term. A lucky few always have good luck. Some are prone to have more bad luck. For 1996, most horses should have experienced more problems or difficulties than normal years. On the other hand, the oxen should have had a smooth year.

To make the system work for you, you need to test the ideas with your life events in order to build up your confidence level and your awareness of the flows. The crucial step is to determine your lucky flows and try to attune to them.

APPROACHES TO A GOOD RELATIONSHIP

The bottom line for a good relationship is harmony: a balance of yang and yin forces. The Meng system has outlined four fundamental principles for establishing a good relationship. The surest bond for a happy relationship is a mutually supportive cosmic system between the individuals. That is, each person possesses the crucial element that the other party desperately needs for best harmony.

How to find one's crucial elements is detailed in *The Path to Good Fortune.* It is a complicated and time-consuming process, not practical for many busy readers. We will have practical examples to find out our crucial benefiting elements in Chapters 5 and 6. Diligent readers who can determine their crucial elements for a good life can make use of such discovery to facilitate their marriage. Others may try some quick tips from the following discussions.

Here are three simple principles: pairing, teaming, and clashing of signs. Pairing signs in the day stems or year branches are most likely to produce a bonding couple; they prosper and produce good children. However, minor conflict and quarrels remain a way of life as they adjust to the changing cosmic flows. In any event, they are unlikely to separate. In order to relate well, always look for signs of opposite genders (i.e., play the game of balancing the yang and yin forces).

We will illustrate how the principles work with the following examples.

George Bush			**Barbara Bush**		
6/12/1924			6/8/1925		
R	M	T	r	R	t
H	F	R	r	F	g

Year branches R and g are a pair; there is root binding the couple; they are not likely to separate. Day stems are both water, one yang and one yin, matching the physical gender of the couple; the yang is leading the yin, i.e., husband leading wife, a traditional natural order.

We can see that there is good fortune, good prosperity, and good children, if not harmony all the time. No marriage is perfect.

Franklin Roosevelt			**Eleanor Roosevelt**		
1/30/1882			10/11/1884		
e	m	m	T	T	T
f	g	f	F	H	M

Year branches M and f are a pair. The spouse palace is f and F respectively, part of the cardinal trio. Day stems T and e are another natural pair, but in the wrong gender order. Ideally, the T yang self should go to the president and vice versa. The marriage was permanently bonded, although interrupted by a persistent affair. There was bond, but not harmony. They have many children together.

Harry Truman			**Bess Truman**		
5/8/1884			2/13/1885		
E	e	T	e	E	t
F	f	M	r	T	m

Year branches are in the trio. Both day stems are the earth in opposite genders properly positioned for the gender, i.e., yang sign goes to the husband and vice versa. They were a devoted couple, according to documents.

Lyndon Johnson			**Lady Bird**		
8/27/1908			12/22/1912		
T	m	E	R	R	R
T	m	M	M	M	R

Both branches are teammates in a trio. There was root. Day stems are both yang. Spouse palace is tiger and monkey, a clashing pair. The bond was shaky. However, the First Lady had plenty of water, which the president desperately needed to maintain his harmony.

The bond disappeared as soon as he got his own, when he entered the water period in his LC. As the dependence was gone, the spousal clashing took effect. He started a long-term affair of seventeen years with another woman. Lady Bird devoted her energy to her gardening hobby. The marriage stayed to the end.

There are various options to handle spousal clashing signs. Separation in some form seems necessary. While many opt to divorce, others keep their vow but wisely avoid the clashing impact of a separate life!

Dwight Eisenhower			**Mamie Eisenhower**		
10/14/1890			11/14/1896		
E	F	M	m	e	F
W	H	T	d	r	M

Both year branches clash with each other. The day stems have different gender, but they are not of the same element. Their bond depended on their cosmic composition. The First Lady has substantial wood, which could restore the harmony in the president's system.

We will explain Eisenhower's system in detail in Chapter 7.

The clashing branches show their impact. Mrs. Eisenhower moved twenty-eight times with her husband. These moves indeed saved their marriage; they absorbed the shock. In fact, the president had a long-term relationship with an Irish woman, starting 1942, and contemplated divorce years later, even though it never materialized.

Prince Charles			**Princess Diana**		
11/14/1948			7/1/1961		
r	r	E	t	T	m
t	r	R	d	F	g

What bonded the couple? There were pairing pairs in both year and day branches, i.e., "Rg" and "td," very strong roots. They did create a relationship of fifteen years and two children, regardless of a great obstacle between them, and many mishaps involved.

By cosmic system, Prince Charles has excessive cold water; he needs plenty of fire to warm up his system and plenty of wood to absorb the roaring water in order to bring peace to his life. Princess Diana's system has abundant wood and fire, which initially attracted the prince. Diana tremendously complemented his needs.

However, starting at age thirty-two, heavy earth flow entered her system, dissipating most of her fire flow and weakening her wood flow. The energy that bonded the couple quickly dwindled.

In conclusions, mutual attraction between partners comes from complementary flows of each other. Pairing signs are helpful in bonding the couple. Clashing signs are likely to cause turmoil. In terms of short-term bad flows, partners can seek temporary retreat from each other to minimize the impact. Cosmic truth dictates that some people are destined for multiple marriages, i.e., people with more than one spouse sign in their BC. Sometimes it is better to live with the flow than to hang onto a painful relationship.

4

Messages from the Flow Pillars

The forms and standing order of the pillars in our Bazi carry interesting and revealing messages of the person. While most of them have proven validity, and many are amazingly accurate, they are, however, by no means golden rules. There are many ways to derive the messages. Let us start with the flow timetable.

FLOW TIMETABLE

In ancient China, before the Western "timing system" concept of the week was introduced, the sixty pillars were organized into six time units to express the time duration between the month and the day. As indicated in Figure 4A, they are grouped into six columns. Each column was comparable to the duration of a week; the cycle has ten days.

Pillars headed by the "T" in the first row were used to name the time period of the ten days in the group. Each pillar in the table represents a day. For example, in the TR column, TR is the first ten-day cycle, TH the second, and TM the third, etc.; there are six ten-day periods, all headed by a "T?" pillar. Within each time period, each day is named by a pillar in the order; for example, in the TR column, TR is the first day and tg the second, etc. For instance, when someone specified a date as a "tg" day during the TR period, it became the second day in the TR period.

This is just to give you some idea of how the pillars are arranged for some reasons. Such a structure, coincidentally, expresses a whole array of messages in our Bazi. Here are some of simple and straightforward messages.

Three of the Four Pillars in One Column

Any Bazi having three of the four pillars falling into the same column, the person will enjoy easy success in life. These people are destined for quick wealth and fame without much effort on their own! Test it for yourself. Many Nobel Prize winners fell into this lucky category. Some examples are as follows. We'll use the example of Princess Diana to illustrate how to locate such pillars.

Column # → Selves ▼	1	2	3	4	5	6
T	TR	TH	TM	TF	TW	TT
***t**	tg	tr	tm	td	tf	tt
F	FT	FR	FH	FM	FF	FW
***f**	fr	fg	fr	fm	fd	ff
E	EW	ET	ER	EH	EM	EF
***e**	ef	et	eg	er	em	ed
M	MF	MW	MT	MR	MH	MM
***m**	md	mf	mt	mg	mr	mm
R	RM	RF	RW	RT	RR	RH
***r**	rm	rd	rf	rt	rg	rr
Void signs	**H, r**	**M, m**	**F, d**	**W, f**	**T, t**	**R, g**

Figure 4A Flow Pillars

Princess Diana—July 1, 1961

F t T m
H d F g

To begin, you can use any pillar in the Bazi and find any two of the other three pillars from the same column. It might be confusing and strenuous for beginners, as you might have to go through a few columns without success. But it is all a matter of finger work. After you are familiar with the pillar arrangement, it becomes easier.

For our illustration, you are better off to begin with TF, since it is the column head, and search for mg, td, or FH. The first three pillars of Diana's Bazi are all found in column four. Below are some exercises for further verification.

Julius Axelrod—May 30, 1912, 1970 NP winner in physiology, all pillars are in column five.

Milton Friedman—July 31, 1912, 1976 NP winner in economics, all pillars are in column five.

Each of the Four Pillars in a Separate Column

This one is for talented people or great achievers who relentlessly work hard to succeed on their own effort, most likely known for their contribution to the wellbeing of mankind. Many great leaders and great scholars have such pillars. President George Washington, of the United States, had the best example. Each pillar of his Bazi is in a separate column as indicated by the numbers below each pillar; what makes it so auspicious is the consecutive sequence of the pillar number.

George Washington

m t R R
f m T R
2 3 4 5

Other examples are President Bill Clinton (August 19, 1946, t hour), shipping tycoon of Greece Aristotle Onassis (January 15, 1906, F hour, MF, ed, eg, tf), and Lee Kwang-Yiu of Singapore (September 16, 1926, T hour). They are all great achievers.

Void Signs

On the bottom row of the table, there are two void signs listed for each column of pillars. They play a special role in our lives. Each of us has two void signs for our Bazi. As all sixty pillars are included in the table, we can all locate our void signs from the table and get some insight of our system.

To find your void signs, check your day pillar from the table. Take the example of President Eisenhower. His day pillar was EW. Locate EW in the first column, and see that it has the void signs of H and r on the bottom row. Thus, his void signs were H and r.

What message do we derive from these void signs? Void means empty. A void sign in the hour branch indicates the possibility of having no children, having a number of daughters but no male heir, not having children close by, or not being benefited by children. On the parent position, it could mean the self is an orphan or has little parental support. In the spouse position, the self might remain single, have a sick or absentee spouse, or have a very loose marital relationship. In the month branch, it could mean an unstable career or a change in jobs.

President Eisenhower had a void (H) sign in the month branch; he had many great careers and moved frequently on jobs. In this case, it just means frequent changes of careers.

In any event, no good sign should fall into a void position. For a male, it would be very difficult to keep a wife when his only or crucial money sign being voided, as a money sign also represents a man's spouse.

On the other hand, void signs can bring blessings. When a bad sign is being voided, it could exempt you from the pain of parental or spousal abuses, or headaches from children, depending on the position of the void sign. Excessive void signs, such as having two in the BC, makes the self bright, as the person develops clear vision; he or she can clearly envision issues and leads an error-free life! Having three void signs could make one rich and powerful. This is the wisdom of the Tao: when you can't shoulder the stress, you surrender to get protection/provision! It is the essence of the natural law! There is light at the end of the tunnel! It could also mean uninterrupted vision.

When the void sign falls into the relationship branch, it eliminates the damaging effect of the signs. When a mentor sign sits on the void signs, it could bring wealth or fame to the person. Just imagine: why would a noble man choose such a bad seat? He foresees some great things happening from the person!

MIXING PILLARS IN A BAZI

Pillars in capital letters are yang, in the masculine gender; in small letters, they are yin, feminine gender. Ideally, yin and yang pillars in the Bazi should be properly mixed in form and in order to ensure harmony in life. However, in reality, this ideal state rarely takes place.

When all the pillars are yang, the person is open, honest, courageous, tenacious, and, of course, stubbornly unyielding as well. They make great martyrs and leaders in big crisis. The following example was the martyr who died in the Chinese Revolution against the corrupt dynasty.

The Chinese revolution martyr

T	T	T	T
H	T	H	H

President D. Eisenhower—(October 14, 1890, T hour), a brave soldier

T	E	F	M
T	W	H	T

The next is Winston Churchill—(November 30, 1874). His great courage to lead the country during the great crisis is well known.

R	M	T	T
F	F	T	H

Isaac Newton, known for his super passion and dedication to the truth, had the following Bazi.

F	M	R	R
R	R	R	F

When all the pillars in the Bazi are yin, people tend to keep their thoughts to themselves and are likely to move forward to achieve their goals without hurting others. Some could be manipulatively ambitious. Others obligingly stay in their domain.

This Bazi hardly made public figures or famous people, as there is not enough yang force to show visibility for the person.

We found the example of a very powerful Chinese official who was very clever and manipulative. All his life he tried desperately to become the emperor, in the modern Chinese era when the emperor was out of fashion. He did succeed to crown himself as an emperor but stayed there for only eighty-three days. Without a trace of yang force in his four pillars, it was difficult for him to stay in the top visible spot.

The short-lived emperor, staying on the throne for eighty-three days.

f	f	r	e
d	f	m	d

People with mixed pillars fall into different categories. Yang pillars in the outer zone (the year and hour pillars) and yin pillars in the inner zone (day and self pillars) are likely to be outgoing, sharing, and caring but keep their desire or thoughts to themselves. They are careful planners who enjoy an active social life.

The following example is of a state secretary of China who was successful and wealthy, commanding great power.

M	r	t	M
M	t	m	W

What happens when this is reversed—yin pillars in the outer zone and yang pillars in the inner? These people appear to be very agreeable but barely change their minds. Don't ever try to convince them to accept a different idea.

Adolf Hitler (April 20, 1889) was a good example. He had small build and looked agreeable but was determined to fight to his last breath.

f	F	E	e
m	T	W	g

A not typical but illustrative example is Jacqueline Kennedy Onassis (July 29, 1929). She demonstrated herself as a person of great inner strength under a docile appearance.

m	T	m	e
d	H	d	f

Having equal numbers of pillars in yin and yang positioned in alternate positions makes a disciplined and responsible person. They carefully weigh options in decision-making and take a stand when circumstances require. They also have good control in their approach and make dependable friends. Most of them do well in their careers.

President A. Lincoln—Feb. 12, 1809

T	e	F	e
H	d	T	f

Founder of Modern Taiwan—Oct. 31, 1887

M	e	M	f
F	f	H	r

Wife (January 27, 1893) of founder of modern China (Dr. Y. S. Sun) was known to show a role model of discipline and dedication to her husband had a similar system.

t	T	r	R
r	R	g	W

OTHER SPECIAL PILLARS

1. Trouble relationship: **FT, fd, rd, md, TF, MF, MH, TH, td**

A Bazi having one or more of these pillars is likely to have some mishaps in relationships; the more such pillars, the higher the casualties. When it falls into the self pillar, it creates the most damage.

People having such pillars in their systems are likely to be attractive and consequently and unintentionally attract unwanted/unhealthy relationship, have more relationships than they need or want, or suffer some oddities in relationships such as engaging in messy battles.

The harm of the pillars varies with the structure of Bazi. A high-profile politician in the United States has three such pillars; he regularly engaged in bisexual and other sexual scandals but he stayed intact in a high position due his great Bazi; he was also fortunate enough to have committed such acts during his high luck cycle, protected by auspicious energy. Below are his three pillars (data on birth hour unavailable); all three fall in the troubled relationship group.

A high profile politician

?	f	M	f
?	d	H	d

The high-profile murder case of Scott Peterson and his wife in Modesto, California, offers an unusual case of inclusive aspects of such pillars.

Scott Peterson and his wife, Laci in Modesto:

Scott (October 24, 1972, no birth hour)

?	E	M	R
	R	H	R

Laci (May 4, 1975)

?	M	M	t
?	H	W	t

Both contain the relationship pillar, MH, in the Bazi; Laci (the wife) was killed by Scott, who in turn was convicted and given a death sentence for the act. The same pillar (MH) killed both husband and wife.

What was more interesting were all the days of the vital events for Scott, carrying a relationship pillar:

Wife disappeared: December 24, 2002, FT (Laci was killed on a relationship day pillar of FT)

Dead body discovered: April 13, 2003, rd (year pillar)

Arrested: April 18, 2003, rd (year pillar)

Sentenced to death: December 13, 2004, FT (day pillar)

Princess Diana had two of such pillars, being in the month and self pillar respectively. Her story spoke for the effects.

F	t	T	m
H	d	F	g

The above were serious cases. In a not-so-harmful case, it could just mean oddities in a relationship or an unhappy marriage. It is not surprising that even Confucius had it in his year pillar (MH). He let go of his wife in his early life; he had a strong distaste for women and put women and non-evolved (indecent, not gentleman-like) individuals into one class. This is well documented.

2. Intelligent Self: **ER, eg, EF, fd, FF, and ed**

Anyone with one of these pillars as a day pillar is most likely to be intelligent. They tend to be at least very resourceful if not very intelligent. Many prominent scholars and Nobel Prize winners have such day pillars.

3. Clever Self: **TW, tr, FW, fm, EF, MH, MT, mr, RT, and rd**

People having a day pillar in this group are likely to be smart and have a smooth and successful life. They make good managers.

4. In-Law Relationship: **mt, RW, rf, FF, fd, EM, mm, RH, rr, FR, ET, and fg**

People having these pillars are likely to have problems with in-laws or are unlikely to find the right marital partner. They are more likely to encounter some odd marriages as well. The magnitude of the effect depends on the position and the number of such pillars one possesses. One of these as a day pillar is the worst. Try to detach from the tangle of the people involved.

5
Message from Special Stars

In the Meng system, each of the twenty-two signs also carries special messages known as *stars*. The way these stars were designed has been a mystery, mostly incorporated from other divination systems after the Meng was invented. Over time, most messages have been amazingly accurate. They are easy and simple to use, and it is so much fun to apply them to our systems.

Many of these stars were discussed in *Easy Ways to Harmony*. In this book, we add more formulas and organize them in a more convenient order for easy use. They are organized into three tables according to their reference point. We'll explain each as we move along.

Special Stars by Year Branch

The year branch is the letter of the alphabet at the bottom of our year pillar, indicating the year we were born. We have chosen five stars as listed in the following table for this reference point. All message stars in the table also refer to only the branches in our birth composite. For example, Linda was born in the year of "R," her talent star is "W," romance star is "m," so on and so forth as shown in the table.

Stars of talent, romance, and mobility can be located by using the day branch as well. We'll illustrate each category with more examples below.

Talent includes outstanding skill in all fields. Successful scholars, scientists, writers, artists, good chefs, and seamstresses are all talented in a special way. Those with a talent star usually excel in literary endeavors or art and hold high positions.

However, there are many ways (in the Meng system) to recognize talents; a talent star (like any stars in the table) is only a simple way. Many talented people were born without a talent star in our BC.

We will touch on some of these complicated procedures in latter part of this book for these messages. In fact, many great talents do not have a talent star. Isaac Newton and Thomas Edison were good examples.

Star → Year Branch ↓	Talent	Romance	Mobility	Solitude	Anxiety
R	W	m	T	T, H	T , H
***g**	g	F	r	T, H	r, t
T	H	t	M	g, f	R, W
***t**	d	R	f	g, f	f, g
W	W	m	T	g, f	T, F
***f**	g	F	r	W, M	t, d
F	H	t	M	W, M	W, M
***d**	d	R	f	W, M	f, m
M	W	m	T	r, d	F, H
***m**	g	F	r	r, d	r, d
H	H	t	M	r, d	R, M
***r**	d	R	f	T, H	g, m

Figure 5A Special Stars by Year Branch

A talent star also functions as a protector/guard to protect us from evil or danger. However, when the star falls in a void sign, the self is likely to be a monk or other spiritual leader, leading an isolated life, or dedicated to metaphysics. Let us illustrate with an example.

Robert Taylor (a movie star)**—August 5, 1911**

?	f	t	m
?	d	d	r

His year branch is "r"; we begin to search this star from all the branches in his birth composite. As we don't have his birth time data, we can only limit our search to his month and day branch. From the row of "r," we found the talent star being "d," which appears in both his month and day branches. Thus, he had two talent stars.

Fortunately, they are located in the vital and intimate position. As the month branch governs our career issues, his talent star truly enhanced his acting career success. The day branch, which represents our spouse and health, would likely bring him a talented wife and satisfaction from being talented. He did marry another talented movie star in his first marriage.

His day branch "d" also shows his talent star as "d." It completes our search.

The following Nobel Prize winners all have a talent star:

Aston William—September 1, 1877

Gabriela Mistral—April 7, 1889

Christian Duve—October 2, 1917

Richard Hicks—April 8, 1904

Harry Martinson—May 6, 1904

A romance star makes some one popular, well liked, attractive, sociable, generous, and smart. Consequently, it is very easy for the selves to attract romantic partners and/or to attract an audience and build up fame. It is crucial for movie stars, singers, authors, and PR personnel to succeed.

A romance star is ideally positioned in the month or day branches so you are protected from an unwanted partner. Those who have this star in the hour branch are likely to pay the price of bad romance; the peripheral position encourages easy access by undiscriminating romance.

A romance star in the void sign is very tricky. The meaning of "void" could be empty, no application, idealistic, philosophic, and metaphysical or something relating to high-mindedness. An empty star (a void position) leads to easy but fruitless romance. People with a romance star falling in a void sign (Figure 4A in Chapter 4, the flow table) need help in getting married. The practice of arranged marriages might not be a bad idea for these people. Some concession or compromise in dating practices might help.

On the other hand, a romance star in the void position could mean blessings. Fruitless romance is inconsequential and therefore would never create an unwanted, troublesome relationship. A void romance with a mentor star is, however, a wonderful thing to have. The self is likely to achieve fame in philosophy or another high-minded, noble pursuit. Knowing the message ahead, it might help to orient our career to the flow.

Here is an example for locating the romance star.

Brooke Shields—May 31, 1965

?	t	R	t
?	m	F	f

In the row for f (her year branch), we locate her romance star as F, which is found at the month branch, a good position. Her outlook and lifestyle speak for itself. Princess Diana, born in the "g" year (July 1, 1961), also had a romance star, F, in the month branch.

The romance star can also be located by the reference of day branch. Let us illustrate with Elizabeth Taylor's system. There is no romance star from her year branch.

Elizabeth Taylor—February 27, 1932

E	r	R
F	t	M

Taylor's day branch is F; we check row F and locate "t" as Taylor's romance star, which is found at her month branch. There is no romance star associated with the year branch. The romance star is commonly found in the systems of successful movie stars.

When the romance star occurs in the luck cycle, the person becomes especially attractive during that period. This occurrence can indicate extramarital affairs sometimes. The system of President Eisenhower provides an interesting illustration. He was born in the year of MT. The romance star for year T is t, not found in his birth composite.

However, it occurred in his luck cycle from 1942 to 1948. He started an affair with an Irish woman (his driver) in 1942 at the age of fifty-two during an overseas assignment. It ended shortly after the WWII, at the last leg of the "t" flow. There was rumor that he contemplated a divorce in order to marry the Irish woman; apparently, the attempt was not supported by the flow.

Dwight Eisenhower—October 14, 1890

E	F	M
W	H	T

8	18	28	38	48
f	E	e	M	m
r	R	g	T	t

For single individuals who are looking for romance, the occurrence of such a star provides a golden period for successful dating, and the magnitude of the success depends on the power and the position of the star. If you are serious about making it work, check out the year, month, and days containing your romance star, and conduct your dating game accordingly.

How to proceed? You get ready in anticipating such an important time period by grooming your outlook and fixing your outfit; keep busy and mingle properly when the romance star occurs.

For example, if your romance star is the "m," you should get ready during the "m" year, focus on the "m" month, and make full use of all the "m" days. Of course, don't forget your "m" luck period if you have one. Please remember, the "m" is on the branch, and such days should be one of the following: tm, fm, em, mm, and rm. Such days come in a twelve-day cycle.

While you are waiting for the best day, don't forget the "m" hour. It comes constantly every day from 5:00 to 7:00 p.m.! You are reinforcing your luck by using the right time with the right day. Make it a rule to contact your date on the great hours! A client changed her calling hour on the enlightenment of this discovery, which concluded a happy romance game.

A word of caution: the impact of these stars varies with individuals, depending on your compatibility with the element of the stars. If your romance star happens to "m," and metal is your beneficial element, you will enjoy such happy times. On the other hand, if metal hurts you, you are likely to encounter courtship in those days, of course. However, your date would be challenging or you would go through a rocky road in courtship!

There are no equal rights in romance! Some have to work harder and get less! We are assigned with different blessings.

The mobility star implies travel or change, either physical or mental. People with such a star in their BC have a mobile life, depending on where the star falls. In the year pillar, the self is more mobile during the first quarter of life; in the month pillar, more mobile in the second quarter, so on so forth. President Nixon had a mobile star at the day branch, and he had a very mobile life, particularly during the third quarter of his life. Bob Hope shared a similar star.

Bob Hope—May 29, 1903

?	f	E	r
?	f	F	t

Sidney Altman (Nobel Prize winner in 1989)—May 7, 1939

?	T	e	e
?	W	f	t

Altman's mobility star occurs at the month pillar, which indicates a mobile life in the twenties. Let us find out what happened during that period. He earned his BS from MIT in 1960, started graduate work at Columbia in 1961, worked in a laboratory in Colorado in 1962, and moved to Harvard a couple of years later. He graduated with a Harvard Ph.D. in 1967 and left Harvard in 1969 after two years of research. Five moves in nine years. Socially, he moved upward four notches in a row.

During 1989 (ef), Altman's mobility was reactivated by the year flow of "f"; he made an overseas trip to Europe to receive his Nobel Prize. He was lucky to be able to make such a long trip so that he could follow the flow. Those under such mobile flow but not making a significant move are likely to fall or stumble, causing a move to a hospital, an involuntary move forced by the flow.

It is very important to be aware of the occurrence of your mobility stars and to follow the flow by making a move in some way. A move can consist of extra exercises; a change of mentality, behaviors, or lifestyle; or simply an outfit. Of course, long physical moves and change in environment are the most effective.

The mobility star can also be located by the day branch as a reference. That is, each person has the chance to have two mobility stars, one by year branch and the other by the day branch. They seem to be both equally powerful. Let us explain with the system of Elizabeth Taylor.

Elizabeth Taylor—February 27, 1932

?	E	r	R
?	F	t	M

Taylor does not have a mobility star by the reference of her year branch. However, using the day branch as a reference, we locate M as the mobility on the F row; it is found in her year branch. Thus, using her day branch F as a reference, she does have a mobility star.

A mobility star at the spouse palace would cause an unstable marriage unless anchored by some other signs in the BC. We'll touch on this issue in a later part of the book.

The solitude star is associated with a socially inactive life. The person may remain unmarried or married with a sick or very detached spouse. In any event, the person has very few close relatives or friends. Some are simply dedicated to a lonely goal. If the star is found only in the luck cycle, it indicates temporary solitude for a few years.

On the positive side, many spiritual leaders and distinguished scholars have powerful solitude stars. It certainly takes a substantial degree of solitude to learn the truth or to communicate with the divine. It is common among Nobel Prize winners, as many work alone diligently in the laboratory. Let us use some examples to illustrate the procedure of locating the star.

Leonie Sachs (Nobel Prize winner in 1966 in literature) December 10, 1891.

Leonie Sachs—December 10, 1891

M	m	m
F	g	t

For those born in a t year, g and f are the solitude stars. Sachs has one in the month branch. He was a devoted writer and was never married.

Pearl Buck (June 26, 1892), a great writer, had a solitude star at the day branch. She married in 1917 and remained single after divorcing in 1935, at age forty-four, the third quarter of her life when the day branch influence came into effect.

When the solitude star occurs over the course of a luck cycle, it influences our lifestyle, causing a prolonged single adulthood or bringing a few years of quiet life. Take a look at this example.

Maurice Allais (Nobel Prize winner in 1988 in economics)**—May 31, 1911**

?	m	T	m
?	g	F	r

10	20	30	40
r	R	m	M
f	W	t	T

Allais married in 1960 at the age of forty-nine. There was no solitude star in his BC, but there was a message in his luck cycle. A solitude star occurred in his LC in the T period between the ages of forty-five and forty-nine. He married at the end of this solitude period, when the solitude flow subsided.

Luis Alvarez (Nobel Prize winner in 1968 in physics)—June 13, 1911

?	T	T	m
?	T	F	r

8	18	28	38
t	F	f	E
d	M	m	H

Sharing a similar destiny, Alvarez married at forty-seven. His solitude stars are T and H, which are found in the third quarter of his BC and in the LC from age forty-three to forty-seven. He married at the end of the ruling dynasty of solitude star H.

Ronald Reagan—February 6, 1911, offered an even more interesting insight into the star.

f	M	m
d	T	r

1	11	21	31	41	51
e	E	f	F	t	T
g	R	r	H	m	M

Ronald Reagan was divorced from his first wife in 1948 (at age thirty-seven). A solitude star, H, occurred in his luck cycle during the period from age thirty-six to forty. He married Nancy in 1952, at age forty-one, as soon as he passed the solitude period.

These are just a few examples of how the solitude star affects our destiny. I have noticed that many inventors have this star in their birth composites. Sometimes, solitude can mean confinement.

While a solitude star can mean temporary peace to some busy people, it can bring disaster to many of us. When confronted with such a fate at any given point in our lives, it is wise to heed the ancient Chinese wisdom, "following the flow." When a solitude star occurs in our own system, we should keep ourselves in solitude for one to two hours a day by staying up late, or go to a quiet place during the entire period.

If a solitude star occurs for a loved one, encourage or help that person to do the same. You might also want to stay away from each other by having separate activities. How well does it work? There are no statistics. The observations seem to be true. It might be the last resort to save a marriage through the difficult times! Successful relationships take planning and vision. It might be worth a try as long as it is carried out properly and doesn't hurt the relationship. Under some compelling circumstance to save a marriage, we might need it. Seek mutual understanding and consent before proceeding!

The anxiety star is associated with worry, sorrow, separation, illness, and funerals. The systems of John Kennedy and his wife, Jacqueline, offer some very interesting insight in interpreting this star.

John Kennedy—May 29, 1917

?	m	t	f
?	d	f	f

7	17	27	37
T	r	R	m
W	t	T	g

The solitude stars of birth year "f" are "d" and "t." They occurred in the period of his early twenties, in his month pillar, and in the third quarter (where d is located) of his BC. He was in the Navy in his late twenties, the t period in his LC, and his back was badly hurt. He died at forty-six in an "rt" year on November 12 ("ed" day). He had "d" and "t" together on this sorrowful day.

Jacqueline Kennedy Onassis—July 28, 1929 to May 19, 1994

m	T	m	e
d	H	d	f

There are two anxiety stars in her BC, the "d." She had more than her share of sorrow and anxiety. She was widowed in both 1963 (rt) and 1975 (tt), with the same anxiety star found in both years. She died during the luck pillar of et. Were these coincidences or messages of fate? We'll leave the answer to our readers.

Quite often, the solitude and the anxiety star go hand in hand. As you can see from Figure 5A, some people have the same signs representing both stars. The system of Aung San Sun Kyi, Nobel Prize winner in 1991, a leader of an opposition political party of former Burma, is a good illustration.

Aung San Sun Kyi—June 19, 1945

?	e	R	t
?	d	F	m

6	16	26	36	46	56
r	T	t	F	f	E
d	M	m	H	r	R

She married to a British professor in England in 1972 and returned home in 1988 to visit her ailing mother. She organized an opposition party the same year and was arrested the next year. She has been separated from her spouse and two sons ever since. What is the message in her system? Let us find out.

She has both a solitude and an anxiety star in the day branch, the spouse position. She has been a political prisoner since 1989, at the age of forty-four, and separated from her husband, who is teaching outside the country. This anxiety star is found in her day pillar, representing the third quarter of her life. She is in sad confinement! Looking ahead, her confinement seems to last until age fifty-five, after her solitude period of r.

After the "r" period, she did have more freedom to associate with her people under the supervision of the government, but she was fighting a losing battle.

Eleanor Roosevelt—October 11, 1884 had an anxiety star at the day branch, her spouse position. Those who are familiar with her biography should be able to draw some insight from this occurrence of the anxiety star.

SPECIAL STARS BY MONTH BRANCH

The *guard* is a great protector, guarding us from evil and danger. It is more powerful and reliable than the scholar star. Practically all great military generals have it, enabling them to survive great battles. Eisenhower had the one combining yin and yang forces in one. Many great people had it, Isaac Newton, Thomas Edison, Albert Einstein, Richard Nixon, and Margaret Thatcher included. It explains why Thatcher escaped the bomb blast in her hotel by a timing of seconds. Such a star is very common in the BC of great military commanders.

Month branch	R	g	T	t	W	f	F	d	M	m	H	r
Guard	R, f*	M	F, f	T	R	M, m	F, r*	T	R, r	M, T*	F	T, t

Figure 5B Special Stars by month branch

Note: On the table, stars with a * are branches, all others are stems.

The two guard signs for the month represent the force of yin and yang. When the guard star stays as only one as shown in the months of g, t, W, H, and d, it is more powerful, as it combines yin and yang forces in one sign.

People with this star are wonderful friends to have: helpful and reliable. Determining the guard is a little tricky. The guard stars found on the day pillar are most powerful. Here is the illustration to locate the star.

Thomas Edison

R	E	R	.f
R	T	T	.d

His birth month branch is "T," and the guard star below the "T" branch is "f" and "F." We located "f" in his year stem. He survived the risk of saving a boy on the rail from an incoming train at fifteen; he also survived the hassles and hardship of inventing on electricity and fighting patent infringement.

People having any guard stars in their birth composite are likely caring and fair, with few exceptions. The Tao says the Almighty protects the good people.

We can enjoy the protection of the guard even if we don't have it in our BC. When it shows up in our LC, the cosmic year, month, or day, we can afford taking some risk to move forward with a bigger goal as we receive extra protection on the guard days.

Here are some rules to read the message from the guard star. Its position in the BC and nature of sign play the key. Let us illustrate with examples. Billionaire Bill Gates has a powerful guard star in his month pillar as shown below:

?	R	F	t
?	H	H	d

Being born in the "H" month, his guard star is the stem "F." It is in the parental pillar, indicating protecting and beneficial parents. Apparently he has great supporting parents. Secondly, being a fire element, it is the money sign for the water "R" self. A guard star in the money sign means money earned/spent within a good cause. Money on the stem indicates generosity; hidden in the branch, great saving. His global charity foundation speaks loudly for the truth of the star. Of course, he has so much more money in the branches as well, as his other money signs reveal.

When the guard star pairs up to the self, the protection is even more intimate and secure. The self is, figuratively speaking, glued to the star; he or she is therefore very benevolent, giving and caring, never deviating from the good deeds the guard star dictates. Here is another example.

T	m	F	f
F	t	F	g

The guard star for the "F" month is the "F" and "Fm," a natural stem pair, making the self part of the guard team, functioning as one unit, and protecting the needy. In this case, as the guard is in the parental position, the principle of parental protection applies. Since the "F" is the ruler and career sign for the self "m," the self is likely getting good protecting bosses or follows the lead of good fair great leaders and/or a great cause.

SPECIAL STARS BY SELF

Relation-Ship	Wealth	Easy Food	**Self**	Mentor	Scholar	Happy career	Easy income
F	R, g	*f	**T**	g,d	f, r	eg, ed	FW, FT
F	g, M	F	**t**	R, M	F	MR, MM	fm, fr
T	T,W	R	**F**	r, m	T, M	mr, mm	ER, EF
d	T, W	*f	**f**	r, m	m	RT, RW	eg, ef
W	R, g	F	**E**	g, d	T, M	rg, rd	MR, MF
W	g, M	M	**e**	R, M	m	TR, TM	mr, md
H	R, g	T	**M**	g, d	f, r	tg, td	RH, RM
m	r, d	F	**m**	T, F	R	FF, FT	rt, rf
R	M, H	*m	**R**	f, t	T, M	ft, ff	TR, TF
M	M, H	*r	**r**	f, t	t	EH	tg, tf

Figure 5C Special Stars by Self

*Except Self stems listed as reference, all alphabets are branches. Effects of all signs (and pillars) apply to signs in the four-pillar, showing up in the LC period, year, month or day as indicated in the lunar calendars.

1. The *relationship* star enhances opportunities to meet romance partners. The flow would make the person attractive; the person is consequently prone to engage in easy relationship. However, the star creates odds and challenges in the relationship (marriage or courtship), which at best is not happily ended. The person can be trapped and suffers as a result.

Let us shed some light on this star with some examples.

Lana Turner (February 8, 1920 to June 29, 1995), a great movie star in the 1940s–1950s.

?	F	E	M
?	M	T	M

As an "F" self, she had a relationship star, "T," at the month branch. Her married life began at twenty and ended in fifty-two, in seven of those years remaining single. Over a period of twenty-five years, she had eight marriages and many affairs. Dividing twenty-five years over the eight marriages, each averages as three years.

Her contemporary counterpart, Elizabeth Taylor matched her in marriage frequency (eight times), but her marriage life was more than twice as long, and she did not commit extramarital affairs. Although frequent marital change remains a rule in the movie star circle, Turner's life is probably the unique, extreme case. Do we blame it on the "T"?

Ingrid Bergman's (August 29, 1915–August 29, 1982), marriages give another perspective on the relationship star.

?	R	T	t
?	W	M	t

23	33	43
f	E	e
r	R	g

As an "R" self, her relationship star is "R" (in the branch, of course); there is no branch "R" in her BC. However, the "R" set in during her LC period from thirty-eight to forty-two.

She first married in 1937 to a physician in the U.S.A., giving birth to a daughter. In 1950, she took off to Italy for a new movie (age thirty-five) and had an affair with the producer in the following year. She was soon divorced by her husband and ended up marrying the producer. As her audience sought revenge over her misconduct, she divorced her second husband and returned to the U.S.A. in 1957 at age forty-two the last leg of the "R" period.

It was Bergman's shortest (five years), most embarrassing, and most costly marriage. Her other two marriages were thirteen and eighteen years, respectively. The star influence from our LC impacted her life during the given period.

Cary Grant's marriages reinforce more or less the above perspectives. Here is his Bazi (January 18, 1904).

?	m	t	r
?	r	g	t

As an "m" self, his relationship is "m," which is not in his BC. However, from thirty-eight to forty-two, he was in the "m" period. He married a wealthy lady in 1942 at thirty-eight and divorced in 1945 (a tm year, the same "m" effects). It was not a happy marriage, even though they remained lifelong friends after the divorce. Their only son died in plane crash.

Princess Diana also got a relationship star at her month branch. Her BC was displayed in Chapter 4, in the section of the troubled relationship pillar.

2. The *wealth* star makes people rich and famous as well. It takes two of these signs to make a star, as indicated in the table. To qualify, the two signs must be found together in either the BC or one in the BC and the other in the luck cycle or in a given year. In the latter case,

prosperity occurs only at that particular point in the person's life. Though the reasons have never been clearly indicated, these observations seem to work very well.

I have personally tested this formula and will share my findings below. Readers are encouraged to test the message for themselves. For convenience, let us use Richard Nixon's BC. He was an M self with both R and g in the branches. Is there is any wonder that he could be so successful?

Richard Nixon

F	M	r	R
H	T	**g**	**R**

Wealth stars are also found in the BC of the following lucky people:

Edgar Adrian—November 30, 1889, NP in 1932

President of Bangladesh—January 19, 1936, seventh president in 1977

Maurice Greenberg—May 4, 1925, Forbes 400 richest list 1995

Mikhail Gorbachev—March 2, 1931, NP 1990 in peace

Octavio Paz—March 31, 1914, NP 1990 in literature.

Halldor Laxneww—April 23, 1902, NP in 1955 in literature

President Bill Clinton—August 19, 1946, U.S. president 1988–1996

Elytis Odysseus—November 2, 1910, NP in 1979

Czeslaw Milosz—June 30, 1911, NP in 1980 in literature

To see how the stars work jointly in the BC and LC, we use examples below.

Jean Dausset (Nobel Prize winner in 1980 in medicine) October 19, 1916

e	e	F
g	r	W

The prosperity stars for e selves are g and M, and there is only a "g" in Dausset's BC. Dausset won the prize in 1980, the year of MM. Year branch M teamed up with g to create prosperity.

Thomas Donnall (Nobel Prize winner in 1990) March 15, 1920

?	R	e	M
?	m	T	M

17	27	37	47	57	67
m	R	r	T	e	F
f	F	d	M	m	H

Donnall is an R self. His prosperity stars are M and H. He won the Nobel Prize when he was seventy, during his "H" luck cycle, when the H joined the M in his BC, creating fame and wealth.

3. *Easy food* leads to good luck in livelihood or just having good food conveniently. It is impractical to get data for discussion. Readers have to do their own tests.
4. A *mentor (guide)* functions like an invisible hand, guiding us to success and good fortune. Having such a sign in our system is extremely blessed: one usually succeeds easily on a

smooth path. The blessing given depends on the strength of the sign. However, even a powerless sign (such as those in a void position) guide makes a happy and decent person.

Most successful people have mentor sign in their BC, as big success needs the help from the Almighty. The person with a mentor star is likely to be kind, fair, and talented, and have a clear sense of life direction.

Readers can check on the examples being discussed in other categories to find out who has the mentor. Thomas Edison, Margaret Thatcher, Princess Margaret, Richard Nixon, J. Kennedy Onassis, and Ronald Reagan all have one. Some have two.

Like the romance star, we can make full use of the mentor effects. Checking out our mentor LC, and the mentor year, month, and days from the calendars, is no doubt the first step. Secondly, we have to remember, and mark down in our action space, our mentor direction. Each mentor occupies a thirty degrees domain as shown in Figure 5D. Each branch is also attached to an animal. The animal school, simple, fun and globally well known, was incorporated into Meng many years ago.

Since everyone has two mentors, it pays to locate both of them and ask for help. Most of us meditate or pray; some pray to God, others to the Almighty or Heaven. It is personal choice. From the metaphysical point, you can ask for additional help when you really need it. The procedure works better when you face your mentor direction on your mentor days. Your mentor hour would enhance the effects, of course. You have to believe it to see the effect.

Each cosmic animal has a cardinal direction that is listed in the following table. You can locate the domain of your mentor animals in your house/room and face such directions for help in your prayer or meditation.

Rat-g-345-15	Rabbit-t-75-105	Horse-F-165-195	Rooster-m-255-285
Ox-g-15-45	Dragon-W-105-135	Goat-d-195-225	Dog-H-285-0315
Tiger-T-45-75	Snake-f-135-165	Monkey-M-225-255	Pig-r-315-345

Figure 5D Locating your mentor animals

Those born into your mentor years are likely to be your mentors, who could unintentionally show you the right thing to do and point to you the right direction to move. Try to associate with these people as much as possible. Seek their insight and observe that they do.

If you happen to like these animal signs, extend it to their figurines. You can display them at home and in your office, carry them in your bag, or wear them as charms. Connect your energy to these figurines by quietly communicating to them. How does it work? Again, there are no statistics. The idea is that everything carries flow/energy. We need to prosper on the right energy. Metaphysical help is always the last resort.

When a mentor is being clashed, disaster is likely to happen. To get ready for the discussion, go to Chapter 3, on the sign interaction and look for the clashing pairs. We display Thomas Edison's system for illustration.

R	E	R	f
R	T	T	d

2	12	22
m	M	e
g	R	r

As "E" self, his mentors are the d and g. He was age seven through eleven at the "g" period. As "g" (LC) and "d "(in BC) clashed onto each other, he was kicked out of school and tutored by his mother at home. At age twelve (1859 another "d" year), one more "d" to join the clashing, he lost most of his hearing. Try by all means to keep your mentor intact and take precautions in anticipation of such an event.

On the other hand, mentor pairing creates some of the best blessings. His luck period "r" (twenty-seven through thirty-one) was the peak of his inventive life; the "r" paired up to his mentor "d." Year 1879, a "t' (rabbit) year, was the banner year during the period. He literally lighted the world with his long-lasting light bulb; there was one more sign to join the mentor pair, reinforcing the effect. Check on the trio of wood from Chapter 3.

If you miss the mentor pairing, there is a better way to make it up. The action takes place in the self pillar. There are sixteen such blessed self pillars: TR, TF, FT, FW, ER EF, MR, MF, RM, RH, tf, tg, ef, eg, mr, md. These selves are likely to enjoy some strokes of unexpected great luck during their mid life; momentum of luck varies with the quality of the BC.

5. The *happy career* star brings in luck in career matters. It is easy for the holders to line up a good job and a good promotion. Readers can test its validity on their own by checking calendars.
6. *Easy income* brings good luck in getting high pay at work. Readers can test its validity on their own by checking calendars.
7. *Scholar:* people with a *scholar star* are either well learned or enjoy artistic pursuits. Even a very weak scholar star will, at the very least, make one look or behave like a scholar—very civilized indeed. However, a self sitting on a powerful scholar sign could spend a lifetime studying without gaining any recognition. The logic? The star is too close to persistently push one to endless study. Why would one engage in endless study? The goal has not been achieved.

In any event, a scholar star also protects one from evil or danger. Most artists or movie stars have good scholar stars. Let us begin with this example.

Lana Turner—February 8, 1920

F	E	M
M	T	M

Self is F, and in the F self row, we see that her scholar stars are T and M. Turner had a T and two "M"s in her branches, and she was extremely talented.

Other celebrities, to name a few, include:

Bob Dole—July 22, 1923

Brooke Shields—May 31, 1965

Ernest Hemingway—July 21, 1899

Linda Evans—November 18, 1942

Joan Collins—May 23, 1933

Elizabeth Taylor—February 27, 1932

Prince Charles—November 14, 1948

Princess Diana—July 1, 1961

6

Types of Energy System by Self

The discussions on reading/analyzing a Bazi in Chapter 4 and 5 cover only the simple and convenient rules. These rules, requiring basically finger walking, offer good clues on the quality of the Bazi. They don't tell us the whole picture, the potential, and how they work together to affect our lives.

The study of Bazi is about the fundamental truth of life, i.e., understanding our potentials and successfully fulfilling God's plan according to God's laws. Given the eight signs from the four pillars assigned by God from our birth, we need to know how these signs interact to affect our lives in various areas, i.e., our endowments and potential to achieve. This is about God's plan.

As the signs interact, we want to target the good flows ahead and get ready to ride on them to achieve, and to stay low to tide over the bad ones. During the process of interaction, we need to identify the mechanism at work and pinpoint the trouble spots or bottleneck causing the malfunction of energy on our temporary down cycle, how to clear the blockage to a smooth passage, and how to attune to such blocks when they become our only options.

Understanding the nature and strength of the self sign is the first step to discover the key for such actions. In the BC, the self represents the person of the birthday, while the other seven signs describe the environment that supports the self. For example, if the self is a tree (yang wood, "T"), born in spring, sitting on some moist warm earth, with some metal signs to trim and refine the tree, some sunlight (the stem "F") to provide opportunities to earn a livelihood and chance to shine, and some extra water to offer irrigation when needed, the self would prosper and succeed as a happy person.

That is the perfect environment for the wood self. This perfect condition varies with different selves, of course. However, practically all Bazi systems are less than perfect. Each has a different nature and strength. Each requires different additional element(s) or sign interactions to make up for the deficit. Consequently, each prospers on a different strategy.

As noted in the *Path to Good Fortune,* people born at the same time and same place, i.e., with the same Bazi, live different lives. Among the many people born at the same time as President Richard Nixon, only one became the president of the United States. It is because the Meng does not account for many other factors such as the genes of the self, its birth environment, and its subsequent living habitat (office and residence), the people associating with the self, its career and hobbies, etc.

As everything in the universe carries different cosmic flows, with everything and everyone interacting with one and other constantly, the cosmic flow impacts each of us in different ways. Due to the variable factors, people with the same Bazi could respond to the same cosmic flow differently, resulting in different luck and a different destiny. How one responds to a certain flow in the past determines our response to the same flow in the future. This is the fundamental procedure to forecast our destiny.

As our energy surges upon the onset of good flows and ebbs at the incoming damaging flows, good flow naturally gives us good luck, while bad flow brings more unhappy events. By checking the timely flows of our key life events, we should have a clear picture on how flows create positive or negative impacts in our lives.

The first step in analyze a Bazi is to classify the strength of the self. We group the different self types into the following categories. In each category, we use key life events of the individual to verify our criteria of classification. These events are grouped as positive and negative to identify the distinctive effects of various flows.

DOMINANT SELVES

Dominant selves have powerful and focused energy, are confident, and are capable of achieving what they want and having clear vision of their life direction. They are mostly powerful leaders in their fields, meeting almost no competitors. They all have special skill, are extremely talented, and are eventually successful. Many are geniuses.

This great energy creates great life. How do we determine a dominant self? There are various grades, such as the quality of a product or a person. A true, stable, dominant self should meet two criteria: (1) born at the right time, such as a wood self born in the spring while a fire self born in the summer, and (2) being in charge of a team in his or her own element, i.e., a water self has a water team, so on and so forth. The ideal one should have good support from the LC.

Let us illustrate with some examples.

Fred Banting (Nobel Prize winner in 1923 for work with insulin) November 14, 1891 to February 21, 1941

?	<u>T</u>	e	m
?	W	r	t

22	32	42	52
F	t	T	r
M	f	F	f

The self (T) is a tree, born in the wood month, and the "r" contains "T" and "R," i.e., wood supported by water, which is the right time. Secondly, there is a wood team of "r" and "t"; the self "T" is in charge of the wood troop; there is no competitor in the environment (his life). He became a great general of all the trees in the wood team. Banting thus met the fundamental requirements of a dominant self.

How do we grade the system? First, there seems to be no water to support the wood, as there are no apparent water signs. We don't know his hour to make a final conclusion. Based on what we see, his trees barely grow big. Since the wood team represents his power and all its rewards, it means his potential for big success is therefore limited.

Secondly, his wood team consists of only two of the three signs to make a full wood team; i.e., a wood trio should consist of "t," "d," and "r." It means he did not have the full strength to be at the top, as his troop is not big enough.

Luckily, there is some hidden water (the "r") in "W"; it moistens the earth immediately beneath the big tree. The tree is also well anchored to grow. Thus, Banting was well supported to be a great leader. All he needed is more opportunities. And, remember, our BC changes with the onset of new flows from our LC. The onset of additional water/wood would put him on the top of the world.

Fortune surely knocked on his door in 1923(rr), at age thirty-two at LC "t." He was awarded the Nobel Prize in medicine for the discovery of insulin. How did the flow orchestrate the event?

First, the "t" from his LC brought in more bush. Secondly, the "rr" from the cosmos in the year of 1923 sent in rain (stem "r") from the sky (could be an automatic irrigation device) to make trees grow tall, and more wood (branch r) to enlarge his wood troop. He stood tall to be recognized.

The following year (1924, TR), with more water and wood, he was awarded a life pension from Canadian government. He also married in same year. All the signs on this great fortune were t, T, and r, basically, wood and water. We therefore conclude his benefiting elements were wood and water, the elements making his life tick! Determining the key benefiting elements is crucial in analyzing the Meng system, as we can harness more of the flow to enhance our lives, promoting our luck.

What could go wrong with a dominant self, as there is no perfect system? Like any powerful dictator, a dominant self does not take slight easily. For a dominant wood self, metal, which chops the wood, is the number one enemy. Fire comes next. How to verify our conclusion? We search for his key life events—his bad years:

- 1917 (ff)—a fire and metal year, hurt arm in military service.
- 1920 (MM) to 1921 (mm)—powerful metal year, great financial loss in surgical (metal business) shop.
- 1932 (RM)—a metal year at the last year of the branch, "f" (containing yang metal) period—divorced.
- 1941 (mf)—year of powerful metal flow, age fifty at the branch "F" period, died in plane (metal) crash. His plane ran out of gas and descended.

Other good examples of dominant self are Ted Turner (November 19, 1938 a dominant wood self) and Warren Buffet (August 30, 1930, a dominant water). The former got rich investing in woodland; the latter succeeded in investing in water (finance).

Concluding criteria to define a dominant self, we have: (1) self being born at the right time and (2) having an alliance or trio of the self element. There are a few exceptions, as life is so complicated.

OVERLY STRONG/STRONG SELVES

Like the dominant selves, strong/overly strong selves have powerful energy, and most are also born leaders. Besides being born in the right time, they are strong for a number of other reasons: they are supported by good grantors or other kin signs that are not so strong. They all are confident and have special skills; some are extremely talented.

There is a key difference between the overly strong and the dominant: the kin signs of the overly strong self are not aligned as a team. As a result, they compete with the self, making them restless; very few strong selves lead a peaceful life. They have to earn everything through their own effort, often through competition. Their luck improves as additional controlling elements show up in their luck cycle.

President D. Eisenhower—October 14, 1890 to March 28, 1969

T	E	F	M
T	W	H	T

8	18	28	38	48	58
f	E	e	M	m	R
r	R	g	T	t	W

The self as yang earth born in the "H" month of powerful earth, he was born in the right time. There is a powerful a fire alliance (from H and T) and another yang fire. A powerful grantor is a wonderful fame factor; most great leaders have it. The person enjoys protected fame. M is another fame factor, as it governs expression of the earth selves, putting the self in a highly visible position. It is standing tall in the BC.

The number one drawback: another yang earth competing for dominance and leadership. There is an "E" hidden in "W." Another "E" in the "H" could get loose occasionally, becoming a competitor as well. It gets more active when additional earth signs come along, making the self fight hard for success.

To keep other earth kin at bay, he needed metal to loosen up and weaken the earth, or wood to anchor and control the earth. Thus, his good elements were metal and wood. The following life events support our conclusion.

He was promoted to five-star general in 1944 (TM), at age fifty-four, a wood and metal year, with metal from the last leg of his "m" period in his LC.

He achieved victory in the Battle of Normandy, 1945 (tm), year of wood and metal, age fifty-five at the LC of "t.'

He served as U.S. president, January 1952 (mt), a year of metal and wood, age sixty-two, the beginning of the "W" period; while mt from the year flow easily won him the honor, the "W" earth made him busy governing a country, fighting among competing countries.

His number one enemy is another yang earth, typically the "E" sign. He lived a good and successful life most of the time. The worst period happened to be from 1909 to 1915, when he had to work to support his brother's college education. During that period, he also had quite a few knee injuries, smoked too much, and studied too little. Such events fell into his "E" period, heavy earth.

In another "e" period, age thirty, his son died, giving him a few years of sorrow. He died March 28, 1969, year of "cm," an earth year.

The criteria to differentiate an overly strong self are not so clear-cut. Basically, the self is very strong—strong enough to win with a hard fight but having no easy control over other competitors, as he or she has no subordinate team (trio or alliance of the self element). They would encounter setbacks when additional signs of the self element set in.

Margaret Thatcher is good example. She is very strong "M" self. She had the most difficult time leading her country from 1980 to 1981 (MM-mm), with a job approval rating of twenty-five percent. She retired in 1990 (MF) and broke her arm in an MF month (June 2009). The additional metal caused the fight. Another "M" acts like a competitor.

SIBLING RIVALRY

Siblings in a family compete and fight among themselves; yet, in some rare occasions, they are close enough to fight as a team. It then becomes a dominant self. It is like we all compete in the society and yet are sensible enough to work together to defend our community against invaders. This reality reflects in the four pillars as well.

When the self encounters other signs of the same element (the kin of the self) in his/her BaZi and does not form a team (alliance or trio), he or she has a sibling rivalry case.

What is the difference between an overly strong self and a sibling rivalry self? An overly strong self is stronger than any other kin sign in the BC, so he or she surely wins in the fight; there is no peace but the self win most of the time, with little loss. Due to their stronger position, they are not being challenged into fights so often; a strong self fights only on the onset of additional kin signs from the LC or the cosmos.

A sibling rivalry self, on the other hand, competes constantly with other kin signs in the BC. Thus, it is quite challenging.

As in any fights, the results of the act can be financial loss, divorce, illness, or other unfortunate mishaps. In severe cases, the self of sibling rivalry frequently suffers from pains, headaches, or shortness of breath, all symbols of bad fights; many often feel very exhausted and suffer from lingering fatigue or mysterious lifelong pain.

There are of different grades, of course. Some sibling rivalry selves make wonderfully great leaders. Let us illustrate with some examples.

Linda Evans—November 18, 1942

?	**t**	m	R
?	r (**T** R)	r (**T** R)	F

3	13	23	33	43	53
M	e	E	f	F	t
H	m	M	d	F	f

The self is a plant born in a month with powerful water and wood flow—the right timing. Secondly, there are two more kin signs in branch "r." Remember, the branch "r" contains "T" and "R." Thus, she is competing with two trees; as yang wood, both are stronger than the self. They are also supported by good water, a winning edge over the yin wood self, "t."

The self "t" is therefore engaging in regular losing battles to survive. Let us see how the reality of her life fits into our analysis. In her early life, she played a supporting role in the TV series "The Big Valley" for many years, riding horses, in constant motion, symbolizing the sibling battles on horseback. With all the hard work, she gained little fame and forever played the supporting role without recognition, riding horses in the same fashion—in circles, symbolizing getting ready to fight. Alas, they are silly fights without gain.

What would be a strategy to win and stop the unending, silly fights? Three ways:

- Joining the wood signs into a wood team
- Using fire to burn up the excessive wood, her competitors
- Using metal to chop down the wood

Her best solution would be to have a wood team, joining all other wood signs into a team under her leadership. All the wood signs pay tribute on her behalf and follow her orders; it means abundant goodies with little effort. Her life eventually proved the validity of this strategy.

Her luck turned around in 1981 (mm) at age thirty-nine, as soon as she entered the "d" period. The "d," joined the "r" in her BC to create a wood team, made her a dominant self in charge of the wood alliance, a wood leader meeting no resistance. She began to star in "Dynasty" as the leading actress. The TV series became a big hit in the 1980s; it ended in 1989, boosting her fame and wealth to an all-time high, reaching the peak of her life.

Metal flow of 1981 (mm) also reinforced the momentum. The metal trimmed and refined the plant (t) for fine performance. All in a sudden, she became very articulate, sophisticated, and attractive!

Now let us see how fire worked in her life. "Dynasty "reached its peak in 1986 and 1987 (FT-ft), years of big fire flow supported by wood. Evans had also entered her stem "F" at about the same time. The sun worked with fire from the cosmos, shining up the leaves and adding huge glamour to the leaves of the plant; glamour translates into fame.

As the sun retreated from her energy system (her life) at age forty-seven, "Dynasty" ended its run in 1989 (ef), a year of moist earth. Being back to her sibling rivalry stage, the onset of earth (representing money for the wood self) triggered sibling fight; she lost the battle to her "T"s.

From age forty-eight to fifty-two, Evans entered the branch "F." This is heat from the ground, and it does not shine the plant. But it certainly helped to curtail the competing effect of wood in her life. The years after the show were comfortable indeed! The heat is, however, best used when combined with the other fire sign.

The effect took place in 1994 (TH), when the "H" joined her "F" to form a fire alliance, burning up and curtailing the other trees. She enjoyed focused energy to set up her fitness center, another big hit to take advantage of the last leg of her fire period. The center has grown into a chain of fifteen centers.

How do we evaluate her marriages? She has had a few unsuccessful relationships and two divorces. The chronology of the events clearly shows the impact of wood, her siblings.

- 1960 (MR) to 1962 (RT)—engaged in a metal time period of 1960, dissolved in a wood year (1962), no marriage involved. One more wood was coming along to fight off her lover, taking away her goodies.
- 1989 (ef) to 1998 (ET)—dating relationship started in the late part of the year 1989, metal time period ("f" contains M) and ended in 1998, the same branch "T" for the cosmic year, i.e. the same sibling.
- 1968 (EM) to 1974 (TT)—married in the "M" time period, divorced in the "T" year again.
- 1975 (tt) to 1981 (mm)—the branch "t" enhances her marriage as it pairs up to her spouse "r," forming a wood team—a good year for dating/marriage.

Unfortunately, strong yin metal would destroy her spouse, the "T" in "r," her spouse palace, even though it stops the competition from other wood signs. She would have a good career in a metal year but mishaps in marriage.

There is a dilemma in her system. That was why she lamented that when she was in love, she stopped working. She could only have one at a time. The only time she can keep both is in her dominant self period. And it is a gift from the Almighty.

The challenge of kin has dramatic effects. Unfortunately, as dictated by the brutal need for survival, sibling rivalry is the most common system in our reality. We like to illustrate on the truth with one an additional example.

Princess Margaret—August 21–1930, f hour

f	r	T	M
f	t	M	F

4	14	24	34	44	54	64
r	R	m	M	e	E	f
d	F	f	W	t	T	g

As yin water (rain) born in metal month, under the strong filtering and cleaning effect of the metal, she was elegant and smart, a glamorous beauty. Wood represent the talent of the water; she got both the yang and yin wood, talented in many things. The "M" on the year pillar, being her grantor element, depicts her long inherited nobility and distinction from her ancestors all the way to her parents, giving her high status.

Fire, as her money sign, stays at the year branch, grounded and secure, extending all the way from her ancestors, ready for her from the very beginning of life. Some more fire on the hour pillar in excessive supply provides more comfort than she needed. She was literally wrapped up in money.

She was protected by a guard and helped by a mentor underneath to doubly insure a good life. With all these blessings, why was she miserable over most of her life? There are two drawbacks. Branch "M" has "M" and "R," including her sibling, which is yang water. This sibling is fatally detrimental to the self.

First, being yang and more powerful, it has a constant winning edge over the self. Secondly, this "M" is more accessible to the financial assets (F), strategically blocking its flow to the self. It controls the livelihood of the princess. This money, besides feeding her, could also choke her to death, depending on the circumstance. Thirdly, this "M" naturally pairs up with the "t," the spouse palace of the princess, a power to fatally dissolve her relationship.

With a powerful sibling, the excessive money (the fire element in her BC) has also become a source of trouble. It triggers sibling battle and tempts the self to seek excessive fun or vices.

What happened in her life? What matters most when one securely possesses every good tangible thing in the world? Naturally, they yearn for love and recognition. The worst scenario for a sibling rivalry self is the battle; what triggers the battle is practically always the money (representing all the vices and the goodies). Siblings get bruises, pains, or other illnesses when they are fighting; when they fight, they end up losing the goodies (spouse, money, etc.) as someone else outside the fighting team always takes the dole away. For Princess Margaret, it was the "F," and "f," her money sign.

During her "F" period, from age nineteen to twenty-three, her sister took the family throne; Queen Elizabeth was crowned in 1952, when the self was twenty-two. In the following year, she fell in love with group captain, Peter Townsend, a divorcee who was deemed unfit for a royal match. Margaret gave up the relationship under a royal order (from her sister) in order to keep her royal financial support.

She was separated from her husband in 1966 (FF), and after numerous extramarital affairs, they divorced in 1978 (EF), the same "F" all along. She died on February 9, 2009 (RF), another "F" year.

She was unhappy most of her life and remained chronically very sick after 1985, after a lung operation; the time frame matched her "f" in her hour pillar and the thick earth of LC "E." Symbolically, she was fighting hard with her sibling for the money and got hurt often. Thick earth choked up her circulation and breathing system; symbolically, earth blocks the water. Her most serious stroke occurred in January 1993, year of RM; it means two more siblings coming along to join the fight. Figuratively speaking, she was beaten to total exhaustion.

How to restore peace to her life? She needed to team up her siblings. It happened in 1960 (MR), when she got married. What happened? During the year, the branch "R" from the year paired up with the "M" to form a water team, under the charge of the self. There was no more sibling rivalry.

Her biggest honorary title from a foreign country (India) came in 1948 (ER); the "R" from the year flow paired the "M" in her BC to form another water team. Another pairing act occurred in 1965 (tf), when both branches of "f" and "M" formed a natural pair to eliminate the sibling effect.

Why did she incur so many extramarital affairs? She got both the troubled relationship pillar in the year, in a peripheral unprotected region, and another relationship sign in her month branch. All the affairs came in double! The excessive fire triggered the desire.

WEAK SELVES

Weak selves are born with weak energy; they need the help of grantor(s) and sometimes kin as well. The best help is from grantor, as a kin might cause sibling rivalry under some circumstances. The criteria to definite a weak self are not clear-cut, as it can be weak for many reasons.

Although being born in the wrong time is the main reason, one could be weak in possessing a great grantor when another draining element in the BC is too overwhelming. Proficiency and experience in analysis helps. The surest way to tell is through verification of key life events of the self; we tell by how the self responds to the flow at a given point. That is the worksheet procedure. If the self benefits from kin, grantor or both, he or she is a weak self.

A weak self is the most common system. Many were born weak, and too many are feeble. Due to their low energy momentum, very few are great leaders. The most blessed weak self is supported by a powerful and reliable grantor. It offers great protection and makes them a strong self without the challenge of sibling rivalry.

With the help from some good stars such as mentor or guard, many can become great achievers too—most commonly, scholars. Most are hard workers, steadily and surely fulfilling their goals. Our illustration is Harry Truman.

President Harry Truman—May 8, 1884, late evening

r	<u>**E**</u>	e	T
r	F	f	M

9	19	29	39	49	59	69	79
M	m	R	r	T	t	F	f
F	d	M	m	H	r	R	g

Self "E" was born in a hot month and on a fire day—right month and right day for a fire person. Flanked by another yin earth, he seems to be strong. However, the "e" is being paired up by the T and the "f" pairs to the "M"; they both lose their original support. The only reliable support is from the day branch; it is weak. On the other hand, the powerful water at the hour pillar is diluting the earth, weakening the self further.

With the energy from birth, he might succeed in a career with strenuous effort over a long-term fight; the momentum is, however, far from enough to carry out his big ambition. Additional water, and metal from his LC or the cosmos, would even weaken him further. To shine, he needs more fire (grantor) or wood (to fire up the grantor). Let us get some feedback from his life events.

We can see that his luck pillars before thirty-nine were all metal or powerful water. The only fire period, "F," was his high school, in which he did very well. He did not go to college until age thirty-nine. Let us chronicle his key events below:

Periods of metal and water flow:

- 1901–1906, age seventeen to twenty-three, after high school graduation, clerks in the railway and mailroom of a newspaper
- 1906–1917, age twenty-two to twenty-three, at stem "m," weak energy, farmer
- 1915, age thirty-one at stem "R," traded in lead and zinc, big loss
- 1917–1918, age thirty-three to thirty-four, military service, captain
- 1919–1921 married, small business, opened shop 1919 (td), closed shop in 1921 (mm), in debt from 1921–1934 at the branch "M" period
- 1921–1922, age thirty-seven to thirty-eight, at branch "M," big loss ($28 thousand) in trading metal commodity
- 1923, age thirty-nine, at the "r" period, hard work to study law in Kansas, was relatively better as the "r" paired to the E, helping him succeed
- Late forties, at the branch "m" metal period, salesman, after two years of being the judge at the last year of the "r" pairing period
- Death, December 26, 1972, a watery year, watery month, and a metal day

Periods of fire and wood:

- 1926 (FT), age forty-two, court judge
- 1934 (TH), age fifty, year of great heat and wood, entering the "T" period, U.S. Senate
- 1945–1953 (tm), age sixty-one at the "t" year during the "tr" period, with wood to boost the fire, vice president and president in the same year, staying for two terms during his stem "F" period.

HELPLESS SELVES

While the dominant self is the most powerful type, at the extreme end, on the other side of the spectrum of self-classification, is the helpless self. The birth environments of such selves are very hostile, totally stripping the self of any possible defense. He or she has to surrender to the dominant flow for total provision/protection for survival, i.e., surviving like an infant.

Is it a good life? Just imagine the full entitlement of what an infant enjoys without the slightest effort on its own: unconditional love and care. Such people enjoy great success easily, with great help. Of course, there are different grades; not all infants have a good life. There are very lucky, less lucky, and unlucky infants. However, regardless of the grading, all helpless selves get some free provisions. A helpless self is protected and provided for by a boss. Nevertheless, a boss also has different grades. As a rule, a powerful, solid boss is generous, and a weak or shaky boss is mean. All bosses demand absolute loyalty, and a powerful boss is even more demanding.

In reality, the analogy applies to anyone born in a totally hostile cosmic environment. That is, you are a fire born in a watery year, wet month and a rainy day, and there is no wood to support the fire and no earth to block the water, leaving you totally helpless to survive on your own. The water, being the dominant flow, is in total control your destiny. You surrender to the dominant flow for protection and livelihood.

While there is no free lunch, you have to meet some conditions to be qualified. First, you have to show loyalty by standing alone in your BC, i.e., there should be no more fire sign in your birth environment. Ideally, you should be stripped from the support of wood as well, i.e., wood signs in your BC should be minimal.

Secondly, you should never anger your boss, such as by hampering its operation in any manner. As your protecting flow is water, any significant earth from your BC, LC, or the cosmic year would hinder the smooth flow of the water; when it happens, you will incur bad luck as punishment from the boss.

On the other hand, if you make your boss happy, you will be rewarded abundantly. For example, if you encounter a metal/water LC, your water boss will be delighted to be empowered. At the same time, water/metal also enfeebles you, making you more faithful. It pleases the boss, and you are subsequently rewarded. That is one way to predict our upcoming luck.

To be born as an infant is the most blessed, as everyone would love the infant unconditionally and wholeheartedly. It means abundant and easy success for the individual. There are different grades of being helpless. Let us explain.

Some helpless are born with energy like a young child. As a young child, one has to perform little chores and is subject to occasional scolding or punishment for misbehaving; it means having assistance to achieve good success in one's struggles; life is always well provided, and the person will never worry for the next meal or shelter.

With increasing energy as a teenager, one is expected to perform and to work, and in poor families, one has to struggle for independence. In a good family, one works hard to succeed. As our energy path changes periodically, a feeble child could be pushed back to the status of an infant by the onset of new enfeebling flow; thus, the person prospers suddenly for a few years or more. On the other hand, a newborn infant could also be pushed up to the status of a child or teenager to experience new challenge or struggle.

Helpless self systems have wide swings of ups and downs in life cycle. The person could swing from an idiot to a genius. They become geniuses when supported by the dominant flow (symbolically, the powerful boss), and idiots when, abandoned by the dominant flow, they have to function on their feeble energy, like a teenager taking full charge of his life.

Let us illustrate with examples.

Thomas Edison—November 11, 1847 to October 18, 1931

R	E	R	f
R	T	T	d

2	12	22	32	42	52	63	73
m	M	e	E	f	F	t	T
g	R	r	H	m	M	d	F

Edison's system is great case to illustrate the fine line between a genius and an idiot.

As an "earth self," undermined by powerful wood (woods in the spring, empowered by abundant water, the three "R"s), without help from other earth, he was a helpless earth self, surrendering to the lead of wood.

There is no way the self could function on his own energy. He had to surrender to the wood flow for protection and provision. However, he was not totally helpless, like an infant, to enjoy unconditional love and care. On his year pillar, there is an "f," fire on the stem, another fire, and earth hidden in "d" to empower him. All this extra fire and earth added up, changing him to the status of a young child. Thus, symbolically, he was not loyal enough to earn the total trust from the wood boss.

Since these elements are found in the year pillar, he was vulnerable to rebelling and being punished in the early quarter of his life. That is, he was inclined toward a bad life during such a period. The effect would show without effects from the LC.

In addition, any onset of metal, fire, or earth from other external sources would further reinforce his bad luck. Any onset of earth would empower him to rebel like a teenager, acting on the illusion of winning over the boss. What do teenagers do? They make lots of noise and waves without achieving results. They pay dearly for the waves.

We conclude his good elements as wood and water and his damaging elements as metal, fire, and earth, with metal as the worst.

Let us find out what the metal did to his life. Metal flow had crept into his life since age two, spoiling his childhood, being the strongest from two to twelve. He was a very sick child and a very slow learner. After only three months of formal schooling, he was labeled as retarded. His mother tutored him at home until age twelve. From age twelve to fifteen, another metal period, he was selling newspapers on a train, and he lost most of his hearing ability in a metal year (1860, MM) within the metal period between ages twelve and thirteen. He set up a print shop within the train. He remained a voracious reader all his life.

As an analogy, the self who previously surrendered, suddenly rebelled, trying to cut the wood with a big knife. He failed, as a single knife cannot fight a wood army, and as a result he was severely punished for rebelling. In the metal year during his metal LC, using the same analogy, he launched a bigger fight using two knives; he incurred the more severe punishment of losing most of his hearing.

In his other metal period "m," age forty-seven to fifty-one (1894 to 1899), he opened and closed three factories, one after the other, in manufacturing cement and/or refining minerals. All resulted in huge losses. Minerals (metal/earth), which angered his wood boss, brought him disasters and losses. The same analogy applies.

What happened in his earth/fire periods? During the "e" period from age twenty-one to twenty-six, he made a wrong move, quitting a prestigious research job with Western Union to start an invention career on his own. He invented the wrong products, which had no market; he led a destitute life. In the mixed period of earth and fire from age thirty-seven to forty-eight, he was busy fighting patent infringement lawsuits. There were no inventions, despite his hard work and experiments.

He died on Oct. 18, 1931, at age eighty-four, on a day of powerful fire and earth, as shown below.

F	E	m
F	H	d

How did good flows contribute to his success? At age fifteen (1862, RH), first half of the year, he saved a child on the rail from an oncoming train. The grateful father of the child taught him the trade of telegraphy over a few months. It became his first step toward becoming an inventor. While the "M" in his LC was still exercising its detrimental effect, the onset of the water cosmic flow of the year gave him an initial big push. To get a better job, he needed help from an additional steady, good flow.

At age seventeen (1864, TR), during LC "R," all wood and water, from his LC and the cosmos he received a double favor: he suddenly landed a telegraphy research job with Western Union. As the momentum of his water ("R") period grew, he swiftly moved to the senior research post in the firm at the age of twenty-two. What a miracle for a handicapped person with only three months of previous schooling!

The peak of his life came at the "r" period; the "r" joined the "d" in his BC to form a wood team. It was like Edison bringing an army of wood soldiers to empower his wood boss. It impressed the big boss, who rewarded him abundantly as a result. Let us see what happened during that five-year period. Below is a chronological summary of his achievements:

- Age twenty-seven (1874, TH), at LC "r," invented the quadruplex telegraph; sold patent at a great profit.
- Age twenty-eight (1875, tr), invented the electric pen.
- Age twenty-nine (1876, FR), built a new lab in New Jersey—the invention factory (the world's first at this time), his kingdom of invention.
- Age thirty-two (1879, et), invented the long-lasting light bulb, lighting up the whole world, creating a shock wave worldwide; this was his landmark invention, the peak of his inventive life. This was the result of a full wood trio among his BC "d," LC, "r," and the cosmic year "t." He got the highest reward from his most powerful wood boss. That was the zenith of his whole life.

The residual flow of the same period, with the help of the year flow of the cosmos, extended his success to a few more years. At thirty-five (1882, RF), he set up light companies in the United States and Europe.

In the other wood period, from his sixties to seventies, he won worldwide recognition and honor from both corporations and government, leading to a happy and peaceful life.

Even a top invention guru is vulnerable to the impact of cosmic flow. Edison felt and admitted the impact. His metaphysical view: "Nature is not merciful and loving but wholly merciless and indifferent. Natural law does not bend in our favor."

This is a typical life motto for a helpless self! Beware of the flow and attune to it!

Our next example is Winston Churchill.

Winston Churchill—November 30, 1874, noon, to January 24, 1965

R	M	T	T
F	F	H	H

2	12	22	32	42	52	62	72	82
t	F	f	E	e	M	m	R	r
r	R	g	T	t	W	f	F	d

He was metal self surrounded by two fire alliances that are supported by abundant yang wood, very dry. The environment is dry and blazingly hostile to the metal self. There is no other metal sign in the BC. Thus, he was a helpless self, following the lead of the fire.

The self surrendered to the dominant flow of fire, which became his protector and provider. As wood fuels the fire, empowering it, it is the second best beneficial element. To be faithful and qualified as helpless for the reward and provision, he needed to avoid metal, which empowers the self. To stay on good terms with the boss, the fire, he had to keep water away. Water and metal then become the harmful elements. Earth, being neutral, protects the fire from the water; it is a good element.

First, let us find out how water affected his life.

- Age seven to twelve, during the "r (T R)" period, his boyhood, besides being a poor student, he was very stubborn; he stuttered.
- Age seventeen to twenty-one, during the branch "R" period, he took the college entrance exam twice before he could attend college.
- In 1923 (rr), he lost a campaign but recovered and won in the beginning of 1924 (TR) when the flow of wood supported his fire.
- In 1939, starting the third year of his stem "m" period, he was the prime minister, leading the country in its struggle to resist an overwhelming invasion by Hitler.
- In 1945 (tm), after the victory, he thought he should succeed in his bid for reelection as prime minister. Instead, he lost in the year of metal, 1945 (tm).
- In June 1953 (rf), at the first half of the year, he suffered a bad stroke but won a Nobel Prize at year end.
- From age seventy-two, in the year of 1946, during the stem "R" period, he remained inactive during the entire water period after losing the 1945 election.

How did he thrive upon the onset of fire?

- Stem "F," period, age twelve to seventeen: In high school, he received high marks in English and history and also was a fencing champion.
- 1895 (td), age twenty-one: He graduated eighth among 150 students, in spite of his poor start in college.
- Stem "f" period, starting at age twenty-two: He completed military assignments for the government, published articles on battles, was hired as a war correspondent by the *Morning Star,* and, in addition to his regular assignments, published a book, *The River War* (1899, age twenty-five).
- Branch "T," fire trio: In charge of a reform committee, he succeeded in launching some of the most important reforms in British history.
- Branch "F" period: He served a second term as prime minister.
- 1953 (rf), age seventy-nine at branch "F": He won the Nobel Prize for literature.

FEEBLE/HELPLESS SELVES

Many systems have mixed energy without a leading flow; there are no definite and permanent good or damaging elements to guide the selves in decision-making. These systems don't fall into any of the above categories, making it hard for the individual to see a direction.

The most dramatic type is the very feeble self; its energy is so feeble that a person cannot function properly on one's own energy. On the other hand, the self is being dragged by some illusive helping element, being disqualified from getting help as a helpless. How do these people survive? Let us illustrate with a typical example.

John Jr. Kennedy—November 25, 1960, around midnight

M	f	f	M	
R	f	r	R	
4	14	24	34	44
E	e	M	m	R
R	g	T	t	W

The self is a yin fire born in wet month of a watery year, and in the totally dark hours. By all these flows, the yin fire cannot survive on its own, as there is not a trace of fire helping him. That is, he is totally helpless like an infant, surrendering to the protection and provision of water and metal.

After the surrender, the self will enjoy a good life of free entitlement. In reality, it translates to easy success and a good life. But there is a fundamental condition: the self has to be sincere and faithful, i.e., he is stripped of any help, with no more fire or wood signs to empower him.

Does Kennedy meet the condition? There are two more fire signs, the "f," in month stem and the day branch, and one wood sign hidden in month branch, "r." They act like a pair of body guards, tagging the self along from all fronts, giving out a clear message that the person is guarded by his trusted people, not ready to surrender. Yet the protection from such guards is very illusive; it barely functions under the overwhelming water. Under such circumstances, the self is put on hold by the boss for observation before he can be trusted.

To seek and gain trust, the self has to find a way to hide or discard the naughty signs. Since it takes great skill to accomplish the job, such as by distracting the attention of the other party, the borderline helpless are normally either stunningly beautiful or smart and alert—and it could be both, depending on the distribution and interactions of the signs in the BC and the LC.

However, such tactics serve only as emergence solutions; they are not reliable and do not go far enough to achieve a permanent impact. When they get help from LC or the cosmos to eliminate the trouble elements in their BC, they will make occasional headway. Other times, they play hide-and-seek in the changing mode of stop-and-go. Their luck swings! Some fare better than others.

Now let us check out how his life responded to the fire and wood.

- In November 1963 (rt), a wood month of a wood year, his father was assassinated.
- In 1975 (tt), a powerful wood year, his stepfather died, losing the home in Greece.
- In 1987 (ft), a fire and wood year, he resigned from his prosecutor job.
- In 1998 (ET), his magazine, *George,* suffered drying-up advertising revenues.
- On July 16, 1999 (et), an earth day, wood month and year, he died in a plane crash. A wood trio from by the t, d, and r from his BC took him to the battlefield, challenging the boss. The rebel was smashed.

His response to the water and metal flow:

- From 1960 (MR) to early 1963, a metal and water period, he was son of the president and lived a happy life in the White House.
- In 1968 (EM), age eight, a metal year at his "R" LC period, his mother remarried, under the provision of a shipping tycoon, and he had a great life in Greek islands.
- From age nineteen to twenty-three (1983 rr), a "g" period, under the influence of metal alliance, he graduated from Harvard Law School and found the prosecutor job.
- In 1996 and 1997 (FR/fg), water and metal influence, published *George* magazine, which was well supported by friends.

From the recorded events, we can see that it takes great extra flow to make great things happen. It is very challenging for beginners to interpret in terms of determining the benefiting flow in order to enhance the luck. The only way to find out is by digging into one's key life events.

Borderline cases between feeble and helpless are very common systems in modern lives among well-to-do families. Many seek help from foreign energy sources such as drugs or alcohol. We'll discuss solutions to such system in later chapters.

This chapter covers almost all self types, covering ninety-nine percent of the population. There are some exceptions that we don't see in our daily encounters. These also require a higher level of perspective for analysis.

7

Selected Bazi Examples

Equipped with the fundamental knowledge of how the system works and the procedure to identify the self types, we are ready to explore more examples. Readers who have questions about the procedure may take this opportunity to learn more from these discussions. Whether you have concerns about charting out the borderline birth composite, trouble in telling the self types, or problems in finding the truth of the four pillars, these examples offer additional guidelines and ample insight to clear up your questions.

While our goal is to expose readers to many various aspects of the reality of life by providing as many different examples as possible, our choice is determined by availability of data rather than personal preference. First, our choices must be well known enough for readers to verify the applications. Second, each example has to stand out as a unique textbook model to illustrate a theme or procedure.

Lastly, since data relating to birth hours are hard to come by, even on well-known births, they have become our first choice for convenient discussions.

We have been lucky enough to find a handful of people who are, for the most part, well-known for different reasons. We deliberately focus on the more challenging ones, since they reflect the prevalent brutal reality of life, offering rich insight and vital lessons that we can share and use. These examples are grouped into three parts.

In all cases, we use the same foolproof procedure by listing positive and negative events for readers to verify how flows impact an event. Keep in mind that the flow of the cosmos and the flow in the individual's LC interact to influence the events. Carefully note how the flows work together to create the change in our life path.

The first group is the weak self, which represents the great majority of lives worldwide—in different grades, of course. Unlike the dominant selves who succeed in having full control over what they want, or the helpless selves who prosper on the full backup of a big boss, weak selves work very hard, very often in circles, and most need help to proceed over a long journey. The fortunate among us get better help with less effort. Others go into a long struggle. Our two examples shed light on different circumstances.

WEAK SELVES

Richard Nixon—January 9, 1913, 7–9 P.M.

guard

F	M	r	R
H	T	g	R

guard mentor

9	19	29	39	49	59	69	79
T	t	F	f	E	e	M	m
T	t	W	f	F	d	M	m

The self is yang metal, metal ore. How to tell his strength? Being born in the winter, not at the right time, he therefore was not born strong. There is plenty of water to drain the metal, weakening it, preventing the yang metal to be refined into a useful tool. He is not a strong tool or a strong person. This is a weak metal self.

Fortunately, his birth month has a powerful grantor, the "g," giving him potential to grow and perform difficult tasks; the "g" is his mentor, guiding him to the right path. Fire is crucial turning the metal ore into a useful tool, i.e., making him a productive person and a high achiever.

Bottom line: fire gives him the best luck; wood, which drains the water and fuels the fire, comes next.

Water is the number one damaging element, as it potentially puts out the fire; in extreme cases, water could make a knife rusty as well.

Let us put his key life events into two groups as shown below.

Positive events

- 1946 (FH), age thirty-three, at stem F, Congress
- 1952 (RW) to 1960 (MR) age thirty-nine to forty-six, at pillar "ff," vice president
- 1968 (EM), age fifty-five, at branch "F," forming a fire trio with "H" and "T", the most fire in his life, president
- 1980 (MM), age sixty-seven, at d, meeting with national leaders overseas, at his retirement.

Negative events

- 1960 (MR), age forty-seven, a watery year, lost election to Kennedy
- 1962 (RT) to 1967, age forty-nine, at E, practiced law and traveled
- 1972 (RR), age fifty-nine, at stem "e," reelected, then Watergate
- 1974 (TT), age sixty-onc, an "e" LC, resigned in August
- 1974 to 1980, at "ed" (moist earth) period, quiet life in San Clemente

Let us start with the positive events to examine how the fire changes his life. At thirty-three (1946, FH) during the stem "F" LC, he entered the Congress, a big step forward. Both the fire in his BC and the grand cosmos worked together to form a fire alliance to sharpen the metal tool. He scored victory.

At thirty-nine, during the LC "ff," additional fire boosted his energy, and he became the vice president. The double "f" (fire) reinforced each other to make it a powerful fire pillar.

When did he become the president? At fifty-five in his branch "F" cycle, a powerful fire under proper chemical interaction put him back in power. This "F" joined the other fire signs in his BC, making the most powerful fire team available in his life; it was a fire trio, a full fire team, and it suddenly put him into the most powerful position in the world.

How did he fall a few times? As the fire dwindled in momentum at the last leg of the "f" cycle, he finished his two-term vice presidency and started to campaign against Kennedy to become the next president. He lost. Why? He campaigned in 1960 (MR), a very wet year; the water put out the meager fire from his own system. He became a rusty, useless sword.

Why did he get into the Watergate incident? First, he was out of his "F" cycle, not supported by the magic energy; second, 1972 (RR), with double water sign, was a very wet year. The following year was "rg," another wet year; he dragged on in great trouble for two more years and left the office in 1974, his LC of moist earth draining away his last trace of fire.

Amazingly, the element of water, which he dreaded most, manifested itself in the Watergate (The name of the place carries energy!) incident, which ruined his presidency.

He died in the winter (watery season for each year) of 1994 (TH) at the age of eighty-one, his metal period, empowering water.

After verifying the nature and strength of the self element, we can proceed with the analysis of the BC. One feature stands out in his BC: all water signs concentrate in his year and month pillars while all fire signs are in the day and hour pillars. Just imagine when all signs are mixing up: what would happen? There would be no usable energy as the fire and water offset each other.

By keeping each group in a separate domain, the fire can perform without obstacles. The person is therefore a well-organized person. Can our readers see why his first part of life was so difficult? The water dominated his first part of life. In his high school days, he had to travel to the wholesaler to pick up groceries and then stocked them in the family store. During his college life in Chicago, he lived in a shack, and shaved and washed in the restroom in the library.

There are some lucky stars in his BC. A guard in the day stem, a mentor in the month branch, two pairing at the branches. He was born to get protection, and received great help when he needed it. The pairing involving the mentor is especially auspicious, bringing fortunate help. All pairings indicate great personal ability to team up help. He was a born great leader.

Could the knowledge on the Bazi of President Nixon's life have helped him steer his life differently so as to avoid Watergate? Although extreme hard work and exceptional and unexpected circumstances could enhance some flow, very few can achieve big goals with weak or unfavorable energy. Improper means of forcing an issue can move part of our goal onto the road. However, it takes the right energy to keep the momentum.

He could have avoided the impeachment, but not the retirement, if he had moved with the flow to forgo the re-election!

Our next weak self example has a weaker flow to move things around; he consequently worked harder over a longer journey to achieve his goal.

Mao Zedong (Tse-Tung)—December 26, 1893 to September 9, 1976

T	**f**	**T**	**r**
W	**m**	**R**	**f**
▼	▼		▼
solitude	mentor. scholar		guard

6	**16**	**26**	**36**	**46**	**56**	**66**	**76**
r	**R**	**m**	**M**	**e**	**E**	**f**	**F**
r	**H**	**m**	**M**	**d**	**F**	**f**	**W**
		▼ mentor					

He was a yin fire born in a water year and a water month, on a metal day, well-qualified as a helpless case to enjoy an easy life with great entitlements. However, there are two "T"s flanking on both sides, empowering and protecting the self. They are powerful, standing tall and up front; the self has no way to hide and pretend to be helpless. He became a weak self under the protection in the struggle toward his goal. Making his life harder is the soaking-wet wood, giving out smoke while burning. He had a long, hard, struggling life.

Having determined the self type, we can surely determine that additional fire would be the best rescue; it evaporates the excessive water and dries the soaking wood. Dry earth comes next, as it blocks and absorbs the water. Water is the last thing he wanted. Keeping this in mind, we can properly assess his luck cycle.

Fortunately, he was born in the bright morning with a rising run, enjoying late success. Like all great leaders, he was born with a natural guard protecting from all danger and evil, and a mentor in his spouse palace guiding him to the right path. He did receive good great help from his wives and father-in-law.

His powerful grantors made him famous worldwide. For a weak self, a grantor is the most precious thing to have, and having a crucial grantor is a sure way to achieve a mark. A grantor works like a stamp to leave a mark.

He loved books, philosophy, and metaphysics, the I Ching in particular. He was sitting on a scholar star, close and intimate enough to make him a great lifelong student but too close for easy success in his career. People having a scholar star at the day branch normally marry late and succeed late in career matters. This is almost a golden rule. Test it for yourself.

The greatest drawback of his BC is the damp wood, which issues great smoke when burning. That translates into frustrations and confusion. He needed plenty of fire to dry up the wood so as to give smooth, strong fire, giving him great usable energy to conquer. Additional water and metal would worsen the situation. Since water fares as the most threatening element, yang dry earth stands as the most effective element to block it.

Let us check out his life events to verify our analysis.

Positive events:

- In 1918 (EF), at age twenty-five, his "H" period, he graduated from a normal university; he cherished the few school years.
- In 1919 (ed), year of earth and wood, he married to the daughter of his beloved and respected professor.

- In 1922 (RH), age twenty-nine, at "m" period, he became a commissioner in the Communist party in Shanghai, in charge of recruiting members.
- In 1934 (TH), age forty-one, at the stem "M" period, he found a permanent, secure home base for the party.
- In 1946 (FH), age fifty-three, at "d" period, additional earth and wood, he forcefully launched the civil war, gaining great momentum.
- In 1949 (eg), age fifty-six, at the "E" period, he won the war.
- From 1954 to 1959, age sixty-one to sixty-six, at the stem "F" period, he was chairman of the country.
- In 1972 (RR), age seventy-nine, at stem "F" period, China gained global recognition; he met with President Nixon and other national leaders.

Negative events:

- Childhood and youth prior to 1918: LC period of r, r, and R, additional water from his LC reinforcing his hardship, he stayed with a destitute family in a poor village.
- 1911 (mg), age eighteen, at stem R period, he became a soldier to earn a living.
- 1930 (MF), at the stem "M," his wife was arrested and executed by the government.
- Branch "M" (water and metal, M joined the R to form a water alliance, adding more hardship) period, he made a long, difficult journey, toiling twenty-five thousand miles from the South to Sian, a province in the northwest country side, struggling to rebuild the party.
- 1976, in a watery day of September, at the age of eighty-three, during his W (W and R to form a water alliance) period, he died.

Checking on his good events, "H," and "F" are the most outstanding signs; others are all earth. There was one exception: Chairman Mao met President Nixon in a watery year. However, the event took place in his "F" period. The accumulative momentum of fire from his LC outweighed the water from the year.

The peak of his life, being the Chairman of the country, did fall into the strongest fire period in his LC. There is one interesting feature in his action plan; the three key actions all took place in dog years: 1922, 1934, and 1946.

As a chief leader, he set off a great campaign to recruit members for the Communist Party, started the fateful journal from the Southwest to a permanent home for the party, and launched the civil war, all in a dog year. Why in a dog year? Mao was a savvy metaphysician. Dogs respond to barking instantly, creating an echoing effect; initially small crowds instantly gather enormous momentum to turn into huge gangs. On the other hand, he could have felt the effect of the dry earth and tried to take advantage of it. He followed the lunar calendars!

Interestingly, dog years have been known to produce widespread, huge demonstrations. Outstanding examples include the campus demonstrations against the Vietnam War in 1970 (MH), starting from Kent State, Ohio, spreading all over other campuses nationwide. Mao tried to make full use of the barking effect to gather momentum from the people when calling for an effective government. The result was a sweeping success!

His negative events clearly demonstrate the water and metal impact. In his early life, strong water from his LC was extinguishing the fire; he had to scramble for a livelihood in a destitute family. Water finally put out the fire in 1976 at his dragon period, when the dragon from 1976 joined the water team in his system, totally putting out the fire.

The above two examples clearly demonstrate how a weak self benefits from the grantor and the kin. For feng shui design, the goal is strengthening the self. The strategy is, however, not as simple and direct. Our priority is to protect/empower such elements rather than enhancing more of the same elements. In the case of Chairman Mao, blocking water is most crucial. That is why "H" had stood out as the most auspicious sign in his life.

HELPLESS AND FEEBLE SELVES

When the self gets too weak or very feeble like a very young child, there is no way to empower the self into becoming a productive or independent adult. The maximum empowering help that could ever appear might be just big enough to turn the person into a fumbling teenager; what can a teenager do?

The person in such circumstance is therefore better off to go to the other extreme, being stripped of the last trace of help so that he or she can be fully qualified for total protection and provision from a capable parent, like any infant. Unfortunately, the option is not up to us. In fact, even a fully qualified helpless infant (by birth energy) could be pushed into the status of a rebellious child at the onset of a new empowering flow from their luck cycles or from the external cosmic flows.

The mischievous child is suddenly disqualified as helpless. He or she then would be stripped of all the provision and protection and kicked out of the house to toil on one's own effort, which means a hard life. How does a child support himself or herself?

The following four examples illustrate different grades of helpless selves and their consequential life journeys.

Jacqueline Kennedy Onassis—July 28, 1929 to May 19, 1994

	▲guard		
m	T	m	e
d	H	d	f
▼mentor		▼mentor	▲scholar

3	13	23	33	43	53	63
R	r	T	t	F	f	E
M	m	H	r	R	g	T

The self is a tree born in late summer, the wrong time; the tree does not grow. There are four metal signs: two on the stem to trim off the branches and two hidden in the earth (H and f) to cut the roots, enfeebling the tree into an infant status, symbolically. There is not a trace of water to moisten the excessive earth, with five of them teaming up all over the tree. The enfeebled tree has to surrender to the earth and metal for survival, protection, and provision.

Her lucky elements are therefore metal and earth. As she had to be faithful to enjoy her provision, there should be no wood or water. It follows that the two "d"s post potential harm, as they could easily turn into a wood team at the onset of a branch "r" or "t."

What does the metal do to benefit her? The stem, "m," is her ruler, her husband, being powerful, up front and standing tall, flanking side by side, fighting for her attention. They make her very attractive to great men who are ready to protect and provide for her. She did have two great husbands.

Her spouse palace, the "H," is basically earth; as there are four (three hidden) more earth signs around in her BC, she was likely having multiple relationships (spouses), all great providers.

Let us check out her life events to verify our analysis and conclusions, starting with the positive ones. Here is the list:

- In 1949 (eg), at branch "m," she had the great opportunity to study in France for the next two years and learn a great language.
- In 1951 (mt), at branch "m," she graduated and had great fun touring Europe.
- In 1953 (rf), she married the future president in September (mm).
- In 1957 (fm) was the birth of her daughter.
- In 1960 (MR), was the birth of her son.
- In 1961 (mg), she became the First Lady.
- In 1968 (EM), she remarried, A. Onassis.
- From 1977 (ff) to 1978 (EF), she received a $26 million settlement from Christina Onassis.

Checking on the cosmic flows for the events, we can see how metal and earth contributed to her good luck. In 1949, at age twenty, she got a chance to gain proficiency with a prestigious foreign language. It greatly enhanced her political and marital status.

In 1951, the metal influence for the first eight to nine months offered a great growing opportunity. She married a great provider (the future president) in a metal month of a metal year; the "f" of the year flow joined the "m" in the month to form a metal alliance.

She bore two children, both in metal years, to secure her position in the Kennedy clan, and she finally became First Lady in the most powerful metal year. Being widowed for a few years, she remarried in another metal year, to another metal boss, Aristotle Onassis, her great provider. Aristotle Onassis was a dominant earth self.

As her money sign is the earth and fire, which empowers the earth, she was awarded a huge sum in the fire and earth year. All these events happened for a cosmic reason.

Her negative events were all amazingly related to water and wood. In 1952 (RW), a watery year, she broke an engagement with a broker. During her "T" LC, from 1953 to 1957, she endured great pressure from the Kennedy family as a member and in the role of a senator's wife, plus she endured continuous anxiety over her sick husband. John Kennedy endured two nearly fatal back surgeries and had a chronic disease during that period.

In 1955 (td), a wood year, she had a miscarriage. In 1963, the year of wood and water working together, she became a widow. In another watery year, January of 1973 (a metal and water month in a watery year), her stepson died in a plane crash. The death turned her husband into a broken and disillusioned person. He died shortly in Paris, in March 1975 (tt), a powerful wood year. A true helpless gets strong backup from a boss to successfully bear the hardship.

The TH pillar from 1994 acted like someone with identical and equal power, setting in to fiercely compete with the self in a tough fight; the self finally gave up. Here comes a question: Why was she widowed in a "t" year twice?

Jacqueline's system provides a uniquely interesting case on marriage. Her spouse palace is the most vulnerable spot. It is earth being penetrated by the tree on the top and subtly pierced by the hidden wood, "t," within the "d"s from both sides. Her spouse would never be comfortable in her life. It is very unstable, even in normal times.

Anytime an additional sign of either "t" or "r" shows up from the LC or the cosmos, the "d" will become a wood team, powerfully piercing the H and eventually killing the spouse. That was exactly what happened in both 1963 and 1975, and during her "r" period from age thirty-seven to forty-two, her first widowhood.

She remarried at thirty-nine in 1968 by the temporary help of metal from the cosmos; it took her couple of years to adjust to a brand new environment before she could fully merge into the marriage. To begin with, the marriage had odd arrangements, above all other concerns, and was different from a traditional marriage by definition, or another union bonded by emotional needs.

Shortly after she entered the stem "t" period, she began her widowhood. Any wood signs would function like another woman competing with her for the husband. She ended up losing, as she could not win over a wood team.

When we view the event from the point of a helpless getting help, the wood self was being empowered by the wood alliance of "td"; she began to rebel and got kicked out of the palace (the grand home of Aristotle Onassis). Since it is a super helpless BC, people in such system would never have to worry about their next meal or good shelter. She was surely compensated $26 million by his daughter on the event of her departure, even though the Greek laws prohibit foreigners from inheriting from a deceased spouse.

This is clearly a standard helpless case in which the BC does not consist of any element helping the self to rebel. The self is fully qualified as helpless. As a result, the self is open minded, flexible, observant, intuitive, pleasing, and accommodating, just like an infant. They are born to enjoy unconditional enormous entitlements, tangible or intangible. If the BC is supported by good LC in all or most of the time periods, it guarantees a good lifetime.

But as a clearly good case, Jacqueline maintained her great fortune regardless of all the mishaps. She bravely and quietly endured the enormous mishaps and hardships from both marriages and stayed until their ends so as to maintain social approval. She fulfilled the job of a good role model and lived a full life.

Our next example is mixing helpless case, the borderline helpless. In the BC, there is either some kin sign or grantor empowering the very feeble self, and the person has a tendency to rebel under some compelling circumstances—normally when additional kin or a grantor sets in to team up with the troubling energy in the BC. When rebelling, they are vulnerable to being stripped of their provision, i.e., incurring bad luck.

Due to such shaky circumstances, these individuals are always on guard and likely to play tricks to keep or gain their free provisions, trying hard to stay in or jump back into the palace, so to speak. To do so, they need to be extremely skillful to distract the watchman with their great looks or smart tricks, figuratively speaking. They are either wizardly smart or stunningly charming in order to skillfully cross the border to fulfill a goal.

As they lack the substance to maintain the energy momentum to succeed, some fail miserably, while many suffer great misfortune at some point in their lives. All have problems in their marriage/relationship, as it takes enduring courage to keep the commitment, something the borderline, vanity helpless selves do not have.

There are different grades of shaky borderline helpless. The one of Princes Diana should be one of the most interesting among them.

Princess Diana—July 1, 1961 to August 31, 1997

guard ▲			
F	**t**	**T**	**m**
H	**d**	**F** ▼	**g**
▼		popularity	
solitude		relationship	
		scholar	

2	**12**	**22**	**32**
t	**F**	**f**	**E**
d	**M**	**m**	**H**

The self was a plant born in hot summer, with a powerful sun shining upon the plant near by; there is a strong metal pillar by the year to trim and refine the plant. The environment creates a feeble plant, with fire and metal as the leading dominant elements. The self therefore surrenders to the fire and metal for protection and provision.

However, the self is not exactly helpless; there are two more wood signs (the "T" and the "t" hidden in "d") dragging its legs to surrender, making her unfaithful and unable to gain the full support and trust of her boss. In fact, these two woods signs are the key trouble spots in her system. Between the two wood signs, "T" posts the biggest threat, as it is up front and more powerful than the yin wood.

She has to deal with powerful competitor neck to neck. It could be a colleague, sibling, or another woman competing for love or attention. Since she did not work and had no competing sibling, it then became another woman competing for her husband.

As "d" would become wood when joining "r" or "t," when the interaction takes place, the self would have to fight on two fronts, with more challenges to face.

Bottom line: metal is her number one beneficial element, as it effectively chops off her competitor, other wood signs in her surroundings. Fire comes next, as it helps to curtail the wood and shines the leaves for glamour. Both wood and water are most damaging, as they empower her competitors to harm her.

Let us check out how her life events corresponding to our analysis.

Positive events:

- In 1977 (ff), age sixteen, at stem "F," LC she met the prince and they started dating.
- In February (fg) 1981 (mm), they became engaged.
- In July 1981 (mm), they married.
- In June 1982 (RH), her son was born.
- On October 23, 1991 (EH, FT, md), she took a last family trip.
- In January 1997 (mg fg), she visited Angola to campaign against landmines. In June 1997 (rg, fg), she sponsored a charity auction of her personal items and raised £4.5 million for AIDS research.
- In August 1997 (FM, fg), she visited Bosnia to campaign against landmines.

Among the happy events, the elements of metal and fire distinctively stand out. The "H," a powerful fire house, and "g," the powerful metal house, were responsible for her most glamorous events. With the summer fire and a powerful metal year, she married the prince (first in line heir to the throne) in a wedding with thirty-five thousand guests, televised globally.

During 1997 (fg), year of fire and metal, after the divorce, in spite of widely publicized affairs, she maintained her respect with the public and was invited to host public charity functions. Surprisingly, she succeeded in raising millions from these functions.

Negative events:

- In 1967 (fd), at six, the "t" period, additional wood stripped her parental love away.
- In 1987 (ft), at twenty-six, "t" and "d" made a wood team to cause loss and suffering, and unofficial separation. Prince Charles moved out to live with the other woman.
- On December 9, 1992 (RR month in RM year), at thirty-one, the last year of her "m" period, an official separation was ordered by the Queen.
- In 1994 (TH, June, November), Prince Charles confessed to adultery and, in a published book, admitted marrying Diana to please his father.
- In November 1994 (TH), a book exposed the love affair of Diana with James Hewitt, her riding trainer.
- In November 1995 (tr), in a televised interview, Diana admitted being unfaithful to her husband.
- On August 28, 1996 (FM month in a FR year), she was divorced.
- On August 31, 1997, she died at midnight, R hour, traveling north in a tunnel over the sea.

Mixing helpless selves have a strong sense of entitlements, occasional illusions, and a tendency to rebel (going across the line). Princess Diana's willful, unpredictable behaviors and unsteady emotional changes truly reflect the unstable mixing energy of her Bazi, the dramatic swings of a mixing helpless life.

As the wife of a prince, she was supposed to respect all decisions from the prince and obey all orders from the royal higher-ups, the Queen in particular. She was awarded all the royal glamour and privilege, rising from the common citizen to the high title without effort of her own. There is a trade-off!

However, she was trying to create an impossible combination: pursuing the right of a common citizen and keeping the royal privileges at the same time. The Queen (her cosmic boss) had to keep her out of the palace, even doing so at a great price. By fighting with the boss, Princess Diana paid a price as well.

While Princess Diana's system interestingly shows a physical boss in reality, many borderline individuals just show some self-inflicted disasters, following the onset of bad flow.

Could she have lived her life differently? She died in 1997 at age thirty-six, at the end of the "E" period, her money sign, when the siblings were battling brutally for the big money. She was indeed wrestling fiercely and succeeded in amassing a huge fortune from both the Prince and the Queen. But she lost her life by holding on to the big dole, too big and slippery for her feeble arms and too tempting to the robbers! The other, stronger sibling ("T" in her BC, standing neck to neck) hit her hard to get it back. She lost in helpless defense!

There was no other reason for her to die so soon! That was a good year. The five years of "H" constitute the best period in her life; the "H" would join the F in her BC to make fire alliance, burning up her biggest enemy, "T," giving her at least of five years of great life. The following five years of "e" would also be auspicious, as they would pair up the "T," her biggest trouble spot.

She needed the wisdom and endurance to tide over the sibling rivalry period. And that was something she had never tried to acquire all her life!

Adolf Hitler—April 20, 1889, 6:30 p.m. to April 30, 1945

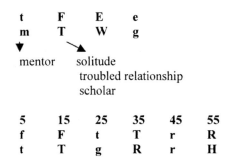

t	**F**	**E**	**e**
m	**T**	**W**	**g**
▼	↘		
mentor	solitude troubled relationship scholar		

5	**15**	**25**	**35**	**45**	**55**
f	**F**	**t**	**T**	**r**	**R**
t	**T**	**g**	**R**	**r**	**H**

Hitler was a yang fire born in the year and month of powerful earth, which drains and enfeebles fire energy; by the year and month pillars, he was qualified as a helpless fire surrendering to the lead of earth, for easy success and entitlement.

But that is only part of the story. The system is very much mixed. First, he was sitting on a sign containing fire, wood, and earth. Second, there is a wood standing tall to challenge the dominance of the earth and empowering the fire as well. He is not to be trusted and is subject to frequent punishment, i.e., a sweet and sour life with frequent surprises, some very nasty.

Like all borderline helpless selves, he aimed high and tried to climb high but always needed help to do so. The helpless self could not succeed on its own. With the troublesome elements dragging his feet to claim his entitlements, he was frequently punished for being dishonest or unfaithful. His twenty-five years of fire and wood put him into many tortured periods.

Symbolically, as a child, his father functioned as his boss; being a poor student and a disobedient child, he was frequently beaten or whipped by his father. Often, he stood silently counting the whipping while his mother was sadly hiding.

On the other hand, like a wizardly smart borderline helpless, he had an amazingly eloquent oratorical talent, an impossible product from a poor student with limited schooling. His speech could swing the most powerful and smartest people to his side and move a big crowd to his calling. It finally landed him the top job.

Bottom line: his good element is earth, the source of all his provision, wealth, and fame; as wood challenges the dominant earth, it is the number one detrimental element. Fire, which empowers the self, disqualifying his helpless status, comes next. Water, which clears all other fire to compete with him, leading him to the helpless path, is another good element.

Let us check on his good life events. All the earth signs brought him wealth, fame, and position. The heavy dose of water from the cosmos and his LC worked together to land him the Chancellor position; it cleared out the last trace of the extra fire, polishing him as a fully helpless, to be trusted for great fortune.

Positive events:

- In 1913 (rg), he received a small inheritance from an aunt.
- In 1918 (EF), he received an award of honor for bravery in military service.
- In July 1919 (ed), he got a job as a police spy.
- In July 1921, at age thirty-two, at "g" period, he became chairman of the German Workers' Party.
- In late December 1924 ("fg" month), he was released from prison.
- In 1933 (rm), at age forty-four, at branch "R" period, he became Chancellor of Germany.

Now let us check on his negative and see how fire and wood impacted his life. Yin wood seemed to be the most detrimental. It took away his bread provider at age fourteen and his life at fifty-six. Other times, it sent him to prison and brought him bodily injuries.

The powerful yang wood in 1923 did not do much harm, because it was associated with powerful water on the same pillars.

Fire comes next, and it took away his support and freedom. Fire acts mainly as a competitor, diminishing his support and resources.

Negative Events:

- He was a poor student and tortured by his father.
- In 1903 (rt) at fourteen, the branch "t" period, his father died.
- In 1907 (fd), at seventeen, fire year in his "F" period, his mother died.
- In 1916 (FW), twenty-seven, at stem "t" period, he was wounded in the left thigh.
- On October 15, 1918 (RH, td, EF), wood day in a fire year, he was temporarily blinded by a gas attack in the military service.
- In November 1923 ("rr" month in an "rr" year, very powerful wood flow), hiding from arrest, he contemplated suicide.
- On April 1, 1924 (ft, TR a fire and wood month in a wood year), he was sentenced to prison for five years.
- On April 30, 1945 (et, ef, tm), heavy wood flow, he committed suicide.

We can see that the borderline helpless could be awarded with enormous great fortune, but it always comes with a catch and is never long in duration. They are always treading on a string. The outcome of misfortune varies with the individuals and is something unpredictable. One thing we know for sure: the stunning beauty or talent comes with great price, which could cost our lives. What is the solution? We'll elaborate in the next chapter.

Christopher Reeve—September 25, 1952 to October 10, 2004

?	T	e	R
?	H	m	W
		↓Popularity	

4	14	24	34	44
M	m	R	r	T
H	r	R	g	T

Christopher Reeve was a tree born in the most powerful metal month. Being supported and empowered by moist earth on the stem and some more moist earth from the "W" nearby, this metal, "m," is super powerful. It has almost full power over the tree.

This tree is further enfeebled by hot earth and some more metal underneath, hurting the root, depriving the tree of growth. The tree is therefore being controlled by the metal on all fronts and prevented from growing.

However, there is a little drawback from the water (R) in the year pillar. As a grantor to a tree, it is trying to empower the tree, with the potential to disqualify its helpless status. How far could the damage go? Fortunately, water, "R," at the year stem is blocked by the "e" from reaching the tree. The system makes it a shaky helpless case.

Like other helpless selves, he was born to enjoy easy great fame and wealth. There are conditions, of course; he has to be faithful to the metal, stripping himself from the support of water and wood. He should never challenge his boss by playing with fire, as it would hurt the metal.

In the Meng system, the horse was classified as the true fire (branch F) and the most powerful fire among all fire signs. Interestingly, Reeve happened to be allergic to horses. He excelled in many sports but not in horseback riding.

However, unaware of the impact of natural laws and cosmic flows, he was adamant about meeting the challenge. He sought medical help to cure the allergy and expended a great effort to practice riding horses, thereby planting the seed of his fatal misfortune.

Any wood sign alone, or wood teams in any form, would create trouble or disaster, depending on the magnitude and momentum in its onset, as it directly teams up with the tree self to challenge the metal.

Among the metal signs, "g" and "f" are the most auspicious, as they pair up with the "m" in his BC to form a metal alliance. Below are his life events to verify our analysis.

Let us start with the good ones.

He was born to wealthy and caring parents, excelled both in academics and sports before eighteen, and was accepted by many great colleges during the metal periods. He selected Cornell. Within this great period, the few metal years fared as the best and most memorable.

But as soon as he entered college, he was torn between a passion for acting and the obligation to focus on academic subjects. He was never at peace; acting had always been his calling, but he worried about social disapproval in doing so. That was the water and wood period of "r." He tried to rebel.

Immediately after graduation, from age twenty-four to thirty-eight, he entered fifteen years of water periods. He actually rebelled by starting his acting career. But he was never happy, fumbling along without a clear direction, traveling over long distances to make films, and was barely happy with the production. His few great films happened to be produced in metal years. The prominent one was shot in May 1979, taking place in a metal month of an earth year where the earth and metal working together reinforcing the result.

The peak of his life occurred in the "g" period at the age of thirty-nine; the "g" paired up to the "m" in his BC to form a powerful metal team. He produced the best film in 1992, at age forty, a metal year in a metal period; it was nominated for eight awards. Two years later, he became the president of the Creative Coalition, urged by his associates to run for Congress.

Below is a summary of his positive life events, showing how the metal boss was rewarding him.

Positive events:

- Born to wealthy, well-educated, and capable parents, he was well loved and properly cared for.
- In childhood (in LC of MH), he excelled in sports and class work.
- In 1961(mg), age nine, he found true passion (to act).
- In 1968 (EM), he first acted in a play.
- In 1970 (MH), with many offers from prestigious universities, he entered Cornell.
- In 1971 (mr), he toured France, a good learning experience.
- In 1973 (rg), he was selected to study in the prestigious Juilliard Advanced Program.
- In May 1979 (ef month of ed year), he shot his favorite film, "Somewhere in Time."

- In 1992 (RM), at age forty, at LC "g," one of his films, "The Remains of the Day," was nominated for eight academy awards.
- In 1994 (TH), at age forty-two, at "g" period, he became co-president of the Creative Coalition and was encouraged to run for Congress.

How did water and wood impact his life? Let us check on his negative events. As the bad impact of our damaging elements would not show much during our good luck cycle, we don't find significant incidences of such impact during his metal LC periods. It showed during his water period, when water joined the attack.

In the powerful year of wood in 1975 (tt), he fainted on stage after a long term (over months) of malnutrition and exhaustion; his bad diet habit started in 1974 (TT), another powerful wood year. Water, acting alone, does not create direct immediate impact; it just created tiring and not so fruitful work.

A powerful wood flow proved most fatal. In the powerful wood year of 1995 (tr), he started to rebel by aggressively practicing horseback riding to prepare for an equestrian event, making a show. In the metal month of May (mf), while the metal boss was ruling, he challenged his metal boss on a fire day (EF) with a galloping fire (F, horse). To his surprise, the horse suddenly stopped, resulting in a force that threw him off, paralyzing him from the head down.

A story stated that a rabbit suddenly spooked the horse. The rabbit is the branch "t," the most powerful wood sign. In any event, we can see how the wood, and fire orchestrated together to create the fateful event!

Negative events:

- In 1975 (tt), at age twenty-three, he fainted onstage from exhaustion and malnutrition.
- From age twenty-four to thirty-eight, periods branch "r," stem "R," and branch "R," struggling to start an acting career, he traveled frequently, over long distances, to produce films.
- On May 27, 1995 (fire day EF, metal month mf in a powerful wood year tr), he was paralyzed.

Could he have avoided the fate of the moment? He got ten years of a powerful wood period starting age forty-four, shortly after his fall; the wood flow would most likely make him rebel violently, leading to some long-term, big disaster or a long, unhappy life. Without the horseback riding, he could have avoided the accident, even though he definitely would have been punished in some other ways. It could be poor health or an unhappy life.

In the ancient Chinese wisdom, one can tide over a bad time or a bad fate by voluntarily going through a planned self-punishment regimen. The practice could include veggie dieting, vigorous exercising, studying difficult books, and engaging in heavy, meaningful charity work. It has worked out fine for many. For young children under such circumstances, caring, knowledgeable parents would send them to a monastery for temporary seclusion to endure some hardship.

The I Ching wisdom consistently warns against pushing to the limit and preaches about appreciation of every little blessing in our possession. While he already excelled and had so much fun in performing many different sports, there was no point for him to ignore his health warning—the allergy to horses. Without the horseback riding, he could have avoided the accident. Playing with fire is his number one forbidden act!

DISTORTED SYSTEMS

Our next two illustrations are extreme mixing case of severely distorted energy. It is common among alcoholics, drug users, and chronic mental patients. The person is in a lifelong or chronic low energy state without the provisions and guidance of a boss like the helpless cases. As they cannot function on low energy to make a living or fulfill a goal, they seek illusive help or conduct illusive acts for self-satisfaction.

Cary Stayner—August 13, 1961

?	E	F	m
	T	M	g
	▼Solitude		▼
	Anxiety		mentor
	mobility		

1	**11**	**21**	**31**	**41**
t	**T**	**r**	**R**	**m**
d	**F**	**f**	**W**	**t**

Speculative explanations abound on the behaviors of Cary Stayner, the serial killer of Yosemite Park in year of 1999. The Meng offers a different set of perspectives.

According to the first edition of the newspaper of April 1999, Cary Stayner was born on August 12. A later version on the Internet shows the day as August 13. He could have been born at midnight on August 12, close enough to August 13. Regardless of the day discrepancy, my analysis on both birth data shows similar truth in the Meng. Since it is the data on prevalent records, we use August 13 as the day.

Being born as the yang earth born in the powerful metal year and a metal month, the earth is highly disintegrated by the infiltration of metal. It is so much loosened up that it becomes almost functionless. In addition, the earth is being curtailed by wood underneath. Symbolically, the self is like an infant, under the total care of the parent. The person therefore enjoys very easy great success and provisions without effort on his own. Again, there are conditions: there should be no other earth or fire to support the self.

Unfortunately, a fire (F) is empowering him on the stem, and another "E" is hidden on the branch "T," performing similar functions. The seemingly helpless earth slowly bounces back as a feeble rebellious child or teenager in different occasions, losing his entitlements, support and guidance from a provider. With limited energy, he fumbled along, doing whatever comes his way.

Individuals in this system have low ability and get no respect from others. They have limited resources to function and are socially restricted. Stayner needed additional metal or water from the LC or the cosmos to eliminate the extra trace of earth and fire to win back the support from the metal boss.

Additional earth or fire would push him to the illusion of empowerment; the self would rebel on illusion and fantasy, doing bizarre acts. His life events speak for our analysis and conclusion.

Positive events:

- In 1968 (EM), second half of the year, age seven at the "t" period, he was a great cartoonist.
- In 1972 (RR), age eleven at "T" period, he was a gifted student.

- In September 2000 (tm month in an MW year), age thirty-nine at "W," a judge changed his death sentence to life in prison without parole.

He became a great cartoonist in 1968 (EM) at age seven. The metal flow from the cosmos during the second half of the year further disintegrated the earth, turning him into a helpless earth; he gained the trust of the metal boss, who rewarded him by rallying behind him, imposing talent into his hands, pushing him into fame.

In 1972 (RR), great water extinguished the fire in his BC and diluted the earth into useless mud. He also became helpless for the year. His helpless status earned him the trust and the backing glamour from the boss.

In a metal month of 2000, a powerful metal year, the judge acted to his favor, changed his death sentence to life prison without parole. Without the flow to render him into an obedient child to admit his crime to show repentance, it would not happen. He was given the death sentence in the early part of the same year in an earth day of the earth month (see record below on negative events). All along, we can clearly see how the enfeebling elements enhanced his life.

Now let find out how additional earth and fire pushed him to the edge.

Negative events:

- His brother was kidnapped, causing grief in his early teens at his LC, "F" period.
- In his late twenties, at "f," he smoked marijuana.
- In 1977 (ff), he stripped in front of a girl.
- In 1989 (ef), age twenty-seven at an "f" period, his brother Steve died.
- In 1990 (md), age twenty-eight at "f," his uncle was shot.
- In 1999 (et), February (FT), being laid off in April (EW), he killed four people.
- On February 11, 2000 (er day in ET of MW year), he was sentenced to death.

At the onset of additional of fire or earth, he incurred loss or illusions. During the fire ("f") period, he and both his parents grieved over the disappearance of his younger brother. Another fire from the cosmos in 1977 (ff) created fantasy for him; he rebelled and stripped in front of a girl.

During his earth and fire ("f" contains E, F, and M) period, in an earth year, his brother died, leaving him with a few years of grieving. His uncle living with him died in the same earth period in a different year. It was suspected that he could have shot him out of distress/illusion.

In 1999, his doomed fateful year, he was laid off in the "F" month and killed four women in separate incidences, all in April, a powerful "E" month. However, he was not arrested until the hot month July of powerful earth flow.

He received a death sentence on an earth day (er) of an earth month (ET). The same sentence was changed to life imprisonment in a metal month in the same year.

Stayner's system is a typical low-energy system but not low enough to be qualified as a helpless to enjoy good life. Although some can enjoy some brief moments of entitlement and good life under special conditions when all flows from different sources orchestrated to his big favor, most aimlessly struggle all their lives. Their low energy allows them to perform only some very simple tasks.

They are incapable of making sound decisions, yet they are not disabled or mentally retarded to qualify for assistance. The relatively capable and resourceful among them retreat to the illusive world of drugs and alcohol; some become sex addicts. All are unhappy. What do we do with this group of people who fell into the cracks? We will elaborate on the solutions in the next chapter.

The next example delivers a special theme on how certain distorted energy constantly affects some behaviors, regardless of the self type.

Ted Kaczynski—May 22, 1942

?	t	t	R
?	r	f	F ▼ scholar troubled relationship

5	15	25	35	45	55	65
F	f	E	e	M	m	R
F	d	M	m	H	r	R

The puzzling, globally shocking story of Ted Kaczynski, known as the Unabomer, happens to be a textbook case in the Meng system. How a hidden underground metal flow in his energy system destroyed a great mathematician!

He is a yin wood, a plant, born in the summer, with little water sharing among three wood signs. He was fortunate enough to have some water underneath. However, branch "r" is being constantly clashed with the "f" nearby, stripping off his support and undermining his roots. There is metal hidden in the "f," serving as a powerful knife; when united with other metal signs, the empowering metal could be fatal to a plant, as it is constantly cutting off its roots.

He led a very insecure life, constantly apprehensive about being rootless. He had a passion for preserving nature, especially trees and plants. Stories indicated that he became furious when a patch of wood was being cleared for housing development in Chicago.

What would ease his life is having a big fire to melt down the metal. It would keep his roots growing to support the plant, giving him a stable life. Sunlight would also add shine to the leaves of the plant, translating to glamour and fame. It was no wonder that, during the great fire period of "FF," he skipped two grades and graduated from high school at sixteen.

His fire momentum declined during the yin fire period of "fd"; he graduated from Harvard (BA) and took his Ph.D. in mathematics from Michigan at twenty-five, not showing any distinction throughout his college life.

A twenty-five, he entered the "E" LC period. While his own fire had dwindled down to the last trace, fire from the year 1967 (fd) offered him a lift. He got a teaching post at U.C. Berkeley. However, without the support of additional fire, the plant began to fade, and he quit in 1969 (em) at age twenty-seven.

The "m" from the year cosmic flow joined the "f" in his BC to form a strong metal alliance, speeding up the cutting effort on his roots. Without the anchoring support of roots, he lost his foothold on livelihood, figuratively speaking. It began his long-lasting metal-torturing life!

By cosmic flow, his official metal period lingered from age thirty to fifty-four, with the peak falling from age forty to forty-four. As you can see from his LC pillars, the metal period started from branch "M" to branch "H," with branch "m" as the peak. By definition, branch "m" is the most powerful metal sign. The "H" included as a damaging sign might require some explanation. It has great heat and sharp metal inside; both damage the roots.

He felt the advancing embedding root-cutting pain after half a dozen years. Being intuitive, he illusively sensed the pain source and probably identified it as metal. As the nonstop, torturing pain finally created illusions in his mentality, he found explosives as an elusive solution to get rid of the metal, blasting it off into pieces. Being a logical mathematician, he ran through a chain formula of elusive analysis, involving other imaginative innocent individuals into the interactions for his misfortune.

What are the grounds for our assumption? From 1978 (age thirty-six) to 1995 (age fifty-three), he mailed out sixteen bombs in seventeen years. Keep in mind that saving up the money to purchase the materials, making the bombs as an amateur without the right tools, and mailing them out would take tremendous effort and resources for a jobless, destitute person in an isolated environment. Targeting recipients for the bomb is another long and tedious process. Each operation serves as a procedure to release his enduring embedded pain, a rewarding endeavor; the total process for each mailing might take a few months.

The mailing date and the recipient of each mailed bomb were all documented. The table below listed the explosion date of the package. While the explosion dates do not necessarily reflect the mental state of the sender, the mailing dates should give us some clues. As we don't have the mailing dates on public record, we allow five to seven days for the package delivery.

Explosion Date	**Flow by year, month, day**	**Day flows prior to explosion**
May 25-1978 Ill.	EF, ff, fr	RF, **mf**, MW (5/20,19, 18)
May 9-1979 Chicago	ed, ef, FR	**md, MF**, ef (5/4, 3, 2)
Nov 15-1979 Chicago	ed, TH, FH	**mf, MW**, et (11/10, 9, 8)
Jun 10-1980 Utah	MM, mf, TT	**em, EM**, fd (6/5, 4, 3)
Oct 8-1981 Tennessee	mm, EH, ed	TT, **rg**, RR (10/3, 2, 1)
May 5-1982 Tennessee	RH, tf, ER	rd, RF, **mf** (4/30, 29, 28)
Jul 2-1982 Berkeley	RH, FF, FH	**mf, MW**, et (6/ 27, 26, 25)
May 15-1985 Berkeley	tg, MW, TT	er, EH, **fm** (4/30, 29, 28)
Jun 13,1985 WA state	tg, mf, rd	ET,**fg**, FR(6/8, 7, 6)
Nov 15-1985 Michigan	tg, fr, EF	**rg**, RR, **mr**(11/10, 9, 8)
Dec 11-1985 SAC, CA	tg, fr, TM	et, ET, **fg** (12/ 6, 5, 4)
Feb 20-1987 Utah	ft, RT, MR	td, TF, **rf** (2/15, 14, 13)
June 22-1993 Calif	rm, EF,TH	**ef**, EW, **ft** (6/17, 16, 15)
Jun 24-1993 Yale U.	rm, EF, FR	**md**, MF, **ef** (6/19, 18, 17)
Dec 10-1994 NJ	TH, FR, MF	**tg**, TR, rr (12/5, 4, 3)
Apr 24-1995 SAC, CA	tr, MW, tm	**MW**, et, ET (4/19,18,17)

Table of Explosion Dates

The dominant cosmic flow of the explosion day tells us the cosmic flow at work for the year and the month, while the flow of the few days prior to the action adds more light on the total energy being at work in the sender's mind for the operation. We check out the cosmic flows for those days from the calendars. All the timely cosmic flows are listed in columns two and three.

For example, in the above table, on the row of May 25, 1978, the year is EF and month flow is ff, while the day flow is fr; however, we don't use the explosion day (mail arrival day) flow, as it does not reflect the state of mind of the sender. Instead, we use one of the three days in column three. They represent the cosmic flows for the fifth, sixth, and the seventh days prior to the explosions—the possible mailing days, the days of great stress from the metal-inflicted pain on the sender. These potential days are in the order RF, mf, and MW, as indicated in column three.

To read the cosmic flow, we need some explanation. Among the metal signs, "m" stands as number one in strength for both stems and branches, and branch "g" the second, with branches

"H" and "f" the third runner-up. Let us count the periods with metal flows, starting with the year. Eleven incidents occurred in metal years and nine in the metal months. Among the potential mailing days, the influence of metal clearly stands out.

Further analysis of the data tells a more revealing story of the metal at work. Among the seventeen years of the bomb-mailing period, half of the bombs mailed out in the few years from 1981 to 1985, i.e., a quarter of the years got half of the bomb explosions. What made it so phenomenal? That period fell into his branch "m" from age thirty-nine to forty-three, the most powerful metal period in his whole life.

Within the five years of the "m" period, half of the eight incidences fell into one single year of 1985. It was the "tg" year within the "m" period, joining the "f" in his BC, making a full score of a metal trio, the most powerful metal underground. He was desperately pained!

Years 1983 (rr) and 1984 (TR) within the heavy "m" period had no bombs mailed out. Why? There were two possible reasons: (1) powerful water and wood empowered him, giving him more energy to endure the hardship, and (2) water also drains and weakens the power of metal.

Interestingly, from 1987 to 1993, there was not a single explosion in a long period of five years. That period fell into his stem "M" period. Metal signs on the stems represent metal flow above ground; unlike the branch metal, which cuts the roots, it only trims the overgrown tree branches, functioning as refinement. It therefore causes no enduring and permanent pain. On the other hand, the stem "M" is the natural ruler for a yin wood self, and it naturally guides/controls the self from misbehaving.

Can feng shui help to avert his destiny, knowing the impact of metal and the course of his metal cycle? If he stayed away from the metal-rich Montana and resided in the woods by a riverside and surrounded himself with floral and water color beddings and clothing, it would have changed his hardship.

However, feng shui starts from the mind of the individual. He needs to believe in the cosmic flows and be willing to attune to it. It is easier to plant something in the mind of a young child. For a high professional with a firm mindset against the superstition of metaphysics, it does not work.

He was arrested on April (mt) 3 (MF), 1996 (FR), when the rat clashed into the horse; being born as a horse, it was a year of mishaps. Both the month and day were dominated with metal as well.

Starting at age fifty-five, at the stem "m" period, he served a jail term. He was sentenced in 1998 at fifty-six, but he has been locked up since he was arrested. This surface metal could mean metal bar. He was well provided with shelter and food, living in peace, and there is no more underground metal to undermine his life.

8

Sailing with the Flow

As a product of cosmic flows, surviving between the heaven and the earth, what do we do to maximize our well-being as human beings?

We cannot change the natural cycle of the cosmic flows; we have no choice of birthdays, our parents, our DNA, our siblings, or any other relatives clinging to our lives. Given the knowledge and means to understand our destiny, we cannot reverse a bad course. This is the brutal natural reality, a golden rule in metaphysics, a proven set record from our predecessors. What are our options?

Our destiny is preset like the genes we inherited; the Almighty has a niche for everyone to keep the world in proper order. However, two areas are left open for our set niche: how we perform our role and how to get there. Some courses leading to the destination are certainly less painful, while some logistic means of getting there are more efficient, resulting in a happier life!

While the options are wide open, they are boiled down to two approaches:

Feng Shui Design

All design starts with a good knowledge of our cosmic energy composition as indicated from our Bazi.

The cosmic truth is: every human and everything in the cosmos is defined by cosmic flows and carries the energy; oceans and rivers carry water flow; trees (fabric and books included), wood; all forms of heat, fire, all minerals, metal; etc. Every person carries a dominant flow of the five elements; there are fire persons, water persons, earth persons, etc. All these flows can be harnessed to enhance our energy.

We can harness water flow by living on the waterfront, using water décor, water color at home and in the workplace, or by associating the water persons. I have seen the luck of wood deficient people surge by living close to a forest, a sick person (a feeble earth person) regaining health by living on a mountain. Even a place or street named after a mountain or hill has shown some improvement.

A mine or steel factory certainly generates metal energy; a hot region gives more fire energy. Holistic energy therapy goes far and beyond, including career, hobby, diet, wardrobe, bedding, art forms, etc. The list can be very creative and endless!

Setting up an action table by flows in the lunar calendar, capitalizing on a good flow day for optimal actions, adds a crucial touch to a feng shui design!

There are some other elaborate systems tracking the move of cosmic energy besides the lunar calendars. They are documented in feng shui literature. Each belongs to a separate field and offers different functions. They all take effort to learn and practice. It is worth our effort to explore.

PRACTICING NATURAL LAWS

Feng shui design only applies to systems with usable energy that could be strong enough to interact with a foreign energy. The very feeble or the severely distorted systems do not have usable energy; there is no leading flow to guide the person. The very feeble get into depression easily.

Distorted energy shows up as birth defects at various levels, mostly in the mental state. Many have limited vision, unable to coordinate details. Under social pressure, some victims import foreign energy, resorting to the stimulus of drugs or alcohol.

The best option for these systems is practicing natural laws; picking the right attitudes. Over the years, I have noticed how attitude impacts lives. Due to environmental quality, people in the Orient should encounter more low-energy systems. We would expect more drug users, alcoholics, and mental problems. Instead, there are just more patient, content workers.

Social philosophy that values hard work, discipline, and self contentment encourages individuals to best use their natural endowments. Many who can't afford or were unable to succeed in their formal education readily pick up a vigorous marketable apprenticeship early on. They all seem to adapt to the COSMIC INJUSTICE naturally!

By vigorously devoting themselves to the same task, people are gathering a consistent harmonious energy, making it their leading life force. Those who have picked the right career to complement their energy from an early start can reap even more benefit as they move along! I have seen a fire-deficient person prosper as an electrician. For the same reason, carpentry would benefit a wood-deficient person. Their self-confidence in turn activates their psychic energy to further invigorate the system.

Good functional attitudes are indeed natural laws. Studies over the world have repeatedly concluded that children who are coached on good values turn out to be happier and more responsible and productive adults. Working hard alone does not guarantee success. In fact, many who fail in life work harder than those who succeed. It is a consistently right approach that finally leads us to success, putting us on the natural course and moving with the infallible natural fabric.

Wise and successful people practice natural laws, e.g., Plato, Isaac Newton, Thomas Edison, and Lao Tzu. Where do we find natural laws? Natural science, history, philosophy, and the Bible are all good sources of natural laws. Being close to nature keeps us in touch with natural laws.

While some were born to embrace natural laws without learning, many pick up a few haphazardly. We can all learn by studying from right sources. Knowledgeable people have concluded that I Ching (Book of Change) has the most complete collection of natural laws. It is the only document to have classified such laws into sixty-four categories, each addressing an independent theme covering social, political, and economic issues. Each theme is a hexagram.

While there are countless versions of I Ching publications worldwide, these laws are only clearly listed by each hexagram in a new book of mine, a breakthrough in I Ching: *Succeed Naturally, the I Ching Way.* While these laws might take further refinement to serve the public, they are a good start, leading us to the proper source of natural laws.

Appendix

Lunar Calendars

Reading the Lunar Calendars

Each page of the appendix represents one lunar calendar year. The cosmic flow of each year, with its cosmic animal, is listed at the top. The twelve lunar months, with their cosmic flows, appear in the first row. Each lunar month can be thirty or twenty-nine days, as indicated in the month columns; the numeric order of these days is listed in the column: "Day of Mon" (Mon for month), between the columns of lunar June and July.

The corresponding months and days in the Western calendar are listed in each month column with the cosmic flow for each day.

For instance, on the calendar for 1965, lunar January 1 is February 2 in the Western calendar, and the cosmic flow for the day is "fr."

Climate Dividers

There are twelve climate dividers in each lunar year, one falling into each month, indicating significant climatic change between the two adjacent month periods. These are listed in the second row, with a preceding number indicating the initial day of the new climatic period in that lunar month.

For instance, in 1965, the first climatic divider is Spring. It falls on lunar January 3 as indicated by its preceding number (February 4 on Western calendar). The beginning time for the new flow to change is indicated in the third row.

As a result of lunar influence, the beginning or ending climate divider of one particular year could fall into the preceding or the following year, resulting in one year with thirteen dividers, and the other, eleven. Years with two Springs are favorable years for weddings and some other celebrations.

Since some months have twenty-nine days, and no month has more than thirty days, there are fewer than 365 days in any given year. These missing days add up to one month every three years. The additional month is added to the third year, making it a thirteen-month year. This additional month is called leap month.

For instance, 1933 has two months of lunar May; the second May is an extension of the first May, and it shares the same cosmic flow. It can be treated as the same month, with its length doubled.

In figuring out luck cycle, the repeating month is treated as an extension of the previous month; its cosmic pillar is used only once. There is no other change in the procedure. If a birthday falls into the leap month, use the cosmic pillar of the preceding month as the month pillar.

Readers having doubts about working out the BC or LC on the borderline birthdays can gain insight and guidance from the examples in the book.

1920 MM MONKEY

JAN ET	FEB et	MAR MW	APR mf	MAY RF	JUN rd	DAY OF MON	JUL TM	AUG tm	SEP FH	OCT fr	NOV ER	DEC eg
16 WARM	17 CLEAR	18 SUMMER	20 GRAIN	22 HEAT	24 FALL		26 DEW	27 C DEW	28 WINTER	28 SNOW	28 CHILL	27 SPRING
4:51	10:15	4:12	9:03	19:19	5:29		7:27	23:33	1:05	17:31	4:34	16:21
2 20 EM	3 20 fg	4 19 fd	5 18 FR	6 16 tf	7 16 tr	1	8 14 TW	9 12 rm	10 12 rt	11 11 rm	12 10 RT	1 9 RM
2 21 em	3 21 ET	4 20 EM	5 19 fg	6 17 FF	7 17 FR	2	8 15 tf	9 13 TH	10 13 TW	11 12 TH	12 11 rt	1 10 rm
2 22 MH	3 22 et	4 21 em	5 20 ET	6 18 fd	7 18 fg	3	8 16 FF	9 14 tr	10 14 tf	11 13 tr	12 12 TW	1 11 TH
2 23 mr	3 23 MW	4 22 MH	5 21 et	6 19 EM	7 19 ET	4	8 17 fd	9 15 FR	10 15 FF	11 14 FR	12 13 tf	1 12 tr
2 24 RR	3 24 mf	4 23 mr	5 22 MW	6 20 em	7 20 et	5	8 18 EM	9 16 fg	10 16 fd	11 15 fg	12 14 FF	1 13 FR
2 25 rg	3 25 RF	4 24 RR	5 23 mf	6 21 MH	7 21 MW	6	8 19 em	9 17 ET	10 17 EM	11 16 ET	12 15 fd	1 14 fg
2 26 TT	3 26 rd	4 25 rg	5 24 RF	6 22 mr	7 22 mf	7	8 20 MH	9 18 et	10 18 em	11 17 et	12 16 EM	1 15 ET
2 27 tt	3 27 TM	4 26 TT	5 25 rd	6 23 RR	7 23 RF	8	8 21 mr	9 19 MW	10 19 MH	11 18 MW	12 17 em	1 16 et
2 28 FW	3 28 tm	4 27 tt	5 26 TM	6 24 rg	7 24 rd	9	8 22 RR	9 20 mf	10 20 mr	11 19 mf	12 18 MH	1 17 MW
2 29 ff	3 29 FH	4 28 FW	5 27 tm	6 25 TT	7 25 TM	10	8 23 rg	9 21 RF	10 21 RR	11 20 RF	12 19 mr	1 18 mf
3 1 EF	3 30 fr	4 29 ff	5 28 FH	6 26 tt	7 26 tm	11	8 24 TT	9 22 rd	10 22 rg	11 21 rd	12 20 RR	1 19 RF
3 2 ed	3 31 ER	4 30 EF	5 29 fr	6 27 FW	7 27 FH	12	8 25 tt	9 23 TM	10 23 TT	11 22 TM	12 21 rg	1 20 rd
3 3 MM	4 1 eg	5 1 ed	5 30 ER	6 28 ff	7 28 fr	13	8 26 FW	9 24 tm	10 24 tt	11 23 tm	12 22 TT	1 21 TM
3 4 mm	4 2 MT	5 2 MM	5 31 eg	6 29 EF	7 29 ER	14	8 27 ff	9 25 FH	10 25 FW	11 24 FH	12 23 tt	1 22 tm
3 5 RH	4 3 mt	5 3 mm	6 1 MT	6 30 ed	7 30 eg	15	8 28 EF	9 26 fr	10 26 ff	11 25 fr	12 24 FW	1 23 FH
3 6 rr	4 4 RW	5 4 RH	6 2 mt	7 1 MM	7 31 MT	16	8 29 ed	9 27 ER	10 27 EF	11 26 ER	12 25 ff	1 24 fr
3 7 TR	4 5 rf	5 5 rr	6 3 RW	7 2 mm	8 1 mt	17	8 30 MM	9 28 eg	10 28 ed	11 27 eg	12 26 EF	1 25 ER
3 8 tg	4 6 TF	5 6 TR	6 4 rf	7 3 RH	8 2 RW	18	8 31 mm	9 29 MT	10 29 MM	11 28 MT	12 27 ed	1 26 eg
3 9 FT	4 7 td	5 7 tg	6 5 TF	7 4 rr	8 3 rf	19	9 1 RH	9 30 mt	10 30 mm	11 29 mt	12 28 MM	1 27 MT
3 10 ft	4 8 FM	5 8 FT	6 6 td	7 5 TR	8 4 TF	20	9 2 rr	10 1 RW	10 31 RH	11 30 RW	12 29 mm	1 28 mt
3 11 EW	4 9 fm	5 9 ft	6 7 FM	7 6 tg	8 5 td	21	9 3 TR	10 2 rf	11 1 rr	12 1 rf	12 30 RH	1 29 RW
3 12 ef	4 10 EH	5 10 EW	6 8 fm	7 7 FT	8 6 FM	22	9 4 tg	10 3 TF	11 2 TR	12 2 TF	12 31 rr	1 30 rf
3 13 MF	4 11 er	5 11 ef	6 9 EH	7 8 ft	8 7 fm	23	9 5 FT	10 4 td	11 3 tg	12 3 td	1 1 TR	1 31 TF
3 14 md	4 12 MR	5 12 MF	6 10 er	7 9 EW	8 8 EH	24	9 6 ft	10 5 FM	11 4 FT	12 4 FM	1 2 tg	2 1 td
3 15 RM	4 13 mg	5 13 md	6 11 MR	7 10 ef	8 9 er	25	9 7 EW	10 6 fm	11 5 ft	12 5 fm	1 3 FT	2 2 FM
3 16 rm	4 14 RT	5 14 RM	6 12 mg	7 11 MF	8 10 MR	26	9 8 ef	10 7 EH	11 6 EW	12 6 EH	1 4 ft	2 3 fm
3 17 TH	4 15 rt	5 15 rm	6 13 RT	7 12 md	8 11 mg	27	9 9 MF	10 8 er	11 7 ef	12 7 er	1 5 EW	2 4 EH
3 18 tr	4 16 TW	5 16 TH	6 14 rt	7 13 RM	8 12 RT	28	9 10 md	10 9 MR	11 8 MF	12 8 MR	1 6 ef	2 5 er
3 19 FR	4 17 tf	5 17 tr	6 15 TW	7 14 rm	8 13 rt	29	9 11 RM	10 10 mg	11 9 md	12 9 mg	1 7 MF	2 6 MR
	4 18 FF			7 15 TH		30		10 11 RT	11 10 RM		1 8 md	2 7 mg

1921 mm ROOSTER

JAN MT	FEB mt	MAR RW	APR rf	MAY TF	JUN td	DAY OF MON	JUL FM	AUG fm	SEP EH	OCT er	NOV MR	DEC mg
27 WARM	27 CLEAR	29 SUMMER		1 GRAIN	4 HEAT		5 FALL	7 DEW	9 C DEW	9 WINTER	10 SNOW	9 CHILL
10:46	16:09	10:05		14:42	18:31		11:17	13:10	5:22	7:58	0:07	10:17
2 8 RT	3 10 RM	4 8 mg	5 8 md	6 6 MR	7 5 ef	1	8 4 er	9 2 EW	10 1 fm	10 31 ft	11 29 FM	12 29 FT
2 9 rt	3 11 rm	4 9 RT	5 9 RM	6 7 mg	7 6 MF	2	8 5 MR	9 3 ef	10 2 EH	11 1 EW	11 30 fm	12 30 ft
2 10 TW	3 12 TH	4 10 rt	5 10 rm	6 8 RT	7 7 md	3	8 6 mg	9 4 MF	10 3 er	11 2 ef	12 1 EH	12 31 EW
2 11 tf	3 13 tr	4 11 TW	5 11 TH	6 9 rt	7 8 RM	4	8 7 RT	9 5 md	10 4 MR	11 3 MF	12 2 er	1 1 ef
2 12 FF	3 14 FR	4 12 tf	5 12 tr	6 10 TW	7 9 rm	5	8 8 rt	9 6 RM	10 5 mg	11 4 md	12 3 MR	1 2 MF
2 13 fd	3 15 fg	4 13 FF	5 13 FR	6 11 tf	7 10 TH	6	8 9 TW	9 7 rm	10 6 RT	11 5 RM	12 4 mg	1 3 md
2 14 EM	3 16 ET	4 14 fd	5 14 fg	6 12 FF	7 11 tr	7	8 10 tf	9 8 TH	10 7 rt	11 6 rm	12 5 RT	1 4 RM
2 15 em	3 17 et	4 15 EM	5 15 ET	6 13 fd	7 12 FR	8	8 11 FF	9 9 tr	10 8 TW	11 7 TH	12 6 rt	1 5 rm
2 16 MH	3 18 MW	4 16 em	5 16 et	6 14 EM	7 13 fg	9	8 12 fd	9 10 FR	10 9 tf	11 8 tr	12 7 TW	1 6 TH
2 17 mr	3 19 mf	4 17 MH	5 17 MW	6 15 em	7 14 ET	10	8 13 EM	9 11 fg	10 10 FF	11 9 FR	12 8 tf	1 7 tr
2 18 RR	3 20 RF	4 18 mr	5 18 mf	6 16 MH	7 15 et	11	8 14 em	9 12 ET	10 11 fd	11 10 fg	12 9 FF	1 8 FR
2 19 rg	3 21 rd	4 19 RR	5 19 RF	6 17 mr	7 16 MW	12	8 15 MH	9 13 et	10 12 EM	11 11 ET	12 10 fd	1 9 fg
2 20 TT	3 22 TM	4 20 rg	5 20 rd	6 18 RR	7 17 mf	13	8 16 mr	9 14 MW	10 13 em	11 12 et	12 11 EM	1 10 ET
2 21 tt	3 23 tm	4 21 TT	5 21 TM	6 19 rg	7 18 RF	14	8 17 RR	9 15 mf	10 14 MH	11 13 MW	12 12 em	1 11 et
2 22 FW	3 24 FH	4 22 tt	5 22 tm	6 20 TT	7 19 rd	15	8 18 rg	9 16 RF	10 15 mr	11 14 mf	12 13 MH	1 12 MW
2 23 ff	3 25 fr	4 23 FW	5 23 FH	6 21 tt	7 20 TM	16	8 19 TT	9 17 rd	10 16 RR	11 15 RF	12 14 mr	1 13 mf
2 24 EF	3 26 ER	4 24 ff	5 24 fr	6 22 FW	7 21 tm	17	8 20 tt	9 18 TM	10 17 rg	11 16 rd	12 15 RR	1 14 RF
2 25 ed	3 27 eg	4 25 EF	5 25 ER	6 23 ff	7 22 FH	18	8 21 FW	9 19 tm	10 18 TT	11 17 TM	12 16 rg	1 15 rd
2 26 MM	3 28 MT	4 26 ed	5 26 eg	6 24 EF	7 23 fr	19	8 22 ff	9 20 FH	10 19 tt	11 18 tm	12 17 TT	1 16 TM
2 27 mm	3 29 mt	4 27 MM	5 27 MT	6 25 ed	7 24 ER	20	8 23 EF	9 21 fr	10 20 FW	11 19 FH	12 18 tt	1 17 tm
2 28 RH	3 30 RW	4 28 mm	5 28 mt	6 26 MM	7 25 eg	21	8 24 ed	9 22 ER	10 21 ff	11 20 fr	12 19 FW	1 18 FH
3 1 rr	3 31 rf	4 29 RH	5 29 RW	6 27 mm	7 26 MT	22	8 25 MM	9 23 eg	10 22 EF	11 21 ER	12 20 ff	1 19 fr
3 2 TR	4 1 TF	4 30 rr	5 30 rf	6 28 RH	7 27 mt	23	8 26 mm	9 24 MT	10 23 ed	11 22 eg	12 21 EF	1 20 ER
3 3 tg	4 2 td	5 1 TR	5 31 TF	6 29 rr	7 28 RW	24	8 27 RH	9 25 mt	10 24 MM	11 23 MT	12 22 ed	1 21 eg
3 4 FT	4 3 FM	5 2 tg	6 1 td	6 30 TR	7 29 rf	25	8 28 rr	9 26 RW	10 25 mm	11 24 mt	12 23 MM	1 22 MT
3 5 ft	4 4 fm	5 3 FT	6 2 FM	7 1 tg	8 30 TF	26	8 29 TR	9 27 rf	10 26 RH	11 25 RW	12 24 mm	1 23 mt
3 6 EW	4 5 EH	5 4 ft	6 3 fm	7 2 FT	7 31 td	27	8 30 tg	9 28 TF	10 27 rr	11 26 rf	12 25 RH	1 24 RW
3 7 ef	4 6 er	5 5 EW	6 4 EH	7 3 ft	8 1 FM	28	8 31 FT	9 29 td	10 28 TR	11 27 TF	12 26 rr	1 25 rf
3 8 MF	4 7 MR	5 6 ef	6 5 er	7 4 EW	8 2 fm	29	9 1 ft	9 30 FM	10 29 tg	11 28 td	12 27 TR	1 26 TF
3 9 md		5 7 MF			8 3 EH	30			10 30 FT		12 28 tg	1 27 td

1922 RH DOG

JAN RT	FEB rt	MAR TW	APR tf	MAY FF	MAY FF	JUN fd	DAY OF	JUL EM	AUG em	SEP MH	OCT mr	NOV RR	DEC rg
8 SPRING	8 WARM	9 CLEAR	10 SUMMER	11 GRAIN	14 HEAT	16 FALL	MON	17 DEW	19 C DEW	20 WINTER	20 SNOW	20 CHILL	20 SPRING
22:07	16:34	21:58	15:53	20:30	7:13	17:05		19:07	11:11	13:47	5:11	16:15	4:01
1 28 FM	2 27 FT	3 28 td	4 27 tg	5 27 td	6 25 TR	7 24 rf	1	8 23 rr	9 21 RW	10 20 mm	11 19 mt	12 18 MM	1 17 MT
1 29 fm	2 28 ft	3 29 FM	4 28 FT	5 28 FM	6 26 tg	7 25 TF	2	8 24 TR	9 22 rf	10 21 RH	11 20 RW	12 19 mm	1 18 mt
1 30 EH	3 1 EW	3 30 fm	4 29 ft	5 29 fm	6 27 FT	7 26 td	3	8 25 tg	9 23 TF	10 22 rr	11 21 rf	12 20 RH	1 19 RW
1 31 er	3 2 ef	3 31 EH	4 30 EW	5 30 EH	6 28 ft	7 27 FM	4	8 26 FT	9 24 td	10 23 TR	11 22 TF	12 21 rr	1 20 rf
2 1 MR	3 3 MF	4 1 er	5 1 ef	5 31 er	6 29 EW	7 28 fm	5	8 27 ft	9 25 FM	10 24 tg	11 23 td	12 22 TR	1 21 TF
2 2 mg	3 4 md	4 2 MR	5 2 MF	6 1 MR	6 30 ef	7 29 EH	6	8 28 EW	9 26 fm	10 25 FT	11 24 FM	12 23 tg	1 22 td
2 3 RT	3 5 RM	4 3 mg	5 3 md	6 2 mg	7 1 MF	7 30 er	7	8 29 ef	9 27 EH	10 26 ft	11 25 fm	12 24 FT	1 23 FM
2 4 rt	3 6 rm	4 4 RT	5 4 RM	6 3 RT	7 2 md	7 31 MR	8	8 30 MF	9 28 er	10 27 EW	11 26 EH	12 25 ft	1 24 fm
2 5 TW	3 7 TH	4 5 rt	5 5 rm	6 4 rt	7 3 RM	8 1 mg	9	8 31 md	9 29 MR	10 28 ef	11 27 er	12 26 EW	1 25 EH
2 6 tf	3 8 tr	4 6 TW	5 6 TH	6 5 TW	7 4 rm	8 2 RT	10	9 1 RM	9 30 mg	10 29 MF	11 28 MR	12 27 ef	1 26 er
2 7 FF	3 9 FR	4 7 tf	5 7 tr	6 6 tf	7 5 TH	8 3 rt	11	9 2 rm	10 1 RT	10 30 md	11 29 mg	12 28 MF	1 27 MR
2 8 fd	3 10 fg	4 8 FF	5 8 FR	6 7 FF	7 6 tr	8 4 TW	12	9 3 TH	10 2 rt	10 31 RM	11 30 RT	12 29 md	1 28 mg
2 9 EM	3 11 ET	4 9 fd	5 9 fg	6 8 fd	7 7 FR	8 5 tf	13	9 4 tr	10 3 TW	11 1 rm	12 1 rt	12 30 RM	1 29 RT
2 10 em	3 12 et	4 10 EM	5 10 ET	6 9 EM	7 8 fg	8 6 FF	14	9 5 FR	10 4 tf	11 2 TH	12 2 TW	12 31 rm	1 30 rt
2 11 MH	3 13 MW	4 11 em	5 11 et	6 10 em	7 9 ET	8 7 fd	15	9 6 fg	10 5 FF	11 3 tr	12 3 tf	1 1 TH	1 31 TW
2 12 mr	3 14 mf	4 12 MH	5 12 MW	6 11 MH	7 10 et	8 8 EM	16	9 7 ET	10 6 fd	11 4 FR	12 4 FF	1 2 tr	2 1 tf
2 13 RR	3 15 RF	4 13 mr	5 13 mf	6 12 mr	7 11 MW	8 9 em	17	9 8 et	10 7 EM	11 5 fg	12 5 fd	1 3 FR	2 2 FF
2 14 rg	3 16 rd	4 14 RR	5 14 RF	6 13 RR	7 12 mf	8 10 MH	18	9 9 MW	10 8 em	11 6 ET	12 6 EM	1 4 fg	2 3 fd
2 15 TT	3 17 TM	4 15 rg	5 15 rd	6 14 rg	7 13 RF	8 11 mr	19	9 10 mf	10 9 MH	11 7 et	12 7 em	1 5 ET	2 4 EM
2 16 tt	3 18 tm	4 16 TT	5 16 TM	6 15 TT	7 14 rd	8 12 RR	20	9 11 RF	10 10 mr	11 8 MW	12 8 MH	1 6 et	2 5 em
2 17 FW	3 19 FH	4 17 tt	5 17 tm	6 16 tt	7 15 TM	8 13 rg	21	9 12 rd	10 11 RR	11 9 mf	12 9 mr	1 7 MW	2 6 MH
2 18 ff	3 20 fr	4 18 FW	5 18 FH	6 17 FW	7 16 tm	8 14 TT	22	9 13 TM	10 12 rg	11 10 RF	12 10 RR	1 8 mf	2 7 mr
2 19 EF	3 21 ER	4 19 ff	5 19 fr	6 18 ff	7 17 FH	8 15 tt	23	9 14 tm	10 13 TT	11 11 rd	12 11 rg	1 9 RF	2 8 RR
2 20 ed	3 22 eg	4 20 EF	5 20 ER	6 19 EF	7 18 fr	8 16 FW	24	9 15 FH	10 14 tt	11 12 TM	12 12 TT	1 10 rd	2 9 rg
2 21 MM	3 23 MT	4 21 ed	5 21 eg	6 20 ed	7 19 ER	8 17 ff	25	9 16 fr	10 15 FW	11 13 tm	12 13 tt	1 11 TM	2 10 TT
2 22 mm	3 24 mt	4 22 MM	5 22 MT	6 21 MM	7 20 eg	8 18 EF	26	9 17 ER	10 16 ff	11 14 FH	12 14 FW	1 12 tm	2 11 tt
2 23 RH	3 25 RW	4 23 mm	5 23 mt	6 22 mm	7 21 MT	8 19 ed	27	9 18 eg	10 17 EF	11 15 fr	12 15 ff	1 13 FH	2 12 FW
2 24 rr	3 26 rf	4 24 RH	5 24 RW	6 23 RH	7 22 mt	8 20 MM	28	9 19 MT	10 18 ed	11 16 ER	12 16 EF	1 14 fr	2 13 ff
2 25 TR	3 27 TF	4 25 rr	5 25 rf	6 24 rr	7 23 RW	8 21 mm	29	9 20 mt	10 19 MM	11 17 eg	12 17 ed	1 15 ER	2 14 EF
2 26 tg		4 26 TR	5 26 TF			8 22 RH	30			11 18 MT		1 16 eg	2 15 ed

1923 rr BOAR

JAN TT	FEB tt	MAR FW	APR ff	MAY EF	JUN ed	DAY OF MON	JUL MM	AUG mm	SEP RH	OCT rr	NOV TR	DEC tg
19 WARM	21 CLEAR	21 SUMMER	23 GRAIN	25 HEAT	26 FALL		29 DEW	29 C DEW		1 WINTER	1 SNOW	1 CHILL
22:25	3:46	21:39	2:15	13:01	22:25		1:41	17:00		19:30	11:05	22:06
2 16 MM	3 17 eg	4 16 ed	5 16 eg	6 14 EF	7 14 ER	1	8 12 ff	9 11 fr	10 10 FW	11 8 tm	12 8 et	1 6 TM
2 17 mm	3 18 MT	4 17 MM	5 17 MT	6 15 ed	7 15 eg	2	8 13 EF	9 12 ER	10 11 ff	11 9 FH	12 9 FW	1 7 tm
2 18 RH	3 19 mt	4 18 mm	5 18 mt	6 16 MM	7 16 MT	3	8 14 ed	9 13 eg	10 12 EF	11 10 fr	12 10 ff	1 8 FH
2 19 rr	3 20 RW	4 19 RH	5 19 RW	6 17 mm	7 17 mt	4	8 15 MM	9 14 MT	10 13 ed	11 11 ER	12 11 EF	1 9 fr
2 20 TR	3 21 rf	4 20 rr	5 20 rf	6 18 RH	7 18 RW	5	8 16 mm	9 15 mt	10 14 MM	11 12 eg	12 12 ed	1 10 ER
2 21 tg	3 22 TF	4 21 TR	5 21 TF	6 19 rr	7 19 rf	6	8 17 RH	9 16 RW	10 15 mm	11 13 MT	12 13 MM	1 11 eg
2 22 FT	3 23 td	4 22 tg	5 22 td	6 20 TR	7 20 TF	7	8 18 rr	9 17 rf	10 16 RH	11 14 mt	12 14 mm	1 12 MT
2 23 ft	3 24 FM	4 23 FT	5 23 FM	6 21 tg	7 21 td	8	8 19 TR	9 18 TF	10 17 rr	11 15 RW	12 15 RH	1 13 mt
2 24 EW	3 25 fm	4 24 ft	5 24 fm	6 22 FT	7 22 FM	9	8 20 tg	9 19 td	10 18 TR	11 16 rf	12 16 rr	1 14 RW
2 25 ef	3 26 EH	4 25 EW	5 25 EH	6 23 ft	7 23 fm	10	8 21 FT	9 20 FM	10 19 tg	11 17 TF	12 17 TR	1 15 rf
2 26 MF	3 27 er	4 26 ef	5 26 er	6 24 EW	7 24 EH	11	8 22 ft	9 21 fm	10 20 FT	11 18 td	12 18 tg	1 16 TF
2 27 md	3 28 MR	4 27 MF	5 27 MR	6 25 ef	7 25 er	12	8 23 EW	9 22 EH	10 21 ft	11 19 FM	12 19 FT	1 17 td
2 28 RM	3 29 mg	4 28 md	5 28 mg	6 26 MF	7 26 MR	13	8 24 ef	9 23 er	10 22 EW	11 20 fm	12 20 ft	1 18 FM
3 1 rm	3 30 RT	4 29 RM	5 29 RT	6 27 md	7 27 mg	14	8 25 MF	9 24 MR	10 23 ef	11 21 EH	12 21 EW	1 19 fm
3 2 TH	3 31 rt	4 30 rm	5 30 rt	6 28 RM	7 28 RT	15	8 26 md	9 25 mg	10 24 MF	11 22 er	12 22 ef	1 20 EH
3 3 tr	4 1 TW	5 1 TH	5 31 TW	6 29 rm	7 29 rt	16	8 27 RM	9 26 RT	10 25 md	11 23 MR	12 23 MF	1 21 er
3 4 FR	4 2 tf	5 2 tr	6 1 tf	6 30 TH	7 30 TW	17	8 28 rm	9 27 rt	10 26 RM	11 24 mg	12 24 md	1 22 MR
3 5 fg	4 3 FF	5 3 FR	6 2 FF	7 1 tr	7 31 tf	18	8 29 TH	9 28 TW	10 27 rm	11 25 RT	12 25 RM	1 23 mg
3 6 ET	4 4 fd	5 4 fg	6 3 fd	7 2 FR	8 1 FF	19	8 30 tr	9 29 tf	10 28 TH	11 26 rt	12 26 rm	1 24 RT
3 7 et	4 5 EM	5 5 ET	6 4 EM	7 3 fg	8 2 fd	20	8 31 FR	9 30 FF	10 29 tr	11 27 TW	12 27 TH	1 25 rt
3 8 MW	4 6 em	5 6 et	6 5 em	7 4 ET	8 3 EM	21	9 1 fg	10 1 fd	10 30 FR	11 28 tf	12 28 tr	1 26 TW
3 9 mf	4 7 MH	5 7 MW	6 6 MH	7 5 et	8 4 em	22	9 2 ET	10 2 EM	10 31 fg	11 29 FF	12 29 FR	1 27 tf
3 10 RF	4 8 mr	5 8 mf	6 7 mr	7 6 MW	8 5 MH	23	9 3 et	10 3 em	11 1 ET	11 30 fd	12 30 fg	1 28 FF
3 11 rd	4 9 RR	5 9 RF	6 8 RR	7 7 mf	8 6 mr	24	9 4 MW	10 4 MH	11 2 et	12 1 EM	12 31 ET	1 29 fd
3 12 TM	4 10 rg	5 10 rd	6 9 rg	7 8 RF	8 7 RR	25	9 5 mf	10 5 mr	11 3 MW	12 2 em	1 1 et	1 30 EM
3 13 tm	4 11 TT	5 11 TM	6 10 TT	7 9 rd	8 8 rg	26	9 6 RF	10 6 RR	11 4 mf	12 3 MH	1 2 MW	1 31 em
3 14 FH	4 12 tt	5 12 tm	6 11 tt	7 10 TM	8 9 TT	27	9 7 rd	10 7 rg	11 5 RF	12 4 mr	1 3 mf	2 1 MH
3 15 fr	4 13 FW	5 13 FH	6 12 FW	7 11 tm	8 10 tt	28	9 8 TM	10 8 TT	11 6 rd	12 5 RR	1 4 RF	2 2 mr
3 16 ER	4 14 ff	5 14 fr	6 13 ff	7 12 FH	8 11 FW	29	9 9 tm	10 9 tt	11 7 TM	12 6 rg	1 5 rd	2 3 RR
	4 15 EF	5 15 ER		7 13 fr		30	9 10 FH			12 7 TT		2 4 rg

1924 TR RAT

JAN FT	FEB ft	MAR EW	APR ef	MAY MF	JUN md	DAY OF MON	JUL RM	AUG rm	SEP TH	OCT tr	NOV FR	DEC fg
1 SPRING	2 WARM	2 CLEAR	3 SUMMER	5 GRAIN	6 HEAT		8 FALL	10 DEW	10 C DEW	12 WINTER	11 SNOW	12 CHILL
9:50	4:13	9:34	3:26	8:02	18:30		4:13	7:30	21:53	1:26	16:54	3:54
2 5 TT	3 5 rd	4 4 rg	5 4 rd	6 2 RR	7 2 RF	1	8 1 RR	8 30 mf	9 29 mr	10 28 MW	11 27 MH	12 26 et
2 6 tt	3 6 TM	4 5 TT	5 5 TM	6 3 rg	7 3 rd	2	8 2 rg	8 31 RF	9 30 RR	10 29 mf	11 28 mr	12 27 MW
2 7 FW	3 7 tm	4 6 tt	5 6 tm	6 4 TT	7 4 TM	3	8 3 TT	9 1 rd	10 1 rg	10 30 RF	11 29 RR	12 28 mf
2 8 ff	3 8 FH	4 7 FW	5 7 FH	6 5 tt	7 5 tm	4	8 4 tt	9 2 TM	10 2 TT	10 31 rd	11 30 rg	12 29 RF
2 9 EF	3 9 fr	4 8 ff	5 8 fr	6 6 FW	7 6 FH	5	8 5 FW	9 3 tm	10 3 tt	11 1 TM	12 1 TT	12 30 rd
2 10 ed	3 10 ER	4 9 EF	5 9 ER	6 7 ff	7 7 fr	6	8 6 ff	9 4 FH	10 4 FW	11 2 tm	12 2 tt	12 31 TM
2 11 MM	3 11 eg	4 10 ed	5 10 eg	6 8 EF	7 8 ER	7	8 7 EF	9 5 fr	10 5 ff	11 3 FH	12 3 FW	1 1 tm
2 12 mm	3 12 MT	4 11 MM	5 11 MT	6 9 ed	7 9 eg	8	8 8 ed	9 6 ER	10 6 EF	11 4 fr	12 4 ff	1 2 FH
2 13 RH	3 13 mt	4 12 mm	5 12 mt	6 10 MM	7 10 MT	9	8 9 MM	9 7 eg	10 7 ed	11 5 ER	12 5 EF	1 3 fr
2 14 rr	3 14 RW	4 13 RH	5 13 RW	6 11 mm	7 11 mt	10	8 10 mm	9 8 MT	10 8 MM	11 6 eg	12 6 ed	1 4 ER
2 15 TR	3 15 rf	4 14 rr	5 14 rf	6 12 RH	7 12 RW	11	8 11 RH	9 9 mt	10 9 mm	11 7 MT	12 7 MM	1 5 eg
2 16 tg	3 16 TF	4 15 TR	5 15 TF	6 13 rr	7 13 rf	12	8 12 rr	9 10 RW	10 10 RH	11 8 mt	12 8 mm	1 6 MT
2 17 FT	3 17 td	4 16 tg	5 16 td	6 14 TR	7 14 TF	13	8 13 TR	9 11 rf	10 11 rr	11 9 RW	12 9 RH	1 7 mt
2 18 ft	3 18 FM	4 17 FT	5 17 FM	6 15 tg	7 15 td	14	8 14 tg	9 12 TF	10 12 TR	11 10 rf	12 10 rr	1 8 RW
2 19 EW	3 19 fm	4 18 ft	5 18 fm	6 16 FT	7 16 FM	15	8 15 FT	9 13 td	10 13 tg	11 11 TF	12 11 TR	1 9 rf
2 20 ef	3 20 EH	4 19 EW	5 19 EH	6 17 ft	7 17 fm	16	8 16 ft	9 14 FM	10 14 FT	11 12 td	12 12 tg	1 10 TF
2 21 MF	3 21 er	4 20 ef	5 20 er	6 18 EW	7 18 EH	17	8 17 EW	9 15 fm	10 15 ft	11 13 FM	12 13 FT	1 11 td
2 22 md	3 22 MR	4 21 MF	5 21 MR	6 19 ef	7 19 er	18	8 18 ef	9 16 EH	10 16 EW	11 14 fm	12 14 ft	1 12 FM
2 23 RM	3 23 mg	4 22 md	5 22 mg	6 20 MF	7 20 MR	19	8 19 MF	9 17 er	10 17 ef	11 15 EH	12 15 EW	1 13 fm
2 24 rm	3 24 RT	4 23 RM	5 23 RT	6 21 md	7 21 mg	20	8 20 md	9 18 MR	10 18 MF	11 16 er	12 16 ef	1 14 EH
2 25 TH	3 25 rt	4 24 rm	5 24 rt	6 22 RM	7 22 RT	21	8 21 RM	9 19 mg	10 19 md	11 17 MR	12 17 MF	1 15 er
2 26 tr	3 26 TW	4 25 TH	5 25 TW	6 23 rm	7 23 rt	22	8 22 rm	9 20 RT	10 20 RM	11 18 mg	12 18 md	1 16 MR
2 27 FR	3 27 tf	4 26 tr	5 26 tf	6 24 TH	7 24 TW	23	8 23 TH	9 21 rt	10 21 rm	11 19 RT	12 19 RM	1 17 mg
2 28 fg	3 28 FF	4 27 FR	5 27 FF	6 25 tr	7 25 tf	24	8 24 tr	9 22 TW	10 22 TH	11 20 rt	12 20 rm	1 18 RT
2 29 ET	3 29 fd	4 28 fg	5 28 fd	6 26 FR	7 26 FF	25	8 25 FR	9 23 tf	10 23 tr	11 21 TW	12 21 TH	1 19 rt
3 1 et	3 30 EM	4 29 ET	5 29 EM	6 27 fg	7 27 fd	26	8 26 fg	9 24 FF	10 24 FR	11 22 tf	12 22 tr	1 20 TW
3 2 MW	3 31 em	4 30 et	5 30 em	6 28 ET	7 28 EM	27	8 27 ET	9 25 fd	10 25 fg	11 23 FF	12 23 FR	1 21 tf
3 3 mf	4 1 MH	5 1 MW	5 31 MH	6 29 et	7 29 em	28	8 28 et	9 26 EM	10 26 ET	11 24 fd	12 24 fg	1 22 FF
3 4 RF	4 2 mr	5 2 mf	6 1 mr	6 30 MW	7 30 MH	29	8 29 MW	9 27 em	10 27 et	11 25 EM	12 25 ET	1 23 fd
	4 3 RR	5 3 RF		7 1 mf	7 31 mr	30		9 28 MH		11 26 em		

1925 tg OX

JAN ET	FEB et	MAR MW	APR mf	APR	MAY RF	JUN rd	DAY OF	JUL TM	AUG tm	SEP FH	OCT tr	NOV ER	DEC er
12 SPRING	12 WARM	13 CLEAR	14 SUMMER	16 GRAIN	18 HEAT	19 FALL	MON	21 DEW	22 C DEW	22 WINTER	22 SNOW	22 CHILL	22 SPRING
15:37	10:00	15:23	9:18	13:57	0:25	10:08		12:40	3:48	7:16	23:26	9:55	21:39
1 24 EM	2 23 ET	3 24 fd	4 23 fg	5 22 FF	6 21 FR	7 21 FF	1	8 19 tr	9 18 tf	10 18 tr	11 16 TW	12 16 TH	1 14 rt
1 25 em	2 24 et	3 25 EM	4 24 ET	5 23 fd	6 22 fg	7 22 fd	2	8 20 FR	9 19 FF	10 19 FR	11 17 tf	12 17 tr	1 15 TW
1 26 MH	2 25 MW	3 26 em	4 25 et	5 24 EM	6 23 ET	7 23 EM	3	8 21 fg	9 20 fd	10 20 fg	11 18 FF	12 18 FR	1 16 tf
1 27 mr	2 26 mf	3 27 MH	4 26 MW	5 25 em	6 24 et	7 24 em	4	8 22 ET	9 21 EM	10 21 ET	11 19 fd	12 19 fg	1 17 FF
1 28 RR	2 27 RF	3 28 mr	4 27 mf	5 26 MH	6 25 MW	7 25 MH	5	8 23 et	9 22 em	10 22 et	11 20 EM	12 20 ET	1 18 fd
1 29 rg	2 28 rd	3 29 RR	4 28 RF	5 27 mr	6 26 mf	7 26 mr	6	8 24 MW	9 23 MH	10 23 MW	11 21 em	12 21 et	1 19 EM
1 30 TT	3 1 TM	3 30 rg	4 29 rd	5 28 RR	6 27 RF	7 27 RR	7	8 25 mf	9 24 mr	10 24 mf	11 22 MH	12 22 MW	1 20 em
1 31 tt	3 2 tm	3 31 TT	4 30 TM	5 29 rg	6 28 rd	7 28 rg	8	8 26 RF	9 25 RR	10 25 RF	11 23 mr	12 23 mf	1 21 MH
2 1 FW	3 3 FH	4 1 tt	5 1 tm	5 30 TT	6 29 TM	7 29 TT	9	8 27 rd	9 26 rg	10 26 rd	11 24 RR	12 24 RF	1 22 mr
2 2 ff	3 4 fr	4 2 FW	5 2 FH	5 31 tt	6 30 tm	7 30 tt	10	8 28 TM	9 27 TT	10 27 TM	11 25 rg	12 25 rd	1 23 RR
2 3 EF	3 5 ER	4 3 ff	5 3 fr	6 1 FW	7 1 FH	7 31 FW	11	8 29 tm	9 28 tt	10 28 tm	11 26 TT	12 26 TM	1 24 rg
2 4 ed	3 6 eg	4 4 EF	5 4 ER	6 2 ff	7 2 fr	8 1 ff	12	8 30 FH	9 29 FW	10 29 FH	11 27 tt	12 27 tm	1 25 TT
2 5 MM	3 7 MT	4 5 ed	5 5 eg	6 3 EF	7 3 ER	8 2 EF	13	8 31 fr	9 30 ff	10 30 fr	11 28 FW	12 28 FH	1 26 tt
2 6 mm	3 8 mt	4 6 MM	5 6 MT	6 4 ed	7 4 eg	8 3 ed	14	9 1 ER	10 1 EF	10 31 ER	11 29 ff	12 29 fr	1 27 FW
2 7 RH	3 9 RW	4 7 mm	5 7 mt	6 5 MM	7 5 MT	8 4 MM	15	9 2 eg	10 2 ed	11 1 eg	11 30 EF	12 30 ER	1 28 ff
2 8 rr	3 10 rf	4 8 RH	5 8 RW	6 6 mm	7 6 mt	8 5 mm	16	9 3 MT	10 3 MM	11 2 MT	12 1 ed	12 31 eg	1 29 EF
2 9 TR	3 11 TF	4 9 rr	5 9 rf	6 7 RH	7 7 RW	8 6 RH	17	9 4 mt	10 4 mm	11 3 mt	12 2 MM	1 1 MT	1 30 ed
2 10 tg	3 12 td	4 10 TR	5 10 TF	6 8 rr	7 8 rf	8 7 rr	18	9 5 RW	10 5 RH	11 4 RW	12 3 mm	1 2 mt	1 31 MM
2 11 FT	3 13 FM	4 11 tg	5 11 td	6 9 TR	7 9 TF	8 8 TR	19	9 6 rf	10 6 rr	11 5 rf	12 4 RH	1 3 RW	2 1 mm
2 12 ft	3 14 fm	4 12 FT	5 12 FM	6 10 tg	7 10 td	8 9 tg	20	9 7 TF	10 7 TR	11 6 TF	12 5 rr	1 4 rf	2 2 RH
2 13 EW	3 15 EH	4 13 ft	5 13 fm	6 11 FT	7 11 FM	8 10 FT	21	9 8 td	10 8 tg	11 7 td	12 6 TR	1 5 TF	2 3 rr
2 14 ef	3 16 er	4 14 EW	5 14 EH	6 12 ft	7 12 fm	8 11 ft	22	9 9 FM	10 9 FT	11 8 FM	12 7 tg	1 6 td	2 4 TR
2 15 MF	3 17 MR	4 15 ef	5 15 er	6 13 EW	7 13 EH	8 12 EW	23	9 10 fm	10 10 ft	11 9 fm	12 8 FT	1 7 FM	2 5 tg
2 16 md	3 18 mg	4 16 MF	5 16 MR	6 14 ef	7 14 er	8 13 ef	24	9 11 EH	10 11 EW	11 10 EH	12 9 ft	1 8 fm	2 6 FT
2 17 RM	3 19 RT	4 17 md	5 17 mg	6 15 MF	7 15 MR	8 14 MF	25	9 12 er	10 12 ef	11 11 er	12 10 EW	1 9 EH	2 7 ft
2 18 rm	3 20 rt	4 18 RM	5 18 RT	6 16 md	7 16 mg	8 15 md	26	9 13 MR	10 13 MF	11 12 MR	12 11 ef	1 10 er	2 8 EW
2 19 TH	3 21 TW	4 19 rm	5 19 rt	6 17 RM	7 17 RT	8 16 RM	27	9 14 mg	10 14 md	11 13 mg	12 12 MF	1 11 MR	2 9 ef
2 20 tr	3 22 tf	4 20 TH	5 20 TW	6 18 rm	7 18 rt	8 17 rm	28	9 15 RT	10 15 RM	11 14 RT	12 13 md	1 12 mg	2 10 MF
2 21 FR	3 23 FF	4 21 tr	5 21 tf	6 19 TH	7 19 TW	8 18 TH	29	9 16 rt	10 16 rm	11 15 rt	12 14 RM	1 13 RT	2 11 md
2 22 fg		4 22 FR		6 20 tr	7 20 tf		30	9 17 TW	10 17 TH		12 15 rm		2 12 RM

1926 FT TIGER

JAN MT	FEB mt	MAR RW	APR rf	MAY FF	JUN td	DAY OF MON	JUL FM	AUG fm	SEP EH	OCT er	NOV MR	DEC mg
22 WARM	23 CLEAR	25 SUMMER	26 GRAIN	29 HEAT			1 FALL	2 DEW	3 C DEW	4 WINTER	4 SNOW	3 CHILL
16:00	21:19	15:09	19:42	6:06			15:45	19:07	9:25	13:05	5:16	15:45
2 13 rm	3 14 RT	4 12 md	5 12 mg	6 10 MF	7 10 MR	1	8 8 ef	9 7 er	10 7 ef	11 5 EH	12 5 EW	1 4 EH
2 14 TH	3 15 rt	4 13 rm	5 13 RT	6 11 md	7 11 mg	2	8 9 MF	9 8 MR	10 8 MF	11 6 er	12 6 ef	1 5 er
2 15 tr	3 16 TW	4 14 rm	5 14 rt	6 12 rm	7 12 RT	3	8 10 md	9 9 mg	10 9 md	11 7 MR	12 7 MF	1 6 MR
2 16 FR	3 17 tf	4 15 TH	5 15 TW	6 13 rm	7 13 rt	4	8 11 rm	9 10 RT	10 10 rm	11 8 mg	12 8 md	1 7 mg
2 17 fg	3 18 FF	4 16 tr	5 16 tf	6 14 TH	7 14 TW	5	8 12 rm	9 11 rt	10 11 rm	11 9 RT	12 9 rm	1 8 RT
2 18 ET	3 19 fd	4 17 FR	5 17 FF	6 15 tr	7 15 tf	6	8 13 TH	9 12 TW	10 12 TH	11 10 rt	12 10 rm	1 9 rt
2 19 et	3 20 EM	4 18 fg	5 18 fd	6 16 FR	7 16 FF	7	8 14 tr	9 13 tf	10 13 tr	11 11 TW	12 11 TH	1 10 TW
2 20 MW	3 21 em	4 19 ET	5 19 EM	6 17 fg	7 17 fd	8	8 15 FR	9 14 FF	10 14 FR	11 12 tf	12 12 tr	1 11 tf
2 21 mf	3 22 MH	4 20 et	5 20 em	6 18 ET	7 18 EM	9	8 16 fg	9 15 fd	10 15 fg	11 13 FF	12 13 FR	1 12 FF
2 22 RF	3 23 mr	4 21 MW	5 21 MH	6 19 et	7 19 em	10	8 17 ET	9 16 EM	10 16 ET	11 14 fd	12 14 fg	1 13 fd
2 23 rd	3 24 RR	4 22 mf	5 22 mr	6 20 MW	7 20 MH	11	8 18 et	9 17 em	10 17 et	11 15 EM	12 15 ET	1 14 EM
2 24 TM	3 25 rg	4 23 RF	5 23 RR	6 21 mf	7 21 mr	12	8 19 MW	9 18 MH	10 18 MW	11 16 em	12 16 et	1 15 em
2 25 tm	3 26 TT	4 24 rd	5 24 rg	6 22 RF	7 22 RR	13	8 20 mf	9 19 mr	10 19 mf	11 17 MH	12 17 MW	1 16 MH
2 26 FH	3 27 tt	4 25 TM	5 25 TT	6 23 rd	7 23 rg	14	8 21 RF	9 20 RR	10 20 RF	11 18 mr	12 18 mf	1 17 mr
2 27 fr	3 28 FW	4 26 tm	5 26 tt	6 24 TM	7 24 TT	15	8 22 rd	9 21 rg	10 21 rd	11 19 RR	12 19 RF	1 18 RR
2 28 ER	3 29 ff	4 27 FH	5 27 FW	6 25 tm	7 25 tt	16	8 23 TM	9 22 TT	10 22 TM	11 20 rg	12 20 rd	1 19 rg
3 1 eg	3 30 EF	4 28 fr	5 28 ff	6 26 FH	7 26 FW	17	8 24 tm	9 23 tt	10 23 tm	11 21 TT	12 21 TM	1 20 TT
3 2 MT	3 31 ed	4 29 ER	5 29 EF	6 27 fr	7 27 ff	18	8 25 FH	9 24 FW	10 24 FH	11 22 tt	12 22 tm	1 21 tt
3 3 mt	4 1 MM	4 30 eg	5 30 ed	6 28 ER	7 28 EF	19	8 26 fr	9 25 ff	10 25 fr	11 23 FW	12 23 FH	1 22 FW
3 4 RW	4 2 mm	5 1 MT	5 31 MM	6 29 eg	7 29 ed	20	8 27 ER	9 26 EF	10 26 ER	11 24 ff	12 24 fr	1 23 ff
3 5 rf	4 3 RH	5 2 mt	6 1 mm	6 30 MT	7 30 MM	21	8 28 eg	9 27 ed	10 27 eg	11 25 EF	12 25 ER	1 24 EF
3 6 TF	4 4 rr	5 3 RW	6 2 RH	7 1 mt	7 31 mm	22	8 29 MT	9 28 MM	10 28 MT	11 26 ed	12 26 eg	1 25 ed
3 7 td	4 5 TR	5 4 rf	6 3 rr	7 2 RW	8 1 RH	23	8 30 mt	9 29 mm	10 29 mt	11 27 MM	12 27 MT	1 26 MM
3 8 FM	4 6 tg	5 5 TF	6 4 TR	7 3 rf	8 2 rr	24	8 31 RW	9 30 RH	10 30 RW	11 28 mm	12 28 mt	1 27 mm
3 9 fm	4 7 FT	5 6 td	6 5 tg	7 4 TF	8 3 TR	25	9 1 rf	10 1 rr	10 31 rf	11 29 RH	12 29 RW	1 28 RH
3 10 EH	4 8 ft	5 7 FM	6 6 FT	7 5 td	8 4 tg	26	9 2 TF	10 2 TR	11 1 TF	11 30 rr	12 30 rf	1 29 rr
3 11 er	4 9 EW	5 8 fm	6 7 ft	7 6 FM	8 5 FT	27	9 3 td	10 3 tg	11 2 td	12 1 TR	12 31 TF	1 30 TR
3 12 MR	4 10 ef	5 9 EH	6 8 EW	7 7 fm	8 6 ft	28	9 4 FM	10 4 FT	11 3 FM	12 2 tg	1 1 td	1 31 tg
3 13 mg	4 11 MF	5 10 er	6 9 ef	7 8 EH	8 7 EW	29	9 5 fm	10 5 ft	11 4 fm	12 3 FT	1 2 FM	2 1 FT
		5 11 MR		7 9 er		30	9 6 EH	10 6 EW		12 4 ft	1 3 fm	

1927 ft RABBIT

JAN RT	FEB rt	MAR TW	APR tf	MAY FF	JUN fd	DAY OF MON	JUL EM	AUG em	SEP MH	OCT mr	NOV RR	DEC rg
4 SPRING	3 WARM	5 CLEAR	6 SUMMER	8 GRAIN	10 HEAT		11 FALL	14 DEW	14 C DEW	13 WINTER	15 SNOW	14 CHILL
3:31	21:51	2:57	20:54	1:25	11:50		21:32	0:06	15:16	17:57	11:05	21:32
2 2 ft	3 4 fm	4 2 FT	5 1 td	5 31 tg	6 29 TF	1	7 29 TR	8 27 rf	9 26 rr	10 25 RW	11 24 RH	12 24 RW
2 3 EW	3 5 EH	4 3 ft	5 2 FM	6 1 FT	6 30 td	2	7 30 tg	8 28 TF	9 27 TR	10 26 rf	11 25 rr	12 25 rf
2 4 ef	3 6 er	4 4 EW	5 3 fm	6 2 ft	7 1 FM	3	7 31 FT	8 29 td	9 28 tg	10 27 TF	11 26 TR	12 26 TF
2 5 MF	3 7 MR	4 5 ef	5 4 EH	6 3 EW	7 2 fm	4	8 1 ft	8 30 FM	9 29 FT	10 28 td	11 27 tg	12 27 td
2 6 md	3 8 mg	4 6 MF	5 5 er	6 4 ef	7 3 EH	5	8 2 EW	8 31 fm	9 30 ft	10 29 FM	11 28 FT	12 28 FM
2 7 RM	3 9 RT	4 7 md	5 6 MR	6 5 MF	7 4 er	6	8 3 ef	9 1 EH	10 1 EW	10 30 fm	11 29 ft	12 29 fm
2 8 rm	3 10 rt	4 8 RM	5 7 mg	6 6 md	7 5 MR	7	8 4 MF	9 2 er	10 2 ef	10 31 EH	11 30 EW	12 30 EH
2 9 TH	3 11 TW	4 9 rm	5 8 RT	6 7 RM	7 6 mg	8	8 5 md	9 3 MR	10 3 MF	11 1 er	12 1 ef	12 31 er
2 10 tr	3 12 tf	4 10 TH	5 9 rt	6 8 rm	7 7 RT	9	8 6 RM	9 4 mg	10 4 md	11 2 MR	12 2 MF	1 1 MR
2 11 FR	3 13 FF	4 11 tr	5 10 TW	6 9 TH	7 8 rt	10	8 7 rm	9 5 RT	10 5 RM	11 3 mg	12 3 md	1 2 mg
2 12 fg	3 14 fd	4 12 FR	5 11 tf	6 10 tr	7 9 TW	11	8 8 TH	9 6 rt	10 6 rm	11 4 RT	12 4 RM	1 3 RT
2 13 ET	3 15 EM	4 13 fg	5 12 FF	6 11 FR	7 10 tf	12	8 9 tr	9 7 TW	10 7 TH	11 5 rt	12 5 rm	1 4 rt
2 14 et	3 16 em	4 14 ET	5 13 fd	6 12 fg	7 11 FF	13	8 10 FR	9 8 tf	10 8 tr	11 6 TW	12 6 TH	1 5 TW
2 15 MW	3 17 MH	4 15 et	5 14 EM	6 13 ET	7 12 fd	14	8 11 fg	9 9 FF	10 9 FR	11 7 tf	12 7 tr	1 6 tf
2 16 mf	3 18 mr	4 16 MW	5 15 em	6 14 et	7 13 EM	15	8 12 ET	9 10 fd	10 10 fg	11 8 FF	12 8 FR	1 7 FF
2 17 RF	3 19 RR	4 17 mf	5 16 MH	6 15 MW	7 14 em	16	8 13 et	9 11 EM	10 11 ET	11 9 fd	12 9 fg	1 8 fd
2 18 rd	3 20 rg	4 18 RF	5 17 mr	6 16 mf	7 15 MH	17	8 14 MW	9 12 em	10 12 et	11 10 EM	12 10 ET	1 9 EM
2 19 TM	3 21 TT	4 19 rd	5 18 RR	6 17 RF	7 16 mr	18	8 15 mf	9 13 MH	10 13 MW	11 11 em	12 11 et	1 10 em
2 20 tm	3 22 tt	4 20 TM	5 19 rg	6 18 rd	7 17 RR	19	8 16 RF	9 14 mr	10 14 mf	11 12 MH	12 12 MW	1 11 MH
2 21 FH	3 23 FW	4 21 tm	5 20 TT	6 19 TM	7 18 rg	20	8 17 rd	9 15 RR	10 15 RF	11 13 mr	12 13 mf	1 12 mr
2 22 fr	3 24 ff	4 22 FH	5 21 tt	6 20 tm	7 19 TT	21	8 18 TM	9 16 rg	10 16 rd	11 14 RR	12 14 RF	1 13 RR
2 23 ER	3 25 EF	4 23 fr	5 22 FW	6 21 FH	7 20 tt	22	8 19 tm	9 17 TT	10 17 TM	11 15 rg	12 15 rd	1 14 rg
2 24 eg	3 26 ed	4 24 ER	5 23 ff	6 22 fr	7 21 FW	23	8 20 FH	9 18 tt	10 18 tm	11 16 TT	12 16 TM	1 15 TT
2 25 MT	3 27 MM	4 25 eg	5 24 EF	6 23 ER	7 22 ff	24	8 21 fr	9 19 FW	10 19 FH	11 17 tt	12 17 tm	1 16 tt
2 26 mt	3 28 mm	4 26 MT	5 25 ed	6 24 eg	7 23 EF	25	8 22 ER	9 20 ff	10 20 fr	11 18 FW	12 18 FH	1 17 FW
2 27 RW	3 29 RH	4 27 mt	5 26 MM	6 25 MT	7 24 ed	26	8 23 eg	9 21 EF	10 21 ER	11 19 ff	12 19 fr	1 18 ff
2 28 rf	3 30 rr	4 28 RW	5 27 mm	6 26 mt	7 25 MM	27	8 24 MT	9 22 ed	10 22 eg	11 20 EF	12 20 ER	1 19 EF
3 1 TF	3 31 TR	4 29 rf	5 28 RH	6 27 RW	7 26 mm	28	8 25 mt	9 23 MM	10 23 MT	11 21 ed	12 21 eg	1 20 ed
3 2 td	4 1 tg	4 30 TF	5 29 rr	6 28 rf	7 27 RH	29	8 26 RW	9 24 mm	10 24 mt	11 22 MM	12 22 MT	1 21 MM
3 3 FM			5 30 TR		7 28 rr	30		9 25 RH		11 23 mm	12 23 mt	1 22 mm

1928 EW DRAGON

JAN TT	FEB tt	FEB tt	MAR FW	APR ff	MAY EF	JUN ed	DAY OF MON	JUL MM	AUG mm	SEP RH	OCT rr	NOV TR	DEC tg
14 SPRING	15 WARM	15 CLEAR	17 SUMMER	19 GRAIN	7 HEAT	23 FALL		25 DEW	25 C DEW	27 WINTER	26 SNOW	26 CHILL	25 SPRING
9:17	3:38	8:55	2:44	7:18	17:45	3:28		6:02	21:11	0:44	16:18	3:23	14:57
1 23 RH	2 21 mt	3 22 mm	4 20 MT	5 19 ed	6 18 eg	7 17 EF	1	8 15 fr	9 14 ff	10 13 FH	11 12 FW	12 12 FH	1 11 FW
1 24 rr	2 22 RW	3 23 RH	4 21 mt	5 20 MM	6 19 MT	7 18 ed	2	8 16 ER	9 15 EF	10 14 fr	11 13 ff	12 13 fr	1 12 ff
1 25 TR	2 23 rf	3 24 rr	4 22 RW	5 21 mm	6 20 mt	7 19 MM	3	8 17 eg	9 16 ed	10 15 ER	11 14 EF	12 14 ER	1 13 EF
1 26 tg	2 24 TF	3 25 TR	4 23 rf	5 22 RH	6 21 RW	7 20 mm	4	8 18 MT	9 17 MM	10 16 eg	11 15 ed	12 15 eg	1 14 ed
1 27 FT	2 25 td	3 26 tg	4 24 TF	5 23 rr	6 22 rf	7 21 RH	5	8 19 mt	9 18 mm	10 17 MT	11 16 MM	12 16 MT	1 15 MM
1 28 ft	2 26 FM	3 27 FT	4 25 td	5 24 TR	6 23 TF	7 22 rr	6	8 20 RW	9 19 RH	10 18 mt	11 17 mm	12 17 mt	1 16 mm
1 29 EW	2 27 fm	3 28 ft	4 26 FM	5 25 tg	6 24 td	7 23 TR	7	8 21 rf	9 20 rr	10 19 RW	11 18 RH	12 18 RW	1 17 RH
1 30 ef	2 28 EH	3 29 EW	4 27 fm	5 26 FT	6 25 FM	7 24 tg	8	8 22 TF	9 21 TR	10 20 rf	11 19 rr	12 19 rf	1 18 rr
1 31 MF	2 29 er	3 30 ef	4 28 EH	5 27 ft	6 26 fm	7 25 FT	9	8 23 td	9 22 tg	10 21 TF	11 20 TR	12 20 TF	1 19 TR
2 1 md	3 1 MR	3 31 MF	4 29 er	5 28 EW	6 27 EH	7 26 ft	10	8 24 FM	9 23 FT	10 22 td	11 21 tg	12 21 td	1 20 tg
2 2 RM	3 2 mg	4 1 md	4 30 MR	5 29 ef	6 28 er	7 27 EW	11	8 25 fm	9 24 ft	10 23 FM	11 22 FT	12 22 FM	1 21 FT
2 3 rm	3 3 RT	4 2 RM	5 1 mg	5 30 MF	6 29 MR	7 28 ef	12	8 26 EH	9 25 EW	10 24 fm	11 23 ft	12 23 fm	1 22 ft
2 4 TH	3 4 rt	4 3 rm	5 2 RT	5 31 md	6 30 mg	7 29 MF	13	8 27 er	9 26 ef	10 25 EH	11 24 EW	12 24 EH	1 23 EW
2 5 tr	3 5 TW	4 4 TH	5 3 rt	6 1 RM	7 1 RT	7 30 md	14	8 28 MR	9 27 MF	10 26 er	11 25 ef	12 25 er	1 24 ef
2 6 FR	3 6 tf	4 5 tr	5 4 TW	6 2 rm	7 2 rt	7 31 RM	15	8 29 mg	9 28 md	10 27 MR	11 26 MF	12 26 MR	1 25 MF
2 7 fg	3 7 FF	4 6 FR	5 5 tf	6 3 TH	7 3 TW	8 1 rm	16	8 30 RT	9 29 RM	10 28 mg	11 27 md	12 27 mg	1 26 md
2 8 ET	3 8 fd	4 7 fg	5 6 FF	6 4 tr	7 4 tf	8 2 TH	17	8 31 rt	9 30 rm	10 29 RT	11 28 RM	12 28 RT	1 27 RM
2 9 et	3 9 EM	4 8 ET	5 7 fd	6 5 FR	7 5 FF	8 3 tr	18	9 1 TW	10 1 TH	10 30 rt	11 29 rm	12 29 rt	1 28 rm
2 10 MW	3 10 em	4 9 et	5 8 EM	6 6 fg	7 6 fd	8 4 FR	19	9 2 tf	10 2 tr	10 31 TW	11 30 TH	12 30 TW	1 29 TH
2 11 mf	3 11 MH	4 10 MW	5 9 em	6 7 ET	7 7 EM	8 5 fg	20	9 3 FF	10 3 FR	11 1 tf	12 1 tr	12 31 tf	1 30 tr
2 12 RF	3 12 mr	4 11 mf	5 10 MH	6 8 et	7 8 em	8 6 ET	21	9 4 fd	10 4 fg	11 2 FF	12 2 FR	1 1 FF	1 31 FR
2 13 rd	3 13 RR	4 12 RF	5 11 mr	6 9 MW	7 9 MH	8 7 et	22	9 5 EM	10 5 ET	11 3 fd	12 3 fg	1 2 fd	2 1 fg
2 14 TM	3 14 rg	4 13 rd	5 12 RR	6 10 mf	7 10 mr	8 8 MW	23	9 6 em	10 6 et	11 4 EM	12 4 ET	1 3 EM	2 2 ET
2 15 tm	3 15 TT	4 14 TM	5 13 rg	6 11 RF	7 11 RR	8 9 mf	24	9 7 MH	10 7 MW	11 5 em	12 5 et	1 4 em	2 3 et
2 16 FH	3 16 tt	4 15 tm	5 14 TT	6 12 rd	7 12 rg	8 10 RF	25	9 8 mr	10 8 mf	11 6 MH	12 6 MW	1 5 MH	2 4 MW
2 17 fr	3 17 FW	4 16 FH	5 15 tt	6 13 TM	7 13 TT	8 11 rd	26	9 9 RR	10 9 RF	11 7 mr	12 7 mf	1 6 mr	2 5 mf
2 18 ER	3 18 ff	4 17 fr	5 16 FW	6 14 tm	7 14 tt	8 12 TM	27	9 10 rg	10 10 rd	11 8 RR	12 8 RF	1 7 RR	2 6 RF
2 19 eg	3 19 EF	4 18 ER	5 17 ff	6 15 FH	7 15 FW	8 13 tm	28	9 11 TT	10 11 TM	11 9 rg	12 9 rd	1 8 rg	2 7 rd
2 20 MT	3 20 ed	4 19 eg	5 18 EF	6 16 fr	7 16 ff	8 14 FH	29	9 12 tt	10 12 tm	11 10 TT	12 10 TM	1 9 TT	2 8 TM
	3 21 MM			6 17 ER			30	9 13 FW		11 11 tt	12 11 tm	1 10 tt	2 9 tm

1929 ef SNAKE

JAN FT	FEB ft	MAR EW	APR ef	MAY MF	JUN md	DAY OF MON	JUL RM	AUG rm	SEP TH	OCT tr	NOV FR	DEC fg
25 WARM	26 CLEAR	27 SUMMER	29 GRAIN		1 HEAT		4 FALL	6 DEW	7 C DEW	8 WINTER	7 SNOW	7 CHILL
9:32	14:52	8:41	13:11		23:32		9:09	11:40	3:55	5:28	21:57	9:03
2 10 FH	3 11 tt	4 10 tm	5 9 TT	6 7 rd	7 7 rg	1	8 5 RF	9 3 mr	10 3 mf	11 1 MH	12 1 MW	12 31 MH
2 11 fr	3 12 FW	4 11 FH	5 10 tt	6 8 TM	7 8 TT	2	8 6 rd	9 4 RR	10 4 RF	11 2 mr	12 2 mf	1 1 mr
2 12 ER	3 13 ff	4 12 fr	5 11 FW	6 9 tm	7 9 tt	3	8 7 TM	9 5 rg	10 5 rd	11 3 RR	12 3 RF	1 2 RR
2 13 eg	3 14 EF	4 13 ER	5 12 ff	6 10 FH	7 10 FW	4	8 8 tm	9 6 TT	10 6 TM	11 4 rg	12 4 rd	1 3 rg
2 14 MT	3 15 ed	4 14 eg	5 13 EF	6 11 fr	7 11 ff	5	8 9 FH	9 7 tt	10 7 tm	11 5 TT	12 5 TM	1 4 TT
2 15 mt	3 16 MM	4 15 MT	5 14 ed	6 12 ER	7 12 EF	6	8 10 fr	9 8 FW	10 8 FH	11 6 tt	12 6 tm	1 5 tt
2 16 RW	3 17 mm	4 16 mt	5 15 MM	6 13 eg	7 13 ed	7	8 11 ER	9 9 ff	10 9 fr	11 7 FW	12 7 FH	1 6 FW
2 17 rf	3 18 RH	4 17 RW	5 16 mm	6 14 MT	7 14 MM	8	8 12 eg	9 10 EF	10 10 ER	11 8 ff	12 8 fr	1 7 ff
2 18 TF	3 19 rr	4 18 rf	5 17 RH	6 15 mt	7 15 mm	9	8 13 MT	9 11 ed	10 11 eg	11 9 EF	12 9 ER	1 8 EF
2 19 td	3 20 TR	4 19 TF	5 18 rr	6 16 RW	7 16 RH	10	8 14 mt	9 12 MM	10 12 MT	11 10 ed	12 10 eg	1 9 ed
2 20 FM	3 21 tg	4 20 td	5 19 TR	6 17 rf	7 17 rr	11	8 15 RW	9 13 mm	10 13 mt	11 11 MM	12 11 MT	1 10 MM
2 21 fm	3 22 FT	4 21 FM	5 20 tg	6 18 TF	7 18 TR	12	8 16 rf	9 14 RH	10 14 RW	11 12 mm	12 12 mt	1 11 mm
2 22 EH	3 23 ft	4 22 fm	5 21 FT	6 19 td	7 19 tg	13	8 17 TF	9 15 rr	10 15 rf	11 13 RH	12 13 RW	1 12 RH
2 23 er	3 24 EW	4 23 EH	5 22 ft	6 20 FM	7 20 FT	14	8 18 td	9 16 TR	10 16 TF	11 14 rr	12 14 rf	1 13 rr
2 24 MR	3 25 ef	4 24 er	5 23 EW	6 21 fm	7 21 ft	15	8 19 FM	9 17 tg	10 17 td	11 15 TR	12 15 TF	1 14 TR
2 25 mg	3 26 MF	4 25 MR	5 24 ef	6 22 EH	7 22 EW	16	8 20 fm	9 18 FT	10 18 FM	11 16 tg	12 16 td	1 15 tg
2 26 RT	3 27 md	4 26 mg	5 25 MF	6 23 er	7 23 ef	17	8 21 EH	9 19 ft	10 19 fm	11 17 FT	12 17 FM	1 16 FT
2 27 rt	3 28 RM	4 27 RT	5 26 md	6 24 MR	7 24 MF	18	8 22 er	9 20 EW	10 20 EH	11 18 ft	12 18 fm	1 17 ft
2 28 TW	3 29 rm	4 28 rt	5 27 RM	6 25 mg	7 25 md	19	8 23 MR	9 21 ef	10 21 er	11 19 EW	12 19 EH	1 18 EW
3 1 tf	3 30 TH	4 29 TW	5 28 rm	6 26 RT	7 26 RM	20	8 24 mg	9 22 MF	10 22 MR	11 20 ef	12 20 er	1 19 ef
3 2 FF	3 31 tr	4 30 tf	5 29 TH	6 27 rt	7 27 rm	21	8 25 RT	9 23 md	10 23 mg	11 21 MF	12 21 MR	1 20 MF
3 3 fd	4 1 FR	5 1 FF	5 30 tr	6 28 TW	7 28 TH	22	8 26 rt	9 24 RM	10 24 RT	11 22 md	12 22 mg	1 21 md
3 4 EM	4 2 fg	5 2 fd	5 31 FR	6 29 tf	7 29 tr	23	8 27 TW	9 25 rm	10 25 rt	11 23 RM	12 23 RT	1 22 RM
3 5 em	4 3 ET	5 3 EM	6 1 fg	6 30 FF	7 30 FR	24	8 28 tf	9 26 TH	10 26 TW	11 24 rm	12 24 rt	1 23 rm
3 6 MH	4 4 et	5 4 em	6 2 ET	7 1 fd	7 31 fg	25	8 29 FF	9 27 tr	10 27 tf	11 25 TH	12 25 TW	1 24 TH
3 7 mr	4 5 MW	5 5 MH	6 3 et	7 2 EM	8 1 ET	26	8 30 fd	9 28 FR	10 28 FF	11 26 tr	12 26 tf	1 25 tr
3 8 RR	4 6 mf	5 6 mr	6 4 MW	7 3 em	8 2 et	27	8 31 EM	9 29 fg	10 29 fd	11 27 FR	12 27 FF	1 26 FR
3 9 rg	4 7 RF	5 7 RR	6 5 mf	7 4 MH	8 3 MW	28	9 1 em	9 30 ET	10 30 EM	11 28 fg	12 28 fd	1 27 fg
3 10 TT	4 8 rd	5 8 rg	6 6 RF	7 5 mr	8 4 mf	29	9 2 MH	10 1 et	10 31 em	11 29 ET	12 29 EM	1 28 ET
	4 9 TM			7 6 RR		30		10 2 MW		11 30 et	12 30 em	1 29 et

1930 MF HORSE

JAN ET	FEB et	MAR MW	APR mf	MAY RF	JUN rd	JUN rd	DAY OF MON	JUL TM	AUG tm	SEP FH	OCT fr	NOV ER	DEC eg
6 SPRING	7 WARM	7 CLEAR	8 SUMMER	10 GRAIN	13 HEAT	14 FALL		16 DEW	18 C DEW	18 WINTER	19 SNOW	18 CHILL	18 SPRING
20:52	15:17	20:38	14:28	19:05	5:20	15:31		17:29	9:44	11:21	9:32	15:12	2:41
1 30 MW	2 28 em	3 30 et	4 29 em	5 28 ET	6 26 fd	7 26 fg	1	8 24 FF	9 22 tr	10 22 tf	11 20 TH	12 20 TW	1 19 TH
1 31 mf	3 1 MH	3 31 MW	4 30 MH	5 29 et	6 27 EM	7 27 ET	2	8 25 fd	9 23 FR	10 23 FF	11 21 tr	12 21 tf	1 20 tr
2 1 RF	3 2 mr	4 1 mf	5 1 mr	5 30 MW	6 28 em	7 28 et	3	8 26 EM	9 24 fg	10 24 fd	11 22 FR	12 22 FF	1 21 FR
2 2 rd	3 3 RR	4 2 RF	5 2 RR	5 31 mf	6 29 MH	7 29 MW	4	8 27 em	9 25 ET	10 25 EM	11 23 fg	12 23 fd	1 22 fg
2 3 TM	3 4 rg	4 3 rd	5 3 rg	6 1 RF	6 30 mr	7 30 mf	5	8 28 MH	9 26 et	10 26 em	11 24 ET	12 24 EM	1 23 ET
2 4 tm	3 5 TT	4 4 TM	5 4 TT	6 2 rd	7 1 RR	7 31 RF	6	8 29 mr	9 27 MW	10 27 MH	11 25 et	12 25 em	1 24 et
2 5 FH	3 6 tt	4 5 tm	5 5 tt	6 3 TM	7 2 rg	8 1 rd	7	8 30 RR	9 28 mf	10 28 mr	11 26 MW	12 26 MH	1 25 MW
2 6 fr	3 7 FW	4 6 FH	5 6 FW	6 4 tm	7 3 TT	8 2 TM	8	8 31 rg	9 29 RF	10 29 RR	11 27 mf	12 27 mr	1 26 mf
2 7 ER	3 8 ff	4 7 fr	5 7 ff	6 5 FH	7 4 tt	8 3 tm	9	9 1 TT	9 30 rd	10 30 rg	11 28 RF	12 28 RR	1 27 RF
2 8 eg	3 9 EF	4 8 ER	5 8 EF	6 6 fr	7 5 FW	8 4 FH	10	9 2 tt	10 1 TM	10 31 TT	11 29 rd	12 29 rg	1 28 rd
2 9 MT	3 10 ed	4 9 eg	5 9 ed	6 7 ER	7 6 ff	8 5 fr	11	9 3 FW	10 2 tm	11 1 tt	11 30 TM	12 30 TT	1 29 TM
2 10 mt	3 11 MM	4 10 MT	5 10 MM	6 8 eg	7 7 EF	8 6 ER	12	9 4 ff	10 3 FH	11 2 FW	12 1 tm	12 31 tt	1 30 tm
2 11 RW	3 12 mm	4 11 mt	5 11 mm	6 9 MT	7 8 ed	8 7 eg	13	9 5 EF	10 4 fr	11 3 ff	12 2 FH	1 1 FW	1 31 FH
2 12 rf	3 13 RH	4 12 RW	5 12 RH	6 10 mt	7 9 MM	8 8 MT	14	9 6 ed	10 5 ER	11 4 EF	12 3 fr	1 2 ff	2 1 fr
2 13 TF	3 14 rr	4 13 rf	5 13 rr	6 11 RW	7 10 mm	8 9 mt	15	9 7 MM	10 6 eg	11 5 ed	12 4 ER	1 3 EF	2 2 ER
2 14 td	3 15 TR	4 14 TF	5 14 TR	6 12 rf	7 11 RH	8 10 RW	16	9 8 mm	10 7 MT	11 6 MM	12 5 eg	1 4 ed	2 3 eg
2 15 FM	3 16 tg	4 15 td	5 15 tg	6 13 TF	7 12 rr	8 11 rf	17	9 9 RH	10 8 mt	11 7 mm	12 6 MT	1 5 MM	2 4 MT
2 16 fm	3 17 FT	4 16 FM	5 16 FT	6 14 td	7 13 TR	8 12 TF	18	9 10 rr	10 9 RW	11 8 RH	12 7 mt	1 6 mm	2 5 mt
2 17 EH	3 18 ft	4 17 fm	5 17 ft	6 15 FM	7 14 tg	8 13 td	19	9 11 TR	10 10 rf	11 9 rr	12 8 RW	1 7 RH	2 6 RW
2 18 er	3 19 EW	4 18 EH	5 18 EW	6 16 fm	7 15 FT	8 14 FM	20	9 12 tg	10 11 TF	11 10 TR	12 9 rf	1 8 rr	2 7 rf
2 19 MR	3 20 ef	4 19 er	5 19 ef	6 17 EH	7 16 ft	8 15 fm	21	9 13 FT	10 12 td	11 11 tg	12 10 TF	1 9 TR	2 8 TF
2 20 mg	3 21 MF	4 20 MR	5 20 MF	6 18 er	7 17 EW	8 16 EH	22	9 14 ft	10 13 FM	11 12 FT	12 11 td	1 10 tg	2 9 td
2 21 RT	3 22 md	4 21 mg	5 21 md	6 19 MR	7 18 ef	8 17 er	23	9 15 EW	10 14 fm	11 13 ft	12 12 FM	1 11 FT	2 10 FM
2 22 rt	3 23 RM	4 22 RT	5 22 RM	6 20 mg	7 19 MF	8 18 MR	24	9 16 ef	10 15 EH	11 14 EW	12 13 fm	1 12 ft	2 11 fm
2 23 TW	3 24 rm	4 23 rt	5 23 rm	6 21 RT	7 20 md	8 19 mg	25	9 17 MF	10 16 er	11 15 ef	12 14 EH	1 13 EW	2 12 EH
2 24 tf	3 25 TH	4 24 TW	5 24 TH	6 22 rt	7 21 RM	8 20 RT	26	9 18 md	10 17 MR	11 16 MF	12 15 er	1 14 ef	2 13 er
2 25 FF	3 26 tr	4 25 tf	5 25 tr	6 23 TW	7 22 rm	8 21 rt	27	9 19 RM	10 18 mg	11 17 md	12 16 MR	1 15 MF	2 14 MR
2 26 fd	3 27 FR	4 26 FF	5 26 FR	6 24 tf	7 23 TH	8 22 TW	28	9 20 rm	10 19 RT	11 18 RM	12 17 mg	1 16 md	2 15 mg
2 27 EM	3 28 fg	4 27 fd	5 27 fg	6 25 FF	7 24 tr	8 23 tf	29	9 21 TH	10 20 rt	11 19 rm	12 18 RT	1 17 RM	2 16 RT
	3 29 ET	4 28 EM			7 25 FR		30		10 21 TW		12 19 rt	1 18 rm	

1931 md RAM

JAN MT	FEB mt	MAR RW	APR rf	MAY TF	JUN ed	DAY OF MON	JUL FM	AUG fm	SEP EH	OCT er	NOV MR	DEC mg
18 WARM	19 CLEAR	19 SUMMER	22 GRAIN	23 HEAT	25 FALL		27 DEW	28 C DEW	29 WINTER	29 SNOW	29 CHILL	29 SPRING
21:03	2:21	20:10	0:42	11:6	21:20		0:10	15:33	17:10	9:41	3:30	8:30
2 17 rt	3 19 rm	4 18 rt	5 17 RM	6 16 RT	7 15 md	1	8 14 mg	9 12 MF	10 11 er	11 10 ef	12 9 EH	1 8 EW
2 18 TW	3 20 TH	4 19 TW	5 18 rm	6 17 rt	7 16 RM	2	8 15 RT	9 13 md	10 12 MR	11 11 MF	12 10 er	1 9 ef
2 19 tf	3 21 tr	4 20 tf	5 19 TH	6 18 TW	7 17 rm	3	8 16 rt	9 14 RM	10 13 mg	11 12 md	12 11 MR	1 10 MF
2 20 FF	3 22 FR	4 21 FF	5 20 tr	6 19 tf	7 18 TH	4	8 17 TW	9 15 rm	10 14 RT	11 13 RM	12 12 mg	1 11 md
2 21 fd	3 23 fg	4 22 fd	5 21 FR	6 20 FF	7 19 tr	5	8 18 tf	9 16 TH	10 15 rt	11 14 rm	12 13 RT	1 12 RM
2 22 EM	3 24 ET	4 23 EM	5 22 fg	6 21 fd	7 20 FR	6	8 19 FF	9 17 tr	10 16 TW	11 15 TH	12 14 rt	1 13 rm
2 23 em	3 25 et	4 24 em	5 23 ET	6 22 EM	7 21 fg	7	8 20 fd	9 18 FR	10 17 tf	11 16 tr	12 15 TW	1 14 TH
2 24 MH	3 26 MW	4 25 MH	5 24 et	6 23 em	7 22 ET	8	8 21 EM	9 19 fg	10 18 FF	11 17 FR	12 16 tf	1 15 tr
2 25 mr	3 27 mf	4 26 mr	5 25 MW	6 24 MH	7 23 et	9	8 22 em	9 20 ET	10 19 fd	11 18 fg	12 17 FF	1 16 FR
2 26 RR	3 28 RF	4 27 RR	5 26 mf	6 25 mr	7 24 MW	10	8 23 MH	9 21 et	10 20 EM	11 19 ET	12 18 fd	1 17 fg
2 27 rg	3 29 rd	4 28 rg	5 27 RF	6 26 RR	7 25 mf	11	8 24 mr	9 22 MW	10 21 em	11 20 et	12 19 EM	1 18 ET
2 28 TT	3 30 TM	4 29 TT	5 28 rd	6 27 rg	7 26 RF	12	8 25 RR	9 23 mf	10 22 MH	11 21 MW	12 20 em	1 19 et
3 1 tt	3 31 tm	4 30 tt	5 29 TM	6 28 TT	7 27 rd	13	8 26 rg	9 24 RF	10 23 mr	11 22 mf	12 21 MH	1 20 MW
3 2 FW	4 1 FH	5 1 FW	5 30 tm	6 29 tt	7 28 TM	14	8 27 TT	9 25 rd	10 24 RR	11 23 RF	12 22 mr	1 21 mf
3 3 ff	4 2 fr	5 2 ff	5 31 FH	6 30 FW	7 29 tm	15	8 28 tt	9 26 TM	10 25 rg	11 24 rd	12 23 RR	1 22 RF
3 4 EF	4 3 ER	5 3 EF	6 1 fr	7 1 ff	7 30 FH	16	8 29 FW	9 27 tm	10 26 TT	11 25 TM	12 24 rg	1 23 rd
3 5 ed	4 4 eg	5 4 ed	6 2 ER	7 2 EF	7 31 fr	17	8 30 ff	9 28 FH	10 27 tt	11 26 tm	12 25 TT	1 24 TM
3 6 MM	4 5 MT	5 5 MM	6 3 eg	7 3 ed	8 1 ER	18	8 31 EF	9 29 fr	10 28 FW	11 27 FH	12 26 tt	1 25 tm
3 7 mm	4 6 mt	5 6 mm	6 4 MT	7 4 MM	8 2 eg	19	9 1 ed	9 30 ER	10 29 ff	11 28 fr	12 27 FW	1 26 FH
3 8 RH	4 7 RW	5 7 RH	6 5 mt	7 5 mm	8 3 MT	20	9 2 MM	10 1 eg	10 30 EF	11 29 ER	12 28 ff	1 27 fr
3 9 rr	4 8 rf	5 8 rr	6 6 RW	7 6 RH	8 4 mt	21	9 3 mm	10 2 MT	10 31 ed	11 30 eg	12 29 EF	1 28 ER
3 10 TR	4 9 TF	5 9 TR	6 7 rf	7 7 rr	8 5 RW	22	9 4 RH	10 3 mt	11 1 MM	12 1 MT	12 30 ed	1 29 eg
3 11 tg	4 10 td	5 10 tg	6 8 TF	7 8 TR	8 6 rf	23	9 5 rr	10 4 RW	11 2 mm	12 2 mt	12 31 MM	1 30 MT
3 12 FT	4 11 FM	5 11 FT	6 9 td	7 9 tg	8 7 TF	24	9 6 TR	10 5 rf	11 3 RH	12 3 RW	1 1 mm	1 31 mt
3 13 ft	4 12 fm	5 12 ft	6 10 FM	7 10 FT	8 8 td	25	9 7 tg	10 6 TF	11 4 rr	12 4 rf	1 2 RH	2 1 RW
3 14 EW	4 13 EH	5 13 EW	6 11 fm	7 11 ft	8 9 FM	26	9 8 FT	10 7 td	11 5 TR	12 5 TF	1 3 rr	2 2 rf
3 15 ef	4 14 er	5 14 ef	6 12 EH	7 12 EW	8 10 fm	27	9 9 ft	10 8 FM	11 6 tg	12 6 td	1 4 TR	2 3 TF
3 16 MF	4 15 MR	5 15 MF	6 13 er	7 13 ef	8 11 EH	28	9 10 EW	10 9 fm	11 7 FT	12 7 FM	1 5 tg	2 4 td
3 17 md	4 16 mg	5 16 md	6 14 MR	7 14 MF	8 12 er	29	9 11 ef	10 10 EH	11 8 ft	12 8 fm	1 6 FT	2 5 FM
3 18 RM	4 17 RT		6 15 mg		8 13 MR	30			11 9 EW		1 7 ft	

1932 RM MONKEY

JAN RT	FEB rt	MAR TW	APR tf	MAY FF	JUN fd	DAY OF MON	JUL EM	AUG em	SEP MH	OCT mr	NOV RR	DEC rg
30 WARM	30 CLEAR		1 SUMMER	3 GRAIN	4 HEAT		7 FALL	8 DEW	9 C DEW	11 WINTER	10 SNOW	11 CHILL
2:50	8:07		1:55	6:28	17:14		3:18	5:03	21:21	0:02	15:19	2:24
2 6 fm	3 7 ft	4 6 fm	5 6 ft	6 4 FM	7 4 FT	1	8 2 td	9 1 tg	9 30 TF	10 29 rr	11 28 rf	12 27 RH
2 7 EH	3 8 EW	4 7 EH	5 7 EW	6 5 fm	7 5 ft	2	8 3 FM	9 2 FT	10 1 td	10 30 TR	11 29 TF	12 28 rr
2 8 er	3 9 ef	4 8 er	5 8 ef	6 6 EH	7 6 EW	3	8 4 fm	9 3 ft	10 2 FM	10 31 tg	11 30 td	12 29 TR
2 9 MR	3 10 MF	4 9 MR	5 9 MF	6 7 er	7 7 ef	4	8 5 EH	9 4 EW	10 3 fm	11 1 FT	12 1 FM	12 30 tg
2 10 mg	3 11 md	4 10 mg	5 10 md	6 8 MR	7 8 MF	5	8 6 er	9 5 ef	10 4 EH	11 2 ft	12 2 fm	12 31 FT
2 11 RT	3 12 RM	4 11 RT	5 11 RM	6 9 mg	7 9 md	6	8 7 MR	9 6 MF	10 5 er	11 3 EW	12 3 EH	1 1 ft
2 12 rt	3 13 rm	4 12 rt	5 12 rm	6 10 RT	7 10 RM	7	8 8 mg	9 7 md	10 6 MR	11 4 ef	12 4 er	1 2 EW
2 13 TW	3 14 TH	4 13 TW	5 13 TH	6 11 rt	7 11 rm	8	8 9 RT	9 8 RM	10 7 mg	11 5 MF	12 5 MR	1 3 ef
2 14 tf	3 15 tr	4 14 tf	5 14 tr	6 12 TW	7 12 TH	9	8 10 rt	9 9 rm	10 8 RT	11 6 md	12 6 mg	1 4 MF
2 15 FF	3 16 FR	4 15 FF	5 15 FR	6 13 tf	7 13 tr	10	8 11 TW	9 10 TH	10 9 rt	11 7 RM	12 7 RT	1 5 md
2 16 fd	3 17 fg	4 16 fd	5 16 fg	6 14 FF	7 14 FR	11	8 12 tf	9 11 tr	10 10 TW	11 8 rm	12 8 rt	1 6 RM
2 17 EM	3 18 ET	4 17 EM	5 17 ET	6 15 fd	7 15 fg	12	8 13 FF	9 12 FR	10 11 tf	11 9 TH	12 9 TW	1 7 rm
2 18 em	3 19 et	4 18 em	5 18 et	6 16 EM	7 16 ET	13	8 14 fd	9 13 fg	10 12 FF	11 10 tr	12 10 tf	1 8 TH
2 19 MH	3 20 MW	4 19 MH	5 19 MW	6 17 em	7 17 et	14	8 15 EM	9 14 ET	10 13 fd	11 11 FR	12 11 FF	1 9 tr
2 20 mr	3 21 mf	4 20 mr	5 20 mf	6 18 MH	7 18 MW	15	8 16 em	9 15 et	10 14 EM	11 12 fg	12 12 fd	1 10 FR
2 21 RR	3 22 RF	4 21 RR	5 21 RF	6 19 mr	7 19 mf	16	8 17 MH	9 16 MW	10 15 em	11 13 ET	12 13 EM	1 11 fg
2 22 rg	3 23 rd	4 22 rg	5 22 rd	6 20 RR	7 20 RF	17	8 18 mr	9 17 mf	10 16 MH	11 14 et	12 14 em	1 12 ET
2 23 TT	3 24 TM	4 23 TT	5 23 TM	6 21 rg	7 21 rd	18	8 19 RR	9 18 RF	10 17 mr	11 15 MW	12 15 MH	1 13 et
2 24 tt	3 25 tm	4 24 tt	5 24 tm	6 22 TT	7 22 TM	19	8 20 rg	9 19 rd	10 18 RR	11 16 mf	12 16 mr	1 14 MW
2 25 FW	3 26 FH	4 25 FW	5 25 FH	6 23 tt	7 23 tm	20	8 21 TT	9 20 TM	10 19 rg	11 17 RF	12 17 RR	1 15 mf
2 26 ff	3 27 fr	4 26 ff	5 26 fr	6 24 FW	7 24 FH	21	8 22 tt	9 21 tm	10 20 TT	11 18 rd	12 18 rg	1 16 RF
2 27 EF	3 28 ER	4 27 EF	5 27 ER	6 25 ff	7 25 fr	22	8 23 FW	9 22 FH	10 21 tt	11 19 TM	12 19 TT	1 17 rd
2 28 ed	3 29 eg	4 28 ed	5 28 eg	6 26 EF	7 26 ER	23	8 24 ff	9 23 fr	10 22 FW	11 20 tm	12 20 tt	1 18 TM
2 29 MM	3 30 MT	4 29 MM	5 29 MT	6 27 ed	7 27 eg	24	8 25 EF	9 24 ER	10 23 ff	11 21 FH	12 21 FW	1 19 tm
3 1 mm	3 31 mt	4 30 mm	5 30 mt	6 28 MM	7 28 MT	25	8 26 ed	9 25 eg	10 24 EF	11 22 fr	12 22 ff	1 20 FH
3 2 RH	4 1 RW	5 1 RH	5 31 RW	6 29 mm	7 29 mt	26	8 27 MM	9 26 MT	10 25 ed	11 23 ER	12 23 EF	1 21 fr
3 3 rr	4 2 rf	5 2 rr	6 1 rf	6 30 RH	7 30 RW	27	8 28 mm	9 27 mt	10 26 MM	11 24 eg	12 24 ed	1 22 ER
3 4 TR	4 3 TF	5 3 TR	6 2 TF	7 1 rr	7 31 rf	28	8 29 RH	9 28 RW	10 27 mm	11 25 MT	12 25 MM	1 23 eg
3 5 tg	4 4 td	5 4 tg	6 3 td	7 2 TR	8 1 TF	29	8 30 rr	9 29 rf	10 28 RH	11 26 mt	12 26 mm	1 24 MT
3 6 FT	4 5 FM	5 5 FT		7 3 tg		30	8 31 TR			11 27 RW		1 25 mt

1933 rm ROOSTER

JAN TT	FEB tt	MAR FW	APR ff	MAY EF	MAY	JUN ed	DAY OF MON	JUL MM	AUG mm	SEP RH	OCT rr	NOV TR	DEC tg
10 SPRING	11 WARM	11 CLEAR	12 SUMMER	14 GRAIN	15 HEAT	18 FALL		19 DEW	20 C DEW	21 WINTER	20 SNOW	21 CHILL	21 SPRING
14:10	8:32	13:51	7:42	12:18	23:02	8:26		11:47	3:11	5:51	14:04	8:17	20:04
1 26 RW	2 24 mm	3 26 mt	4 25 mm	5 24 MT	6 23 MM	7 23 MT	1	8 21 ed	9 20 eg	10 19 EF	11 18 RR	12 17 ff	1 15 FH
1 27 rf	2 25 RH	3 27 RW	4 26 RH	5 25 mt	6 24 mm	7 24 mt	2	8 22 MM	9 21 MT	10 20 ed	11 19 eg	12 18 EF	1 16 fr
1 28 TF	2 26 rr	3 28 rf	4 27 rr	5 26 RW	6 25 RH	7 25 RW	3	8 23 mm	9 22 mt	10 21 MM	11 20 MT	12 19 ed	1 17 RR
1 29 td	2 27 TR	3 29 TF	4 28 TR	5 27 rf	6 26 rr	7 26 rf	4	8 24 RH	9 23 RW	10 22 mm	11 21 mt	12 20 MM	1 18 eg
1 30 FM	2 28 tg	3 30 td	4 29 tg	5 28 TF	6 27 TR	7 27 TF	5	8 25 rr	9 24 rf	10 23 RH	11 22 RW	12 21 mm	1 19 MT
1 31 fm	3 1 FT	3 31 FM	4 30 FT	5 29 td	6 28 tg	7 28 td	6	8 26 TR	9 25 TF	10 24 rr	11 23 rf	12 22 RH	1 20 mt
2 1 EH	3 2 ft	4 1 fm	5 1 ft	5 30 FM	6 29 FT	7 29 FM	7	8 27 tg	9 26 td	10 25 TR	11 24 TF	12 23 rr	1 21 RW
2 2 er	3 3 EW	4 2 EH	5 2 EW	5 31 fm	6 30 ft	7 30 fm	8	8 28 FT	9 27 FM	10 26 tg	11 25 td	12 24 TR	1 22 rf
2 3 MR	3 4 ef	4 3 er	5 3 ef	6 1 EH	7 1 EW	7 31 EH	9	8 29 ft	9 28 fm	10 27 FT	11 26 FM	12 25 tg	1 23 TF
2 4 mg	3 5 MF	4 4 MR	5 4 MF	6 2 er	7 2 ef	8 1 er	10	8 30 EW	9 29 EH	10 28 ft	11 27 fm	12 26 FT	1 24 td
2 5 RT	3 6 md	4 5 mg	5 5 md	6 3 MR	7 3 MF	8 2 MR	11	8 31 ef	9 30 er	10 29 EW	11 28 EH	12 27 ft	1 25 FM
2 6 rt	3 7 RM	4 6 RT	5 6 RM	6 4 mg	7 4 md	8 3 mg	12	9 1 MF	10 1 MR	10 30 ef	11 29 er	12 28 EW	1 26 fm
2 7 TW	3 8 rm	4 7 rt	5 7 rm	6 5 RT	7 5 RM	8 4 RT	13	9 2 md	10 2 mg	10 31 MF	11 30 MR	12 29 ef	1 27 EH
2 8 tf	3 9 TH	4 8 TW	5 8 TH	6 6 rt	7 6 rm	8 5 rt	14	9 3 RM	10 3 RT	11 1 md	12 1 mg	12 30 MF	1 28 er
2 9 FF	3 10 tr	4 9 tf	5 9 tr	6 7 TW	7 7 TH	8 6 TW	15	9 4 rm	10 4 rt	11 2 RM	12 2 RT	12 31 md	1 29 MR
2 10 fd	3 11 FR	4 10 FF	5 10 FR	6 8 tf	7 8 tr	8 7 tf	16	9 5 TH	10 5 TW	11 3 rm	12 3 rt	1 1 RM	1 30 mg
2 11 EM	3 12 fg	4 11 fd	5 11 fg	6 9 FF	7 9 FR	8 8 FF	17	9 6 tr	10 6 tf	11 4 TH	12 4 TW	1 2 rm	1 31 RT
2 12 em	3 13 ET	4 12 EM	5 12 ET	6 10 fd	7 10 fg	8 9 fd	18	9 7 FR	10 7 FF	11 5 tr	12 5 tf	1 3 TH	2 1 rt
2 13 MH	3 14 et	4 13 em	5 13 et	6 11 EM	7 11 ET	8 10 EM	19	9 8 fg	10 8 fd	11 6 FR	12 6 FF	1 4 tr	2 2 TW
2 14 mr	3 15 MW	4 14 MH	5 14 MW	6 12 em	7 12 et	8 11 em	20	9 9 ET	10 9 EM	11 7 fg	12 7 fd	1 5 FR	2 3 tf
2 15 RR	3 16 mf	4 15 mr	5 15 mf	6 13 MH	7 13 MW	8 12 MH	21	9 10 et	10 10 em	11 8 ET	12 8 EM	1 6 fg	2 4 FF
2 16 rg	3 17 RF	4 16 RR	5 16 RF	6 14 mr	7 14 mf	8 13 mr	22	9 11 MW	10 11 MH	11 9 et	12 9 em	1 7 ET	2 5 fd
2 17 TT	3 18 rd	4 17 rg	5 17 rd	6 15 RR	7 15 RF	8 14 RR	23	9 12 mf	10 12 mr	11 10 MW	12 10 MH	1 8 et	2 6 EM
2 18 tt	3 19 TM	4 18 TT	5 18 TM	6 16 rg	7 16 rd	8 15 rg	24	9 13 RF	10 13 RR	11 11 mf	12 11 mr	1 9 MW	2 7 em
2 19 FW	3 20 tm	4 19 tt	5 19 tm	6 17 TT	7 17 TM	8 16 TT	25	9 14 rd	10 14 rg	11 12 RF	12 12 RR	1 10 mf	2 8 MH
2 20 ff	3 21 FH	4 20 FW	5 20 FH	6 18 tt	7 18 tm	8 17 tt	26	9 15 TM	10 15 TT	11 13 rd	12 13 rg	1 11 RF	2 9 mr
2 21 EF	3 22 fr	4 21 ff	5 21 fr	6 19 FW	7 19 FH	8 18 FW	27	9 16 tm	10 16 tt	11 14 TM	12 14 TT	1 12 rd	2 10 RR
2 22 ed	3 23 ER	4 22 EF	5 22 ER	6 20 ff	7 20 fr	8 19 ff	28	9 17 FH	10 17 FW	11 15 tm	12 15 tt	1 13 TM	2 11 rg
2 23 MM	3 24 eg	4 23 ed	5 23 eg	6 21 EF	7 21 ER	8 20 EF	29	9 18 fr	10 18 ff	11 16 FH	12 16 FW	1 14 tm	2 12 TT
	3 25 MT	4 24 MM		6 22 ed	7 22 eg		30	9 19 ER		11 17 fr			2 13 tt

1934 TH DOG

JAN FT			FEB ft			MAR EW			APR ef			MAY MF			JUN md			DAY OF MON
21 WARM			22 CLEAR			23 SUMMER			25 GRAIN			27 HEAT			28 FALL			
14:27			22:44			13:31			18:02			4:25			14:04			
2	14	FW	3	15	tm	4	14	et	5	13	TM	6	12	TT	7	12	TM	1
2	15	ff	3	16	FH	4	15	FW	5	14	tm	6	13	et	7	13	tm	2
2	16	EF	3	17	fr	4	16	ff	5	15	FH	6	14	FW	7	14	FH	3
2	17	ed	3	18	ER	4	17	EF	5	16	fr	6	15	ff	7	15	fr	4
2	18	MM	3	19	eg	4	18	ed	5	17	ER	6	16	EF	7	16	ER	5
2	19	mm	3	20	MT	4	19	MM	5	18	eg	6	17	ed	7	17	eg	6
2	20	RH	3	21	mt	4	20	mm	5	19	MT	6	18	MM	7	18	MT	7
2	21	rr	3	22	RW	4	21	RH	5	20	mt	6	19	mm	7	19	mt	8
2	22	TR	3	23	rf	4	22	rr	5	21	RW	6	20	RH	7	20	RW	9
2	23	tg	3	24	TF	4	23	TR	5	22	rf	6	21	rr	7	21	rf	10
2	24	FT	3	25	td	4	24	tg	5	23	TF	6	22	TR	7	22	TF	11
2	25	ft	3	26	FM	4	25	FT	5	24	td	6	23	tg	7	23	td	12
2	26	EW	3	27	fm	4	26	ft	5	25	FM	6	24	FT	7	24	FM	13
2	27	ef	3	28	EH	4	27	EW	5	26	fm	6	25	ft	7	25	fm	14
2	28	MF	3	29	er	4	28	ef	5	27	EH	6	26	EW	7	26	EH	15
3	1	md	3	30	MR	4	29	MF	5	28	er	6	27	ef	7	27	er	16
3	2	RM	3	31	mg	4	30	md	5	29	MR	6	28	MF	7	28	MR	17
3	3	rm	4	1	RT	5	1	RM	5	30	mg	6	29	md	7	29	mg	18
3	4	TH	4	2	rt	5	2	rm	5	31	RT	6	30	RM	7	30	RT	19
3	5	tr	4	3	TW	5	3	TH	6	1	rt	7	1	rm	7	31	rt	20
3	6	FR	4	4	tf	5	4	tr	6	2	TW	7	2	TH	8	1	TW	21
3	7	fg	4	5	FF	5	5	FR	6	3	tf	7	3	tr	8	2	tf	22
3	8	ET	4	6	fd	5	6	fg	6	4	FF	7	4	FR	8	3	FF	23
3	9	et	4	7	EM	5	7	ET	6	5	fd	7	5	fg	8	4	fd	24
3	10	MW	4	8	em	5	8	et	6	6	EM	7	6	ET	8	5	EM	25
3	11	mf	4	9	MH	5	9	MW	6	7	em	7	7	et	8	6	em	26
3	12	RF	4	10	mr	5	10	mf	6	8	MH	7	8	MW	8	7	MH	27
3	13	rd	4	11	RR	5	11	RF	6	9	mr	7	9	mf	8	8	mr	28
3	14	TM	4	12	rg	5	12	rd	6	10	RR	7	10	RF	8	9	RR	29
			4	13	TT				6	11	rg	7	11	rd				30

DAY OF MON	JUL RM			AUG rm			SEP TH			OCT tr			NOV FR			DEC fg		
	30 DEW						2 C DEW			20 WINTER			2 SNOW			2 CHILL		
	17:36						7:45			11:41			3:53			14:03		
1	8	10	rg	9	9	rd	10	8	RR	11	7	RF	12	7	RR	1	5	mf
2	8	11	TT	9	10	TM	10	9	rg	11	8	rd	12	8	rg	1	6	RF
3	8	12	et	9	11	tm	10	10	TT	11	9	TM	12	9	TT	1	7	rd
4	8	13	FW	9	12	FH	10	11	et	11	10	tm	12	10	et	1	8	TM
5	8	14	ff	9	13	fr	10	12	FW	11	11	FH	12	11	FW	1	9	tm
6	8	15	EF	9	14	ER	10	13	ff	11	12	fr	12	12	ff	1	10	FH
7	8	16	ed	9	15	eg	10	14	EF	11	13	ER	12	13	EF	1	11	fr
8	8	17	MM	9	16	MT	10	15	ed	11	14	eg	12	14	ed	1	12	ER
9	8	18	mm	9	17	mt	10	16	MM	11	15	MT	12	15	MM	1	13	eg
10	8	19	RH	9	18	RW	10	17	mm	11	16	mt	12	16	mm	1	14	MT
11	8	20	rr	9	19	rf	10	18	RH	11	17	RW	12	17	RH	1	15	mt
12	8	21	TR	9	20	TF	10	19	rr	11	18	rf	12	18	rr	1	16	RW
13	8	22	tg	9	21	td	10	20	TR	11	19	TF	12	19	TR	1	17	rf
14	8	23	FT	9	22	FM	10	21	tg	11	20	td	12	20	tg	1	18	TF
15	8	24	ft	9	23	fm	10	22	FT	11	21	FM	12	21	FT	1	19	td
16	8	25	EW	9	24	EH	10	23	ft	11	22	fm	12	22	ft	1	20	FM
17	8	26	ef	9	25	er	10	24	EW	11	23	EH	12	23	EW	1	21	fm
18	8	27	MF	9	26	MR	10	25	ef	11	24	er	12	24	ef	1	22	EH
19	8	28	md	9	27	mg	10	26	MF	11	25	MR	12	25	MF	1	23	er
20	8	29	RM	9	28	RT	10	27	md	11	26	mg	12	26	md	1	24	MR
21	8	30	rm	9	29	rt	10	28	RM	11	27	RT	12	27	RM	1	25	mg
22	8	31	TH	9	30	TW	10	29	rm	11	28	rt	12	28	rm	1	26	RT
23	9	1	tr	10	1	tf	10	30	TH	11	29	TW	12	29	TH	1	27	rt
24	9	2	FR	10	2	FF	10	31	tr	11	30	tf	12	30	tr	1	28	TW
25	9	3	fg	10	3	fd	11	1	FR	12	1	FF	12	31	FR	1	29	tf
26	9	4	ET	10	4	EM	11	2	fg	12	2	fd	1	1	fg	1	30	FF
27	9	5	et	10	5	em	11	3	ET	12	3	EM	1	2	ET	1	31	fd
28	9	6	MW	10	6	MH	11	4	et	12	4	em	1	3	et	2	1	EM
29	9	7	mf	10	7	mr	11	5	MW	12	5	MH	1	4	MW	2	2	em
30	9	8	RF				11	6	mf	12	6	mr				2	3	MH

1935 tr BOAR

JAN ET	FEB et	MAR MW	APR mf	MAY RF	JUN rd	DAY OF MON	JUL TM	AUG tm	SEP FH	OCT fr	NOV ER	DEC eg
2 SPRING	2 WARM	4 CLEAR	4 SUMMER	7 GRAIN	8 HEAT		10 FALL	11 DEW	12 C DEW	13 WINTER	13 SNOW	12 CHILL
1:49	20:11	1:27	19:12	0:06	10:06		19:48	23:25	13:36	17:30	9:43	19:47
2 4 mr	3 5 MW	4 3 em	5 3 et	6 1 EM	7 1 ET	1	7 30 fd	8 29 fg	9 28 fd	10 27 FR	11 26 FF	12 26 FR
2 5 RR	3 6 mf	4 4 MH	5 4 MW	6 2 em	7 2 et	2	7 31 EM	8 30 ET	9 29 EM	10 28 fg	11 27 fd	12 27 fg
2 6 rg	3 7 RF	4 5 mr	5 5 mf	6 3 MH	7 3 MW	3	8 1 em	8 31 et	9 30 em	10 29 ET	11 28 EM	12 28 ET
2 7 TT	3 8 rd	4 6 RR	5 6 RF	6 4 mr	7 4 mf	4	8 2 MH	9 1 MW	10 1 MH	10 30 et	11 29 em	12 29 et
2 8 tt	3 9 TM	4 7 rg	5 7 rd	6 5 RR	7 5 RF	5	8 3 mr	9 2 mf	10 2 mr	10 31 MW	11 30 MH	12 30 MW
2 9 FW	3 10 tm	4 8 TT	5 8 TM	6 6 rg	7 6 rd	6	8 4 RR	9 3 RF	10 3 RR	11 1 mf	12 1 mr	12 31 mf
2 10 ff	3 11 FH	4 9 tt	5 9 tm	6 7 TT	7 7 TM	7	8 5 rg	9 4 rd	10 4 rg	11 2 RF	12 2 RR	1 1 RF
2 11 EF	3 12 fr	4 10 FW	5 10 FH	6 8 tt	7 8 tm	8	8 6 TT	9 5 TM	10 5 TT	11 3 rd	12 3 rg	1 2 rd
2 12 ed	3 13 ER	4 11 ff	5 11 fr	6 9 FW	7 9 FH	9	8 7 tt	9 6 tm	10 6 tt	11 4 TM	12 4 TT	1 3 TM
2 13 MM	3 14 eg	4 12 EF	5 12 ER	6 10 ff	7 10 fr	10	8 8 FW	9 7 FH	10 7 FW	11 5 tm	12 5 tt	1 4 tm
2 14 mm	3 15 MT	4 13 ed	5 13 eg	6 11 EF	7 11 ER	11	8 9 ff	9 8 fr	10 8 ff	11 6 FH	12 6 FW	1 5 FH
2 15 RH	3 16 mt	4 14 MM	5 14 MT	6 12 ed	7 12 eg	12	8 10 EF	9 9 ER	10 9 EF	11 7 fr	12 7 ff	1 6 fr
2 16 rr	3 17 RW	4 15 mm	5 15 mt	6 13 MM	7 13 MT	13	8 11 ed	9 10 eg	10 10 ed	11 8 ER	12 8 EF	1 7 ER
2 17 TR	3 18 rf	4 16 RH	5 16 RW	6 14 mm	7 14 mt	14	8 12 MM	9 11 MT	10 11 MM	11 9 eg	12 9 ed	1 8 eg
2 18 tg	3 19 TF	4 17 rr	5 17 rf	6 15 RH	7 15 RW	15	8 13 mm	9 12 mt	10 12 mm	11 10 MT	12 10 MM	1 9 MT
2 19 FT	3 20 td	4 18 TR	5 18 TF	6 16 rr	7 16 rf	16	8 14 RH	9 13 RW	10 13 RH	11 11 mt	12 11 mm	1 10 mt
2 20 ft	3 21 FM	4 19 tg	5 19 td	6 17 TR	7 17 TF	17	8 15 rr	9 14 rf	10 14 rr	11 12 RW	12 12 RH	1 11 RW
2 21 EW	3 22 fm	4 20 FT	5 20 FM	6 18 tg	7 18 td	18	8 16 TR	9 15 TF	10 15 TR	11 13 rf	12 13 rr	1 12 rf
2 22 ef	3 23 EH	4 21 ft	5 21 fm	6 19 FT	7 19 FM	19	8 17 tg	9 16 td	10 16 tg	11 14 TF	12 14 TR	1 13 TF
2 23 MF	3 24 er	4 22 EW	5 22 EH	6 20 ft	7 20 fm	20	8 18 FT	9 17 FM	10 17 FT	11 15 td	12 15 tg	1 14 td
2 24 md	3 25 MR	4 23 ef	5 23 er	6 21 EW	7 21 EH	21	8 19 ft	9 18 fm	10 18 ft	11 16 FM	12 16 FT	1 15 FM
2 25 RM	3 26 mg	4 24 MF	5 24 MR	6 22 ef	7 22 er	22	8 20 EW	9 19 EH	10 19 EW	11 17 fm	12 17 ft	1 16 fm
2 26 rm	3 27 RT	4 25 md	5 25 mg	6 23 MF	7 23 MR	23	8 21 ef	9 20 er	10 20 ef	11 18 EH	12 18 EW	1 17 EH
2 27 TH	3 28 rt	4 26 RM	5 26 RT	6 24 md	7 24 mg	24	8 22 MF	9 21 MR	10 21 MF	11 19 er	12 19 ef	1 18 er
2 28 tr	3 29 TW	4 27 rm	5 27 rt	6 25 RM	7 25 RT	25	8 23 md	9 22 mg	10 22 md	11 20 MR	12 20 MF	1 19 MR
3 1 FR	3 30 tf	4 28 TH	5 28 TW	6 26 rm	7 26 rt	26	8 24 RM	9 23 RT	10 23 RM	11 21 mg	12 21 md	1 20 mg
3 2 fg	3 31 FF	4 29 tr	5 29 tf	6 27 TH	7 27 TW	27	8 25 rm	9 24 rt	10 24 rm	11 22 RT	12 22 RM	1 21 RT
3 3 ET	4 1 fd	4 30 FR	5 30 FF	6 28 tr	7 28 tf	28	8 26 TH	9 25 TW	10 25 TH	11 23 rt	12 23 rm	1 22 rt
3 4 et	4 2 EM	5 1 fg	5 31 fd	6 29 FR	7 29 FF	29	8 27 tr	9 26 tf	10 26 tr	11 24 TW	12 24 TH	1 23 TW
		5 2 ET		6 30 fg		30	8 28 FR	9 27 FF		11 25 tf	12 25 tr	

1936 FR RAT

JAN MT	FEB mt	MAR RW	MAR RW	APR rf	MAY FF	JUN td	DAY OF MON	JUL FM	AUG fm	SEP EH	OCT er	NOV MR	DEC mg
13 SPRING	13 WARM	14 CLEAR	16 SUMMER	17 GRAIN	19 HEAT	22 FALL		23 DEW	23 C DEW	24 WINTER	24 SNOW	24 CHILL	23 SPRING
7:30	1:50	7:07	1:14	5:31	15:59	1:43		5:13	19:33	23:19	15:33	1:44	13:26
1 24 tf	2 23 tr	3 23 TW	4 21 rm	5 21 rt	6 19 RM	7 18 mg	1	8 17 md	9 16 mg	10 15 MF	11 14 MR	12 14 MF	1 13 MR
1 25 FF	2 24 FR	3 24 tf	4 22 TH	5 22 TW	6 20 rm	7 19 RT	2	8 18 RM	9 17 RT	10 16 md	11 15 mg	12 15 md	1 14 mg
1 26 fd	2 25 fg	3 25 FF	4 23 tr	5 23 tf	6 21 TH	7 20 rt	3	8 19 rm	9 18 rt	10 17 RM	11 16 RT	12 16 RM	1 15 RT
1 27 EM	2 26 ET	3 26 fd	4 24 FR	5 24 FF	6 22 tr	7 21 TW	4	8 20 TH	9 19 TW	10 18 rm	11 17 rt	12 17 rm	1 16 rt
1 28 em	2 27 et	3 27 EM	4 25 fg	5 25 fd	6 23 FR	7 22 tf	5	8 21 tr	9 20 tf	10 19 TH	11 18 TW	12 18 TH	1 17 TW
1 29 MH	2 28 MW	3 28 em	4 26 ET	5 26 EM	6 24 fg	7 23 FF	6	8 22 FR	9 21 FF	10 20 tr	11 19 tf	12 19 tr	1 18 tf
1 30 mr	2 29 mf	3 29 MH	4 27 et	5 27 em	6 25 ET	7 24 fd	7	8 23 fg	9 22 fd	10 21 FR	11 20 FF	12 20 FR	1 19 FF
1 31 RR	3 1 RF	3 30 mr	4 28 MW	5 28 MH	6 26 et	7 25 EM	8	8 24 ET	9 23 EM	10 22 fg	11 21 fd	12 21 fg	1 20 fd
2 1 rg	3 2 rd	3 31 RR	4 29 mf	5 29 mr	6 27 MW	7 26 em	9	8 25 et	9 24 em	10 23 ET	11 22 EM	12 22 ET	1 21 EM
2 2 TT	3 3 TM	4 1 rg	4 30 RF	5 30 RR	6 28 mf	7 27 MH	10	8 26 MW	9 25 MH	10 24 et	11 23 em	12 23 et	1 22 em
2 3 tt	3 4 tm	4 2 TT	5 1 rd	5 31 rg	6 29 RF	7 28 mr	11	8 27 mf	9 26 mr	10 25 MW	11 24 MH	12 24 MW	1 23 MH
2 4 FW	3 5 FH	4 3 tt	5 2 TM	6 1 TT	6 30 rd	7 29 RR	12	8 28 RF	9 27 RR	10 26 mf	11 25 mr	12 25 mf	1 24 mr
2 5 ff	3 6 fr	4 4 FW	5 3 tm	6 2 tt	7 1 TM	7 30 rg	13	8 29 rd	9 28 rg	10 27 RF	11 26 RR	12 26 RF	1 25 RR
2 6 EF	3 7 ER	4 5 ff	5 4 FH	6 3 FW	7 2 tm	7 31 TT	14	8 30 TM	9 29 TT	10 28 rd	11 27 rg	12 27 rd	1 26 rg
2 7 ed	3 8 eg	4 6 EF	5 5 fr	6 4 ff	7 3 FH	8 1 tt	15	8 31 tm	9 30 tt	10 29 TM	11 28 TT	12 28 TM	1 27 TT
2 8 MM	3 9 MT	4 7 ed	5 6 ER	6 5 EF	7 4 fr	8 2 FW	16	9 1 FH	10 1 FW	10 30 tm	11 29 tt	12 29 tm	1 28 tt
2 9 mm	3 10 mt	4 8 MM	5 7 eg	6 6 ed	7 5 ER	8 3 ff	17	9 2 fr	10 2 ff	10 31 FH	11 30 FW	12 30 FH	1 29 FW
2 10 RH	3 11 RW	4 9 mm	5 8 MT	6 7 MM	7 6 eg	8 4 EF	18	9 3 ER	10 3 EF	11 1 fr	12 1 ff	12 31 fr	1 30 ff
2 11 rr	3 12 rf	4 10 RH	5 9 mt	6 8 mm	7 7 MT	8 5 ed	19	9 4 eg	10 4 ed	11 2 ER	12 2 EF	1 1 ER	1 31 EF
2 12 TR	3 13 TF	4 11 rr	5 10 RW	6 9 RH	7 8 mt	8 6 MM	20	9 5 MT	10 5 MM	11 3 eg	12 3 ed	1 2 eg	2 1 ed
2 13 tg	3 14 td	4 12 TR	5 11 rf	6 10 rr	7 9 RW	8 7 mm	21	9 6 mt	10 6 mm	11 4 MT	12 4 MM	1 3 MT	2 2 MM
2 14 FT	3 15 FM	4 13 tg	5 12 TF	6 11 TR	7 10 rf	8 8 RH	22	9 7 RW	10 7 RH	11 5 mt	12 5 mm	1 4 mt	2 3 mm
2 15 ft	3 16 fm	4 14 FT	5 13 td	6 12 tg	7 11 TF	8 9 rr	23	9 8 rf	10 8 rr	11 6 RW	12 6 RH	1 5 RW	2 4 RH
2 16 EW	3 17 EH	4 15 ft	5 14 FM	6 13 FT	7 12 td	8 10 TR	24	9 9 TF	10 9 TR	11 7 rf	12 7 rr	1 6 rf	2 5 rr
2 17 ef	3 18 er	4 16 EW	5 15 fm	6 14 ft	7 13 FM	8 11 tg	25	9 10 td	10 10 tg	11 8 TF	12 8 TR	1 7 TF	2 6 TR
2 18 MF	3 19 MR	4 17 ef	5 16 EH	6 15 EW	7 14 fm	8 12 FT	26	9 11 FM	10 11 FT	11 9 td	12 9 tg	1 8 td	2 7 tg
2 19 md	3 20 mg	4 18 MF	5 17 er	6 16 ef	7 15 EH	8 13 ft	27	9 12 fm	10 12 ft	11 10 FM	12 10 FT	1 9 FM	2 8 FT
2 20 RM	3 21 RT	4 19 md	5 18 MR	6 17 MF	7 16 er	8 14 EW	28	9 13 EH	10 13 EW	11 11 fm	12 11 ft	1 10 fm	2 9 ft
2 21 rm	3 22 rt	4 20 RM	5 19 mg	6 18 md	7 17 MR	8 15 ef	29	9 14 er	10 14 ef	11 12 EH	12 12 EW	1 11 EH	2 10 EW
2 22 TH			5 20 RT			8 16 MF	30	9 15 MR		11 13 er	12 13 ef	1 12 er	

1937 fg OX

JAN RT	FEB et	MAR TW	APR tf	MAY FF	JUN fd	DAY OF	JUL EM	AUG em	SEP MH	OCT mr	NOV RR	DEC rg
24 WARM	24 CLEAR	26 SUMMER	28 GRAIN	29 HEAT		MON	3 FALL	4 DEW	6 C DEW	6 WINTER	5 SNOW	5 CHILL
7:45	13:02	7:02	11:23	21:46			7:26	11:01	1:12	5:09	21:22	7:32
2 11 ef	3 13 er	4 11 EW	5 10 fm	6 9 ft	7 8 FM	1	8 6 tg	9 5 td	10 4 TR	11 3 TF	12 3 TR	1 2 TF
2 12 MF	3 14 MR	4 12 ef	5 11 EH	6 10 EW	7 9 fm	2	8 7 FT	9 6 FM	10 5 tg	11 4 td	12 4 tg	1 3 td
2 13 md	3 15 mg	4 13 MF	5 12 er	6 11 ef	7 10 EH	3	8 8 ft	9 7 fm	10 6 FT	11 5 FM	12 5 FT	1 4 FM
2 14 RM	3 16 RT	4 14 md	5 13 MR	6 12 MF	7 11 er	4	8 9 EW	9 8 EH	10 7 ft	11 6 fm	12 6 ft	1 5 fm
2 15 rm	3 17 rt	4 15 RM	5 14 mg	6 13 md	7 12 MR	5	8 10 ef	9 9 er	10 8 EW	11 7 EH	12 7 EW	1 6 EH
2 16 TH	3 18 TW	4 16 rm	5 15 RT	6 14 RM	7 13 mg	6	8 11 MF	9 10 MR	10 9 ef	11 8 er	12 8 ef	1 7 er
2 17 tr	3 19 tf	4 17 TH	5 16 rt	6 15 rm	7 14 RT	7	8 12 md	9 11 mg	10 10 MF	11 9 MR	12 9 MF	1 8 MR
2 18 FR	3 20 FF	4 18 tr	5 17 TW	6 16 TH	7 15 rt	8	8 13 RM	9 12 RT	10 11 md	11 10 mg	12 10 md	1 9 mg
2 19 fg	3 21 fd	4 19 FR	5 18 tf	6 17 tr	7 16 TW	9	8 14 rm	9 13 rt	10 12 RM	11 11 RT	12 11 RM	1 10 RT
2 20 ET	3 22 EM	4 20 fg	5 19 FF	6 18 FR	7 17 tf	10	8 15 TH	9 14 TW	10 13 rm	11 12 rt	12 12 rm	1 11 rt
2 21 et	3 23 em	4 21 ET	5 20 fd	6 19 fg	7 18 FF	11	8 16 tr	9 15 tf	10 14 TH	11 13 TW	12 13 TH	1 12 TW
2 22 MW	3 24 MH	4 22 et	5 21 EM	6 20 ET	7 19 fd	12	8 17 FR	9 16 FF	10 15 tr	11 14 tf	12 14 tr	1 13 tf
2 23 mf	3 25 mr	4 23 MW	5 22 em	6 21 et	7 20 EM	13	8 18 fg	9 17 fd	10 16 FR	11 15 FF	12 15 FR	1 14 FF
2 24 RF	3 26 RR	4 24 mf	5 23 MH	6 22 MW	7 21 em	14	8 19 ET	9 18 EM	10 17 fg	11 16 fd	12 16 fg	1 15 fd
2 25 rd	3 27 rg	4 25 RF	5 24 mr	6 23 mf	7 22 MH	15	8 20 et	9 19 em	10 18 ET	11 17 EM	12 17 ET	1 16 EM
2 26 TM	3 28 TT	4 26 rd	5 25 RR	6 24 RF	7 23 mr	16	8 21 MW	9 20 MH	10 19 et	11 18 em	12 18 et	1 17 em
2 27 tm	3 29 tt	4 27 TM	5 26 rg	6 25 rd	7 24 RR	17	8 22 mf	9 21 mr	10 20 MW	11 19 MH	12 19 MW	1 18 MH
2 28 FH	3 30 FW	4 28 tm	5 27 TT	6 26 TM	7 25 rg	18	8 23 RF	9 22 RR	10 21 mf	11 20 mr	12 20 mf	1 19 mr
3 1 fr	3 31 ff	4 29 FH	5 28 tt	6 27 tm	7 26 TT	19	8 24 rd	9 23 rg	10 22 RF	11 21 RR	12 21 RF	1 20 RR
3 2 ER	4 1 EF	4 30 fr	5 29 FW	6 28 FH	7 27 tt	20	8 25 TM	9 24 TT	10 23 rd	11 22 rg	12 22 rd	1 21 rg
3 3 eg	4 2 ed	5 1 ER	5 30 ff	6 29 fr	7 28 FW	21	8 26 tm	9 25 tt	10 24 TM	11 23 TT	12 23 TM	1 22 TT
3 4 MT	4 3 MM	5 2 eg	5 31 EF	6 30 ER	7 29 ff	22	8 27 FH	9 26 FW	10 25 tm	11 24 tt	12 24 tm	1 23 tt
3 5 mt	4 4 mm	5 3 MT	6 1 ed	7 1 eg	7 30 EF	23	8 28 fr	9 27 ff	10 26 FH	11 25 FW	12 25 FH	1 24 FW
3 6 RW	4 5 RH	5 4 mt	6 2 MM	7 2 MT	7 31 ed	24	8 29 ER	9 28 EF	10 27 fr	11 26 ff	12 26 fr	1 25 ff
3 7 rf	4 6 rr	5 5 RW	6 3 mm	7 3 mt	8 1 MM	25	8 30 eg	9 29 ed	10 28 ER	11 27 EF	12 27 ER	1 26 EF
3 8 TF	4 7 TR	5 6 rf	6 4 RH	7 4 RW	8 2 mm	26	8 31 MT	9 30 MM	10 29 eg	11 28 ed	12 28 eg	1 27 ed
3 9 td	4 8 tg	5 7 TF	6 5 rr	7 5 rf	8 3 RH	27	9 1 mt	10 1 mm	10 30 MT	11 29 MM	12 29 MT	1 28 MM
3 10 FM	4 9 FT	5 8 td	6 6 TR	7 6 TF	8 4 rr	28	9 2 RW	10 2 RH	10 31 mt	11 30 mm	12 30 mt	1 29 mm
3 11 fm	4 10 ft	5 9 FM	6 7 tg	7 7 td	8 5 TR	29	9 3 rf	10 3 rr	11 1 RW	12 1 RH	12 31 RW	1 30 RH
3 12 EH			6 8 FT			30	9 4 TF		11 2 rf	12 2 rr	1 1 rf	

1938 ET TIGER

JAN TT	FEB tt	MAR FW	APR ff	MAY EF	JUN ed	DAY OF MON	JUL MM	JUL MM	AUG mm	SEP RH	OCT rr	NOV TR	DEC tg
5 SPRING	5 WARM	5 CLEAR	7 SUMMER	9 GRAIN	11 HEAT		13 FALL	15 DEW	16 C DEW	17 WINTER	17 SNOW	16 CHILL	17 SPRING
19:15	13:34	18:49	12:36	17:07	3:32		13:13	15:49	7:02	9:49	3:13	13:28	1:11
1 31 rr	3 2 rf	4 1 rr	4 30 RW	5 29 mm	6 28 mt	1	7 27 MM	8 25 eg	9 24 ed	10 23 ER	11 22 EF	12 22 ER	1 20 ff
2 1 TR	3 3 TF	4 2 TR	5 1 rf	5 30 RH	6 29 RW	2	7 28 mm	8 26 MT	9 25 MM	10 24 eg	11 23 ed	12 23 eg	1 21 EF
2 2 tg	3 4 td	4 3 tg	5 2 TF	5 31 rr	6 30 rf	3	7 29 RH	8 27 mt	9 26 mm	10 25 MT	11 24 MM	12 24 MT	1 22 ed
2 3 FT	3 5 FM	4 4 FT	5 3 td	6 1 TR	7 1 TF	4	7 30 rr	8 28 RW	9 27 RH	10 26 mt	11 25 mm	12 25 mt	1 23 MM
2 4 ft	3 6 fm	4 5 ft	5 4 FM	6 2 tg	7 2 td	5	7 31 TR	8 29 rf	9 28 rr	10 27 RW	11 26 RH	12 26 RW	1 24 mm
2 5 EW	3 7 EH	4 6 EW	5 5 fm	6 3 FT	7 3 FM	6	8 1 tg	8 30 TF	9 29 TR	10 28 rf	11 27 rr	12 27 rf	1 25 RH
2 6 ef	3 8 er	4 7 ef	5 6 EH	6 4 ft	7 4 fm	7	8 2 FT	8 31 td	9 30 tg	10 29 TF	11 28 TR	12 28 TF	1 26 rr
2 7 MF	3 9 MR	4 8 MF	5 7 er	6 5 EW	7 5 EH	8	8 3 ft	9 1 FM	10 1 FT	10 30 td	11 29 tg	12 29 td	1 27 TR
2 8 md	3 10 mg	4 9 md	5 8 MR	6 6 ef	7 6 er	9	8 4 EW	9 2 fm	10 2 ft	10 31 FM	11 30 FT	12 30 FM	1 28 tg
2 9 RM	3 11 RT	4 10 RM	5 9 mg	6 7 MF	7 7 MR	10	8 5 ef	9 3 EH	10 3 EW	11 1 fm	12 1 ft	12 31 fm	1 29 FT
2 10 rm	3 12 rt	4 11 rm	5 10 RT	6 8 md	7 8 mg	11	8 6 MF	9 4 er	10 4 ef	11 2 EH	12 2 EW	1 1 EH	1 30 ft
2 11 TH	3 13 TW	4 12 TH	5 11 rt	6 9 RM	7 9 RT	12	8 7 md	9 5 MR	10 5 MF	11 3 er	12 3 ef	1 2 er	1 31 EW
2 12 tr	3 14 tf	4 13 tr	5 12 TW	6 10 rm	7 10 rt	13	8 8 RM	9 6 mg	10 6 md	11 4 MR	12 4 MF	1 3 MR	2 1 ef
2 13 FR	3 15 FF	4 14 FR	5 13 tf	6 11 TH	7 11 TW	14	8 9 rm	9 7 RT	10 7 RM	11 5 mg	12 5 md	1 4 mg	2 2 MF
2 14 fg	3 16 fd	4 15 fg	5 14 FF	6 12 tr	7 12 tf	15	8 10 TH	9 8 rt	10 8 rm	11 6 RT	12 6 RM	1 5 RT	2 3 md
2 15 ET	3 17 EM	4 16 ET	5 15 fd	6 13 FR	7 13 FF	16	8 11 tr	9 9 TW	10 9 TH	11 7 rt	12 7 rm	1 6 rt	2 4 RM
2 16 et	3 18 em	4 17 et	5 16 EM	6 14 fg	7 14 fd	17	8 12 FR	9 10 tf	10 10 tr	11 8 TW	12 8 TH	1 7 TW	2 5 rm
2 17 MW	3 19 MH	4 18 MW	5 17 em	6 15 ET	7 15 EM	18	8 13 fg	9 11 FF	10 11 FR	11 9 tf	12 9 tr	1 8 tf	2 6 TH
2 18 mf	3 20 mr	4 19 mf	5 18 MH	6 16 et	7 16 em	19	8 14 ET	9 12 fd	10 12 fg	11 10 FF	12 10 FR	1 9 FF	2 7 tr
2 19 RF	3 21 RR	4 20 RF	5 19 mr	6 17 MW	7 17 MH	20	8 15 et	9 13 EM	10 13 ET	11 11 fd	12 11 fg	1 10 fd	2 8 FR
2 20 rd	3 22 rg	4 21 rd	5 20 RR	6 18 mf	7 18 mr	21	8 16 MW	9 14 em	10 14 et	11 12 EM	12 12 ET	1 11 EM	2 9 fg
2 21 TM	3 23 TT	4 22 TM	5 21 rg	6 19 RF	7 19 RR	22	8 17 mf	9 15 MH	10 15 MW	11 13 em	12 13 et	1 12 em	2 10 ET
2 22 tm	3 24 tt	4 23 tm	5 22 TT	6 20 rd	7 20 rg	23	8 18 RF	9 16 mr	10 16 mf	11 14 MH	12 14 MW	1 13 MH	2 11 et
2 23 FH	3 25 FW	4 24 FH	5 23 tt	6 21 TM	7 21 TT	24	8 19 rd	9 17 RR	10 17 RF	11 15 mr	12 15 mf	1 14 mr	2 12 MW
2 24 fr	3 26 ff	4 25 fr	5 24 FW	6 22 tm	7 22 tt	25	8 20 TM	9 18 rg	10 18 rd	11 16 RR	12 16 RF	1 15 RR	2 13 mf
2 25 ER	3 27 EF	4 26 ER	5 25 ff	6 23 FH	7 23 FW	26	8 21 tm	9 19 TT	10 19 TM	11 17 rg	12 17 rd	1 16 rg	2 14 RF
2 26 eg	3 28 ed	4 27 eg	5 26 EF	6 24 fr	7 24 ff	27	8 22 FH	9 20 tt	10 20 tm	11 18 TT	12 18 TM	1 17 TT	2 15 rd
2 27 MT	3 29 MM	4 28 MT	5 27 ed	6 25 ER	7 25 EF	28	8 23 fr	9 21 FW	10 21 FH	11 19 tt	12 19 tm	1 18 tt	2 16 TM
2 28 mt	3 30 mm	4 29 mt	5 28 MM	6 26 eg	7 26 ed	29	8 24 ER	9 22 ff	10 22 fr	11 20 FW	12 20 FH	1 19 FW	2 17 tm
3 1 RW	3 31 RH			6 27 MT		30		9 23 EF		11 21 ff	12 21 fr		2 18 FH

1939 et RABBIT

JAN FT	FEB ft	MAR EW	APR ef	MAY MF	JUN md	DAY OF MON	JUL RM	AUG rm	SEP TH	OCT tr	NOV FR	DEC fg
16 WARM	17 CLEAR	17 SUMMER	19 GRAIN	22 HEAT	23 FALL		25 DEW	27 C DEW	27 WINTER	28 SNOW	27 CHILL	28 SPRING
19:27	0:38	18:21	23:19	9:19	19:04		20:39	14:05	15:40	9:02	19:24	7:08
2 19 fr	3 21 ff	4 20 fr	5 19 FW	6 17 tm	7 17 tt	1	8 15 TM	9 13 rg	10 13 rd	11 11 RR	12 11 RF	1 9 mr
2 20 ER	3 22 EF	4 21 ER	5 20 ff	6 18 FH	7 18 FW	2	8 16 tm	9 14 TT	10 14 TM	11 12 rg	12 12 rd	1 10 RR
2 21 eg	3 23 ed	4 22 eg	5 21 EF	6 19 fr	7 19 ff	3	8 17 FH	9 15 tt	10 15 tm	11 13 TT	12 13 TM	1 11 rg
2 22 MT	3 24 MM	4 23 MT	5 22 ed	6 20 ER	7 20 EF	4	8 18 fr	9 16 FW	10 16 FH	11 14 tt	12 14 tm	1 12 TT
2 23 mt	3 25 mm	4 24 mt	5 23 MM	6 21 eg	7 21 ed	5	8 19 ER	9 17 ff	10 17 fr	11 15 FW	12 15 FH	1 13 tt
2 24 RW	3 26 RH	4 25 RW	5 24 mm	6 22 MT	7 22 MM	6	8 20 eg	9 18 EF	10 18 ER	11 16 ff	12 16 fr	1 14 FW
2 25 rf	3 27 rr	4 26 rf	5 25 RH	6 23 mt	7 23 mm	7	8 21 MT	9 19 ed	10 19 eg	11 17 EF	12 17 ER	1 15 ff
2 26 TF	3 28 TR	4 27 TF	5 26 rr	6 24 RW	7 24 RH	8	8 22 mt	9 20 MM	10 20 MT	11 18 ed	12 18 eg	1 16 EF
2 27 td	3 29 tg	4 28 td	5 27 TR	6 25 rf	7 25 rr	9	8 23 RW	9 21 mm	10 21 mt	11 19 MM	12 19 MT	1 17 ed
2 28 FM	3 30 FT	4 29 FM	5 28 tg	6 26 TF	7 26 TR	10	8 24 rf	9 22 RH	10 22 RW	11 20 mm	12 20 mt	1 18 MM
3 1 fm	3 31 ft	4 30 fm	5 29 FT	6 27 td	7 27 tg	11	8 25 TF	9 23 rr	10 23 rf	11 21 RH	12 21 RW	1 19 mm
3 2 EH	4 1 EW	5 1 EH	5 30 ft	6 28 FM	7 28 FT	12	8 26 td	9 24 TR	10 24 TF	11 22 rr	12 22 rf	1 20 RH
3 3 er	4 2 ef	5 2 er	5 31 EW	6 29 fm	7 29 ft	13	8 27 FM	9 25 tg	10 25 td	11 23 TR	12 23 TF	1 21 rr
3 4 MR	4 3 MF	5 3 MR	6 1 ef	6 30 EH	7 30 EW	14	8 28 fm	9 26 FT	10 26 FM	11 24 tg	12 24 td	1 22 TR
3 5 mg	4 4 md	5 4 mg	6 2 MF	7 1 er	7 31 ef	15	8 29 EH	9 27 ft	10 27 fm	11 25 FT	12 25 FM	1 23 tg
3 6 RT	4 5 RM	5 5 RT	6 3 md	7 2 MR	8 1 MF	16	8 30 er	9 28 EW	10 28 EH	11 26 ft	12 26 fm	1 24 FT
3 7 rt	4 6 rm	5 6 rt	6 4 RM	7 3 mg	8 2 md	17	8 31 MR	9 29 ef	10 29 er	11 27 EW	12 27 EH	1 25 ft
3 8 TW	4 7 TH	5 7 TW	6 5 rm	7 4 RT	8 3 RM	18	9 1 mg	9 30 MF	10 30 MR	11 28 ef	12 28 er	1 26 EW
3 9 tf	4 8 tr	5 8 tf	6 6 TH	7 5 rt	8 4 rm	19	9 2 RT	10 1 md	10 31 mg	11 29 MF	12 29 MR	1 27 ef
3 10 FF	4 9 FR	5 9 FF	6 7 tr	7 6 TW	8 5 TH	20	9 3 rt	10 2 RM	11 1 RT	11 30 md	12 30 mg	1 28 MF
3 11 fd	4 10 fg	5 10 fd	6 8 FR	7 7 tf	8 6 tr	21	9 4 TW	10 3 rm	11 2 rt	12 1 RM	12 31 RT	1 29 md
3 12 EM	4 11 ET	5 11 EM	6 9 fg	7 8 FF	8 7 FR	22	9 5 tf	10 4 TH	11 3 TW	12 2 rm	1 1 rt	1 30 RM
3 13 em	4 12 et	5 12 em	6 10 ET	7 9 fd	8 8 fg	23	9 6 FF	10 5 tr	11 4 tf	12 3 TH	1 2 TW	1 31 rm
3 14 MH	4 13 MW	5 13 MH	6 11 et	7 10 EM	8 9 ET	24	9 7 fd	10 6 FR	11 5 FF	12 4 tr	1 3 tf	2 1 TH
3 15 mr	4 14 mf	5 14 mr	6 12 MW	7 11 em	8 10 et	25	9 8 EM	10 7 fg	11 6 fd	12 5 FR	1 4 FF	2 2 tr
3 16 RR	4 15 RF	5 15 RR	6 13 mf	7 12 MH	8 11 MW	26	9 9 em	10 8 ET	11 7 EM	12 6 fg	1 5 fd	2 3 FR
3 17 rg	4 16 rd	5 16 rg	6 14 RF	7 13 mr	8 12 mf	27	9 10 MH	10 9 et	11 8 em	12 7 ET	1 6 EM	2 4 fg
3 18 TT	4 17 TM	5 17 TT	6 15 rd	7 14 RR	8 13 RF	28	9 11 mr	10 10 MW	11 9 MH	12 8 et	1 7 em	2 5 ET
3 19 tt	4 18 tm	5 18 tt	6 16 TM	7 15 rg	8 14 rd	29	9 12 RR	10 11 mf	11 10 mr	12 9 MW	1 8 MH	2 6 et
3 20 FW	4 19 FH			7 16 TT		30		10 12 RF		12 10 mf		2 7 MW

1940 MW DRAGON

JAN ET	FEB et	MAR MW	APR mf	MAY RF	JUN rd	DAY OF MON	JUL TM	AUG tm	SEP FH	OCT fr	NOV ER	DEC eg
28 WARM	28 CLEAR	29 SUMMER		1 GRAIN	3 HEAT		5 FALL	7 DEW	8 C DEW	8 WINTER	9 SNOW	9 CHILL
1:24	6:35	0:16		5:07	15:08		1:34	3:30	19:54	21:27	13:58	1:04
2 8 mf	3 9 mr	4 8 mf	5 7 MH	6 6 MW	7 5 em	1	8 4 et	9 2 EM	10 1 fg	10 31 fd	11 29 FR	12 29 FF
2 9 RF	3 10 RR	4 9 RF	5 8 mr	6 7 mf	7 6 MH	2	8 5 MW	9 3 em	10 2 ET	11 1 EM	11 30 fg	12 30 fd
2 10 rd	3 11 rg	4 10 rd	5 9 RR	6 8 RF	7 7 mr	3	8 6 mf	9 4 MH	10 3 et	11 2 em	12 1 ET	12 31 EM
2 11 TM	3 12 TT	4 11 TM	5 10 rg	6 9 rd	7 8 RR	4	8 7 RF	9 5 mr	10 4 MW	11 3 MH	12 2 et	1 1 em
2 12 tm	3 13 tt	4 12 tm	5 11 TT	6 10 TM	7 9 rg	5	8 8 rd	9 6 RR	10 5 mf	11 4 mr	12 3 MW	1 2 MH
2 13 FH	3 14 FW	4 13 FH	5 12 tt	6 11 tm	7 10 TT	6	8 9 TM	9 7 rg	10 6 RF	11 5 RR	12 4 mf	1 3 mr
2 14 fr	3 15 ff	4 14 fr	5 13 FW	6 12 FH	7 11 tt	7	8 10 tm	9 8 TT	10 7 rd	11 6 rg	12 5 RF	1 4 RR
2 15 ER	3 16 EF	4 15 ER	5 14 ff	6 13 fr	7 12 FW	8	8 11 FH	9 9 tt	10 8 TM	11 7 TT	12 6 rd	1 5 rg
2 16 eg	3 17 ed	4 16 eg	5 15 EF	6 14 ER	7 13 ff	9	8 12 fr	9 10 FW	10 9 tm	11 8 tt	12 7 TM	1 6 TT
2 17 MT	3 18 MM	4 17 MT	5 16 ed	6 15 eg	7 14 EF	10	8 13 ER	9 11 ff	10 10 FH	11 9 FW	12 8 tm	1 7 tt
2 18 mt	3 19 mm	4 18 mt	5 17 MM	6 16 MT	7 15 ed	11	8 14 eg	9 12 EF	10 11 fr	11 10 ff	12 9 FH	1 8 FW
2 19 RW	3 20 RH	4 19 RW	5 18 mm	6 17 mt	7 16 MM	12	8 15 MT	9 13 ed	10 12 ER	11 11 EF	12 10 fr	1 9 ff
2 20 rf	3 21 rr	4 20 rf	5 19 RH	6 18 RW	7 17 mm	13	8 16 mt	9 14 MM	10 13 eg	11 12 ed	12 11 ER	1 10 EF
2 21 TF	3 22 TR	4 21 TF	5 20 rr	6 19 rf	7 18 RH	14	8 17 RW	9 15 mm	10 14 MT	11 13 MM	12 12 eg	1 11 ed
2 22 td	3 23 tg	4 22 td	5 21 TR	6 20 TF	7 19 rr	15	8 18 rf	9 16 RH	10 15 mt	11 14 mm	12 13 MT	1 12 MM
2 23 FM	3 24 FT	4 23 FM	5 22 tg	6 21 td	7 20 TR	16	8 19 TF	9 17 rr	10 16 RW	11 15 RH	12 14 mt	1 13 mm
2 24 fm	3 25 ft	4 24 fm	5 23 FT	6 22 FM	7 21 tg	17	8 20 td	9 18 TR	10 17 rf	11 16 rr	12 15 RW	1 14 RH
2 25 EH	3 26 EW	4 25 EH	5 24 ft	6 23 fm	7 22 FT	18	8 21 FM	9 19 tg	10 18 TF	11 17 TR	12 16 rf	1 15 rr
2 26 er	3 27 ef	4 26 er	5 25 EW	6 24 EH	7 23 ft	19	8 22 fm	9 20 FT	10 19 td	11 18 tg	12 17 TF	1 16 TR
2 27 MR	3 28 MF	4 27 MR	5 26 ef	6 25 er	7 24 EW	20	8 23 EH	9 21 ft	10 20 FM	11 19 FT	12 18 td	1 17 tg
2 28 mg	3 29 md	4 28 mg	5 27 MF	6 26 MR	7 25 ef	21	8 24 er	9 22 EW	10 21 fm	11 20 ft	12 19 FM	1 18 FT
2 29 RT	3 30 RM	4 29 RT	5 28 md	6 27 mg	7 26 MF	22	8 25 MR	9 23 ef	10 22 EH	11 21 EW	12 20 fm	1 19 ft
3 1 rt	3 31 rm	4 30 rt	5 29 RM	6 28 RT	7 27 md	23	8 26 mg	9 24 MF	10 23 er	11 22 ef	12 21 EH	1 20 EW
3 2 TW	4 1 TH	5 1 TW	5 30 rm	6 29 rt	7 28 RM	24	8 27 RT	9 25 md	10 24 MR	11 23 MF	12 22 er	1 21 ef
3 3 tf	4 2 tr	5 2 tf	5 31 TH	6 30 TW	7 29 rm	25	8 28 rt	9 26 RM	10 25 mg	11 24 md	12 23 MR	1 22 MF
3 4 FF	4 3 FR	5 3 FF	6 1 tr	7 1 tf	7 30 TH	26	8 29 TW	9 27 rm	10 26 RT	11 25 RM	12 24 mg	1 23 md
3 5 fd	4 4 fg	5 4 fd	6 2 FR	7 2 FF	7 31 tr	27	8 30 tf	9 28 TH	10 27 rt	11 26 rm	12 25 RT	1 24 RM
3 6 EM	4 5 ET	5 5 EM	6 3 fg	7 3 fd	8 1 FR	28	8 31 FF	9 29 tr	10 28 TW	11 27 TH	12 26 rt	1 25 rm
3 7 em	4 6 et	5 6 em	6 4 ET	7 4 EM	8 2 fg	29	9 1 fd	9 30 FR	10 29 tf	11 28 tr	12 27 TW	1 26 TH
3 8 MH	4 7 MW		6 5 et		8 3 ET	30			10 30 FF		12 28 tf	

1941 mf SNAKE

JAN MT	FEB mt	MAR RW	APR rf	MAY FF	JUN td	JUN td	DAY OF MON	JUL FM	AUG fm	SEP EH	OCT er	NOV MR	DEC mg
9 SPRING	9 WARM	9 CLEAR	11 SUMMER	12 GRAIN	13 HEAT	16 FALL	-	17 DEW	19 C DEW	20 WINTER	19 SNOW	20 CHILL	19 SPRING
12:50	7:10	12:25	6:10	10:40	31:03	7:22		9:24	1:43	3:25	19:57	7:03	18:49
1 27 tr	2 26 tf	3 28 tr	4 26 TW	5 26 TH	6 25 TW	7 24 rm	1	8 23 rt	9 21 RM	10 20 mg	11 19 md	12 18 MR	1 17 MF
1 28 FR	2 27 FF	3 29 FR	4 27 tf	5 27 tr	6 26 tf	7 25 TH	2	8 24 TW	9 22 rm	10 21 RT	11 20 RM	12 19 mg	1 18 md
1 29 fg	2 28 fd	3 30 fg	4 28 FF	5 28 FR	6 27 FF	7 26 tr	3	8 25 tf	9 23 TH	10 22 rt	11 21 rm	12 20 RT	1 19 RM
1 30 ET	3 1 EM	3 31 ET	4 29 fd	5 29 fg	6 28 fd	7 27 FR	4	8 26 FF	9 24 tr	10 23 TW	11 22 TH	12 21 rt	1 20 rm
1 31 et	3 2 em	4 1 et	4 30 EM	5 30 ET	6 29 EM	7 28 fg	5	8 27 fd	9 25 FR	10 24 tf	11 23 tr	12 22 TW	1 21 TH
2 1 MW	3 3 MH	4 2 MW	5 1 em	5 31 et	6 30 em	7 29 ET	6	8 28 EM	9 26 fg	10 25 FF	11 24 FR	12 23 tf	1 22 tr
2 2 mf	3 4 mr	4 3 mf	5 2 MH	6 1 MW	7 1 MH	7 30 et	7	8 29 em	9 27 ET	10 26 fd	11 25 fg	12 24 FF	1 23 FR
2 3 RF	3 5 RR	4 4 RF	5 3 mr	6 2 mf	7 2 mr	7 31 MW	8	8 30 MH	9 28 et	10 27 EM	11 26 ET	12 25 fd	1 24 fg
2 4 rd	3 6 rg	4 5 rd	5 4 RR	6 3 RF	7 3 RR	8 1 mf	9	8 31 mr	9 29 MW	10 28 em	11 27 et	12 26 EM	1 25 ET
2 5 TM	3 7 TT	4 6 TM	5 5 rg	6 4 rd	7 4 rg	8 2 RF	10	9 1 RR	9 30 mf	10 29 MH	11 28 MW	12 27 em	1 26 et
2 6 tm	3 8 tt	4 7 tm	5 6 TT	6 5 TM	7 5 TT	8 3 rd	11	9 2 rg	10 1 RF	10 30 mr	11 29 mf	12 28 MH	1 27 MW
2 7 FH	3 9 FW	4 8 FH	5 7 tt	6 6 tm	7 6 tt	8 4 TM	12	9 3 TT	10 2 rd	10 31 RR	11 30 RF	12 29 mr	1 28 mf
2 8 fr	3 10 ff	4 9 fr	5 8 FW	6 7 FH	7 7 FW	8 5 tm	13	9 4 tt	10 3 TM	11 1 rg	12 1 rd	12 30 RR	1 29 RF
2 9 ER	3 11 EF	4 10 ER	5 9 ff	6 8 fr	7 8 ff	8 6 FH	14	9 5 FW	10 4 tm	11 2 TT	12 2 TM	12 31 rg	1 30 rd
2 10 eg	3 12 ed	4 11 eg	5 10 EF	6 9 ER	7 9 EF	8 7 fr	15	9 6 ff	10 5 FH	11 3 tt	12 3 tm	1 1 TT	1 31 TM
2 11 MT	3 13 MM	4 12 MT	5 11 ed	6 10 eg	7 10 ed	8 8 ER	16	9 7 EF	10 6 fr	11 4 FW	12 4 FH	1 2 tt	2 1 tm
2 12 mt	3 14 mm	4 13 mt	5 12 MM	6 11 MT	7 11 MM	8 9 eg	17	9 8 ed	10 7 ER	11 5 ff	12 5 fr	1 3 FW	2 2 FH
2 13 RW	3 15 RH	4 14 RW	5 13 mm	6 12 mt	7 12 mm	8 10 MT	18	9 9 MM	10 8 eg	11 6 EF	12 6 ER	1 4 ff	2 3 fr
2 14 rf	3 16 rr	4 15 rf	5 14 RH	6 13 RW	7 13 RH	8 11 mt	19	9 10 mm	10 9 MT	11 7 ed	12 7 eg	1 5 EF	2 4 ER
2 15 TF	3 17 TR	4 16 TF	5 15 rr	6 14 rf	7 14 rr	8 12 RW	20	9 11 RH	10 10 mt	11 8 MM	12 8 MT	1 6 ed	2 5 eg
2 16 td	3 18 tg	4 17 td	5 16 TR	6 15 TF	7 15 TR	8 13 rf	21	9 12 rr	10 11 RW	11 9 mm	12 9 mt	1 7 MM	2 6 MT
2 17 FM	3 19 FT	4 18 FM	5 17 tg	6 16 td	7 16 tg	8 14 TF	22	9 13 TR	10 12 rf	11 10 RH	12 10 RW	1 8 mm	2 7 mt
2 18 fm	3 20 ft	4 19 fm	5 18 FT	6 17 FM	7 17 FT	8 15 td	23	9 14 tg	10 13 TF	11 11 rr	12 11 rf	1 9 RH	2 8 RW
2 19 EH	3 21 EW	4 20 EH	5 19 ft	6 18 fm	7 18 ft	8 16 FM	24	9 15 FT	10 14 td	11 12 TR	12 12 TF	1 10 rr	2 9 rf
2 20 er	3 22 ef	4 21 er	5 20 EW	6 19 EH	7 19 EW	8 17 fm	25	9 16 ft	10 15 FM	11 13 tg	12 13 td	1 11 TR	2 10 TF
2 21 MR	3 23 MF	4 22 MR	5 21 ef	6 20 er	7 20 ef	8 18 EH	26	9 17 EW	10 16 fm	11 14 FT	12 14 FM	1 12 tg	2 11 td
2 22 mg	3 24 md	4 23 mg	5 22 MF	6 21 MR	7 21 MF	8 19 er	27	9 18 ef	10 17 EH	11 15 ft	12 15 fm	1 13 FT	2 12 FM
2 23 RT	3 25 RM	4 24 RT	5 23 md	6 22 mg	7 22 md	8 20 MR	28	9 19 MF	10 18 er	11 16 EW	12 16 EH	1 14 ft	2 13 fm
2 24 rt	3 26 rm	4 25 rt	5 24 RM	6 23 RT	7 23 RM	8 21 mg	29	9 20 md	10 19 MR	11 17 ef	12 17 er	1 15 EW	2 14 EH
2 25 TW	3 27 TH		5 25 rm	6 24 rt		8 22 RT	30			11 18 MF		1 16 ef	

1942 RF HORSE

JAN RT	FEB rt	MAR TW	APR tf	MAY FF	JUN fd	DAY OF MON	JUL EM	AUG em	SEP MH	OCT mr	NOV RR	DEC rg
20 WARM	20 CLEAR	22 SUMMER	23 GRAIN	25 HEAT	27 FALL		28 DEW	30 C DEW		1 WINTER	1 SNOW	1 CHILL
12:53	18:24	12:07	16:37	3:14	13:10		15:07	7:32		9:12	1:47	13:10
2 15 er	3 17 ef	4 15 EH	5 15 EW	6 14 EH	7 13 ft	1	8 12 fm	9 10 FT	10 10 FM	11 8 tg	12 8 td	1 6 TR
2 16 MR	3 18 MF	4 16 er	5 16 ef	6 15 er	7 14 EW	2	8 13 EH	9 11 ft	10 11 fm	11 9 FT	12 9 FM	1 7 tg
2 17 mg	3 19 md	4 17 MR	5 17 MF	6 16 MR	7 15 ef	3	8 14 er	9 12 EW	10 12 EH	11 10 ft	12 10 fm	1 8 FT
2 18 RT	3 20 RM	4 18 mg	5 18 md	6 17 mg	7 16 MF	4	8 15 MR	9 13 ef	10 13 er	11 11 EW	12 11 EH	1 9 ft
2 19 rt	3 21 rm	4 19 RT	5 19 RM	6 18 RT	7 17 md	5	8 16 mg	9 14 MF	10 14 MR	11 12 ef	12 12 er	1 10 EW
2 20 TW	3 22 TH	4 20 rt	5 20 rm	6 19 rt	7 18 RM	6	8 17 RT	9 15 md	10 15 mg	11 13 MF	12 13 MR	1 11 ef
2 21 tf	3 23 tr	4 21 TW	5 21 TH	6 20 TW	7 19 rm	7	8 18 rt	9 16 RM	10 16 RT	11 14 md	12 14 mg	1 12 MF
2 22 FF	3 24 FR	4 22 tf	5 22 tr	6 21 tf	7 20 TH	8	8 19 TW	9 17 rm	10 17 rt	11 15 RM	12 15 RT	1 13 md
2 23 fd	3 25 fg	4 23 FF	5 23 FR	6 22 FF	7 21 tr	9	8 20 tf	9 18 TH	10 18 TW	11 16 rm	12 16 rt	1 14 RM
2 24 EM	3 26 ET	4 24 fd	5 24 fg	6 23 fd	7 22 FR	10	8 21 FF	9 19 tr	10 19 tf	11 17 TH	12 17 TW	1 15 rm
2 25 em	3 27 et	4 25 EM	5 25 ET	6 24 EM	7 23 fg	11	8 22 fd	9 20 FR	10 20 FF	11 18 tr	12 18 tf	1 16 TH
2 26 MH	3 28 MW	4 26 em	5 26 et	6 25 em	7 24 ET	12	8 23 EM	9 21 fg	10 21 fd	11 19 FR	12 19 FF	1 17 tr
2 27 mr	3 29 mf	4 27 MH	5 27 MW	6 26 MH	7 25 et	13	8 24 em	9 22 ET	10 22 EM	11 20 fg	12 20 fd	1 18 FR
2 28 RR	3 30 RF	4 28 mr	5 28 mf	6 27 mr	7 26 MW	14	8 25 MH	9 23 et	10 23 em	11 21 ET	12 21 EM	1 19 fg
3 1 rg	3 31 rd	4 29 RR	5 29 RF	6 28 RR	7 27 mf	15	8 26 mr	9 24 MW	10 24 MH	11 22 et	12 22 em	1 20 ET
3 2 TT	4 1 TM	4 30 rg	5 30 rd	6 29 rg	7 28 RF	16	8 27 RR	9 25 mf	10 25 mr	11 23 MW	12 23 MH	1 21 et
3 3 tt	4 2 tm	5 1 TT	5 31 TM	6 30 TT	7 29 rd	17	8 28 rg	9 26 RF	10 26 RR	11 24 mf	12 24 mr	1 22 MW
3 4 FW	4 3 FH	5 2 tt	6 1 tm	7 1 tt	7 30 TM	18	8 29 TT	9 27 rd	10 27 rg	11 25 RF	12 25 RR	1 23 mf
3 5 ff	4 4 fr	5 3 FW	6 2 FH	7 2 FW	7 31 tm	19	8 30 tt	9 28 TM	10 28 TT	11 26 rd	12 26 rg	1 24 RF
3 6 EF	4 5 ER	5 4 ff	6 3 fr	7 3 ff	8 1 FH	20	8 31 FW	9 29 tm	10 29 tt	11 27 TM	12 27 TT	1 25 rd
3 7 ed	4 6 eg	5 5 EF	6 4 ER	7 4 EF	8 2 fr	21	9 1 ff	9 30 FH	10 30 FW	11 28 tm	12 28 tt	1 26 TM
3 8 MM	4 7 MT	5 6 ed	6 5 eg	7 5 ed	8 3 ER	22	9 2 EF	10 1 fr	10 31 ff	11 29 FH	12 29 FW	1 27 tm
3 9 mm	4 8 mt	5 7 MM	6 6 MT	7 6 MM	8 4 eg	23	9 3 ed	10 2 ER	11 1 EF	11 30 fr	12 30 ff	1 28 FH
3 10 RH	4 9 RW	5 8 mm	6 7 mt	7 7 mm	8 5 MT	24	9 4 MM	10 3 eg	11 2 ed	12 1 ER	12 31 EF	1 29 fr
3 11 rr	4 10 rf	5 9 RH	6 8 RW	7 8 RH	8 6 mt	25	9 5 mm	10 4 MT	11 3 MM	12 2 eg	1 1 ed	1 30 ER
3 12 TR	4 11 TF	5 10 rr	6 9 rf	7 9 rr	8 7 RW	26	9 6 RH	10 5 mt	11 4 mm	12 3 MT	1 2 MM	1 31 eg
3 13 tg	4 12 td	5 11 TR	6 10 TF	7 10 TR	8 8 rf	27	9 7 rr	10 6 RW	11 5 RH	12 4 mt	1 3 mm	2 1 MT
3 14 FT	4 13 FM	5 12 tg	6 11 td	7 11 tg	8 9 TF	28	9 8 TR	10 7 rf	11 6 rr	12 5 RW	1 4 RH	2 2 mt
3 15 ft	4 14 fm	5 13 FT	6 12 FM	7 12 FT	8 10 td	29	9 9 tg	10 8 TF	11 7 TR	12 6 rf	1 5 rr	2 3 RW
3 16 EW		5 14 ft	6 13 fm		8 11 FM	30		10 9 td		12 7 TF		2 4 rf

1943 rd RAM

JAN TT			FEB tt			MAR FW			APR ff			MAY EF			JUN ed			DAY OF MON	JUL MM			AUG mm			SEP RH			OCT rr			NOV TR			DEC tg		
1 SPRING			1 WARM			1 CLEAR			3 SUMMER			4 GRAIN			7 HEAT				8 FALL			9 DEW			11 C DEW			11 WINTER			12 SNOW			11 CHILL		
0:41			18:59			23:59			17:54			23:19			9:03				18:19			21:53			13:21			16:06			7:33			19:00		
2	5	TF	3	6	rr	4	5	rf	5	4	RH	6	3	RW	7	2	mm	1	8	1	mt	8	31	mm	9	29	MT	10	29	MM	11	27	eg	12	27	ed
2	6	td	3	7	TR	4	6	TF	5	5	rr	6	4	rf	7	3	RH	2	8	2	RW	9	1	RH	9	30	mt	10	30	mm	11	28	MT	12	28	MM
2	7	FM	3	8	tg	4	7	td	5	6	TR	6	5	TF	7	4	rr	3	8	3	rf	9	2	rr	10	1	RW	10	31	RH	11	29	mt	12	29	mm
2	8	fm	3	9	FT	4	8	FM	5	7	tg	6	6	td	7	5	TR	4	8	4	TF	9	3	TR	10	2	rf	11	1	rr	11	30	RW	12	30	RH
2	9	EH	3	10	ft	4	9	fm	5	8	FT	6	7	FM	7	6	tg	5	8	5	td	9	4	tg	10	3	TF	11	2	TR	12	1	rf	12	31	rr
2	10	er	3	11	EW	4	10	EH	5	9	ft	6	8	fm	7	7	FT	6	8	6	FM	9	5	FT	10	4	td	11	3	tg	12	2	TF	1	1	TR
2	11	MR	3	12	ef	4	11	er	5	10	EW	6	9	EH	7	8	ft	7	8	7	fm	9	6	ft	10	5	FM	11	4	FT	12	3	td	1	2	tg
2	12	mg	3	13	MF	4	12	MR	5	11	ef	6	10	er	7	9	EW	8	8	8	EH	9	7	EW	10	6	fm	11	5	ft	12	4	FM	1	3	FT
2	13	RT	3	14	md	4	13	mg	5	12	MF	6	11	MR	7	10	ef	9	8	9	er	9	8	ef	10	7	EH	11	6	EW	12	5	fm	1	4	ft
2	14	rt	3	15	RM	4	14	RT	5	13	md	6	12	mg	7	11	MF	10	8	10	MR	9	9	MF	10	8	er	11	7	ef	12	6	EH	1	5	EW
2	15	TW	3	16	rm	4	15	rt	5	14	RM	6	13	RT	7	12	md	11	8	11	mg	9	10	md	10	9	MR	11	8	MF	12	7	er	1	6	ef
2	16	tf	3	17	TH	4	16	TW	5	15	rm	6	14	rt	7	13	RM	12	8	12	RT	9	11	RM	10	10	mg	11	9	md	12	8	MR	1	7	MF
2	17	FF	3	18	tr	4	17	tf	5	16	TH	6	15	TW	7	14	rm	13	8	13	rt	9	12	rm	10	11	RT	11	10	RM	12	9	mg	1	8	md
2	18	fd	3	19	FR	4	18	FF	5	17	tr	6	16	tf	7	15	TH	14	8	14	TW	9	13	TH	10	12	rt	11	11	rm	12	10	RT	1	9	RM
2	19	EM	3	20	fg	4	19	fd	5	18	FR	6	17	FF	7	16	tr	15	8	15	tf	9	14	tr	10	13	TW	11	12	TH	12	11	rt	1	10	rm
2	20	em	3	21	ET	4	20	EM	5	19	fg	6	18	fd	7	17	FR	16	8	16	FF	9	15	FR	10	14	tf	11	13	tr	12	12	TW	1	11	TH
2	21	MH	3	22	et	4	21	em	5	20	ET	6	19	EM	7	18	fg	17	8	17	fd	9	16	fg	10	15	FF	11	14	FR	12	13	tf	1	12	tr
2	22	mr	3	23	MW	4	22	MH	5	21	et	6	20	em	7	19	ET	18	8	18	EM	9	17	ET	10	16	fd	11	15	fg	12	14	FF	1	13	FR
2	23	RR	3	24	mf	4	23	mr	5	22	MW	6	21	MH	7	20	et	19	8	19	em	9	18	et	10	17	EM	11	16	ET	12	15	fd	1	14	fg
2	24	rg	3	25	RF	4	24	RR	5	23	mf	6	22	mr	7	21	MW	20	8	20	MH	9	19	MW	10	18	em	11	17	et	12	16	EM	1	15	ET
2	25	TT	3	26	rd	4	25	rg	5	24	RF	6	23	RR	7	22	mf	21	8	21	mr	9	20	mf	10	19	MH	11	18	MW	12	17	em	1	16	et
2	26	tt	3	27	TM	4	26	TT	5	25	rd	6	24	rg	7	23	RF	22	8	22	RR	9	21	RF	10	20	mr	11	19	mf	12	18	MH	1	17	MW
2	27	FW	3	28	tm	4	27	tt	5	26	TM	6	25	TT	7	24	rd	23	8	23	rg	9	22	rd	10	21	RR	11	20	RF	12	19	mr	1	18	mf
2	28	ff	3	29	FH	4	28	FW	5	27	tm	6	26	tt	7	25	TM	24	8	24	TT	9	23	TM	10	22	rg	11	21	rd	12	20	RR	1	19	RF
3	1	EF	3	30	fr	4	29	ff	5	28	FH	6	27	FW	7	26	tm	25	8	25	tt	9	24	tm	10	23	TT	11	22	TM	12	21	rg	1	20	rd
3	2	ed	3	31	ER	4	30	EF	5	29	fr	6	28	ff	7	27	FH	26	8	26	FW	9	25	FH	10	24	tt	11	23	tm	12	22	TT	1	21	TM
3	3	MM	4	1	eg	5	1	ed	5	30	ER	6	29	EF	7	28	fr	27	8	27	ff	9	26	fr	10	25	FW	11	24	FH	12	23	tt	1	22	tm
3	4	mm	4	2	MT	5	2	MM	5	31	eg	6	30	ed	7	29	ER	28	8	28	EF	9	27	ER	10	26	ff	11	25	fr	12	24	FW	1	23	FH
3	5	RH	4	3	mt	5	3	mm	6	1	MT	7	1	MM	7	30	eg	29	8	29	ed	9	28	eg	10	27	EF	11	26	ER	12	25	ff	1	24	fr
			4	4	RW				6	2	mt				7	31	MT	30	8	30	MM				10	28	ed				12	26	EF			

1944 TM MONKEY

JAN FT	FEB ft	MAR EW	APR ef	APR ef	MAY MF	JUN md	DAY OF MON	JUL TM	AUG rm	SEP TH	OCT tr	NOV FR	DEC fg
12 SPRING	12 WARM	13 CLEAR	13 SUMMER	16 GRAIN	17 HEAT	20 FALL		21 DEW	22 C DEW	22 WINTER	22 SNOW	23 CHILL	22 SPRING
6:23	0:41	5:54	23:40	4:11	14:37	0:19		3:42	19:10	21:55	13:28	0:35	21:20
1 25 ER	2 24 EF	3 24 fr	4 23 ff	5 22 FH	6 21 FW	7 20 tm	1	8 19 tt	9 17 TM	10 17 TT	11 16 TM	12 15 rd	1 14 rd
1 26 eg	2 25 ed	3 25 ER	4 24 EF	5 23 fr	6 22 ff	7 21 FH	2	8 20 FW	9 18 tm	10 18 tt	11 17 tm	12 16 TT	1 15 TM
1 27 MT	2 26 MM	3 26 eg	4 25 ed	5 24 ER	6 23 EF	7 22 fr	3	8 21 ff	9 19 FH	10 19 FW	11 18 FH	12 17 tt	1 16 tm
1 28 mt	2 27 mm	3 27 MT	4 26 MM	5 25 eg	6 24 ed	7 23 ER	4	8 22 EF	9 20 fr	10 20 ff	11 19 fr	12 18 FW	1 17 FH
1 29 RW	2 28 RH	3 28 mt	4 27 mm	5 26 MT	6 25 MM	7 24 eg	5	8 23 ed	9 21 ER	10 21 EF	11 20 ER	12 19 ff	1 18 fr
1 30 rf	2 29 rr	3 29 RW	4 28 RH	5 27 mt	6 26 mm	7 25 MT	6	8 24 MM	9 22 eg	10 22 ed	11 21 eg	12 20 EF	1 19 ER
1 31 TF	3 1 TR	3 30 rf	4 29 rr	5 28 RW	6 27 RH	7 26 mt	7	8 25 mm	9 23 MT	10 23 MM	11 22 MT	12 21 ed	1 20 eg
2 1 td	3 2 tg	3 31 TF	4 30 TR	5 29 rf	6 28 rr	7 27 RW	8	8 26 RH	9 24 mt	10 24 mm	11 23 mt	12 22 MM	1 21 MT
2 2 FM	3 3 FT	4 1 td	5 1 tg	5 30 TF	6 29 TR	7 28 rf	9	8 27 rr	9 25 RW	10 25 RH	11 24 RW	12 23 mm	1 22 mt
2 3 fm	3 4 ft	4 2 FM	5 2 FT	5 31 td	6 30 tg	7 29 TF	10	8 28 TR	9 26 rf	10 26 rr	11 25 rf	12 24 RH	1 23 RW
2 4 EH	3 5 EW	4 3 fm	5 3 ft	6 1 FM	7 1 FT	7 30 td	11	8 29 tg	9 27 TF	10 27 TR	11 26 TF	12 25 rr	1 24 rf
2 5 er	3 6 ef	4 4 EH	5 4 EW	6 2 fm	7 2 ft	7 31 FM	12	8 30 FT	9 28 td	10 28 tg	11 27 td	12 26 TR	1 25 TF
2 6 MR	3 7 MF	4 5 er	5 5 ef	6 3 EH	7 3 EW	8 1 fm	13	8 31 ft	9 29 FM	10 29 FT	11 28 FM	12 27 tg	1 26 td
2 7 mg	3 8 md	4 6 MR	5 6 MF	6 4 er	7 4 ef	8 2 EH	14	9 1 EW	9 30 fm	10 30 ft	11 29 fm	12 28 FT	1 27 FM
2 8 RT	3 9 RM	4 7 mg	5 7 md	6 5 MR	7 5 MF	8 3 er	15	9 2 ef	10 1 EH	10 31 EW	11 30 EH	12 29 ft	1 28 fm
2 9 rt	3 10 rm	4 8 RT	5 8 RM	6 6 mg	7 6 md	8 4 MR	16	9 3 MF	10 2 er	11 1 ef	12 1 er	12 30 EW	1 29 EH
2 10 TW	3 11 TH	4 9 rt	5 9 rm	6 7 RT	7 7 RM	8 5 mg	17	9 4 md	10 3 MR	11 2 MF	12 2 MR	12 31 ef	1 30 er
2 11 tf	3 12 tr	4 10 TW	5 10 TH	6 8 rt	7 8 rm	8 6 RT	18	9 5 RM	10 4 mg	11 3 md	12 3 mg	1 1 MF	1 31 MR
2 12 FF	3 13 FR	4 11 tf	5 11 tr	6 9 TW	7 9 TH	8 7 rt	19	9 6 rm	10 5 RT	11 4 RM	12 4 RT	1 2 md	2 1 mg
2 13 fd	3 14 fg	4 12 FF	5 12 FR	6 10 tf	7 10 tr	8 8 TW	20	9 7 TH	10 6 rt	11 5 rm	12 5 rt	1 3 RM	2 2 RT
2 14 EM	3 15 ET	4 13 fd	5 13 fg	6 11 FF	7 11 FR	8 9 tf	21	9 8 tr	10 7 TW	11 6 TH	12 6 TW	1 4 rm	2 3 rt
2 15 em	3 16 et	4 14 EM	5 14 ET	6 12 fd	7 12 fg	8 10 FF	22	9 9 FR	10 8 tf	11 7 tr	12 7 tf	1 5 TH	2 4 TW
2 16 MH	3 17 MW	4 15 em	5 15 et	6 13 EM	7 13 ET	8 11 fd	23	9 10 fg	10 9 FF	11 8 FR	12 8 FF	1 6 tr	2 5 tf
2 17 mr	3 18 mf	4 16 MH	5 16 MW	6 14 em	7 14 et	8 12 EM	24	9 11 ET	10 10 fd	11 9 fg	12 9 fd	1 7 FR	2 6 FF
2 18 RR	3 19 RF	4 17 mr	5 17 mf	6 15 MH	7 15 MW	8 13 em	25	9 12 et	10 11 EM	11 10 ET	12 10 EM	1 8 fg	2 7 fd
2 19 rg	3 20 rd	4 18 RR	5 18 RF	6 16 mr	7 16 mf	8 14 MH	26	9 13 MW	10 12 em	11 11 et	12 11 em	1 9 ET	2 8 EM
2 20 TT	3 21 TM	4 19 rg	5 19 rd	6 17 RR	7 17 RF	8 15 mr	27	9 14 mf	10 13 MH	11 12 MW	12 12 MH	1 10 et	2 9 em
2 21 tt	3 22 tm	4 20 TT	5 20 TM	6 18 rg	7 18 rd	8 16 RR	28	9 15 RF	10 14 mr	11 13 mf	12 13 mr	1 11 MW	2 10 MH
2 22 FW	3 23 FH	4 21 tt	5 21 tm	6 19 TT	7 19 TM	8 17 rg	29	9 16 rd	10 15 RR	11 14 RF	12 14 RR	1 12 mf	2 11 mr
2 23 ff		4 22 FW		6 20 tt		8 18 TT	30		10 16 rg	11 15 rd		1 13 RF	2 12 RR

1945 tm ROOSTER

JAN ET			FEB et			MAR MW			APR mf			MAY RF			JUN rd			DAY OF MON	JUL TM			AUG tm			SEP FH			OCT fr			NOV ER			DEC eg		
22 WARM			23 CLEAR			25 SUMMER			26 GRAIN			28 HEAT							1 FALL			3 DEW			4 C DEW			4 WINTER			3 SNOW			4 CHILL		
6:38			11:52			5:37			10:06			20:27							6:06			9:30			0:59			3:44			19:18			6:17		
2	13	rg	3	14	RF	4	12	mr	5	12	mf	6	10	MH	7	9	et	1	8	8	em	9	6	ET	10	6	EM	11	5	ET	12	5	EM	1	3	fg
2	14	TT	3	15	rd	4	13	RR	5	13	RF	6	11	mr	7	10	MW	2	8	9	MH	9	7	et	10	7	em	11	6	et	12	6	em	1	4	ET
2	15	tt	3	16	TM	4	14	rg	5	14	rd	6	12	RR	7	11	mf	3	8	10	mr	9	8	MW	10	8	MH	11	7	MW	12	7	MH	1	5	et
2	16	FW	3	17	tm	4	15	TT	5	15	TM	6	13	rg	7	12	RF	4	8	11	RR	9	9	mf	10	9	mr	11	8	mf	12	8	mr	1	6	MW
2	17	ff	3	18	FH	4	16	tt	5	16	tm	6	14	TT	7	13	rd	5	8	12	rg	9	10	RF	10	10	RR	11	9	RF	12	9	RR	1	7	mf
2	18	EF	3	19	fr	4	17	FW	5	17	FH	6	15	tt	7	14	TM	6	8	13	TT	9	11	rd	10	11	rg	11	10	rd	12	10	rg	1	8	RF
2	19	ed	3	20	ER	4	18	ff	5	18	fr	6	16	FW	7	15	tm	7	8	14	tt	9	12	TM	10	12	TT	11	11	TM	12	11	TT	1	9	rd
2	20	MM	3	21	eg	4	19	EF	5	19	ER	6	17	ff	7	16	FH	8	8	15	FW	9	13	tm	10	13	tt	11	12	tm	12	12	tt	1	10	TM
2	21	mm	3	22	MT	4	20	ed	5	20	eg	6	18	EF	7	17	fr	9	8	16	ff	9	14	FH	10	14	FW	11	13	FH	12	13	FW	1	11	tm
2	22	RH	3	23	mt	4	21	MM	5	21	MT	6	19	ed	7	18	ER	10	8	17	EF	9	15	fr	10	15	ff	11	14	fr	12	14	ff	1	12	FH
2	23	rr	3	24	RW	4	22	mm	5	22	mt	6	20	MM	7	19	eg	11	8	18	ed	9	16	ER	10	16	EF	11	15	ER	12	15	EF	1	13	fr
2	24	TR	3	25	rf	4	23	RH	5	23	RW	6	21	mm	7	20	MT	12	8	19	MM	9	17	eg	10	17	ed	11	16	eg	12	16	ed	1	14	ER
2	25	tg	3	26	TF	4	24	rr	5	24	rf	6	22	RH	7	21	mt	13	8	20	mm	9	18	MT	10	18	MM	11	17	MT	12	17	MM	1	15	eg
2	26	FT	3	27	td	4	25	TR	5	25	TF	6	23	rr	7	22	RW	14	8	21	RH	9	19	mt	10	19	mm	11	18	mt	12	18	mm	1	16	MT
2	27	ft	3	28	FM	4	26	tg	5	26	td	6	24	TR	7	23	rf	15	8	22	rr	9	20	RW	10	20	RH	11	19	RW	12	19	RH	1	17	mt
2	28	EW	3	29	fm	4	27	FT	5	27	FM	6	25	tg	7	24	TF	16	8	23	TR	9	21	rf	10	21	rr	11	20	rf	12	20	rr	1	18	RW
3	1	ef	3	30	EH	4	28	ft	5	28	fm	6	26	FT	7	25	td	17	8	24	tg	9	22	TF	10	22	TR	11	21	TF	12	21	TR	1	19	rf
3	2	MF	3	31	er	4	29	EW	5	29	EH	6	27	ft	7	26	FM	18	8	25	FT	9	23	td	10	23	tg	11	22	td	12	22	tg	1	20	TF
3	3	md	4	1	MR	4	30	ef	5	30	er	6	28	EW	7	27	fm	19	8	26	ft	9	24	FM	10	24	FT	11	23	FM	12	23	FT	1	21	td
3	4	RM	4	2	mg	5	1	MF	5	31	MR	6	29	ef	7	28	EH	20	8	27	EW	9	25	fm	10	25	ft	11	24	fm	12	24	ft	1	22	FM
3	5	rm	4	3	RT	5	2	md	6	1	mg	6	30	MF	7	29	er	21	8	28	ef	9	26	EH	10	26	EW	11	25	EH	12	25	EW	1	23	fm
3	6	TH	4	4	rt	5	3	RM	6	2	RT	7	1	md	7	30	MR	22	8	29	MF	9	27	er	10	27	ef	11	26	er	12	26	ef	1	24	EH
3	7	tr	4	5	TW	5	4	rm	6	3	rt	7	2	RM	7	31	mg	23	8	30	md	9	28	MR	10	28	MF	11	27	MR	12	27	MF	1	25	er
3	8	FR	4	6	tf	5	5	TH	6	4	TW	7	3	rm	8	1	RT	24	8	31	RM	9	29	mg	10	29	md	11	28	mg	12	28	md	1	26	MR
3	9	fg	4	7	FF	5	6	tr	6	5	tf	7	4	TH	8	2	rt	25	9	1	rm	9	30	RT	10	30	RM	11	29	RT	12	29	RM	1	27	mg
3	10	ET	4	8	fd	5	7	FR	6	6	FF	7	5	tr	8	3	TW	26	9	2	TH	10	1	rt	10	31	rm	11	30	rt	12	30	rm	1	28	RT
3	11	et	4	9	EM	5	8	fg	6	7	fd	7	6	FR	8	4	tf	27	9	3	tr	10	2	TW	11	1	TH	12	1	TW	12	31	TH	1	29	rt
3	12	MW	4	10	em	5	9	ET	6	8	EM	7	7	fg	8	5	FF	28	9	4	FR	10	3	tf	11	2	tr	12	2	tf	1	1	tr	1	30	TW
3	13	mf	4	11	MH	5	10	et	6	9	em	7	8	ET	8	6	fd	29	9	5	fg	10	4	FF	11	3	FR	12	3	FF	1	2	FR	1	31	tf
						5	11	MW							8	7	EM	30				10	5	fd	11	4	fg	12	4	fd				2	1	FF

1946 FH DOG

JAN MT	FEB mt	MAR RW	APR rf	MAY TF	JUN td	DAY OF MON	JUL FM	AUG fm	SEP EH	OCT er	NOV MR	DEC mg
3 SPRING	3 WARM	4 CLEAR	6 SUMMER	7 GRAIN	10 HEAT		12 FALL	13 DEW	15 C DEW	15 WINTER	15 SNOW	15 CHILL
18:05	12:25	17:39	11:22	15:49	2:11		11:52	15:18	5:42	9:34	1:01	12:11
2 2 fd	3 4 fg	4 2 FF	5 1 tr	5 31 tf	6 29 FH	1	7 28 rt	8 27 rm	9 25 RT	10 25 RM	11 24 RT	12 23 md
2 3 EM	3 5 ET	4 3 fd	5 2 FR	6 1 FF	6 30 tr	2	7 29 TW	8 28 FH	9 26 rt	10 26 rm	11 25 rt	12 24 RM
2 4 em	3 6 et	4 4 EM	5 3 fg	6 2 fd	7 1 FF	3	7 30 tf	8 29 tr	9 27 TW	10 27 FH	11 26 TW	12 25 rm
2 5 MH	3 7 MW	4 5 em	5 4 ET	6 3 EM	7 2 fg	4	7 31 FF	8 30 FF	9 28 tf	10 28 tr	11 27 tf	12 26 FH
2 6 mr	3 8 mf	4 6 MH	5 5 et	6 4 em	7 3 ET	5	8 1 fd	8 31 fg	9 29 FF	10 29 FF	11 28 FF	12 27 tr
2 7 RR	3 9 RF	4 7 mr	5 6 MW	6 5 MH	7 4 et	6	8 2 EM	9 1 ET	9 30 fd	10 30 fg	11 29 fd	12 28 FF
2 8 rg	3 10 rd	4 8 RR	5 7 mf	6 6 mr	7 5 MW	7	8 3 em	9 2 et	10 1 EM	10 31 ET	11 30 EM	12 29 fg
2 9 TT	3 11 TM	4 9 rg	5 8 RF	6 7 RR	7 6 mf	8	8 4 MH	9 3 MW	10 2 em	11 1 et	12 1 em	12 30 ET
2 10 tt	3 12 tm	4 10 TT	5 9 rd	6 8 rg	7 7 RF	9	8 5 mr	9 4 mf	10 3 MH	11 2 MW	12 2 MH	12 31 et
2 11 FW	3 13 FH	4 11 tt	5 10 TM	6 9 TT	7 8 rd	10	8 6 RR	9 5 RF	10 4 mr	11 3 mf	12 3 mr	1 1 MW
2 12 ff	3 14 fr	4 12 FW	5 11 tm	6 10 tt	7 9 TM	11	8 7 rg	9 6 rd	10 5 RR	11 4 RF	12 4 RR	1 2 mf
2 13 EF	3 15 ER	4 13 ff	5 12 FH	6 11 FW	7 10 tm	12	8 8 TT	9 7 TM	10 6 rg	11 5 rd	12 5 rg	1 3 RF
2 14 ed	3 16 eg	4 14 EF	5 13 fr	6 12 ff	7 11 FH	13	8 9 tt	9 8 tm	10 7 TT	11 6 TM	12 6 TT	1 4 rd
2 15 MM	3 17 MT	4 15 ed	5 14 ER	6 13 EF	7 12 fr	14	8 10 FW	9 9 FH	10 8 tt	11 7 tm	12 7 tt	1 5 TM
2 16 mm	3 18 mt	4 16 MM	5 15 eg	6 14 ed	7 13 ER	15	8 11 ff	9 10 fr	10 9 FW	11 8 FH	12 8 FW	1 6 tm
2 17 RH	3 19 RW	4 17 mm	5 16 MT	6 15 MM	7 14 eg	16	8 12 EF	9 11 ER	10 10 ff	11 9 fr	12 9 ff	1 7 FH
2 18 rr	3 20 rf	4 18 RH	5 17 mt	6 16 mm	7 15 MT	17	8 13 ed	9 12 eg	10 11 EF	11 10 ER	12 10 EF	1 8 fr
2 19 TR	3 21 TF	4 19 rr	5 18 RW	6 17 RH	7 16 mt	18	8 14 MM	9 13 MT	10 12 ed	11 11 eg	12 11 ed	1 9 ER
2 20 tg	3 22 td	4 20 TR	5 19 rf	6 18 rr	7 17 RW	19	8 15 mm	9 14 mt	10 13 MM	11 12 MT	12 12 MM	1 10 eg
2 21 FT	3 23 FM	4 21 tg	5 20 TF	6 19 TR	7 18 rf	20	8 16 RH	9 15 RW	10 14 mm	11 13 mt	12 13 mm	1 11 MT
2 22 ft	3 24 fm	4 22 FT	5 21 td	6 20 tg	7 19 TF	21	8 17 rr	9 16 rf	10 15 RH	11 14 RW	12 14 RH	1 12 mt
2 23 EW	3 25 EH	4 23 ft	5 22 FM	6 21 FT	7 20 td	22	8 18 TR	9 17 TF	10 16 rr	11 15 rf	12 15 rr	1 13 RW
2 24 ef	3 26 er	4 24 EW	5 23 fm	6 22 ft	7 21 FM	23	8 19 tg	9 18 td	10 17 TR	11 16 TF	12 16 TR	1 14 rf
2 25 MF	3 27 MR	4 25 ef	5 24 EH	6 23 EW	7 22 fm	24	8 20 FT	9 19 FM	10 18 tg	11 17 td	12 17 tg	1 15 TF
2 26 md	3 28 mg	4 26 MF	5 25 er	6 24 ef	7 23 EH	25	8 21 ft	9 20 fm	10 19 FT	11 18 FM	12 18 FT	1 16 td
2 27 RM	3 29 RT	4 27 md	5 26 MR	6 25 MF	7 24 er	26	8 22 EW	9 21 EH	10 20 ft	11 19 fm	12 19 ft	1 17 FM
2 28 rm	3 30 rt	4 28 RM	5 27 mg	6 26 md	7 25 MR	27	8 23 ef	9 22 er	10 21 EW	11 20 EH	12 20 EW	1 18 fm
3 1 TH	3 31 TW	4 29 rm	5 28 RT	6 27 RM	7 26 mg	28	8 24 MF	9 23 MR	10 22 ef	11 21 er	12 21 ef	1 19 EH
3 2 tr	4 1 tf	4 30 TH	5 29 rt	6 28 rm	7 27 RT	29	8 25 md	9 24 mg	10 23 MF	11 22 MR	12 22 MF	1 20 er
3 3 FR			5 30 TW			30	8 26 RM		10 24 md	11 23 mg		1 21 MR

1947 fr BOAR

JAN RT	FEB et	FEB et	MAR TW	APR tf	MAY RF	JUN fd	DAY OF MON	JUL EM	AUG em	SEP MH	OCT mr	NOV RR	DEC rg
14 SPRING	14 WARM	14 CLEAR	16 SUMMER	18 GRAIN	20 HEAT	22 FALL		24 DEW	25 C DEW	26 WINTER	26 SNOW	26 CHILL	26 SPRING
23:55	18:12	23:23	17:05	21:33	7:56	17:39		21:07	11:32	15:23	7:40	18:01	5:43
1 22 mg	2 21 md	3 23 mg	4 21 MF	5 20 er	6 19 ef	7 18 EH	1	8 16 ft	9 15 fm	10 14 FT	11 13 FM	12 12 tg	1 11 td
1 23 RT	2 22 RM	3 24 RT	4 22 md	5 21 MR	6 20 MF	7 19 er	2	8 17 EW	9 16 EH	10 15 ft	11 14 fm	12 13 FT	1 12 FM
1 24 rt	2 23 rm	3 25 rt	4 23 RM	5 22 mg	6 21 md	7 20 MR	3	8 18 ef	9 17 er	10 16 EW	11 15 EH	12 14 ft	1 13 fm
1 25 TW	2 24 TH	3 26 TW	4 24 rm	5 23 RT	6 22 RM	7 21 mg	4	8 19 MF	9 18 MR	10 17 ef	11 16 er	12 15 EW	1 14 EH
1 26 tf	2 25 tr	3 27 tf	4 25 TH	5 24 rt	6 23 rm	7 22 RT	5	8 20 md	9 19 mg	10 18 MF	11 17 MR	12 16 ef	1 15 er
1 27 FF	2 26 FR	3 28 FF	4 26 tr	5 25 TW	6 24 TH	7 23 rt	6	8 21 RM	9 20 RT	10 19 md	11 18 mg	12 17 MF	1 16 MR
1 28 fd	2 27 fg	3 29 fd	4 27 FR	5 26 tf	6 25 tr	7 24 TW	7	8 22 rm	9 21 rt	10 20 RM	11 19 RT	12 18 md	1 17 mg
1 29 EM	2 28 ET	3 30 EM	4 28 fg	5 27 FF	6 26 FR	7 25 tf	8	8 23 TH	9 22 TW	10 21 rm	11 20 rt	12 19 RM	1 18 RT
1 30 em	3 1 et	3 31 em	4 29 ET	5 28 fd	6 27 fg	7 26 FF	9	8 24 tr	9 23 tf	10 22 TH	11 21 TW	12 20 rm	1 19 rt
1 31 MH	3 2 MW	4 1 MH	4 30 et	5 29 EM	6 28 ET	7 27 fd	10	8 25 FR	9 24 FF	10 23 tr	11 22 tf	12 21 TH	1 20 TW
2 1 mr	3 3 mf	4 2 mr	5 1 MW	5 30 em	6 29 et	7 28 EM	11	8 26 fg	9 25 fd	10 24 FR	11 23 FF	12 22 tr	1 21 tf
2 2 RR	3 4 RF	4 3 RR	5 2 mf	5 31 MH	6 30 MW	7 29 em	12	8 27 ET	9 26 EM	10 25 fg	11 24 fd	12 23 FR	1 22 FF
2 3 rg	3 5 rd	4 4 rg	5 3 RF	6 1 mr	7 1 mf	7 30 MH	13	8 28 et	9 27 em	10 26 ET	11 25 EM	12 24 fg	1 23 fd
2 4 TT	3 6 TM	4 5 TT	5 4 rd	6 2 RR	7 2 RF	7 31 mr	14	8 29 MW	9 28 MH	10 27 et	11 26 em	12 25 ET	1 24 EM
2 5 tt	3 7 tm	4 6 tt	5 5 TM	6 3 rg	7 3 rd	8 1 RR	15	8 30 mf	9 29 mr	10 28 MW	11 27 MH	12 26 et	1 25 em
2 6 FW	3 8 FH	4 7 FW	5 6 tm	6 4 TT	7 4 TM	8 2 rg	16	8 31 RF	9 30 RR	10 29 mf	11 28 mr	12 27 MW	1 26 MH
2 7 ff	3 9 fr	4 8 ff	5 7 FH	6 5 tt	7 5 tm	8 3 TT	17	9 1 rd	10 1 rg	10 30 RF	11 29 RR	12 28 mf	1 27 mr
2 8 EF	3 10 ER	4 9 EF	5 8 fr	6 6 FW	7 6 FH	8 4 tt	18	9 2 TM	10 2 TT	10 31 rd	11 30 rg	12 29 RF	1 28 RR
2 9 ed	3 11 eg	4 10 ed	5 9 ER	6 7 ff	7 7 fr	8 5 FW	19	9 3 tm	10 3 tt	11 1 TM	12 1 TT	12 30 rd	1 29 rg
2 10 MM	3 12 MT	4 11 MM	5 10 eg	6 8 EF	7 8 ER	8 6 ff	20	9 4 FH	10 4 FW	11 2 tm	12 2 tt	12 31 TM	1 30 TT
2 11 mm	3 13 mt	4 12 mm	5 11 MT	6 9 ed	7 9 eg	8 7 EF	21	9 5 fr	10 5 ff	11 3 FH	12 3 FW	1 1 tm	1 31 tt
2 12 RH	3 14 RW	4 13 RH	5 12 mt	6 10 MM	7 10 MT	8 8 ed	22	9 6 ER	10 6 EF	11 4 fr	12 4 ff	1 2 FH	2 1 FW
2 13 rr	3 15 rf	4 14 rr	5 13 RW	6 11 mm	7 11 mt	8 9 MM	23	9 7 eg	10 7 ed	11 5 ER	12 5 EF	1 3 fr	2 2 ff
2 14 TR	3 16 TF	4 15 TR	5 14 rf	6 12 RH	7 12 RW	8 10 mm	24	9 8 MT	10 8 MM	11 6 eg	12 6 ed	1 4 ER	2 3 EF
2 15 tg	3 17 td	4 16 tg	5 15 TF	6 13 rr	7 13 rf	8 11 RH	25	9 9 mt	10 9 mm	11 7 MT	12 7 MM	1 5 eg	2 4 ed
2 16 FT	3 18 FM	4 17 FT	5 16 td	6 14 TR	7 14 TF	8 12 rr	26	9 10 RW	10 10 RH	11 8 mt	12 8 mm	1 6 MT	2 5 MM
2 17 ft	3 19 fm	4 18 ft	5 17 FM	6 15 tg	7 15 td	8 13 TR	27	9 11 rf	10 11 rr	11 9 RW	12 9 RH	1 7 mt	2 6 mm
2 18 EW	3 20 EH	4 19 EW	5 18 fm	6 16 FT	7 16 FM	8 14 tg	28	9 12 TF	10 12 TR	11 10 rf	12 10 rr	1 8 RW	2 7 RH
2 19 ef	3 21 er	4 20 ef	5 19 EH	6 17 ft	7 17 fm	8 15 FT	29	9 13 td	10 13 tg	11 11 TF	12 11 TR	1 9 rf	2 8 rr
2 20 MF	3 22 MR			6 18 EW			30	9 14 FM		11 12 td		1 10 TF	2 9 TR

1948 ER RAT

JAN TT	FEB tt	MAR FW	APR ff	MAY EF	JUN ed	DAY OF MON	JUL MM	AUG mm	SEP RH	OCT rr	NOV TR	DEC tg
25 WARM	26 CLEAR	27 SUMMER	29 GRAIN		1 HEAT		3 FALL	6 DEW	6 C DEW	7 WINTER	7 SNOW	8 CHILL
23:58	5:10	22:53	3:21		13:44		23:27	2:06	17:21	21:12	13:29	0:08
2 10 tg	3 11 td	4 9 TR	5 9 TF	6 7 rr	7 7 rf	1	8 5 RH	9 3 mt	10 3 mm	11 1 MT	12 1 MM	12 30 eg
2 11 FT	3 12 FM	4 10 tg	5 10 td	6 8 TR	7 8 TF	2	8 6 rr	9 4 RW	10 4 RH	11 2 mt	12 2 mm	12 31 MT
2 12 ft	3 13 fm	4 11 FT	5 11 FM	6 9 tg	7 9 td	3	8 7 TR	9 5 rf	10 5 rr	11 3 RW	12 3 RH	1 1 mt
2 13 EW	3 14 EH	4 12 ft	5 12 fm	6 10 FT	7 10 FM	4	8 8 tg	9 6 TF	10 6 TR	11 4 rf	12 4 rr	1 2 RW
2 14 ef	3 15 er	4 13 EW	5 13 EH	6 11 ft	7 11 fm	5	8 9 FT	9 7 td	10 7 tg	11 5 TF	12 5 TR	1 3 rf
2 15 MF	3 16 MR	4 14 ef	5 14 er	6 12 EW	7 12 EH	6	8 10 ft	9 8 FM	10 8 FT	11 6 td	12 6 tg	1 4 TF
2 16 md	3 17 mg	4 15 MF	5 15 MR	6 13 ef	7 13 er	7	8 11 EW	9 9 fm	10 9 ft	11 7 FM	12 7 FT	1 5 td
2 17 RM	3 18 RT	4 16 md	5 16 mg	6 14 MF	7 14 MR	8	8 12 ef	9 10 EH	10 10 EW	11 8 fm	12 8 ft	1 6 FM
2 18 rm	3 19 rt	4 17 RM	5 17 RT	6 15 md	7 15 mg	9	8 13 MF	9 11 er	10 11 ef	11 9 EH	12 9 EW	1 7 fm
2 19 TH	3 20 TW	4 18 rm	5 18 rt	6 16 RM	7 16 RT	10	8 14 md	9 12 MR	10 12 MF	11 10 er	12 10 ef	1 8 EH
2 20 tr	3 21 tf	4 19 TH	5 19 TW	6 17 rm	7 17 rt	11	8 15 RM	9 13 mg	10 13 md	11 11 MR	12 11 MF	1 9 er
2 21 FR	3 22 FF	4 20 tr	5 20 tf	6 18 TH	7 18 TW	12	8 16 rm	9 14 RT	10 14 RM	11 12 mg	12 12 md	1 10 MR
2 22 fg	3 23 fd	4 21 FR	5 21 FF	6 19 tr	7 19 tf	13	8 17 TH	9 15 rt	10 15 rm	11 13 RT	12 13 RM	1 11 mg
2 23 ET	3 24 EM	4 22 fg	5 22 fd	6 20 FR	7 20 FF	14	8 18 tr	9 16 TW	10 16 TH	11 14 rt	12 14 rm	1 12 RT
2 24 et	3 25 em	4 23 ET	5 23 EM	6 21 fg	7 21 fd	15	8 19 FR	9 17 tf	10 17 tr	11 15 TW	12 15 TH	1 13 rt
2 25 MW	3 26 MH	4 24 et	5 24 em	6 22 ET	7 22 EM	16	8 20 fg	9 18 FF	10 18 FR	11 16 tf	12 16 tr	1 14 TW
2 26 mf	3 27 mr	4 25 MW	5 25 MH	6 23 et	7 23 em	17	8 21 ET	9 19 fd	10 19 fg	11 17 FF	12 17 FR	1 15 tf
2 27 RF	3 28 RR	4 26 mf	5 26 mr	6 24 MW	7 24 MH	18	8 22 et	9 20 EM	10 20 ET	11 18 fd	12 18 fg	1 16 FF
2 28 rd	3 29 rg	4 27 RF	5 27 RR	6 25 mf	7 25 mr	19	8 23 MW	9 21 em	10 21 et	11 19 EM	12 19 ET	1 17 fd
2 29 TM	3 30 TT	4 28 rd	5 28 rg	6 26 RF	7 26 RR	20	8 24 mf	9 22 MH	10 22 MW	11 20 em	12 20 et	1 18 EM
3 1 tm	3 31 tt	4 29 TM	5 29 TT	6 27 rd	7 27 rg	21	8 25 RF	9 23 mr	10 23 mf	11 21 MH	12 21 MW	1 19 em
3 2 FH	4 1 FW	4 30 tm	5 30 tt	6 28 TM	7 28 TT	22	8 26 rd	9 24 RR	10 24 RF	11 22 mr	12 22 mf	1 20 MH
3 3 fr	4 2 ff	5 1 FH	5 31 FW	6 29 tm	7 29 tt	23	8 27 TM	9 25 rg	10 25 rd	11 23 RR	12 23 RF	1 21 mr
3 4 ER	4 3 EF	5 2 fr	6 1 ff	6 30 FH	7 30 FW	24	8 28 tm	9 26 TT	10 26 TM	11 24 rg	12 24 rd	1 22 RR
3 5 eg	4 4 ed	5 3 ER	6 2 EF	7 1 fr	7 31 ff	25	8 29 FH	9 27 tt	10 27 tm	11 25 TT	12 25 TM	1 23 rg
3 6 MT	4 5 MM	5 4 eg	6 3 ed	7 2 ER	8 1 EF	26	8 30 fr	9 28 FW	10 28 FH	11 26 tt	12 26 tm	1 24 TT
3 7 mt	4 6 mm	5 5 MT	6 4 MM	7 3 eg	8 2 ed	27	8 31 ER	9 29 ff	10 29 fr	11 27 FW	12 27 FH	1 25 tt
3 8 RW	4 7 RH	5 6 mt	6 5 mm	7 4 MT	8 3 MM	28	9 1 eg	9 30 EF	10 30 ER	11 28 ff	12 28 fr	1 26 FW
3 9 rf	4 8 rr	5 7 RW	6 6 RH	7 5 mt	8 4 mm	29	9 2 MT	10 1 ed	10 31 eg	11 29 EF	12 29 ER	1 27 ff
3 10 TF		5 8 rf		7 6 RW		30		10 2 MM		11 30 ed		1 28 EF

1949 eg OX

JAN FT	FEB ft	MAR EW	APR ef	MAY MF	JUN md	DAY OF MON	JUL RM	JUL RM	AUG rm	SEP TH	OCT tr	NOV FR	DEC fg
7 SPRING	7 WARM	8 CLEAR	9 SUMMER	10 GRAIN	12 HEAT		14 FALL	16 DEW	18 C DEW	18 WINTER	18 SNOW	18 CHILL	18 SPRING
11:23	5:40	10:52	4:37	9:07	19:32		5:16	7:55	0:15	3:02	19:20	5:39	17:21
1 29 ed	2 28 eg	3 29 EF	4 28 ER	5 28 EF	6 26 fr	1	7 26 ff	8 24 FH	9 22 tt	10 22 tm	11 20 TT	12 20 TM	1 18 rg
1 30 MM	3 1 MT	3 30 ed	4 29 eg	5 29 ed	6 27 ER	2	7 27 EF	8 25 fr	9 23 FW	10 23 FH	11 21 tt	12 21 tm	1 19 TT
1 31 mm	3 2 mt	3 31 MM	4 30 MT	5 30 MM	6 28 eg	3	7 28 ed	8 26 ER	9 24 ff	10 24 fr	11 22 FW	12 22 FH	1 20 tt
2 1 RH	3 3 RW	4 1 mm	5 1 mt	5 31 mm	6 29 MT	4	7 29 MM	8 27 eg	9 25 EF	10 25 ER	11 23 ff	12 23 fr	1 21 FW
2 2 rr	3 4 rf	4 2 RH	5 2 RW	6 1 RH	6 30 mt	5	7 30 mm	8 28 MT	9 26 ed	10 26 eg	11 24 EF	12 24 ER	1 22 ff
2 3 TR	3 5 TF	4 3 rr	5 3 rf	6 2 rr	7 1 RW	6	7 31 RH	8 29 mt	9 27 MM	10 27 MT	11 25 ed	12 25 eg	1 23 EF
2 4 tg	3 6 td	4 4 TR	5 4 TF	6 3 TR	7 2 rf	7	8 1 rr	8 30 RW	9 28 mm	10 28 mt	11 26 MM	12 26 MT	1 24 ed
2 5 FT	3 7 FM	4 5 tg	5 5 td	6 4 tg	7 3 TF	8	8 2 TR	8 31 rf	9 29 RH	10 29 RW	11 27 mm	12 27 mt	1 25 MM
2 6 ft	3 8 fm	4 6 FT	5 6 FM	6 5 FT	7 4 td	9	8 3 tg	9 1 TF	9 30 rr	10 30 rf	11 28 RH	12 28 RW	1 26 mm
2 7 EW	3 9 EH	4 7 ft	5 7 fm	6 6 ft	7 5 FM	10	8 4 FT	9 2 td	10 1 TR	10 31 TF	11 29 rr	12 29 rf	1 27 RH
2 8 ef	3 10 er	4 8 EW	5 8 EH	6 7 EW	7 6 fm	11	8 5 ft	9 3 FM	10 2 tg	11 1 td	11 30 TR	12 30 TF	1 28 rr
2 9 MF	3 11 MR	4 9 ef	5 9 er	6 8 ef	7 7 EH	12	8 6 EW	9 4 fm	10 3 FT	11 2 FM	12 1 tg	12 31 td	1 29 TR
2 10 md	3 12 mg	4 10 MF	5 10 MR	6 9 MF	7 8 er	13	8 7 ef	9 5 EH	10 4 ft	11 3 fm	12 2 FT	1 1 FM	1 30 tg
2 11 RM	3 13 RT	4 11 md	5 11 mg	6 10 md	7 9 MR	14	8 8 MF	9 6 er	10 5 EW	11 4 EH	12 3 ft	1 2 fm	1 31 FT
2 12 rm	3 14 rt	4 12 RM	5 12 RT	6 11 RM	7 10 mg	15	8 9 md	9 7 MR	10 6 ef	11 5 er	12 4 EW	1 3 EH	2 1 ft
2 13 TH	3 15 TW	4 13 rm	5 13 rt	6 12 rm	7 11 RT	16	8 10 RM	9 8 mg	10 7 MF	11 6 MR	12 5 ef	1 4 er	2 2 EW
2 14 tr	3 16 tf	4 14 TH	5 14 TW	6 13 TH	7 12 rt	17	8 11 rm	9 9 RT	10 8 md	11 7 mg	12 6 MF	1 5 MR	2 3 ef
2 15 FR	3 17 FF	4 15 tr	5 15 tf	6 14 tr	7 13 TW	18	8 12 TH	9 10 rt	10 9 RM	11 8 RT	12 7 md	1 6 mg	2 4 MF
2 16 fg	3 18 fd	4 16 FR	5 16 FF	6 15 FR	7 14 tf	19	8 13 tr	9 11 TW	10 10 rm	11 9 rt	12 8 RM	1 7 RT	2 5 md
2 17 ET	3 19 EM	4 17 fg	5 17 fd	6 16 fg	7 15 FF	20	8 14 FR	9 12 tf	10 11 TH	11 10 TW	12 9 rm	1 8 rt	2 6 RM
2 18 et	3 20 em	4 18 ET	5 18 EM	6 17 ET	7 16 fd	21	8 15 fg	9 13 FF	10 12 tr	11 11 tf	12 10 TH	1 9 TW	2 7 rm
2 19 MW	3 21 MH	4 19 et	5 19 em	6 18 et	7 17 EM	22	8 16 ET	9 14 fd	10 13 FR	11 12 FF	12 11 tr	1 10 tf	2 8 TH
2 20 mf	3 22 mr	4 20 MW	5 20 MH	6 19 MW	7 18 em	23	8 17 et	9 15 EM	10 14 fg	11 13 fd	12 12 FR	1 11 FF	2 9 tr
2 21 RF	3 23 RR	4 21 mf	5 21 mr	6 20 mf	7 19 MH	24	8 18 MW	9 16 em	10 15 ET	11 14 EM	12 13 fg	1 12 fd	2 10 FR
2 22 rd	3 24 rg	4 22 RF	5 22 RR	6 21 RF	7 20 mr	25	8 19 mf	9 17 MH	10 16 et	11 15 em	12 14 ET	1 13 EM	2 11 fg
2 23 TM	3 25 TT	4 23 rd	5 23 rg	6 22 rd	7 21 RR	26	8 20 RF	9 18 mr	10 17 MW	11 16 MH	12 15 et	1 14 em	2 12 ET
2 24 tm	3 26 tt	4 24 TM	5 24 TT	6 23 TM	7 22 rg	27	8 21 rd	9 19 RR	10 18 mf	11 17 mr	12 16 MW	1 15 MH	2 13 et
2 25 FH	3 27 FW	4 25 tm	5 25 tt	6 24 tm	7 23 TT	28	8 22 TM	9 20 rg	10 19 RF	11 18 RR	12 17 mf	1 16 mr	2 14 MW
2 26 fr	3 28 ff	4 26 FH	5 26 FW	6 25 FH	7 24 tt	29	8 23 tm	9 21 TT	10 20 rd	11 19 rg	12 18 RF	1 17 RR	2 15 mf
2 27 ER		4 27 fr	5 27 ff		7 25 FW	30			10 21 TM		12 19 rd		2 16 RF

1950 MT TIGER

JAN ET	FEB ef	MAR MW	APR mf	MAY RF	JUN rd	DAY OF MON	JUL TM	AUG tm	SEP FH	OCT fr	NOV ER	DEC eg
18 WARM	19 CLEAR	20 SUMMER	21 GRAIN	24 HEAT	25 FALL		26 DEW	28 C DEW	29 WINTER	29 SNOW	29 CHILL	28 SPRING
11:36	16:45	10:25	15:09	1:14	11:36		13:34	6:04	7:44	1:10	11:31	23:14
2 17 rd	3 18 RR	4 17 RF	5 17 RR	6 15 mf	7 15 mr	1	8 14 mf	9 12 MH	10 11 er	11 10 em	12 9 ET	1 8 EM
2 18 TM	3 19 rg	4 18 rd	5 18 rg	6 16 RF	7 16 RR	2	8 15 RF	9 13 mr	10 12 MW	11 11 MH	12 10 et	1 9 em
2 19 tm	3 20 TT	4 19 TM	5 19 TT	6 17 rd	7 17 rg	3	8 16 rd	9 14 RR	10 13 mf	11 12 mr	12 11 MW	1 10 MH
2 20 FH	3 21 tt	4 20 tm	5 20 tt	6 18 TM	7 18 TT	4	8 17 TM	9 15 rg	10 14 RF	11 13 RR	12 12 mf	1 11 mr
2 21 fr	3 22 FW	4 21 FH	5 21 FW	6 19 tm	7 19 tt	5	8 18 tm	9 16 TT	10 15 rd	11 14 rg	12 13 RF	1 12 RR
2 22 ER	3 23 ff	4 22 fr	5 22 ff	6 20 FH	7 20 FW	6	8 19 FH	9 17 tt	10 16 TM	11 15 TT	12 14 rd	1 13 rg
2 23 eg	3 24 EF	4 23 ER	5 23 EF	6 21 fr	7 21 ff	7	8 20 fr	9 18 FW	10 17 tm	11 16 tt	12 15 TM	1 14 TT
2 24 MT	3 25 ed	4 24 eg	5 24 ed	6 22 ER	7 22 EF	8	8 21 ER	9 19 ff	10 18 FH	11 17 FW	12 16 tm	1 15 tt
2 25 mt	3 26 MM	4 25 MT	5 25 MM	6 23 eg	7 23 ed	9	8 22 eg	9 20 EF	10 19 fr	11 18 ff	12 17 FH	1 16 FW
2 26 RW	3 27 mm	4 26 mt	5 26 mm	6 24 MT	7 24 MM	10	8 23 MT	9 21 ed	10 20 ER	11 19 EF	12 18 fr	1 17 ff
2 27 rf	3 28 RH	4 27 RW	5 27 RH	6 25 mt	7 25 mm	11	8 24 mt	9 22 MM	10 21 eg	11 20 ed	12 19 ER	1 18 EF
2 28 TF	3 29 rr	4 28 rf	5 28 rr	6 26 RW	7 26 RH	12	8 25 RW	9 23 mm	10 22 MT	11 21 MM	12 20 eg	1 19 ed
3 1 td	3 30 TR	4 29 TF	5 29 TR	6 27 rf	7 27 rr	13	8 26 rf	9 24 RH	10 23 mt	11 22 mm	12 21 MT	1 20 MM
3 2 FM	3 31 tg	4 30 td	5 30 tg	6 28 TF	7 28 TR	14	8 27 TF	9 25 rr	10 24 RW	11 23 RH	12 22 mt	1 21 mm
3 3 fm	4 1 FT	5 1 FM	5 31 FT	6 29 td	7 29 tg	15	8 28 td	9 26 TR	10 25 rf	11 24 rr	12 23 RW	1 22 RH
3 4 EH	4 2 ft	5 2 fm	6 1 ft	6 30 FM	7 30 FT	16	8 29 FM	9 27 tg	10 26 TF	11 25 TR	12 24 rf	1 23 rr
3 5 er	4 3 EW	5 3 EH	6 2 EW	7 1 fm	7 31 ft	17	8 30 fm	9 28 FT	10 27 td	11 26 tg	12 25 TF	1 24 TR
3 6 MR	4 4 ef	5 4 er	6 3 ef	7 2 EH	8 1 EW	18	8 31 EH	9 29 ft	10 28 FM	11 27 FT	12 26 td	1 25 tg
3 7 mg	4 5 MF	5 5 MR	6 4 MF	7 3 er	8 2 ef	19	9 1 er	9 30 EW	10 29 fm	11 28 ft	12 27 FM	1 26 FT
3 8 RT	4 6 md	5 6 mg	6 5 md	7 4 MR	8 3 MF	20	9 2 MR	10 1 ef	10 30 EH	11 29 EW	12 28 fm	1 27 ft
3 9 rt	4 7 RM	5 7 RT	6 6 RM	7 5 mg	8 4 md	21	9 3 mg	10 2 MF	10 31 er	11 30 ef	12 29 EH	1 28 EW
3 10 TW	4 8 rm	5 8 rt	6 7 rm	7 6 RT	8 5 RM	22	9 4 RT	10 3 md	11 1 MR	12 1 MF	12 30 er	1 29 ef
3 11 tf	4 9 TH	5 9 TW	6 8 TH	7 7 rt	8 6 rm	23	9 5 rt	10 4 RM	11 2 mg	12 2 md	12 31 MR	1 30 MF
3 12 FF	4 10 tr	5 10 tf	6 9 tr	7 8 TW	8 7 TH	24	9 6 TW	10 5 rm	11 3 RT	12 3 RM	1 1 mg	1 31 md
3 13 fd	4 11 FR	5 11 FF	6 10 FR	7 9 tf	8 8 tr	25	9 7 tf	10 6 TH	11 4 rt	12 4 rm	1 2 RT	2 1 RM
3 14 EM	4 12 fg	5 12 fd	6 11 fg	7 10 FF	8 9 FR	26	9 8 FF	10 7 tr	11 5 TW	12 5 TH	1 3 rt	2 2 rm
3 15 em	4 13 ET	5 13 EM	6 12 ET	7 11 fd	8 10 fg	27	9 9 fd	10 8 FR	11 6 tf	12 6 tr	1 4 TW	2 3 TH
3 16 MH	4 14 et	5 14 em	6 13 et	7 12 EM	8 11 ET	28	9 10 EM	10 9 fg	11 7 FF	12 7 FR	1 5 tf	2 4 tr
3 17 mr	4 15 MW	5 15 MH	6 14 MW	7 13 em	8 12 et	29	9 11 em	10 10 ET	11 8 fd	12 8 fg	1 6 FF	2 5 FR
	4 16 mf	5 16 mr		7 14 MH	8 13 MW	30			11 9 EM		1 7 fd	

1951 mt RABBIT

JAN MT	FEB mt	MAR RW	APR rf	MAY TF	JUN td	DAY OF MON	JUL FM	AUG fm	SEP EH	OCT er	NOV MR	DEC mg
29 WARM	29 CLEAR		1 SUMMER	2 GRAIN	5 HEAT		6 FALL	8 DEW	9 C DEW	10 WINTER	10 SNOW	10 CHILL
17:27	22:33		16:10	20:33	7:28		17:24	19:19	11:53	13:27	6:03	17:10
2 6 fg	3 8 fd	4 6 FR	5 6 FF	6 5 FR	7 4 tf	1	8 3 tr	9 1 TW	10 1 TH	10 30 rt	11 29 rm	12 28 RT
2 7 ET	3 9 EM	4 7 fg	5 7 fd	6 6 fg	7 5 FF	2	8 4 FR	9 2 tf	10 2 tr	10 31 TW	11 30 TH	12 29 rt
2 8 et	3 10 em	4 8 ET	5 8 EM	6 7 ET	7 6 fd	3	8 5 fg	9 3 FF	10 3 FR	11 1 tf	12 1 tr	12 30 TW
2 9 MW	3 11 MH	4 9 et	5 9 em	6 8 et	7 7 EM	4	8 6 ET	9 4 fd	10 4 fg	11 2 FF	12 2 FR	12 31 tf
2 10 mf	3 12 mr	4 10 MW	5 10 MH	6 9 MW	7 8 em	5	8 7 et	9 5 EM	10 5 ET	11 3 fd	12 3 fg	1 1 FF
2 11 RF	3 13 RR	4 11 mf	5 11 mr	6 10 mf	7 9 MH	6	8 8 MW	9 6 em	10 6 et	11 4 EM	12 4 ET	1 2 fd
2 12 rd	3 14 rg	4 12 RF	5 12 RR	6 11 RF	7 10 mr	7	8 9 mf	9 7 MH	10 7 MW	11 5 em	12 5 et	1 3 EM
2 13 TM	3 15 TT	4 13 rd	5 13 rg	6 12 rd	7 11 RR	8	8 10 RF	9 8 mr	10 8 mf	11 6 MH	12 6 MW	1 4 em
2 14 tm	3 16 tt	4 14 TM	5 14 TT	6 13 TM	7 12 rg	9	8 11 rd	9 9 RR	10 9 RF	11 7 mr	12 7 mf	1 5 MH
2 15 FH	3 17 FW	4 15 tm	5 15 tt	6 14 tm	7 13 TT	10	8 12 TM	9 10 rg	10 10 rd	11 8 RR	12 8 RF	1 6 mr
2 16 fr	3 18 ff	4 16 FH	5 16 FW	6 15 FH	7 14 tt	11	8 13 tm	9 11 TT	10 11 TM	11 9 rg	12 9 rd	1 7 RR
2 17 ER	3 19 EF	4 17 fr	5 17 ff	6 16 fr	7 15 FW	12	8 14 FH	9 12 tt	10 12 tm	11 10 TT	12 10 TM	1 8 rg
2 18 eg	3 20 ed	4 18 ER	5 18 EF	6 17 ER	7 16 ff	13	8 15 fr	9 13 FW	10 13 FH	11 11 tt	12 11 tm	1 9 TT
2 19 MT	3 21 MM	4 19 eg	5 19 ed	6 18 eg	7 17 EF	14	8 16 ER	9 14 ff	10 14 fr	11 12 FW	12 12 FH	1 10 tt
2 20 mt	3 22 mm	4 20 MT	5 20 MM	6 19 MT	7 18 ed	15	8 17 eg	9 15 EF	10 15 ER	11 13 ff	12 13 fr	1 11 FW
2 21 RW	3 23 RH	4 21 mt	5 21 mm	6 20 mt	7 19 MM	16	8 18 MT	9 16 ed	10 16 eg	11 14 EF	12 14 ER	1 12 ff
2 22 rf	3 24 rr	4 22 RW	5 22 RH	6 21 RW	7 20 mm	17	8 19 mt	9 17 MM	10 17 MT	11 15 ed	12 15 eg	1 13 EF
2 23 TF	3 25 TR	4 23 rf	5 23 rr	6 22 rf	7 21 RH	18	8 20 RW	9 18 mm	10 18 mt	11 16 MM	12 16 MT	1 14 ed
2 24 td	3 26 tg	4 24 TF	5 24 TR	6 23 TF	7 22 rr	19	8 21 rf	9 19 RH	10 19 RW	11 17 mm	12 17 mt	1 15 MM
2 25 FM	3 27 FT	4 25 td	5 25 tg	6 24 td	7 23 TR	20	8 22 TF	9 20 rr	10 20 rf	11 18 RH	12 18 RW	1 16 mm
2 26 fm	3 28 ft	4 26 FM	5 26 FT	6 25 FM	7 24 tg	21	8 23 td	9 21 TR	10 21 TF	11 19 rr	12 19 rf	1 17 RH
2 27 EH	3 29 EW	4 27 fm	5 27 ft	6 26 fm	7 25 FT	22	8 24 FM	9 22 tg	10 22 td	11 20 TR	12 20 TF	1 18 rr
2 28 er	3 30 ef	4 28 EH	5 28 EW	6 27 EH	7 26 ft	23	8 25 fm	9 23 FT	10 23 FM	11 21 tg	12 21 td	1 19 TR
3 1 MR	3 31 MF	4 29 er	5 29 ef	6 28 er	7 27 EW	24	8 26 EH	9 24 ft	10 24 fm	11 22 FT	12 22 FM	1 20 tg
3 2 mg	4 1 md	4 30 MR	5 30 MF	6 29 MR	7 28 ef	25	8 27 er	9 25 EW	10 25 EH	11 23 ft	12 23 fm	1 21 FT
3 3 RT	4 2 RM	5 1 mg	5 31 md	6 30 mg	7 29 MF	26	8 28 MR	9 26 ef	10 26 er	11 24 EW	12 24 EH	1 22 ft
3 4 rt	4 3 rm	5 2 RT	6 1 RM	7 1 RT	7 30 md	27	8 29 mg	9 27 MF	10 27 MR	11 25 ef	12 25 er	1 23 EW
3 5 TW	4 4 TH	5 3 rt	6 2 rm	7 2 rt	7 31 RM	28	8 30 RT	9 28 md	10 28 mg	11 26 MF	12 26 MR	1 24 ef
3 6 tf	4 5 tr	5 4 TW	6 3 TH	7 3 TW	8 1 rm	29	8 31 rt	9 29 RM	10 29 RT	11 27 md	12 27 mg	1 25 MF
3 7 FF		5 5 tf	6 4 tr		8 2 TH	30		9 30 rm		11 28 RM		1 26 md

1952 RW DRAGON

JAN RT	FEB et	MAR TW	APR tf	MAY FF	MAY FF	JUN fd	DAY OF MON	JUL EM	AUG em	SEP MH	OCT mr	NOV RR	DEC rg
10 SPRING	10 WARM	11 CLEAR	12 SUMMER	14 GRAIN	16 HEAT	17 FALL		20 DEW	20 C DEW	20 WINTER	21 SNOW	20 CHILL	21 SPRING
4:54	23:08	4:16	21:54	2:21	13:15	23:12		1:14	17:42	19:22	11:56	23:03	10:46
1 27 RM	2 25 mg	3 26 md	4 24 MR	5 24 MF	6 22 er	7 22 ef	1	8 20 EH	9 19 EW	10 19 EH	11 17 ft	12 17 fm	1 15 FT
1 28 rm	2 26 RT	3 27 RM	4 25 mg	5 25 md	6 23 MR	7 23 MF	2	8 21 er	9 20 ef	10 20 er	11 18 EW	12 18 EH	1 16 ft
1 29 TH	2 27 rt	3 28 rm	4 26 RT	5 26 RM	6 24 mg	7 24 md	3	8 22 MR	9 21 MF	10 21 MR	11 19 ef	12 19 er	1 17 EW
1 30 tr	2 28 TW	3 29 TH	4 27 rt	5 27 rm	6 25 RT	7 25 RM	4	8 23 mg	9 22 md	10 22 mg	11 20 MF	12 20 MR	1 18 ef
1 31 FR	2 29 tf	3 30 tr	4 28 TW	5 28 TH	6 26 rt	7 26 rm	5	8 24 RT	9 23 RM	10 23 RT	11 21 md	12 21 mg	1 19 MF
2 1 fg	3 1 FF	3 31 FR	4 29 tf	5 29 tr	6 27 TW	7 27 TH	6	8 25 rt	9 24 rm	10 24 rt	11 22 RM	12 22 RT	1 20 md
2 2 ET	3 2 fd	4 1 fg	4 30 FF	5 30 FR	6 28 tf	7 28 tr	7	8 26 TW	9 25 TH	10 25 TW	11 23 rm	12 23 rt	1 21 RM
2 3 et	3 3 EM	4 2 ET	5 1 fd	5 31 fg	6 29 FF	7 29 FR	8	8 27 tf	9 26 tr	10 26 tf	11 24 TH	12 24 TW	1 22 rm
2 4 MW	3 4 em	4 3 et	5 2 EM	6 1 ET	6 30 fd	7 30 fg	9	8 28 FF	9 27 FR	10 27 FF	11 25 tr	12 25 tf	1 23 TH
2 5 mf	3 5 MH	4 4 MW	5 3 em	6 2 et	7 1 EM	7 31 ET	10	8 29 fd	9 28 fg	10 28 fd	11 26 FR	12 26 FF	1 24 tr
2 6 RF	3 6 mr	4 5 mf	5 4 MH	6 3 MW	7 2 em	8 1 et	11	8 30 EM	9 29 ET	10 29 EM	11 27 fg	12 27 fd	1 25 FR
2 7 rd	3 7 RR	4 6 RF	5 5 mr	6 4 mf	7 3 MH	8 2 MW	12	8 31 em	9 30 et	10 30 em	11 28 ET	12 28 EM	1 26 fg
2 8 TM	3 8 rg	4 7 rd	5 6 RR	6 5 RF	7 4 mr	8 3 mf	13	9 1 MH	10 1 MW	10 31 MH	11 29 et	12 29 em	1 27 ET
2 9 tm	3 9 TT	4 8 TM	5 7 rg	6 6 rd	7 5 RR	8 4 RF	14	9 2 mr	10 2 mf	11 1 mr	11 30 MW	12 30 MH	1 28 et
2 10 FH	3 10 tt	4 9 tm	5 8 TT	6 7 TM	7 6 rg	8 5 rd	15	9 3 RR	10 3 RF	11 2 RR	12 1 mf	12 31 mr	1 29 MW
2 11 fr	3 11 FW	4 10 FH	5 9 tt	6 8 tm	7 7 TT	8 6 TM	16	9 4 rg	10 4 rd	11 3 rg	12 2 RF	1 1 RR	1 30 mf
2 12 ER	3 12 ff	4 11 fr	5 10 FW	6 9 FH	7 8 tt	8 7 tm	17	9 5 TT	10 5 TM	11 4 TT	12 3 rd	1 2 rg	1 31 RF
2 13 eg	3 13 EF	4 12 ER	5 11 ff	6 10 fr	7 9 FW	8 8 FH	18	9 6 tt	10 6 tm	11 5 tt	12 4 TM	1 3 TT	2 1 rd
2 14 MT	3 14 ed	4 13 eg	5 12 EF	6 11 ER	7 10 ff	8 9 fr	19	9 7 FW	10 7 FH	11 6 FW	12 5 tm	1 4 tt	2 2 TM
2 15 mt	3 15 MM	4 14 MT	5 13 ed	6 12 eg	7 11 EF	8 10 ER	20	9 8 ff	10 8 fr	11 7 ff	12 6 FH	1 5 FW	2 3 tm
2 16 RW	3 16 mm	4 15 mt	5 14 MM	6 13 MT	7 12 ed	8 11 eg	21	9 9 EF	10 9 ER	11 8 EF	12 7 fr	1 6 ff	2 4 FH
2 17 rf	3 17 RH	4 16 RW	5 15 mm	6 14 mt	7 13 MM	8 12 MT	22	9 10 ed	10 10 eg	11 9 ed	12 8 ER	1 7 EF	2 5 fr
2 18 TF	3 18 rr	4 17 rf	5 16 RH	6 15 RW	7 14 mm	8 13 mt	23	9 11 MM	10 11 MT	11 10 MM	12 9 eg	1 8 ed	2 6 ER
2 19 td	3 19 TR	4 18 TF	5 17 rr	6 16 rf	7 15 RH	8 14 RW	24	9 12 mm	10 12 mt	11 11 mm	12 10 MT	1 9 MM	2 7 eg
2 20 FM	3 20 tg	4 19 td	5 18 TR	6 17 TF	7 16 rr	8 15 rf	25	9 13 RH	10 13 RW	11 12 RH	12 11 mt	1 10 mm	2 8 MT
2 21 fm	3 21 FT	4 20 FM	5 19 tg	6 18 td	7 17 TR	8 16 TF	26	9 14 rr	10 14 rf	11 13 rr	12 12 RW	1 11 RH	2 9 mt
2 22 EH	3 22 ft	4 21 fm	5 20 FT	6 19 FM	7 18 tg	8 17 td	27	9 15 TR	10 15 TF	11 14 TR	12 13 rf	1 12 rr	2 10 RW
2 23 er	3 23 EW	4 22 EH	5 21 ft	6 20 fm	7 19 FT	8 18 FM	28	9 16 tg	10 16 td	11 15 tg	12 14 TF	1 13 TR	2 11 rf
2 24 MR	3 24 ef	4 23 er	5 22 EW	6 21 EH	7 20 ft	8 19 fm	29	9 17 FT	10 17 FM	11 16 FT	12 15 td	1 14 tg	2 12 TF
	3 25 MF		5 23 ef		7 21 EW		30	9 18 ft	10 18 fm		12 16 FM		2 13 td

1953 rf SNAKE

JAN TT	FEB tt	MAR FW	APR ff	MAY EF	JUN ed	DAY OF MON	JUL MM	AUG mm	SEP RH	OCT rr	NOV TR	DEC tg
21 WARM	22 CLEAR	23 SUMMER	25 GRAIN	27 HEAT	29 FALL			1 DEW	1 C DEW	2 WINTER	2 SNOW	2 CHILL
4:56	10:13	3:53	8:17	19:03	5:00			7:59	23:31	1:02	17:38	5:18
2 14 FM	3 15 tg	4 14 td	5 13 TR	6 11 rf	7 11 rr	1	8 10 rf	9 8 RH	10 8 RH	11 7 RH	12 6 mt	1 5 mm
2 15 fm	3 16 FT	4 15 FM	5 14 tg	6 12 TF	7 12 TR	2	8 11 TF	9 9 rr	10 9 rf	11 8 rr	12 7 RH	1 6 RH
2 16 EH	3 17 ft	4 16 fm	5 15 FT	6 13 td	7 13 tg	3	8 12 td	9 10 TR	10 10 TF	11 9 TR	12 8 rf	1 7 rr
2 17 er	3 18 EW	4 17 EH	5 16 ft	6 14 FM	7 14 FT	4	8 13 FM	9 11 tg	10 11 td	11 10 tg	12 9 TF	1 8 TR
2 18 MR	3 19 ef	4 18 er	5 17 EW	6 15 fm	7 15 ft	5	8 14 fm	9 12 FT	10 12 FM	11 11 FT	12 10 td	1 9 tg
2 19 mg	3 20 MF	4 19 MR	5 18 ef	6 16 EH	7 16 EW	6	8 15 EH	9 13 ft	10 13 fm	11 12 ft	12 11 FM	1 10 FT
2 20 RT	3 21 md	4 20 mg	5 19 MF	6 17 er	7 17 ef	7	8 16 er	9 14 EW	10 14 EH	11 13 EW	12 12 fm	1 11 ft
2 21 rt	3 22 RM	4 21 RT	5 20 md	6 18 MR	7 18 MF	8	8 17 MR	9 15 ef	10 15 er	11 14 ef	12 13 EH	1 12 EW
2 22 TW	3 23 rm	4 22 rt	5 21 RM	6 19 mg	7 19 md	9	8 18 mg	9 16 MF	10 16 MR	11 15 MF	12 14 er	1 13 ef
2 23 fm	3 24 TH	4 23 TW	5 22 rm	6 20 RT	7 20 RM	10	8 19 RT	9 17 md	10 17 mg	11 16 md	12 15 MR	1 14 MF
2 24 EH	3 25 tr	4 24 fm	5 23 TH	6 21 rt	7 21 rm	11	8 20 rt	9 18 RM	10 18 RT	11 17 RM	12 16 mg	1 15 md
2 25 er	3 26 FR	4 25 EH	5 24 tr	6 22 TW	7 22 TH	12	8 21 TW	9 19 rm	10 19 rt	11 18 rm	12 17 RT	1 16 RM
2 26 MR	3 27 fg	4 26 er	5 25 FR	6 23 fm	7 23 tr	13	8 22 fm	9 20 TH	10 20 TW	11 19 TH	12 18 rt	1 17 rm
2 27 mg	3 28 ET	4 27 MR	5 26 fg	6 24 EH	7 24 FR	14	8 23 EH	9 21 tr	10 21 fm	11 20 tr	12 19 TW	1 18 TH
2 28 RT	3 29 et	4 28 mg	5 27 ET	6 25 er	7 25 fg	15	8 24 er	9 22 FR	10 22 EH	11 21 FR	12 20 fm	1 19 tr
3 1 rt	3 30 MW	4 29 RT	5 28 et	6 26 MR	7 26 ET	16	8 25 MR	9 23 fg	10 23 er	11 22 fg	12 21 EH	1 20 FR
3 2 TW	3 31 mf	4 30 rt	5 29 MW	6 27 mg	7 27 et	17	8 26 mg	9 24 ET	10 24 MR	11 23 ET	12 22 er	1 21 fg
3 3 rg	4 1 RF	5 1 TW	5 30 mf	6 28 RT	7 28 MW	18	8 27 RT	9 25 et	10 25 mg	11 24 et	12 23 MR	1 22 ET
3 4 TT	4 2 rd	5 2 rg	5 31 RF	6 29 rt	7 29 mf	19	8 28 rt	9 26 MW	10 26 RT	11 25 MW	12 24 mg	1 23 et
3 5 tt	4 3 TM	5 3 TT	6 1 rd	6 30 TW	7 30 RF	20	8 29 TW	9 27 mf	10 27 rt	11 26 mf	12 25 RT	1 24 MW
3 6 FW	4 4 tm	5 4 tt	6 2 TM	7 1 rg	7 31 rd	21	8 30 rg	9 28 RF	10 28 TW	11 27 RF	12 26 rt	1 25 mf
3 7 ff	4 5 FH	5 5 FW	6 3 tm	7 2 TT	8 1 TM	22	8 31 TT	9 29 rd	10 29 rg	11 28 rd	12 27 TW	1 26 RF
3 8 EF	4 6 fr	5 6 ff	6 4 FH	7 3 tt	8 2 tm	23	9 1 tt	9 30 TM	10 30 TT	11 29 TM	12 28 rg	1 27 rd
3 9 ed	4 7 ER	5 7 EF	6 5 fr	7 4 FW	8 3 FH	24	9 2 FW	10 1 tm	10 31 tt	11 30 tm	12 29 TT	1 28 TM
3 10 MM	4 8 eg	5 8 ed	6 6 ER	7 5 ff	8 4 fr	25	9 3 ff	10 2 FH	11 1 FW	12 1 FH	12 30 tt	1 29 tm
3 11 mm	4 9 MT	5 9 MM	6 7 eg	7 6 EF	8 5 ER	26	9 4 EF	10 3 fr	11 2 ff	12 2 fr	12 31 FW	1 30 FH
3 12 RH	4 10 mt	5 10 mm	6 8 MT	7 7 ed	8 6 eg	27	9 5 ed	10 4 ER	11 3 EF	12 3 ER	1 1 ff	1 31 fr
3 13 rr	4 11 RW	5 11 RH	6 9 mt	7 8 MM	8 7 MT	28	9 6 MM	10 5 eg	11 4 ed	12 4 eg	1 2 EF	2 1 ER
3 14 TR	4 12 rf	5 12 rr	6 10 RW	7 9 mm	8 8 mt	29	9 7 mm	10 6 MT	11 5 MM	12 5 MT	1 3 ed	2 2 eg
	4 13 TF			7 10 RH	8 9 RW	30		10 7 mt	11 6 mm		1 4 MM	

1954 TF HORSE

DAY OF MON	JAN FT			FEB ft			MAR EW			APR ef			MAY MF			JUN md		
	2 SPRING			2 WARM			3 CLEAR			4 SUMMER			6 GRAIN			9 HEAT		
	16:31			10:29			16:00			9:39			14:02			0:20		
1	2	3	MT	3	5	MM	4	3	eg	5	3	ed	6	1	ER	6	30	ff
2	2	4	mt	3	6	mm	4	4	MT	5	4	MM	6	2	eg	7	1	EF
3	2	5	RW	3	7	RH	4	5	mt	5	5	mm	6	3	MT	7	2	ed
4	2	6	rf	3	8	rr	4	6	RW	5	6	RH	6	4	mt	7	3	MM
5	2	7	TF	3	9	TR	4	7	rf	5	7	rr	6	5	RW	7	4	mm
6	2	8	td	3	10	tg	4	8	TF	5	8	TR	6	6	rf	7	5	RH
7	2	9	FM	3	11	FT	4	9	td	5	9	tg	6	7	TF	7	6	rr
8	2	10	fm	3	12	ft	4	10	FM	5	10	FT	6	8	td	7	7	TR
9	2	11	EH	3	13	EW	4	11	fm	5	11	ft	6	9	FM	7	8	tg
10	2	12	er	3	14	ef	4	12	EH	5	12	EW	6	10	fm	7	9	FT
11	2	13	MR	3	15	MF	4	13	er	5	13	ef	6	11	EH	7	10	ft
12	2	14	mg	3	16	md	4	14	MR	5	14	MF	6	12	er	7	11	EW
13	2	15	RT	3	17	RM	4	15	mg	5	15	md	6	13	MR	7	12	ef
14	2	16	rt	3	18	rm	4	16	RT	5	16	RM	6	14	mg	7	13	MF
15	2	17	TW	3	19	TH	4	17	rt	5	17	rm	6	15	RT	7	14	md
16	2	18	tf	3	20	tr	4	18	TW	5	18	TH	6	16	rt	7	15	RM
17	2	19	FF	3	21	FR	4	19	tf	5	19	tr	6	17	TW	7	16	rm
18	2	20	fd	3	22	fg	4	20	FF	5	20	FR	6	18	tf	7	17	TH
19	2	21	EM	3	23	ET	4	21	fd	5	21	fg	6	19	FF	7	18	tr
20	2	22	em	3	24	et	4	22	EM	5	22	ET	6	20	fd	7	19	FR
21	2	23	MH	3	25	MW	4	23	em	5	23	et	6	21	EM	7	20	fg
22	2	24	mr	3	26	mf	4	24	MH	5	24	MW	6	22	em	7	21	ET
23	2	25	RR	3	27	RF	4	25	mr	5	25	mf	6	23	MH	7	22	et
24	2	26	rg	3	28	rd	4	26	RR	5	26	RF	6	24	mr	7	23	MW
25	2	27	TT	3	29	TM	4	27	rg	5	27	rd	6	25	RR	7	24	mf
26	2	28	tt	3	30	tm	4	28	TT	5	28	TM	6	26	rg	7	25	RF
27	3	1	FW	3	31	FH	4	29	tt	5	29	tm	6	27	TT	7	26	rd
28	3	2	ff	4	1	fr	4	30	FW	5	30	FH	6	28	tt	7	27	TM
29	3	3	EF	4	2	ER	5	1	ff	5	31	fr	6	29	FW	7	28	tm
30	3	4	ed				5	2	EF							7	29	FH

DAY OF MON	JUL RM			AUG rm			SEP TH			OCT tr			NOV FR			DEC fg		
	10 FALL			12 DEW			13 C DEW			13 WINTER			14 SNOW			13 CHILL		
	10:00			13:47			5:20			8:09			0:28			11:08		
1	7	30	fr	8	28	FW	9	27	FH	10	27	FW	11	25	tm	12	25	tt
2	7	31	ER	8	29	ff	9	28	fr	10	28	ff	11	26	FH	12	26	FW
3	8	1	eg	8	30	EF	9	29	ER	10	29	EF	11	27	fr	12	27	ff
4	8	2	MT	8	31	ed	9	30	eg	10	30	ed	11	28	ER	12	28	EF
5	8	3	mt	9	1	MM	10	1	MT	10	31	MM	11	29	eg	12	29	ed
6	8	4	RW	9	2	mm	10	2	mt	11	1	mm	11	30	MT	12	30	MM
7	8	5	rf	9	3	RH	10	3	RW	11	2	RH	12	1	mt	12	31	mm
8	8	6	TF	9	4	rr	10	4	rf	11	3	rr	12	2	RW	1	1	RH
9	8	7	td	9	5	TR	10	5	TF	11	4	TR	12	3	rf	1	2	rr
10	8	8	FM	9	6	tg	10	6	td	11	5	tg	12	4	TF	1	3	TR
11	8	9	fm	9	7	FT	10	7	FM	11	6	FT	12	5	td	1	4	tg
12	8	10	EH	9	8	ft	10	8	fm	11	7	ft	12	6	FM	1	5	FT
13	8	11	er	9	9	EW	10	9	EH	11	8	EW	12	7	fm	1	6	ft
14	8	12	MR	9	10	ef	10	10	er	11	9	ef	12	8	EH	1	7	EW
15	8	13	mg	9	11	MF	10	11	MR	11	10	MF	12	9	er	1	8	ef
16	8	14	RT	9	12	md	10	12	mg	11	11	md	12	10	MR	1	9	MF
17	8	15	rt	9	13	RM	10	13	RT	11	12	RM	12	11	mg	1	10	md
18	8	16	TW	9	14	rm	10	14	rt	11	13	rm	12	12	RT	1	11	RM
19	8	17	tf	9	15	TH	10	15	TW	11	14	TH	12	13	rt	1	12	rm
20	8	18	FF	9	16	tr	10	16	tf	11	15	tr	12	14	TW	1	13	TH
21	8	19	fd	9	17	FR	10	17	FF	11	16	FR	12	15	tf	1	14	tr
22	8	20	EM	9	18	fg	10	18	fd	11	17	fg	12	16	FF	1	15	FR
23	8	21	em	9	19	ET	10	19	EM	11	18	ET	12	17	fd	1	16	fg
24	8	22	MH	9	20	et	10	20	em	11	19	et	12	18	EM	1	17	ET
25	8	23	mr	9	21	MW	10	21	MH	11	20	MW	12	19	em	1	18	et
26	8	24	RR	9	22	mf	10	22	mr	11	21	mf	12	20	MH	1	19	MW
27	8	25	rg	9	23	RF	10	23	RR	11	22	RF	12	21	mr	1	20	mf
28	8	26	TT	9	24	rd	10	24	rg	11	23	rd	12	22	RR	1	21	RF
29	8	27	tt	9	25	TM	10	25	TT	11	24	TM	12	23	rg	1	22	rd
30				9	26	tm	10	26	tt				12	24	TT	1	23	TM

1955 td RAM

JAN ET	FEB et	MAR MW	MAR MW	APR mf	MAY RF	JUN rd	DAY OF MON	JUL TM	AUG tm	SEP FH	OCT fr	NOV ER	DEC eg
12 SPRING	13 WARM	13 CLEAR	15 SUMMER	16 GRAIN	19 HEAT	21 FALL		22 DEW	24 C DEW	24 WINTER	25 SNOW	24 CHILL	24 SPRING
22:18	16:32	21:39	15:18	19:44	6:07	15:50		19:36	11:09	13:49	5:23	16:31	4:13
1 24 tm	2 22 TT	3 24 TM	4 22 rg	5 22 rd	6 20 RR	7 19 mg	1	8 18 mr	9 16 MW	10 16 MH	11 14 et	12 14 em	1 13 et
1 25 FH	2 23 tt	3 25 tm	4 23 TT	5 23 TM	6 21 rg	7 20 RF	2	8 19 RR	9 17 mg	10 17 mr	11 15 MW	12 15 MH	1 14 MW
1 26 fr	2 24 FW	3 26 FH	4 24 tt	5 24 tm	6 22 TT	7 21 rd	3	8 20 rg	9 18 RF	10 18 RR	11 16 mg	12 16 mr	1 15 mg
1 27 ER	2 25 ff	3 27 fr	4 25 FW	5 25 FH	6 23 tt	7 22 TM	4	8 21 TT	9 19 rd	10 19 rg	11 17 RF	12 17 RR	1 16 RF
1 28 eg	2 26 EF	3 28 ER	4 26 ff	5 26 fr	6 24 FW	7 23 tm	5	8 22 tt	9 20 TM	10 20 TT	11 18 rd	12 18 rg	1 17 rd
1 29 MT	2 27 ed	3 29 eg	4 27 EF	5 27 ER	6 25 ff	7 24 FH	6	8 23 FW	9 21 tm	10 21 tt	11 19 TM	12 19 TT	1 18 TM
1 30 mt	2 28 MM	3 30 MT	4 28 ed	5 28 eg	6 26 EF	7 25 fr	7	8 24 ff	9 22 FH	10 22 FW	11 20 tm	12 20 tt	1 19 tm
1 31 RW	3 1 mm	3 31 mt	4 29 MM	5 29 MT	6 27 ed	7 26 ER	8	8 25 EF	9 23 fr	10 23 ff	11 21 FH	12 21 FW	1 20 FH
2 1 rf	3 2 RH	4 1 RW	4 30 mm	5 30 mt	6 28 MM	7 27 eg	9	8 26 ed	9 24 ER	10 24 EF	11 22 fr	12 22 ff	1 21 fr
2 2 TF	3 3 rr	4 2 rf	5 1 RH	5 31 RW	6 29 mm	7 28 MT	10	8 27 MM	9 25 eg	10 25 ed	11 23 ER	12 23 EF	1 22 ER
2 3 td	3 4 TR	4 3 TF	5 2 rr	6 1 rf	6 30 RH	7 29 mt	11	8 28 mm	9 26 MT	10 26 MM	11 24 eg	12 24 ed	1 23 eg
2 4 FM	3 5 tg	4 4 td	5 3 TR	6 2 TF	7 1 rr	7 30 RW	12	8 29 RH	9 27 mt	10 27 mm	11 25 MT	12 25 MM	1 24 MT
2 5 fm	3 6 FT	4 5 FM	5 4 tg	6 3 td	7 2 TR	7 31 rf	13	8 30 rr	9 28 RW	10 28 RH	11 26 mt	12 26 mm	1 25 mt
2 6 EH	3 7 ft	4 6 fm	5 5 FT	6 4 FM	7 3 tg	8 1 TF	14	8 31 TR	9 29 rf	10 29 rr	11 27 RW	12 27 RH	1 26 RW
2 7 er	3 8 EW	4 7 EH	5 6 ft	6 5 fm	7 4 FT	8 2 td	15	9 1 tg	9 30 TF	10 30 TR	11 28 rf	12 28 rr	1 27 rf
2 8 MR	3 9 ef	4 8 er	5 7 EW	6 6 EH	7 5 ft	8 3 FM	16	9 2 FT	10 1 td	10 31 tg	11 29 TF	12 29 TR	1 28 TF
2 9 mg	3 10 MF	4 9 MR	5 8 ef	6 7 er	7 6 EW	8 4 fm	17	9 3 ft	10 2 FM	11 1 FT	11 30 td	12 30 tg	1 29 td
2 10 RT	3 11 md	4 10 mg	5 9 MF	6 8 MR	7 7 ef	8 5 EH	18	9 4 EW	10 3 fm	11 2 ft	12 1 FM	12 31 FT	1 30 FM
2 11 rt	3 12 RM	4 11 RT	5 10 md	6 9 mg	7 8 MF	8 6 er	19	9 5 ef	10 4 EH	11 3 EW	12 2 fm	1 1 ft	1 31 fm
2 12 TW	3 13 rm	4 12 rt	5 11 RM	6 10 RT	7 9 md	8 7 MR	20	9 6 MF	10 5 er	11 4 ef	12 3 EH	1 2 EW	2 1 EH
2 13 tf	3 14 TH	4 13 TW	5 12 rm	6 11 rt	7 10 RM	8 8 mg	21	9 7 md	10 6 MR	11 5 MF	12 4 er	1 3 ef	2 2 er
2 14 FF	3 15 tr	4 14 tf	5 13 TH	6 12 TW	7 11 rm	8 9 RT	22	9 8 RM	10 7 mg	11 6 md	12 5 MR	1 4 MF	2 3 MR
2 15 fd	3 16 FR	4 15 FF	5 14 tr	6 13 tf	7 12 TH	8 10 rt	23	9 9 rm	10 8 RT	11 7 RM	12 6 mg	1 5 md	2 4 mg
2 16 EM	3 17 fg	4 16 fd	5 15 FR	6 14 FF	7 13 tr	8 11 TW	24	9 10 TH	10 9 rt	11 8 rm	12 7 RT	1 6 RM	2 5 RT
2 17 em	3 18 ET	4 17 EM	5 16 fg	6 15 fd	7 14 FR	8 12 tf	25	9 11 tr	10 10 TW	11 9 TH	12 8 rt	1 7 rm	2 6 rt
2 18 MH	3 19 et	4 18 em	5 17 ET	6 16 EM	7 15 fg	8 13 FF	26	9 12 FR	10 11 tf	11 10 tr	12 9 TW	1 8 TH	2 7 TW
2 19 mr	3 20 MW	4 19 MH	5 18 et	6 17 em	7 16 ET	8 14 fd	27	9 13 fg	10 12 FF	11 11 FR	12 10 tf	1 9 tr	2 8 tf
2 20 RR	3 21 mf	4 20 mr	5 19 MW	6 18 MH	7 17 et	8 15 EM	28	9 14 ET	10 13 fd	11 12 fg	12 11 FF	1 10 FR	2 9 FF
2 21 rg	3 22 RF	4 21 RR	5 20 mf	6 19 mr	7 18 MW	8 16 em	29	9 15 et	10 14 EM	11 13 ET	12 12 fd	1 11 fg	2 10 fd
	3 23 rd		5 21 RF			8 17 MH	30		10 15 em		12 13 EM	1 12 ET	2 11 EM

1956 FM MONKEY

JAN MT	FEB mt	MAR RW	APR rf	MAY TF	JUN td	DAY OF MON	JUL FM	AUG fm	SEP EH	OCT er	NOV MR	DEC mg
23 WARM	25 CLEAR	25 SUMMER	28 GRAIN	29 HEAT			2 FALL	4 DEW	5 C DEW	5 WINTER	6 SNOW	5 CHILL
22:25	3:32	21:11	1:36	11:59			21:41	1:24	15:37	19:48	11:03	22:11
2 12 em	3 12 ET	4 11 EM	5 10 fg	6 9 fd	7 8 FR	1	8 6 tf	9 5 tr	10 4 TW	11 3 TH	12 2 rt	1 1 rm
2 13 MH	3 13 et	4 12 em	5 11 ET	6 10 EM	7 9 fg	2	8 7 FF	9 6 FR	10 5 tf	11 4 tr	12 3 TW	1 2 TH
2 14 mr	3 14 MW	4 13 MH	5 12 et	6 11 em	7 10 ET	3	8 8 fd	9 7 fg	10 6 FF	11 5 FR	12 4 tf	1 3 tr
2 15 RR	3 15 mf	4 14 mr	5 13 MW	6 12 MH	7 11 et	4	8 9 EM	9 8 ET	10 7 fd	11 6 fg	12 5 FF	1 4 FR
2 16 rg	3 16 RF	4 15 RR	5 14 mf	6 13 mr	7 12 MW	5	8 10 em	9 9 et	10 8 EM	11 7 ET	12 6 fd	1 5 fg
2 17 TT	3 17 rd	4 16 rg	5 15 RF	6 14 RR	7 13 mf	6	8 11 MH	9 10 MW	10 9 em	11 8 et	12 7 EM	1 6 ET
2 18 tt	3 18 TM	4 17 TT	5 16 rd	6 15 rg	7 14 RF	7	8 12 mr	9 11 mf	10 10 MH	11 9 MW	12 8 em	1 7 et
2 19 FW	3 19 tm	4 18 tt	5 17 TM	6 16 TT	7 15 rd	8	8 13 RR	9 12 RF	10 11 mr	11 10 mf	12 9 MH	1 8 MW
2 20 ff	3 20 FH	4 19 FW	5 18 tm	6 17 tt	7 16 TM	9	8 14 rg	9 13 rd	10 12 RR	11 11 RF	12 10 mr	1 9 mf
2 21 EF	3 21 fr	4 20 ff	5 19 FH	6 18 FW	7 17 tm	10	8 15 TT	9 14 TM	10 13 rg	11 12 rd	12 11 RR	1 10 RF
2 22 ed	3 22 ER	4 21 EF	5 20 fr	6 19 ff	7 18 FH	11	8 16 tt	9 15 tm	10 14 TT	11 13 TM	12 12 rg	1 11 rd
2 23 MM	3 23 eg	4 22 ed	5 21 ER	6 20 EF	7 19 fr	12	8 17 FW	9 16 FH	10 15 tt	11 14 tm	12 13 TT	1 12 TM
2 24 mm	3 24 MT	4 23 MM	5 22 eg	6 21 ed	7 20 ER	13	8 18 ff	9 17 fr	10 16 FW	11 15 FH	12 14 tt	1 13 tm
2 25 RH	3 25 mt	4 24 mm	5 23 MT	6 22 MM	7 21 eg	14	8 19 EF	9 18 ER	10 17 ff	11 16 fr	12 15 FW	1 14 FH
2 26 rr	3 26 RW	4 25 RH	5 24 mt	6 23 mm	7 22 MT	15	8 20 ed	9 19 eg	10 18 EF	11 17 ER	12 16 ff	1 15 fr
2 27 TR	3 27 rf	4 26 rr	5 25 RW	6 24 RH	7 23 mt	16	8 21 MM	9 20 MT	10 19 ed	11 18 eg	12 17 EF	1 16 ER
2 28 tg	3 28 TF	4 27 TR	5 26 rf	6 25 rr	7 24 RW	17	8 22 mm	9 21 mt	10 20 MM	11 19 MT	12 18 ed	1 17 eg
2 29 FT	3 29 td	4 28 tg	5 27 TF	6 26 TR	7 25 rf	18	8 23 RH	9 22 RW	10 21 mm	11 20 mt	12 19 MM	1 18 MT
3 1 ft	3 30 FM	4 29 FT	5 28 td	6 27 tg	7 26 TF	19	8 24 rr	9 23 rf	10 22 RH	11 21 RW	12 20 mm	1 19 mt
3 2 EW	3 31 fm	4 30 ft	5 29 FM	6 28 FT	7 27 td	20	8 25 TR	9 24 TF	10 23 rr	11 22 rf	12 21 RH	1 20 RW
3 3 ef	4 1 EH	5 1 EW	5 30 fm	6 29 ft	7 28 FM	21	8 26 tg	9 25 td	10 24 TR	11 23 TF	12 22 rr	1 21 rf
3 4 MF	4 2 er	5 2 ef	5 31 EH	6 30 EW	7 29 fm	22	8 27 FT	9 26 FM	10 25 tg	11 24 td	12 23 TR	1 22 TF
3 5 md	4 3 MR	5 3 MF	6 1 er	7 1 ef	7 30 EH	23	8 28 ft	9 27 fm	10 26 FT	11 25 FM	12 24 tg	1 23 td
3 6 RM	4 4 mg	5 4 md	6 2 MR	7 2 MF	7 31 er	24	8 29 EW	9 28 EH	10 27 ft	11 26 fm	12 25 FT	1 24 FM
3 7 rm	4 5 RT	5 5 RM	6 3 mg	7 3 md	8 1 MR	25	8 30 ef	9 29 er	10 28 EW	11 27 EH	12 26 ft	1 25 fm
3 8 TH	4 6 rt	5 6 rm	6 4 RT	7 4 RM	8 2 mg	26	8 31 MF	9 30 MR	10 29 ef	11 28 er	12 27 EW	1 26 EH
3 9 tr	4 7 TW	5 7 TH	6 5 rt	7 5 rm	8 3 RT	27	9 1 md	10 1 mg	10 30 MF	11 29 MR	12 28 ef	1 27 er
3 10 FR	4 8 tf	5 8 tr	6 6 TW	7 6 TH	8 4 rt	28	9 2 RM	10 2 RT	10 31 md	11 30 mg	12 29 MF	1 28 MR
3 11 fg	4 9 FF	5 9 FR	6 7 tf	7 7 tr	8 5 TW	29	9 3 rm	10 3 rt	11 1 RM	12 1 RT	12 30 md	1 29 mg
	4 10 fd		6 8 FF			30	9 4 TH		11 2 rm		12 31 RM	1 30 RT

1957 fm ROOSTER

JAN RT	FEB rt	MAR TW	APR tf	MAY FF	JUN fd	DAY OF MON	JUL EM	AUG em	AUG em	SEP MH	OCT mr	NOV RR	DEC rg
5 SPRING	5 WARM	6 CLEAR	7 SUMMER	9 GRAIN	10 HEAT		13 FALL	15 DEW	15 C DEW	17 WINTER	16 SNOW	17 CHILL	16 SPRING
9:55	4:11	9:19	3:11	7:25	17:49		3:33	7:03	21:31	1:37	17:57	4:05	15:50
1 31 rt	3 2 rm	3 31 RT	4 30 RM	5 29 mg	6 28 md	1	7 27 MR	8 25 ef	9 24 er	10 23 EW	11 22 EH	12 21 ft	1 20 fm
2 1 TW	3 3 TH	4 1 rt	5 1 rm	5 30 RT	6 29 RM	2	7 28 mg	8 26 MF	9 25 MR	10 24 ef	11 23 er	12 22 EW	1 21 EH
2 2 tf	3 4 tr	4 2 tw	5 2 TH	5 31 RT	6 30 rm	3	7 29 RT	8 27 md	9 26 mg	10 25 MF	11 24 MR	12 23 ef	1 22 er
2 3 FF	3 5 FR	4 3 tf	5 3 tr	6 1 tw	7 1 TH	4	7 30 RT	8 28 RM	9 27 RT	10 26 md	11 25 mg	12 24 MF	1 23 MR
2 4 fd	3 6 fg	4 4 FF	5 4 FR	6 2 tf	7 2 tr	5	7 31 tw	8 29 rm	9 28 RT	10 27 RM	11 26 RT	12 25 md	1 24 mg
2 5 EM	3 7 ET	4 5 fd	5 5 fg	6 3 FF	7 3 FR	6	8 1 tf	8 30 TH	9 29 tw	10 28 rm	11 27 RT	12 26 RM	1 25 RT
2 6 em	3 8 et	4 6 EM	5 6 ET	6 4 fd	7 4 fg	7	8 2 FF	8 31 tr	9 30 tf	10 29 TH	11 28 tw	12 27 rm	1 26 RT
2 7 MH	3 9 MW	4 7 em	5 7 et	6 5 EM	7 5 ET	8	8 3 fd	9 1 FR	10 1 FF	10 30 tr	11 29 tf	12 28 TH	1 27 tw
2 8 mr	3 10 mf	4 8 MH	5 8 MW	6 6 em	7 6 et	9	8 4 EM	9 2 fg	10 2 fd	10 31 FR	11 30 FF	12 29 tr	1 28 tf
2 9 RR	3 11 RF	4 9 mr	5 9 mf	6 7 MH	7 7 MW	10	8 5 em	9 3 ET	10 3 EM	11 1 fg	12 1 fd	12 30 FR	1 29 FF
2 10 rg	3 12 rd	4 10 RR	5 10 RF	6 8 mr	7 8 mf	11	8 6 MH	9 4 et	10 4 em	11 2 ET	12 2 EM	12 31 fg	1 30 fd
2 11 TT	3 13 TM	4 11 rg	5 11 rd	6 9 RR	7 9 RF	12	8 7 mr	9 5 MW	10 5 MH	11 3 et	12 3 em	1 1 ET	1 31 EM
2 12 tt	3 14 tm	4 12 TT	5 12 TM	6 10 rg	7 10 rd	13	8 8 RR	9 6 mf	10 6 mr	11 4 MW	12 4 MH	1 2 et	2 1 em
2 13 FW	3 15 FH	4 13 tt	5 13 tm	6 11 TT	7 11 TM	14	8 9 rg	9 7 RF	10 7 RR	11 5 mf	12 5 mr	1 3 MW	2 2 MH
2 14 ff	3 16 fr	4 14 FW	5 14 FH	6 12 tt	7 12 tm	15	8 10 TT	9 8 rd	10 8 rg	11 6 RF	12 6 RR	1 4 mf	2 3 mr
2 15 EF	3 17 ER	4 15 ff	5 15 fr	6 13 FW	7 13 FH	16	8 11 tt	9 9 TM	10 9 TT	11 7 rd	12 7 rg	1 5 RF	2 4 RR
2 16 ed	3 18 eg	4 16 EF	5 16 ER	6 14 ff	7 14 fr	17	8 12 FW	9 10 tm	10 10 tt	11 8 TM	12 8 TT	1 6 rd	2 5 rg
2 17 MM	3 19 MT	4 17 ed	5 17 eg	6 15 EF	7 15 ER	18	8 13 ff	9 11 FH	10 11 FW	11 9 tm	12 9 tt	1 7 TM	2 6 TT
2 18 mm	3 20 mt	4 18 MM	5 18 MT	6 16 ed	7 16 eg	19	8 14 EF	9 12 fr	10 12 ff	11 10 FH	12 10 FW	1 8 tm	2 7 tt
2 19 RH	3 21 RW	4 19 mm	5 19 mt	6 17 MM	7 17 MT	20	8 15 ed	9 13 ER	10 13 EF	11 11 fr	12 11 ff	1 9 FH	2 8 FW
2 20 rr	3 22 rf	4 20 RH	5 20 RW	6 18 mm	7 18 mt	21	8 16 MM	9 14 eg	10 14 ed	11 12 ER	12 12 EF	1 10 fr	2 9 ff
2 21 TR	3 23 TF	4 21 rr	5 21 rf	6 19 RH	7 19 RW	22	8 17 mm	9 15 MT	10 15 MM	11 13 eg	12 13 ed	1 11 ER	2 10 EF
2 22 tg	3 24 td	4 22 TR	5 22 TF	6 20 rr	7 20 rf	23	8 18 RH	9 16 mt	10 16 mm	11 14 MT	12 14 MM	1 12 eg	2 11 ed
2 23 FT	3 25 FM	4 23 tg	5 23 td	6 21 TR	7 21 TF	24	8 19 rr	9 17 RW	10 17 RH	11 15 mt	12 15 mm	1 13 MT	2 12 MM
2 24 ft	3 26 fm	4 24 FT	5 24 FM	6 22 tg	7 22 td	25	8 20 TR	9 18 rf	10 18 rr	11 16 RW	12 16 RH	1 14 mt	2 13 mm
2 25 EW	3 27 EH	4 25 ft	5 25 fm	6 23 FT	7 23 FM	26	8 21 tg	9 19 TF	10 19 TR	11 17 rf	12 17 rr	1 15 RW	2 14 RH
2 26 ef	3 28 er	4 26 EW	5 26 EH	6 24 ft	7 24 fm	27	8 22 FT	9 20 td	10 20 tg	11 18 TF	12 18 TR	1 16 rf	2 15 rr
2 27 MF	3 29 MR	4 27 ef	5 27 er	6 25 EW	7 25 EH	28	8 23 ft	9 21 FM	10 21 FT	11 19 td	12 19 tg	1 17 TF	2 16 TR
2 28 md	3 30 mg	4 28 MF	5 28 MR	6 26 ef	7 26 er	29	8 24 EW	9 22 fm	10 22 ft	11 20 FM	12 20 FT	1 18 td	2 17 tg
3 1 RM		4 29 md		6 27 MF		30		9 23 EH		11 21 fm		1 19 FM	

1958 EH DOG

JAN TT	FEB tt	MAR FW	APR ff	MAY EF	JUN ed	DAY OF MON	JUL MM	AUG mm	SEP RH	OCT rr	NOV TR	DEC tg
17 WARM	17 CLEAR	18 SUMMER	19 GRAIN	22 HEAT	23 FALL		25 DEW	27 C DEW	27 WINTER	27 SNOW	27 CHILL	27 SPRING
10:06	15:13	9:01	13:13	0:03	9:18		13:01	3:20	7:26	23:47	9:59	21:43
2 18 FT	3 20 FM	4 19 FT	5 19 FM	6 17 tg	7 17 td	1	8 15 TR	9 13 rf	10 13 rr	11 11 RW	12 11 RH	1 9 mt
2 19 ft	3 21 fm	4 20 ft	5 20 fm	6 18 FT	7 18 FM	2	8 16 tg	9 14 TF	10 14 TR	11 12 rf	12 12 rr	1 10 RW
2 20 EW	3 22 EH	4 21 EW	5 21 EH	6 19 ft	7 19 fm	3	8 17 FT	9 15 td	10 15 tg	11 13 TF	12 13 TR	1 11 rf
2 21 ef	3 23 er	4 22 ef	5 22 er	6 20 EW	7 20 EH	4	8 18 ft	9 16 FM	10 16 FT	11 14 td	12 14 tg	1 12 TF
2 22 MF	3 24 MR	4 23 MF	5 23 MR	6 21 ef	7 21 er	5	8 19 EW	9 17 fm	10 17 ft	11 15 FM	12 15 FT	1 13 td
2 23 md	3 25 mg	4 24 md	5 24 mg	6 22 MF	7 22 MR	6	8 20 ef	9 18 EH	10 18 EW	11 16 fm	12 16 ft	1 14 FM
2 24 RM	3 26 RT	4 25 RM	5 25 RT	6 23 md	7 23 mg	7	8 21 MF	9 19 er	10 19 ef	11 17 EH	12 17 EW	1 15 fm
2 25 rm	3 27 rt	4 26 rm	5 26 rt	6 24 RM	7 24 RT	8	8 22 md	9 20 MR	10 20 MF	11 18 er	12 18 ef	1 16 EH
2 26 TH	3 28 TW	4 27 TH	5 27 TW	6 25 rm	7 25 rt	9	8 23 RM	9 21 mg	10 21 md	11 19 MR	12 19 MF	1 17 er
2 27 tr	3 29 tf	4 28 tr	5 28 tf	6 26 TH	7 26 TW	10	8 24 rm	9 22 RT	10 22 RM	11 20 mg	12 20 md	1 18 MR
2 28 FR	3 30 FF	4 29 FR	5 29 FF	6 27 tr	7 27 tf	11	8 25 TH	9 23 rt	10 23 rm	11 21 RT	12 21 RM	1 19 mg
3 1 fg	3 31 fd	4 30 fg	5 30 fd	6 28 FR	7 28 FF	12	8 26 tr	9 24 TW	10 24 TH	11 22 rt	12 22 rm	1 20 RT
3 2 ET	4 1 EM	5 1 ET	5 31 EM	6 29 fg	7 29 fd	13	8 27 FR	9 25 tf	10 25 tr	11 23 TW	12 23 TH	1 21 rt
3 3 et	4 2 em	5 2 et	6 1 em	6 30 ET	7 30 EM	14	8 28 fg	9 26 FF	10 26 FR	11 24 tf	12 24 tr	1 22 TW
3 4 MW	4 3 MH	5 3 MW	6 2 MH	7 1 et	7 31 em	15	8 29 ET	9 27 fd	10 27 fg	11 25 FF	12 25 FR	1 23 tf
3 5 mf	4 4 mr	5 4 mf	6 3 mr	7 2 MW	8 1 MH	16	8 30 et	9 28 EM	10 28 ET	11 26 fd	12 26 fg	1 24 FF
3 6 RF	4 5 RR	5 5 RF	6 4 RR	7 3 mf	8 2 mr	17	8 31 MW	9 29 em	10 29 et	11 27 EM	12 27 ET	1 25 fd
3 7 rd	4 6 rg	5 6 rd	6 5 rg	7 4 RF	8 3 RR	18	9 1 mf	9 30 MH	10 30 MW	11 28 em	12 28 et	1 26 EM
3 8 TM	4 7 TT	5 7 TM	6 6 TT	7 5 rd	8 4 rg	19	9 2 RF	10 1 mr	10 31 mf	11 29 MH	12 29 MW	1 27 em
3 9 tm	4 8 tt	5 8 tm	6 7 tt	7 6 TM	8 5 TT	20	9 3 rd	10 2 RR	11 1 RF	11 30 mr	12 30 mf	1 28 MH
3 10 FH	4 9 FW	5 9 FH	6 8 FW	7 7 tm	8 6 tt	21	9 4 TM	10 3 rg	11 2 rd	12 1 RR	12 31 RF	1 29 mr
3 11 fr	4 10 ff	5 10 fr	6 9 ff	7 8 FH	8 7 FW	22	9 5 tm	10 4 TT	11 3 TM	12 2 rg	1 1 rd	1 30 RR
3 12 ER	4 11 EF	5 11 ER	6 10 EF	7 9 fr	8 8 ff	23	9 6 FH	10 5 tt	11 4 tm	12 3 TT	1 2 TM	1 31 rg
3 13 eg	4 12 ed	5 12 eg	6 11 ed	7 10 ER	8 9 EF	24	9 7 fr	10 6 FW	11 5 FH	12 4 tt	1 3 tm	2 1 TT
3 14 MT	4 13 MM	5 13 MT	6 12 MM	7 11 eg	8 10 ed	25	9 8 ER	10 7 ff	11 6 fr	12 5 FW	1 4 FH	2 2 tt
3 15 mt	4 14 mm	5 14 mt	6 13 mm	7 12 MT	8 11 MM	26	9 9 eg	10 8 EF	11 7 ER	12 6 ff	1 5 fr	2 3 FW
3 16 RW	4 15 RH	5 15 RW	6 14 RH	7 13 mt	8 12 mm	27	9 10 MT	10 9 ed	11 8 eg	12 7 EF	1 6 ER	2 4 ff
3 17 rf	4 16 rr	5 16 rf	6 15 rr	7 14 RW	8 13 RH	28	9 11 mt	10 10 MM	11 9 MT	12 8 ed	1 7 eg	2 5 EF
3 18 TF	4 17 TR	5 17 TF	6 16 TR	7 15 rf	8 14 rr	29	9 12 RW	10 11 mm	11 10 mt	12 9 MM	1 8 MT	2 6 ed
3 19 td	4 18 tg	5 18 td		7 16 TF		30		10 12 RH		12 10 mm		2 7 MM

1959 er BOAR

JAN FT	FEB ft	MAR EW	APR ef	MAY MF	JUN md	DAY OF MON	JUL RM	AUG rm	SEP TH	OCT tr	NOV FR	DEC fg
27 WARM	28 CLEAR	29 SUMMER		1 GRAIN	3 HEAT		5 FALL	6 DEW	8 C DEW	8 WINTER	9 SNOW	8 CHILL
15:57	21:04	14:39		19:01	5:21		15:05	17:49	9:11	13:16	5:37	15:43
2 8 mm	3 9 MT	4 8 MM	5 8 MT	6 6 ed	7 6 eg	1	8 4 EF	9 3 ER	10 2 ff	11 1 fr	11 30 FW	12 30 FH
2 9 RH	3 10 mt	4 9 mm	5 9 mt	6 7 MM	7 7 MT	2	8 5 ed	9 4 eg	10 3 EF	11 2 ER	12 1 ff	12 31 fr
2 10 rr	3 11 RW	4 10 RH	5 10 RW	6 8 mm	7 8 mt	3	8 6 MM	9 5 MT	10 4 ed	11 3 eg	12 2 EF	1 1 ER
2 11 TR	3 12 rf	4 11 rr	5 11 rf	6 9 RH	7 9 RW	4	8 7 mm	9 6 mt	10 5 MM	11 4 MT	12 3 ed	1 2 eg
2 12 tg	3 13 TF	4 12 TR	5 12 TF	6 10 rr	7 10 rf	5	8 8 RH	9 7 RW	10 6 mm	11 5 mt	12 4 MM	1 3 MT
2 13 FT	3 14 td	4 13 tg	5 13 td	6 11 TR	7 11 TF	6	8 9 rr	9 8 rf	10 7 RH	11 6 RW	12 5 mm	1 4 mt
2 14 ft	3 15 FM	4 14 FT	5 14 FM	6 12 tg	7 12 td	7	8 10 TR	9 9 TF	10 8 rr	11 7 rf	12 6 RH	1 5 RW
2 15 EW	3 16 fm	4 15 ft	5 15 fm	6 13 FT	7 13 FM	8	8 11 tg	9 10 td	10 9 TR	11 8 TF	12 7 rr	1 6 rf
2 16 ef	3 17 EH	4 16 EW	5 16 EH	6 14 ft	7 14 fm	9	8 12 FT	9 11 FM	10 10 tg	11 9 td	12 8 TR	1 7 TF
2 17 MF	3 18 er	4 17 ef	5 17 er	6 15 EW	7 15 EH	10	8 13 ft	9 12 fm	10 11 FT	11 10 FM	12 9 tg	1 8 td
2 18 md	3 19 MR	4 18 MF	5 18 MR	6 16 ef	7 16 er	11	8 14 EW	9 13 EH	10 12 ft	11 11 fm	12 10 FT	1 9 FM
2 19 RM	3 20 mg	4 19 md	5 19 mg	6 17 MF	7 17 MR	12	8 15 ef	9 14 er	10 13 EW	11 12 EH	12 11 ft	1 10 fm
2 20 rm	3 21 RT	4 20 RM	5 20 RT	6 18 md	7 18 mg	13	8 16 MF	9 15 MR	10 14 ef	11 13 er	12 12 EW	1 11 EH
2 21 TH	3 22 rt	4 21 rm	5 21 rt	6 19 RM	7 19 RT	14	8 17 md	9 16 mg	10 15 MF	11 14 MR	12 13 ef	1 12 er
2 22 tr	3 23 TW	4 22 TH	5 22 TW	6 20 rm	7 20 rt	15	8 18 RM	9 17 RT	10 16 md	11 15 mg	12 14 MF	1 13 MR
2 23 FR	3 24 tf	4 23 tr	5 23 tf	6 21 TH	7 21 TW	16	8 19 rm	9 18 rt	10 17 RM	11 16 RT	12 15 md	1 14 mg
2 24 fg	3 25 FF	4 24 FR	5 24 FF	6 22 tr	7 22 tf	17	8 20 TH	9 19 TW	10 18 rm	11 17 rt	12 16 RM	1 15 RT
2 25 ET	3 26 fd	4 25 fg	5 25 fd	6 23 FR	7 23 FF	18	8 21 tr	9 20 tf	10 19 TH	11 18 TW	12 17 rm	1 16 rt
2 26 et	3 27 EM	4 26 ET	5 26 EM	6 24 fg	7 24 fd	19	8 22 FR	9 21 FF	10 20 tr	11 19 tf	12 18 TH	1 17 TW
2 27 MW	3 28 em	4 27 et	5 27 em	6 25 ET	7 25 EM	20	8 23 fg	9 22 fd	10 21 FR	11 20 FF	12 19 tr	1 18 tf
2 28 mf	3 29 MH	4 28 MW	5 28 MH	6 26 et	7 26 em	21	8 24 ET	9 23 EM	10 22 fg	11 21 fd	12 20 FR	1 19 FF
3 1 RF	3 30 mr	4 29 mf	5 29 mr	6 27 MW	7 27 MH	22	8 25 et	9 24 em	10 23 ET	11 22 EM	12 21 fg	1 20 fd
3 2 rd	3 31 RR	4 30 RF	5 30 RR	6 28 mf	7 28 mr	23	8 26 MW	9 25 MH	10 24 et	11 23 em	12 22 ET	1 21 EM
3 3 TM	4 1 rg	5 1 rd	5 31 rg	6 29 RF	7 29 RR	24	8 27 mf	9 26 mr	10 25 MW	11 24 MH	12 23 et	1 22 em
3 4 tm	4 2 TT	5 2 TM	6 1 TT	6 30 rd	7 30 rg	25	8 28 RF	9 27 RR	10 26 mf	11 25 mr	12 24 MW	1 23 MH
3 5 FH	4 3 tt	5 3 tm	6 2 tt	7 1 TM	7 31 TT	26	8 29 rd	9 28 rg	10 27 RF	11 26 RR	12 25 mf	1 24 mr
3 6 fr	4 4 FW	5 4 FH	6 3 FW	7 2 tm	8 1 tt	27	8 30 TM	9 29 TT	10 28 rd	11 27 rg	12 26 RF	1 25 RR
3 7 ER	4 5 ff	5 5 fr	6 4 ff	7 3 FH	8 2 FW	28	8 31 tm	9 30 tt	10 29 TM	11 28 TT	12 27 rd	1 26 rg
3 8 eg	4 6 EF	5 6 ER	6 5 EF	7 4 fr	8 3 ff	29	9 1 FH	10 1 FW	10 30 tm	11 29 tt	12 28 TM	1 27 TT
	4 7 ed	5 7 eg		7 5 ER		30	9 2 fr		10 31 FH		12 29 tm	

1960 MR RAT

JAN ET			FEB et			MAR MW			APR mf			MAY RF			JUN rd			JUN rd			DAY OF MON	JUL TM			AUG tm			SEP FH			OCT fr			NOV ER			DEC eg		
9 SPRING			8 WARM			10 CLEAR			10 SUMMER			13 GRAIN			14 HEAT			15 FALL				18 DEW			18 C DEW			19 WINTER			19 SNOW			19 CHILL			19 SPRING		
3:23			21:36			2:44			20:23			1:11			11:13			21:00				0:39			15:09			19:06			11:26			21:43			9:23		
1	28	tt	2	27	tm	3	27	TT	4	26	TM	5	25	rg	6	24	rd	7	24	rg	1	8	22	RF	9	21	RR	10	20	mf	11	19	mr	12	18	MW	1	17	MH
1	29	FW	2	28	FH	3	28	tt	4	27	tm	5	26	TT	6	25	TM	7	25	TT	2	8	23	rd	9	22	rg	10	21	RF	11	20	RR	12	19	mf	1	18	mr
1	30	ff	2	29	fr	3	29	FW	4	28	FH	5	27	tt	6	26	tm	7	26	tt	3	8	24	TM	9	23	TT	10	22	rd	11	21	rg	12	20	RF	1	19	RR
1	31	EF	3	1	ER	3	30	ff	4	29	fr	5	28	FW	6	27	FH	7	27	FW	4	8	25	tm	9	24	tt	10	23	TM	11	22	TT	12	21	rd	1	20	rg
2	1	ed	3	2	eg	3	31	EF	4	30	ER	5	29	ff	6	28	fr	7	28	ff	5	8	26	FH	9	25	FW	10	24	tm	11	23	tt	12	22	TM	1	21	TT
2	2	MM	3	3	MT	4	1	ed	5	1	eg	5	30	EF	6	29	ER	7	29	EF	6	8	27	fr	9	26	ff	10	25	FH	11	24	FW	12	23	tm	1	22	tt
2	3	mm	3	4	mt	4	2	MM	5	2	MT	5	31	ed	6	30	eg	7	30	ed	7	8	28	ER	9	27	EF	10	26	fr	11	25	ff	12	24	FH	1	23	FW
2	4	RH	3	5	RW	4	3	mm	5	3	mt	6	1	MM	7	1	MT	7	31	MM	8	8	29	eg	9	28	ed	10	27	ER	11	26	EF	12	25	fr	1	24	ff
2	5	rr	3	6	rf	4	4	RH	5	4	RW	6	2	mm	7	2	mt	8	1	mm	9	8	30	MT	9	29	MM	10	28	eg	11	27	ed	12	26	ER	1	25	EF
2	6	TR	3	7	TF	4	5	rr	5	5	rf	6	3	RH	7	3	RW	8	2	RH	10	8	31	mt	9	30	mm	10	29	MT	11	28	MM	12	27	eg	1	26	ed
2	7	tg	3	8	td	4	6	TR	5	6	TF	6	4	rr	7	4	rf	8	3	rr	11	9	1	RW	10	1	RH	10	30	mt	11	29	mm	12	28	MT	1	27	MM
2	8	FT	3	9	FM	4	7	tg	5	7	td	6	5	TR	7	5	TF	8	4	TR	12	9	2	rf	10	2	rr	10	31	RW	11	30	RH	12	29	mt	1	28	mm
2	9	ft	3	10	fm	4	8	FT	5	8	FM	6	6	tg	7	6	td	8	5	tg	13	9	3	TF	10	3	TR	11	1	rf	12	1	rr	12	30	RW	1	29	RH
2	10	EW	3	11	EH	4	9	ft	5	9	fm	6	7	FT	7	7	FM	8	6	FT	14	9	4	td	10	4	tg	11	2	TF	12	2	TR	12	31	rf	1	30	rr
2	11	ef	3	12	er	4	10	EW	5	10	EH	6	8	ft	7	8	fm	8	7	ft	15	9	5	FM	10	5	FT	11	3	td	12	3	tg	1	1	TF	1	31	TR
2	12	MF	3	13	MR	4	11	ef	5	11	er	6	9	EW	7	9	EH	8	8	EW	16	9	6	fm	10	6	ft	11	4	FM	12	4	FT	1	2	td	2	1	tg
2	13	md	3	14	mg	4	12	MF	5	12	MR	6	10	ef	7	10	er	8	9	ef	17	9	7	EH	10	7	EW	11	5	fm	12	5	ft	1	3	FM	2	2	FT
2	14	RM	3	15	RT	4	13	md	5	13	mg	6	11	MF	7	11	MR	8	10	MF	18	9	8	er	10	8	ef	11	6	EH	12	6	EW	1	4	fm	2	3	ft
2	15	rm	3	16	rt	4	14	RM	5	14	RT	6	12	md	7	12	mg	8	11	md	19	9	9	MR	10	9	MF	11	7	er	12	7	ef	1	5	EH	2	4	EW
2	16	TH	3	17	TW	4	15	rm	5	15	rt	6	13	RM	7	13	RT	8	12	RM	20	9	10	mg	10	10	md	11	8	MR	12	8	MF	1	6	er	2	5	ef
2	17	tr	3	18	tf	4	16	TH	5	16	TW	6	14	rm	7	14	rt	8	13	rm	21	9	11	RT	10	11	RM	11	9	mg	12	9	md	1	7	MR	2	6	MF
2	18	FR	3	19	FF	4	17	tr	5	17	tf	6	15	TH	7	15	TW	8	14	TH	22	9	12	rt	10	12	rm	11	10	RT	12	10	RM	1	8	mg	2	7	md
2	19	fg	3	20	fd	4	18	FR	5	18	FF	6	16	tr	7	16	tf	8	15	tr	23	9	13	TW	10	13	TH	11	11	rt	12	11	rm	1	9	RT	2	8	RM
2	20	ET	3	21	EM	4	19	fg	5	19	fd	6	17	FR	7	17	FF	8	16	FR	24	9	14	tf	10	14	tr	11	12	TW	12	12	TH	1	10	rt	2	9	rm
2	21	et	3	22	em	4	20	ET	5	20	EM	6	18	fg	7	18	fd	8	17	fg	25	9	15	FF	10	15	FR	11	13	tf	12	13	tr	1	11	TW	2	10	TH
2	22	MW	3	23	MH	4	21	et	5	21	em	6	19	ET	7	19	EM	8	18	ET	26	9	16	fd	10	16	fg	11	14	FF	12	14	FR	1	12	tf	2	11	tr
2	23	mf	3	24	mr	4	22	MW	5	22	MH	6	20	et	7	20	em	8	19	et	27	9	17	EM	10	17	ET	11	15	fd	12	15	fg	1	13	FF	2	12	FR
2	24	RF	3	25	RR	4	23	mf	5	23	mr	6	21	MW	7	21	MH	8	20	MW	28	9	18	em	10	18	et	11	16	EM	12	16	ET	1	14	fd	2	13	fg
2	25	rd	3	26	rg	4	24	RF	5	24	RR	6	22	mf	7	22	mr	8	21	mf	29	9	19	MH	10	19	MW	11	17	em	12	17	et	1	15	EM	2	14	ET
2	26	TM				4	25	rd				6	23	RF	7	23	RR				30	9	20	mr				11	18	MH				1	16	em			

1961 mg OX

JAN MT	FEB mt	MAR RW	APR rf	MAY TF	JUN td	DAY OF MON	JUL FM	AUG fm	SEP EH	OCT er	NOV MR	DEC mg
20 WARM	20 CLEAR	22 SUMMER	23 GRAIN	25 HEAT	27 FALL		29 DEW	29 C DEW		1 WINTER		1 CHILL
										0:55		3:35
										30 SNOW		30 SPRING
3:35	8:42	2:21	6:46	17:07	3:27		5:29	22:03		17:16		15:18
2 15 et	3 17 em	4 15 ET	5 15 EM	6 13 fg	7 13 fd	1	8 11 FR	9 10 FF	10 10 FR	11 8 tf	12 8 tr	1 6 TW
2 16 MW	3 18 MH	4 16 et	5 16 em	6 14 ET	7 14 EM	2	8 12 fg	9 11 fd	10 11 fg	11 9 FF	12 9 FR	1 7 tf
2 17 mf	3 19 mr	4 17 MW	5 17 MH	6 15 et	7 15 em	3	8 13 ET	9 12 EM	10 12 ET	11 10 fd	12 10 fg	1 8 FF
2 18 RF	3 20 RR	4 18 mf	5 18 mr	6 16 MW	7 16 MH	4	8 14 et	9 13 em	10 13 et	11 11 EM	12 11 ET	1 9 fd
2 19 rd	3 21 rg	4 19 RF	5 19 RR	6 17 mf	7 17 mr	5	8 15 MW	9 14 MH	10 14 MW	11 12 em	12 12 et	1 10 EM
2 20 TM	3 22 TT	4 20 rd	5 20 rg	6 18 RF	7 18 RR	6	8 16 mf	9 15 mr	10 15 mf	11 13 MH	12 13 MW	1 11 em
2 21 tm	3 23 tt	4 21 TM	5 21 TT	6 19 rd	7 19 rg	7	8 17 RF	9 16 RR	10 16 RF	11 14 mr	12 14 mf	1 12 MH
2 22 FH	3 24 FW	4 22 tm	5 22 tt	6 20 TM	7 20 TT	8	8 18 rd	9 17 rg	10 17 rd	11 15 RR	12 15 RF	1 13 mr
2 23 fr	3 25 ff	4 23 FH	5 23 FW	6 21 tm	7 21 tt	9	8 19 TM	9 18 TT	10 18 TM	11 16 rg	12 16 rd	1 14 RR
2 24 ER	3 26 EF	4 24 fr	5 24 ff	6 22 FH	7 22 FW	10	8 20 tm	9 19 tt	10 19 tm	11 17 TT	12 17 TM	1 15 rg
2 25 eg	3 27 ed	4 25 ER	5 25 EF	6 23 fr	7 23 ff	11	8 21 FH	9 20 FW	10 20 FH	11 18 tt	12 18 tm	1 16 TT
2 26 MT	3 28 MM	4 26 eg	5 26 ed	6 24 ER	7 24 EF	12	8 22 fr	9 21 ff	10 21 fr	11 19 FW	12 19 FH	1 17 tt
2 27 mt	3 29 mm	4 27 MT	5 27 MM	6 25 eg	7 25 ed	13	8 23 ER	9 22 EF	10 22 ER	11 20 ff	12 20 fr	1 18 FW
2 28 RW	3 30 RH	4 28 mt	5 28 mm	6 26 MT	7 26 MM	14	8 24 eg	9 23 ed	10 23 eg	11 21 EF	12 21 ER	1 19 ff
3 1 rf	3 31 rr	4 29 RW	5 29 RH	6 27 mt	7 27 mm	15	8 25 MT	9 24 MM	10 24 MT	11 22 ed	12 22 eg	1 20 EF
3 2 TF	4 1 TR	4 30 rf	5 30 rr	6 28 RW	7 28 RH	16	8 26 mt	9 25 mm	10 25 mt	11 23 MM	12 23 MT	1 21 ed
3 3 td	4 2 tg	5 1 TF	5 31 TR	6 29 rf	7 29 rr	17	8 27 RW	9 26 RH	10 26 RW	11 24 mm	12 24 mt	1 22 MM
3 4 FM	4 3 FT	5 2 td	6 1 tg	6 30 TF	7 30 TR	18	8 28 rf	9 27 rr	10 27 rf	11 25 RH	12 25 RW	1 23 mm
3 5 fm	4 4 ft	5 3 FM	6 2 FT	7 1 td	7 31 tg	19	8 29 TF	9 28 TR	10 28 TF	11 26 rr	12 26 rf	1 24 RH
3 6 EH	4 5 EW	5 4 fm	6 3 ft	7 2 FM	8 1 FT	20	8 30 td	9 29 tg	10 29 td	11 27 TR	12 27 TF	1 25 rr
3 7 er	4 6 ef	5 5 EH	6 4 EW	7 3 fm	8 2 ft	21	8 31 FM	9 30 FT	10 30 FM	11 28 tg	12 28 td	1 26 TR
3 8 MR	4 7 MF	5 6 er	6 5 ef	7 4 EH	8 3 EW	22	9 1 fm	10 1 ft	10 31 fm	11 29 FT	12 29 FM	1 27 tg
3 9 mg	4 8 md	5 7 MR	6 6 MF	7 5 er	8 4 ef	23	9 2 EH	10 2 EW	11 1 EH	11 30 ft	12 30 fm	1 28 FT
3 10 RT	4 9 RM	5 8 mg	6 7 md	7 6 MR	8 5 MF	24	9 3 er	10 3 ef	11 2 er	12 1 EW	12 31 EH	1 29 ft
3 11 rt	4 10 rm	5 9 RT	6 8 RM	7 7 mg	8 6 md	25	9 4 MR	10 4 MF	11 3 MR	12 2 ef	1 1 er	1 30 EW
3 12 TW	4 11 TH	5 10 rt	6 9 rm	7 8 RT	8 7 RM	26	9 5 mg	10 5 md	11 4 mg	12 3 MF	1 2 MR	1 31 ef
3 13 tf	4 12 tr	5 11 TW	6 10 TH	7 9 rt	8 8 rm	27	9 6 RT	10 6 RM	11 5 RT	12 4 md	1 3 mg	2 1 MF
3 14 FF	4 13 FR	5 12 tf	6 11 tr	7 10 TW	8 9 TH	28	9 7 rt	10 7 rm	11 6 rt	12 5 RM	1 4 RT	2 2 md
3 15 fd	4 14 fg	5 13 FF	6 12 FR	7 11 tf	8 10 tr	29	9 8 TW	10 8 TH	11 7 TW	12 6 rm	1 5 rt	2 3 RM
3 16 EM		5 14 fd		7 12 FF		30	9 9 tf	10 9 tr		12 7 TH		2 4 rm

1962 RT TIGER

JAN RT	FEB rt	MAR TW	APR tf	MAY FF	JUN fd	DAY OF MON	JUL EM	AUG em	SEP MH	OCT mr	NOV RR	DEC rg
	1 WARM	1 CLEAR	3 SUMMER	5 GRAIN	6 HEAT		9 FALL	10 DEW	11 C DEW	12 WINTER	11 SNOW	11 CHILL
	9:30	14:34	8:10	12:31	23:16		9:34	11:16	3:57	5:35	23:06	9:27
2 5 TH	3 6 rt	4 5 rm	5 4 RT	6 2 md	7 2 mg	1	7 31 MF	8 30 MR	9 29 MF	10 28 er	11 27 ef	12 27 er
2 6 tr	3 7 TW	4 6 TH	5 5 rt	6 3 RM	7 3 RT	2	8 1 md	8 31 mg	9 30 md	10 29 MR	11 28 MF	12 28 MR
2 7 FR	3 8 tf	4 7 tr	5 6 TW	6 4 rm	7 4 rt	3	8 2 RM	9 1 RT	10 1 RM	10 30 mg	11 29 md	12 29 mg
2 8 fg	3 9 FF	4 8 FR	5 7 tf	6 5 TH	7 5 TW	4	8 3 rm	9 2 rt	10 2 rm	10 31 RT	11 30 RM	12 30 RT
2 9 ET	3 10 fd	4 9 fg	5 8 FF	6 6 tr	7 6 tf	5	8 4 TH	9 3 TW	10 3 TH	11 1 rt	12 1 rm	12 31 rt
2 10 et	3 11 EM	4 10 ET	5 9 fd	6 7 FR	7 7 FF	6	8 5 tr	9 4 tf	10 4 tr	11 2 TW	12 2 TH	1 1 TW
2 11 MW	3 12 em	4 11 et	5 10 EM	6 8 fg	7 8 fd	7	8 6 FR	9 5 FF	10 5 FR	11 3 tf	12 3 tr	1 2 tf
2 12 mf	3 13 MH	4 12 MW	5 11 em	6 9 ET	7 9 EM	8	8 7 fg	9 6 fd	10 6 fg	11 4 FF	12 4 FR	1 3 FF
2 13 RF	3 14 mr	4 13 mf	5 12 MH	6 10 et	7 10 em	9	8 8 ET	9 7 EM	10 7 ET	11 5 fd	12 5 fg	1 4 fd
2 14 rd	3 15 RR	4 14 RF	5 13 mr	6 11 MW	7 11 MH	10	8 9 et	9 8 em	10 8 et	11 6 EM	12 6 ET	1 5 EM
2 15 TM	3 16 rg	4 15 rd	5 14 RR	6 12 mf	7 12 mr	11	8 10 MW	9 9 MH	10 9 MW	11 7 em	12 7 et	1 6 em
2 16 tm	3 17 TT	4 16 TM	5 15 rg	6 13 RF	7 13 RR	12	8 11 mf	9 10 mr	10 10 mf	11 8 MH	12 8 MW	1 7 MH
2 17 FH	3 18 tt	4 17 tm	5 16 TT	6 14 rd	7 14 rg	13	8 12 RF	9 11 RR	10 11 RF	11 9 mr	12 9 mf	1 8 mr
2 18 fr	3 19 FW	4 18 FH	5 17 tt	6 15 TM	7 15 TT	14	8 13 rd	9 12 rg	10 12 rd	11 10 RR	12 10 RF	1 9 RR
2 19 ER	3 20 ff	4 19 fr	5 18 FW	6 16 tm	7 16 tt	15	8 14 TM	9 13 TT	10 13 TM	11 11 rg	12 11 rd	1 10 rg
2 20 eg	3 21 EF	4 20 ER	5 19 ff	6 17 FH	7 17 FW	16	8 15 tm	9 14 tt	10 14 tm	11 12 TT	12 12 TM	1 11 TT
2 21 MT	3 22 ed	4 21 eg	5 20 EF	6 18 fr	7 18 ff	17	8 16 FH	9 15 FW	10 15 FH	11 13 tt	12 13 tm	1 12 tt
2 22 mt	3 23 MM	4 22 MT	5 21 ed	6 19 ER	7 19 EF	18	8 17 fr	9 16 ff	10 16 fr	11 14 FW	12 14 FH	1 13 FW
2 23 RW	3 24 mm	4 23 mt	5 22 MM	6 20 eg	7 20 ed	19	8 18 ER	9 17 EF	10 17 ER	11 15 ff	12 15 fr	1 14 ff
2 24 rf	3 25 RH	4 24 RW	5 23 mm	6 21 MT	7 21 MM	20	8 19 eg	9 18 ed	10 18 eg	11 16 EF	12 16 ER	1 15 EF
2 25 TF	3 26 rr	4 25 rf	5 24 RH	6 22 mt	7 22 mm	21	8 20 MT	9 19 MM	10 19 MT	11 17 ed	12 17 eg	1 16 ed
2 26 td	3 27 TR	4 26 TF	5 25 rr	6 23 RW	7 23 RH	22	8 21 mt	9 20 mm	10 20 mt	11 18 MM	12 18 MT	1 17 MM
2 27 FM	3 28 tg	4 27 td	5 26 TR	6 24 rf	7 24 rr	23	8 22 RW	9 21 RH	10 21 RW	11 19 mm	12 19 mt	1 18 mm
2 28 fm	3 29 FT	4 28 FM	5 27 tg	6 25 TF	7 25 TR	24	8 23 rf	9 22 rr	10 22 rf	11 20 RH	12 20 RW	1 19 RH
3 1 EH	3 30 ft	4 29 fm	5 28 FT	6 26 td	7 26 tg	25	8 24 TF	9 23 TR	10 23 TF	11 21 rr	12 21 rf	1 20 rr
3 2 er	3 31 EW	4 30 EH	5 29 ft	6 27 FM	7 27 FT	26	8 25 td	9 24 tg	10 24 td	11 22 TR	12 22 TF	1 21 TR
3 3 MR	4 1 ef	5 1 er	5 30 EW	6 28 fm	7 28 ft	27	8 26 FM	9 25 FT	10 25 FM	11 23 tg	12 23 td	1 22 tg
3 4 mg	4 2 MF	5 2 MR	5 31 ef	6 29 EH	7 29 EW	28	8 27 fm	9 26 ft	10 26 fm	11 24 FT	12 24 FM	1 23 FT
3 5 RT	4 3 md	5 3 mg	6 1 MF	6 30 er	7 30 ef	29	8 28 EH	9 27 EW	10 27 EH	11 25 ft	12 25 fm	1 24 ft
	4 4 RM			7 1 MR		30	8 29 er	9 28 ef		11 26 EW	12 26 EH	

1963 rt RABBIT

JAN TT	FEB tt	MAR FW	APR ff	APR ff	MAY EF	JUN ed	DAY OF	JUL MM	AUG mm	SEP RH	OCT rr	NOV TR	DEC tg
11 SPRING	11 WARM	12 CLEAR	13 SUMMER	15 GRAIN	18 HEAT	19 FALL	MON	21 DEW	22 C DEW	23 WINTER	23 SNOW	22 CHILL	22 SPRING
21:08	15:17	20:19	13:52	18:15	5:05	15:18		17:12	9:41	11:32	4:13	15:22	2:56
1 25 EW	2 24 EH	3 25 ft	4 24 fm	5 23 FT	6 21 td	7 21 tg	1	8 19 TF	9 18 TR	10 17 rf	11 16 rr	12 16 rf	1 15 rr
1 26 ef	2 25 er	3 26 EW	4 25 EH	5 24 ft	6 22 FM	7 22 FT	2	8 20 td	9 19 tg	10 18 TF	11 17 TR	12 17 TF	1 16 TR
1 27 MF	2 26 MR	3 27 ef	4 26 er	5 25 EW	6 23 fm	7 23 ft	3	8 21 FM	9 20 FT	10 19 td	11 18 tg	12 18 td	1 17 tg
1 28 md	2 27 mg	3 28 MF	4 27 MR	5 26 ef	6 24 EH	7 24 EW	4	8 22 fm	9 21 ft	10 20 FM	11 19 FT	12 19 FM	1 18 FT
1 29 RM	2 28 RT	3 29 md	4 28 mg	5 27 MF	6 25 er	7 25 ef	5	8 23 EH	9 22 EW	10 21 fm	11 20 ft	12 20 fm	1 19 ft
1 30 rm	3 1 rt	3 30 RM	4 29 RT	5 28 md	6 26 MR	7 26 MF	6	8 24 er	9 23 ef	10 22 EH	11 21 EW	12 21 EH	1 20 EW
1 31 TH	3 2 TW	3 31 rm	4 30 rt	5 29 RM	6 27 mg	7 27 md	7	8 25 MR	9 24 MF	10 23 er	11 22 ef	12 22 er	1 21 ef
2 1 tr	3 3 tf	4 1 TH	5 1 TW	5 30 rm	6 28 RT	7 28 RM	8	8 26 mg	9 25 md	10 24 MR	11 23 MF	12 23 MR	1 22 MF
2 2 FR	3 4 FF	4 2 tr	5 2 tf	5 31 TH	6 29 rt	7 29 rm	9	8 27 RT	9 26 RM	10 25 mg	11 24 md	12 24 mg	1 23 md
2 3 fg	3 5 fd	4 3 FR	5 3 FF	6 1 tr	6 30 TW	7 30 TH	10	8 28 rt	9 27 rm	10 26 RT	11 25 RM	12 25 RT	1 24 RM
2 4 ET	3 6 EM	4 4 fg	5 4 fd	6 2 FR	7 1 tf	7 31 tr	11	8 29 TW	9 28 TH	10 27 rt	11 26 rm	12 26 rt	1 25 rm
2 5 et	3 7 em	4 5 ET	5 5 EM	6 3 fg	7 2 FF	8 1 FR	12	8 30 tf	9 29 tr	10 28 TW	11 27 TH	12 27 TW	1 26 TH
2 6 MW	3 8 MH	4 6 et	5 6 em	6 4 ET	7 3 fd	8 2 fg	13	8 31 FF	9 30 FR	10 29 tf	11 28 tr	12 28 tf	1 27 tr
2 7 mf	3 9 mr	4 7 MW	5 7 MH	6 5 et	7 4 EM	8 3 ET	14	9 1 fd	10 1 fg	10 30 FF	11 29 FR	12 29 FF	1 28 FR
2 8 RF	3 10 RR	4 8 mf	5 8 mr	6 6 MW	7 5 em	8 4 et	15	9 2 EM	10 2 ET	10 31 fd	11 30 fg	12 30 fd	1 29 fg
2 9 rd	3 11 rg	4 9 RF	5 9 RR	6 7 mf	7 6 MH	8 5 MW	16	9 3 em	10 3 et	11 1 EM	12 1 ET	12 31 EM	1 30 ET
2 10 TM	3 12 TT	4 10 rd	5 10 rg	6 8 RF	7 7 mr	8 6 mf	17	9 4 MH	10 4 MW	11 2 em	12 2 et	1 1 em	1 31 et
2 11 tm	3 13 tt	4 11 TM	5 11 TT	6 9 rd	7 8 RR	8 7 RF	18	9 5 mr	10 5 mf	11 3 MH	12 3 MW	1 2 MH	2 1 MW
2 12 FH	3 14 FW	4 12 tm	5 12 tt	6 10 TM	7 9 rg	8 8 rd	19	9 6 RR	10 6 RF	11 4 mr	12 4 mf	1 3 mr	2 2 mf
2 13 fr	3 15 ff	4 13 FH	5 13 FW	6 11 tm	7 10 TT	8 9 TM	20	9 7 rg	10 7 rd	11 5 RR	12 5 RF	1 4 RR	2 3 RF
2 14 ER	3 16 EF	4 14 fr	5 14 ff	6 12 FH	7 11 tt	8 10 tm	21	9 8 TT	10 8 TM	11 6 rg	12 6 rd	1 5 rg	2 4 rd
2 15 eg	3 17 ed	4 15 ER	5 15 EF	6 13 fr	7 12 FW	8 11 FH	22	9 9 tt	10 9 tm	11 7 TT	12 7 TM	1 6 TT	2 5 TM
2 16 MT	3 18 MM	4 16 eg	5 16 ed	6 14 ER	7 13 ff	8 12 fr	23	9 10 FW	10 10 FH	11 8 tt	12 8 tm	1 7 tt	2 6 tm
2 17 mt	3 19 mm	4 17 MT	5 17 MM	6 15 eg	7 14 EF	8 13 ER	24	9 11 ff	10 11 fr	11 9 FW	12 9 FH	1 8 FW	2 7 FH
2 18 RW	3 20 RH	4 18 mt	5 18 mm	6 16 MT	7 15 ed	8 14 eg	25	9 12 EF	10 12 ER	11 10 ff	12 10 fr	1 9 ff	2 8 fr
2 19 rf	3 21 rr	4 19 RW	5 19 RH	6 17 mt	7 16 MM	8 15 MT	26	9 13 ed	10 13 eg	11 11 EF	12 11 ER	1 10 EF	2 9 ER
2 20 TF	3 22 TR	4 20 rf	5 20 rr	6 18 RW	7 17 mm	8 16 mt	27	9 14 MM	10 14 MT	11 12 ed	12 12 eg	1 11 ed	2 10 eg
2 21 td	3 23 tg	4 21 TF	5 21 TR	6 19 rf	7 18 RH	8 17 RW	28	9 15 mm	10 15 mt	11 13 MM	12 13 MT	1 12 MM	2 11 MT
2 22 FM	3 24 FT	4 22 td	5 22 tg	6 20 TF	7 19 rr	8 18 rf	29	9 16 RH	10 16 RW	11 14 mm	12 14 mt	1 13 mm	2 12 mt
2 23 fm		4 23 FM			7 20 TR		30	9 17 rr		11 15 RH	12 15 RW	1 14 RH	

1964 TW DRAGON

JAN FT			FEB ft			MAR EW			APR ef			MAY MF			JUN md			DAY OF MON	JUL RM			AUG rm			SEP TH			OCT tr			NOV FR			DEC fg		
22 WARM			23 CLEAR			24 SUMMER			26 GRAIN			28 HEAT			30 FALL							2 DEW			3 C DEW			4 WINTER			4 SNOW			3 CHILL		
20:58			2:18			19:51			0:12			10:32			20:16							23:00			15:30			17:15			9:53			21:02		
2	13	RW	3	14	RH	4	12	mt	5	12	mm	6	10	MT	7	9	ed	1	8	8	eg	9	6	EF	10	6	ER	11	4	ff	12	4	fr	1	3	ff
2	14	rf	3	15	rr	4	13	RW	5	13	RH	6	11	mt	7	10	MM	2	8	9	MT	9	7	ed	10	7	eg	11	5	EF	12	5	ER	1	4	EF
2	15	TF	3	16	TR	4	14	rf	5	14	rr	6	12	RW	7	11	mm	3	8	10	mt	9	8	MM	10	8	MT	11	6	ed	12	6	eg	1	5	ed
2	16	td	3	17	tg	4	15	TF	5	15	TR	6	13	rf	7	12	RH	4	8	11	RW	9	9	mm	10	9	mt	11	7	MM	12	7	MT	1	6	MM
2	17	FM	3	18	FT	4	16	td	5	16	tg	6	14	TF	7	13	rr	5	8	12	rf	9	10	RH	10	10	RW	11	8	mm	12	8	mt	1	7	mm
2	18	fm	3	19	ft	4	17	FM	5	17	FT	6	15	td	7	14	TR	6	8	13	TF	9	11	rr	10	11	rf	11	9	RH	12	9	RW	1	8	RH
2	19	EH	3	20	EW	4	18	fm	5	18	ft	6	16	FM	7	15	tg	7	8	14	td	9	12	TR	10	12	TF	11	10	rr	12	10	rf	1	9	rr
2	20	er	3	21	ef	4	19	EH	5	19	EW	6	17	fm	7	16	FT	8	8	15	FM	9	13	tg	10	13	td	11	11	TR	12	11	TF	1	10	TR
2	21	MR	3	22	MF	4	20	er	5	20	ef	6	18	EH	7	17	ft	9	8	16	fm	9	14	FT	10	14	FM	11	12	tg	12	12	td	1	11	tg
2	22	mg	3	23	md	4	21	MR	5	21	MF	6	19	er	7	18	EW	10	8	17	EH	9	15	ft	10	15	fm	11	13	FT	12	13	FM	1	12	FT
2	23	RT	3	24	RM	4	22	mg	5	22	md	6	20	MR	7	19	ef	11	8	18	er	9	16	EW	10	16	EH	11	14	ft	12	14	fm	1	13	ft
2	24	rt	3	25	rm	4	23	RT	5	23	RM	6	21	mg	7	20	MF	12	8	19	MR	9	17	ef	10	17	er	11	15	EW	12	15	EH	1	14	EW
2	25	TW	3	26	TH	4	24	rt	5	24	rm	6	22	RT	7	21	md	13	8	20	mg	9	18	MF	10	18	MR	11	16	ef	12	16	er	1	15	ef
2	26	tf	3	27	tr	4	25	TW	5	25	TH	6	23	rt	7	22	RM	14	8	21	RT	9	19	md	10	19	mg	11	17	MF	12	17	MR	1	16	MF
2	27	FF	3	28	FR	4	26	tf	5	26	tr	6	24	TW	7	23	rm	15	8	22	rt	9	20	RM	10	20	RT	11	18	md	12	18	mg	1	17	md
2	28	fd	3	29	fg	4	27	FF	5	27	FR	6	25	tf	7	24	TH	16	8	23	TW	9	21	rm	10	21	rt	11	19	RM	12	19	RT	1	18	RM
2	29	EM	3	30	ET	4	28	fd	5	28	fg	6	26	FF	7	25	tr	17	8	24	tf	9	22	TH	10	22	TW	11	20	rm	12	20	rt	1	19	rm
3	1	em	3	31	et	4	29	EM	5	29	ET	6	27	fd	7	26	FR	18	8	25	FF	9	23	tr	10	23	tf	11	21	TH	12	21	TW	1	20	TH
3	2	MH	4	1	MW	4	30	em	5	30	et	6	28	EM	7	27	fg	19	8	26	fd	9	24	FR	10	24	FF	11	22	tr	12	22	tf	1	21	tr
3	3	mr	4	2	mf	5	1	MH	5	31	MW	6	29	em	7	28	ET	20	8	27	EM	9	25	fg	10	25	fd	11	23	FR	12	23	FF	1	22	FR
3	4	RR	4	3	RF	5	2	mr	6	1	mf	6	30	MH	7	29	et	21	8	28	em	9	26	ET	10	26	EM	11	24	fg	12	24	fd	1	23	fg
3	5	rg	4	4	rd	5	3	RR	6	2	RF	7	1	mr	7	30	MW	22	8	29	MH	9	27	et	10	27	em	11	25	ET	12	25	EM	1	24	ET
3	6	TT	4	5	TM	5	4	rg	6	3	rd	7	2	RR	7	31	mf	23	8	30	mr	9	28	MW	10	28	MH	11	26	et	12	26	em	1	25	et
3	7	tt	4	6	tm	5	5	TT	6	4	TM	7	3	rg	8	1	RF	24	8	31	RR	9	29	mf	10	29	mr	11	27	MW	12	27	MH	1	26	MW
3	8	FW	4	7	FH	5	6	tt	6	5	tm	7	4	TT	8	2	rd	25	9	1	rg	9	30	RF	10	30	RR	11	28	mf	12	28	mr	1	27	mf
3	9	ff	4	8	fr	5	7	FW	6	6	FH	7	5	tt	8	3	TM	26	9	2	TT	10	1	rd	10	31	rg	11	29	RF	12	29	RR	1	28	RF
3	10	EF	4	9	ER	5	8	ff	6	7	fr	7	6	FW	8	4	tm	27	9	3	tt	10	2	TM	11	1	TT	11	30	rd	12	30	rg	1	29	rd
3	11	ed	4	10	eg	5	9	EF	6	8	ER	7	7	ff	8	5	FH	28	9	4	FW	10	3	tm	11	2	tt	12	1	TM	12	31	TT	1	30	TM
3	12	MM	4	11	MT	5	10	ed	6	9	eg	7	8	EF	8	6	fr	29	9	5	ff	10	4	FH	11	3	FW	12	2	tm	1	1	tt	1	31	tm
3	13	mm				5	11	MM							8	7	ER	30				10	5	fr				12	3	FH	1	2	FW	2	1	FH

1965 tf SNAKE

JAN ET	FEB et	MAR MW	APR mf	MAY RF	JUN rd	DAY OF MON	JUL TM	AUG tm	SEP FH	OCT tr	NOV ER	DEC eg
3 SPRING	4 WARM	4 CLEAR	6 SUMMER	7 GRAIN	9 HEAT		12 FALL	13 DEW	14 C DEW	16 WINTER	15 SNOW	15 CHILL
8:46	2:48	8:07	1:42	6:02	16:22		2:05	5:41	21:19	0:13	15:46	3:16
2 2 fr	3 3 FW	4 2 FH	5 1 tt	5 31 tm	6 29 TT	1	7 28 rd	8 27 rg	9 25 RF	10 24 mr	11 23 mf	12 23 mr
2 3 ER	3 4 ff	4 3 fr	5 2 FW	6 1 FH	6 30 tt	2	7 29 TM	8 28 TT	9 26 rd	10 25 RR	11 24 RF	12 24 RR
2 4 eg	3 5 EF	4 4 ER	5 3 ff	6 2 fr	7 1 FW	3	7 30 tm	8 29 tt	9 27 TM	10 26 rg	11 25 rd	12 25 rg
2 5 MT	3 6 ed	4 5 eg	5 4 EF	6 3 ER	7 2 ff	4	7 31 FH	8 30 FW	9 28 tm	10 27 TT	11 26 TM	12 26 TT
2 6 mt	3 7 MM	4 6 MT	5 5 ed	6 4 eg	7 3 EF	5	8 1 fr	8 31 ff	9 29 FH	10 28 tt	11 27 tm	12 27 tt
2 7 RW	3 8 mm	4 7 mt	5 6 MM	6 5 MT	7 4 ed	6	8 2 ER	9 1 EF	9 30 fr	10 29 FW	11 28 FH	12 28 FW
2 8 rf	3 9 RH	4 8 RW	5 7 mm	6 6 mt	7 5 MM	7	8 3 eg	9 2 ed	10 1 ER	10 30 ff	11 29 fr	12 29 ff
2 9 TF	3 10 rr	4 9 rf	5 8 RH	6 7 RW	7 6 mm	8	8 4 MT	9 3 MM	10 2 eg	10 31 EF	11 30 ER	12 30 EF
2 10 td	3 11 TR	4 10 TF	5 9 rr	6 8 rf	7 7 RH	9	8 5 mt	9 4 mm	10 3 MT	11 1 ed	12 1 eg	12 31 ed
2 11 FM	3 12 tg	4 11 td	5 10 TR	6 9 TF	7 8 rr	10	8 6 RW	9 5 RH	10 4 mt	11 2 MM	12 2 MT	1 1 MM
2 12 fm	3 13 FT	4 12 FM	5 11 tg	6 10 td	7 9 TR	11	8 7 rf	9 6 rr	10 5 RW	11 3 mm	12 3 mt	1 2 mm
2 13 EH	3 14 ft	4 13 fm	5 12 FT	6 11 FM	7 10 tg	12	8 8 TF	9 7 TR	10 6 rf	11 4 RH	12 4 RW	1 3 RH
2 14 er	3 15 EW	4 14 EH	5 13 ft	6 12 fm	7 11 FT	13	8 9 td	9 8 tg	10 7 TF	11 5 rr	12 5 rf	1 4 rr
2 15 MR	3 16 ef	4 15 er	5 14 EW	6 13 EH	7 12 ft	14	8 10 FM	9 9 FT	10 8 td	11 6 TR	12 6 TF	1 5 TR
2 16 mg	3 17 MF	4 16 MR	5 15 ef	6 14 er	7 13 EW	15	8 11 fm	9 10 ft	10 9 FM	11 7 tg	12 7 td	1 6 tg
2 17 RT	3 18 md	4 17 mg	5 16 MF	6 15 MR	7 14 ef	16	8 12 EH	9 11 EW	10 10 fm	11 8 FT	12 8 FM	1 7 FT
2 18 rt	3 19 RM	4 18 RT	5 17 md	6 16 mg	7 15 MF	17	8 13 er	9 12 ef	10 11 EH	11 9 ft	12 9 fm	1 8 ft
2 19 TW	3 20 rm	4 19 rt	5 18 RM	6 17 RT	7 16 md	18	8 14 MR	9 13 MF	10 12 er	11 10 EW	12 10 EH	1 9 EW
2 20 tf	3 21 TH	4 20 TW	5 19 rm	6 18 rt	7 17 RM	19	8 15 mg	9 14 md	10 13 MR	11 11 ef	12 11 er	1 10 ef
2 21 FF	3 22 tr	4 21 tf	5 20 TH	6 19 TW	7 18 rm	20	8 16 RT	9 15 RM	10 14 mg	11 12 MF	12 12 MR	1 11 MF
2 22 fd	3 23 FR	4 22 FF	5 21 tr	6 20 tf	7 19 TH	21	8 17 rt	9 16 rm	10 15 RT	11 13 md	12 13 mg	1 12 md
2 23 EM	3 24 fg	4 23 fd	5 22 FR	6 21 FF	7 20 tr	22	8 18 TW	9 17 TH	10 16 rt	11 14 RM	12 14 RT	1 13 RM
2 24 em	3 25 ET	4 24 EM	5 23 fg	6 22 fd	7 21 FR	23	8 19 tf	9 18 tr	10 17 TW	11 15 rm	12 15 rt	1 14 rm
2 25 MH	3 26 et	4 25 em	5 24 ET	6 23 EM	7 22 fg	24	8 20 FF	9 19 FR	10 18 tf	11 16 TH	12 16 TW	1 15 TH
2 26 mr	3 27 MW	4 26 MH	5 25 et	6 24 em	7 23 ET	25	8 21 fd	9 20 fg	10 19 FF	11 17 tr	12 17 tf	1 16 tr
2 27 RR	3 28 mf	4 27 mr	5 26 MW	6 25 MH	7 24 et	26	8 22 EM	9 21 ET	10 20 fd	11 18 FR	12 18 FF	1 17 FR
2 28 rg	3 29 RF	4 28 RR	5 27 mf	6 26 mr	7 25 MW	27	8 23 em	9 22 et	10 21 EM	11 19 fg	12 19 fd	1 18 fg
3 1 TT	3 30 rd	4 29 rg	5 28 RF	6 27 RR	7 26 mf	28	8 24 MH	9 23 MW	10 22 em	11 20 ET	12 20 EM	1 19 ET
3 2 tt	3 31 TM	4 30 TT	5 29 rd	6 28 rg	7 27 RF	29	8 25 mr	9 24 mf	10 23 MH	11 21 et	12 21 em	1 20 et
	4 1 tm		5 30 TM			30	8 26 RR			11 22 MW	12 22 MH	

1966 FF HORSE

JAN MT	FEB mt	MAR RW	MAR RW	APR rf	MAY FF	JUN td	DAY OF MON	JUL FM	AUG fm	SEP EH	OCT er	NOV MR	DEC mg
15 SPRING	15 WARM	15 CLEAR	16 SUMMER	18 GRAIN	19 HEAT	22 FALL		24 DEW	25 C DEW	26 WINTER	26 SNOW	26 CHILL	25 SPRING
14:38	8:51	13: 57	7:31	11:50	22:07	7:49		11:30	3:08	6:02	21:38	9:06	20:31
1 21 MW	2 20 MH	3 22 MW	4 21 MH	5 20 et	6 19 em	7 18 ET	1	8 16 fd	9 15 fg	10 14 FF	11 12 tr	12 12 tf	1 11 tr
1 22 mf	2 21 mr	3 23 mf	4 22 mr	5 21 MW	6 20 MH	7 19 et	2	8 17 EM	9 16 ET	10 15 fd	11 13 FR	12 13 FF	1 12 FR
1 23 RF	2 22 RR	3 24 RF	4 23 RR	5 22 mf	6 21 mr	7 20 MW	3	8 18 em	9 17 et	10 16 EM	11 14 fg	12 14 fd	1 13 fg
1 24 rd	2 23 rg	3 25 rd	4 24 rg	5 23 RF	6 22 RR	7 21 mf	4	8 19 MH	9 18 MW	10 17 em	11 15 ET	12 15 EM	1 14 ET
1 25 TM	2 24 TT	3 26 TM	4 25 TT	5 24 rd	6 23 rg	7 22 RF	5	8 20 mr	9 19 mf	10 18 MH	11 16 et	12 16 em	1 15 et
1 26 tm	2 25 tt	3 27 tm	4 26 tt	5 25 TM	6 24 TT	7 23 rd	6	8 21 RR	9 20 RF	10 19 mr	11 17 MW	12 17 MH	1 16 MW
1 27 FH	2 26 FW	3 28 FH	4 27 FW	5 26 tm	6 25 tt	7 24 TM	7	8 22 rg	9 21 rd	10 20 RR	11 18 mf	12 18 mr	1 17 mf
1 28 fr	2 27 ff	3 29 fr	4 28 ff	5 27 FH	6 26 FW	7 25 tm	8	8 23 TT	9 22 TM	10 21 rg	11 19 RF	12 19 RR	1 18 RF
1 29 ER	2 28 EF	3 30 ER	4 29 EF	5 28 fr	6 27 ff	7 26 FH	9	8 24 tt	9 23 tm	10 22 TT	11 20 rd	12 20 rg	1 19 rd
1 30 eg	3 1 ed	3 31 eg	4 30 ed	5 29 ER	6 28 EF	7 27 fr	10	8 25 FW	9 24 FH	10 23 tt	11 21 TM	12 21 TT	1 20 TM
1 31 MT	3 2 MM	4 1 MT	5 1 MM	5 30 eg	6 29 ed	7 28 ER	11	8 26 ff	9 25 fr	10 24 FW	11 22 tm	12 22 tt	1 21 tm
2 1 mt	3 3 mm	4 2 mt	5 2 mm	5 31 MT	6 30 MM	7 29 eg	12	8 27 EF	9 26 ER	10 25 ff	11 23 FH	12 23 FW	1 22 FH
2 2 RW	3 4 RH	4 3 RW	5 3 RH	6 1 mt	7 1 mm	7 30 MT	13	8 28 ed	9 27 eg	10 26 EF	11 24 fr	12 24 ff	1 23 fr
2 3 rf	3 5 rr	4 4 rf	5 4 rr	6 2 RW	7 2 RH	7 31 mt	14	8 29 MM	9 28 MT	10 27 ed	11 25 ER	12 25 EF	1 24 ER
2 4 TF	3 6 TR	4 5 TF	5 5 TR	6 3 rf	7 3 rr	8 1 RW	15	8 30 mm	9 29 mt	10 28 MM	11 26 eg	12 26 ed	1 25 eg
2 5 td	3 7 tg	4 6 td	5 6 tg	6 4 TF	7 4 TR	8 2 rf	16	8 31 RH	9 30 RW	10 29 mm	11 27 MT	12 27 MM	1 26 MT
2 6 FM	3 8 FT	4 7 FM	5 7 FT	6 5 td	7 5 tg	8 3 TF	17	9 1 rr	10 1 rf	10 30 RH	11 28 mt	12 28 mm	1 27 mt
2 7 fm	3 9 ft	4 8 fm	5 8 ft	6 6 FM	7 6 FT	8 4 td	18	9 2 TR	10 2 TF	10 31 rr	11 29 RW	12 29 RH	1 28 RW
2 8 EH	3 10 EW	4 9 EH	5 9 EW	6 7 fm	7 7 ft	8 5 FM	19	9 3 tg	10 3 td	11 1 TR	11 30 rf	12 30 rr	1 29 rf
2 9 er	3 11 ef	4 10 er	5 10 ef	6 8 EH	7 8 EW	8 6 fm	20	9 4 FT	10 4 FM	11 2 tg	12 1 TF	12 31 TR	1 30 TF
2 10 MR	3 12 MF	4 11 MR	5 11 MF	6 9 er	7 9 ef	8 7 EH	21	9 5 ft	10 5 fm	11 3 FT	12 2 td	1 1 tg	1 31 td
2 11 mg	3 13 md	4 12 mg	5 12 md	6 10 MR	7 10 MF	8 8 er	22	9 6 EW	10 6 EH	11 4 ft	12 3 FM	1 2 FT	2 1 FM
2 12 RT	3 14 RM	4 13 RT	5 13 RM	6 11 mg	7 11 md	8 9 MR	23	9 7 ef	10 7 er	11 5 EW	12 4 fm	1 3 ft	2 2 fm
2 13 rt	3 15 rm	4 14 rt	5 14 rm	6 12 RT	7 12 RM	8 10 mg	24	9 8 MF	10 8 MR	11 6 ef	12 5 EH	1 4 EW	2 3 EH
2 14 TW	3 16 TH	4 15 TW	5 15 TH	6 13 rt	7 13 rm	8 11 RT	25	9 9 md	10 9 mg	11 7 MF	12 6 er	1 5 ef	2 4 er
2 15 tf	3 17 tr	4 16 tf	5 16 tr	6 14 TW	7 14 TH	8 12 rt	26	9 10 RM	10 10 RT	11 8 md	12 7 MR	1 6 MF	2 5 MR
2 16 FF	3 18 FR	4 17 FF	5 17 FR	6 15 tf	7 15 tr	8 13 TW	27	9 11 rm	10 11 rt	11 9 RM	12 8 mg	1 7 md	2 6 mg
2 17 fd	3 19 fg	4 18 fd	5 18 fg	6 16 FF	7 16 FR	8 14 tf	28	9 12 TH	10 12 TW	11 10 rm	12 9 RT	1 8 RM	2 7 RT
2 18 EM	3 20 ET	4 19 EM	5 19 ET	6 17 fd	7 17 fg	8 15 FF	29	9 13 tr	10 13 tf	11 11 TH	12 10 rt	1 9 rm	2 8 rt
2 19 em	3 21 et	4 20 em		6 18 EM			30	9 14 FR			12 11 TW	1 10 TH	

1967 fd RAM

JAN RT	FEB rt	MAR TW	APR tf	MAY FF	JUN fd	DAY OF MON	JUL EM	AUG em	SEP MH	OCT mr	NOV RR	DEC rg
26 WARM	26 CLEAR	27 SUMMER	29 GRAIN		1 HEAT		3 FALL	5 DEW	6 C DEW	7 WINTER	7 SNOW	7 CHILL
14:42	19:42	13:18	17:36		3:54		13:35	17:18	7:42	11:52	3:18	14:26
2 9 TW	3 11 TH	4 10 TW	5 9 rm	6 8 rt	7 8 rm	1	8 6 RT	9 4 md	10 4 mg	11 2 MF	12 2 MR	12 31 ef
2 10 tf	3 12 tr	4 11 tf	5 10 TH	6 9 TW	7 9 TH	2	8 7 rt	9 5 RM	10 5 RT	11 3 md	12 3 mg	1 1 MF
2 11 FF	3 13 FR	4 12 FF	5 11 tr	6 10 tf	7 10 tr	3	8 8 TW	9 6 rm	10 6 rt	11 4 RM	12 4 RT	1 2 md
2 12 fd	3 14 fg	4 13 fd	5 12 FR	6 11 FF	7 11 FR	4	8 9 tf	9 7 TH	10 7 TW	11 5 rm	12 5 rt	1 3 RM
2 13 EM	3 15 ET	4 14 EM	5 13 fg	6 12 fd	7 12 fg	5	8 10 FF	9 8 tr	10 8 tf	11 6 TH	12 6 TW	1 4 rm
2 14 em	3 16 et	4 15 em	5 14 ET	6 13 EM	7 13 ET	6	8 11 fd	9 9 FR	10 9 FF	11 7 tr	12 7 tf	1 5 TH
2 15 MH	3 17 MW	4 16 MH	5 15 et	6 14 em	7 14 et	7	8 12 EM	9 10 fg	10 10 fd	11 8 FR	12 8 FF	1 6 tr
2 16 mr	3 18 mf	4 17 mr	5 16 MW	6 15 MH	7 15 MW	8	8 13 em	9 11 ET	10 11 EM	11 9 fg	12 9 fd	1 7 FR
2 17 RR	3 19 RF	4 18 RR	5 17 mf	6 16 mr	7 16 mf	9	8 14 MH	9 12 et	10 12 em	11 10 ET	12 10 EM	1 8 fg
2 18 rg	3 20 rd	4 19 rg	5 18 RF	6 17 RR	7 17 RF	10	8 15 mr	9 13 MW	10 13 MH	11 11 et	12 11 em	1 9 ET
2 19 TT	3 21 TM	4 20 TT	5 19 rd	6 18 rg	7 18 rd	11	8 16 RR	9 14 mf	10 14 mr	11 12 MW	12 12 MH	1 10 et
2 20 tt	3 22 tm	4 21 tt	5 20 TM	6 19 TT	7 19 TM	12	8 17 rg	9 15 RF	10 15 RR	11 13 mf	12 13 mr	1 11 MW
2 21 FW	3 23 FH	4 22 FW	5 21 tm	6 20 tt	7 20 tm	13	8 18 TT	9 16 rd	10 16 rg	11 14 RF	12 14 RR	1 12 mf
2 22 ff	3 24 fr	4 23 ff	5 22 FH	6 21 FW	7 21 FH	14	8 19 tt	9 17 TM	10 17 TT	11 15 rd	12 15 rg	1 13 RF
2 23 EF	3 25 ER	4 24 EF	5 23 fr	6 22 ff	7 22 fr	15	8 20 FW	9 18 tm	10 18 tt	11 16 TM	12 16 TT	1 14 rd
2 24 ed	3 26 eg	4 25 ed	5 24 ER	6 23 EF	7 23 ER	16	8 21 ff	9 19 FH	10 19 FW	11 17 tm	12 17 tt	1 15 TM
2 25 MM	3 27 MT	4 26 MM	5 25 eg	6 24 ed	7 24 eg	17	8 22 EF	9 20 fr	10 20 ff	11 18 FH	12 18 FW	1 16 tm
2 26 mm	3 28 mt	4 27 mm	5 26 MT	6 25 MM	7 25 MT	18	8 23 ed	9 21 ER	10 21 EF	11 19 fr	12 19 ff	1 17 FH
2 27 RH	3 29 RW	4 28 RH	5 27 mt	6 26 mm	7 26 mt	19	8 24 MM	9 22 eg	10 22 ed	11 20 ER	12 20 EF	1 18 fr
2 28 rr	3 30 rf	4 29 rr	5 28 RW	6 27 RH	7 27 RW	20	8 25 mm	9 23 MT	10 23 MM	11 21 eg	12 21 ed	1 19 ER
3 1 TR	3 31 TF	4 30 TR	5 29 rf	6 28 rr	7 28 rf	21	8 26 RH	9 24 mt	10 24 mm	11 22 MT	12 22 MM	1 20 eg
3 2 tg	4 1 td	5 1 tg	5 30 TF	6 29 TR	7 29 TF	22	8 27 rr	9 25 RW	10 25 RH	11 23 mt	12 23 mm	1 21 MT
3 3 FT	4 2 FM	5 2 FT	5 31 td	6 30 tg	7 30 td	23	8 28 TR	9 26 rf	10 26 rr	11 24 RW	12 24 RH	1 22 mt
3 4 ft	4 3 fm	5 3 ft	6 1 FM	7 1 FT	7 31 FM	24	8 29 tg	9 27 TF	10 27 TR	11 25 rf	12 25 rr	1 23 RW
3 5 EW	4 4 EH	5 4 EW	6 2 fm	7 2 ft	8 1 fm	25	8 30 FT	9 28 td	10 28 tg	11 26 TF	12 26 TR	1 24 rf
3 6 ef	4 5 er	5 5 ef	6 3 EH	7 3 EW	8 2 EH	26	8 31 ft	9 29 FM	10 29 FT	11 27 td	12 27 tg	1 25 TF
3 7 MF	4 6 MR	5 6 MF	6 4 er	7 4 ef	8 3 er	27	9 1 EW	9 30 fm	10 30 ft	11 28 FM	12 28 FT	1 26 td
3 8 md	4 7 mg	5 7 md	6 5 MR	7 5 MF	8 4 MR	28	9 2 ef	10 1 EH	10 31 EW	11 29 fm	12 29 ft	1 27 FM
3 9 RM	4 8 RT	5 8 RM	6 6 mg	7 6 md	8 5 mg	29	9 3 MF	10 2 er	11 1 ef	11 30 EH	12 30 EW	1 28 fm
3 10 rm	4 9 rt		6 7 RT	7 7 RM		30		10 3 MR		12 1 er		1 29 EH

1968 EM MONKEY

JAN TT	FEB tt	MAR FW	APR ff	MAY EF	JUN ed	DAY OF MON	JUL MM	JUL MM	AUG mm	SEP RH	OCT rr	NOV TR	DEC tg
7 SPRING	7 WARM	8 CLEAR	9 SUMMER	10 GRAIN	12 HEAT		14 FALL	15 DEW	17 C DEW	17 WINTER	18 SNOW	17 CHILL	18 SPRING
2:08	20:18	1:21	19:50	23:19	9:42		19:27	23:07	13:35	17:41	9:09	20:17	7:59
1 30 er	2 28 EW	3 29 EH	4 27 ft	5 27 fm	6 26 ft	1	7 25 FM	8 24 FT	9 22 td	10 22 tg	11 20 TF	12 20 TR	1 18 rf
1 31 MR	2 29 ef	3 30 er	4 28 EW	5 28 EH	6 27 EW	2	7 26 fm	8 25 ft	9 23 FM	10 23 FT	11 21 td	12 21 tg	1 19 TF
2 1 mg	3 1 MF	3 31 MR	4 29 ef	5 29 er	6 28 ef	3	7 27 EH	8 26 EW	9 24 fm	10 24 ft	11 22 FM	12 22 FT	1 20 td
2 2 RT	3 2 md	4 1 mg	4 30 MF	5 30 MR	6 29 MF	4	7 28 er	8 27 ef	9 25 EH	10 25 EW	11 23 fm	12 23 ft	1 21 FM
2 3 rt	3 3 RM	4 2 RT	5 1 md	5 31 mg	6 30 md	5	7 29 MR	8 28 MF	9 26 er	10 26 ef	11 24 EH	12 24 EW	1 22 fm
2 4 TW	3 4 rm	4 3 rt	5 2 RM	6 1 RT	7 1 RM	6	7 30 mg	8 29 md	9 27 MR	10 27 MF	11 25 er	12 25 ef	1 23 EH
2 5 tf	3 5 TH	4 4 TW	5 3 rm	6 2 rt	7 2 rm	7	7 31 RT	8 30 RM	9 28 mg	10 28 md	11 26 MR	12 26 MF	1 24 er
2 6 FF	3 6 tr	4 5 tf	5 4 TH	6 3 TW	7 3 TH	8	8 1 rt	8 31 rm	9 29 RT	10 29 RM	11 27 mg	12 27 md	1 25 MR
2 7 fd	3 7 FR	4 6 FF	5 5 tr	6 4 tf	7 4 tr	9	8 2 TW	9 1 TH	9 30 rt	10 30 rm	11 28 RT	12 28 RM	1 26 mg
2 8 EM	3 8 fg	4 7 fd	5 6 FR	6 5 FF	7 5 FR	10	8 3 tf	9 2 tr	10 1 TW	10 31 TH	11 29 rt	12 29 rm	1 27 RT
2 9 em	3 9 ET	4 8 EM	5 7 fg	6 6 fd	7 6 fg	11	8 4 FF	9 3 FR	10 2 tf	11 1 tr	11 30 TW	12 30 TH	1 28 rt
2 10 MH	3 10 et	4 9 em	5 8 ET	6 7 EM	7 7 ET	12	8 5 fd	9 4 fg	10 3 FF	11 2 FR	12 1 tf	12 31 tr	1 29 TW
2 11 mr	3 11 MW	4 10 MH	5 9 et	6 8 em	7 8 et	13	8 6 EM	9 5 ET	10 4 fd	11 3 fg	12 2 FF	1 1 FR	1 30 tf
2 12 RR	3 12 mf	4 11 mr	5 10 MW	6 9 MH	7 9 MW	14	8 7 em	9 6 et	10 5 EM	11 4 ET	12 3 fd	1 2 fg	1 31 FF
2 13 rg	3 13 RF	4 12 RR	5 11 mf	6 10 mr	7 10 mf	15	8 8 MH	9 7 MW	10 6 em	11 5 et	12 4 EM	1 3 ET	2 1 fd
2 14 TT	3 14 rd	4 13 rg	5 12 RF	6 11 RR	7 11 RF	16	8 9 mr	9 8 mf	10 7 MH	11 6 MW	12 5 em	1 4 et	2 2 EM
2 15 tt	3 15 TM	4 14 TT	5 13 rd	6 12 rg	7 12 rd	17	8 10 RR	9 9 RF	10 8 mr	11 7 mf	12 6 MH	1 5 MW	2 3 em
2 16 FW	3 16 tm	4 15 tt	5 14 TM	6 13 TT	7 13 TM	18	8 11 rg	9 10 rd	10 9 RR	11 8 RF	12 7 mr	1 6 mf	2 4 MH
2 17 ff	3 17 FH	4 16 FW	5 15 tm	6 14 tt	7 14 tm	19	8 12 TT	9 11 TM	10 10 rg	11 9 rd	12 8 RR	1 7 RF	2 5 mr
2 18 EF	3 18 fr	4 17 ff	5 16 FH	6 15 FW	7 15 FH	20	8 13 tt	9 12 tm	10 11 TT	11 10 TM	12 9 rg	1 8 rd	2 6 RR
2 19 ed	3 19 ER	4 18 EF	5 17 fr	6 16 ff	7 16 fr	21	8 14 FW	9 13 FH	10 12 tt	11 11 tm	12 10 TT	1 9 TM	2 7 rg
2 20 MM	3 20 eg	4 19 ed	5 18 ER	6 17 EF	7 17 ER	22	8 15 ff	9 14 fr	10 13 FW	11 12 FH	12 11 tt	1 10 tm	2 8 TT
2 21 mm	3 21 MT	4 20 MM	5 19 eg	6 18 ed	7 18 eg	23	8 16 EF	9 15 ER	10 14 ff	11 13 fr	12 12 FW	1 11 FH	2 9 tt
2 22 RH	3 22 mt	4 21 mm	5 20 MT	6 19 MM	7 19 MT	24	8 17 ed	9 16 eg	10 15 EF	11 14 ER	12 13 ff	1 12 fr	2 10 FW
2 23 rr	3 23 RW	4 22 RH	5 21 mt	6 20 mm	7 20 mt	25	8 18 MM	9 17 MT	10 16 ed	11 15 eg	12 14 EF	1 13 ER	2 11 ff
2 24 TR	3 24 rf	4 23 rr	5 22 RW	6 21 RH	7 21 RW	26	8 19 mm	9 18 mt	10 17 MM	11 16 MT	12 15 ed	1 14 eg	2 12 EF
2 25 tg	3 25 TF	4 24 TR	5 23 rf	6 22 rr	7 22 rf	27	8 20 RH	9 19 RW	10 18 mm	11 17 mt	12 16 MM	1 15 MT	2 13 ed
2 26 FT	3 26 td	4 25 tg	5 24 TF	6 23 TR	7 23 TF	28	8 21 rr	9 20 rf	10 19 RH	11 18 RW	12 17 mm	1 16 mt	2 14 MM
2 27 ft	3 27 FM	4 26 FT	5 25 td	6 24 tg	7 24 td	29	8 22 TR	9 21 TF	10 20 rr	11 19 rf	12 18 RH	1 17 RW	2 15 mm
	3 28 fm		5 26 FM	6 25 FT		30	8 23 tg		10 21 TR		12 19 rr		2 16 RH

1969 em ROOSTER

JAN FT	FEB ft	MAR EW	APR ef	MAY MF	JUN md	DAY OF	JUL RM	AUG rm	SEP TH	OCT tr	NOV FR	DEC fg
18 WARM	19 CLEAR	20 SUMMER	22 GRAIN	23 HEAT	26 FALL	MON	27 DEW	27 C DEW	28 WINTER	28 SNOW	29 CHILL	28 SPRING
2:11	7:15	0:50	5:12	15:32	1:14		3:56	19:17	23:31	15:54	1:59	13:46
2 17 rr	3 18 RW	4 17 RH	5 16 mt	6 15 mm	7 14 MT	1	8 13 MM	9 12 MT	10 11 ed	11 10 eg	12 9 EF	1 8 ER
2 18 TR	3 19 rf	4 18 rr	5 17 RW	6 16 RH	7 15 mt	2	8 14 mm	9 13 mt	10 12 MM	11 11 MT	12 10 ed	1 9 eg
2 19 tg	3 20 TF	4 19 TR	5 18 rf	6 17 rr	7 16 RW	3	8 15 RH	9 14 RW	10 13 mm	11 12 mt	12 11 MM	1 10 MT
2 20 FT	3 21 td	4 20 tg	5 19 TF	6 18 TR	7 17 rf	4	8 16 rr	9 15 rf	10 14 RH	11 13 RW	12 12 mm	1 11 mt
2 21 ft	3 22 FM	4 21 FT	5 20 td	6 19 tg	7 18 TF	5	8 17 TR	9 16 TF	10 15 rr	11 14 rf	12 13 RH	1 12 RW
2 22 EW	3 23 fm	4 22 ft	5 21 FM	6 20 FT	7 19 td	6	8 18 tg	9 17 td	10 16 TR	11 15 TF	12 14 rr	1 13 rf
2 23 ef	3 24 EH	4 23 EW	5 22 fm	6 21 ft	7 20 FM	7	8 19 FT	9 18 FM	10 17 tg	11 16 td	12 15 TR	1 14 TF
2 24 MF	3 25 er	4 24 ef	5 23 EH	6 22 EW	7 21 fm	8	8 20 ft	9 19 fm	10 18 FT	11 17 FM	12 16 tg	1 15 td
2 25 md	3 26 MR	4 25 MF	5 24 er	6 23 ef	7 22 EH	9	8 21 EW	9 20 EH	10 19 ft	11 18 fm	12 17 FT	1 16 FM
2 26 RM	3 27 mg	4 26 md	5 25 MR	6 24 MF	7 23 er	10	8 22 ef	9 21 er	10 20 EW	11 19 EH	12 18 ft	1 17 fm
2 27 rm	3 28 RT	4 27 RM	5 26 mg	6 25 md	7 24 MR	11	8 23 MF	9 22 MR	10 21 ef	11 20 er	12 19 EW	1 18 EH
2 28 TH	3 29 rt	4 28 rm	5 27 RT	6 26 RM	7 25 mg	12	8 24 md	9 23 mg	10 22 MF	11 21 MR	12 20 ef	1 19 er
3 1 tr	3 30 TW	4 29 TH	5 28 rt	6 27 rm	7 26 RT	13	8 25 RM	9 24 RT	10 23 md	11 22 mg	12 21 MF	1 20 MR
3 2 FR	3 31 tf	4 30 tr	5 29 TW	6 28 TH	7 27 rt	14	8 26 rm	9 25 rt	10 24 RM	11 23 RT	12 22 md	1 21 mg
3 3 fg	4 1 FF	5 1 FR	5 30 tf	6 29 tr	7 28 TW	15	8 27 TH	9 26 TW	10 25 rm	11 24 rt	12 23 RM	1 22 RT
3 4 ET	4 2 fd	5 2 fg	5 31 FF	6 30 FR	7 29 tf	16	8 28 tr	9 27 tf	10 26 TH	11 25 TW	12 24 rm	1 23 rt
3 5 et	4 3 EM	5 3 ET	6 1 fd	7 1 fg	7 30 FF	17	8 29 FR	9 28 FF	10 27 tr	11 26 tf	12 25 TH	1 24 TW
3 6 MW	4 4 em	5 4 et	6 2 EM	7 2 ET	7 31 fd	18	8 30 fg	9 29 fd	10 28 FR	11 27 FF	12 26 tr	1 25 tf
3 7 mf	4 5 MH	5 5 MW	6 3 em	7 3 et	8 1 EM	19	8 31 ET	9 30 EM	10 29 fg	11 28 fd	12 27 FR	1 26 FF
3 8 RF	4 6 mr	5 6 mf	6 4 MH	7 4 MW	8 2 em	20	9 1 et	10 1 em	10 30 ET	11 29 EM	12 28 fg	1 27 fd
3 9 rd	4 7 RR	5 7 RF	6 5 mr	7 5 mf	8 3 MH	21	9 2 MW	10 2 MH	10 31 et	11 30 em	12 29 ET	1 28 EM
3 10 TM	4 8 rg	5 8 rd	6 6 RR	7 6 RF	8 4 mr	22	9 3 mf	10 3 mr	11 1 MW	12 1 MH	12 30 et	1 29 em
3 11 tm	4 9 TT	5 9 TM	6 7 rg	7 7 rd	8 5 RR	23	9 4 RF	10 4 RR	11 2 mf	12 2 mr	12 31 MW	1 30 MH
3 12 FH	4 10 tt	5 10 tm	6 8 TT	7 8 TM	8 6 rg	24	9 5 rd	10 5 rg	11 3 RF	12 3 RR	1 1 mf	1 31 mr
3 13 fr	4 11 FW	5 11 FH	6 9 tt	7 9 tm	8 7 TT	25	9 6 TM	10 6 TT	11 4 rd	12 4 rg	1 2 RF	2 1 RR
3 14 ER	4 12 ff	5 12 fr	6 10 FW	7 10 FH	8 8 tt	26	9 7 tm	10 7 tt	11 5 TM	12 5 TT	1 3 rd	2 2 rg
3 15 eg	4 13 EF	5 13 ER	6 11 ff	7 11 fr	8 9 FW	27	9 8 FH	10 8 FW	11 6 tm	12 6 tt	1 4 TM	2 3 TT
3 16 MT	4 14 ed	5 14 eg	6 12 EF	7 12 ER	8 10 ff	28	9 9 fr	10 9 ff	11 7 FH	12 7 FW	1 5 tm	2 4 tt
3 17 mt	4 15 MM	5 15 MT	6 13 ed	7 13 eg	8 11 EF	29	9 10 ER	10 10 EF	11 8 fr	12 8 ff	1 6 FH	2 5 FW
	4 16 mm		6 14 MM		8 12 ed	30	9 11 eg		11 9 ER		1 7 fr	

1970 MH DOG

JAN ET	FEB et	MAR MW	APR mf	MAY RF	JUN rd	DAY OF MON	JUL TM	AUG tm	SEP FH	OCT fr	NOV ER	DEC eg
29 WARM	29 CLEAR		2 SUMMER	3 GRAIN	5 HEAT		7 FALL	8 DEW	10 C DEW	10 WINTER	9 SNOW	10 CHILL
7:51	13:00		6:28	11:13	21:14		7:20	9:42	1:06	5:20	21:43	7:45
2 6 ff	3 8 fr	4 6 FW	5 5 tm	6 4 tt	7 3 TM	1	8 2 TT	9 1 TM	9 30 rg	10 30 rd	11 29 rg	12 28 RF
2 7 EF	3 9 ER	4 7 ff	5 6 FH	6 5 FW	7 4 tm	2	8 3 tt	9 2 tm	10 1 TT	10 31 TM	11 30 TT	12 29 rd
2 8 ed	3 10 eg	4 8 EF	5 7 fr	6 6 ff	7 5 FH	3	8 4 FW	9 3 FH	10 2 tt	11 1 tm	12 1 tt	12 30 TM
2 9 MM	3 11 MT	4 9 ed	5 8 ER	6 7 EF	7 6 fr	4	8 5 ff	9 4 fr	10 3 FW	11 2 FH	12 2 FW	12 31 tm
2 10 mm	3 12 mt	4 10 MM	5 9 eg	6 8 ed	7 7 ER	5	8 6 EF	9 5 ER	10 4 ff	11 3 fr	12 3 ff	1 1 FH
2 11 RH	3 13 RW	4 11 mm	5 10 MT	6 9 MM	7 8 eg	6	8 7 ed	9 6 eg	10 5 EF	11 4 ER	12 4 EF	1 2 fr
2 12 rr	3 14 rf	4 12 RH	5 11 mt	6 10 mm	7 9 MT	7	8 8 MM	9 7 MT	10 6 ed	11 5 eg	12 5 ed	1 3 ER
2 13 TR	3 15 TF	4 13 rr	5 12 RW	6 11 RH	7 10 mt	8	8 9 mm	9 8 mt	10 7 MM	11 6 MT	12 6 MM	1 4 eg
2 14 tg	3 16 td	4 14 TR	5 13 rf	6 12 rr	7 11 RW	9	8 10 RH	9 9 RW	10 8 mm	11 7 mt	12 7 mm	1 5 MT
2 15 FT	3 17 FM	4 15 tg	5 14 TF	6 13 TR	7 12 rf	10	8 11 rr	9 10 rf	10 9 RH	11 8 RW	12 8 RH	1 6 mt
2 16 ft	3 18 fm	4 16 FT	5 15 td	6 14 tg	7 13 TF	11	8 12 TR	9 11 TF	10 10 rr	11 9 rf	12 9 rr	1 7 RW
2 17 EW	3 19 EH	4 17 ft	5 16 FM	6 15 FT	7 14 td	12	8 13 tg	9 12 td	10 11 TR	11 10 TF	12 10 TR	1 8 rf
2 18 ef	3 20 er	4 18 EW	5 17 fm	6 16 ft	7 15 FM	13	8 14 FT	9 13 FM	10 12 tg	11 11 td	12 11 tg	1 9 TF
2 19 MF	3 21 MR	4 19 ef	5 18 EH	6 17 EW	7 16 fm	14	8 15 ft	9 14 fm	10 13 FT	11 12 FM	12 12 FT	1 10 td
2 20 md	3 22 mg	4 20 MF	5 19 er	6 18 ef	7 17 EH	15	8 16 EW	9 15 EH	10 14 ft	11 13 fm	12 13 ft	1 11 FM
2 21 RM	3 23 RT	4 21 md	5 20 MR	6 19 MF	7 18 er	16	8 17 ef	9 16 er	10 15 EW	11 14 EH	12 14 EW	1 12 fm
2 22 rm	3 24 rt	4 22 RM	5 21 mg	6 20 md	7 19 MR	17	8 18 MF	9 17 MR	10 16 ef	11 15 er	12 15 ef	1 13 EH
2 23 TH	3 25 TW	4 23 rm	5 22 RT	6 21 RM	7 20 mg	18	8 19 md	9 18 mg	10 17 MF	11 16 MR	12 16 MF	1 14 er
2 24 tr	3 26 tf	4 24 TH	5 23 rt	6 22 rm	7 21 RT	19	8 20 RM	9 19 RT	10 18 md	11 17 mg	12 17 md	1 15 MR
2 25 FR	3 27 FF	4 25 tr	5 24 TW	6 23 TH	7 22 rt	20	8 21 rm	9 20 rt	10 19 RM	11 18 RT	12 18 RM	1 16 mg
2 26 fg	3 28 fd	4 26 FR	5 25 tf	6 24 tr	7 23 TW	21	8 22 TH	9 21 TW	10 20 rm	11 19 rt	12 19 rm	1 17 RT
2 27 ET	3 29 EM	4 27 fg	5 26 FF	6 25 FR	7 24 tf	22	8 23 tr	9 22 tf	10 21 TH	11 20 TW	12 20 TH	1 18 rt
2 28 et	3 30 em	4 28 ET	5 27 fd	6 26 fg	7 25 FF	23	8 24 FR	9 23 FF	10 22 tr	11 21 tf	12 21 tr	1 19 TW
3 1 MW	3 31 MH	4 29 et	5 28 EM	6 27 ET	7 26 fd	24	8 25 fg	9 24 fd	10 23 FR	11 22 FF	12 22 FR	1 20 tf
3 2 mf	4 1 mr	4 30 MW	5 29 em	6 28 et	7 27 EM	25	8 26 ET	9 25 EM	10 24 fg	11 23 fd	12 23 fg	1 21 FF
3 3 RF	4 2 RR	5 1 mf	5 30 MH	6 29 MW	7 28 em	26	8 27 et	9 26 em	10 25 ET	11 24 EM	12 24 ET	1 22 fd
3 4 rd	4 3 rg	5 2 RF	5 31 mr	6 30 mf	7 29 MH	27	8 28 MW	9 27 MH	10 26 et	11 25 em	12 25 et	1 23 EM
3 5 TM	4 4 TT	5 3 rd	6 1 RR	7 1 RF	7 30 mr	28	8 29 mf	9 28 mr	10 27 MW	11 26 MH	12 26 MW	1 24 em
3 6 tm	4 5 tt	5 4 TM	6 2 rg	7 2 rd	7 31 RR	29	8 30 RF	9 29 RR	10 28 mf	11 27 mr	12 27 mf	1 25 MH
3 7 FH			6 3 TT		8 1 rg	30	8 31 rd		10 29 RF	11 28 RR		1 26 mr

1971 mr BOAR

JAN MT	FEB mt	MAR RW	APR rf	MAY TF	MAY TF	JUN td	DAY OF	JUL FM	AUG fm	SEP EH	OCT er	NOV MR	DEC mg
9 SPRING	10 WARM	10 CLEAR	12 SUMMER	14 GRAIN	16 HEAT	18 FALL	MON	19 DEW	21 C DEW	21 WINTER	21 SNOW	20 CHILL	21 SPRING
19:26	13:35	18:36	12:08	17:00	3:29	13:29		17:30	8:13	11:10	3:33	13:43	1:20
1 27 RR	2 25 mf	3 27 mr	4 25 MW	5 24 em	6 23 et	7 22 EM	1	8 21 ET	9 19 fd	10 19 fg	11 18 fd	12 18 fg	1 16 FF
1 28 rg	2 26 RF	3 28 RR	4 26 mf	5 25 MH	6 24 MW	7 23 em	2	8 22 et	9 20 EM	10 20 ET	11 19 EM	12 19 ET	1 17 fd
1 29 TT	2 27 rd	3 29 rg	4 27 RF	5 26 mr	6 25 mf	7 24 MH	3	8 23 MW	9 21 em	10 21 et	11 20 em	12 20 et	1 18 EM
1 30 tt	2 28 TM	3 30 TT	4 28 rd	5 27 RR	6 26 RF	7 25 mr	4	8 24 mf	9 22 MH	10 22 MW	11 21 MH	12 21 MW	1 19 em
1 31 FW	3 1 tm	3 31 tt	4 29 TM	5 28 rg	6 27 rd	7 26 RR	5	8 25 RF	9 23 mr	10 23 mf	11 22 mr	12 22 mf	1 20 MH
2 1 ff	3 2 FH	4 1 FW	4 30 tm	5 29 TT	6 28 TM	7 27 rg	6	8 26 rd	9 24 RR	10 24 RF	11 23 RR	12 23 RF	1 21 mr
2 2 EF	3 3 fr	4 2 ff	5 1 FH	5 30 tt	6 29 tm	7 28 TT	7	8 27 TM	9 25 rg	10 25 rd	11 24 rg	12 24 rd	1 22 RR
2 3 ed	3 4 ER	4 3 EF	5 2 fr	5 31 FW	6 30 FH	7 29 tt	8	8 28 tm	9 26 TT	10 26 TM	11 25 TT	12 25 TM	1 23 rg
2 4 MM	3 5 eg	4 4 ed	5 3 ER	6 1 ff	7 1 fr	7 30 FW	9	8 29 FH	9 27 tt	10 27 tm	11 26 tt	12 26 tm	1 24 TT
2 5 mm	3 6 MT	4 5 MM	5 4 eg	6 2 EF	7 2 ER	7 31 ff	10	8 30 fr	9 28 FW	10 28 FH	11 27 FW	12 27 FH	1 25 tt
2 6 RH	3 7 mt	4 6 mm	5 5 MT	6 3 ed	7 3 eg	8 1 EF	11	8 31 ER	9 29 ff	10 29 fr	11 28 ff	12 28 fr	1 26 FW
2 7 rr	3 8 RW	4 7 RH	5 6 mt	6 4 MM	7 4 MT	8 2 ed	12	9 1 eg	9 30 EF	10 30 ER	11 29 EF	12 29 ER	1 27 ff
2 8 TR	3 9 rf	4 8 rr	5 7 RW	6 5 mm	7 5 mt	8 3 MM	13	9 2 MT	10 1 ed	10 31 eg	11 30 ed	12 30 eg	1 28 EF
2 9 tg	3 10 TF	4 9 TR	5 8 rf	6 6 RH	7 6 RW	8 4 mm	14	9 3 mt	10 2 MM	11 1 MT	12 1 MM	12 31 MT	1 29 ed
2 10 FT	3 11 td	4 10 tg	5 9 TF	6 7 rr	7 7 rf	8 5 RH	15	9 4 RW	10 3 mm	11 2 mt	12 2 mm	1 1 mt	1 30 MM
2 11 ft	3 12 FM	4 11 FT	5 10 td	6 8 TR	7 8 TF	8 6 rr	16	9 5 rf	10 4 RH	11 3 RW	12 3 RH	1 2 RW	1 31 mm
2 12 EW	3 13 fm	4 12 ft	5 11 FM	6 9 tg	7 9 td	8 7 TR	17	9 6 TF	10 5 rr	11 4 rf	12 4 rr	1 3 rf	2 1 RH
2 13 ef	3 14 EH	4 13 EW	5 12 fm	6 10 FT	7 10 FM	8 8 tg	18	9 7 td	10 6 TR	11 5 TF	12 5 TR	1 4 TF	2 2 rr
2 14 MF	3 15 er	4 14 ef	5 13 EH	6 11 ft	7 11 fm	8 9 FT	19	9 8 FM	10 7 tg	11 6 td	12 6 tg	1 5 td	2 3 TR
2 15 md	3 16 MR	4 15 MF	5 14 er	6 12 EW	7 12 EH	8 10 ft	20	9 9 fm	10 8 FT	11 7 FM	12 7 FT	1 6 FM	2 4 tg
2 16 RM	3 17 mg	4 16 md	5 15 MR	6 13 ef	7 13 er	8 11 EW	21	9 10 EH	10 9 ft	11 8 fm	12 8 ft	1 7 fm	2 5 FT
2 17 rm	3 18 RT	4 17 RM	5 16 mg	6 14 MF	7 14 MR	8 12 ef	22	9 11 er	10 10 EW	11 9 EH	12 9 EW	1 8 EH	2 6 ft
2 18 TH	3 19 rt	4 18 rm	5 17 RT	6 15 md	7 15 mg	8 13 MF	23	9 12 MR	10 11 ef	11 10 er	12 10 ef	1 9 er	2 7 EW
2 19 tr	3 20 TW	4 19 TH	5 18 rt	6 16 RM	7 16 RT	8 14 md	24	9 13 mg	10 12 MF	11 11 MR	12 11 MF	1 10 MR	2 8 ef
2 20 FR	3 21 tf	4 20 tr	5 19 TW	6 17 rm	7 17 rt	8 15 RM	25	9 14 RT	10 13 md	11 12 mg	12 12 md	1 11 mg	2 9 MF
2 21 fg	3 22 FF	4 21 FR	5 20 tf	6 18 TH	7 18 TW	8 16 rm	26	9 15 rt	10 14 RM	11 13 RT	12 13 RM	1 12 RT	2 10 md
2 22 ET	3 23 fd	4 22 fg	5 21 FF	6 19 tr	7 19 tf	8 17 TH	27	9 16 TW	10 15 rm	11 14 rt	12 14 rm	1 13 rt	2 11 RM
2 23 et	3 24 EM	4 23 ET	5 22 fd	6 20 FR	7 20 FF	8 18 tr	28	9 17 tf	10 16 TH	11 15 TW	12 15 TH	1 14 TW	2 12 rm
2 24 MW	3 25 em	4 24 et	5 23 EM	6 21 fg	7 21 fd	8 19 FR	29	9 18 FF	10 17 tr	11 16 tf	12 16 tr	1 15 tf	2 13 TH
	3 26 MH			6 22 ET		8 20 fg	30		10 18 FR	11 17 FF	12 17 FR		2 14 tr

1972 RR RAT

JAN RT	FEB rt	MAR TW	APR tf	MAY FF	JUN fd	DAY OF MON	JUL EM	AUG em	SEP MH	OCT mr	NOV RR	DEC rg
20 WARM	22 CLEAR	22 SUMMER	24 GRAIN	27 HEAT	28 FALL		30 DEW		2 C DEW	2 WINTER	2 SNOW	2 CHILL
19:28	0:36	18:26	22:22	9:17	19:17		21:15		14:02	15:40	9:23	19:26
2 15 FR	3 15 tf	4 14 tr	5 13 TW	6 11 rm	7 11 rt	1	8 9 RM	9 8 RT	10 7 md	11 6 mg	12 6 md	1 4 MR
2 16 fg	3 16 FF	4 15 FR	5 14 tf	6 12 TH	7 12 TW	2	8 10 rm	9 9 rt	10 8 RM	11 7 RT	12 7 RM	1 5 mg
2 17 ET	3 17 fd	4 16 fg	5 15 FF	6 13 tr	7 13 tf	3	8 11 TH	9 10 TW	10 9 rm	11 8 rt	12 8 rm	1 6 RT
2 18 et	3 18 EM	4 17 ET	5 16 fd	6 14 FR	7 14 FF	4	8 12 tr	9 11 tf	10 10 TH	11 9 TW	12 9 TH	1 7 rt
2 19 MW	3 19 em	4 18 et	5 17 EM	6 15 fg	7 15 fd	5	8 13 FR	9 12 FF	10 11 tr	11 10 tf	12 10 tr	1 8 TW
2 20 mf	3 20 MH	4 19 MW	5 18 em	6 16 ET	7 16 EM	6	8 14 fg	9 13 fd	10 12 FR	11 11 FF	12 11 FR	1 9 tf
2 21 RF	3 21 mr	4 20 mf	5 19 MH	6 17 et	7 17 em	7	8 15 ET	9 14 EM	10 13 fg	11 12 fd	12 12 fg	1 10 FF
2 22 rd	3 22 RR	4 21 RF	5 20 mr	6 18 MW	7 18 MH	8	8 16 et	9 15 em	10 14 ET	11 13 EM	12 13 ET	1 11 fd
2 23 TM	3 23 rg	4 22 rd	5 21 RR	6 19 mf	7 19 mr	9	8 17 MW	9 16 MH	10 15 et	11 14 em	12 14 et	1 12 EM
2 24 tm	3 24 TT	4 23 TM	5 22 rg	6 20 RF	7 20 RR	10	8 18 mf	9 17 mr	10 16 MW	11 15 MH	12 15 MW	1 13 em
2 25 FH	3 25 tt	4 24 tm	5 23 TT	6 21 rd	7 21 rg	11	8 19 RF	9 18 RR	10 17 mf	11 16 mr	12 16 mf	1 14 MH
2 26 fr	3 26 FW	4 25 FH	5 24 tt	6 22 TM	7 22 TT	12	8 20 rd	9 19 rg	10 18 RF	11 17 RR	12 17 RF	1 15 mr
2 27 ER	3 27 ff	4 26 fr	5 25 FW	6 23 tm	7 23 tt	13	8 21 TM	9 20 TT	10 19 rd	11 18 rg	12 18 rd	1 16 RR
2 28 eg	3 28 EF	4 27 ER	5 26 ff	6 24 FH	7 24 FW	14	8 22 tm	9 21 tt	10 20 TM	11 19 TT	12 19 TM	1 17 rg
2 29 MT	3 29 ed	4 28 eg	5 27 EF	6 25 fr	7 25 ff	15	8 23 FH	9 22 FW	10 21 tm	11 20 tt	12 20 tm	1 18 TT
3 1 mt	3 30 MM	4 29 MT	5 28 ed	6 26 ER	7 26 EF	16	8 24 fr	9 23 ff	10 22 FH	11 21 FW	12 21 FH	1 19 tt
3 2 RW	3 31 mm	4 30 mt	5 29 MM	6 27 eg	7 27 ed	17	8 25 ER	9 24 EF	10 23 fr	11 22 ff	12 22 fr	1 20 FW
3 3 rf	4 1 RH	5 1 RW	5 30 mm	6 28 MT	7 28 MM	18	8 26 eg	9 25 ed	10 24 ER	11 23 EF	12 23 ER	1 21 ff
3 4 TF	4 2 rr	5 2 rf	5 31 RH	6 29 mt	7 29 mm	19	8 27 MT	9 26 MM	10 25 eg	11 24 ed	12 24 eg	1 22 EF
3 5 td	4 3 TR	5 3 TF	6 1 rr	6 30 RW	7 30 RH	20	8 28 mt	9 27 mm	10 26 MT	11 25 MM	12 25 MT	1 23 ed
3 6 FM	4 4 tg	5 4 td	6 2 TR	7 1 rf	7 31 rr	21	8 29 RW	9 28 RH	10 27 mt	11 26 mm	12 26 mt	1 24 MM
3 7 fm	4 5 FT	5 5 FM	6 3 tg	7 2 TF	8 1 TR	22	8 30 rf	9 29 rr	10 28 RW	11 27 RH	12 27 RW	1 25 mm
3 8 EH	4 6 ft	5 6 fm	6 4 FT	7 3 td	8 2 tg	23	8 31 TF	9 30 TR	10 29 rf	11 28 rr	12 28 rf	1 26 RH
3 9 er	4 7 EW	5 7 EH	6 5 ft	7 4 FM	8 3 FT	24	9 1 td	10 1 tg	10 30 TF	11 29 TR	12 29 TF	1 27 rr
3 10 MR	4 8 ef	5 8 er	6 6 EW	7 5 fm	8 4 ft	25	9 2 FM	10 2 FT	10 31 td	11 30 tg	12 30 td	1 28 TR
3 11 mg	4 9 MF	5 9 MR	6 7 ef	7 6 EH	8 5 EW	26	9 3 fm	10 3 ft	11 1 FM	12 1 FT	12 31 FM	1 29 tg
3 12 RT	4 10 md	5 10 mg	6 8 MF	7 7 er	8 6 ef	27	9 4 EH	10 4 EW	11 2 fm	12 2 ft	1 1 fm	1 30 FT
3 13 rt	4 11 RM	5 11 RT	6 9 md	7 8 MR	8 7 MF	28	9 5 er	10 5 ef	11 3 EH	12 3 EW	1 2 EH	1 31 ft
3 14 TW	4 12 rm	5 12 rt	6 10 RM	7 9 mg	8 8 md	29	9 6 MR	10 6 MF	11 4 er	12 4 ef	1 3 er	2 1 EW
	4 13 TH			7 10 RT		30	9 7 mg		11 5 MR	12 5 MF		2 2 ef

1973 rg OX

JAN TT	FEB tt	MAR FW	APR ff	MAY EF	JUN ed	DAY OF MON	JUL MM	AUG mm	SEP RH	OCT rr	NOV TR	DEC tg
2 SPRING	2 WARM	3 CLEAR	4 SUMMER	6 GRAIN	8 HEAT		10 FALL	12 DEW	13 C DEW	13 WINTER	13 SNOW	14 CHILL
7:04	1:13	6:14	0:08	4:07	15:05		1:05	3:00	22:48	21:28	15:13	1:20
2 3 MF	3 5 MR	4 3 ef	5 3 er	6 1 EW	6 30 fm	1	7 30 ft	8 28 FM	9 26 tg	10 26 td	11 25 tg	12 24 TF
2 4 md	3 6 mg	4 4 MF	5 4 MR	6 2 ef	7 1 EH	2	7 31 EW	8 29 fm	9 27 FT	10 27 FM	11 26 FT	12 25 td
2 5 RM	3 7 RT	4 5 md	5 5 mg	6 3 MF	7 2 er	3	8 1 ef	8 30 EH	9 28 ft	10 28 fm	11 27 ft	12 26 FM
2 6 rm	3 8 rt	4 6 RM	5 6 RT	6 4 md	7 3 MR	4	8 2 MF	8 31 er	9 29 EW	10 29 EH	11 28 EW	12 27 fm
2 7 TH	3 9 TW	4 7 rm	5 7 rt	6 5 RM	7 4 mg	5	8 3 md	9 1 MR	9 30 ef	10 30 er	11 29 ef	12 28 EH
2 8 tr	3 10 tf	4 8 TH	5 8 TW	6 6 rm	7 5 RT	6	8 4 RM	9 2 mg	10 1 MF	10 31 MR	11 30 MF	12 29 er
2 9 FR	3 11 FF	4 9 tr	5 9 tf	6 7 TH	7 6 rt	7	8 5 rm	9 3 RT	10 2 md	11 1 mg	12 1 md	12 30 MR
2 10 fg	3 12 fd	4 10 FR	5 10 FF	6 8 tr	7 7 TW	8	8 6 TH	9 4 rt	10 3 RM	11 2 RT	12 2 RM	12 31 mg
2 11 ET	3 13 EM	4 11 fg	5 11 fd	6 9 FR	7 8 tf	9	8 7 tr	9 5 TW	10 4 rm	11 3 rt	12 3 rm	1 1 RT
2 12 et	3 14 em	4 12 ET	5 12 EM	6 10 fg	7 9 FF	10	8 8 FR	9 6 tf	10 5 TH	11 4 TW	12 4 TH	1 2 rt
2 13 MW	3 15 MH	4 13 et	5 13 em	6 11 ET	7 10 fd	11	8 9 fg	9 7 FF	10 6 tr	11 5 tf	12 5 tr	1 3 TW
2 14 mf	3 16 mr	4 14 MW	5 14 MH	6 12 et	7 11 EM	12	8 10 ET	9 8 fd	10 7 FR	11 6 FF	12 6 FR	1 4 tf
2 15 RF	3 17 RR	4 15 mf	5 15 mr	6 13 MW	7 12 em	13	8 11 et	9 9 EM	10 8 fg	11 7 fd	12 7 fg	1 5 FF
2 16 rd	3 18 rg	4 16 RF	5 16 RR	6 14 mf	7 13 MH	14	8 12 MW	9 10 em	10 9 ET	11 8 EM	12 8 ET	1 6 fd
2 17 TM	3 19 TT	4 17 rd	5 17 rg	6 15 RF	7 14 mr	15	8 13 mf	9 11 MH	10 10 et	11 9 em	12 9 et	1 7 EM
2 18 tm	3 20 tt	4 18 TM	5 18 TT	6 16 rd	7 15 RR	16	8 14 RF	9 12 mr	10 11 MW	11 10 MH	12 10 MW	1 8 em
2 19 FH	3 21 FW	4 19 tm	5 19 tt	6 17 TM	7 16 rg	17	8 15 rd	9 13 RR	10 12 mf	11 11 mr	12 11 mf	1 9 MH
2 20 fr	3 22 ff	4 20 FH	5 20 FW	6 18 tm	7 17 TT	18	8 16 TM	9 14 rg	10 13 RF	11 12 RR	12 12 RF	1 10 mr
2 21 ER	3 23 EF	4 21 fr	5 21 ff	6 19 FH	7 18 tt	19	8 17 tm	9 15 TT	10 14 rd	11 13 rg	12 13 rd	1 11 RR
2 22 eg	3 24 ed	4 22 ER	5 22 EF	6 20 fr	7 19 FW	20	8 18 FH	9 16 tt	10 15 TM	11 14 TT	12 14 TM	1 12 rg
2 23 MT	3 25 MM	4 23 eg	5 23 ed	6 21 ER	7 20 ff	21	8 19 fr	9 17 FW	10 16 tm	11 15 tt	12 15 tm	1 13 TT
2 24 mt	3 26 mm	4 24 MT	5 24 MM	6 22 eg	7 21 EF	22	8 20 ER	9 18 ff	10 17 FH	11 16 FW	12 16 FH	1 14 tt
2 25 RW	3 27 RH	4 25 mt	5 25 mm	6 23 MT	7 22 ed	23	8 21 eg	9 19 EF	10 18 fr	11 17 ff	12 17 fr	1 15 FW
2 26 rf	3 28 rr	4 26 RW	5 26 RH	6 24 mt	7 23 MM	24	8 22 MT	9 20 ed	10 19 ER	11 18 EF	12 18 ER	1 16 ff
2 27 TF	3 29 TR	4 27 rf	5 27 rr	6 25 RW	7 24 mm	25	8 23 mt	9 21 MM	10 20 eg	11 19 ed	12 19 eg	1 17 EF
2 28 td	3 30 tg	4 28 TF	5 28 TR	6 26 rf	7 25 RH	26	8 24 RW	9 22 mm	10 21 MT	11 20 MM	12 20 MT	1 18 ed
3 1 FM	3 31 FT	4 29 td	5 29 tg	6 27 TF	7 26 rr	27	8 25 rf	9 23 RH	10 22 mt	11 21 mm	12 21 mt	1 19 MM
3 2 fm	4 1 ft	4 30 FM	5 30 FT	6 28 td	7 27 TR	28	8 26 TF	9 24 rr	10 23 RW	11 22 RH	12 22 RW	1 20 mm
3 3 EH	4 2 EW	5 1 fm	5 31 ft	6 29 FM	7 28 tg	29	8 27 td	9 25 TR	10 24 rf	11 23 rr	12 23 rf	1 21 RH
3 4 er		5 2 EH			7 29 FT	30			10 25 TF	11 24 TR		1 22 rr

1974 TT TIGER

JAN FT	FEB ft	MAR EW	APR ef	APR ef	MAY MF	JUN md	DAY OF MON	JUL RM	AUG rm	SEP TH	OCT tr	NOV FR	DEC fg
13 SPRING	13 WARM	13 CLEAR	15 SUMMER	16 GRAIN	18 HEAT	21 FALL		22 DEW	24 C DEW	25 WINTER	24 SNOW	24 CHILL	24 SPRING
13:00	7:07	12:05	5:34	9:52	20:13	5:57		9:58	1:40	3:18	21:02	0:36	19:02
1 23 TR	2 22 TF	3 24 TR	4 22 rf	5 22 rr	6 20 RW	7 19 mm	1	8 18 mt	9 16 MM	10 15 eg	11 14 ed	12 14 eg	1 12 EF
1 24 tg	2 23 td	3 25 tg	4 23 TF	5 23 TR	6 21 rf	7 20 RH	2	8 19 RW	9 17 mm	10 16 MT	11 15 MM	12 15 MT	1 13 ed
1 25 FT	2 24 FM	3 26 FT	4 24 td	5 24 tg	6 22 TF	7 21 rr	3	8 20 rf	9 18 RH	10 17 mt	11 16 mm	12 16 mt	1 14 MM
1 26 ft	2 25 fm	3 27 ft	4 25 FM	5 25 FT	6 23 td	7 22 TR	4	8 21 TF	9 19 rr	10 18 RW	11 17 RH	12 17 RW	1 15 mm
1 27 EW	2 26 EH	3 28 EW	4 26 fm	5 26 ft	6 24 FM	7 23 tg	5	8 22 td	9 20 TR	10 19 rf	11 18 rr	12 18 rf	1 16 RH
1 28 ef	2 27 er	3 29 ef	4 27 EH	5 27 EW	6 25 fm	7 24 FT	6	8 23 FM	9 21 tg	10 20 TF	11 19 TR	12 19 TF	1 17 rr
1 29 MF	2 28 MR	3 30 MF	4 28 er	5 28 ef	6 26 EH	7 25 ft	7	8 24 fm	9 22 FT	10 21 td	11 20 tg	12 20 td	1 18 TR
1 30 md	3 1 mg	3 31 md	4 29 MR	5 29 MF	6 27 er	7 26 EW	8	8 25 EH	9 23 ft	10 22 FM	11 21 FT	12 21 FM	1 19 tg
1 31 RM	3 2 RT	4 1 RM	4 30 mg	5 30 md	6 28 MR	7 27 ef	9	8 26 er	9 24 EW	10 23 fm	11 22 ft	12 22 fm	1 20 FT
2 1 rm	3 3 rt	4 2 rm	5 1 RT	5 31 RM	6 29 mg	7 28 MF	10	8 27 MR	9 25 ef	10 24 EH	11 23 EW	12 23 EH	1 21 ft
2 2 TH	3 4 TW	4 3 TH	5 2 rt	6 1 rm	6 30 RT	7 29 md	11	8 28 mg	9 26 MF	10 25 er	11 24 ef	12 24 er	1 22 EW
2 3 tr	3 5 tf	4 4 tr	5 3 TW	6 2 TH	7 1 rt	7 30 RM	12	8 29 RT	9 27 md	10 26 MR	11 25 MF	12 25 MR	1 23 ef
2 4 FR	3 6 FF	4 5 FR	5 4 tf	6 3 tr	7 2 TW	7 31 rm	13	8 30 rt	9 28 RM	10 27 mg	11 26 md	12 26 mg	1 24 MF
2 5 fg	3 7 fd	4 6 fg	5 5 FF	6 4 FR	7 3 tf	8 1 TH	14	8 31 TW	9 29 rm	10 28 RT	11 27 RM	12 27 RT	1 25 md
2 6 ET	3 8 EM	4 7 ET	5 6 fd	6 5 fg	7 4 FF	8 2 tr	15	9 1 tf	9 30 TH	10 29 rt	11 28 rm	12 28 rt	1 26 RM
2 7 et	3 9 em	4 8 et	5 7 EM	6 6 ET	7 5 fd	8 3 FR	16	9 2 FF	10 1 tr	10 30 TW	11 29 TH	12 29 TW	1 27 rm
2 8 MW	3 10 MH	4 9 MW	5 8 em	6 7 et	7 6 EM	8 4 fg	17	9 3 fd	10 2 FR	10 31 tf	11 30 tr	12 30 tf	1 28 TH
2 9 mf	3 11 mr	4 10 mf	5 9 MH	6 8 MW	7 7 em	8 5 ET	18	9 4 EM	10 3 fg	11 1 FF	12 1 FR	12 31 FF	1 29 tr
2 10 RF	3 12 RR	4 11 RF	5 10 mr	6 9 mf	7 8 MH	8 6 et	19	9 5 em	10 4 ET	11 2 fd	12 2 fg	1 1 fd	1 30 FR
2 11 rd	3 13 rg	4 12 rd	5 11 RR	6 10 RF	7 9 mr	8 7 MW	20	9 6 MH	10 5 et	11 3 EM	12 3 ET	1 2 EM	1 31 fg
2 12 TM	3 14 TT	4 13 TM	5 12 rg	6 11 rd	7 10 RR	8 8 mf	21	9 7 mr	10 6 MW	11 4 em	12 4 et	1 3 em	2 1 ET
2 13 tm	3 15 tt	4 14 tm	5 13 TT	6 12 TM	7 11 rg	8 9 RF	22	9 8 RR	10 7 mf	11 5 MH	12 5 MW	1 4 MH	2 2 et
2 14 FH	3 16 FW	4 15 FH	5 14 tt	6 13 tm	7 12 TT	8 10 rd	23	9 9 rg	10 8 RF	11 6 mr	12 6 mf	1 5 mr	2 3 MW
2 15 fr	3 17 ff	4 16 fr	5 15 FW	6 14 FH	7 13 tt	8 11 TM	24	9 10 TT	10 9 rd	11 7 RR	12 7 RF	1 6 RR	2 4 mf
2 16 ER	3 18 EF	4 17 ER	5 16 ff	6 15 fr	7 14 FW	8 12 tm	25	9 11 tt	10 10 TM	11 8 rg	12 8 rd	1 7 rg	2 5 RF
2 17 eg	3 19 ed	4 18 eg	5 17 EF	6 16 ER	7 15 ff	8 13 FH	26	9 12 FW	10 11 tm	11 9 TT	12 9 TM	1 8 TT	2 6 rd
2 18 MT	3 20 MM	4 19 MT	5 18 ed	6 17 eg	7 16 EF	8 14 fr	27	9 13 ff	10 12 FH	11 10 tt	12 10 tm	1 9 tt	2 7 TM
2 19 mt	3 21 mm	4 20 mt	5 19 MM	6 18 MT	7 17 ed	8 15 ER	28	9 14 EF	10 13 fr	11 11 FW	12 11 FH	1 10 FW	2 8 tm
2 20 RW	3 22 RH	4 21 RW	5 20 mm	6 19 mt	7 18 MM	8 16 eg	29	9 15 ed	10 14 ER	11 12 ff	12 12 fr	1 11 ff	2 9 FH
2 21 rf	3 23 rr		5 21 RH			8 17 MT	30			11 13 EF	12 13 ER		2 10 fr

1975 tt RABBIT

JAN ET	FEB et	MAR MW	APR mf	MAY RF	JUN rd	DAY OF MON	JUL TM	AUG tm	SEP FH	OCT fr	NOV ER	DEC eg
24 WARM	24 CLEAR	25 SUMMER	27 GRAIN	29 HEAT			2 FALL	3 DEW	5 C DEW	6 WINTER	6 SNOW	6 CHILL
13:07	18:02	11:27	15:42	2:00			11:45	15:47	7:29	9:03	1:46	13:34
2 11 ER	3 13 EF	4 12 ER	5 11 ff	6 10 fr	7 9 FW	1	8 7 tm	9 6 tt	10 5 TM	11 3 rg	12 3 rd	1 1 RR
2 12 eg	3 14 ed	4 13 eg	5 12 EF	6 11 ER	7 10 ff	2	8 8 FH	9 7 FW	10 6 tm	11 4 TT	12 4 TM	1 2 rg
2 13 MT	3 15 MM	4 14 MT	5 13 ed	6 12 eg	7 11 EF	3	8 9 fr	9 8 ff	10 7 FH	11 5 tt	12 5 tm	1 3 TT
2 14 mt	3 16 mm	4 15 mt	5 14 MM	6 13 MT	7 12 ed	4	8 10 ER	9 9 EF	10 8 fr	11 6 FW	12 6 FH	1 4 tt
2 15 RW	3 17 RH	4 16 RW	5 15 mm	6 14 mt	7 13 MM	5	8 11 eg	9 10 ed	10 9 ER	11 7 ff	12 7 fr	1 5 FW
2 16 rf	3 18 rr	4 17 rf	5 16 RH	6 15 RW	7 14 mm	6	8 12 MT	9 11 MM	10 10 eg	11 8 EF	12 8 ER	1 6 ff
2 17 TF	3 19 TR	4 18 TF	5 17 rr	6 16 rf	7 15 RH	7	8 13 mt	9 12 mm	10 11 MT	11 9 ed	12 9 eg	1 7 EF
2 18 td	3 20 tg	4 19 td	5 18 TR	6 17 TF	7 16 rr	8	8 14 RW	9 13 RH	10 12 mt	11 10 MM	12 10 MT	1 8 ed
2 19 FM	3 21 FT	4 20 FM	5 19 tg	6 18 td	7 17 TR	9	8 15 rf	9 14 rr	10 13 RW	11 11 mm	12 11 mt	1 9 MM
2 20 fm	3 22 ft	4 21 fm	5 20 FT	6 19 FM	7 18 tg	10	8 16 TF	9 15 TR	10 14 rf	11 12 RH	12 12 RW	1 10 mm
2 21 EH	3 23 EW	4 22 EH	5 21 ft	6 20 fm	7 19 FT	11	8 17 td	9 16 tg	10 15 TF	11 13 rr	12 13 rf	1 11 RH
2 22 er	3 24 ef	4 23 er	5 22 EW	6 21 EH	7 20 ft	12	8 18 FM	9 17 FT	10 16 td	11 14 TR	12 14 TF	1 12 RR
2 23 MR	3 25 MF	4 24 MR	5 23 ef	6 22 er	7 21 EW	13	8 19 fm	9 18 ft	10 17 FM	11 15 tg	12 15 td	1 13 TR
2 24 mg	3 26 md	4 25 mg	5 24 MF	6 23 MR	7 22 ef	14	8 20 EH	9 19 EW	10 18 fm	11 16 FT	12 16 FM	1 14 tg
2 25 RT	3 27 RM	4 26 RT	5 25 md	6 24 mg	7 23 MF	15	8 21 er	9 20 ef	10 19 EH	11 17 ft	12 17 fm	1 15 FT
2 26 rt	3 28 rm	4 27 rt	5 26 RM	6 25 RT	7 24 md	16	8 22 MR	9 21 MF	10 20 er	11 18 EW	12 18 EH	1 16 ft
2 27 TW	3 29 TH	4 28 TW	5 27 rm	6 26 rt	7 25 RM	17	8 23 mg	9 22 md	10 21 MR	11 19 ef	12 19 er	1 17 EW
2 28 tf	3 30 tr	4 29 tf	5 28 TH	6 27 TW	7 26 rm	18	8 24 RT	9 23 RM	10 22 mg	11 20 MF	12 20 MR	1 18 ef
3 1 FF	3 31 FR	4 30 FF	5 29 tr	6 28 tf	7 27 TH	19	8 25 rt	9 24 rm	10 23 RT	11 21 md	12 21 mg	1 19 MF
3 2 fd	4 1 fg	5 1 fd	5 30 FR	6 29 FF	7 28 tr	20	8 26 TW	9 25 TH	10 24 rt	11 22 RM	12 22 RT	1 20 md
3 3 EM	4 2 ET	5 2 EM	5 31 fg	6 30 fd	7 29 FR	21	8 27 tf	9 26 tr	10 25 TW	11 23 rm	12 23 rt	1 21 RM
3 4 em	4 3 et	5 3 em	6 1 ET	7 1 EM	7 30 fg	22	8 28 FF	9 27 FR	10 26 tf	11 24 TH	12 24 TW	1 22 rm
3 5 MH	4 4 MW	5 4 MH	6 2 et	7 2 em	7 31 ET	23	8 29 fd	9 28 fg	10 27 FF	11 25 tr	12 25 tf	1 23 TH
3 6 mr	4 5 mf	5 5 mr	6 3 MW	7 3 MH	8 1 et	24	8 30 EM	9 29 ET	10 28 fd	11 26 FR	12 26 FF	1 24 tr
3 7 RR	4 6 RF	5 6 RR	6 4 mf	7 4 mr	8 2 MW	25	8 31 em	9 30 et	10 29 EM	11 27 fg	12 27 fd	1 25 FR
3 8 rg	4 7 rd	5 7 rg	6 5 RF	7 5 RR	8 3 mf	26	9 1 MH	10 1 MW	10 30 em	11 28 ET	12 28 EM	1 26 fg
3 9 TT	4 8 TM	5 8 TT	6 6 rd	7 6 rg	8 4 RF	27	9 2 mr	10 2 mf	10 31 MH	11 29 et	12 29 em	1 27 ET
3 10 tt	4 9 tm	5 9 tt	6 7 TM	7 7 TT	8 5 rd	28	9 3 RR	10 3 RF	11 1 mr	11 30 MW	12 30 MH	1 28 et
3 11 FW	4 10 FH	5 10 FW	6 8 tm	7 8 tt	8 6 TM	29	9 4 rg	10 4 rd	11 2 RR	12 1 mf	12 31 mr	1 29 MW
3 12 ff	4 11 fr		6 9 FH			30	9 5 TT			12 2 RF		1 30 mf

1976 FW DRAGON

JAN MT	FEB mt	MAR RW	APR rf	MAY TF	JUN td	DAY OF MON	JUL FM	AUG fm	AUG fm	SEP EH	OCT er	NOV MR	DEC mg
6 SPRING	5 WARM	5 CLEAR	7 SUMMER	8 GRAIN	11 HEAT		12 FALL	14 DEW	15 C DEW	16 WINTER	17 SNOW	16 CHILL	17 SPRING
0:40	18:48	23:47	17:15	21:31	7:51		17:38	21:36	13:18	16:17	7:41	19:24	6:34
1 31 RF	3 1 RR	3 31 RF	4 29 mr	5 29 mf	6 27 MH	1	7 27 MW	8 25 em	9 24 et	10 23 EM	11 21 fg	12 21 fd	1 19 FR
2 1 rd	3 2 rg	4 1 rd	4 30 RR	5 30 RF	6 28 mr	2	7 28 mf	8 26 MH	9 25 MW	10 24 em	11 22 ET	12 22 EM	1 20 fg
2 2 TM	3 3 TT	4 2 TM	5 1 rg	5 31 rd	6 29 RR	3	7 29 RF	8 27 mr	9 26 mf	10 25 MH	11 23 et	12 23 em	1 21 ET
2 3 tm	3 4 tt	4 3 tm	5 2 TT	6 1 TM	6 30 rg	4	7 30 rd	8 28 RR	9 27 RF	10 26 mr	11 24 MW	12 24 MH	1 22 et
2 4 FH	3 5 FW	4 4 FH	5 3 tt	6 2 tm	7 1 TT	5	7 31 TM	8 29 rg	9 28 rd	10 27 RR	11 25 mf	12 25 mr	1 23 MW
2 5 fr	3 6 ff	4 5 fr	5 4 FW	6 3 FH	7 2 tt	6	8 1 tm	8 30 TT	9 29 TM	10 28 rg	11 26 RF	12 26 RR	1 24 mf
2 6 ER	3 7 EF	4 6 ER	5 5 ff	6 4 fr	7 3 FW	7	8 2 FH	8 31 tt	9 30 tm	10 29 TT	11 27 rd	12 27 rg	1 25 RF
2 7 eg	3 8 ed	4 7 eg	5 6 EF	6 5 ER	7 4 ff	8	8 3 fr	9 1 FW	10 1 FH	10 30 tt	11 28 TM	12 28 TT	1 26 rd
2 8 MT	3 9 MM	4 8 MT	5 7 ed	6 6 eg	7 5 EF	9	8 4 ER	9 2 ff	10 2 fr	10 31 FW	11 29 tm	12 29 tt	1 27 TM
2 9 mt	3 10 mm	4 9 mt	5 8 MM	6 7 MT	7 6 ed	10	8 5 eg	9 3 EF	10 3 ER	11 1 ff	11 30 FH	12 30 FW	1 28 tm
2 10 RW	3 11 RH	4 10 RW	5 9 mm	6 8 mt	7 7 MM	11	8 6 MT	9 4 ed	10 4 eg	11 2 EF	12 1 fr	12 31 ff	1 29 FH
2 11 rf	3 12 rr	4 11 rf	5 10 RH	6 9 RW	7 8 mm	12	8 7 mt	9 5 MM	10 5 MT	11 3 ed	12 2 ER	1 1 EF	1 30 fr
2 12 TF	3 13 TR	4 12 TF	5 11 rr	6 10 rf	7 9 RH	13	8 8 RW	9 6 mm	10 6 mt	11 4 MM	12 3 eg	1 2 ed	1 31 ER
2 13 td	3 14 tg	4 13 td	5 12 TR	6 11 TF	7 10 rr	14	8 9 rf	9 7 RH	10 7 RW	11 5 mm	12 4 MT	1 3 MM	2 1 eg
2 14 FM	3 15 FT	4 14 FM	5 13 tg	6 12 td	7 11 TR	15	8 10 TF	9 8 rr	10 8 rf	11 6 RH	12 5 mt	1 4 mm	2 2 MT
2 15 fm	3 16 ft	4 15 fm	5 14 FT	6 13 FM	7 12 tg	16	8 11 td	9 9 TR	10 9 TF	11 7 rr	12 6 RW	1 5 RH	2 3 mt
2 16 EH	3 17 EW	4 16 EH	5 15 ft	6 14 fm	7 13 FT	17	8 12 FM	9 10 tg	10 10 td	11 8 TR	12 7 rf	1 6 rr	2 4 RW
2 17 er	3 18 ef	4 17 er	5 16 EW	6 15 EH	7 14 ft	18	8 13 fm	9 11 FT	10 11 FM	11 9 tg	12 8 TF	1 7 TR	2 5 rf
2 18 MR	3 19 MF	4 18 MR	5 17 ef	6 16 er	7 15 EW	19	8 14 EH	9 12 ft	10 12 fm	11 10 FT	12 9 td	1 8 tg	2 6 TF
2 19 mg	3 20 md	4 19 mg	5 18 MF	6 17 MR	7 16 ef	20	8 15 er	9 13 EW	10 13 EH	11 11 ft	12 10 FM	1 9 FT	2 7 td
2 20 RT	3 21 RM	4 20 RT	5 19 md	6 18 mg	7 17 MF	21	8 16 MR	9 14 ef	10 14 er	11 12 EW	12 11 fm	1 10 ft	2 8 FM
2 21 rt	3 22 rm	4 21 rt	5 20 RM	6 19 RT	7 18 md	22	8 17 mg	9 15 MF	10 15 MR	11 13 ef	12 12 EH	1 11 EW	2 9 fm
2 22 TW	3 23 TH	4 22 TW	5 21 rm	6 20 rt	7 19 RM	23	8 18 RT	9 16 md	10 16 mg	11 14 MF	12 13 er	1 12 ef	2 10 EH
2 23 tf	3 24 tr	4 23 tf	5 22 TH	6 21 TW	7 20 rm	24	8 19 rt	9 17 RM	10 17 RT	11 15 md	12 14 MR	1 13 MF	2 11 er
2 24 FF	3 25 FR	4 24 FF	5 23 tr	6 22 tf	7 21 TH	25	8 20 TW	9 18 rm	10 18 rt	11 16 RM	12 15 mg	1 14 md	2 12 MR
2 25 fd	3 26 fg	4 25 fd	5 24 FR	6 23 FF	7 22 tr	26	8 21 tf	9 19 TH	10 19 TW	11 17 rm	12 16 RT	1 15 RM	2 13 mg
2 26 EM	3 27 ET	4 26 EM	5 25 fg	6 24 fd	7 23 FR	27	8 22 FF	9 20 tr	10 20 tf	11 18 TH	12 17 rt	1 16 rm	2 14 RT
2 27 em	3 28 et	4 27 em	5 26 ET	6 25 EM	7 24 fg	28	8 23 fd	9 21 FR	10 21 FF	11 19 tr	12 18 TW	1 17 TH	2 15 rt
2 28 MH	3 29 MW	4 28 MH	5 27 et	6 26 em	7 25 ET	29	8 24 EM	9 22 fg	10 22 fd	11 20 FR	12 19 tf	1 18 tr	2 16 TW
2 29 mr	3 30 mf		5 28 MW		7 26 et	30		9 23 ET			12 20 FF		2 17 tf

1977 ff SNAKE

JAN RT	FEB rt	MAR TW	APR tf	MAY FF	JUN fd	DAY OF MON	JUL EM	AUG em	SEP MH	OCT mr	NOV RR	DEC rg
17 WARM	17 CLEAR	18 SUMMER	20 GRAIN	21 HEAT	24 FALL		25 DEW	26 C DEW	26 WINTER	27 SNOW	27 CHILL	27 SPRING
0:44	5:40	23:16	3:32	13:48	0:18		3:24	19:07	22:06	13:31	1:13	12:27
2 18 FF	3 20 FR	4 18 tf	5 18 tr	6 17 tf	7 16 TH	1	8 15 TW	9 13 rm	10 13 rt	11 11 RM	12 11 RT	1 9 md
2 19 fd	3 21 fg	4 19 FF	5 19 FR	6 18 FF	7 17 tr	2	8 16 tf	9 14 TH	10 14 TW	11 12 rm	12 12 rt	1 10 RM
2 20 EM	3 22 ET	4 20 fd	5 20 fg	6 19 fd	7 18 FR	3	8 17 FF	9 15 tr	10 15 tf	11 13 TH	12 13 TW	1 11 rm
2 21 em	3 23 et	4 21 EM	5 21 ET	6 20 EM	7 19 fg	4	8 18 fd	9 16 FR	10 16 FF	11 14 tr	12 14 tf	1 12 TH
2 22 MH	3 24 MW	4 22 em	5 22 et	6 21 em	7 20 ET	5	8 19 EM	9 17 fg	10 17 fd	11 15 FR	12 15 FF	1 13 tr
2 23 mr	3 25 mf	4 23 MH	5 23 MW	6 22 MH	7 21 et	6	8 20 em	9 18 ET	10 18 EM	11 16 fg	12 16 fd	1 14 FR
2 24 RR	3 26 RF	4 24 mr	5 24 mf	6 23 mr	7 22 MW	7	8 21 MH	9 19 et	10 19 em	11 17 ET	12 17 EM	1 15 fg
2 25 rg	3 27 rd	4 25 RR	5 25 RF	6 24 RR	7 23 mf	8	8 22 mr	9 20 MW	10 20 MH	11 18 et	12 18 em	1 16 ET
2 26 TT	3 28 TM	4 26 rg	5 26 rd	6 25 rg	7 24 RF	9	8 23 RR	9 21 mf	10 21 mr	11 19 MW	12 19 MH	1 17 et
2 27 tt	3 29 tm	4 27 TT	5 27 TM	6 26 TT	7 25 rd	10	8 24 rg	9 22 RF	10 22 RR	11 20 mf	12 20 mr	1 18 MW
2 28 FW	3 30 FH	4 28 tt	5 28 tm	6 27 tt	7 26 TM	11	8 25 TT	9 23 rd	10 23 rg	11 21 RF	12 21 RR	1 19 mf
3 1 ff	3 31 fr	4 29 FW	5 29 FH	6 28 FW	7 27 tm	12	8 26 tt	9 24 TM	10 24 TT	11 22 rd	12 22 rg	1 20 RF
3 2 EF	4 1 ER	4 30 ff	5 30 fr	6 29 ff	7 28 FH	13	8 27 FW	9 25 tm	10 25 tt	11 23 TM	12 23 TT	1 21 rd
3 3 ed	4 2 eg	5 1 EF	5 31 ER	6 30 EF	7 29 fr	14	8 28 ff	9 26 FH	10 26 FW	11 24 tm	12 24 tt	1 22 TM
3 4 MM	4 3 MT	5 2 ed	6 1 eg	7 1 ed	7 30 ER	15	8 29 EF	9 27 fr	10 27 ff	11 25 FH	12 25 FW	1 23 tm
3 5 mm	4 4 mt	5 3 MM	6 2 MT	7 2 MM	7 31 eg	16	8 30 ed	9 28 ER	10 28 EF	11 26 fr	12 26 ff	1 24 FH
3 6 RH	4 5 RW	5 4 mm	6 3 mt	7 3 mm	8 1 MT	17	8 31 MM	9 29 eg	10 29 ed	11 27 ER	12 27 EF	1 25 fr
3 7 rr	4 6 rf	5 5 RH	6 4 RW	7 4 RH	8 2 mt	18	9 1 mm	9 30 MT	10 30 MM	11 28 eg	12 28 ed	1 26 ER
3 8 TR	4 7 TF	5 6 rr	6 5 rf	7 5 rr	8 3 RW	19	9 2 RH	10 1 mt	10 31 mm	11 29 MT	12 29 MM	1 27 eg
3 9 tg	4 8 td	5 7 TR	6 6 TF	7 6 TR	8 4 rf	20	9 3 rr	10 2 RW	11 1 RH	11 30 mt	12 30 mm	1 28 MT
3 10 FT	4 9 FM	5 8 tg	6 7 td	7 7 tg	8 5 TF	21	9 4 TR	10 3 rf	11 2 rr	12 1 RW	12 31 RH	1 29 mt
3 11 ft	4 10 fm	5 9 FT	6 8 FM	7 8 FT	8 6 td	22	9 5 tg	10 4 TF	11 3 TR	12 2 rf	1 1 rr	1 30 RW
3 12 EW	4 11 EH	5 10 ft	6 9 fm	7 9 ft	8 7 FM	23	9 6 FT	10 5 td	11 4 tg	12 3 TF	1 2 TR	1 31 rf
3 13 ef	4 12 er	5 11 EW	6 10 EH	7 10 EW	8 8 fm	24	9 7 ft	10 6 FM	11 5 FT	12 4 td	1 3 tg	2 1 TF
3 14 MF	4 13 MR	5 12 ef	6 11 er	7 11 ef	8 9 EH	25	9 8 EW	10 7 fm	11 6 ft	12 5 FM	1 4 FT	2 2 td
3 15 md	4 14 mg	5 13 MF	6 12 MR	7 12 MF	8 10 er	26	9 9 ef	10 8 EH	11 7 EW	12 6 fm	1 5 ft	2 3 FM
3 16 RM	4 15 RT	5 14 md	6 13 mg	7 13 md	8 11 MR	27	9 10 MF	10 9 er	11 8 ef	12 7 EH	1 6 EW	2 4 fm
3 17 rm	4 16 rt	5 15 RM	6 14 RT	7 14 RM	8 12 mg	28	9 11 md	10 10 MR	11 9 MF	12 8 er	1 7 ef	2 5 EH
3 18 TH	4 17 TW	5 16 rm	6 15 rt	7 15 rm	8 13 RT	29	9 12 RM	10 11 mg	11 10 md	12 9 MR	1 8 MF	2 6 er
3 19 tr		5 17 TH	6 16 TW		8 14 rt	30		10 12 RT		12 10 mg		

1978 EF HORSE

JAN TT	FEB tt	MAR FW	APR ff	MAY EF	JUN ed	DAY OF MON	JUL MM	AUG mm	SEP RH	OCT rr	NOV TR	DEC tg
28 WARM	28 CLEAR	30 SUMMER		1 GRAIN	3 HEAT		5 FALL	7 DEW	8 C DEW	8 WINTER	8 : SNOW	8 CHILL
6:38	11:39	5:09		9:23	19:37		5:18	8:08	23:31	2:34	19:20	6:32
2 7 MR	3 9 MF	4 7 er	5 7 ef	6 6 er	7 5 EW	1	8 4 EH	9 3 EW	10 2 fm	11 1 ft	11 30 FM	12 30 FT
2 8 mg	3 10 md	4 8 MR	5 8 MF	6 7 MR	7 6 ef	2	8 5 er	9 4 ef	10 3 EH	11 2 EW	12 1 fm	12 31 ft
2 9 RT	3 11 RM	4 9 mg	5 9 md	6 8 mg	7 7 MF	3	8 6 MR	9 5 MF	10 4 er	11 3 ef	12 2 EH	1 1 EW
2 10 rt	3 12 rm	4 10 RT	5 10 RM	6 9 RT	7 8 md	4	8 7 mg	9 6 md	10 5 MR	11 4 MF	12 3 er	1 2 ef
2 11 TW	3 13 TH	4 11 rt	5 11 rm	6 10 rt	7 9 RM	5	8 8 RT	9 7 RM	10 6 mg	11 5 md	12 4 MR	1 3 MF
2 12 tf	3 14 tr	4 12 TW	5 12 TH	6 11 TW	7 10 rm	6	8 9 rt	9 8 rm	10 7 RT	11 6 RM	12 5 mg	1 4 md
2 13 FF	3 15 FR	4 13 tf	5 13 tr	6 12 tf	7 11 TH	7	8 10 TW	9 9 TH	10 8 rt	11 7 rm	12 6 RT	1 5 RM
2 14 fd	3 16 fg	4 14 FF	5 14 FR	6 13 FF	7 12 tr	8	8 11 tf	9 10 tr	10 9 TW	11 8 TH	12 7 rt	1 6 rm
2 15 EM	3 17 ET	4 15 fd	5 15 fg	6 14 fd	7 13 FR	9	8 12 FF	9 11 FR	10 10 tf	11 9 tr	12 8 TW	1 7 TH
2 16 em	3 18 et	4 16 EM	5 16 ET	6 15 EM	7 14 fg	10	8 13 fd	9 12 fg	10 11 FF	11 10 FR	12 9 tf	1 8 tr
2 17 MH	3 19 MW	4 17 em	5 17 et	6 16 em	7 15 ET	11	8 14 EM	9 13 ET	10 12 fd	11 11 fg	12 10 FF	1 9 FR
2 18 mr	3 20 mf	4 18 MH	5 18 MW	6 17 MH	7 16 et	12	8 15 em	9 14 et	10 13 EM	11 12 ET	12 11 fd	1 10 fg
2 19 RR	3 21 RF	4 19 mr	5 19 mf	6 18 mr	7 17 MW	13	8 16 MH	9 15 MW	10 14 em	11 13 et	12 12 EM	1 11 ET
2 20 rg	3 22 rd	4 20 RR	5 20 RF	6 19 RR	7 18 mf	14	8 17 mr	9 16 mf	10 15 MH	11 14 MW	12 13 em	1 12 et
2 21 TT	3 23 TM	4 21 rg	5 21 rd	6 20 rg	7 19 RF	15	8 18 RR	9 17 RF	10 16 mr	11 15 mf	12 14 MH	1 13 MW
2 22 tt	3 24 tm	4 22 TT	5 22 TM	6 21 TT	7 20 rd	16	8 19 rg	9 18 rd	10 17 RR	11 16 RF	12 15 mr	1 14 mf
2 23 FW	3 25 FH	4 23 tt	5 23 tm	6 22 tt	7 21 TM	17	8 20 TT	9 19 TM	10 18 rg	11 17 rd	12 16 RR	1 15 RF
2 24 ff	3 26 fr	4 24 FW	5 24 FH	6 23 FW	7 22 tm	18	8 21 tt	9 20 tm	10 19 TT	11 18 TM	12 17 rg	1 16 rd
2 25 EF	3 27 ER	4 25 ff	5 25 fr	6 24 ff	7 23 FH	19	8 22 FW	9 21 FH	10 20 tt	11 19 tm	12 18 TT	1 17 TM
2 26 ed	3 28 eg	4 26 EF	5 26 ER	6 25 EF	7 24 fr	20	8 23 ff	9 22 fr	10 21 FW	11 20 FH	12 19 tt	1 18 tm
2 27 MM	3 29 MT	4 27 ed	5 27 eg	6 26 ed	7 25 ER	21	8 24 EF	9 23 ER	10 22 ff	11 21 fr	12 20 FW	1 19 FH
2 28 mm	3 30 mt	4 28 MM	5 28 MT	6 27 MM	7 26 eg	22	8 25 ed	9 24 eg	10 23 EF	11 22 ER	12 21 ff	1 20 fr
3 1 RH	3 31 RW	4 29 mm	5 29 mt	6 28 mm	7 27 MT	23	8 26 MM	9 25 MT	10 24 ed	11 23 eg	12 22 EF	1 21 ER
3 2 rr	4 1 rf	4 30 RH	5 30 RW	6 29 RH	7 28 mt	24	8 27 mm	9 26 mt	10 25 MM	11 24 MT	12 23 ed	1 22 eg
3 3 TR	4 2 TF	5 1 rr	5 31 rf	6 30 rr	7 29 RW	25	8 28 RH	9 27 RW	10 26 mm	11 25 mt	12 24 MM	1 23 MT
3 4 tg	4 3 td	5 2 TR	6 1 TF	7 1 TR	7 30 rf	26	8 29 rr	9 28 rf	10 27 RH	11 26 RW	12 25 mm	1 24 mt
3 5 FT	4 4 FM	5 3 tg	6 2 td	7 2 tg	7 31 TF	27	8 30 TR	9 29 TF	10 28 rr	11 27 rf	12 26 RH	1 25 RW
3 6 ft	4 5 fm	5 4 FT	6 3 FM	7 3 FT	8 1 td	28	8 31 tg	9 30 td	10 29 TR	11 28 TF	12 27 rr	1 26 rf
3 7 EW	4 6 EH	5 5 ft	6 4 fm	7 4 ft	8 2 FM	29	9 1 FT	10 1 FM	10 30 tg	11 29 td	12 28 TR	1 27 TF
3 8 ef		5 6 EW	6 5 EH		8 3 fm	30	9 2 ft		10 31 FT		12 29 tg	

1979 ed RAM

JAN FT	FEB ft	MAR EW	APR ef	MAY MF	JUN md	JUN md	DAY OF MON	JUL RM	AUG rm	SEP TH	OCT tr	NOV FR	DEC fg
8 SPRING	8 WARM	9 CLEAR	11 SUMMER	12 GRAIN	15 HEAT	16 FALL		17 DEW	19 C DEW	19 WINTER	19 SNOW	19 CHILL	19 SPRING
18:13	12:20	17:18	10:47	15:05	1:25	11:11		15:01	5:30	9:45	1:18	12:29	0:10
1 28 td	2 27 tg	3 28 TF	4 26 rr	5 26 rf	6 24 RH	7 24 RW	1	8 23 RH	9 21 mt	10 21 mm	11 20 mt	12 19 MM	1 18 MT
1 29 FM	2 28 FT	3 29 td	4 27 TR	5 27 TF	6 25 rr	7 25 rf	2	8 24 rr	9 22 RW	10 22 RH	11 21 RW	12 20 mm	1 19 mt
1 30 fm	3 1 ft	3 30 FM	4 28 tg	5 28 td	6 26 TR	7 26 TF	3	8 25 TR	9 23 rf	10 23 rr	11 22 rf	12 21 RH	1 20 RW
1 31 EH	3 2 EW	3 31 fm	4 29 FT	5 29 FM	6 27 tg	7 27 td	4	8 26 tg	9 24 TF	10 24 TR	11 23 TF	12 22 rr	1 21 rf
2 1 er	3 3 ef	4 1 EH	4 30 ft	5 30 fm	6 28 FT	7 28 FM	5	8 27 FT	9 25 td	10 25 tg	11 24 td	12 23 TR	1 22 TF
2 2 MR	3 4 MF	4 2 er	5 1 EW	5 31 EH	6 29 ft	7 29 fm	6	8 28 ft	9 26 FM	10 26 FT	11 25 FM	12 24 tg	1 23 td
2 3 mg	3 5 md	4 3 MR	5 2 ef	6 1 er	6 30 EW	7 30 EH	7	8 29 EW	9 27 fm	10 27 ft	11 26 fm	12 25 FT	1 24 FM
2 4 RT	3 6 RM	4 4 mg	5 3 MF	6 2 MR	7 1 ef	7 31 er	8	8 30 ef	9 28 EH	10 28 EW	11 27 EH	12 26 ft	1 25 fm
2 5 rt	3 7 rm	4 5 RT	5 4 md	6 3 mg	7 2 MF	8 1 MR	9	8 31 MF	9 29 er	10 29 ef	11 28 er	12 27 EW	1 26 EH
2 6 TW	3 8 TH	4 6 rt	5 5 RM	6 4 RT	7 3 md	8 2 mg	10	9 1 md	9 30 MR	10 30 MF	11 29 MR	12 28 ef	1 27 er
2 7 tf	3 9 tr	4 7 TW	5 6 rm	6 5 rt	7 4 RM	8 3 RT	11	9 2 RM	10 1 mg	10 31 md	11 30 mg	12 29 MF	1 28 MR
2 8 FF	3 10 FR	4 8 tf	5 7 TH	6 6 TW	7 5 rm	8 4 rt	12	9 3 rm	10 2 RT	11 1 RM	12 1 RT	12 30 md	1 29 mg
2 9 fd	3 11 fg	4 9 FF	5 8 tr	6 7 tf	7 6 TH	8 5 TW	13	9 4 TH	10 3 rt	11 2 rm	12 2 rt	12 31 RM	1 30 RT
2 10 EM	3 12 ET	4 10 fd	5 9 FR	6 8 FF	7 7 tr	8 6 tf	14	9 5 tr	10 4 TW	11 3 TH	12 3 TW	1 1 rm	1 31 rt
2 11 em	3 13 et	4 11 EM	5 10 fg	6 9 fd	7 8 FR	8 7 FF	15	9 6 FR	10 5 tf	11 4 tr	12 4 tf	1 2 TH	2 1 TW
2 12 MH	3 14 MW	4 12 em	5 11 ET	6 10 EM	7 9 fg	8 8 fd	16	9 7 fg	10 6 FF	11 5 FR	12 5 FF	1 3 tr	2 2 tf
2 13 mr	3 15 mf	4 13 MH	5 12 et	6 11 em	7 10 ET	8 9 EM	17	9 8 ET	10 7 fd	11 6 fg	12 6 fd	1 4 FR	2 3 FF
2 14 RR	3 16 RF	4 14 mr	5 13 MW	6 12 MH	7 11 et	8 10 em	18	9 9 et	10 8 EM	11 7 ET	12 7 EM	1 5 fg	2 4 fd
2 15 rg	3 17 rd	4 15 RR	5 14 mf	6 13 mr	7 12 MW	8 11 MH	19	9 10 MW	10 9 em	11 8 et	12 8 em	1 6 ET	2 5 EM
2 16 TT	3 18 TM	4 16 rg	5 15 RF	6 14 RR	7 13 mf	8 12 mr	20	9 11 mf	10 10 MH	11 9 MW	12 9 MH	1 7 et	2 6 em
2 17 tt	3 19 tm	4 17 TT	5 16 rd	6 15 rg	7 14 RF	8 13 RR	21	9 12 RF	10 11 mr	11 10 mf	12 10 mr	1 8 MW	2 7 MH
2 18 FW	3 20 FH	4 18 tt	5 17 TM	6 16 TT	7 15 rd	8 14 rg	22	9 13 rd	10 12 RR	11 11 RF	12 11 RR	1 9 mf	2 8 mr
2 19 ff	3 21 fr	4 19 FW	5 18 tm	6 17 tt	7 16 TM	8 15 TT	23	9 14 TM	10 13 rg	11 12 rd	12 12 rg	1 10 RF	2 9 RR
2 20 EF	3 22 ER	4 20 ff	5 19 FH	6 18 FW	7 17 tm	8 16 tt	24	9 15 tm	10 14 TT	11 13 TM	12 13 TT	1 11 rd	2 10 rg
2 21 ed	3 23 eg	4 21 EF	5 20 fr	6 19 ff	7 18 FH	8 17 FW	25	9 16 FH	10 15 tt	11 14 tm	12 14 tt	1 12 TM	2 11 TT
2 22 MM	3 24 MT	4 22 ed	5 21 ER	6 20 EF	7 19 fr	8 18 ff	26	9 17 fr	10 16 FW	11 15 FH	12 15 FW	1 13 tm	2 12 tt
2 23 mm	3 25 mt	4 23 MM	5 22 eg	6 21 ed	7 20 ER	8 19 EF	27	9 18 ER	10 17 ff	11 16 fr	12 16 ff	1 14 FH	2 13 FW
2 24 RH	3 26 RW	4 24 mm	5 23 MT	6 22 MM	7 21 eg	8 20 ed	28	9 19 eg	10 18 EF	11 17 ER	12 17 EF	1 15 fr	2 14 ff
2 25 rr	3 27 rf	4 25 RH	5 24 mt	6 23 mm	7 22 MT	8 21 MM	29	9 20 MT	10 19 ed	11 18 eg	12 18 ed	1 16 ER	2 15 EF
2 26 TR			5 25 RW		7 23 mt	8 22 mm	30		10 20 MM	11 19 MT		1 17 eg	

1980 MM MONKEY

JAN ET	FEB et	MAR MW	APR mf	MAY RF	JUN rd	DAY OF MON	JUL TM	AUG tm	SEP FH	OCT fr	NOV ER	DEC eg
19 WARM	19 CLEAR	21 SUMMER	23 GRAIN	25 HEAT	27 FALL		28 DEW	30 C DEW	30 WINTER		1 SNOW	30 SPRING
18:17	23:15	16:45	21:14	7:24	17:09		19:54	11:20	15:35		7:02	5:56
											30 CHILL	
											18:13	
2 16 ed	3 17 eg	4 15 EF	5 14 fr	6 13 ff	7 12 FH	1	8 11 FW	9 9 tm	10 9 tt	11 8 tm	12 7 TT	1 6 TM
2 17 MM	3 18 MT	4 16 ed	5 15 ER	6 14 EF	7 13 fr	2	8 12 ff	9 10 FH	10 10 FW	11 9 FH	12 8 tt	1 7 tm
2 18 mm	3 19 mt	4 17 MM	5 16 eg	6 15 ed	7 14 ER	3	8 13 EF	9 11 fr	10 11 ff	11 10 fr	12 9 FW	1 8 FH
2 19 RH	3 20 RW	4 18 mm	5 17 MT	6 16 MM	7 15 eg	4	8 14 ed	9 12 ER	10 12 EF	11 11 ER	12 10 ff	1 9 fr
2 20 rr	3 21 rf	4 19 RH	5 18 mt	6 17 mm	7 16 MT	5	8 15 MM	9 13 eg	10 13 ed	11 12 eg	12 11 EF	1 10 ER
2 21 TR	3 22 TF	4 20 rr	5 19 RW	6 18 RH	7 17 mt	6	8 16 mm	9 14 MT	10 14 MM	11 13 MT	12 12 ed	1 11 eg
2 22 tg	3 23 td	4 21 TR	5 20 rf	6 19 rr	7 18 RW	7	8 17 RH	9 15 mt	10 15 mm	11 14 mt	12 13 MM	1 12 MT
2 23 FT	3 24 FM	4 22 tg	5 21 TF	6 20 TR	7 19 rf	8	8 18 rr	9 16 RW	10 16 RH	11 15 RW	12 14 mm	1 13 mt
2 24 ft	3 25 fm	4 23 FT	5 22 td	6 21 tg	7 20 TF	9	8 19 TR	9 17 rf	10 17 rr	11 16 rf	12 15 RH	1 14 RW
2 25 EW	3 26 EH	4 24 ft	5 23 FM	6 22 FT	7 21 td	10	8 20 tg	9 18 TF	10 18 TR	11 17 TF	12 16 rr	1 15 rf
2 26 ef	3 27 er	4 25 EW	5 24 fm	6 23 ft	7 22 FM	11	8 21 FT	9 19 td	10 19 tg	11 18 td	12 17 TR	1 16 TF
2 27 MF	3 28 MR	4 26 ef	5 25 EH	6 24 EW	7 23 fm	12	8 22 ft	9 20 FM	10 20 FT	11 19 FM	12 18 tg	1 17 td
2 28 md	3 29 mg	4 27 MF	5 26 er	6 25 ef	7 24 EH	13	8 23 EW	9 21 fm	10 21 ft	11 20 fm	12 19 FT	1 18 FM
2 29 RM	3 30 RT	4 28 md	5 27 MR	6 26 MF	7 25 er	14	8 24 ef	9 22 EH	10 22 EW	11 21 EH	12 20 ft	1 19 fm
3 1 rm	3 31 rt	4 29 RM	5 28 mg	6 27 md	7 26 MR	15	8 25 MF	9 23 er	10 23 ef	11 22 er	12 21 EW	1 20 EH
3 2 TH	4 1 TW	4 30 rm	5 29 RT	6 28 RM	7 27 mg	16	8 26 md	9 24 MR	10 24 MF	11 23 MR	12 22 ef	1 21 er
3 3 tr	4 2 tf	5 1 TH	5 30 rt	6 29 rm	7 28 RT	17	8 27 RM	9 25 mg	10 25 md	11 24 mg	12 23 MF	1 22 MR
3 4 FR	4 3 TF	5 2 tr	5 31 TW	6 30 TH	7 29 rt	18	8 28 rm	9 26 RT	10 26 RM	11 25 RT	12 24 md	1 23 mg
3 5 fg	4 4 td	5 3 FR	6 1 tf	7 1 tr	7 30 TW	19	8 29 TH	9 27 rt	10 27 rm	11 26 rt	12 25 RM	1 24 RT
3 6 ET	4 5 EM	5 4 fg	6 2 TF	7 2 FR	7 31 tf	20	8 30 tr	9 28 TW	10 28 TH	11 27 TW	12 26 rm	1 25 rt
3 7 et	4 6 em	5 5 ET	6 3 td	7 3 fg	8 1 TF	21	8 31 FR	9 29 tf	10 29 tr	11 28 tf	12 27 TH	1 26 TW
3 8 MW	4 7 MH	5 6 et	6 4 EM	7 4 ET	8 2 td	22	9 1 fg	9 30 TF	10 30 FR	11 29 TF	12 28 tr	1 27 tf
3 9 mf	4 8 mr	5 7 MW	6 5 em	7 5 et	8 3 EM	23	9 2 ET	10 1 td	10 31 fg	11 30 td	12 29 FR	1 28 TF
3 10 RF	4 9 RR	5 8 mf	6 6 MH	7 6 MW	8 4 em	24	9 3 et	10 2 EM	11 1 ET	12 1 EM	12 30 fg	1 29 td
3 11 rd	4 10 rg	5 9 RF	6 7 mr	7 7 mf	8 5 MH	25	9 4 MW	10 3 em	11 2 et	12 2 em	12 31 ET	1 30 EM
3 12 TM	4 11 TT	5 10 rd	6 8 RR	7 8 RF	8 6 mr	26	9 5 mf	10 4 MH	11 3 MW	12 3 MH	1 1 et	1 31 em
3 13 tm	4 12 tt	5 11 TM	6 9 rg	7 9 rd	8 7 RR	27	9 6 RF	10 5 mr	11 4 mf	12 4 mr	1 2 MW	2 1 MH
3 14 FH	4 13 FW	5 12 tm	6 10 TT	7 10 TM	8 8 rg	28	9 7 rd	10 6 RR	11 5 RF	12 5 RR	1 3 mf	2 2 mr
3 15 fr	4 14 ff	5 13 FH	6 11 tt	7 11 tm	8 9 TT	29	9 8 TM	10 7 rg	11 6 rd	12 6 rg	1 4 RF	2 3 RR
3 16 ER			6 12 FW		8 10 tt	30		10 8 TT	11 7 TM		1 5 rd	2 4 rg

1981 mm ROOSTER

JAN MT	FEB mt	MAR RW	APR rf	MAY TF	JUN td	DAY OF MON	JUL FM	AUG fm	SEP EH	OCT er	NOV MR	DEC mg
29 WARM		1 CLEAR	2 SUMMER	5 GRAIN	6 HEAT		8 FALL	11 DEW	11 C DEW	11 WINTER	12 SNOW	12 CHILL
23:58		4:59	22:35	3:03	13:12		23:31	1:43	17:10	21:24	13:51	0:02
2 5 TT	3 6 rd	4 5 rg	5 4 RF	6 2 mr	7 2 mf	1	7 31 MH	8 29 et	9 28 em	10 28 et	11 26 EM	12 26 ET
2 6 tt	3 7 TM	4 6 TT	5 5 rd	6 3 RR	7 3 RF	2	8 1 mr	8 30 MW	9 29 MH	10 29 MW	11 27 em	12 27 et
2 7 FW	3 8 tm	4 7 tt	5 6 TM	6 4 rg	7 4 rd	3	8 2 RR	8 31 mf	9 30 mr	10 30 mf	11 28 MH	12 28 MW
2 8 ff	3 9 FH	4 8 FW	5 7 tm	6 5 TT	7 5 TM	4	8 3 rg	9 1 RF	10 1 RR	10 31 RF	11 29 mr	12 29 mf
2 9 EF	3 10 fr	4 9 ff	5 8 FH	6 6 tt	7 6 tm	5	8 4 TT	9 2 rd	10 2 rg	11 1 rd	11 30 RR	12 30 RF
2 10 ed	3 11 ER	4 10 EF	5 9 fr	6 7 FW	7 7 FH	6	8 5 tt	9 3 TM	10 3 TT	11 2 TM	12 1 rg	12 31 rd
2 11 MM	3 12 eg	4 11 ed	5 10 ER	6 8 ff	7 8 fr	7	8 6 FW	9 4 tm	10 4 tt	11 3 tm	12 2 TT	1 1 TM
2 12 mm	3 13 MT	4 12 MM	5 11 eg	6 9 EF	7 9 ER	8	8 7 ff	9 5 FH	10 5 FW	11 4 FH	12 3 tt	1 2 tm
2 13 RH	3 14 mt	4 13 mm	5 12 MT	6 10 ed	7 10 eg	9	8 8 EF	9 6 fr	10 6 ff	11 5 fr	12 4 FW	1 3 FH
2 14 rr	3 15 RW	4 14 RH	5 13 mt	6 11 MM	7 11 MT	10	8 9 ed	9 7 ER	10 7 EF	11 6 ER	12 5 ff	1 4 fr
2 15 TR	3 16 rf	4 15 rr	5 14 RW	6 12 mm	7 12 mt	11	8 10 MM	9 8 eg	10 8 ed	11 7 eg	12 6 EF	1 5 ER
2 16 tg	3 17 TF	4 16 TR	5 15 rf	6 13 RH	7 13 RW	12	8 11 mm	9 9 MT	10 9 MM	11 8 MT	12 7 ed	1 6 eg
2 17 FT	3 18 td	4 17 tg	5 16 TF	6 14 rr	7 14 rf	13	8 12 RH	9 10 mt	10 10 mm	11 9 mt	12 8 MM	1 7 MT
2 18 ft	3 19 FM	4 18 FT	5 17 td	6 15 TR	7 15 TF	14	8 13 rr	9 11 RW	10 11 RH	11 10 RW	12 9 mm	1 8 mt
2 19 EW	3 20 fm	4 19 ft	5 18 FM	6 16 tg	7 16 td	15	8 14 TR	9 12 rf	10 12 rr	11 11 rf	12 10 RH	1 9 RW
2 20 ef	3 21 EH	4 20 EW	5 19 fm	6 17 FT	7 17 FM	16	8 15 tg	9 13 TF	10 13 TR	11 12 TF	12 11 rr	1 10 rf
2 21 MF	3 22 er	4 21 ef	5 20 EH	6 18 ft	7 18 fm	17	8 16 FT	9 14 td	10 14 tg	11 13 td	12 12 TR	1 11 TF
2 22 md	3 23 MR	4 22 MF	5 21 er	6 19 EW	7 19 EH	18	8 17 ft	9 15 FM	10 15 FT	11 14 FM	12 13 tg	1 12 td
2 23 RM	3 24 mg	4 23 md	5 22 MR	6 20 ef	7 20 er	19	8 18 EW	9 16 fm	10 16 ft	11 15 fm	12 14 FT	1 13 FM
2 24 rm	3 25 RT	4 24 RM	5 23 mg	6 21 MF	7 21 MR	20	8 19 ef	9 17 EH	10 17 EW	11 16 EH	12 15 ft	1 14 fm
2 25 TH	3 26 rt	4 25 rm	5 24 RT	6 22 md	7 22 mg	21	8 20 MF	9 18 er	10 18 ef	11 17 er	12 16 EW	1 15 EH
2 26 tr	3 27 TW	4 26 TH	5 25 rt	6 23 RM	7 23 RT	22	8 21 md	9 19 MR	10 19 MF	11 18 MR	12 17 ef	1 16 er
2 27 FR	3 28 tf	4 27 tr	5 26 TW	6 24 rm	7 24 rt	23	8 22 RM	9 20 mg	10 20 md	11 19 mg	12 18 MF	1 17 MR
2 28 fg	3 29 FF	4 28 FR	5 27 tf	6 25 TH	7 25 TW	24	8 23 rm	9 21 RT	10 21 RM	11 20 RT	12 19 md	1 18 mg
3 1 ET	3 30 fd	4 29 fg	5 28 FF	6 26 tr	7 26 tf	25	8 24 TH	9 22 rt	10 22 rm	11 21 rt	12 20 RM	1 19 RT
3 2 et	3 31 EM	4 30 ET	5 29 fd	6 27 FR	7 27 FF	26	8 25 tr	9 23 TW	10 23 TH	11 22 TW	12 21 rm	1 20 rt
3 3 MW	4 1 em	5 1 et	5 30 EM	6 28 fg	7 28 fd	27	8 26 FR	9 24 tf	10 24 tr	11 23 tf	12 22 TH	1 21 TW
3 4 mf	4 2 MH	5 2 MW	5 31 em	6 29 ET	7 29 EM	28	8 27 fg	9 25 FF	10 25 FR	11 24 FF	12 23 tr	1 22 tf
3 5 RF	4 3 mr	5 3 mf	6 1 MH	6 30 et	7 30 em	29	8 28 ET	9 26 fd	10 26 fg	11 25 fd	12 24 FR	1 23 FF
	4 4 RR			7 1 MW		30		9 27 EM	10 27 ET		12 25 fg	1 24 fd

1982 RH DOG

JAN RT	FEB rt	MAR TW	APR tf	APR tf	MAY FF	JUN fd	DAY OF	JUL EM	AUG em	SEP MH	OCT mr	NOV RR	DEC rg
11 SPRING	11 WARM	12 CLEAR	13 SUMMER	15 GRAIN	17 HEAT	19 FALL	MON	21 DEW	23 C DEW	23 WINTER	23 SNOW	23 CHILL	22 SPRING
11:46	5:57	10:54	4:21	8:36	19:19	5:19		7:32	0:12	3:13	19:40	5:59	17:40
1 25 EM	2 24 ET	3 25 fd	4 24 fg	5 23 FF	6 21 tr	7 21 tf	1	8 19 TH	9 17 rt	10 17 rm	11 15 RT	12 15 RM	1 14 RT
1 26 em	2 25 et	3 26 EM	4 25 ET	5 24 fd	6 22 FR	7 22 FF	2	8 20 tr	9 18 TW	10 18 TH	11 16 rt	12 16 rm	1 15 rt
1 27 MH	2 26 MW	3 27 em	4 26 et	5 25 EM	6 23 fg	7 23 fd	3	8 21 FR	9 19 tf	10 19 tr	11 17 TW	12 17 TH	1 16 TW
1 28 mr	2 27 mf	3 28 MH	4 27 MW	5 26 em	6 24 ET	7 24 EM	4	8 22 fg	9 20 FF	10 20 FR	11 18 tf	12 18 tr	1 17 tf
1 29 RR	2 28 RF	3 29 mr	4 28 mf	5 27 MH	6 25 et	7 25 em	5	8 23 ET	9 21 fd	10 21 fg	11 19 FF	12 19 FR	1 18 FF
1 30 rg	3 1 rd	3 30 RR	4 29 RF	5 28 mr	6 26 MW	7 26 MH	6	8 24 et	9 22 EM	10 22 ET	11 20 fd	12 20 fg	1 19 fd
1 31 TT	3 2 TM	3 31 rg	4 30 rd	5 29 RR	6 27 mf	7 27 mr	7	8 25 MW	9 23 em	10 23 et	11 21 EM	12 21 ET	1 20 EM
2 1 tt	3 3 tm	4 1 TT	5 1 TM	5 30 rg	6 28 RF	7 28 RR	8	8 26 mf	9 24 MH	10 24 MW	11 22 em	12 22 et	1 21 em
2 2 FW	3 4 FH	4 2 tt	5 2 tm	5 31 TT	6 29 rd	7 29 rg	9	8 27 RF	9 25 mr	10 25 mf	11 23 MH	12 23 MW	1 22 MH
2 3 ff	3 5 fr	4 3 FW	5 3 FH	6 1 tt	6 30 TM	7 30 TT	10	8 28 rd	9 26 RR	10 26 RF	11 24 mr	12 24 mf	1 23 mr
2 4 EF	3 6 ER	4 4 ff	5 4 fr	6 2 FW	7 1 tm	7 31 tt	11	8 29 TM	9 27 rg	10 27 rd	11 25 RR	12 25 RF	1 24 RR
2 5 ed	3 7 eg	4 5 EF	5 5 ER	6 3 ff	7 2 FH	8 1 FW	12	8 30 tm	9 28 TT	10 28 TM	11 26 rg	12 26 rd	1 25 rg
2 6 MM	3 8 MT	4 6 ed	5 6 eg	6 4 EF	7 3 fr	8 2 ff	13	8 31 FH	9 29 tt	10 29 tm	11 27 TT	12 27 TM	1 26 TT
2 7 mm	3 9 mt	4 7 MM	5 7 MT	6 5 ed	7 4 ER	8 3 EF	14	9 1 fr	9 30 FW	10 30 FH	11 28 tt	12 28 tm	1 27 tt
2 8 RH	3 10 RW	4 8 mm	5 8 mt	6 6 MM	7 5 eg	8 4 ed	15	9 2 ER	10 1 ff	10 31 fr	11 29 FW	12 29 FH	1 28 FW
2 9 rr	3 11 rf	4 9 RH	5 9 RW	6 7 mm	7 6 MT	8 5 MM	16	9 3 eg	10 2 EF	11 1 ER	11 30 ff	12 30 fr	1 29 ff
2 10 TR	3 12 TF	4 10 rr	5 10 rf	6 8 RH	7 7 mt	8 6 mm	17	9 4 MT	10 3 ed	11 2 eg	12 1 EF	12 31 ER	1 30 EF
2 11 tg	3 13 td	4 11 TR	5 11 TF	6 9 rr	7 8 RW	8 7 RH	18	9 5 mt	10 4 MM	11 3 MT	12 2 ed	1 1 eg	1 31 ed
2 12 FT	3 14 FM	4 12 tg	5 12 td	6 10 TR	7 9 rf	8 8 rr	19	9 6 RW	10 5 mm	11 4 mt	12 3 MM	1 2 MT	2 1 MM
2 13 ft	3 15 fm	4 13 FT	5 13 FM	6 11 tg	7 10 TF	8 9 TR	20	9 7 rf	10 6 RH	11 5 RW	12 4 mm	1 3 mt	2 2 mm
2 14 EW	3 16 EH	4 14 ft	5 14 fm	6 12 FT	7 11 td	8 10 tg	21	9 8 TF	10 7 rr	11 6 rf	12 5 RH	1 4 RW	2 3 RH
2 15 ef	3 17 er	4 15 EW	5 15 EH	6 13 ft	7 12 FM	8 11 FT	22	9 9 td	10 8 TR	11 7 TF	12 6 rr	1 5 rf	2 4 rr
2 16 MF	3 18 MR	4 16 ef	5 16 er	6 14 EW	7 13 fm	8 12 ft	23	9 10 FM	10 9 tg	11 8 td	12 7 TR	1 6 TF	2 5 TR
2 17 md	3 19 mg	4 17 MF	5 17 MR	6 15 ef	7 14 EH	8 13 EW	24	9 11 fm	10 10 FT	11 9 FM	12 8 tg	1 7 td	2 6 tg
2 18 RM	3 20 RT	4 18 md	5 18 mg	6 16 MF	7 15 er	8 14 ef	25	9 12 EH	10 11 ft	11 10 fm	12 9 FT	1 8 FM	2 7 FT
2 19 rm	3 21 rt	4 19 RM	5 19 RT	6 17 md	7 16 MR	8 15 MF	26	9 13 er	10 12 EW	11 11 EH	12 10 ft	1 9 fm	2 8 ft
2 20 TH	3 22 TW	4 20 rm	5 20 rt	6 18 RM	7 17 mg	8 16 md	27	9 14 MR	10 13 ef	11 12 er	12 11 EW	1 10 EH	2 9 EW
2 21 tr	3 23 tf	4 21 TH	5 21 TW	6 19 rm	7 18 RT	8 17 RM	28	9 15 mg	10 14 MF	11 13 MR	12 12 ef	1 11 er	2 10 ef
2 22 FR	3 24 FF	4 22 tr	5 22 tf	6 20 TH	7 19 rt	8 18 rm	29	9 16 RT	10 15 md	11 14 mg	12 13 MF	1 12 MR	2 11 MF
2 23 fg		4 23 FR			7 20 TW		30		10 16 RM		12 14 md	1 13 mg	2 12 md

1983 rr BOAR

JAN TT	FEB tt	MAR FW	APR ff	MAY EF	JUN ed	DAY OF MON	JUL MM	AUG mm	SEP RH	OCT rr	NOV TR	DEC tg
22 WARM	22 CLEAR	24 SUMMER	25 GRAIN	28 HEAT	30 FALL			2 DEW	4 C DEW	4 WINTER	5 SNOW	4 CHILL
11:48	16:45	10:12	14:27	1:06	11:07			13:21	6:01	9:03	1:30	11:42
2 13 RM	3 15 RT	4 13 md	5 13 mg	6 11 MF	7 10 er	1	8 9 ef	9 7 EH	10 6 ft	11 5 fm	12 4 FT	1 3 FM
2 14 rm	3 16 rt	4 14 RM	5 14 RT	6 12 md	7 11 MR	2	8 10 MF	9 8 er	10 7 EW	11 6 EH	12 5 ft	1 4 fm
2 15 TH	3 17 TW	4 15 rm	5 15 rt	6 13 RM	7 12 mg	3	8 11 md	9 9 MR	10 8 ef	11 7 er	12 6 EW	1 5 EH
2 16 tr	3 18 tf	4 16 TH	5 16 TW	6 14 rm	7 13 RT	4	8 12 RM	9 10 mg	10 9 MF	11 8 MR	12 7 ef	1 6 er
2 17 FR	3 19 FF	4 17 tr	5 17 tf	6 15 TH	7 14 rt	5	8 13 rm	9 11 RT	10 10 md	11 9 mg	12 8 MF	1 7 MR
2 18 fg	3 20 fd	4 18 FR	5 18 FF	6 16 tr	7 15 TW	6	8 14 TH	9 12 rt	10 11 RM	11 10 RT	12 9 md	1 8 mg
2 19 ET	3 21 EM	4 19 fg	5 19 fd	6 17 FR	7 16 tf	7	8 15 tr	9 13 TW	10 12 rm	11 11 rt	12 10 RM	1 9 RT
2 20 et	3 22 em	4 20 ET	5 20 EM	6 18 fg	7 17 FF	8	8 16 FR	9 14 tf	10 13 TH	11 12 TW	12 11 rm	1 10 rt
2 21 MW	3 23 MH	4 21 et	5 21 em	6 19 ET	7 18 fd	9	8 17 fg	9 15 FF	10 14 tr	11 13 tf	12 12 TH	1 11 TW
2 22 mf	3 24 mr	4 22 MW	5 22 MH	6 20 et	7 19 EM	10	8 18 ET	9 16 fd	10 15 FR	11 14 FF	12 13 tr	1 12 tf
2 23 RF	3 25 RR	4 23 mf	5 23 mr	6 21 MW	7 20 em	11	8 19 et	9 17 EM	10 16 fg	11 15 fd	12 14 FR	1 13 FF
2 24 rd	3 26 rg	4 24 RF	5 24 RR	6 22 mf	7 21 MH	12	8 20 MW	9 18 em	10 17 ET	11 16 EM	12 15 fg	1 14 fd
2 25 TM	3 27 TT	4 25 rd	5 25 rg	6 23 RF	7 22 mr	13	8 21 mf	9 19 MH	10 18 et	11 17 em	12 16 ET	1 15 EM
2 26 tm	3 28 tt	4 26 TM	5 26 TT	6 24 rd	7 23 RR	14	8 22 RF	9 20 mr	10 19 MW	11 18 MH	12 17 et	1 16 em
2 27 FH	3 29 FW	4 27 tm	5 27 tt	6 25 TM	7 24 rg	15	8 23 rd	9 21 RR	10 20 mf	11 19 mr	12 18 MW	1 17 MH
2 28 fr	3 30 ff	4 28 FH	5 28 FW	6 26 tm	7 25 TT	16	8 24 TM	9 22 rg	10 21 RF	11 20 RR	12 19 mf	1 18 mr
3 1 ER	3 31 EF	4 29 fr	5 29 ff	6 27 FH	7 26 tt	17	8 25 tm	9 23 TT	10 22 rd	11 21 rg	12 20 RF	1 19 RR
3 2 eg	4 1 ed	4 30 ER	5 30 EF	6 28 fr	7 27 FW	18	8 26 FH	9 24 tt	10 23 TM	11 22 TT	12 21 rd	1 20 rg
3 3 MT	4 2 MM	5 1 eg	5 31 ed	6 29 ER	7 28 ff	19	8 27 fr	9 25 FW	10 24 tm	11 23 tt	12 22 TM	1 21 TT
3 4 mt	4 3 mm	5 2 MT	6 1 MM	6 30 eg	7 29 EF	20	8 28 ER	9 26 ff	10 25 FH	11 24 FW	12 23 tm	1 22 tt
3 5 RW	4 4 RH	5 3 mt	6 2 mm	7 1 MT	7 30 ed	21	8 29 eg	9 27 EF	10 26 fr	11 25 ff	12 24 FH	1 23 FW
3 6 rf	4 5 rr	5 4 RW	6 3 RH	7 2 mt	7 31 MM	22	8 30 MT	9 28 ed	10 27 ER	11 26 EF	12 25 fr	1 24 ff
3 7 TF	4 6 TR	5 5 rf	6 4 rr	7 3 RW	8 1 mm	23	8 31 mt	9 29 MM	10 28 eg	11 27 ed	12 26 ER	1 25 EF
3 8 td	4 7 tg	5 6 TF	6 5 TR	7 4 rf	8 2 RH	24	9 1 RW	9 30 mm	10 29 MT	11 28 MM	12 27 eg	1 26 ed
3 9 FM	4 8 FT	5 7 td	6 6 tg	7 5 TF	8 3 rr	25	9 2 rf	10 1 RH	10 30 mt	11 29 mm	12 28 MT	1 27 MM
3 10 fm	4 9 ft	5 8 FM	6 7 FT	7 6 td	8 4 TR	26	9 3 TF	10 2 rr	10 31 RW	11 30 RH	12 29 mt	1 28 mm
3 11 EH	4 10 EW	5 9 fm	6 8 ft	7 7 FM	8 5 tg	27	9 4 td	10 3 TR	11 1 rf	12 1 rr	12 30 RW	1 29 RH
3 12 er	4 11 ef	5 10 EH	6 9 EW	7 8 fm	8 6 FT	28	9 5 FM	10 4 tg	11 2 TF	12 2 TR	12 31 rf	1 30 rr
3 13 MR	4 12 MF	5 11 er	6 10 ef	7 9 EH	8 7 ft	29	9 6 fm	10 5 FT	11 3 td	12 3 tg	1 1 TF	1 31 TR
3 14 mg		5 12 MR			8 8 EW	30			11 4 FM		1 2 td	2 1 tg

1984 TR RAT

JAN FT	FEB ft	MAR EW	APR ef	MAY MF	JUN md	DAY OF MON	JUL RM	AUG rm	SEP TH	OCT tr	OCT tr	NOV FR	DEC fg
3 SPRING	3 WARM	4 CLEAR	5 SUMMER	6 GRAIN	9 HEAT		11 FALL	12 DEW	14 C DEW	15 WINTER	15 SNOW	15 CHILL	15 SPRING
23:19	17:25	22:23	15:51	20:09	6:29		16:18	19:10	11:50	13:46	7:20	18:36	6:12
2 2 FT	3 3 FM	4 1 tg	5 1 td	5 31 tg	6 29 TF	1	7 28 rr	8 27 rf	9 25 RH	10 24 mt	11 23 mm	12 22 MT	1 21 MM
2 3 ft	3 4 fm	4 2 FT	5 2 FM	6 1 FT	6 30 td	2	7 29 TR	8 28 TF	9 26 rr	10 25 RW	11 24 RH	12 23 mt	1 22 mm
2 4 EW	3 5 EH	4 3 ft	5 3 fm	6 2 ft	7 1 FM	3	7 30 tg	8 29 td	9 27 TR	10 26 rf	11 25 rr	12 24 RH	1 23 RH
2 5 ef	3 6 er	4 4 EW	5 4 EH	6 3 EW	7 2 fm	4	7 31 FT	8 30 FM	9 28 tg	10 27 TF	11 26 TR	12 25 rf	1 24 rr
2 6 MF	3 7 MR	4 5 ef	5 5 er	6 4 ef	7 3 EH	5	8 1 ft	8 31 fm	9 29 FT	10 28 td	11 27 tg	12 26 TF	1 25 TR
2 7 md	3 8 mg	4 6 MF	5 6 MR	6 5 MF	7 4 er	6	8 2 EW	9 1 EH	9 30 ft	10 29 FM	11 28 FT	12 27 td	1 26 tg
2 8 RM	3 9 RT	4 7 md	5 7 mg	6 6 md	7 5 MR	7	8 3 ef	9 2 er	10 1 EW	10 30 fm	11 29 ft	12 28 FM	1 27 FT
2 9 rm	3 10 rt	4 8 RM	5 8 RT	6 7 RM	7 6 mg	8	8 4 MF	9 3 MR	10 2 ef	10 31 EH	11 30 EW	12 29 fm	1 28 ft
2 10 TH	3 11 TW	4 9 rm	5 9 rt	6 8 rm	7 7 RT	9	8 5 md	9 4 mg	10 3 MF	11 1 er	12 1 ef	12 30 EH	1 29 EW
2 11 tr	3 12 tf	4 10 TH	5 10 TW	6 9 TH	7 8 rt	10	8 6 RM	9 5 RT	10 4 md	11 2 MR	12 2 MF	12 31 er	1 30 ef
2 12 FR	3 13 FF	4 11 tr	5 11 tf	6 10 tr	7 9 TW	11	8 7 rm	9 6 rt	10 5 RM	11 3 mg	12 3 md	1 1 MR	1 31 MF
2 13 fg	3 14 fd	4 12 FR	5 12 FF	6 11 FR	7 10 tf	12	8 8 TH	9 7 TW	10 6 rm	11 4 RT	12 4 RM	1 2 mg	2 1 md
2 14 ET	3 15 EM	4 13 fg	5 13 fd	6 12 fg	7 11 FF	13	8 9 tr	9 8 tf	10 7 TH	11 5 rt	12 5 rm	1 3 RT	2 2 RM
2 15 et	3 16 em	4 14 ET	5 14 EM	6 13 ET	7 12 fd	14	8 10 FR	9 9 FF	10 8 tr	11 6 TW	12 6 TH	1 4 rt	2 3 rm
2 16 MW	3 17 MH	4 15 et	5 15 em	6 14 et	7 13 EM	15	8 11 fg	9 10 fd	10 9 FR	11 7 tf	12 7 tr	1 5 TW	2 4 TH
2 17 mf	3 18 mr	4 16 MW	5 16 MH	6 15 MW	7 14 em	16	8 12 ET	9 11 EM	10 10 fg	11 8 FF	12 8 FR	1 6 tf	2 5 tr
2 18 RF	3 19 RR	4 17 mf	5 17 mr	6 16 mf	7 15 MH	17	8 13 et	9 12 em	10 11 ET	11 9 fd	12 9 fg	1 7 FF	2 6 FR
2 19 rd	3 20 rg	4 18 RF	5 18 RR	6 17 RF	7 16 mr	18	8 14 MW	9 13 MH	10 12 et	11 10 EM	12 10 ET	1 8 fd	2 7 fg
2 20 TM	3 21 TT	4 19 rd	5 19 rg	6 18 rd	7 17 RR	19	8 15 mf	9 14 mr	10 13 MW	11 11 em	12 11 et	1 9 EM	2 8 ET
2 21 tm	3 22 tt	4 20 TM	5 20 TT	6 19 TM	7 18 rg	20	8 16 RF	9 15 RR	10 14 mf	11 12 MH	12 12 MW	1 10 em	2 9 et
2 22 FH	3 23 FW	4 21 tm	5 21 tt	6 20 tm	7 19 TT	21	8 17 rd	9 16 rg	10 15 RF	11 13 mr	12 13 mf	1 11 MH	2 10 MW
2 23 fr	3 24 ff	4 22 FH	5 22 FW	6 21 FH	7 20 tt	22	8 18 TM	9 17 TT	10 16 rd	11 14 RR	12 14 RF	1 12 mr	2 11 mf
2 24 ER	3 25 EF	4 23 fr	5 23 ff	6 22 fr	7 21 FW	23	8 19 tm	9 18 tt	10 17 TM	11 15 rg	12 15 rd	1 13 RR	2 12 RF
2 25 eg	3 26 ed	4 24 ER	5 24 EF	6 23 ER	7 22 ff	24	8 20 FH	9 19 FW	10 18 tm	11 16 TT	12 16 TM	1 14 rg	2 13 rd
2 26 MT	3 27 MM	4 25 eg	5 25 ed	6 24 eg	7 23 EF	25	8 21 fr	9 20 ff	10 19 FH	11 17 tt	12 17 tm	1 15 TT	2 14 TM
2 27 mt	3 28 mm	4 26 MT	5 26 MM	6 25 MT	7 24 ed	26	8 22 ER	9 21 EF	10 20 fr	11 18 FW	12 18 FH	1 16 tt	2 15 tm
2 28 RW	3 29 RH	4 27 mt	5 27 mm	6 26 mt	7 25 MM	27	8 23 eg	9 22 ed	10 21 ER	11 19 ff	12 19 fr	1 17 FW	2 16 FH
2 29 rf	3 30 rr	4 28 RW	5 28 RH	6 27 RW	7 26 mm	28	8 24 MT	9 23 MM	10 22 eg	11 20 EF	12 20 ER	1 18 ff	2 17 fr
3 1 TF	3 31 TR	4 29 rf	5 29 rr	6 28 rf	7 27 RH	29	8 25 mt	9 24 mm	10 23 MT	11 21 ed	12 21 eg	1 19 EF	2 18 ER
3 2 td		4 30 TF	5 30 TR			30	8 26 RW			11 22 MM		1 20 ed	2 19 eg

1985 tg OX

JAN ET			FEB et			MAR MW			APR mf			MAY RF			JUN rd			DAY OF MON	JUL TM			AUG tm			SEP FH			OCT fr			NOV ER			DEC eg		
14 WARM			16 CLEAR			16 SUMMER			18 GRAIN			20 HEAT			21 FALL				24 DEW			24 C DEW			25 WINTER			26 SNOW			25 CHILL			26 SPRING		
23:16			4:14			21:43			2:00			12:19			22:04				1:53			17:39			19:29			13:09			23:21			11:03		
2	20	MT	3	21	ed	4	20	eg	5	20	ed	6	18	ER	7	18	EF	1	8	16	fr	9	15	ff	10	14	FH	11	12	tt	12	12	tm	1	10	TT
2	21	mt	3	22	MM	4	21	MT	5	21	MM	6	19	eg	7	19	ed	2	8	17	ER	9	16	EF	10	15	fr	11	13	FW	12	13	FH	1	11	tt
2	22	RW	3	23	mm	4	22	mt	5	22	mm	6	20	MT	7	20	MM	3	8	18	eg	9	17	ed	10	16	ER	11	14	ff	12	14	fr	1	12	FW
2	23	rf	3	24	RH	4	23	RW	5	23	RH	6	21	mt	7	21	mm	4	8	19	MT	9	18	MM	10	17	eg	11	15	EF	12	15	ER	1	13	ff
2	24	TF	3	25	rr	4	24	rf	5	24	rr	6	22	RW	7	22	RH	5	8	20	mt	9	19	mm	10	18	MT	11	16	ed	12	16	eg	1	14	EF
2	25	fd	3	26	TR	4	25	TF	5	25	TR	6	23	rf	7	23	rr	6	8	21	RW	9	20	RH	10	19	mt	11	17	MM	12	17	MT	1	15	ed
2	26	FM	3	27	tg	4	26	fd	5	26	tg	6	24	TF	7	24	TR	7	8	22	rf	9	21	rr	10	20	RW	11	18	mm	12	18	mt	1	16	MM
2	27	fm	3	28	FT	4	27	FM	5	27	FT	6	25	fd	7	25	tg	8	8	23	TF	9	22	TR	10	21	rf	11	19	RH	12	19	RW	1	17	mm
2	28	EH	3	29	ft	4	28	fm	5	28	ft	6	26	FM	7	26	FT	9	8	24	fd	9	23	tg	10	22	TF	11	20	rr	12	20	rf	1	18	RH
3	1	er	3	30	EW	4	29	EH	5	29	EW	6	27	fm	7	27	ft	10	8	25	FM	9	24	FT	10	23	fd	11	21	TR	12	21	TF	1	19	rr
3	2	MR	3	31	ef	4	30	er	5	30	ef	6	28	EH	7	28	EW	11	8	26	fm	9	25	ft	10	24	FM	11	22	tg	12	22	fd	1	20	TR
3	3	mg	4	1	MF	5	1	MR	5	31	MF	6	29	er	7	29	ef	12	8	27	EH	9	26	EW	10	25	fm	11	23	FT	12	23	FM	1	21	tg
3	4	RT	4	2	md	5	2	mg	6	1	md	6	30	MR	7	30	MF	13	8	28	er	9	27	ef	10	26	EH	11	24	ft	12	24	fm	1	22	FT
3	5	rt	4	3	RM	5	3	RT	6	2	RM	7	1	mg	7	31	md	14	8	29	MR	9	28	MF	10	27	er	11	25	EW	12	25	EH	1	23	ft
3	6	TW	4	4	rm	5	4	rt	6	3	rm	7	2	RT	8	1	RM	15	8	30	mg	9	29	md	10	28	MR	11	26	ef	12	26	er	1	24	EW
3	7	tf	4	5	TH	5	5	TW	6	4	TH	7	3	rt	8	2	rm	16	8	31	RT	9	30	RM	10	29	mg	11	27	MF	12	27	MR	1	25	ef
3	8	FF	4	6	tr	5	6	tf	6	5	tr	7	4	TW	8	3	TH	17	9	1	rt	10	1	rm	10	30	RT	11	28	md	12	28	mg	1	26	MF
3	9	fd	4	7	FR	5	7	FF	6	6	FR	7	5	tf	8	4	tr	18	9	2	TW	10	2	TH	10	31	rt	11	29	RM	12	29	RT	1	27	md
3	10	EM	4	8	fg	5	8	fd	6	7	fg	7	6	FF	8	5	FR	19	9	3	tf	10	3	tr	11	1	TW	11	30	rm	12	30	rt	1	28	RM
3	11	em	4	9	ET	5	9	EM	6	8	ET	7	7	fd	8	6	fg	20	9	4	FF	10	4	FR	11	2	tf	12	1	TH	12	31	TW	1	29	rm
3	12	MH	4	10	et	5	10	em	6	9	et	7	8	EM	8	7	ET	21	9	5	fd	10	5	fg	11	3	FF	12	2	tr	1	1	tf	1	30	TH
3	13	mr	4	11	MW	5	11	MH	6	10	MW	7	9	em	8	8	et	22	9	6	EM	10	6	ET	11	4	fd	12	3	FR	1	2	FF	1	31	tr
3	14	RR	4	12	mf	5	12	mr	6	11	mf	7	10	MH	8	9	MW	23	9	7	em	10	7	et	11	5	EM	12	4	fg	1	3	fd	2	1	FR
3	15	rg	4	13	RF	5	13	RR	6	12	RF	7	11	mr	8	10	mf	24	9	8	MH	10	8	MW	11	6	em	12	5	ET	1	4	EM	2	2	fg
3	16	TT	4	14	rd	5	14	rg	6	13	rd	7	12	RR	8	11	RF	25	9	9	mr	10	9	mf	11	7	MH	12	6	et	1	5	em	2	3	ET
3	17	tt	4	15	TM	5	15	TT	6	14	TM	7	13	rg	8	12	rd	26	9	10	RR	10	10	RF	11	8	mr	12	7	MW	1	6	MH	2	4	et
3	18	FW	4	16	tm	5	16	tt	6	15	tm	7	14	TT	8	13	TM	27	9	11	rg	10	11	rd	11	9	RR	12	8	mf	1	7	mr	2	5	MW
3	19	ff	4	17	FH	5	17	FW	6	16	FH	7	15	tt	8	14	tm	28	9	12	TT	10	12	TM	11	10	rg	12	9	RF	1	8	RR	2	6	mf
3	20	EF	4	18	fr	5	18	ff	6	17	fr	7	16	FW	8	15	FH	29	9	13	tt	10	13	tm	11	11	TT	12	10	rd	1	9	rg	2	7	RF
			4	19	ER	5	19	EF				7	17	ff				30	9	14	FW							12	11	TM				2	8	rd

1986 FT TIGER

JAN MT	FEB mt	MAR RW	APR rf	MAY TF	JUN td	DAY OF MON	JUL FM	AUG tm	SEP EH	OCT er	NOV MR	DEC mg
26 WARM	27 CLEAR	28 SUMMER	29 GRAIN		1 HEAT		3 FALL	5 DEW	5 C DEW	7 WINTER	6 SNOW	7 CHILL
5:13	10:16	3:50	8:12		18:35		4:17	7:10	23:28	1:20	18:01	5:09
2 9 TM	3 10 rg	4 9 rd	5 9 rg	6 7 RF	7 7 RR	1	8 6 RF	9 4 mr	10 4 mf	11 2 MH	12 2 MW	12 31 em
2 10 tm	3 11 TT	4 10 TM	5 10 TT	6 8 rd	7 8 rg	2	8 7 rd	9 5 RR	10 5 RF	11 3 mr	12 3 mf	1 1 MH
2 11 FH	3 12 tt	4 11 tm	5 11 tt	6 9 TM	7 9 TT	3	8 8 TM	9 6 rg	10 6 rd	11 4 RR	12 4 RF	1 2 mr
2 12 fr	3 13 FW	4 12 FH	5 12 FW	6 10 tm	7 10 tt	4	8 9 tm	9 7 TT	10 7 TM	11 5 rg	12 5 rd	1 3 RR
2 13 ER	3 14 ff	4 13 fr	5 13 ff	6 11 FH	7 11 FW	5	8 10 FH	9 8 tt	10 8 tm	11 6 TT	12 6 TM	1 4 rg
2 14 eg	3 15 EF	4 14 ER	5 14 EF	6 12 fr	7 12 ff	6	8 11 fr	9 9 FW	10 9 FH	11 7 tt	12 7 tm	1 5 TT
2 15 MT	3 16 ed	4 15 eg	5 15 ed	6 13 ER	7 13 EF	7	8 12 ER	9 10 ff	10 10 fr	11 8 FW	12 8 FH	1 6 tt
2 16 mt	3 17 MM	4 16 MT	5 16 MM	6 14 eg	7 14 ed	8	8 13 eg	9 11 EF	10 11 ER	11 9 ff	12 9 fr	1 7 FW
2 17 RW	3 18 mm	4 17 mt	5 17 mm	6 15 MT	7 15 MM	9	8 14 MT	9 12 ed	10 12 eg	11 10 EF	12 10 ER	1 8 ff
2 18 rf	3 19 RH	4 18 RW	5 18 RH	6 16 mt	7 16 mm	10	8 15 mt	9 13 MM	10 13 MT	11 11 ed	12 11 eg	1 9 EF
2 19 TF	3 20 rr	4 19 rf	5 19 rr	6 17 RW	7 17 RH	11	8 16 RW	9 14 mm	10 14 mt	11 12 MM	12 12 MT	1 10 ed
2 20 td	3 21 TR	4 20 TF	5 20 TR	6 18 rf	7 18 rr	12	8 17 rf	9 15 RH	10 15 RW	11 13 mm	12 13 mt	1 11 MM
2 21 FM	3 22 tg	4 21 td	5 21 tg	6 19 TF	7 19 TR	13	8 18 TF	9 16 rr	10 16 rf	11 14 RH	12 14 RW	1 12 mm
2 22 fm	3 23 FT	4 22 FM	5 22 FT	6 20 td	7 20 tg	14	8 19 td	9 17 TR	10 17 TF	11 15 rr	12 15 rf	1 13 RH
2 23 EH	3 24 ft	4 23 fm	5 23 ft	6 21 FM	7 21 FT	15	8 20 FM	9 18 tg	10 18 td	11 16 TR	12 16 TF	1 14 rr
2 24 er	3 25 EW	4 24 EH	5 24 EW	6 22 fm	7 22 ft	16	8 21 fm	9 19 FT	10 19 FM	11 17 tg	12 17 td	1 15 TR
2 25 MR	3 26 ef	4 25 er	5 25 ef	6 23 EH	7 23 EW	17	8 22 EH	9 20 ft	10 20 fm	11 18 FT	12 18 FM	1 16 tg
2 26 mg	3 27 MF	4 26 MR	5 26 MF	6 24 er	7 24 ef	18	8 23 er	9 21 EW	10 21 EH	11 19 ft	12 19 fm	1 17 FT
2 27 RT	3 28 md	4 27 mg	5 27 md	6 25 MR	7 25 MF	19	8 24 MR	9 22 ef	10 22 er	11 20 EW	12 20 EH	1 18 ft
2 28 rt	3 29 RM	4 28 RT	5 28 RM	6 26 mg	7 26 md	20	8 25 mg	9 23 MF	10 23 MR	11 21 ef	12 21 er	1 19 EW
3 1 TW	3 30 rm	4 29 rt	5 29 rm	6 27 RT	7 27 RM	21	8 26 RT	9 24 md	10 24 mg	11 22 MF	12 22 MR	1 20 ef
3 2 tf	3 31 TH	4 30 TW	5 30 TH	6 28 rt	7 28 rm	22	8 27 rt	9 25 RM	10 25 RT	11 23 md	12 23 mg	1 21 MF
3 3 FF	4 1 tr	5 1 tf	5 31 tr	6 29 TW	7 29 TH	23	8 28 TW	9 26 rm	10 26 rt	11 24 RM	12 24 RT	1 22 md
3 4 fd	4 2 FR	5 2 FF	6 1 FR	6 30 tf	7 30 tr	24	8 29 tf	9 27 TH	10 27 TW	11 25 rm	12 25 rt	1 23 RM
3 5 EM	4 3 fg	5 3 fd	6 2 fg	7 1 FF	7 31 FR	25	8 30 FF	9 28 tr	10 28 tf	11 26 TH	12 26 TW	1 24 rm
3 6 em	4 4 ET	5 4 EM	6 3 ET	7 2 fd	8 1 fg	26	8 31 fd	9 29 FR	10 29 FF	11 27 tr	12 27 tf	1 25 TH
3 7 MH	4 5 et	5 5 em	6 4 et	7 3 EM	8 2 ET	27	9 1 EM	9 30 fg	10 30 fd	11 28 FR	12 28 FF	1 26 tr
3 8 mr	4 6 MW	5 6 MH	6 5 MW	7 4 em	8 3 et	28	9 2 em	10 1 ET	10 31 EM	11 29 fg	12 29 fd	1 27 FR
3 9 RR	4 7 mf	5 7 mr	6 6 mf	7 5 MH	8 4 MW	29	9 3 MH	10 2 et	11 1 em	11 30 ET	12 30 EM	1 28 fg
	4 8 RF	5 8 RR		7 6 mr	8 5 mf	30		10 3 MW		12 1 et		

1987 ft RAT

JAN RT	FEB rt	MAR TW	APR tf	MAY FF	JUN fd	JUN fd	DAY OF MON	JUL EM	AUG em	SEP MH	OCT mr	NOV RR	DEC rg
7 SPRING	7 WARM	8 CLEAR	9 SUMMER	11 GRAIN	13 HEAT	14 FALL		16 DEW	17 C DEW	17 WINTER	18 SNOW	17 CHILL	17 SPRING
16:50	10:59	16:03	9:37	13:59	0:22	10:04		13:33	5:17	7:07	0:49	11:32	22:38
1 29 ET	2 28 EM	3 29 fg	4 28 fd	5 27 FR	6 26 FF	7 26 FR	1	8 24 tf	9 23 tr	10 23 tf	11 21 TH	12 21 TW	1 19 rm
1 30 et	3 1 em	3 30 ET	4 29 EM	5 28 fg	6 27 fd	7 27 fg	2	8 25 FF	9 24 FR	10 24 FF	11 22 tr	12 22 tf	1 20 TH
1 31 MW	3 2 MH	3 31 et	4 30 em	5 29 ET	6 28 EM	7 28 ET	3	8 26 fd	9 25 fg	10 25 fd	11 23 FR	12 23 FF	1 21 tr
2 1 mf	3 3 mr	4 1 MW	5 1 MH	5 30 et	6 29 em	7 29 et	4	8 27 EM	9 26 ET	10 26 EM	11 24 fg	12 24 fd	1 22 FR
2 2 RF	3 4 RR	4 2 mf	5 2 mr	5 31 MW	6 30 MH	7 30 MW	5	8 28 em	9 27 et	10 27 em	11 25 ET	12 25 EM	1 23 fg
2 3 rd	3 5 rg	4 3 RF	5 3 RR	6 1 mf	7 1 mr	7 31 mf	6	8 29 MH	9 28 MW	10 28 MH	11 26 et	12 26 em	1 24 ET
2 4 TM	3 6 TT	4 4 rd	5 4 rg	6 2 RF	7 2 RR	8 1 RF	7	8 30 mr	9 29 mf	10 29 mr	11 27 MW	12 27 MH	1 25 et
2 5 tm	3 7 tt	4 5 TM	5 5 TT	6 3 rd	7 3 rg	8 2 rd	8	8 31 RR	9 30 RF	10 30 RR	11 28 mf	12 28 mr	1 26 MW
2 6 FH	3 8 FW	4 6 tm	5 6 tt	6 4 TM	7 4 TT	8 3 TM	9	9 1 rg	10 1 rd	10 31 rg	11 29 RF	12 29 RR	1 27 mf
2 7 fr	3 9 ff	4 7 FH	5 7 FW	6 5 tm	7 5 tt	8 4 tm	10	9 2 TT	10 2 TM	11 1 TT	11 30 rd	12 30 rg	1 28 RF
2 8 ER	3 10 EF	4 8 fr	5 8 ff	6 6 FH	7 6 FW	8 5 FH	11	9 3 tt	10 3 tm	11 2 tt	12 1 TM	12 31 TT	1 29 rd
2 9 eg	3 11 ed	4 9 ER	5 9 EF	6 7 fr	7 7 ff	8 6 fr	12	9 4 FW	10 4 FH	11 3 FW	12 2 tm	1 1 tt	1 30 TM
2 10 MT	3 12 MM	4 10 eg	5 10 ed	6 8 ER	7 8 EF	8 7 ER	13	9 5 ff	10 5 fr	11 4 ff	12 3 FH	1 2 FW	1 31 tm
2 11 mt	3 13 mm	4 11 MT	5 11 MM	6 9 eg	7 9 ed	8 8 eg	14	9 6 EF	10 6 ER	11 5 EF	12 4 fr	1 3 ff	2 1 FH
2 12 RW	3 14 RH	4 12 mt	5 12 mm	6 10 MT	7 10 MM	8 9 MT	15	9 7 ed	10 7 eg	11 6 ed	12 5 ER	1 4 EF	2 2 fr
2 13 rf	3 15 rr	4 13 RW	5 13 RH	6 11 mt	7 11 mm	8 10 mt	16	9 8 MM	10 8 MT	11 7 MM	12 6 eg	1 5 ed	2 3 ER
2 14 TF	3 16 TR	4 14 rf	5 14 rr	6 12 RW	7 12 RH	8 11 RW	17	9 9 mm	10 9 mt	11 8 mm	12 7 MT	1 6 MM	2 4 eg
2 15 td	3 17 tg	4 15 TF	5 15 TR	6 13 rf	7 13 rr	8 12 rf	18	9 10 RH	10 10 RW	11 9 RH	12 8 mt	1 7 mm	2 5 MT
2 16 FM	3 18 FT	4 16 td	5 16 tg	6 14 TF	7 14 TR	8 13 TF	19	9 11 rr	10 11 rf	11 10 rr	12 9 RW	1 8 RH	2 6 mt
2 17 fm	3 19 ft	4 17 FM	5 17 FT	6 15 td	7 15 tg	8 14 td	20	9 12 TR	10 12 TF	11 11 TR	12 10 rf	1 9 rr	2 7 RW
2 18 EH	3 20 EW	4 18 fm	5 18 ft	6 16 FM	7 16 FT	8 15 FM	21	9 13 tg	10 13 td	11 12 tg	12 11 TF	1 10 TR	2 8 rf
2 19 er	3 21 ef	4 19 EH	5 19 EW	6 17 fm	7 17 ft	8 16 fm	22	9 14 FT	10 14 FM	11 13 FT	12 12 td	1 11 tg	2 9 TF
2 20 MR	3 22 MF	4 20 er	5 20 ef	6 18 EH	7 18 EW	8 17 EH	23	9 15 ft	10 15 fm	11 14 ft	12 13 FM	1 12 FT	2 10 fd
2 21 mg	3 23 md	4 21 MR	5 21 MF	6 19 er	7 19 ef	8 18 er	24	9 16 EW	10 16 EH	11 15 EW	12 14 fm	1 13 ft	2 11 FM
2 22 RT	3 24 RM	4 22 mg	5 22 md	6 20 MR	7 20 MF	8 19 MR	25	9 17 ef	10 17 er	11 16 ef	12 15 EH	1 14 EW	2 12 fm
2 23 rt	3 25 rm	4 23 RT	5 23 RM	6 21 mg	7 21 md	8 20 mg	26	9 18 MF	10 18 MR	11 17 MF	12 16 er	1 15 ef	2 13 EH
2 24 TW	3 26 TH	4 24 rt	5 24 rm	6 22 RT	7 22 RM	8 21 RT	27	9 19 md	10 19 mg	11 18 md	12 17 MR	1 16 MF	2 14 er
2 25 tf	3 27 tr	4 25 TW	5 25 TH	6 23 rt	7 23 rm	8 22 rt	28	9 20 RM	10 20 RT	11 19 RM	12 18 mg	1 17 md	2 15 MR
2 26 FF	3 28 FR	4 26 tf	5 26 tr	6 24 TW	7 24 TH	8 23 TW	29	9 21 rm	10 21 rt	11 20 rm	12 19 RT	1 18 RM	2 16 mg
2 27 fd		4 27 FF		6 25 tf	7 25 tr		30	9 22 TH	10 22 TW		12 20 rt		

1988 EW DRAGON

JAN TT	FEB tt	MAR FW	APR ff	MAY EF	JUN ed	DAY OF MON	JUL MM	AUG mm	SEP RH	OCT rr	NOV TR	DEC tg
18 WARM	18 CLEAR	20 SUMMER	21 GRAIN	24 HEAT	25 FALL		27 DEW	28 C DEW	28 WINTER	29 SNOW	28 CHILL	28 SPRING
16:48	21:51	15:25	19:47	6:10	15:52		19:18	11:06	14:10	5:35	17:21	4:36
2 17 RT	3 18 RM	4 16 mg	5 16 md	6 14 MR	7 14 MF	1	8 12 er	9 11 ef	10 11 er	11 9 EW	12 9 EH	1 8 EW
2 18 rt	3 19 rm	4 17 RT	5 17 RM	6 15 mg	7 15 md	2	8 13 MR	9 12 MF	10 12 MR	11 10 ef	12 10 er	1 9 ef
2 19 TW	3 20 TH	4 18 rt	5 18 rm	6 16 RT	7 16 RM	3	8 14 mg	9 13 md	10 13 mg	11 11 MF	12 11 MR	1 10 MF
2 20 tf	3 21 tr	4 19 TW	5 19 TH	6 17 rt	7 17 rm	4	8 15 RT	9 14 RM	10 14 RT	11 12 md	12 12 mg	1 11 md
2 21 FF	3 22 FR	4 20 tf	5 20 tr	6 18 TW	7 18 TH	5	8 16 rt	9 15 rm	10 15 rt	11 13 RM	12 13 RT	1 12 RM
2 22 fd	3 23 fg	4 21 FF	5 21 FR	6 19 tf	7 19 tr	6	8 17 TW	9 16 TH	10 16 TW	11 14 rm	12 14 rt	1 13 rm
2 23 EM	3 24 ET	4 22 fd	5 22 fg	6 20 FF	7 20 FR	7	8 18 tf	9 17 tr	10 17 tf	11 15 TH	12 15 TW	1 14 TH
2 24 em	3 25 et	4 23 EM	5 23 ET	6 21 fd	7 21 fg	8	8 19 FF	9 18 FR	10 18 FF	11 16 tr	12 16 tf	1 15 tr
2 25 MH	3 26 MW	4 24 em	5 24 et	6 22 EM	7 22 ET	9	8 20 fd	9 19 fg	10 19 fd	11 17 FR	12 17 FF	1 16 FR
2 26 mr	3 27 mf	4 25 MH	5 25 MW	6 23 em	7 23 et	10	8 21 EM	9 20 ET	10 20 EM	11 18 fg	12 18 fd	1 17 fg
2 27 RR	3 28 RF	4 26 mr	5 26 mf	6 24 MH	7 24 MW	11	8 22 em	9 21 et	10 21 em	11 19 ET	12 19 EM	1 18 ET
2 28 rg	3 29 rd	4 27 RR	5 27 RF	6 25 mr	7 25 mf	12	8 23 MH	9 22 MW	10 22 MH	11 20 et	12 20 em	1 19 et
2 29 TT	3 30 TM	4 28 rg	5 28 rd	6 26 RR	7 26 RF	13	8 24 mr	9 23 mf	10 23 mr	11 21 MW	12 21 MH	1 20 MW
3 1 tt	3 31 tm	4 29 TT	5 29 TM	6 27 rg	7 27 rd	14	8 25 RR	9 24 RF	10 24 RR	11 22 mf	12 22 mr	1 21 mf
3 2 FW	4 1 FH	4 30 tt	5 30 tm	6 28 TT	7 28 TM	15	8 26 rg	9 25 rd	10 25 rg	11 23 RF	12 23 RR	1 22 RF
3 3 ff	4 2 fr	5 1 FW	5 31 FH	6 29 tt	7 29 tm	16	8 27 TT	9 26 TM	10 26 TT	11 24 rd	12 24 rg	1 23 rd
3 4 EF	4 3 ER	5 2 ff	6 1 fr	6 30 FW	7 30 FH	17	8 28 tt	9 27 tm	10 27 tt	11 25 TM	12 25 TT	1 24 TM
3 5 ed	4 4 eg	5 3 EF	6 2 ER	7 1 ff	7 31 fr	18	8 29 FW	9 28 FH	10 28 FW	11 26 tm	12 26 tt	1 25 tm
3 6 MM	4 5 MT	5 4 ed	6 3 eg	7 2 EF	8 1 ER	19	8 30 ff	9 29 fr	10 29 ff	11 27 FH	12 27 FW	1 26 FH
3 7 mm	4 6 mt	5 5 MM	6 4 MT	7 3 ed	8 2 eg	20	8 31 EF	9 30 ER	10 30 EF	11 28 fr	12 28 ff	1 27 fr
3 8 RH	4 7 RW	5 6 mm	6 5 mt	7 4 MM	8 3 MT	21	9 1 ed	10 1 eg	10 31 ed	11 29 ER	12 29 EF	1 28 ER
3 9 rr	4 8 rf	5 7 RH	6 6 RW	7 5 mm	8 4 mt	22	9 2 MM	10 2 MT	11 1 MM	11 30 eg	12 30 ed	1 29 eg
3 10 TR	4 9 TF	5 8 rr	6 7 rf	7 6 RH	8 5 RW	23	9 3 mm	10 3 mt	11 2 mm	12 1 MT	12 31 MM	1 30 MT
3 11 tg	4 10 td	5 9 TR	6 8 TF	7 7 rr	8 6 rf	24	9 4 RH	10 4 RW	11 3 RH	12 2 mt	1 1 mm	1 31 mt
3 12 FT	4 11 FM	5 10 tg	6 9 td	7 8 TR	8 7 TF	25	9 5 rr	10 5 rf	11 4 rr	12 3 RW	1 2 RH	2 1 RW
3 13 ft	4 12 fm	5 11 FT	6 10 FM	7 9 tg	8 8 td	26	9 6 TR	10 6 TF	11 5 TR	12 4 rf	1 3 rr	2 2 rf
3 14 EW	4 13 EH	5 12 ft	6 11 fm	7 10 FT	8 9 FM	27	9 7 tg	10 7 td	11 6 tg	12 5 TF	1 4 TR	2 3 TF
3 15 ef	4 14 er	5 13 EW	6 12 EH	7 11 ft	8 10 fm	28	9 8 FT	10 8 FM	11 7 FT	12 6 td	1 5 tg	2 4 td
3 16 MF	4 15 MR	5 14 ef	6 13 er	7 12 EW	8 11 EH	29	9 9 ft	10 9 fm	11 8 ft	12 7 FM	1 6 FT	2 5 FM
3 17 md		5 15 MF		7 13 ef		30	9 10 EW	10 10 EH		12 8 fm	1 7 ft	

1989 ef SNAKE

JAN FT	FEB ft	MAR EW	APR ef	MAY MF	JUN md	DAY OF MON	JUL RM	AUG rm	SEP TH	OCT tr	NOV FR	DEC fg
28 WARM	29 CLEAR		1 SUMMER	3 GRAIN	5 HEAT		7 FALL	9 DEW	9 C DEW	10 WINTER	10 SNOW	9 CHILL
22:36	3:39		21:13	1:35	11:58		21:41	1:07	15:49	19:59	11:24	23:12
2 6 fm	3 8 ft	4 6 FM	5 5 tg	6 4 td	7 3 TR	1	8 1 rf	8 31 rr	9 30 rf	10 29 RH	11 28 RW	12 28 RH
2 7 EH	3 9 EW	4 7 fm	5 6 FT	6 5 FM	7 4 tg	2	8 2 TF	9 1 TR	10 1 TF	10 30 rr	11 29 rf	12 29 rr
2 8 er	3 10 ef	4 8 EH	5 7 ft	6 6 fm	7 5 FT	3	8 3 td	9 2 tg	10 2 td	10 31 TR	11 30 TF	12 30 TR
2 9 MR	3 11 MF	4 9 er	5 8 EW	6 7 EH	7 6 ft	4	8 4 FM	9 3 FT	10 3 FM	11 1 tg	12 1 td	12 31 tg
2 10 mg	3 12 md	4 10 MR	5 9 ef	6 8 er	7 7 EW	5	8 5 fm	9 4 ft	10 4 fm	11 2 FT	12 2 FM	1 1 FT
2 11 RT	3 13 RM	4 11 mg	5 10 MF	6 9 MR	7 8 ef	6	8 6 EH	9 5 EW	10 5 EH	11 3 ft	12 3 fm	1 2 ft
2 12 rt	3 14 rm	4 12 RT	5 11 md	6 10 mg	7 9 MF	7	8 7 er	9 6 ef	10 6 er	11 4 EW	12 4 EH	1 3 EW
2 13 TW	3 15 TH	4 13 rt	5 12 RM	6 11 RT	7 10 md	8	8 8 MR	9 7 MF	10 7 MR	11 5 ef	12 5 er	1 4 ef
2 14 tf	3 16 tr	4 14 TW	5 13 rm	6 12 rt	7 11 RM	9	8 9 mg	9 8 md	10 8 mg	11 6 MF	12 6 MR	1 5 MF
2 15 FF	3 17 FR	4 15 tf	5 14 TH	6 13 TW	7 12 rm	10	8 10 RT	9 9 RM	10 9 RT	11 7 md	12 7 mg	1 6 md
2 16 fd	3 18 fg	4 16 FF	5 15 tr	6 14 tf	7 13 TH	11	8 11 rt	9 10 rm	10 10 rt	11 8 RM	12 8 RT	1 7 RM
2 17 EM	3 19 ET	4 17 fd	5 16 FR	6 15 FF	7 14 tr	12	8 12 TW	9 11 TH	10 11 TW	11 9 rm	12 9 rt	1 8 rm
2 18 em	3 20 et	4 18 EM	5 17 fg	6 16 fd	7 15 FR	13	8 13 tf	9 12 tr	10 12 tf	11 10 TH	12 10 TW	1 9 TH
2 19 MH	3 21 MW	4 19 em	5 18 ET	6 17 EM	7 16 fg	14	8 14 FF	9 13 FR	10 13 FF	11 11 tr	12 11 tf	1 10 tr
2 20 mr	3 22 mf	4 20 MH	5 19 et	6 18 em	7 17 ET	15	8 15 fd	9 14 fg	10 14 fd	11 12 FR	12 12 FF	1 11 FR
2 21 RR	3 23 RF	4 21 mr	5 20 MW	6 19 MH	7 18 et	16	8 16 EM	9 15 ET	10 15 EM	11 13 fg	12 13 fd	1 12 fg
2 22 rg	3 24 rd	4 22 RR	5 21 mf	6 20 mr	7 19 MW	17	8 17 em	9 16 et	10 16 em	11 14 ET	12 14 EM	1 13 ET
2 23 TT	3 25 TM	4 23 rg	5 22 RF	6 21 RR	7 20 mf	18	8 18 MH	9 17 MW	10 17 MH	11 15 et	12 15 em	1 14 et
2 24 tt	3 26 tm	4 24 TT	5 23 rd	6 22 rg	7 21 RF	19	8 19 mr	9 18 mf	10 18 mr	11 16 MW	12 16 MH	1 15 MW
2 25 FW	3 27 FH	4 25 tt	5 24 TM	6 23 TT	7 22 rd	20	8 20 RR	9 19 RF	10 19 RR	11 17 mf	12 17 mr	1 16 mf
2 26 ff	3 28 fr	4 26 FW	5 25 tm	6 24 tt	7 23 TM	21	8 21 rg	9 20 rd	10 20 rg	11 18 RF	12 18 RR	1 17 RF
2 27 EF	3 29 ER	4 27 ff	5 26 FH	6 25 FW	7 24 tm	22	8 22 TT	9 21 TM	10 21 TT	11 19 rd	12 19 rg	1 18 rd
2 28 ed	3 30 eg	4 28 EF	5 27 fr	6 26 ff	7 25 FH	23	8 23 tt	9 22 tm	10 22 tt	11 20 TM	12 20 TT	1 19 TM
3 1 MM	3 31 MT	4 29 ed	5 28 ER	6 27 EF	7 26 fr	24	8 24 FW	9 23 FH	10 23 FW	11 21 tm	12 21 tt	1 20 tm
3 2 mm	4 1 mt	4 30 MM	5 29 eg	6 28 ed	7 27 ER	25	8 25 ff	9 24 fr	10 24 ff	11 22 FH	12 22 FW	1 21 FH
3 3 RH	4 2 RW	5 1 mm	5 30 MT	6 29 MM	7 28 eg	26	8 26 EF	9 25 ER	10 25 EF	11 23 fr	12 23 ff	1 22 fr
3 4 rr	4 3 rf	5 2 RH	5 31 mt	6 30 mm	7 29 MT	27	8 27 ed	9 26 eg	10 26 ed	11 24 ER	12 24 EF	1 23 ER
3 5 TR	4 4 TF	5 3 rr	6 1 RW	7 1 RH	7 30 mt	28	8 28 MM	9 27 MT	10 27 MM	11 25 eg	12 25 ed	1 24 eg
3 6 tg	4 5 td	5 4 TR	6 2 rf	7 2 rr	7 31 RW	29	8 29 mm	9 28 mt	10 28 mm	11 26 MT	12 26 MM	1 25 MT
3 7 FT			6 3 TF			30	8 30 RH	9 29 RW		11 27 mt	12 27 mm	1 26 mt

1990 MF HORSE

JAN ET	FEB et	MAR MW	APR mf	MAY RF	MAY RF	JUN rd	DAY OF MON	JUL TM	AUG fm	SEP FH	OCT fr	NOV ER	DEC eg
9 SPRING	10 WARM	10 CLEAR	12 SUMMER	14 GRAIN	15 HEAT	18 FALL		20 DEW	20 C DEW	22 WINTER	21 SNOW	21 CHILL	20 SPRING
10:15	4:25	9:28	2:53	7:24	17:47	3:30		6:14	21:38	1:49	17:13	5:01	16:04
1 27 RW	2 25 mm	3 27 mt	4 25 MM	5 24 eg	6 23 ed	7 22 ER	1	8 20 ff	9 19 fr	10 18 FW	11 17 FH	12 17 FW	1 16 FH
1 28 rf	2 26 RH	3 28 RW	4 26 mm	5 25 MT	6 24 MM	7 23 eg	2	8 21 EF	9 20 ER	10 19 ff	11 18 fr	12 18 ff	1 17 fr
1 29 TF	2 27 rr	3 29 rf	4 27 RH	5 26 mt	6 25 mm	7 24 MT	3	8 22 ed	9 21 eg	10 20 EF	11 19 ER	12 19 EF	1 18 ER
1 30 td	2 28 TR	3 30 TF	4 28 rr	5 27 RW	6 26 RH	7 25 mt	4	8 23 MM	9 22 MT	10 21 ed	11 20 eg	12 20 ed	1 19 eg
1 31 FM	3 1 tg	3 31 td	4 29 TR	5 28 rf	6 27 rr	7 26 RW	5	8 24 mm	9 23 mt	10 22 MM	11 21 MT	12 21 MM	1 20 MT
2 1 fm	3 2 FT	4 1 FM	4 30 tg	5 29 TF	6 28 TR	7 27 rf	6	8 25 RH	9 24 RW	10 23 mm	11 22 mt	12 22 mm	1 21 mt
2 2 EH	3 3 ft	4 2 fm	5 1 FT	5 30 td	6 29 tg	7 28 TF	7	8 26 rr	9 25 rf	10 24 RH	11 23 RW	12 23 RH	1 22 RW
2 3 er	3 4 EW	4 3 EH	5 2 ft	5 31 FM	6 30 FT	7 29 td	8	8 27 TR	9 26 TF	10 25 rr	11 24 rf	12 24 rr	1 23 rf
2 4 MR	3 5 ef	4 4 er	5 3 EW	6 1 fm	7 1 ft	7 30 FM	9	8 28 tg	9 27 td	10 26 TR	11 25 TF	12 25 TR	1 24 TF
2 5 mg	3 6 MF	4 5 MR	5 4 ef	6 2 EH	7 2 EW	7 31 fm	10	8 29 FT	9 28 FM	10 27 tg	11 26 td	12 26 tg	1 25 td
2 6 RT	3 7 md	4 6 mg	5 5 MF	6 3 er	7 3 ef	8 1 EH	11	8 30 ft	9 29 fm	10 28 FT	11 27 FM	12 27 FT	1 26 FM
2 7 rt	3 8 RM	4 7 RT	5 6 md	6 4 MR	7 4 MF	8 2 er	12	8 31 EW	9 30 EH	10 29 ft	11 28 fm	12 28 ft	1 27 fm
2 8 TW	3 9 rm	4 8 rt	5 7 RM	6 5 mg	7 5 md	8 3 MR	13	9 1 ef	10 1 er	10 30 EW	11 29 EH	12 29 EW	1 28 EH
2 9 tf	3 10 TH	4 9 TW	5 8 rm	6 6 RT	7 6 RM	8 4 mg	14	9 2 MF	10 2 MR	10 31 ef	11 30 er	12 30 ef	1 29 er
2 10 FF	3 11 tr	4 10 tf	5 9 TH	6 7 rt	7 7 rm	8 5 RT	15	9 3 md	10 3 mg	11 1 MF	12 1 MR	12 31 MF	1 30 MR
2 11 fd	3 12 FR	4 11 FF	5 10 tr	6 8 TW	7 8 TH	8 6 rt	16	9 4 RM	10 4 RT	11 2 md	12 2 mg	1 1 md	1 31 mg
2 12 EM	3 13 fg	4 12 fd	5 11 FR	6 9 tf	7 9 tr	8 7 TW	17	9 5 rm	10 5 rt	11 3 RM	12 3 RT	1 2 RM	2 1 RT
2 13 em	3 14 ET	4 13 EM	5 12 fg	6 10 FF	7 10 FR	8 8 tf	18	9 6 TH	10 6 TW	11 4 rm	12 4 rt	1 3 rm	2 2 rt
2 14 MH	3 15 et	4 14 em	5 13 ET	6 11 fd	7 11 fg	8 9 FF	19	9 7 tr	10 7 tf	11 5 TH	12 5 TW	1 4 TH	2 3 TW
2 15 mr	3 16 MW	4 15 MH	5 14 et	6 12 EM	7 12 ET	8 10 fd	20	9 8 FR	10 8 FF	11 6 tr	12 6 tf	1 5 tr	2 4 tf
2 16 RR	3 17 mf	4 16 mr	5 15 MW	6 13 em	7 13 et	8 11 EM	21	9 9 fg	10 9 fd	11 7 FR	12 7 FF	1 6 FR	2 5 FF
2 17 rg	3 18 RF	4 17 RR	5 16 mf	6 14 MH	7 14 MW	8 12 em	22	9 10 ET	10 10 EM	11 8 fg	12 8 fd	1 7 fg	2 6 fd
2 18 TT	3 19 rd	4 18 rg	5 17 RF	6 15 mr	7 15 mf	8 13 MH	23	9 11 et	10 11 em	11 9 ET	12 9 EM	1 8 ET	2 7 EM
2 19 tt	3 20 TM	4 19 TT	5 18 rd	6 16 RR	7 16 RF	8 14 mr	24	9 12 MW	10 12 MH	11 10 et	12 10 em	1 9 et	2 8 em
2 20 FW	3 21 tm	4 20 tt	5 19 TM	6 17 rg	7 17 rd	8 15 RR	25	9 13 mf	10 13 mr	11 11 MW	12 11 MH	1 10 MW	2 9 MH
2 21 ff	3 22 FH	4 21 FW	5 20 tm	6 18 TT	7 18 TM	8 16 rg	26	9 14 RF	10 14 RR	11 12 mf	12 12 mr	1 11 mf	2 10 mr
2 22 EF	3 23 fr	4 22 ff	5 21 FH	6 19 tt	7 19 tm	8 17 TT	27	9 15 rd	10 15 rg	11 13 RF	12 13 RR	1 12 RF	2 11 RR
2 23 ed	3 24 ER	4 23 EF	5 22 fr	6 20 FW	7 20 FH	8 18 tt	28	9 16 TM	10 16 TT	11 14 rd	12 14 rg	1 13 rd	2 12 rg
2 24 MM	3 25 eg	4 24 ed	5 23 ER	6 21 ff	7 21 fr	8 19 FW	29	9 17 tm	10 17 tt	11 15 TM	12 15 TT	1 14 TM	2 13 TT
	3 26 MT			6 22 EF			30	9 18 FH		11 16 tm	12 16 tt	1 15 tm	2 14 tt

1991 md RAM

JAN MT	FEB mt	MAR RW	APR rf	MAY TF	JUN td	DAY OF MON	JUL FM	AUG fm	SEP EH	OCT er	NOV MR	DEC mg
20 WARM	21 CLEAR	22 SUMMER	24 GRAIN	26 HEAT	28 FALL			1 DEW	2 C DEW	3 WINTER	3 SNOW	2 CHILL
10:14	15:17	8:51	13:14	23:37	9:20			12:04	3:28	7:39	0:08	10:12
2 15 FW	3 16 tm	4 15 tt	5 14 TM	6 12 rg	7 12 rd	1	8 10 RR	9 8 mf	10 8 mr	11 6 MW	12 6 MH	1 5 MW
2 16 ff	3 17 FH	4 16 FW	5 15 tm	6 13 TT	7 13 TM	2	8 11 rg	9 9 RF	10 9 RR	11 7 mf	12 7 mr	1 6 mf
2 17 EF	3 18 fr	4 17 ff	5 16 FH	6 14 tt	7 14 tm	3	8 12 TT	9 10 rd	10 10 rg	11 8 RF	12 8 RR	1 7 RF
2 18 ed	3 19 ER	4 18 EF	5 17 fr	6 15 FW	7 15 FH	4	8 13 tt	9 11 TM	10 11 TT	11 9 rd	12 9 rg	1 8 rd
2 19 MM	3 20 eg	4 19 ed	5 18 ER	6 16 ff	7 16 fr	5	8 14 FW	9 12 tm	10 12 tt	11 10 TM	12 10 TT	1 9 TM
2 20 mm	3 21 MT	4 20 MM	5 19 eg	6 17 EF	7 17 ER	6	8 15 ff	9 13 FH	10 13 FW	11 11 tm	12 11 tt	1 10 tm
2 21 RH	3 22 mt	4 21 mm	5 20 MT	6 18 ed	7 18 eg	7	8 16 EF	9 14 fr	10 14 ff	11 12 FH	12 12 FW	1 11 FH
2 22 rr	3 23 RW	4 22 RH	5 21 mt	6 19 MM	7 19 MT	8	8 17 ed	9 15 ER	10 15 EF	11 13 fr	12 13 ff	1 12 fr
2 23 TR	3 24 rf	4 23 rr	5 22 RW	6 20 mm	7 20 mt	9	8 18 MM	9 16 eg	10 16 ed	11 14 ER	12 14 EF	1 13 ER
2 24 tg	3 25 TF	4 24 TR	5 23 rf	6 21 RH	7 21 RW	10	8 19 mm	9 17 MT	10 17 MM	11 15 eg	12 15 ed	1 14 eg
2 25 FT	3 26 td	4 25 tg	5 24 TF	6 22 rr	7 22 rf	11	8 20 RH	9 18 mt	10 18 mm	11 16 MT	12 16 MM	1 15 MT
2 26 ft	3 27 FM	4 26 FT	5 25 td	6 23 TR	7 23 TF	12	8 21 rr	9 19 RW	10 19 RH	11 17 mt	12 17 mm	1 16 mt
2 27 EW	3 28 fm	4 27 ft	5 26 FM	6 24 tg	7 24 td	13	8 22 TR	9 20 rf	10 20 rr	11 18 RW	12 18 RH	1 17 RW
2 28 ef	3 29 EH	4 28 EW	5 27 fm	6 25 FT	7 25 FM	14	8 23 tg	9 21 TF	10 21 TR	11 19 rf	12 19 rr	1 18 rf
3 1 MF	3 30 er	4 29 ef	5 28 EH	6 26 ft	7 26 fm	15	8 24 FT	9 22 td	10 22 tg	11 20 TF	12 20 TR	1 19 TF
3 2 md	3 31 MR	4 30 MF	5 29 er	6 27 EW	7 27 EH	16	8 25 ft	9 23 FM	10 23 FT	11 21 td	12 21 tg	1 20 td
3 3 RM	4 1 mg	5 1 md	5 30 MR	6 28 ef	7 28 er	17	8 26 EW	9 24 fm	10 24 ft	11 22 FM	12 22 FT	1 21 FM
3 4 rm	4 2 RT	5 2 RM	5 31 mg	6 29 MF	7 29 MR	18	8 27 ef	9 25 EH	10 25 EW	11 23 fm	12 23 ft	1 22 fm
3 5 TH	4 3 rt	5 3 rm	6 1 RT	6 30 md	7 30 mg	19	8 28 MF	9 26 er	10 26 ef	11 24 EH	12 24 EW	1 23 EH
3 6 tr	4 4 TW	5 4 TH	6 2 rt	7 1 RM	7 31 RT	20	8 29 md	9 27 MR	10 27 MF	11 25 er	12 25 ef	1 24 er
3 7 FR	4 5 tf	5 5 tr	6 3 TW	7 2 rm	8 1 rt	21	8 30 RM	9 28 mg	10 28 md	11 26 MR	12 26 MF	1 25 MR
3 8 fg	4 6 FF	5 6 FR	6 4 tf	7 3 TH	8 2 TW	22	8 31 rm	9 29 RT	10 29 RM	11 27 mg	12 27 md	1 26 mg
3 9 ET	4 7 fd	5 7 fg	6 5 FF	7 4 tr	8 3 tf	23	9 1 TH	9 30 rt	10 30 rm	11 28 RT	12 28 RM	1 27 RT
3 10 et	4 8 EM	5 8 ET	6 6 fd	7 5 FR	8 4 FF	24	9 2 tr	10 1 TW	10 31 TH	11 29 rt	12 29 rm	1 28 rt
3 11 MW	4 9 em	5 9 et	6 7 EM	7 6 fg	8 5 fd	25	9 3 FR	10 2 tf	11 1 tr	11 30 TW	12 30 TH	1 29 TW
3 12 mf	4 10 MH	5 10 MW	6 8 em	7 7 ET	8 6 EM	26	9 4 fg	10 3 FF	11 2 FR	12 1 tf	12 31 tr	1 30 tf
3 13 RF	4 11 mr	5 11 mf	6 9 MH	7 8 et	8 7 em	27	9 5 ET	10 4 fd	11 3 fg	12 2 FF	1 1 FR	1 31 FF
3 14 rd	4 12 RR	5 12 RF	6 10 mr	7 9 MW	8 8 MH	28	9 6 et	10 5 EM	11 4 ET	12 3 fd	1 2 fg	2 1 fd
3 15 TM	4 13 rg	5 13 rd	6 11 RR	7 10 mf	8 9 mr	29	9 7 MW	10 6 em	11 5 et	12 4 EM	1 3 ET	2 2 EM
	4 14 TT			7 11 RF		30		10 7 MH		12 5 em	1 4 et	2 3 em

1992 RM MONKEY

JAN RT	FEB rt	MAR TW	APR tf	MAY FF	JUN fd	DAY OF MON	JUL EM	AUG em	SEP MH	OCT mr	NOV RR	DEC rg
1 SPRING	2 WARM	2 CLEAR	3 SUMMER	5 GRAIN	8 HEAT		9 FALL	11 DEW	13 C DEW	13 WINTER	14 SNOW	13 CHILL
21:54	16:04	20:57	14:41	18:52	5:26		15:09	17:53	9:17	13:28	5:58	16:01
2 4 MH	3 4 et	4 3 em	5 3 et	6 1 EM	6 30 fg	1	7 30 fd	8 28 FR	9 26 tf	10 26 tr	11 24 TW	12 24 TH
2 5 mr	3 5 MW	4 4 MH	5 4 MW	6 2 em	7 1 ET	2	7 31 EM	8 29 fg	9 27 FF	10 27 FR	11 25 tf	12 25 tr
2 6 RR	3 6 mf	4 5 mr	5 5 mf	6 3 MH	7 2 et	3	8 1 em	8 30 ET	9 28 fd	10 28 fg	11 26 FF	12 26 FR
2 7 rg	3 7 RF	4 6 RR	5 6 RF	6 4 mr	7 3 MW	4	8 2 MH	8 31 et	9 29 EM	10 29 ET	11 27 fd	12 27 fg
2 8 TT	3 8 rd	4 7 rg	5 7 rd	6 5 RR	7 4 mf	5	8 3 mr	9 1 MW	9 30 em	10 30 et	11 28 EM	12 28 ET
2 9 tt	3 9 TM	4 8 TT	5 8 TM	6 6 rg	7 5 RF	6	8 4 RR	9 2 mf	10 1 MH	10 31 MW	11 29 em	12 29 et
2 10 FW	3 10 tm	4 9 tt	5 9 tm	6 7 TT	7 6 rd	7	8 5 rg	9 3 RF	10 2 mr	11 1 mf	11 30 MH	12 30 MW
2 11 ff	3 11 FH	4 10 FW	5 10 FH	6 8 tt	7 7 TM	8	8 6 TT	9 4 rd	10 3 RR	11 2 RF	12 1 mr	12 31 mf
2 12 EF	3 12 fr	4 11 ff	5 11 fr	6 9 FW	7 8 tm	9	8 7 tt	9 5 TM	10 4 rg	11 3 rd	12 2 RR	1 1 RF
2 13 ed	3 13 ER	4 12 EF	5 12 ER	6 10 ff	7 9 FH	10	8 8 FW	9 6 tm	10 5 TT	11 4 TM	12 3 rg	1 2 rd
2 14 MM	3 14 eg	4 13 ed	5 13 eg	6 11 EF	7 10 fr	11	8 9 ff	9 7 FH	10 6 tt	11 5 tm	12 4 TT	1 3 TM
2 15 mm	3 15 MT	4 14 MM	5 14 MT	6 12 ed	7 11 ER	12	8 10 EF	9 8 fr	10 7 FW	11 6 FH	12 5 tt	1 4 tm
2 16 RH	3 16 mt	4 15 mm	5 15 mt	6 13 MM	7 12 eg	13	8 11 ed	9 9 ER	10 8 ff	11 7 fr	12 6 FW	1 5 FH
2 17 rr	3 17 RW	4 16 RH	5 16 RW	6 14 mm	7 13 MT	14	8 12 MM	9 10 eg	10 9 EF	11 8 ER	12 7 ff	1 6 fr
2 18 TR	3 18 rf	4 17 rr	5 17 rf	6 15 RH	7 14 mt	15	8 13 mm	9 11 MT	10 10 ed	11 9 eg	12 8 EF	1 7 ER
2 19 tg	3 19 TF	4 18 TR	5 18 TF	6 16 rr	7 15 RW	16	8 14 RH	9 12 mt	10 11 MM	11 10 MT	12 9 ed	1 8 eg
2 20 FT	3 20 td	4 19 tg	5 19 td	6 17 TR	7 16 rf	17	8 15 rr	9 13 RW	10 12 mm	11 11 mt	12 10 MM	1 9 MT
2 21 ft	3 21 FM	4 20 FT	5 20 FM	6 18 tg	7 17 TF	18	8 16 TR	9 14 rf	10 13 RH	11 12 RW	12 11 mm	1 10 mt
2 22 EW	3 22 fm	4 21 ft	5 21 fm	6 19 FT	7 18 td	19	8 17 tg	9 15 TF	10 14 rr	11 13 rf	12 12 RH	1 11 RW
2 23 ef	3 23 EH	4 22 EW	5 22 EH	6 20 ft	7 19 FM	20	8 18 FT	9 16 td	10 15 TR	11 14 TF	12 13 rr	1 12 rf
2 24 MF	3 24 er	4 23 ef	5 23 er	6 21 EW	7 20 fm	21	8 19 ft	9 17 FM	10 16 tg	11 15 td	12 14 TR	1 13 TF
2 25 md	3 25 MR	4 24 MF	5 24 MR	6 22 ef	7 21 EH	22	8 20 EW	9 18 fm	10 17 FT	11 16 FM	12 15 tg	1 14 td
2 26 RM	3 26 mg	4 25 md	5 25 mg	6 23 MF	7 22 er	23	8 21 ef	9 19 EH	10 18 ft	11 17 fm	12 16 FT	1 15 FM
2 27 rm	3 27 RT	4 26 RM	5 26 RT	6 24 md	7 23 MR	24	8 22 MF	9 20 er	10 19 EW	11 18 EH	12 17 ft	1 16 fm
2 28 TH	3 28 rt	4 27 rm	5 27 rt	6 25 RM	7 24 mg	25	8 23 md	9 21 MR	10 20 ef	11 19 er	12 18 EW	1 17 EH
2 29 tr	3 29 TW	4 28 TH	5 28 TW	6 26 rm	7 25 RT	26	8 24 RM	9 22 mg	10 21 MF	11 20 MR	12 19 ef	1 18 er
3 1 FR	3 30 tf	4 29 tr	5 29 tf	6 27 TH	7 26 rt	27	8 25 rm	9 23 RT	10 22 md	11 21 mg	12 20 MF	1 19 MR
3 2 fg	3 31 FF	4 30 FR	5 30 FF	6 28 tr	7 27 TW	28	8 26 TH	9 24 rt	10 23 RM	11 22 RT	12 21 md	1 20 mg
3 3 ET	4 1 fd	5 1 fg	5 31 fd	6 29 FR	7 28 tf	29	8 27 tr	9 25 TW	10 24 rm	11 23 rt	12 22 RM	1 21 RT
	4 2 EM	5 2 ET			7 29 FF	30			10 25 TH		12 23 rm	1 22 rt

1993 rm ROOSTER

JAN TT	FEB tt	MAR FW	MAR FW	APR ff	MAY EF	JUN ed	DAY OF MON	JUL MM	AUG mm	SEP RH	OCT rr	NOV TR	DEC tg
13 SPRING	13 WARM	14 CLEAR	14 SUMMER	17 GRAIN	18 HEAT	20 FALL		22 DEW	23 C DEW	24 WINTER	24 SNOW	24 CHILL	24 SPRING
3:43	21:53	2:56	20:30	23:40	11:15	21:10		0:20	15:07	19:17	11:47	21:57	9:33
1 23 TW	2 21 rm	3 23 rt	4 22 rm	5 21 RT	6 20 RM	7 19 mg	1	8 18 md	9 16 MR	10 15 ef	11 14 er	12 13 EW	1 12 EH
1 24 tf	2 22 TH	3 24 TW	4 23 TH	5 22 rt	6 21 rm	7 20 RT	2	8 19 RM	9 17 mg	10 16 MF	11 15 MR	12 14 ef	1 13 er
1 25 FF	2 23 tr	3 25 tf	4 24 tr	5 23 TW	6 22 TH	7 21 rt	3	8 20 rm	9 18 RT	10 17 md	11 16 mg	12 15 MF	1 14 MR
1 26 fd	2 24 FR	3 26 FF	4 25 FR	5 24 tf	6 23 tr	7 22 TW	4	8 21 TH	9 19 rt	10 18 RM	11 17 RT	12 16 md	1 15 mg
1 27 EM	2 25 fg	3 27 fd	4 26 fg	5 25 FF	6 24 FR	7 23 tf	5	8 22 tr	9 20 TW	10 19 rm	11 18 rt	12 17 RM	1 16 RT
1 28 em	2 26 ET	3 28 EM	4 27 ET	5 26 fd	6 25 fg	7 24 FF	6	8 23 FR	9 21 tf	10 20 TH	11 19 TW	12 18 rm	1 17 rt
1 29 MH	2 27 et	3 29 em	4 28 et	5 27 EM	6 26 ET	7 25 fd	7	8 24 fg	9 22 FF	10 21 tr	11 20 tf	12 19 TH	1 18 TW
1 30 mr	2 28 MW	3 30 MH	4 29 MW	5 28 em	6 27 et	7 26 EM	8	8 25 ET	9 23 fd	10 22 FR	11 21 FF	12 20 tr	1 19 tf
1 31 RR	3 1 mf	3 31 mr	4 30 mf	5 29 MH	6 28 MW	7 27 em	9	8 26 et	9 24 EM	10 23 fg	11 22 fd	12 21 FR	1 20 FF
2 1 rg	3 2 RF	4 1 RR	5 1 RF	5 30 mr	6 29 mf	7 28 MH	10	8 27 MW	9 25 em	10 24 ET	11 23 EM	12 22 fg	1 21 fd
2 2 TT	3 3 rd	4 2 rg	5 2 rd	5 31 RR	6 30 RF	7 29 mr	11	8 28 mf	9 26 MH	10 25 et	11 24 em	12 23 ET	1 22 EM
2 3 tt	3 4 TM	4 3 TT	5 3 TM	6 1 rg	7 1 rd	7 30 RR	12	8 29 RF	9 27 mr	10 26 MW	11 25 MH	12 24 et	1 23 em
2 4 FW	3 5 tm	4 4 tt	5 4 tm	6 2 TT	7 2 TM	7 31 rg	13	8 30 rd	9 28 RR	10 27 mf	11 26 mr	12 25 MW	1 24 MH
2 5 ff	3 6 FH	4 5 FW	5 5 FH	6 3 tt	7 3 tm	8 1 TT	14	8 31 TM	9 29 rg	10 28 RF	11 27 RR	12 26 mf	1 25 mr
2 6 EF	3 7 fr	4 6 ff	5 6 fr	6 4 FW	7 4 FH	8 2 tt	15	9 1 tm	9 30 TT	10 29 rd	11 28 rg	12 27 RF	1 26 RR
2 7 ed	3 8 ER	4 7 EF	5 7 ER	6 5 ff	7 5 fr	8 3 FW	16	9 2 FH	10 1 tt	10 30 TM	11 29 TT	12 28 rd	1 27 rg
2 8 MM	3 9 eg	4 8 ed	5 8 eg	6 6 EF	7 6 ER	8 4 ff	17	9 3 fr	10 2 FW	10 31 tm	11 30 tt	12 29 TM	1 28 TT
2 9 mm	3 10 MT	4 9 MM	5 9 MT	6 7 ed	7 7 eg	8 5 EF	18	9 4 ER	10 3 ff	11 1 FH	12 1 FW	12 30 tm	1 29 tt
2 10 RH	3 11 mt	4 10 mm	5 10 mt	6 8 MM	7 8 MT	8 6 ed	19	9 5 eg	10 4 EF	11 2 fr	12 2 ff	12 31 FH	1 30 FW
2 11 rr	3 12 RW	4 11 RH	5 11 RW	6 9 mm	7 9 mt	8 7 MM	20	9 6 MT	10 5 ed	11 3 ER	12 3 EF	1 1 fr	1 31 ff
2 12 TR	3 13 rf	4 12 rr	5 12 rf	6 10 RH	7 10 RW	8 8 mm	21	9 7 mt	10 6 MM	11 4 eg	12 4 ed	1 2 ER	2 1 EF
2 13 tg	3 14 TF	4 13 TR	5 13 TF	6 11 rr	7 11 rf	8 9 RH	22	9 8 RW	10 7 mm	11 5 MT	12 5 MM	1 3 eg	2 2 ed
2 14 FT	3 15 td	4 14 tg	5 14 td	6 12 TR	7 12 TF	8 10 rr	23	9 9 rf	10 8 RH	11 6 mt	12 6 mm	1 4 MT	2 3 MM
2 15 ft	3 16 FM	4 15 FT	5 15 FM	6 13 tg	7 13 td	8 11 TR	24	9 10 TF	10 9 rr	11 7 RW	12 7 RH	1 5 mt	2 4 mm
2 16 EW	3 17 fm	4 16 ft	5 16 fm	6 14 FT	7 14 FM	8 12 tg	25	9 11 td	10 10 TR	11 8 rf	12 8 rr	1 6 RW	2 5 RH
2 17 ef	3 18 EH	4 17 EW	5 17 EH	6 15 ft	7 15 fm	8 13 FT	26	9 12 FM	10 11 tg	11 9 TF	12 9 TR	1 7 rf	2 6 rr
2 18 MF	3 19 er	4 18 ef	5 18 er	6 16 EW	7 16 EH	8 14 ft	27	9 13 fm	10 12 FT	11 10 td	12 10 tg	1 8 TF	2 7 TR
2 19 md	3 20 MR	4 19 MF	5 19 MR	6 17 ef	7 17 er	8 15 EW	28	9 14 EH	10 13 ft	11 11 FM	12 11 FT	1 9 td	2 8 tg
2 20 RM	3 21 mg	4 20 md	5 20 mg	6 18 MF	7 18 MR	8 16 ef	29	9 15 er	10 14 EW	11 12 fm	12 12 ft	1 10 FM	2 9 FT
	3 22 RT	4 21 RM		6 19 md		8 17 MF	30			11 13 EH		1 11 fm	

1994 TH DOG

JAN FT	FEB ft	MAR EW	APR ef	MAY MF	JUN md	DAY OF MON	JUL RM	AUG rm	SEP TH	OCT tr	NOV FR	DEC fg
25 WARM	25 CLEAR	26 SUMMER	27 GRAIN	29 HEAT			2 FALL	3 DEW	4 C DEW	6 WINTER	5 SNOW	6 CHILL
3:43	8:46	2:20	6:43	16:55			2:50	5:34	22:00	1:06	17:36	3:42
2 10 ft	3 12 fm	4 11 ft	5 11 fm	6 9 FT	7 9 FM	1	8 7 tg	9 6 td	10 5 FR	11 3 rf	12 3 rr	1 1 RW
2 11 EW	3 13 EH	4 12 EW	5 12 EH	6 10 ft	7 10 fm	2	8 8 FT	9 7 FM	10 6 tg	11 4 TF	12 4 FR	1 2 rf
2 12 ef	3 14 er	4 13 ef	5 13 er	6 11 EW	7 11 EH	3	8 9 ft	9 8 fm	10 7 FT	11 5 td	12 5 tg	1 3 TF
2 13 MF	3 15 MR	4 14 MF	5 14 MR	6 12 ef	7 12 er	4	8 10 EW	9 9 EH	10 8 ft	11 6 FM	12 6 FT	1 4 td
2 14 md	3 16 mg	4 15 md	5 15 mg	6 13 MF	7 13 MR	5	8 11 ef	9 10 er	10 9 EW	11 7 fm	12 7 ft	1 5 FM
2 15 RM	3 17 RT	4 16 RM	5 16 RT	6 14 md	7 14 mg	6	8 12 MF	9 11 MR	10 10 ef	11 8 EH	12 8 EW	1 6 fm
2 16 rm	3 18 rt	4 17 rm	5 17 rt	6 15 RM	7 15 RT	7	8 13 md	9 12 mg	10 11 MF	11 9 er	12 9 ef	1 7 EH
2 17 TH	3 19 TW	4 18 TH	5 18 TW	6 16 rm	7 16 rt	8	8 14 RM	9 13 RT	10 12 md	11 10 MR	12 10 MF	1 8 er
2 18 tr	3 20 tf	4 19 tr	5 19 tf	6 17 TH	7 17 TW	9	8 15 rm	9 14 rt	10 13 RM	11 11 mg	12 11 md	1 9 MR
2 19 FR	3 21 FF	4 20 FR	5 20 FF	6 18 tr	7 18 tf	10	8 16 TH	9 15 TW	10 14 rm	11 12 RT	12 12 RM	1 10 mg
2 20 fg	3 22 fd	4 21 fg	5 21 fd	6 19 FR	7 19 FF	11	8 17 tr	9 16 tf	10 15 TH	11 13 rt	12 13 rm	1 11 RT
2 21 ET	3 23 EM	4 22 ET	5 22 EM	6 20 fg	7 20 fd	12	8 18 FR	9 17 FF	10 16 tr	11 14 TW	12 14 TH	1 12 rt
2 22 et	3 24 em	4 23 et	5 23 em	6 21 ET	7 21 EM	13	8 19 fg	9 18 fd	10 17 FR	11 15 tf	12 15 tr	1 13 TW
2 23 MW	3 25 MH	4 24 MW	5 24 MH	6 22 et	7 22 em	14	8 20 ET	9 19 EM	10 18 fg	11 16 FF	12 16 FR	1 14 tf
2 24 mf	3 26 mr	4 25 mf	5 25 mr	6 23 MW	7 23 MH	15	8 21 et	9 20 em	10 19 ET	11 17 fd	12 17 fg	1 15 FF
2 25 RF	3 27 RR	4 26 RF	5 26 RR	6 24 mf	7 24 mr	16	8 22 MW	9 21 MH	10 20 et	11 18 EM	12 18 ET	1 16 fd
2 26 rd	3 28 rg	4 27 rd	5 27 rg	6 25 RF	7 25 RR	17	8 23 mf	9 22 mr	10 21 MW	11 19 em	12 19 et	1 17 EM
2 27 TM	3 29 TT	4 28 TM	5 28 TT	6 26 rd	7 26 rg	18	8 24 RF	9 23 RR	10 22 mf	11 20 MH	12 20 MW	1 18 em
2 28 tm	3 30 tt	4 29 tm	5 29 tt	6 27 TM	7 27 TT	19	8 25 rd	9 24 rg	10 23 RF	11 21 mr	12 21 mf	1 19 MH
3 1 FH	3 31 FW	4 30 FH	5 30 FW	6 28 tm	7 28 tt	20	8 26 TM	9 25 TT	10 24 rd	11 22 RR	12 22 RF	1 20 mr
3 2 fr	4 1 ff	5 1 fr	5 31 ff	6 29 FH	7 29 FW	21	8 27 tm	9 26 tt	10 25 TM	11 23 rg	12 23 rd	1 21 RR
3 3 ER	4 2 EF	5 2 ER	6 1 EF	6 30 fr	7 30 ff	22	8 28 FH	9 27 FW	10 26 tm	11 24 TT	12 24 TM	1 22 rg
3 4 eg	4 3 ed	5 3 eg	6 2 ed	7 1 ER	7 31 EF	23	8 29 fr	9 28 ff	10 27 FH	11 25 tt	12 25 tm	1 23 TT
3 5 MT	4 4 MM	5 4 MT	6 3 MM	7 2 eg	8 1 ed	24	8 30 ER	9 29 EF	10 28 fr	11 26 FW	12 26 FH	1 24 tt
3 6 mt	4 5 mm	5 5 mt	6 4 mm	7 3 MT	8 2 MM	25	8 31 eg	9 30 ed	10 29 ER	11 27 ff	12 27 fr	1 25 FW
3 7 RW	4 6 RH	5 6 RW	6 5 RH	7 4 mt	8 3 mm	26	9 1 MT	10 1 MM	10 30 eg	11 28 EF	12 28 ER	1 26 ff
3 8 rf	4 7 rr	5 7 rf	6 6 rr	7 5 RW	8 4 RH	27	9 2 mt	10 2 mm	10 31 MT	11 29 ed	12 29 eg	1 27 EF
3 9 TF	4 8 TR	5 8 TF	6 7 TR	7 6 rf	8 5 rr	28	9 3 RW	10 3 RH	11 1 mt	11 30 MM	12 30 MT	1 28 ed
3 10 td	4 9 tg	5 9 td	6 8 tg	7 7 TF	8 6 TR	29	9 4 rf	10 4 rr	11 2 RW	12 1 mm	12 31 mt	1 29 MM
3 11 FM	4 10 FT	5 10 FM		7 8 td		30	9 5 TF			12 2 RH		1 30 mm

1995 tr BOAR

JAN ET	FEB et	MAR MW	APR mf	MAY RF	JUN rd	DAY OF MON	JUL TM	AUG tm	AUG tm	SEP FH	OCT fr	NOV RR	DEC eg
5 SPRING	6 WARM	6 CLEAR	7 SUMMER	9 GRAIN	10 HEAT		13 FALL	14 DEW	15 C DEW	16 WINTER	16 SNOW	16 CHILL	16 SPRING
15:24	9:34	14:37	8:11	12:34	22:57		22:57	11:25	3:50	5:44	23:27	9:23	3:26
1 31 RH	3 1 mt	3 31 mm	4 30 mt	5 29 MM	6 28 MT	1	7 27 ed	8 26 eg	9 25 ed	10 24 ER	11 22 ff	12 22 fr	1 20 FW
2 1 rr	3 2 RW	4 1 RH	5 1 RW	5 30 mm	6 29 mt	2	7 28 MM	8 27 MT	9 26 MM	10 35 eg	11 23 EF	12 23 ER	1 21 ff
2 2 TR	3 3 rf	4 2 rr	5 2 rf	5 31 RH	6 30 RW	3	7 29 mm	8 28 mt	9 27 mm	10 26 MT	11 24 ed	12 24 eg	1 22 EF
2 3 tg	3 4 TF	4 3 TR	5 3 TF	6 1 rr	7 1 rf	4	7 30 RH	8 29 RW	9 28 RH	10 27 mt	11 25 MM	12 25 MT	1 23 ed
2 4 FT	3 5 td	4 4 tg	5 4 td	6 2 TR	7 2 TF	5	7 31 rr	8 30 rf	9 29 rr	10 28 RW	11 26 mm	12 26 mt	1 24 MM
2 5 ft	3 6 FM	4 5 FT	5 5 FM	6 3 tg	7 3 td	6	8 1 TR	8 31 TF	9 30 TR	10 29 rf	11 27 RH	12 27 RW	1 25 mm
2 6 EW	3 7 fm	4 6 ft	5 6 fm	6 4 FT	7 4 FM	7	8 2 tg	9 1 td	10 1 tg	10 30 TF	11 28 rr	12 28 rf	1 26 RH
2 7 ef	3 8 EH	4 7 EW	5 7 EH	6 5 ft	7 5 fm	8	8 3 FT	9 2 FM	10 2 FT	10 31 td	11 29 TR	12 29 TF	1 27 rr
2 8 MF	3 9 er	4 8 ef	5 8 er	6 6 EW	7 6 EH	9	8 4 ft	9 3 fm	10 3 ft	11 1 FM	11 30 tg	12 30 td	1 28 TR
2 9 md	3 10 MR	4 9 MF	5 9 MR	6 7 ef	7 7 er	10	8 5 EW	9 4 EH	10 4 EW	11 2 fm	12 1 FT	12 31 FM	1 29 tg
2 10 RM	3 11 mg	4 10 md	5 10 mg	6 8 MF	7 8 MR	11	8 6 ef	9 5 er	10 5 ef	11 3 EH	12 2 ft	1 1 fm	1 30 FT
2 11 rm	3 12 RT	4 11 RM	5 11 RT	6 9 md	7 9 mg	12	8 7 MF	9 6 MR	10 6 MF	11 4 er	12 3 EW	1 2 EH	1 31 ft
2 12 TH	3 13 rt	4 12 rm	5 12 rt	6 10 RM	7 10 RT	13	8 8 md	9 7 mg	10 7 md	11 5 MR	12 4 ef	1 3 er	2 1 EW
2 13 tr	3 14 TW	4 13 TH	5 13 TW	6 11 rm	7 11 rt	14	8 9 RM	9 8 RT	10 8 RM	11 6 mg	12 5 MF	1 4 MR	2 2 ef
2 14 FR	3 15 tf	4 14 tr	5 14 tf	6 12 TH	7 12 TW	15	8 10 rm	9 9 rt	10 9 rm	11 7 RT	12 6 md	1 5 mg	2 3 MF
2 15 fg	3 16 FF	4 15 FR	5 15 FF	6 13 tr	7 13 tf	16	8 11 TH	9 10 TW	10 10 TH	11 8 rt	12 7 RM	1 6 RT	2 4 md
2 16 ET	3 17 fd	4 16 fg	5 16 fd	6 14 FR	7 14 FF	17	8 12 tr	9 11 tf	10 11 tr	11 9 TW	12 8 rm	1 7 rt	2 5 RM
2 17 et	3 18 EM	4 17 ET	5 17 EM	6 15 fg	7 15 fd	18	8 13 FR	9 12 FF	10 12 FR	11 10 tf	12 9 TH	1 8 TW	2 6 rm
2 18 MW	3 19 em	4 18 et	5 18 em	6 16 ET	7 16 EM	19	8 14 fg	9 13 fd	10 13 fg	11 11 FF	12 10 tr	1 9 tf	2 7 TH
2 19 mf	3 20 MH	4 19 MW	5 19 MH	6 17 et	7 17 em	20	8 15 ET	9 14 EM	10 14 ET	11 12 fd	12 11 FR	1 10 FF	2 8 tr
2 20 RF	3 21 mr	4 20 mf	5 20 mr	6 18 MW	7 18 MH	21	8 16 et	9 15 em	10 15 et	11 13 EM	12 12 fg	1 11 fd	2 9 FR
2 21 rd	3 22 RR	4 21 RF	5 21 RR	6 19 mf	7 19 mr	22	8 17 MW	9 16 MH	10 16 MW	11 14 em	12 13 ET	1 12 EM	2 10 fg
2 22 TM	3 23 rg	4 22 rd	5 22 rg	6 20 RF	7 20 RR	23	8 18 mf	9 17 mr	10 17 mf	11 15 MH	12 14 et	1 13 em	2 11 ET
2 23 tm	3 24 TT	4 23 TM	5 23 TT	6 21 rd	7 21 rg	24	8 19 RF	9 18 RR	10 18 RF	11 16 mr	12 15 MW	1 14 MH	2 12 et
2 24 FH	3 25 tt	4 24 tm	5 24 tt	6 22 TM	7 22 TT	25	8 20 rd	9 19 rg	10 19 rd	11 17 RR	12 16 mf	1 15 mr	2 13 MW
2 25 fr	3 26 FW	4 25 FH	5 25 FW	6 23 tm	7 23 tt	26	8 21 TM	9 20 TT	10 20 TM	11 18 rg	12 17 RF	1 16 RR	2 14 mf
2 26 ER	3 27 ff	4 26 fr	5 26 ff	6 24 FH	7 24 FW	27	8 22 tm	9 21 tt	10 21 tm	11 19 TT	12 18 rd	1 17 rg	2 15 RF
2 27 eg	3 28 EF	4 27 ER	5 27 EF	6 25 fr	7 25 ff	28	8 23 FH	9 22 FW	10 22 FH	11 20 tt	12 19 TM	1 18 TT	2 16 rd
2 28 MT	3 29 ed	4 28 eg	5 28 ed	6 26 ER	7 26 EF	29	8 24 fr	9 23 ff	10 23 fr	11 21 FW	12 20 tm	1 19 tt	2 17 TM
	3 30 MM	4 29 MT		6 27 eg		30	8 25 ER	9 24 EF			12 21 FH		2 18 tm

1996 FR RAT

JAN MT	FEB mt	MAR RW	APR rf	MAY TF	JUN td	DAY OF MON	JUL FM	AUG fm	SEP MH	OCT er	NOV MR	DEC mg
16 WARM	17 CLEAR	17 SUMMER	20 GRAIN	22 HEAT	23 FALL		25 DEW	26 C DEW	27 WINTER	27 SNOW	26 CHILL	27 SPRING
15:25	20:28	14:02	18:14	4:47	14:30		17:14	9:38	11:32	5:17	15:22	3:04
2 19 FH	3 19 tt	4 18 tm	5 17 TT	6 16 TM	7 16 TT	1	8 14 rd	9 13 rg	10 12 RF	11 11 RR	12 11 RF	1 9 mr
2 20 fr	3 20 FW	4 19 FH	5 18 tt	6 17 tm	7 17 tt	2	8 15 TM	9 14 TT	10 13 rd	11 12 rg	12 12 rd	1 10 RR
2 21 ER	3 21 ff	4 20 fr	5 19 FW	6 18 FH	7 18 FW	3	8 16 tm	9 15 tt	10 14 TM	11 13 TT	12 13 TM	1 11 rg
2 22 eg	3 22 EF	4 21 ER	5 20 ff	6 19 fr	7 19 ff	4	8 17 FH	9 16 FW	10 15 tm	11 14 tt	12 14 tm	1 12 TT
2 23 MT	3 23 ed	4 22 eg	5 21 EF	6 20 ER	7 20 EF	5	8 18 fr	9 17 ff	10 16 FH	11 15 FW	12 15 FH	1 13 tt
2 24 mt	3 24 MM	4 23 MT	5 22 ed	6 21 eg	7 21 ed	6	8 19 ER	9 18 EF	10 17 fr	11 16 ff	12 16 fr	1 14 FW
2 25 RW	3 25 mm	4 24 mt	5 23 MM	6 22 MT	7 22 MM	7	8 20 eg	9 19 ed	10 18 ER	11 17 EF	12 17 ER	1 15 ff
2 26 rf	3 26 RH	4 25 RW	5 24 mm	6 23 mt	7 23 mm	8	8 21 MT	9 20 MM	10 19 eg	11 18 ed	12 18 eg	1 16 EF
2 27 TF	3 27 rr	4 26 rf	5 25 RH	6 24 RW	7 24 RH	9	8 22 mt	9 21 mm	10 20 MT	11 19 MM	12 19 MT	1 17 ed
2 28 td	3 28 TR	4 27 TF	5 26 rr	6 25 rf	7 25 rr	10	8 23 RW	9 22 RH	10 21 mt	11 20 mm	12 20 mt	1 18 MM
2 29 FM	3 29 tg	4 28 td	5 27 TR	6 26 TF	7 26 TR	11	8 24 rf	9 23 rr	10 22 RW	11 21 RH	12 21 RW	1 19 mm
3 1 fm	3 30 FT	4 29 FM	5 28 tg	6 27 td	7 27 tg	12	8 25 TF	9 24 TR	10 23 rf	11 22 rr	12 22 rf	1 20 RH
3 2 EH	3 31 ft	4 30 fm	5 29 FT	6 28 FM	7 28 FT	13	8 26 td	9 25 tg	10 24 TF	11 23 TR	12 23 TF	1 21 rr
3 3 er	4 1 EW	5 1 EH	5 30 ft	6 29 fm	7 29 ft	14	8 27 FM	9 26 FT	10 25 td	11 24 tg	12 24 td	1 22 TR
3 4 MR	4 2 ef	5 2 er	5 31 EW	6 30 EH	7 30 EW	15	8 28 fm	9 27 ft	10 26 FM	11 25 FT	12 25 FM	1 23 tg
3 5 mg	4 3 MF	5 3 MR	6 1 ef	7 1 er	7 31 ef	16	8 29 EH	9 28 EW	10 27 fm	11 26 ft	12 26 fm	1 24 FT
3 6 RT	4 4 md	5 4 mg	6 2 MF	7 2 MR	8 1 MF	17	8 30 er	9 29 ef	10 28 EH	11 27 EW	12 27 EH	1 25 ft
3 7 rt	4 5 RM	5 5 RT	6 3 md	7 3 mg	8 2 md	18	8 31 MR	9 30 MF	10 29 er	11 28 ef	12 28 er	1 26 EW
3 8 TW	4 6 rm	5 6 rt	6 4 RM	7 4 RT	8 3 RM	19	9 1 mg	10 1 md	10 30 MR	11 29 MF	12 29 MR	1 27 ef
3 9 tf	4 7 TH	5 7 TW	6 5 rm	7 5 rt	8 4 rm	20	9 2 RT	10 2 RM	10 31 mg	11 30 md	12 30 mg	1 28 MF
3 10 FF	4 8 tr	5 8 tf	6 6 TH	7 6 TW	8 5 TH	21	9 3 rt	10 3 rm	11 1 RT	12 1 RM	12 31 RT	1 29 md
3 11 fd	4 9 FR	5 9 FF	6 7 tr	7 7 tf	8 6 tr	22	9 4 TW	10 4 TH	11 2 rt	12 2 rm	1 1 rt	1 30 RM
3 12 EM	4 10 fg	5 10 fd	6 8 FR	7 8 FF	8 7 FR	23	9 5 tf	10 5 tr	11 3 TW	12 3 TH	1 2 TW	1 31 rm
3 13 em	4 11 ET	5 11 EM	6 9 fg	7 9 fd	8 8 fg	24	9 6 FF	10 6 FR	11 4 tf	12 4 tr	1 3 tf	2 1 TH
3 14 MH	4 12 et	5 12 em	6 10 ET	7 10 EM	8 9 ET	25	9 7 fd	10 7 fg	11 5 FF	12 5 FR	1 4 FF	2 2 tr
3 15 mr	4 13 MW	5 13 MH	6 11 et	7 11 em	8 10 et	26	9 8 EM	10 8 ET	11 6 fd	12 6 fg	1 5 fd	2 3 FR
3 16 RR	4 14 mf	5 14 mr	6 12 MW	7 12 MH	8 11 MW	27	9 9 em	10 9 et	11 7 EM	12 7 ET	1 6 EM	2 4 fg
3 17 rg	4 15 RF	5 15 RR	6 13 mf	7 13 mr	8 12 mf	28	9 10 MH	10 10 MW	11 8 em	12 8 et	1 7 em	2 5 ET
3 18 TT	4 16 rd	5 16 rg	6 14 RF	7 14 RR	8 13 RF	29	9 11 mr	10 11 mf	11 9 MH	12 9 MW	1 8 MH	2 6 et
	4 17 TM		6 15 rd	7 15 rg		30	9 12 RR		11 10 mr	12 10 mf		

1997 fg OX

JAN RT	FEB rt	MAR TW	APR tf	MAY FF	JUN fd	DAY OF MON	JUL EM	AUG em	SEP MH	OCT mr	NOV RR	DEC rg
27 WARM	28 CLEAR	29 SUMMER		1 GRAIN	3 HEAT		5 FALL	6 DEW	7 C DEW	8 WINTER	8 SNOW	7 CHILL
21:14	2:17	19:50		23:53	10:36		20:19	23:03	15:27	17:22	11:05	21:11
2 7 MW	3 9 MH	4 7 et	5 7 em	6 5 ET	7 5 EM	1	8 3 fg	9 2 fd	10 2 fg	10 31 FF	11 30 FR	12 30 FF
2 8 mf	3 10 mr	4 8 MW	5 8 MH	6 6 et	7 6 em	2	8 4 ET	9 3 EM	10 3 ET	11 1 fd	12 1 fg	12 31 fd
2 9 RF	3 11 RR	4 9 mf	5 9 mr	6 7 MW	7 7 MH	3	8 5 et	9 4 em	10 4 et	11 2 EM	12 2 ET	1 1 EM
2 10 rd	3 12 rg	4 10 RF	5 10 RR	6 8 mf	7 8 mr	4	8 6 MW	9 5 MH	10 5 MW	11 3 em	12 3 et	1 2 em
2 11 TM	3 13 TT	4 11 rd	5 11 rg	6 9 RF	7 9 RR	5	8 7 mf	9 6 mr	10 6 mf	11 4 MH	12 4 MW	1 3 MH
2 12 tm	3 14 tt	4 12 TM	5 12 TT	6 10 rd	7 10 rg	6	8 8 RF	9 7 RR	10 7 RF	11 5 mr	12 5 mf	1 4 mr
2 13 FH	3 15 FW	4 13 tm	5 13 tt	6 11 TM	7 11 TT	7	8 9 rd	9 8 rg	10 8 rd	11 6 RR	12 6 RF	1 5 RR
2 14 fr	3 16 ff	4 14 FH	5 14 FW	6 12 tm	7 12 tt	8	8 10 TM	9 9 TT	10 9 TM	11 7 rg	12 7 rd	1 6 rg
2 15 ER	3 17 EF	4 15 fr	5 15 ff	6 13 FH	7 13 FW	9	8 11 tm	9 10 tt	10 10 tm	11 8 TT	12 8 TM	1 7 TT
2 16 eg	3 18 ed	4 16 ER	5 16 EF	6 14 fr	7 14 ff	10	8 12 FH	9 11 FW	10 11 FH	11 9 tt	12 9 tm	1 8 tt
2 17 MT	3 19 MM	4 17 eg	5 17 ed	6 15 ER	7 15 EF	11	8 13 fr	9 12 ff	10 12 fr	11 10 FW	12 10 FH	1 9 FW
2 18 mt	3 20 mm	4 18 MT	5 18 MM	6 16 eg	7 16 ed	12	8 14 ER	9 13 EF	10 13 ER	11 11 ff	12 11 fr	1 10 ff
2 19 RW	3 21 RH	4 19 mt	5 19 mm	6 17 MT	7 17 MM	13	8 15 eg	9 14 ed	10 14 eg	11 12 EF	12 12 ER	1 11 EF
2 20 rf	3 22 rr	4 20 RW	5 20 RH	6 18 mt	7 18 mm	14	8 16 MT	9 15 MM	10 15 MT	11 13 ed	12 13 eg	1 12 ed
2 21 TF	3 23 TR	4 21 rf	5 21 rr	6 19 RW	7 19 RH	15	8 17 mt	9 16 mm	10 16 mt	11 14 MM	12 14 MT	1 13 MM
2 22 td	3 24 tg	4 22 TF	5 22 TR	6 20 rf	7 20 rr	16	8 18 RW	9 17 RH	10 17 RW	11 15 mm	12 15 mt	1 14 mm
2 23 FM	3 25 FT	4 23 td	5 23 tg	6 21 TF	7 21 TR	17	8 19 rf	9 18 rr	10 18 rf	11 16 RH	12 16 RW	1 15 RH
2 24 fm	3 26 ft	4 24 FM	5 24 FT	6 22 td	7 22 tg	18	8 20 TF	9 19 TR	10 19 TF	11 17 rr	12 17 rf	1 16 rr
2 25 EH	3 27 EW	4 25 fm	5 25 ft	6 23 FM	7 23 FT	19	8 21 td	9 20 tg	10 20 td	11 18 TR	12 18 TF	1 17 TR
2 26 er	3 28 ef	4 26 EH	5 26 EW	6 24 fm	7 24 ft	20	8 22 FM	9 21 FT	10 21 FM	11 19 tg	12 19 td	1 18 tg
2 27 MR	3 29 MF	4 27 er	5 27 ef	6 25 EH	7 25 EW	21	8 23 fm	9 22 ft	10 22 fm	11 20 FT	12 20 FM	1 19 FT
2 28 mg	3 30 md	4 28 MR	5 28 MF	6 26 er	7 26 ef	22	8 24 EH	9 23 EW	10 23 EH	11 21 ft	12 21 fm	1 20 ft
3 1 RT	3 31 RM	4 29 mg	5 29 md	6 27 MR	7 27 MF	23	8 25 er	9 24 ef	10 24 er	11 22 EW	12 22 EH	1 21 EW
3 2 rt	4 1 rm	4 30 RT	5 30 RM	6 28 mg	7 28 md	24	8 26 MR	9 25 MF	10 25 MR	11 23 ef	12 23 er	1 22 ef
3 3 TW	4 2 TH	5 1 rt	5 31 rm	6 29 RT	7 29 RM	25	8 27 mg	9 26 md	10 26 mg	11 24 MF	12 24 MR	1 23 MF
3 4 tf	4 3 tr	5 2 TW	6 1 TH	6 30 rt	7 30 rm	26	8 28 RT	9 27 RM	10 27 RT	11 25 md	12 25 mg	1 24 md
3 5 FF	4 4 FR	5 3 tf	6 2 tr	7 1 TW	7 31 TH	27	8 29 rt	9 28 rm	10 28 rt	11 26 RM	12 26 RT	1 25 RM
3 6 fd	4 5 fg	5 4 FF	6 3 FR	7 2 tf	8 1 tr	28	8 30 TW	9 29 TH	10 29 TW	11 27 rm	12 27 rt	1 26 rm
3 7 EM	4 6 ET	5 5 fd	6 4 fg	7 3 FF	8 2 FR	29	8 31 tf	9 30 tr	10 30 tf	11 28 TH	12 28 TW	1 27 TH
3 8 em		5 6 EM		7 4 fd		30	9 1 FF	10 1 FR		11 29 tr	12 29 tf	

1998 ET TIGER

JAN TT	FEB tt	MAR FW	APR ff	MAY EF	MAY EF	JUN ed	DAY	JUL MM	AUG mm	SEP RH	OCT rr	NOV TR	DEC tg
8 SPRING	8 WARM	9 CLEAR	11 SUMMER	12 GRAIN	14 HEAT	17 FALL	OF MON	18 DEW	18 C DEW	20 WINTER	19 SNOW	19 CHILL	19 SPRING
9:05	2:57	8:06	1:40	6:02	22:44	16:25		5:24	21:16	0:24	15:51	3:00	14:42
1 28 tr	2 27 tf	3 28 TH	4 26 rt	5 26 rm	6 24 RT	7 23 md	1	8 22 mg	9 21 md	10 20 MR	11 19 MF	12 19 MR	1 17 ef
1 29 FR	2 28 FF	3 29 tr	4 27 TW	5 27 TH	6 25 rt	7 24 RM	2	8 23 RT	9 22 RM	10 21 mg	11 20 md	12 20 mg	1 18 MF
1 30 fg	3 1 fd	3 30 FR	4 28 tf	5 28 tr	6 26 TW	7 25 rm	3	8 24 rt	9 23 rm	10 22 RT	11 21 RM	12 21 RT	1 19 md
1 31 ET	3 2 EM	3 31 fg	4 29 FF	5 29 FR	6 27 tf	7 26 TH	4	8 25 TW	9 24 TH	10 23 rt	11 22 rm	12 22 rt	1 20 RM
2 1 et	3 3 em	4 1 ET	4 30 fd	5 30 fg	6 28 FF	7 27 tr	5	8 26 tf	9 25 tr	10 24 TW	11 23 TH	12 23 TW	1 21 rm
2 2 MW	3 4 MH	4 2 et	5 1 EM	5 31 ET	6 29 fd	7 28 FR	6	8 27 FF	9 26 FR	10 25 tf	11 24 tr	12 24 tf	1 22 TH
2 3 mf	3 5 mr	4 3 MW	5 2 em	6 1 et	6 30 EM	7 29 fg	7	8 28 fd	9 27 fg	10 26 FF	11 25 FR	12 25 FF	1 23 tr
2 4 RF	3 6 RR	4 4 mf	5 3 MH	6 2 MW	7 1 em	7 30 ET	8	8 29 EM	9 28 ET	10 27 fd	11 26 fg	12 26 fd	1 24 FR
2 5 rd	3 7 rg	4 5 RF	5 4 mr	6 3 mf	7 2 MH	7 31 et	9	8 30 em	9 29 et	10 28 EM	11 27 ET	12 27 EM	1 25 fg
2 6 TM	3 8 TT	4 6 rd	5 5 RR	6 4 RF	7 3 mr	8 1 MW	10	8 31 MH	9 30 MW	10 29 em	11 28 et	12 28 em	1 26 ET
2 7 tm	3 9 tt	4 7 TM	5 6 rg	6 5 rd	7 4 RR	8 2 mf	11	9 1 mr	10 1 mf	10 30 MH	11 29 MW	12 29 MH	1 27 et
2 8 FH	3 10 FW	4 8 tm	5 7 TT	6 6 TM	7 5 rg	8 3 RF	12	9 2 RR	10 2 RF	10 31 mr	11 30 mf	12 30 mr	1 28 MW
2 9 fr	3 11 ff	4 9 FH	5 8 tt	6 7 tm	7 6 TT	8 4 rd	13	9 3 rg	10 3 rd	11 1 RR	12 1 RF	12 31 RR	1 29 mf
2 10 ER	3 12 EF	4 10 fr	5 9 FW	6 8 FH	7 7 tt	8 5 TM	14	9 4 TT	10 4 TM	11 2 rg	12 2 rd	1 1 rg	1 30 RF
2 11 eg	3 13 ed	4 11 ER	5 10 ff	6 9 fr	7 8 FW	8 6 tm	15	9 5 tt	10 5 tm	11 3 TT	12 3 TM	1 2 TT	1 31 rd
2 12 MT	3 14 MM	4 12 eg	5 11 EF	6 10 ER	7 9 ff	8 7 FH	16	9 6 FW	10 6 FH	11 4 tt	12 4 tm	1 3 tt	2 1 TM
2 13 mt	3 15 mm	4 13 MT	5 12 ed	6 11 eg	7 10 EF	8 8 fr	17	9 7 ff	10 7 fr	11 5 FW	12 5 FH	1 4 FW	2 2 tm
2 14 RW	3 16 RH	4 14 mt	5 13 MM	6 12 MT	7 11 ed	8 9 ER	18	9 8 EF	10 8 ER	11 6 ff	12 6 fr	1 5 ff	2 3 FH
2 15 rf	3 17 rr	4 15 RW	5 14 mm	6 13 mt	7 12 MM	8 10 eg	19	9 9 ed	10 9 eg	11 7 EF	12 7 ER	1 6 EF	2 4 fr
2 16 TF	3 18 TR	4 16 rf	5 15 RH	6 14 RW	7 13 mm	8 11 MT	20	9 10 MM	10 10 MT	11 8 ed	12 8 eg	1 7 ed	2 5 ER
2 17 td	3 19 tg	4 17 TF	5 16 rr	6 15 rf	7 14 RH	8 12 mt	21	9 11 mm	10 11 mt	11 9 MM	12 9 MT	1 8 MM	2 6 eg
2 18 FM	3 20 FT	4 18 td	5 17 TR	6 16 TF	7 15 rr	8 13 RW	22	9 12 RH	10 12 RW	11 10 mm	12 10 mt	1 9 mm	2 7 MT
2 19 fm	3 21 ft	4 19 FM	5 18 tg	6 17 td	7 16 TR	8 14 rf	23	9 13 rr	10 13 rf	11 11 RH	12 11 RW	1 10 RH	2 8 mt
2 20 EH	3 22 EW	4 20 fm	5 19 FT	6 18 FM	7 17 tg	8 15 TF	24	9 14 TR	10 14 TF	11 12 rr	12 12 rf	1 11 rr	2 9 RW
2 21 er	3 23 ef	4 21 EH	5 20 ft	6 19 fm	7 18 FT	8 16 td	25	9 15 tg	10 15 td	11 13 TR	12 13 TF	1 12 TR	2 10 rf
2 22 MR	3 24 MF	4 22 er	5 21 EW	6 20 EH	7 19 ft	8 17 FM	26	9 16 FT	10 16 FM	11 14 tg	12 14 td	1 13 tg	2 11 TF
2 23 mg	3 25 md	4 23 MR	5 22 ef	6 21 er	7 20 EW	8 18 fm	27	9 17 ft	10 17 fm	11 15 FT	12 15 FM	1 14 FT	2 12 td
2 24 RT	3 26 RM	4 24 mg	5 23 MF	6 22 MR	7 21 ef	8 19 EH	28	9 18 EW	10 18 EH	11 16 ft	12 16 fm	1 15 ft	2 13 FM
2 25 rt	3 27 rm	4 25 RT	5 24 md	6 23 mg	7 22 MF	8 20 er	29	9 19 ef	10 19 er	11 17 EW	12 17 EH	1 16 EW	2 14 fm
2 26 TW			5 25 RM			8 21 MR	30	9 20 MF		11 18 ef	12 18 er		2 15 EH

1999 et RABBIT

JAN FT	FEB ft	MAR EW	APR ef	MAY MF	JUN md	DAY	JUL RM	AUG rm	SEP TH	OCT tr	NOV FR	DEC fg
19 WARM	19 CLEAR	21 SUMMER	23 GRAIN	24 HEAT	27 FALL	OF MON	29 DEW		1 C DEW	1 WINTER 6:14	30 CHILL	29 SPRING
8:52	13:55	7:29	11:51	22:14	7:57		11:13		3:06	30 SNOW 21:14	9:30	20:32
2 16 er	3 18 ef	4 16 EH	5 15 ft	6 14 fm	7 13 FT	1	8 11 td	9 10 tg	10 9 TF	11 8 TR	12 8 TF	1 7 TR
2 17 MR	3 19 MF	4 17 er	5 16 EW	6 15 EH	7 14 ft	2	8 12 FM	9 11 FT	10 10 td	11 9 tg	12 9 td	1 8 tg
2 18 mg	3 20 md	4 18 MR	5 17 ef	6 16 er	7 15 EW	3	8 13 fm	9 12 ft	10 11 FM	11 10 FT	12 10 FM	1 9 FT
2 19 RT	3 21 RM	4 19 mg	5 18 MF	6 17 MR	7 16 ef	4	8 14 EH	9 13 EW	10 12 fm	11 11 ft	12 11 fm	1 10 ft
2 20 rt	3 22 rm	4 20 RT	5 19 md	6 18 mg	7 17 MF	5	8 15 er	9 14 ef	10 13 EH	11 12 EW	12 12 EH	1 11 EW
2 21 TW	3 23 TH	4 21 rt	5 20 RM	6 19 RT	7 18 md	6	8 16 MR	9 15 MF	10 14 er	11 13 ef	12 13 er	1 12 ef
2 22 tf	3 24 tr	4 22 TW	5 21 rm	6 20 rt	7 19 RM	7	8 17 mg	9 16 md	10 15 MR	11 14 MF	12 14 MR	1 13 MF
2 23 FF	3 25 FR	4 23 tf	5 22 TH	6 21 TW	7 20 rm	8	8 18 RT	9 17 RM	10 16 mg	11 15 md	12 15 mg	1 14 md
2 24 fd	3 26 fg	4 24 FF	5 23 tr	6 22 tf	7 21 TH	9	8 19 rt	9 18 rm	10 17 RT	11 16 RM	12 16 RT	1 15 RM
2 25 EM	3 27 ET	4 25 fd	5 24 FR	6 23 FF	7 22 tr	10	8 20 TW	9 19 TH	10 18 rt	11 17 rm	12 17 rt	1 16 rm
2 26 em	3 28 et	4 26 EM	5 25 fg	6 24 fd	7 23 FR	11	8 21 tf	9 20 tr	10 19 TW	11 18 TH	12 18 TW	1 17 TH
2 27 MH	3 29 MW	4 27 em	5 26 ET	6 25 EM	7 24 fg	12	8 22 FF	9 21 FR	10 20 tf	11 19 tr	12 19 tf	1 18 tr
2 28 mr	3 30 mf	4 28 MH	5 27 et	6 26 em	7 25 ET	13	8 23 fd	9 22 fg	10 21 FF	11 20 FR	12 20 FF	1 19 FR
3 1 RR	3 31 RF	4 29 mr	5 28 MW	6 27 MH	7 26 et	14	8 24 EM	9 23 ET	10 22 fd	11 21 fg	12 21 fd	1 20 fg
3 2 rg	4 1 rd	4 30 RR	5 29 mf	6 28 mr	7 27 MW	15	8 25 em	9 24 et	10 23 EM	11 22 ET	12 22 EM	1 21 ET
3 3 TT	4 2 TM	5 1 rg	5 30 RF	6 29 RR	7 28 mf	16	8 26 MH	9 25 MW	10 24 em	11 23 et	12 23 em	1 22 et
3 4 tt	4 3 tm	5 2 TT	5 31 rd	6 30 rg	7 29 RF	17	8 27 mr	9 26 mf	10 25 MH	11 24 MW	12 24 MH	1 23 MW
3 5 FW	4 4 FH	5 3 tt	6 1 TM	7 1 TT	7 30 rd	18	8 28 RR	9 27 RF	10 26 mr	11 25 mf	12 25 mr	1 24 mf
3 6 ff	4 5 fr	5 4 FW	6 2 tm	7 2 tt	7 31 TM	19	8 29 rg	9 28 rd	10 27 RR	11 26 RF	12 26 RR	1 25 RF
3 7 EF	4 6 ER	5 5 ff	6 3 FH	7 3 FW	8 1 tm	20	8 30 TT	9 29 TM	10 28 rg	11 27 rd	12 27 rg	1 26 rd
3 8 ed	4 7 eg	5 6 EF	6 4 fr	7 4 ff	8 2 FH	21	8 31 tt	9 30 tm	10 29 TT	11 28 TM	12 28 TT	1 27 TM
3 9 MM	4 8 MT	5 7 ed	6 5 ER	7 5 EF	8 3 fr	22	9 1 FW	10 1 FH	10 30 tt	11 29 tm	12 29 tt	1 28 tm
3 10 mm	4 9 mt	5 8 MM	6 6 eg	7 6 ed	8 4 ER	23	9 2 ff	10 2 fr	10 31 FW	11 30 FH	12 30 FW	1 29 FH
3 11 RH	4 10 RW	5 9 mm	6 7 MT	7 7 MM	8 5 eg	24	9 3 EF	10 3 ER	11 1 ff	12 1 fr	12 31 ff	1 30 fr
3 12 rr	4 11 rf	5 10 RH	6 8 mt	7 8 mm	8 6 MT	25	9 4 ed	10 4 eg	11 2 EF	12 2 ER	1 1 EF	1 31 ER
3 13 TR	4 12 TF	5 11 rr	6 9 RW	7 9 RH	8 7 mt	26	9 5 MM	10 5 MT	11 3 ed	12 3 eg	1 2 ed	2 1 eg
3 14 tg	4 13 td	5 12 TR	6 10 rf	7 10 rr	8 8 RW	27	9 6 mm	10 6 mt	11 4 MM	12 4 MT	1 3 MM	2 2 MT
3 15 FT	4 14 FM	5 13 tg	6 11 TF	7 11 TR	8 9 rf	28	9 7 RH	10 7 RW	11 5 mm	12 5 mt	1 4 mm	2 3 mt
3 16 ft	4 15 fm	5 14 FT	6 12 td	7 12 tg	8 10 TF	29	9 8 rr	10 8 rf	11 6 RH	12 6 RW	1 5 RH	2 4 RW
3 17 EW			6 13 FM			30	9 9 TR		11 7 rr	12 7 rf	1 6 rr	

2000 MW DRAGON

JAN ET			FEB et			MAR MW			APR mf			MAY RF			JUN rd			DAY OF MON	JUL TM			AUG tm			SEP FH			OCT fr			NOV ER			DEC eg		
30 WARM			30 CLEAR						2 SUMMER			4 GRAIN			6 HEAT				8 FALL			10 DEW			11 C DEW			12 WINTER			12 SNOW			11 CHILL		
14:42			19:45						12:58			17:41			4:04				13:36			17:01			7:56			12:03			3:29			3:19		
2	5	rf	3	6	rr	4	5	rf	5	4	RH	6	2	mt	7	2	mm	1	7	31	MT	8	29	ed	9	28	eg	10	27	EF	11	26	ER	12	26	EF
2	6	TF	3	7	TR	4	6	TF	5	5	rr	6	3	RW	7	3	RH	2	8	1	mt	8	30	MM	9	29	MT	10	28	ed	11	27	eg	12	27	ed
2	7	td	3	8	tg	4	7	td	5	6	TR	6	4	rf	7	4	rr	3	8	2	RW	8	31	mm	9	30	mt	10	29	MM	11	28	MT	12	28	MM
2	8	FM	3	9	FT	4	8	FM	5	7	tg	6	5	TF	7	5	TR	4	8	3	rf	9	1	RH	10	1	RW	10	30	mm	11	29	mt	12	29	mm
2	9	fm	3	10	ft	4	9	fm	5	8	FT	6	6	td	7	6	tg	5	8	4	TF	9	2	rr	10	2	rf	10	31	RH	11	30	RW	12	30	RH
2	10	EH	3	11	EW	4	10	EH	5	9	ft	6	7	FM	7	7	FT	6	8	5	td	9	3	TR	10	3	TF	11	1	rr	12	1	rf	12	31	rr
2	11	er	3	12	ef	4	11	er	5	10	EW	6	8	fm	7	8	ft	7	8	6	FM	9	4	tg	10	4	td	11	2	TR	12	2	TF	1	1	TR
2	12	MR	3	13	MF	4	12	MR	5	11	ef	6	9	EH	7	9	EW	8	8	7	fm	9	5	FT	10	5	FM	11	3	tg	12	3	td	1	2	tg
2	13	mg	3	14	md	4	13	mg	5	12	MF	6	10	er	7	10	ef	9	8	8	EH	9	6	ft	10	6	fm	11	4	FT	12	4	FM	1	3	FT
2	14	RT	3	15	RM	4	14	RT	5	13	md	6	11	MR	7	11	MF	10	8	9	er	9	7	EW	10	7	EH	11	5	ft	12	5	fm	1	4	ft
2	15	rt	3	16	rm	4	15	rt	5	14	RM	6	12	mg	7	12	md	11	8	10	MR	9	8	ef	10	8	er	11	6	EW	12	6	EH	1	5	EW
2	16	TW	3	17	TH	4	16	TW	5	15	rm	6	13	RT	7	13	RM	12	8	11	mg	9	9	MF	10	9	MR	11	7	ef	12	7	er	1	6	ef
2	17	tf	3	18	tr	4	17	tf	5	16	TH	6	14	rt	7	14	rm	13	8	12	RT	9	10	md	10	10	mg	11	8	MF	12	8	MR	1	7	MF
2	18	FF	3	19	FR	4	18	FF	5	17	tr	6	15	TW	7	15	TH	14	8	13	rt	9	11	RM	10	11	RT	11	9	md	12	9	mg	1	8	md
2	19	fd	3	20	fg	4	19	fd	5	18	FR	6	16	tf	7	16	tr	15	8	14	TW	9	12	rm	10	12	rt	11	10	RM	12	10	RT	1	9	RM
2	20	EM	3	21	ET	4	20	EM	5	19	fg	6	17	FF	7	17	FR	16	8	15	tf	9	13	TH	10	13	TW	11	11	rm	12	11	rt	1	10	rm
2	21	em	3	22	et	4	21	em	5	20	ET	6	18	fd	7	18	fg	17	8	16	FF	9	14	tr	10	14	tf	11	12	TH	12	12	TW	1	11	TH
2	22	MH	3	23	MW	4	22	MH	5	21	et	6	19	EM	7	19	ET	18	8	17	fd	9	15	FR	10	15	FF	11	13	tr	12	13	tf	1	12	tr
2	23	mr	3	24	mf	4	23	mr	5	22	MW	6	20	em	7	20	et	19	8	18	EM	9	16	fg	10	16	fd	11	14	FR	12	14	FF	1	13	FR
2	24	RR	3	25	RF	4	24	RR	5	23	mf	6	21	MH	7	21	MW	20	8	19	em	9	17	ET	10	17	EM	11	15	fg	12	15	fd	1	14	fg
2	25	rg	3	26	rd	4	25	rg	5	24	RF	6	22	mr	7	22	mf	21	8	20	MH	9	18	et	10	18	em	11	16	ET	12	16	EM	1	15	ET
2	26	TT	3	27	TM	4	26	TT	5	25	rd	6	23	RR	7	23	RF	22	8	21	mr	9	19	MW	10	19	MH	11	17	et	12	17	em	1	16	et
2	27	tt	3	28	tm	4	27	tt	5	26	TM	6	24	rg	7	24	rd	23	8	22	RR	9	20	mf	10	20	mr	11	18	MW	12	18	MH	1	17	MW
2	28	FW	3	29	FH	4	28	FW	5	27	tm	6	25	TT	7	25	TM	24	8	23	rg	9	21	RF	10	21	RR	11	19	mf	12	19	mr	1	18	mf
2	29	ff	3	30	fr	4	29	ff	5	28	FH	6	26	tt	7	26	tm	25	8	24	TT	9	22	rd	10	22	rg	11	20	RF	12	20	RR	1	19	RF
3	1	EF	3	31	ER	4	30	EF	5	29	fr	6	27	FW	7	27	FH	26	8	25	tt	9	23	TM	10	23	TT	11	21	rd	12	21	rg	1	20	rd
3	2	ed	4	1	eg	5	1	ed	5	30	ER	6	28	ff	7	28	fr	27	8	26	FW	9	24	tm	10	24	tt	11	22	TM	12	22	TT	1	21	TM
3	3	MM	4	2	MT	5	2	MM	5	31	eg	6	29	EF	7	29	ER	28	8	27	ff	9	25	FH	10	25	FW	11	23	tm	12	23	tt	1	22	tm
3	4	mm	4	3	mt	5	3	mm	6	1	MT	6	30	ed	7	30	eg	29	8	28	EF	9	26	fr	10	26	ff	11	24	FH	12	24	FW	1	23	FH
3	5	RH	4	4	RW							7	1	MM				30				9	27	ER				11	25	fr	12	25	ff			

2001 mf SNAKE

JAN MT	FEB mt	MAR RW	APR rf	APR rf	MAY TF	DAY OF MON	JUN td	JUL FM	AUG fm	SEP EH	OCT er	NOV MR	DEC mg
12 SPRING	11 WARM	12 CLEAR	13 SUMMER	14 GRAIN	17 HEAT		18 FALL	20 DEW	22 C DEW	22 WINTER	23 SNOW	22 CHILL	23 SPRING
2:20	20:30	1:33	18:46	23:29	9:52		19:34	22:18	13:42	17:53	9:17	21:10	8:08
1 24 fr	2 23 ff	3 25 fr	4 23 FW	5 23 FH	6 21 tt	1	7 21 tm	8 19 TT	9 17 rd	10 17 rg	11 15 RF	12 15 RR	1 13 mf
1 25 ER	2 24 EF	3 26 ER	4 24 ff	5 24 fr	6 22 FW	2	7 22 FH	8 20 tt	9 18 TM	10 18 TT	11 16 rd	12 16 rg	1 14 RF
1 26 eg	2 25 ed	3 27 eg	4 25 EF	5 25 ER	6 23 ff	3	7 23 fr	8 21 FW	9 19 tm	10 19 tt	11 17 TM	12 17 TT	1 15 rd
1 27 MT	2 26 MM	3 28 MT	4 26 ed	5 26 eg	6 24 EF	4	7 24 ER	8 22 ff	9 20 FH	10 20 FW	11 18 tm	12 18 tt	1 16 TM
1 28 mt	2 27 mm	3 29 mt	4 27 MM	5 27 MT	6 25 ed	5	7 25 eg	8 23 EF	9 21 fr	10 21 ff	11 19 FH	12 19 FW	1 17 tm
1 29 RW	2 28 RH	3 30 RW	4 28 mm	5 28 mt	6 26 MM	6	7 26 MT	8 24 ed	9 22 ER	10 22 EF	11 20 fr	12 20 ff	1 18 FH
1 30 rf	3 1 rr	3 31 rf	4 29 RH	5 29 RW	6 27 mm	7	7 27 mt	8 25 MM	9 23 eg	10 23 ed	11 21 ER	12 21 EF	1 19 fr
1 31 TF	3 2 TR	4 1 TF	4 30 rr	5 30 rf	6 28 RH	8	7 28 RW	8 26 mm	9 24 MT	10 24 MM	11 22 eg	12 22 ed	1 20 ER
2 1 td	3 3 tg	4 2 td	5 1 TR	5 31 TF	6 29 rr	9	7 29 rf	8 27 RH	9 25 mt	10 25 mm	11 23 MT	12 23 MM	1 21 eg
2 2 FM	3 4 FT	4 3 FM	5 2 tg	6 1 td	6 30 TR	10	7 30 TF	8 28 rr	9 26 RW	10 26 RH	11 24 mt	12 24 mm	1 22 MT
2 3 fm	3 5 ft	4 4 fm	5 3 FT	6 2 FM	7 1 tg	11	7 31 td	8 29 TR	9 27 rf	10 27 rr	11 25 RW	12 25 RH	1 23 mt
2 4 EH	3 6 EW	4 5 EH	5 4 ft	6 3 fm	7 2 FT	12	8 1 FM	8 30 tg	9 28 TF	10 28 TR	11 26 rf	12 26 rr	1 24 RW
2 5 er	3 7 ef	4 6 er	5 5 EW	6 4 EH	7 3 ft	13	8 2 fm	8 31 FT	9 29 td	10 29 tg	11 27 TF	12 27 TR	1 25 rf
2 6 MR	3 8 MF	4 7 MR	5 6 ef	6 5 er	7 4 EW	14	8 3 EH	9 1 ft	9 30 FM	10 30 FT	11 28 td	12 28 tg	1 26 TF
2 7 mg	3 9 md	4 8 mg	5 7 MF	6 6 MR	7 5 ef	15	8 4 er	9 2 EW	10 1 fm	10 31 ft	11 29 FM	12 29 FT	1 27 td
2 8 RT	3 10 RM	4 9 RT	5 8 md	6 7 mg	7 6 MF	16	8 5 MR	9 3 ef	10 2 EH	11 1 EW	11 30 fm	12 30 ft	1 28 FM
2 9 rt	3 11 rm	4 10 rt	5 9 RM	6 8 RT	7 7 md	17	8 6 mg	9 4 MF	10 3 er	11 2 ef	12 1 EH	12 31 EW	1 29 fm
2 10 TW	3 12 TH	4 11 TW	5 10 rm	6 9 rt	7 8 RM	18	8 7 RT	9 5 md	10 4 MR	11 3 MF	12 2 er	1 1 ef	1 30 EH
2 11 tf	3 13 tr	4 12 tf	5 11 TH	6 10 TW	7 9 rm	19	8 8 rt	9 6 RM	10 5 mg	11 4 md	12 3 MR	1 2 MF	1 31 er
2 12 FF	3 14 FR	4 13 FF	5 12 tr	6 11 tf	7 10 TH	20	8 9 TW	9 7 rm	10 6 RT	11 5 RM	12 4 mg	1 3 md	2 1 MR
2 13 fd	3 15 fg	4 14 fd	5 13 FR	6 12 FF	7 11 tr	21	8 10 tf	9 8 TH	10 7 rt	11 6 rm	12 5 RT	1 4 RM	2 2 mg
2 14 EM	3 16 ET	4 15 EM	5 14 fg	6 13 fd	7 12 FR	22	8 11 FF	9 9 tr	10 8 TW	11 7 TH	12 6 rt	1 5 rm	2 3 RT
2 15 em	3 17 et	4 16 em	5 15 ET	6 14 EM	7 13 fg	23	8 12 fd	9 10 FR	10 9 tf	11 8 tr	12 7 TW	1 6 TH	2 4 rt
2 16 MH	3 18 MW	4 17 MH	5 16 et	6 15 em	7 14 ET	24	8 13 EM	9 11 fg	10 10 FF	11 9 FR	12 8 tf	1 7 tr	2 5 TW
2 17 mr	3 19 mf	4 18 mr	5 17 MW	6 16 MH	7 15 et	25	8 14 em	9 12 ET	10 11 fd	11 10 fg	12 9 FF	1 8 FR	2 6 tf
2 18 RR	3 20 RF	4 19 RR	5 18 mf	6 17 mr	7 16 MW	26	8 15 MH	9 13 et	10 12 EM	11 11 ET	12 10 fd	1 9 fg	2 7 FF
2 19 rg	3 21 rd	4 20 rg	5 19 RF	6 18 RR	7 17 mf	27	8 16 mr	9 14 MW	10 13 em	11 12 et	12 11 EM	1 10 ET	2 8 fd
2 20 TT	3 22 TM	4 21 TT	5 20 rd	6 19 rg	7 18 RF	28	8 17 RR	9 15 mf	10 14 MH	11 13 MW	12 12 em	1 11 et	2 9 EM
2 21 tt	3 23 tm	4 22 tt	5 21 TM	6 20 TT	7 19 rd	29	8 18 rg	9 16 RF	10 15 mr	11 14 mf	12 13 MH	1 12 MW	2 10 em
2 22 FW	3 24 FH		5 22 tm		7 20 TM	30			10 16 RR		12 14 mr		2 11 MH

2002 RF HORSE

JAN RF	FEB rt	MAR TW	APR tf	MAY FF	JUN fd	DAY OF MON	JUL EM	AUG em	SEP MH	OCT mr	NOV RR	DEC rg
23 WARM	23 CLEAR	24 SUMMER	26 GRAIN	27 HEAT	30 FALL			2 DEW	18 C DEW	3 WINTER	4 SNOW	4 CHILL
2:18	7:21	0:55	4:54	15:40	1:23			4:07	19:31	23:43	15:16	2:15
2 12 mr	3 14 mf	4 13 mr	5 12 MW	6 11 MH	7 10 et	1	8 9 em	9 7 ET	10 6 fd	11 5 fg	12 4 FF	1 3 FR
2 13 RR	3 15 RF	4 14 RR	5 13 mf	6 12 mr	7 11 MW	2	8 10 MH	9 8 et	10 7 EM	11 6 ET	12 5 fd	1 4 fg
2 14 rg	3 16 rd	4 15 rg	5 14 RF	6 13 RR	7 12 mf	3	8 11 mr	9 9 MW	10 8 em	11 7 et	12 6 EM	1 5 ET
2 15 TT	3 17 TM	4 16 TT	5 15 rd	6 14 rg	7 13 RF	4	8 12 RR	9 10 mf	10 9 MH	11 8 MW	12 7 em	1 6 et
2 16 tt	3 18 tm	4 17 tt	5 16 TM	6 15 TT	7 14 rd	5	8 13 rg	9 11 RF	10 10 mr	11 9 mf	12 8 MH	1 7 MW
2 17 FW	3 19 FH	4 18 FW	5 17 tm	6 16 tt	7 15 TM	6	8 14 TT	9 12 rd	10 11 RR	11 10 RF	12 9 mr	1 8 mf
2 18 ff	3 20 fr	4 19 ff	5 18 FH	6 17 FW	7 16 tm	7	8 15 tt	9 13 TM	10 12 rg	11 11 rd	12 10 RR	1 9 RF
2 19 EF	3 21 ER	4 20 EF	5 19 fr	6 18 ff	7 17 FH	8	8 16 FW	9 14 tm	10 13 TT	11 12 TM	12 11 rg	1 10 rd
2 20 ed	3 22 eg	4 21 ed	5 20 ER	6 19 EF	7 18 fr	9	8 17 ff	9 15 FH	10 14 tt	11 13 tm	12 12 TT	1 11 TM
2 21 MM	3 23 MT	4 22 MM	5 21 eg	6 20 ed	7 19 ER	10	8 18 EF	9 16 fr	10 15 FW	11 14 FH	12 13 tt	1 12 tm
2 22 mm	3 24 mt	4 23 mm	5 22 MT	6 21 MM	7 20 eg	11	8 19 ed	9 17 ER	10 16 ff	11 15 fr	12 14 FW	1 13 FH
2 23 RH	3 25 RW	4 24 RH	5 23 mt	6 22 mm	7 21 MT	12	8 20 MM	9 18 eg	10 17 EF	11 16 ER	12 15 ff	1 14 fr
2 24 rr	3 26 rf	4 25 rr	5 24 RW	6 23 RH	7 22 mt	13	8 21 mm	9 19 MT	10 18 ed	11 17 eg	12 16 EF	1 15 ER
2 25 TR	3 27 TF	4 26 TR	5 25 rf	6 24 rr	7 23 RW	14	8 22 RH	9 20 mt	10 19 MM	11 18 MT	12 17 ed	1 16 eg
2 26 tg	3 28 td	4 27 tg	5 26 TF	6 25 TR	7 24 rf	15	8 23 rr	9 21 RW	10 20 mm	11 19 mt	12 18 MM	1 17 MT
2 27 FT	3 29 FM	4 28 FT	5 27 td	6 26 tg	7 25 TF	16	8 24 TR	9 22 rf	10 21 RH	11 20 RW	12 19 mm	1 18 mt
2 28 ft	3 30 fm	4 29 ft	5 28 FM	6 27 FT	7 26 td	17	8 25 tg	9 23 TF	10 22 rr	11 21 rf	12 20 RH	1 19 RW
3 1 EW	3 31 EH	4 30 EW	5 29 fm	6 28 ft	7 27 FM	18	8 26 FT	9 24 td	10 23 TR	11 22 TF	12 21 rr	1 20 rf
3 2 ef	4 1 er	5 1 ef	5 30 EH	6 29 EW	7 28 fm	19	8 27 ft	9 25 FM	10 24 tg	11 23 td	12 22 TR	1 21 TF
3 3 MF	4 2 MR	5 2 MF	5 31 er	6 30 ef	7 29 EH	20	8 28 EW	9 26 fm	10 25 FT	11 24 FM	12 23 tg	1 22 td
3 4 md	4 3 mg	5 3 md	6 1 MR	7 1 MF	7 30 er	21	8 29 ef	9 27 EH	10 26 ft	11 25 fm	12 24 FT	1 23 FM
3 5 RM	4 4 RT	5 4 RM	6 2 mg	7 2 md	7 31 MR	22	8 30 MF	9 28 er	10 27 EW	11 26 EH	12 25 ft	1 24 fm
3 6 rm	4 5 rt	5 5 rm	6 3 RT	7 3 RM	8 1 mg	23	8 31 md	9 29 MR	10 28 ef	11 27 er	12 26 EW	1 25 EH
3 7 TH	4 6 TW	5 6 TH	6 4 rt	7 4 rm	8 2 RT	24	9 1 RM	9 30 mg	10 29 MF	11 28 MR	12 27 ef	1 26 er
3 8 tr	4 7 tf	5 7 tr	6 5 TW	7 5 TH	8 3 rt	25	9 2 rm	10 1 RT	10 30 md	11 29 mg	12 28 MF	1 27 MR
3 9 FR	4 8 FF	5 8 FR	6 6 tf	7 6 tr	8 4 TW	26	9 3 TH	10 2 rt	10 31 RM	11 30 RT	12 29 md	1 28 mg
3 10 fg	4 9 fd	5 9 fg	6 7 FF	7 7 FR	8 5 tf	27	9 4 tr	10 3 TW	11 1 rm	12 1 rt	12 30 RM	1 29 RT
3 11 ET	4 10 EM	5 10 ET	6 8 fd	7 8 fg	8 6 FF	28	9 5 FR	10 4 tf	11 2 TH	12 2 TW	12 31 rm	1 30 rt
3 12 et	4 11 em	5 11 et	6 9 EM	7 9 ET	8 7 fd	29	9 6 fg	10 5 FF	11 3 tr	12 3 tf	1 1 TH	1 31 TW
3 13 MW	4 12 MH		6 10 em		8 8 EM	30			11 4 FR		1 2 tr	

2003 rd RAM

JAN TT	FEB tt	MAR FW	APR ff	MAY EF	JUN ed	DAY OF MON	JUL MM	AUG mm	SEP RH	OCT rr	NOV TR	DEC tg
4 SPRING	4 WARM	4 CLEAR	6 SUMMER	7 GRAIN	8 HEAT		11 FALL	12 DEW	14 C DEW	15 WINTER	14 SNOW	15 CHILL
13:57	8:07	12:55	6:44	10:42	21:29		7:12	9:56	1:20	5:31	22:04	8:04
2 1 tf	3 3 tr	4 2 tf	5 1 TH	5 31 TW	6 30 TH	1	7 29 rt	8 28 rm	9 26 RT	10 25 md	11 24 mg	12 23 MF
2 2 FF	3 4 FR	4 3 FF	5 2 tr	6 1 tf	7 1 tr	2	7 30 TW	8 29 TH	9 27 rt	10 26 RM	11 25 RT	12 24 md
2 3 fd	3 5 fg	4 4 fd	5 3 FR	6 2 FF	7 2 FR	3	7 31 tf	8 30 tr	9 28 TW	10 27 rm	11 26 rt	12 25 RM
2 4 EM	3 6 ET	4 5 EM	5 4 fg	6 3 fd	7 3 fg	4	8 1 FF	8 31 FR	9 29 tf	10 28 TH	11 27 TW	12 26 rm
2 5 em	3 7 et	4 6 em	5 5 ET	6 4 EM	7 4 ET	5	8 2 fd	9 1 fg	9 30 FF	10 29 tr	11 28 tf	12 27 TH
2 6 MH	3 8 MW	4 7 MH	5 6 et	6 5 em	7 5 et	6	8 3 EM	9 2 ET	10 1 fd	10 30 FR	11 29 FF	12 28 tr
2 7 mr	3 9 mf	4 8 mr	5 7 MW	6 6 MH	7 6 MW	7	8 4 em	9 3 et	10 2 EM	10 31 fg	11 30 fd	12 29 FR
2 8 RR	3 10 RF	4 9 RR	5 8 mf	6 7 mr	7 7 mf	8	8 5 MH	9 4 MW	10 3 em	11 1 ET	12 1 EM	12 30 fg
2 9 rg	3 11 rd	4 10 rg	5 9 RF	6 8 RR	7 8 RF	9	8 6 mr	9 5 mf	10 4 MH	11 2 et	12 2 em	12 31 ET
2 10 TT	3 12 TM	4 11 TT	5 10 rd	6 9 rg	7 9 rd	10	8 7 RR	9 6 RF	10 5 mr	11 3 MW	12 3 MH	1 1 et
2 11 tt	3 13 tm	4 12 tt	5 11 TM	6 10 TT	7 10 TM	11	8 8 rg	9 7 rd	10 6 RR	11 4 mf	12 4 mr	1 2 MW
2 12 FW	3 14 FH	4 13 FW	5 12 tm	6 11 tt	7 11 tm	12	8 9 TT	9 8 TM	10 7 rg	11 5 RF	12 5 RR	1 3 mf
2 13 ff	3 15 fr	4 14 ff	5 13 FH	6 12 FW	7 12 FH	13	8 10 tt	9 9 tm	10 8 TT	11 6 rd	12 6 rg	1 4 RF
2 14 EF	3 16 ER	4 15 EF	5 14 fr	6 13 ff	7 13 fr	14	8 11 FW	9 10 FH	10 9 tt	11 7 TM	12 7 TT	1 5 rd
2 15 ed	3 17 eg	4 16 ed	5 15 ER	6 14 EF	7 14 ER	15	8 12 ff	9 11 fr	10 10 FW	11 8 tm	12 8 tt	1 6 TM
2 16 MM	3 18 MT	4 17 MM	5 16 eg	6 15 ed	7 15 eg	16	8 13 EF	9 12 ER	10 11 ff	11 9 FH	12 9 FW	1 7 tm
2 17 mm	3 19 mt	4 18 mm	5 17 MT	6 16 MM	7 16 MT	17	8 14 ed	9 13 eg	10 12 EF	11 10 fr	12 10 ff	1 8 FH
2 18 RH	3 20 RW	4 19 RH	5 18 mt	6 17 mm	7 17 mt	18	8 15 MM	9 14 MT	10 13 ed	11 11 ER	12 11 EF	1 9 fr
2 19 rr	3 21 rf	4 20 rr	5 19 RW	6 18 RH	7 18 RW	19	8 16 mm	9 15 mt	10 14 MM	11 12 eg	12 12 ed	1 10 ER
2 20 TR	3 22 TF	4 21 TR	5 20 rf	6 19 rr	7 19 rf	20	8 17 RH	9 16 RW	10 15 mm	11 13 MT	12 13 MM	1 11 eg
2 21 tg	3 23 td	4 22 tg	5 21 TF	6 20 TR	7 20 TF	21	8 18 rr	9 17 rf	10 16 RH	11 14 mt	12 14 mm	1 12 MT
2 22 FT	3 24 FM	4 23 FT	5 22 td	6 21 tg	7 21 td	22	8 19 TR	9 18 TF	10 17 rr	11 15 RW	12 15 RH	1 13 mt
2 23 ft	3 25 fm	4 24 ft	5 23 FM	6 22 FT	7 22 FM	23	8 20 tg	9 19 td	10 18 TR	11 16 rf	12 16 rr	1 14 RW
2 24 EW	3 26 EH	4 25 EW	5 24 fm	6 23 ft	7 23 fm	24	8 21 FT	9 20 FM	10 19 tg	11 17 TF	12 17 TR	1 15 rf
2 25 ef	3 27 er	4 26 ef	5 25 EH	6 24 EW	7 24 EH	25	8 22 ft	9 21 fm	10 20 FT	11 18 td	12 18 tg	1 16 TF
2 26 MF	3 28 MR	4 27 MF	5 26 er	6 25 ef	7 25 er	26	8 23 EW	9 22 EH	10 21 ft	11 19 FM	12 19 FT	1 17 td
2 27 md	3 29 mg	4 28 md	5 27 MR	6 26 MF	7 26 MR	27	8 24 ef	9 23 er	10 22 EW	11 20 fm	12 20 ft	1 18 FM
2 28 RM	3 30 RT	4 29 RM	5 28 mg	6 27 md	7 27 mg	28	8 25 MF	9 24 MR	10 23 ef	11 21 EH	12 21 EW	1 19 fm
3 1 rm	3 31 rt	4 30 rm	5 29 RT	6 28 RM	7 28 RT	29	8 26 md	9 25 mg	10 24 MF	11 22 er	12 22 ef	1 20 EH
3 2 TH	4 1 TW		5 30 rt	6 29 rm		30	8 27 RM			11 23 MR		1 21 er

2004 TM MONKEY

JAN FT	FEB ft	FEB ft	MAR EW	APR ef	MAY MF	DAY OF MON	JUN md	JUL RM	AUG rm	SEP TH	OCT tr	NOV FR	DEC fg
14 SPRING	15 WARM	15 CLEAR	17 SUMMER	18 GRAIN	20 HEAT		22 FALL	23 DEW	25 C DEW	25 WINTER	26 SNOW	25 CHILL	26 SPRING
19:46	13:56	18:59	12:33	16:55	2:56		13:00	15:44	7:08	11:21	3:54	13:52	1:34
1 22 MR	2 20 ef	3 21 er	4 19 EW	5 19 EH	6 18 EW	1	7 17 fm	8 16 ft	9 14 FM	10 14 FT	11 12 td	12 12 tg	1 10 TR
1 23 mg	2 21 MF	3 22 MR	4 20 ef	5 20 er	6 19 ef	2	7 18 EH	8 17 EW	9 15 fm	10 15 ft	11 13 FM	12 13 FT	1 11 td
1 24 RT	2 22 md	3 23 mg	4 21 MF	5 21 MR	6 20 MF	3	7 19 er	8 18 ef	9 16 EH	10 16 EW	11 14 fm	12 14 ft	1 12 FM
1 25 rt	2 23 RM	3 24 RT	4 22 md	5 22 mg	6 21 md	4	7 20 MR	8 19 MF	9 17 er	10 17 ef	11 15 EH	12 15 EW	1 13 fm
1 26 TW	2 24 rm	3 25 rt	4 23 RM	5 23 RT	6 22 RM	5	7 21 mg	8 20 md	9 18 MR	10 18 MF	11 16 er	12 16 ef	1 14 EH
1 27 tf	2 25 TH	3 26 TW	4 24 rm	5 24 rt	6 23 rm	6	7 22 RT	8 21 RM	9 19 mg	10 19 md	11 17 MR	12 17 MF	1 15 er
1 28 FF	2 26 tr	3 27 tf	4 25 TH	5 25 TW	6 24 TH	7	7 23 rt	8 22 rm	9 20 RT	10 20 RM	11 18 mg	12 18 md	1 16 MR
1 29 fd	2 27 FR	3 28 FF	4 26 tr	5 26 tf	6 25 tr	8	7 24 TW	8 23 TH	9 21 rt	10 21 rm	11 19 RT	12 19 RM	1 17 mg
1 30 EM	2 28 fg	3 29 fd	4 27 FR	5 27 FF	6 26 FR	9	7 25 tf	8 24 tr	9 22 TW	10 22 TH	11 20 rt	12 20 rm	1 18 RT
1 31 em	2 29 ET	3 30 EM	4 28 fg	5 28 fd	6 27 fg	10	7 26 FF	8 25 FR	9 23 tf	10 23 tr	11 21 TW	12 21 TH	1 19 rt
2 1 MH	3 1 et	3 31 em	4 29 ET	5 29 EM	6 28 ET	11	7 27 fd	8 26 fg	9 24 FF	10 24 FR	11 22 tf	12 22 tr	1 20 TW
2 2 mr	3 2 MW	4 1 MH	4 30 et	5 30 em	6 29 et	12	7 28 EM	8 27 ET	9 25 fd	10 25 fg	11 23 FF	12 23 FR	1 21 tf
2 3 RR	3 3 mf	4 2 mr	5 1 MW	5 31 MH	6 30 MW	13	7 29 em	8 28 et	9 26 EM	10 26 ET	11 24 fd	12 24 fg	1 22 FF
2 4 rg	3 4 RF	4 3 RR	5 2 mf	6 1 mr	7 1 mf	14	7 30 MH	8 29 MW	9 27 em	10 27 et	11 25 EM	12 25 ET	1 23 fd
2 5 TT	3 5 rd	4 4 rg	5 3 RF	6 2 RR	7 2 RF	15	7 31 mr	8 30 mf	9 28 MH	10 28 MW	11 26 em	12 26 et	1 24 EM
2 6 tt	3 6 TM	4 5 TT	5 4 rd	6 3 rg	7 3 rd	16	8 1 RR	8 31 RF	9 29 mr	10 29 mf	11 27 MH	12 27 MW	1 25 em
2 7 FW	3 7 tm	4 6 tt	5 5 TM	6 4 TT	7 4 TM	17	8 2 rg	9 1 rd	9 30 RR	10 30 RF	11 28 mr	12 28 mf	1 26 MH
2 8 ff	3 8 FH	4 7 FW	5 6 tm	6 5 tt	7 5 tm	18	8 3 TT	9 2 TM	10 1 rg	10 31 rd	11 29 RR	12 29 RF	1 27 mr
2 9 EF	3 9 fr	4 8 ff	5 7 FH	6 6 FW	7 6 FH	19	8 4 tt	9 3 tm	10 2 TT	11 1 TM	11 30 rg	12 30 rd	1 28 RR
2 10 ed	3 10 ER	4 9 EF	5 8 fr	6 7 ff	7 7 fr	20	8 5 FW	9 4 FH	10 3 tt	11 2 tm	12 1 TT	12 31 TM	1 29 rg
2 11 MM	3 11 eg	4 10 ed	5 9 ER	6 8 EF	7 8 ER	21	8 6 ff	9 5 fr	10 4 FW	11 3 FH	12 2 tt	1 1 tm	1 30 TT
2 12 mm	3 12 MT	4 11 MM	5 10 eg	6 9 ed	7 9 eg	22	8 7 EF	9 6 ER	10 5 ff	11 4 fr	12 3 FW	1 2 FH	1 31 tt
2 13 RH	3 13 mt	4 12 mm	5 11 MT	6 10 MM	7 10 MT	23	8 8 ed	9 7 eg	10 6 EF	11 5 ER	12 4 ff	1 3 fr	2 1 FW
2 14 rr	3 14 RW	4 13 RH	5 12 mt	6 11 mm	7 11 mt	24	8 9 MM	9 8 MT	10 7 ed	11 6 eg	12 5 EF	1 4 ER	2 2 ff
2 15 TR	3 15 rf	4 14 rr	5 13 RW	6 12 RH	7 12 RW	25	8 10 mm	9 9 mt	10 8 MM	11 7 MT	12 6 ed	1 5 eg	2 3 EF
2 16 tg	3 16 TF	4 15 TR	5 14 rf	6 13 rr	7 13 rf	26	8 11 RH	9 10 RW	10 9 mm	11 8 mt	12 7 MM	1 6 MT	2 4 ed
2 17 FT	3 17 td	4 16 tg	5 15 TF	6 14 TR	7 14 TF	27	8 12 rr	9 11 rf	10 10 RH	11 9 RW	12 8 mm	1 7 mt	2 5 MM
2 18 ft	3 18 FM	4 17 FT	5 16 td	6 15 tg	7 15 td	28	8 13 TR	9 12 TF	10 11 rr	11 10 rf	12 9 RH	1 8 RW	2 6 mm
2 19 EW	3 19 fm	4 18 ft	5 17 FM	6 16 FT	7 16 FM	29	8 14 tg	9 13 td	10 12 TR	11 11 TF	12 10 rr	1 9 rf	2 7 RH
	3 20 EH		5 18 fm	6 17 ft		30	8 15 FT		10 13 tg		12 11 TR		2 8 rr

2005 tm ROOSTER

JAN ET	FEB et	MAR MW	APR mf	MAY RF	JUN rd	DAY OF MON	JUL TM	AUG tm	SEP FH	OCT fr	NOV ER	DEC eg
25 WARM	27 CLEAR	27 SUMMER	29 GRAIN		2 HEAT		3 FALL	4 DEW	6 C DEW	6 WINTER	7 SNOW	6 CHILL
19:45	0:48	18:23	22:45		8:44		18:51	21:35	13:59	17:10	9:44	20:29
2 9 TR	3 10 rf	4 9 rr	5 8 RW	6 7 RH	7 6 mt	1	8 5 mm	9 4 mt	10 3 MM	11 2 MT	12 1 ed	12 31 eg
2 10 tg	3 11 TF	4 10 TR	5 9 rf	6 8 rr	7 7 RW	2	8 6 RH	9 5 RW	10 4 mm	11 3 mt	12 2 MM	1 1 MT
2 11 FT	3 12 td	4 11 tg	5 10 TF	6 9 TR	7 8 rf	3	8 7 rr	9 6 rf	10 5 RH	11 4 RW	12 3 mm	1 2 mt
2 12 ft	3 13 FM	4 12 FT	5 11 td	6 10 tg	7 9 TF	4	8 8 TR	9 7 TF	10 6 rr	11 5 rf	12 4 RH	1 3 RW
2 13 EW	3 14 fm	4 13 ft	5 12 FM	6 11 FT	7 10 td	5	8 9 tg	9 8 td	10 7 TR	11 6 TF	12 5 rr	1 4 rf
2 14 ef	3 15 EH	4 14 EW	5 13 fm	6 12 ft	7 11 FM	6	8 10 FT	9 9 FM	10 8 tg	11 7 td	12 6 TR	1 5 TF
2 15 MF	3 16 er	4 15 ef	5 14 EH	6 13 EW	7 12 fm	7	8 11 ft	9 10 fm	10 9 FT	11 8 FM	12 7 tg	1 6 td
2 16 md	3 17 MR	4 16 MF	5 15 er	6 14 ef	7 13 EH	8	8 12 EW	9 11 EH	10 10 ft	11 9 fm	12 8 FT	1 7 FM
2 17 RM	3 18 mg	4 17 md	5 16 MR	6 15 MF	7 14 er	9	8 13 ef	9 12 er	10 11 EW	11 10 EH	12 9 ft	1 8 fm
2 18 rm	3 19 RT	4 18 RM	5 17 mg	6 16 md	7 15 MR	10	8 14 MF	9 13 MR	10 12 ef	11 11 er	12 10 EW	1 9 EH
2 19 TH	3 20 rt	4 19 rm	5 18 RT	6 17 RM	7 16 mg	11	8 15 md	9 14 mg	10 13 MF	11 12 MR	12 11 ef	1 10 er
2 20 tr	3 21 TW	4 20 TH	5 19 rt	6 18 rm	7 17 RT	12	8 16 RM	9 15 RT	10 14 md	11 13 mg	12 12 MF	1 11 MR
2 21 FR	3 22 tf	4 21 tr	5 20 TW	6 19 TH	7 18 rt	13	8 17 rm	9 16 rt	10 15 RM	11 14 RT	12 13 md	1 12 mg
2 22 fg	3 23 FF	4 22 FR	5 21 tf	6 20 tr	7 19 TW	14	8 18 TH	9 17 TW	10 16 rm	11 15 rt	12 14 RM	1 13 RT
2 23 ET	3 24 fd	4 23 fg	5 22 FF	6 21 FR	7 20 tf	15	8 19 tr	9 18 tf	10 17 TH	11 16 TW	12 15 rm	1 14 rt
2 24 et	3 25 EM	4 24 ET	5 23 fd	6 22 fg	7 21 FF	16	8 20 FR	9 19 FF	10 18 tr	11 17 tf	12 16 TH	1 15 TW
2 25 MW	3 26 em	4 25 et	5 24 EM	6 23 ET	7 22 fd	17	8 21 fg	9 20 fd	10 19 FR	11 18 FF	12 17 tr	1 16 tf
2 26 mf	3 27 MH	4 26 MW	5 25 em	6 24 et	7 23 EM	18	8 22 ET	9 21 EM	10 20 fg	11 19 fd	12 18 FR	1 17 FF
2 27 RF	3 28 mr	4 27 mf	5 26 MH	6 25 MW	7 24 em	19	8 23 et	9 22 em	10 21 ET	11 20 EM	12 19 fg	1 18 fd
2 28 rd	3 29 RR	4 28 RF	5 27 mr	6 26 mf	7 25 MH	20	8 24 MW	9 23 MH	10 22 et	11 21 em	12 20 ET	1 19 EM
3 1 TM	3 30 rg	4 29 rd	5 28 RR	6 27 RF	7 26 mr	21	8 25 mf	9 24 mr	10 23 MW	11 22 MH	12 21 et	1 20 em
3 2 tm	3 31 TT	4 30 TM	5 29 rg	6 28 rd	7 27 RR	22	8 26 RF	9 25 RR	10 24 mf	11 23 mr	12 22 MW	1 21 MH
3 3 FH	4 1 tt	5 1 tm	5 30 TT	6 29 TM	7 28 rg	23	8 27 rd	9 26 rg	10 25 RF	11 24 RR	12 23 mf	1 22 mr
3 4 fr	4 2 FW	5 2 FH	5 31 tt	6 30 tm	7 29 TT	24	8 28 TM	9 27 TT	10 26 rd	11 25 rg	12 24 RF	1 23 RR
3 5 ER	4 3 ff	5 3 fr	6 1 FW	7 1 FH	7 30 tt	25	8 29 tm	9 28 tt	10 27 TM	11 26 TT	12 25 rd	1 24 rg
3 6 eg	4 4 EF	5 4 ER	6 2 ff	7 2 fr	7 31 FW	26	8 30 FH	9 29 FW	10 28 tm	11 27 tt	12 26 TM	1 25 TT
3 7 MT	4 5 ed	5 5 eg	6 3 EF	7 3 ER	8 1 ff	27	8 31 fr	9 30 ff	10 29 FH	11 28 FW	12 27 tm	1 26 tt
3 8 mt	4 6 MM	5 6 MT	6 4 ed	7 4 eg	8 2 EF	28	9 1 ER	10 1 EF	10 30 fr	11 29 ff	12 28 FH	1 27 FW
3 9 RW	4 7 mm	5 7 mt	6 5 MM	7 5 MT	8 3 ed	29	9 2 eg	10 2 ed	10 31 ER	11 30 EF	12 29 fr	1 28 ff
	4 8 RH		6 6 mm		8 4 MM	30	9 3 MT		11 1 eg		12 30 ER	

2006 FH DOG

JAN MT	FEB mt	MAR RW	APR rf	MAY TF	JUN td	DAY OF MON	JUL FM	JUL FM	AUG fm	SEP EH	OCT er	NOV MR	DEC mg
7 SPRING	7 WARM	8 CLEAR	8 SUMMER	11 GRAIN	12 HEAT		15 FALL	16 DEW	17 C DEW	17 WINTER	17 SNOW	18 CHILL	17 SPRING
7:25	1:35	6:38	23:49	4:34	14:57		0:40	3:32	19:48	23:00	15:33	1:32	13:14
1 29 EF	2 28 ER	3 29 ff	4 28 fr	5 27 FW	6 26 FH	1	7 25 tt	8 24 tm	9 22 TT	10 22 TM	11 21 TT	12 20 rd	1 19 rg
1 30 ed	3 1 eg	3 30 EF	4 29 ER	5 28 ff	6 27 fr	2	7 26 FW	8 25 FH	9 23 tt	10 23 tm	11 22 tt	12 21 TM	1 20 TT
1 31 MM	3 2 MT	3 31 ed	4 30 eg	5 29 EF	6 28 ER	3	7 27 ff	8 26 fr	9 24 FW	10 24 FH	11 23 FW	12 22 tm	1 21 tt
2 1 mm	3 3 mt	4 1 MM	5 1 MT	5 30 ed	6 29 eg	4	7 28 EF	8 27 ER	9 25 ff	10 25 fr	11 24 ff	12 23 FH	1 22 FW
2 2 RH	3 4 RW	4 2 mm	5 2 mt	5 31 MM	6 30 MT	5	7 29 ed	8 28 eg	9 26 EF	10 26 ER	11 25 EF	12 24 fr	1 23 ff
2 3 rr	3 5 rf	4 3 RH	5 3 RW	6 1 mm	7 1 mt	6	7 30 MM	8 29 MT	9 27 ed	10 27 eg	11 26 ed	12 25 ER	1 24 EF
2 4 TR	3 6 TF	4 4 rr	5 4 rf	6 2 RH	7 2 RW	7	7 31 mm	8 30 mt	9 28 MM	10 28 MT	11 27 MM	12 26 eg	1 25 ed
2 5 tg	3 7 td	4 5 TR	5 5 TF	6 3 rr	7 3 rf	8	8 1 RH	8 31 RW	9 29 mm	10 29 mt	11 28 mm	12 27 MT	1 26 MM
2 6 FT	3 8 FM	4 6 tg	5 6 td	6 4 TR	7 4 TF	9	8 2 rr	9 1 rf	9 30 RH	10 30 RW	11 29 RH	12 28 mt	1 27 mm
2 7 ft	3 9 fm	4 7 FT	5 7 FM	6 5 tg	7 5 td	10	8 3 TR	9 2 TF	10 1 rr	10 31 rf	11 30 rr	12 29 RW	1 28 RH
2 8 EW	3 10 EH	4 8 ft	5 8 fm	6 6 FT	7 6 FM	11	8 4 tg	9 3 td	10 2 TR	11 1 TF	12 1 TR	12 30 rf	1 29 rr
2 9 ef	3 11 er	4 9 EW	5 9 EH	6 7 ft	7 7 fm	12	8 5 FT	9 4 FM	10 3 tg	11 2 td	12 2 tg	12 31 TF	1 30 TR
2 10 MF	3 12 MR	4 10 ef	5 10 er	6 8 EW	7 8 EH	13	8 6 ft	9 5 fm	10 4 FT	11 3 FM	12 3 FT	1 1 td	1 31 tg
2 11 md	3 13 mg	4 11 MF	5 11 MR	6 9 ef	7 9 er	14	8 7 EW	9 6 EH	10 5 ft	11 4 fm	12 4 ft	1 2 FM	2 1 FT
2 12 RM	3 14 RT	4 12 md	5 12 mg	6 10 MF	7 10 MR	15	8 8 ef	9 7 er	10 6 EW	11 5 EH	12 5 EW	1 3 fm	2 2 ft
2 13 rm	3 15 rt	4 13 RM	5 13 RT	6 11 md	7 11 mg	16	8 9 MF	9 8 MR	10 7 ef	11 6 er	12 6 ef	1 4 EH	2 3 EW
2 14 TH	3 16 TW	4 14 rm	5 14 rt	6 12 RM	7 12 RT	17	8 10 md	9 9 mg	10 8 MF	11 7 MR	12 7 MF	1 5 er	2 4 ef
2 15 tr	3 17 tf	4 15 TH	5 15 TW	6 13 rm	7 13 rt	18	8 11 RM	9 10 RT	10 9 md	11 8 mg	12 8 md	1 6 MR	2 5 MF
2 16 FR	3 18 FF	4 16 tr	5 16 tf	6 14 TH	7 14 TW	19	8 12 rm	9 11 rt	10 10 RM	11 9 RT	12 9 RM	1 7 mg	2 6 md
2 17 fg	3 19 fd	4 17 FR	5 17 FF	6 15 tr	7 15 tf	20	8 13 TH	9 12 TW	10 11 rm	11 10 rt	12 10 rm	1 8 RT	2 7 RM
2 18 ET	3 20 EM	4 18 fg	5 18 fd	6 16 FR	7 16 FF	21	8 14 tr	9 13 tf	10 12 TH	11 11 TW	12 11 TH	1 9 rt	2 8 rm
2 19 et	3 21 em	4 19 ET	5 19 EM	6 17 fg	7 17 fd	22	8 15 FR	9 14 FF	10 13 tr	11 12 tf	12 12 tr	1 10 TW	2 9 TH
2 20 MW	3 22 MH	4 20 et	5 20 em	6 18 ET	7 18 EM	23	8 16 fg	9 15 fd	10 14 FR	11 13 FF	12 13 FR	1 11 tf	2 10 tr
2 21 mf	3 23 mr	4 21 MW	5 21 MH	6 19 et	7 19 em	24	8 17 ET	9 16 EM	10 15 fg	11 14 fd	12 14 fg	1 12 FF	2 11 FR
2 22 RF	3 24 RR	4 22 mf	5 22 mr	6 20 MW	7 20 MH	25	8 18 et	9 17 em	10 16 ET	11 15 EM	12 15 ET	1 13 fd	2 12 fg
2 23 rd	3 25 rg	4 23 RF	5 23 RR	6 21 mf	7 21 mr	26	8 19 MW	9 18 MH	10 17 et	11 16 em	12 16 et	1 14 EM	2 13 ET
2 24 TM	3 26 TT	4 24 rd	5 24 rg	6 22 RF	7 22 RR	27	8 20 mf	9 19 mr	10 18 MW	11 17 MH	12 17 MW	1 15 em	2 14 et
2 25 tm	3 27 tt	4 25 TM	5 25 TT	6 23 rd	7 23 rg	28	8 21 RF	9 20 RR	10 19 mf	11 18 mr	12 18 mf	1 16 MH	2 15 MW
2 26 FH	3 28 FW	4 26 tm	5 26 tt	6 24 TM	7 24 TT	29	8 22 rd	9 21 rg	10 20 RF	11 19 RR	12 19 RF	1 17 mr	2 16 mf
2 27 fr		4 27 FH		6 25 tm		30	8 23 TM		10 21 rd	11 20 rg		1 18 RR	2 17 RF

2007 fr BOAR

JAN RT	FEB rt	MAR TW	APR tf	MAY FF	JUN fd	DAY OF MON	JUL EM	AUG em	SEP MH	OCT mr	NOV RR	DEC rg
17 WARM	18 CLEAR	20 SUMMER	21 GRAIN	23 HEAT	26 FALL		27 DEW	29 C DEW	29 WINTER	28 SNOW	28 CHILL	28 SPRING
7:24	12:27	6:01	10:23	20:46	6:29		9:13	1:37	3:32	21:23	7:21	19:03
2 18 rd	3 19 RR	4 17 mf	5 17 mr	6 15 MW	7 14 em	1	8 13 et	9 11 EM	10 11 ET	11 10 EM	12 10 ET	1 8 fd
2 19 TM	3 20 rg	4 18 RF	5 18 RR	6 16 mf	7 15 MH	2	8 14 MW	9 12 em	10 12 et	11 11 em	12 11 et	1 9 EM
2 20 tm	3 21 TT	4 19 rd	5 19 rg	6 17 RF	7 16 mr	3	8 15 mf	9 13 MH	10 13 MW	11 12 MH	12 12 MW	1 10 em
2 21 FH	3 22 tt	4 20 TM	5 20 TT	6 18 rd	7 17 RR	4	8 16 RF	9 14 mr	10 14 mf	11 13 mr	12 13 mf	1 11 MH
2 22 fr	3 23 FW	4 21 tm	5 21 tt	6 19 TM	7 18 rg	5	8 17 rd	9 15 RR	10 15 RF	11 14 RR	12 14 RF	1 12 mr
2 23 ER	3 24 ff	4 22 FH	5 22 FW	6 20 tm	7 19 TT	6	8 18 TM	9 16 rg	10 16 rd	11 15 rg	12 15 rd	1 13 RR
2 24 eg	3 25 EF	4 23 fr	5 23 ff	6 21 FH	7 20 tt	7	8 19 tm	9 17 TT	10 17 TM	11 16 TT	12 16 TM	1 14 rg
2 25 MT	3 26 ed	4 24 ER	5 24 EF	6 22 fr	7 21 FW	8	8 20 FH	9 18 tt	10 18 tm	11 17 tt	12 17 tm	1 15 TT
2 26 mt	3 27 MM	4 25 eg	5 25 ed	6 23 ER	7 22 ff	9	8 21 fr	9 19 FW	10 19 FH	11 18 FW	12 18 FH	1 16 tt
2 27 RW	3 28 mm	4 26 MT	5 26 MM	6 24 eg	7 23 EF	10	8 22 ER	9 20 ff	10 20 fr	11 19 ff	12 19 fr	1 17 FW
2 28 rf	3 29 RH	4 27 mt	5 27 mm	6 25 MT	7 24 ed	11	8 23 eg	9 21 EF	10 21 ER	11 20 EF	12 20 ER	1 18 ff
3 1 TF	3 30 rr	4 28 RW	5 28 RH	6 26 mt	7 25 MM	12	8 24 MT	9 22 ed	10 22 eg	11 21 ed	12 21 eg	1 19 EF
3 2 td	3 31 TR	4 29 rf	5 29 rr	6 27 RW	7 26 mm	13	8 25 mt	9 23 MM	10 23 MT	11 22 MM	12 22 MT	1 20 ed
3 3 FM	4 1 tg	4 30 TF	5 30 TR	6 28 rf	7 27 RH	14	8 26 RW	9 24 mm	10 24 mt	11 23 mm	12 23 mt	1 21 MM
3 4 fm	4 2 FT	5 1 td	5 31 tg	6 29 TF	7 28 rr	15	8 27 rf	9 25 RH	10 25 RW	11 24 RH	12 24 RW	1 22 mm
3 5 EH	4 3 ft	5 2 FM	6 1 FT	6 30 td	7 29 TR	16	8 28 TF	9 26 rr	10 26 rf	11 25 rr	12 25 rf	1 23 RH
3 6 er	4 4 EW	5 3 fm	6 2 ft	7 1 FM	7 30 tg	17	8 29 td	9 27 TR	10 27 TF	11 26 TR	12 26 TF	1 24 rr
3 7 MR	4 5 ef	5 4 EH	6 3 EW	7 2 fm	7 31 FT	18	8 30 FM	9 28 tg	10 28 td	11 27 tg	12 27 td	1 25 TR
3 8 mg	4 6 MF	5 5 er	6 4 ef	7 3 EH	8 1 ft	19	8 31 fm	9 29 FT	10 29 FM	11 28 FT	12 28 FM	1 26 tg
3 9 RT	4 7 md	5 6 MR	6 5 MF	7 4 er	8 2 EW	20	9 1 EH	9 30 ft	10 30 fm	11 29 ft	12 29 fm	1 27 FT
3 10 rt	4 8 RM	5 7 mg	6 6 md	7 5 MR	8 3 ef	21	9 2 er	10 1 EW	10 31 EH	11 30 EW	12 30 EH	1 28 ft
3 11 TW	4 9 rm	5 8 RT	6 7 RM	7 6 mg	8 4 MF	22	9 3 MR	10 2 ef	11 1 er	12 1 ef	12 31 er	1 29 EW
3 12 tf	4 10 TH	5 9 rt	6 8 rm	7 7 RT	8 5 md	23	9 4 mg	10 3 MF	11 2 MR	12 2 MF	1 1 MR	1 30 ef
3 13 FF	4 11 tr	5 10 TW	6 9 TH	7 8 rt	8 6 RM	24	9 5 RT	10 4 md	11 3 mg	12 3 md	1 2 mg	1 31 MF
3 14 fd	4 12 FR	5 11 tf	6 10 tr	7 9 TW	8 7 rm	25	9 6 rt	10 5 RM	11 4 RT	12 4 RM	1 3 RT	2 1 md
3 15 EM	4 13 fg	5 12 FF	6 11 FR	7 10 tf	8 8 TH	26	9 7 TW	10 6 rm	11 5 rt	12 5 rm	1 4 rt	2 2 RM
3 16 em	4 14 ET	5 13 fd	6 12 fg	7 11 FF	8 9 tr	27	9 8 tf	10 7 TH	11 6 TW	12 6 TH	1 5 TW	2 3 rm
3 17 MH	4 15 et	5 14 EM	6 13 ET	7 12 fd	8 10 FR	28	9 9 FF	10 8 tr	11 7 tf	12 7 tr	1 6 tf	2 4 TH
3 18 mr	4 16 MW	5 15 em	6 14 et	7 13 EM	8 11 fg	29	9 10 fd	10 9 FR	11 8 FF	12 8 FR	1 7 FF	2 5 tr
		5 16 MH			8 12 ET	30		10 10 fg	11 9 fd	12 9 fg		2 6 FR

2008 ER RAT

JAN TT	FEB tt	MAR FW	APR ff	MAY EF	JUN ed	DAY OF MON	JUL MM	AUG mm	SEP RH	OCT rr	NOV TR	DEC tg
28 WARM	28 CLEAR		1 SUMMER	2 GRAIN	5 HEAT		7 FALL	8 DEW	10 C DEW	10 WINTER	10 SNOW	10 CHILL
13:13	28:16		11:50	16:12	2:35		12:18	15:02	7:26	9:21	3:13	13:10
2 7 fg	3 8 fd	4 6 FR	5 5 tf	6 4 tr	7 3 TW	1	8 1 rm	8 31 rt	9 29 RM	10 29 RT	11 28 RM	12 27 mg
2 8 ET	3 9 EM	4 7 fg	5 6 FF	6 5 FR	7 4 tf	2	8 2 TH	9 1 TW	9 30 rm	10 30 rt	11 29 rm	12 28 RT
2 9 et	3 10 em	4 8 ET	5 7 fd	6 6 fg	7 5 FF	3	8 3 tr	9 2 tf	10 1 TH	10 31 TW	11 30 TH	12 29 rt
2 10 MW	3 11 MH	4 9 et	5 8 EM	6 7 ET	7 6 fd	4	8 4 FR	9 3 FF	10 2 tr	11 1 tf	12 1 tr	12 30 TW
2 11 mf	3 12 mr	4 10 MW	5 9 em	6 8 et	7 7 EM	5	8 5 fg	9 4 fd	10 3 FR	11 2 FF	12 2 FR	12 31 tf
2 12 RF	3 13 RR	4 11 mf	5 10 MH	6 9 MW	7 8 em	6	8 6 ET	9 5 EM	10 4 fg	11 3 fd	12 3 fg	1 1 FF
2 13 rd	3 14 rg	4 12 RF	5 11 mr	6 10 mf	7 9 MH	7	8 7 et	9 6 em	10 5 ET	11 4 EM	12 4 ET	1 2 fd
2 14 TM	3 15 TT	4 13 rd	5 12 RR	6 11 RF	7 10 mr	8	8 8 MW	9 7 MH	10 6 et	11 5 em	12 5 et	1 3 EM
2 15 tm	3 16 tt	4 14 TM	5 13 rg	6 12 rd	7 11 RR	9	8 9 mf	9 8 mr	10 7 MW	11 6 MH	12 6 MW	1 4 em
2 16 FH	3 17 FW	4 15 tm	5 14 TT	6 13 TM	7 12 rg	10	8 10 RF	9 9 RR	10 8 mf	11 7 mr	12 7 mf	1 5 MH
2 17 fr	3 18 ff	4 16 FH	5 15 tt	6 14 tm	7 13 TT	11	8 11 rd	9 10 rg	10 9 RF	11 8 RR	12 8 RF	1 6 mr
2 18 ER	3 19 EF	4 17 fr	5 16 FW	6 15 FH	7 14 tt	12	8 12 TM	9 11 TT	10 10 rd	11 9 rg	12 9 rd	1 7 RR
2 19 eg	3 20 ed	4 18 ER	5 17 ff	6 16 fr	7 15 FW	13	8 13 tm	9 12 tt	10 11 TM	11 10 TT	12 10 TM	1 8 rg
2 20 MT	3 21 MM	4 19 eg	5 18 EF	6 17 ER	7 16 ff	14	8 14 FH	9 13 FW	10 12 tm	11 11 tt	12 11 tm	1 9 TT
2 21 mt	3 22 mm	4 20 MT	5 19 ed	6 18 eg	7 17 EF	15	8 15 fr	9 14 ff	10 13 FH	11 12 FW	12 12 FH	1 10 tt
2 22 RW	3 23 RH	4 21 mt	5 20 MM	6 19 MT	7 18 ed	16	8 16 ER	9 15 EF	10 14 fr	11 13 ff	12 13 fr	1 11 FW
2 23 rf	3 24 rr	4 22 RW	5 21 mm	6 20 mt	7 19 MM	17	8 17 eg	9 16 ed	10 15 ER	11 14 EF	12 14 ER	1 12 ff
2 24 TF	3 25 TR	4 23 rf	5 22 RH	6 21 RW	7 20 mm	18	8 18 MT	9 17 MM	10 16 eg	11 15 ed	12 15 eg	1 13 EF
2 25 td	3 26 tg	4 24 TF	5 23 rr	6 22 rf	7 21 RH	19	8 19 mt	9 18 mm	10 17 MT	11 16 MM	12 16 MT	1 14 ed
2 26 FM	3 27 FT	4 25 td	5 24 TR	6 23 TF	7 22 rr	20	8 20 RW	9 19 RH	10 18 mt	11 17 mm	12 17 mt	1 15 MM
2 27 fm	3 28 ft	4 26 FM	5 25 tg	6 24 td	7 23 TR	21	8 21 rf	9 20 rr	10 19 RW	11 18 RH	12 18 RW	1 16 mm
2 28 EH	3 29 EW	4 27 fm	5 26 FT	6 25 FM	7 24 tg	22	8 22 TF	9 21 TR	10 20 rf	11 19 rr	12 19 rf	1 17 RH
2 29 er	3 30 ef	4 28 EH	5 27 ft	6 26 fm	7 25 FT	23	8 23 td	9 22 tg	10 21 TF	11 20 TR	12 20 TF	1 18 rr
3 1 MR	3 31 MF	4 29 er	5 28 EW	6 27 EH	7 26 ft	24	8 24 FM	9 23 FT	10 22 td	11 21 tg	12 21 td	1 19 TR
3 2 mg	4 1 md	4 30 MR	5 29 ef	6 28 er	7 27 EW	25	8 25 fm	9 24 ft	10 23 FM	11 22 FT	12 22 FM	1 20 tg
3 3 RT	4 2 RM	5 1 mg	5 30 MF	6 29 MR	7 28 ef	26	8 26 EH	9 25 EW	10 24 fm	11 23 ft	12 23 fm	1 21 FT
3 4 rt	4 3 rm	5 2 RT	5 31 md	6 30 mg	7 29 MF	27	8 27 er	9 26 ef	10 25 EH	11 24 EW	12 24 EH	1 22 ft
3 5 TW	4 4 TH	5 3 rt	6 1 RM	7 1 RT	7 30 md	28	8 28 MR	9 27 MF	10 26 er	11 25 ef	12 25 er	1 23 EW
3 6 tf	4 5 tr	5 4 TW	6 2 rm	7 2 rt	7 31 RM	29	8 29 mg	9 28 md	10 27 MR	11 26 MF	12 26 MR	1 24 ef
3 7 FF			6 3 TH			30	8 30 RT		10 28 mg	11 27 md		1 25 MF

2009 eg OX

JAN FT	FEB ft	MAR EW	APR ef	MAY MF	MAY MF	DAY OF MON	JUN md	JUL RM	AUG rm	SEP TH	OCT tr	NOV FR	DEC fg
12 SPRING	9 WARM	9 CLEAR	11 SUMMER	13 GRAIN	15 HEAT		17 FALL	19 DEW	20 C DEW	21 WINTER	21 SNOW	21 CHILL	21 SPRING
1:12	19:02	23:49	17:39	22:01	8:24		18:07	21:18	13:15	15:10	9:03	19:00	7:01
1 26 md	2 25 mg	3 27 md	4 25 MR	5 24 ef	6 23 er	1	7 22 EW	8 20 fm	9 19 ft	10 18 FM	11 17 FT	12 16 td	1 15 tg
1 27 RM	2 26 RT	3 28 RM	4 26 mg	5 25 MF	6 24 MR	2	7 23 ef	8 21 EH	9 20 EW	10 19 fm	11 18 ft	12 17 FM	1 16 FT
1 28 rm	2 27 rt	3 29 rm	4 27 RT	5 26 md	6 25 mg	3	7 24 MF	8 22 er	9 21 ef	10 20 EH	11 19 EW	12 18 fm	1 17 ft
1 29 TH	2 28 TW	3 30 TH	4 28 rt	5 27 RM	6 26 RT	4	7 25 md	8 23 MR	9 22 MF	10 21 er	11 20 ef	12 19 EH	1 18 EW
1 30 tr	3 1 tf	3 31 tr	4 29 TW	5 28 rm	6 27 rt	5	7 26 RM	8 24 mg	9 23 md	10 22 MR	11 21 MF	12 20 er	1 19 ef
1 31 FR	3 2 FF	4 1 FR	4 30 tf	5 29 TH	6 28 TW	6	7 27 rm	8 25 RT	9 24 RM	10 23 mg	11 22 md	12 21 MR	1 20 MF
2 1 fg	3 3 fd	4 2 fg	5 1 FF	5 30 tr	6 29 tf	7	7 28 TH	8 26 rt	9 25 rm	10 24 RT	11 23 RM	12 22 mg	1 21 md
2 2 ET	3 4 EM	4 3 ET	5 2 fd	5 31 FR	6 30 FF	8	7 29 tr	8 27 TW	9 26 TH	10 25 rt	11 24 rm	12 23 RT	1 22 RM
2 3 et	3 5 em	4 4 et	5 3 EM	6 1 fg	7 1 fd	9	7 30 FR	8 28 tf	9 27 tr	10 26 TW	11 25 TH	12 24 rt	1 23 rm
2 4 MW	3 6 MH	4 5 MW	5 4 em	6 2 ET	7 2 EM	10	7 31 fg	8 29 FF	9 28 FR	10 27 tf	11 26 tr	12 25 TW	1 24 TH
2 5 mf	3 7 mr	4 6 mf	5 5 MH	6 3 et	7 3 em	11	8 1 ET	8 30 fd	9 29 fg	10 28 FF	11 27 FR	12 26 tf	1 25 tr
2 6 RF	3 8 RR	4 7 RF	5 6 mr	6 4 MW	7 4 MH	12	8 2 et	8 31 EM	9 30 ET	10 29 fd	11 28 fg	12 27 FF	1 26 FR
2 7 rd	3 9 rg	4 8 rd	5 7 RR	6 5 mf	7 5 mr	13	8 3 MW	9 1 em	10 1 et	10 30 EM	11 29 ET	12 28 fd	1 27 fg
2 8 TM	3 10 TT	4 9 TM	5 8 rg	6 6 RF	7 6 RR	14	8 4 mf	9 2 MH	10 2 MW	10 31 em	11 30 et	12 29 EM	1 28 ET
2 9 tm	3 11 tt	4 10 tm	5 9 TT	6 7 rd	7 7 rg	15	8 5 RF	9 3 mr	10 3 mf	11 1 MH	12 1 MW	12 30 em	1 29 et
2 10 FH	3 12 FW	4 11 FH	5 10 tt	6 8 TM	7 8 TT	16	8 6 rd	9 4 RR	10 4 RF	11 2 mr	12 2 mf	12 31 MH	1 30 MW
2 11 fr	3 13 ff	4 12 fr	5 11 FW	6 9 tm	7 9 tt	17	8 7 TM	9 5 rg	10 5 rd	11 3 RR	12 3 RF	1 1 mr	1 31 mf
2 12 ER	3 14 EF	4 13 ER	5 12 ff	6 10 FH	7 10 FW	18	8 8 tm	9 6 TT	10 6 TM	11 4 rg	12 4 rd	1 2 RR	2 1 RF
2 13 eg	3 15 ed	4 14 eg	5 13 EF	6 11 fr	7 11 ff	19	8 9 FH	9 7 tt	10 7 tm	11 5 TT	12 5 TM	1 3 rg	2 2 rd
2 14 MT	3 16 MM	4 15 MT	5 14 ed	6 12 ER	7 12 EF	20	8 10 fr	9 8 FW	10 8 FH	11 6 tt	12 6 tm	1 4 TT	2 3 TM
2 15 mt	3 17 mm	4 16 mt	5 15 MM	6 13 eg	7 13 ed	21	8 11 ER	9 9 ff	10 9 fr	11 7 FW	12 7 FH	1 5 tt	2 4 tm
2 16 RW	3 18 RH	4 17 RW	5 16 mm	6 14 MT	7 14 MM	22	8 12 eg	9 10 EF	10 10 ER	11 8 ff	12 8 fr	1 6 FW	2 5 FH
2 17 rf	3 19 rr	4 18 rf	5 17 RH	6 15 mt	7 15 mm	23	8 13 MT	9 11 ed	10 11 eg	11 9 EF	12 9 ER	1 7 ff	2 6 fr
2 18 TF	3 20 TR	4 19 TF	5 18 rr	6 16 RW	7 16 RH	24	8 14 mt	9 12 MM	10 12 MT	11 10 ed	12 10 eg	1 8 EF	2 7 ER
2 19 td	3 21 tg	4 20 td	5 19 TR	6 17 rf	7 17 rr	25	8 15 RW	9 13 mm	10 13 mt	11 11 MM	12 11 MT	1 9 ed	2 8 eg
2 20 FM	3 22 FT	4 21 FM	5 20 tg	6 18 TF	7 18 TR	26	8 16 rf	9 14 RH	10 14 RW	11 12 mm	12 12 mt	1 10 MM	2 9 MT
2 21 fm	3 23 ft	4 22 fm	5 21 FT	6 19 td	7 19 tg	27	8 17 TF	9 15 rr	10 15 rf	11 13 RH	12 13 RW	1 11 mm	2 10 mt
2 22 EH	3 24 EW	4 23 EH	5 22 ft	6 20 FM	7 20 FT	28	8 18 td	9 16 TR	10 16 TF	11 14 rr	12 14 rf	1 12 RH	2 11 RW
2 23 er	3 25 ef	4 24 er	5 23 EW	6 21 fm	7 21 ft	29	8 19 FM	9 17 tg	10 17 td	11 15 TR	12 15 TF	1 13 rr	2 12 rf
2 24 MR	3 26 MF			6 22 EH		30		9 18 FT	10	11 16 tg		1 14 TR	2 13 TF

2010 MT TIGER

JAN ET			FEB et			MAR MW			APR mf			MAY RF			JUN rd			DAY OF MON	JUL TM			AUG tm			SEP FH			OCT tr			NOV ER			DEC eg		
21 WARM			21 CLEAR			22 SUMMER			24 GRAIN			26 HEAT			27 FALL							1 DEW			1 C DEW			2 WINTER			2 SNOW			3 CHILL		
0:35			5:55			23:29			3:51			14:14			23:57							3:04			19:04			21:01			13:41			1:38		
2	14	td	3	16	tg	4	14	TF	5	14	TR	6	12	rf	7	12	rr	1	8	10	RW	9	8	mm	10	8	mt	11	6	MM	12	6	MT	1	4	ed
2	15	FM	3	17	FT	4	15	td	5	15	tg	6	13	TF	7	13	TR	2	8	11	rf	9	9	RH	10	9	RW	11	7	mm	12	7	mt	1	5	MM
2	16	fm	3	18	ft	4	16	FM	5	16	FT	6	14	td	7	14	tg	3	8	12	TF	9	10	rr	10	10	rf	11	8	RH	12	8	RW	1	6	mm
2	17	EH	3	19	EW	4	17	fm	5	17	ft	6	15	FM	7	15	FT	4	8	13	td	9	11	TR	10	11	TF	11	9	rr	12	9	rf	1	7	RH
2	18	er	3	20	ef	4	18	EH	5	18	EW	6	16	fm	7	16	ft	5	8	14	FM	9	12	tg	10	12	td	11	10	TR	12	10	TF	1	8	rr
2	19	MR	3	21	MF	4	19	er	5	19	ef	6	17	EH	7	17	EW	6	8	15	fm	9	13	FT	10	13	FM	11	11	tg	12	11	td	1	9	TR
2	20	mg	3	22	md	4	20	MR	5	20	MF	6	18	er	7	18	ef	7	8	16	EH	9	14	ft	10	14	fm	11	12	FT	12	12	FM	1	10	tg
2	21	RT	3	23	RM	4	21	mg	5	21	md	6	19	MR	7	19	MF	8	8	17	er	9	15	EW	10	15	EH	11	13	ft	12	13	fm	1	11	FT
2	22	rt	3	24	rm	4	22	RT	5	22	RM	6	20	mg	7	20	md	9	8	18	MR	9	16	ef	10	16	er	11	14	EW	12	14	EH	1	12	ft
2	23	TW	3	25	TH	4	23	rt	5	23	rm	6	21	RT	7	21	RM	10	8	19	mg	9	17	MF	10	17	MR	11	15	ef	12	15	er	1	13	EW
2	24	tf	3	26	tr	4	24	TW	5	24	TH	6	22	rt	7	22	rm	11	8	20	RT	9	18	md	10	18	mg	11	16	MF	12	16	MR	1	14	ef
2	25	FF	3	27	FR	4	25	tf	5	25	tr	6	23	TW	7	23	TH	12	8	21	rt	9	19	RM	10	19	RT	11	17	md	12	17	mg	1	15	MF
2	26	fd	3	28	fg	4	26	FF	5	26	FR	6	24	tf	7	24	tr	13	8	22	TW	9	20	rm	10	20	rt	11	18	RM	12	18	RT	1	16	md
2	27	EM	3	29	ET	4	27	fd	5	27	fg	6	25	FF	7	25	FR	14	8	23	tf	9	21	TH	10	21	TW	11	19	rm	12	19	rt	1	17	RM
2	28	em	3	30	et	4	28	EM	5	28	ET	6	26	fd	7	26	fg	15	8	24	FF	9	22	tr	10	22	tf	11	20	TH	12	20	TW	1	18	rm
3	1	MH	3	31	MW	4	29	em	5	29	et	6	27	EM	7	27	ET	16	8	25	fd	9	23	FR	10	23	FF	11	21	tr	12	21	tf	1	19	TH
3	2	mr	4	1	mf	4	30	MH	5	30	MW	6	28	em	7	28	et	17	8	26	EM	9	24	fg	10	24	fd	11	22	FR	12	22	FF	1	20	tr
3	3	RR	4	2	RF	5	1	mr	5	31	mf	6	29	MH	7	29	MW	18	8	27	em	9	25	ET	10	25	EM	11	23	fg	12	23	fd	1	21	FR
3	4	rg	4	3	rd	5	2	RR	6	1	RF	6	30	mr	7	30	mf	19	8	28	MH	9	26	et	10	26	em	11	24	ET	12	24	EM	1	22	fg
3	5	TT	4	4	TM	5	3	rg	6	2	rd	7	1	RR	7	31	RF	20	8	29	mr	9	27	MW	10	27	MH	11	25	et	12	25	em	1	23	ET
3	6	tt	4	5	tm	5	4	TT	6	3	TM	7	2	rg	8	1	rd	21	8	30	RR	9	28	mf	10	28	mr	11	26	MW	12	26	MH	1	24	et
3	7	FW	4	6	FH	5	5	tt	6	4	tm	7	3	TT	8	2	TM	22	8	31	rg	9	29	RF	10	29	RR	11	27	mf	12	27	mr	1	25	MW
3	8	ff	4	7	fr	5	6	FW	6	5	FH	7	4	tt	8	3	tm	23	9	1	TT	9	30	rd	10	30	rg	11	28	RF	12	28	RR	1	26	mf
3	9	EF	4	8	ER	5	7	ff	6	6	fr	7	5	FW	8	4	FH	24	9	2	tt	10	1	TM	10	31	TT	11	29	rd	12	29	rg	1	27	RF
3	10	ed	4	9	eg	5	8	EF	6	7	ER	7	6	ff	8	5	fr	25	9	3	FW	10	2	tm	11	1	tt	11	30	TM	12	30	TT	1	28	rd
3	11	MM	4	10	MT	5	9	ed	6	8	eg	7	7	EF	8	6	ER	26	9	4	ff	10	3	FH	11	2	FW	12	1	tm	12	31	tt	1	29	TM
3	12	mm	4	11	mt	5	10	MM	6	9	MT	7	8	ed	8	7	eg	27	9	5	EF	10	4	fr	11	3	ff	12	2	FH	1	1	FW	1	30	tm
3	13	RH	4	12	RW	5	11	mm	6	10	mt	7	9	MM	8	8	MT	28	9	6	ed	10	5	ER	11	4	EF	12	3	fr	1	2	ff	1	31	FH
3	14	rr	4	13	rf	5	12	RH	6	11	RW	7	10	mm	8	9	mt	29	9	7	MM	10	6	eg	11	5	ed	12	4	ER	1	3	EF	2	1	fr
3	15	TR				5	13	rr				7	11	RH				30				10	7	MT				12	5	eg				2	2	ER

2011 mt RABBIT

JAN MT	FEB mt	MAR RW	APR rf	MAY TF	JUN td	DAY OF MON	JUL FM	AUG fm	SEP FH	OCT er	NOV MR	DEC mg
2 SPRING	2 WARM	3 CLEAR	4 SUMMER	5 GRAIN	7 HEAT		9 FALL	11 DEW	13 C DEW	13 WINTER	13 SNOW	13 CHILL
12:32	6:43	11:46	4:51	9:43	20:06		5:49	8:33	0:54	4:07	19:32	7:27
2 3 eg	3 5 ed	4 3 ER	5 3 EF	6 2 ER	7 1 ff	1	7 31 fr	8 29 FW	9 27 tm	10 27 tt	11 25 TM	12 25 TT
2 4 MT	3 6 MM	4 4 eg	5 4 ed	6 3 eg	7 2 EF	2	8 1 ER	8 30 ff	9 28 FH	10 28 FW	11 26 tm	12 26 tt
2 5 mt	3 7 mm	4 5 MT	5 5 MM	6 4 MT	7 3 ed	3	8 2 eg	8 31 EF	9 29 fr	10 29 ff	11 27 FH	12 27 FW
2 6 RW	3 8 RH	4 6 mt	5 6 mm	6 5 mt	7 4 MM	4	8 3 MT	9 1 ed	9 30 ER	10 30 EF	11 28 fr	12 28 ff
2 7 rf	3 9 rr	4 7 RW	5 7 RH	6 6 RW	7 5 mm	5	8 4 mt	9 2 MM	10 1 eg	10 31 ed	11 29 ER	12 29 EF
2 8 TF	3 10 TR	4 8 rf	5 8 rr	6 7 rf	7 6 RH	6	8 5 RW	9 3 mm	10 2 MT	11 1 MM	11 30 eg	12 30 ed
2 9 td	3 11 tg	4 9 TF	5 9 TR	6 8 TF	7 7 rr	7	8 6 rf	9 4 RH	10 3 mt	11 2 mm	12 1 MT	12 31 MM
2 10 FM	3 12 FT	4 10 td	5 10 tg	6 9 td	7 8 TR	8	8 7 TF	9 5 rr	10 4 RW	11 3 RH	12 2 mt	1 1 mm
2 11 fm	3 13 ft	4 11 FM	5 11 FT	6 10 FM	7 9 tg	9	8 8 td	9 6 TR	10 5 rf	11 4 rr	12 3 RW	1 2 RH
2 12 EH	3 14 EW	4 12 fm	5 12 ft	6 11 fm	7 10 FT	10	8 9 FM	9 7 tg	10 6 TF	11 5 TR	12 4 rf	1 3 rr
2 13 er	3 15 ef	4 13 EH	5 13 EW	6 12 EH	7 11 ft	11	8 10 fm	9 8 FT	10 7 td	11 6 tg	12 5 TF	1 4 TR
2 14 MR	3 16 MF	4 14 er	5 14 ef	6 13 er	7 12 EW	12	8 11 EH	9 9 ft	10 8 FM	11 7 FT	12 6 td	1 5 tg
2 15 mg	3 17 md	4 15 MR	5 15 MF	6 14 MR	7 13 ef	13	8 12 er	9 10 EW	10 9 fm	11 8 ft	12 7 FM	1 6 FT
2 16 RT	3 18 RM	4 16 mg	5 16 md	6 15 mg	7 14 MF	14	8 13 MR	9 11 ef	10 10 EH	11 9 EW	12 8 fm	1 7 ft
2 17 rt	3 19 rm	4 17 RT	5 17 RM	6 16 RT	7 15 md	15	8 14 mg	9 12 MF	10 11 er	11 10 ef	12 9 EH	1 8 EW
2 18 TW	3 20 TH	4 18 rt	5 18 rm	6 17 rt	7 16 RM	16	8 15 RT	9 13 md	10 12 MR	11 11 MF	12 10 er	1 9 ef
2 19 tf	3 21 tr	4 19 TW	5 19 TH	6 18 TW	7 17 rm	17	8 16 rt	9 14 RM	10 13 mg	11 12 md	12 11 MR	1 10 MF
2 20 FF	3 22 FR	4 20 tf	5 20 tr	6 19 tf	7 18 TH	18	8 17 TW	9 15 rm	10 14 RT	11 13 RM	12 12 mg	1 11 md
2 21 fd	3 23 fg	4 21 FF	5 21 FR	6 20 FF	7 19 tr	19	8 18 tf	9 16 TH	10 15 rt	11 14 rm	12 13 RT	1 12 RM
2 22 EM	3 24 ET	4 22 fd	5 22 fg	6 21 fd	7 20 FR	20	8 19 FF	9 17 tr	10 16 TW	11 15 TH	12 14 rt	1 13 rm
2 23 em	3 25 et	4 23 EM	5 23 ET	6 22 EM	7 21 fg	21	8 20 fd	9 18 FR	10 17 tf	11 16 tr	12 15 TW	1 14 TH
2 24 MH	3 26 MW	4 24 em	5 24 et	6 23 em	7 22 ET	22	8 21 EM	9 19 fg	10 18 FF	11 17 FR	12 16 tf	1 15 tr
2 25 mr	3 27 mf	4 25 MH	5 25 MW	6 24 MH	7 23 et	23	8 22 em	9 20 ET	10 19 fd	11 18 fg	12 17 FF	1 16 FR
2 26 RR	3 28 RF	4 26 mr	5 26 mf	6 25 mr	7 24 MW	24	8 23 MH	9 21 et	10 20 EM	11 19 ET	12 18 fd	1 17 fg
2 27 rg	3 29 rd	4 27 RR	5 27 RF	6 26 RR	7 25 mf	25	8 24 mr	9 22 MW	10 21 em	11 20 et	12 19 EM	1 18 ET
2 28 TT	3 30 TM	4 28 rg	5 28 rd	6 27 rg	7 26 RF	26	8 25 RR	9 23 mf	10 22 MH	11 21 MW	12 20 em	1 19 et
3 1 tt	3 31 tm	4 29 TT	5 29 TM	6 28 TT	7 27 rd	27	8 26 rg	9 24 RF	10 23 mr	11 22 mf	12 21 MH	1 20 MW
3 2 FW	4 1 FH	4 30 tt	5 30 tm	6 29 tt	7 28 TM	28	8 27 TT	9 25 rd	10 24 RR	11 23 RF	12 22 mr	1 21 mf
3 3 ff	4 2 fr	5 1 FW	5 31 FH	6 30 FW	7 29 tm	29	8 28 tt	9 26 TM	10 25 rg	11 24 rd	12 23 RR	1 22 RF
3 4 EF		5 2 ff	6 1 fr		7 30 FH	30			10 26 TT		12 24 rg	

2012 RW DRAGON

JAN RT	FEB rt	MAR TW	APR tf	APR tf	MAY FF	DAY OF MON	JUN fd	JUL EM	AUG em	SEP MH	OCT mr	NOV RR	DEC rg
13 SPRING	13 WARM	14 CLEAR	15 SUMMER	16 GRAIN	19 HEAT		20 FALL	22 DEW	23 C DEW	24 WINTER	24 SNOW	24 CHILL	24 SPRING
18:40	12:28	17:16	10:40	14:50	1:21		11:26	14:44	6:42	9:56	2:32	13:16	0:31
1 23 rd	2 22 rg	3 22 RF	4 21 RR	5 21 RF	6 19 mr	1	7 19 mf	8 17 MH	9 16 MW	10 15 em	11 14 et	12 13 EM	1 12 ET
1 24 TM	2 23 TT	3 23 rd	4 22 rg	5 22 rd	6 20 RR	2	7 20 RF	8 18 mr	9 17 mf	10 16 MH	11 15 MW	12 14 em	1 13 et
1 25 tm	2 24 tt	3 24 TM	4 23 TT	5 23 TM	6 21 rg	3	7 21 rd	8 19 RR	9 18 RF	10 17 mr	11 16 mf	12 15 MH	1 14 MW
1 26 FH	2 25 FW	3 25 tm	4 24 tt	5 24 tm	6 22 TT	4	7 22 TM	8 20 rg	9 19 rd	10 18 RR	11 17 RF	12 16 mr	1 15 mf
1 27 fr	2 26 ff	3 26 FH	4 25 FW	5 25 FH	6 23 tt	5	7 23 tm	8 21 TT	9 20 TM	10 19 rg	11 18 rd	12 17 RR	1 16 RF
1 28 ER	2 27 EF	3 27 fr	4 26 ff	5 26 fr	6 24 FW	6	7 24 FH	8 22 tt	9 21 tm	10 20 TT	11 19 TM	12 18 rg	1 17 rd
1 29 eg	2 28 ed	3 28 ER	4 27 EF	5 27 ER	6 25 ff	7	7 25 fr	8 23 FW	9 22 FH	10 21 tt	11 20 tm	12 19 TT	1 18 TM
1 30 MT	2 29 MM	3 29 eg	4 28 ed	5 28 eg	6 26 EF	8	7 26 ER	8 24 ff	9 23 fr	10 22 FW	11 21 FH	12 20 tt	1 19 tm
1 31 mt	3 1 mm	3 30 MT	4 29 MM	5 29 MT	6 27 ed	9	7 27 eg	8 25 EF	9 24 ER	10 23 ff	11 22 fr	12 21 FW	1 20 FH
2 1 RW	3 2 RH	3 31 mt	4 30 mm	5 30 mt	6 28 MM	10	7 28 MT	8 26 ed	9 25 eg	10 24 EF	11 23 ER	12 22 ff	1 21 fr
2 2 rf	3 3 rr	4 1 RW	5 1 RH	5 31 RW	6 29 mm	11	7 29 mt	8 27 MM	9 26 MT	10 25 ed	11 24 eg	12 23 EF	1 22 ER
2 3 TF	3 4 TR	4 2 rf	5 2 rr	6 1 rf	6 30 RH	12	7 30 RW	8 28 mm	9 27 mt	10 26 MM	11 25 MT	12 24 ed	1 23 eg
2 4 td	3 5 tg	4 3 TF	5 3 TR	6 2 TF	7 1 rr	13	7 31 rf	8 29 RH	9 28 RW	10 27 mm	11 26 mt	12 25 MM	1 24 MT
2 5 FM	3 6 FT	4 4 td	5 4 tg	6 3 td	7 2 TR	14	8 1 TF	8 30 rr	9 29 rf	10 28 RH	11 27 RW	12 26 mm	1 25 mt
2 6 fm	3 7 ft	4 5 FM	5 5 FT	6 4 FM	7 3 tg	15	8 2 td	8 31 TR	9 30 TF	10 29 rr	11 28 rf	12 27 RH	1 26 RW
2 7 EH	3 8 EW	4 6 fm	5 6 ft	6 5 fm	7 4 FT	16	8 3 FM	9 1 tg	10 1 td	10 30 TR	11 29 TF	12 28 rr	1 27 rf
2 8 er	3 9 ef	4 7 EH	5 7 EW	6 6 EH	7 5 ft	17	8 4 fm	9 2 FT	10 2 FM	10 31 tg	11 30 td	12 29 TR	1 28 TF
2 9 MR	3 10 MF	4 8 er	5 8 ef	6 7 er	7 6 EW	18	8 5 EH	9 3 ft	10 3 fm	11 1 FT	12 1 FM	12 30 tg	1 29 td
2 10 mg	3 11 md	4 9 MR	5 9 MF	6 8 MR	7 7 ef	19	8 6 er	9 4 EW	10 4 EH	11 2 ft	12 2 fm	12 31 FT	1 30 FM
2 11 RT	3 12 RM	4 10 mg	5 10 md	6 9 mg	7 8 MF	20	8 7 MR	9 5 ef	10 5 er	11 3 EW	12 3 EH	1 1 ft	1 31 fm
2 12 rt	3 13 rm	4 11 RT	5 11 RM	6 10 RT	7 9 md	21	8 8 mg	9 6 MF	10 6 MR	11 4 ef	12 4 er	1 2 EW	2 1 EH
2 13 TW	3 14 TH	4 12 rt	5 12 rm	6 11 rt	7 10 RM	22	8 9 RT	9 7 md	10 7 mg	11 5 MF	12 5 MR	1 3 ef	2 2 er
2 14 tf	3 15 tr	4 13 TW	5 13 TH	6 12 TW	7 11 rm	23	8 10 rt	9 8 RM	10 8 RT	11 6 md	12 6 mg	1 4 MF	2 3 MR
2 15 FF	3 16 FR	4 14 tf	5 14 tr	6 13 tf	7 12 TH	24	8 11 TW	9 9 rm	10 9 rt	11 7 RM	12 7 RT	1 5 md	2 4 mg
2 16 fd	3 17 fg	4 15 FF	5 15 FR	6 14 FF	7 13 tr	25	8 12 tf	9 10 TH	10 10 TW	11 8 rm	12 8 rt	1 6 RM	2 5 RT
2 17 EM	3 18 ET	4 16 fd	5 16 fg	6 15 fd	7 14 FR	26	8 13 FF	9 11 tr	10 11 tf	11 9 TH	12 9 TW	1 7 rm	2 6 rt
2 18 em	3 19 et	4 17 EM	5 17 ET	6 16 EM	7 15 fg	27	8 14 fd	9 12 FR	10 12 FF	11 10 tr	12 10 tf	1 8 TH	2 7 TW
2 19 MH	3 20 MW	4 18 em	5 18 et	6 17 em	7 16 ET	28	8 15 EM	9 13 fg	10 13 fd	11 11 FR	12 11 FF	1 9 tr	2 8 tf
2 20 mr	3 21 mf	4 19 MH	5 19 MW	6 18 MH	7 17 et	29	8 16 em	9 14 ET	10 14 EM	11 12 fg	12 12 fd	1 10 FR	2 9 FF
2 21 RR		4 20 mr	5 20 mf		7 18 MW	30		9 15 et		11 13 ET		1 11 fg	

2013 rf SNAKE

JAN TT	FEB tt	MAR FW	APR ff	MAY EF	JUN ed	DAY OF MON	JUL MM	AUG mm	SEP RH	OCT rr	NOV TR	DEC tr
24 WARM	24 CLEAR	26 SUMMER	27 GRAIN	29 HEAT			1 FALL	3 DEW	4 C DEW	5 WINTER	5 SNOW	5 CHILL
18:19	23:05	16:28	20:44	7:09			17:14	20:33	12:31	15:45	8:21	20:07
2 10 fd	3 12 fg	4 10 FF	5 10 FR	6 9 FF	7 8 tr	1	8 7 tf	9 5 TH	10 5 TW	11 3 rm	12 3 rt	1 1 RM
2 11 EM	3 13 ET	4 11 fd	5 11 fg	6 10 fd	7 9 FR	2	8 8 FF	9 6 tr	10 6 tf	11 4 TH	12 4 TW	1 2 rm
2 12 em	3 14 et	4 12 EM	5 12 ET	6 11 EM	7 10 fg	3	8 9 fd	9 7 FR	10 7 FF	11 5 tr	12 5 tf	1 3 TH
2 13 MH	3 15 MW	4 13 em	5 13 et	6 12 em	7 11 ET	4	8 10 EM	9 8 fg	10 8 fd	11 6 FR	12 6 FF	1 4 tr
2 14 mr	3 16 mf	4 14 MH	5 14 MW	6 13 MH	7 12 et	5	8 11 em	9 9 ET	10 9 EM	11 7 fg	12 7 fd	1 5 FR
2 15 RR	3 17 RF	4 15 mr	5 15 mf	6 14 mr	7 13 MW	6	8 12 MH	9 10 et	10 10 em	11 8 ET	12 8 EM	1 6 fg
2 16 rg	3 18 rd	4 16 RR	5 16 RF	6 15 RR	7 14 mf	7	8 13 mr	9 11 MW	10 11 MH	11 9 et	12 9 em	1 7 ET
2 17 TT	3 19 TM	4 17 rg	5 17 rd	6 16 rg	7 15 RF	8	8 14 RR	9 12 mf	10 12 mr	11 10 MW	12 10 MH	1 8 et
2 18 tt	3 20 tm	4 18 TT	5 18 TM	6 17 TT	7 16 rd	9	8 15 rg	9 13 RF	10 13 RR	11 11 mf	12 11 mr	1 9 MW
2 19 FW	3 21 FH	4 19 tt	5 19 tm	6 18 tt	7 17 TM	10	8 16 TT	9 14 rd	10 14 rg	11 12 RF	12 12 RR	1 10 mf
2 20 ff	3 22 fr	4 20 FW	5 20 FH	6 19 FW	7 18 tm	11	8 17 tt	9 15 TM	10 15 TT	11 13 rd	12 13 rg	1 11 RF
2 21 EF	3 23 ER	4 21 ff	5 21 fr	6 20 ff	7 19 FH	12	8 18 FW	9 16 tm	10 16 tt	11 14 TM	12 14 TT	1 12 rd
2 22 ed	3 24 eg	4 22 EF	5 22 ER	6 21 EF	7 20 fr	13	8 19 ff	9 17 FH	10 17 FW	11 15 tm	12 15 tt	1 13 TM
2 23 MM	3 25 MT	4 23 ed	5 23 eg	6 22 ed	7 21 ER	14	8 20 EF	9 18 fr	10 18 ff	11 16 FH	12 16 FW	1 14 tm
2 24 mm	3 26 mt	4 24 MM	5 24 MT	6 23 MM	7 22 eg	15	8 21 ed	9 19 ER	10 19 EF	11 17 fr	12 17 ff	1 15 FH
2 25 RH	3 27 RW	4 25 mm	5 25 mt	6 24 mm	7 23 MT	16	8 22 MM	9 20 eg	10 20 ed	11 18 ER	12 18 EF	1 16 fr
2 26 rr	3 28 rf	4 26 RH	5 26 RW	6 25 RH	7 24 mt	17	8 23 mm	9 21 MT	10 21 MM	11 19 eg	12 19 ed	1 17 ER
2 27 TR	3 29 TF	4 27 rr	5 27 rf	6 26 rr	7 25 RW	18	8 24 RH	9 22 mt	10 22 mm	11 20 MT	12 20 MM	1 18 eg
2 28 tg	3 30 td	4 28 TR	5 28 TF	6 27 TR	7 26 rf	19	8 25 rr	9 23 RW	10 23 RH	11 21 mt	12 21 mm	1 19 MT
3 1 FT	3 31 FM	4 29 tg	5 29 td	6 28 tg	7 27 TF	20	8 26 TR	9 24 rf	10 24 rr	11 22 RW	12 22 RH	1 20 mt
3 2 ft	4 1 fm	4 30 FT	5 30 FM	6 29 FT	7 28 td	21	8 27 tg	9 25 TF	10 25 TR	11 23 rf	12 23 rr	1 21 RW
3 3 EW	4 2 EH	5 1 ft	5 31 fm	6 30 ft	7 29 FM	22	8 28 FT	9 26 td	10 26 tg	11 24 TF	12 24 TR	1 22 rf
3 4 ef	4 3 er	5 2 EW	6 1 EH	7 1 EW	7 30 fm	23	8 29 ft	9 27 FM	10 27 FT	11 25 td	12 25 tg	1 23 TF
3 5 MF	4 4 MR	5 3 ef	6 2 er	7 2 ef	7 31 EH	24	8 30 EW	9 28 fm	10 28 ft	11 26 FM	12 26 FT	1 24 td
3 6 md	4 5 mg	5 4 MF	6 3 MR	7 3 MF	8 1 er	25	8 31 ef	9 29 EH	10 29 EW	11 27 fm	12 27 ft	1 25 FM
3 7 RM	4 6 RT	5 5 md	6 4 mg	7 4 md	8 2 MR	26	9 1 MF	9 30 er	10 30 ef	11 28 EH	12 28 EW	1 26 fm
3 8 rm	4 7 rt	5 6 RM	6 5 RT	7 5 RM	8 3 mg	27	9 2 md	10 1 MR	10 31 MF	11 29 er	12 29 ef	1 27 EH
3 9 TH	4 8 TW	5 7 rm	6 6 rt	7 6 rm	8 4 RT	28	9 3 RM	10 2 mg	11 1 md	11 30 MR	12 30 MF	1 28 er
3 10 tr	4 9 tf	5 8 TH	6 7 TW	7 7 TH	8 5 rt	29	9 4 rm	10 3 RT	11 2 RM	12 1 mg	12 31 md	1 29 MR
3 11 FR		5 9 tr	6 8 tf		8 6 TW	30		10 4 rt		12 2 RT		1 30 mg

2014 TF HORSE

JAN FT	FEB ft	MAR EW	APR ef	MAY MF	JUN md	DAY OF MON	JUL RM	AUG rm	SEP TH	SEP TH	OCT tr	NOV FR	DEC fg
5 SPRING	6 WARM	6 CLEAR	7 SUMMER	9 GRAIN	11 HEAT		12 FALL	15 DEW	15 C DEW	15 WINTER	16 SNOW	16 CHILL	16 SPRING
6:21	0:07	4:50	22:16	2:32	12:57		23:02	2:21	18:20	21:36	14:11	0:57	12:09
1 31 RT	3 1 md	3 31 mg	4 29 MF	5 29 MR	6 27 ef	1	7 27 er	8 25 EW	9 24 EH	10 24 EW	11 22 fm	12 22 ft	1 20 FM
2 1 rt	3 2 RM	4 1 RT	4 30 md	5 30 mg	6 28 MF	2	7 28 MR	8 26 ef	9 25 er	10 25 ef	11 23 EH	12 23 EW	1 21 fm
2 2 TW	3 3 rm	4 2 rt	5 1 RM	5 31 RT	6 29 md	3	7 29 mg	8 27 MF	9 26 MR	10 26 MF	11 24 er	12 24 ef	1 22 EH
2 3 tf	3 4 TH	4 3 TW	5 2 rm	6 1 rt	6 30 RM	4	7 30 RT	8 28 md	9 27 mg	10 27 md	11 25 MR	12 25 MF	1 23 er
2 4 FF	3 5 tr	4 4 tf	5 3 TH	6 2 TW	7 1 rm	5	7 31 rt	8 29 RM	9 28 RT	10 28 RM	11 26 mg	12 26 md	1 24 MR
2 5 fd	3 6 FR	4 5 FF	5 4 tr	6 3 tf	7 2 TH	6	8 1 TW	8 30 rm	9 29 rt	10 29 rm	11 27 RT	12 27 RM	1 25 mg
2 6 EM	3 7 fg	4 6 fd	5 5 FR	6 4 FF	7 3 tr	7	8 2 tf	8 31 TH	9 30 TW	10 30 TH	11 28 rt	12 28 rm	1 26 RT
2 7 em	3 8 ET	4 7 EM	5 6 fg	6 5 fd	7 4 FR	8	8 3 FF	9 1 tr	10 1 tf	10 31 tr	11 29 TW	12 29 TH	1 27 rt
2 8 MH	3 9 et	4 8 em	5 7 ET	6 6 EM	7 5 fg	9	8 4 fd	9 2 FR	10 2 FF	11 1 FR	11 30 tf	12 30 tr	1 28 TW
2 9 mr	3 10 MW	4 9 MH	5 8 et	6 7 em	7 6 ET	10	8 5 EM	9 3 fg	10 3 fd	11 2 fg	12 1 FF	12 31 FR	1 29 tf
2 10 RR	3 11 mf	4 10 mr	5 9 MW	6 8 MH	7 7 et	11	8 6 em	9 4 ET	10 4 EM	11 3 ET	12 2 fd	1 1 fg	1 30 FF
2 11 rg	3 12 RF	4 11 RR	5 10 mf	6 9 mr	7 8 MW	12	8 7 MH	9 5 et	10 5 em	11 4 et	12 3 EM	1 2 ET	1 31 fd
2 12 TT	3 13 rd	4 12 rg	5 11 RF	6 10 RR	7 9 mf	13	8 8 mr	9 6 MW	10 6 MH	11 5 MW	12 4 em	1 3 et	2 1 EM
2 13 tt	3 14 TM	4 13 TT	5 12 rd	6 11 rg	7 10 RF	14	8 9 RR	9 7 mf	10 7 mr	11 6 mf	12 5 MH	1 4 MW	2 2 em
2 14 FW	3 15 tm	4 14 tt	5 13 TM	6 12 TT	7 11 rd	15	8 10 rg	9 8 RF	10 8 RR	11 7 RF	12 6 mr	1 5 mf	2 3 MH
2 15 ff	3 16 FH	4 15 FW	5 14 tm	6 13 tt	7 12 TM	16	8 11 TT	9 9 rd	10 9 rg	11 8 rd	12 7 RR	1 6 RF	2 4 mr
2 16 EF	3 17 fr	4 16 ff	5 15 FH	6 14 FW	7 13 tm	17	8 12 tt	9 10 TM	10 10 TT	11 9 TM	12 8 rg	1 7 rd	2 5 RR
2 17 ed	3 18 ER	4 17 EF	5 16 fr	6 15 ff	7 14 FH	18	8 13 FW	9 11 tm	10 11 tt	11 10 tm	12 9 TT	1 8 TM	2 6 rg
2 18 MM	3 19 eg	4 18 ed	5 17 ER	6 16 EF	7 15 fr	19	8 14 ff	9 12 FH	10 12 FW	11 11 FH	12 10 tt	1 9 tm	2 7 TT
2 19 mm	3 20 MT	4 19 MM	5 18 eg	6 17 ed	7 16 ER	20	8 15 EF	9 13 fr	10 13 ff	11 12 fr	12 11 FW	1 10 FH	2 8 tt
2 20 RH	3 21 mt	4 20 mm	5 19 MT	6 18 MM	7 17 eg	21	8 16 ed	9 14 ER	10 14 EF	11 13 ER	12 12 ff	1 11 fr	2 9 FW
2 21 rr	3 22 RW	4 21 RH	5 20 mt	6 19 mm	7 18 MT	22	8 17 MM	9 15 eg	10 15 ed	11 14 eg	12 13 EF	1 12 ER	2 10 ff
2 22 TR	3 23 rf	4 22 rr	5 21 RW	6 20 RH	7 19 mt	23	8 18 mm	9 16 MT	10 16 MM	11 15 MT	12 14 ed	1 13 eg	2 11 EF
2 23 tg	3 24 TF	4 23 TR	5 22 rf	6 21 rr	7 20 RW	24	8 19 RH	9 17 mt	10 17 mm	11 16 mt	12 15 MM	1 14 MT	2 12 ed
2 24 FT	3 25 td	4 24 tg	5 23 TF	6 22 TR	7 21 rf	25	8 20 rr	9 18 RW	10 18 RH	11 17 RW	12 16 mm	1 15 mt	2 13 MM
2 25 ft	3 26 FM	4 25 FT	5 24 td	6 23 tg	7 22 TF	26	8 21 TR	9 19 rf	10 19 rr	11 18 rf	12 17 RH	1 16 RW	2 14 mm
2 26 EW	3 27 fm	4 26 ft	5 25 FM	6 24 FT	7 23 td	27	8 22 tg	9 20 TF	10 20 TR	11 19 TF	12 18 rr	1 17 rf	2 15 RH
2 27 ef	3 28 EH	4 27 EW	5 26 fm	6 25 ft	7 24 FM	28	8 23 FT	9 21 td	10 21 tg	11 20 td	12 19 TR	1 18 TF	2 16 rr
2 28 MF	3 29 er	4 28 ef	5 27 EH	6 26 EW	7 25 fm	29	8 24 ft	9 22 FM	10 22 FT	11 21 FM	12 20 tg	1 19 td	2 17 TR
	3 30 MR		5 28 er		7 26 EH	30		9 23 fm	10 23 ft		12 21 FT		2 18 tg

2015 td RAM

JAN ET	FEB et	MAR MW	APR mf	MAY RF	JUN rd	DAY OF MON	JUL TM	AUG tm	SEP FH	OCT tr	NOV ER	DEC eg
16 WARM	17 CLEAR	18 SUMMER	20 GRAIN	22 HEAT	24 FALL		26 DEW	27 C DEW	27 WINTER	26 SNOW	27 CHILL	26 SPRING
5:56	10:58	4:00	8:20	18:30	4:51		8:10	0:09	3:25	20:01	6:47	18:00
2 19 FT	3 20 td	4 19 tg	5 18 TF	6 16 rr	7 16 rf	1	8 14 RH	9 13 RW	10 13 RH	11 12 RW	12 11 mm	1 10 mt
2 20 ft	3 21 FM	4 20 FT	5 19 td	6 17 TR	7 17 TF	2	8 15 rr	9 14 rf	10 14 rr	11 13 rf	12 12 RH	1 11 RW
2 21 EW	3 22 fm	4 21 ft	5 20 FM	6 18 tg	7 18 td	3	8 16 TR	9 15 TF	10 15 TR	11 14 TF	12 13 rr	1 12 rf
2 22 ef	3 23 EH	4 22 EW	5 21 fm	6 19 FT	7 19 FM	4	8 17 tg	9 16 td	10 16 tg	11 15 td	12 14 TR	1 13 TF
2 23 MF	3 24 er	4 23 ef	5 22 EH	6 20 ft	7 20 fm	5	8 18 FT	9 17 FM	10 17 FT	11 16 FM	12 15 tg	1 14 td
2 24 md	3 25 MR	4 24 MF	5 23 er	6 21 EW	7 21 EH	6	8 19 ft	9 18 fm	10 18 ft	11 17 fm	12 16 FT	1 15 FM
2 25 RM	3 26 mg	4 25 md	5 24 MR	6 22 ef	7 22 er	7	8 20 EW	9 19 EH	10 19 EW	11 18 EH	12 17 ft	1 16 fm
2 26 rm	3 27 RT	4 26 RM	5 25 mg	6 23 MF	7 23 MR	8	8 21 ef	9 20 er	10 20 ef	11 19 er	12 18 EW	1 17 EH
2 27 TH	3 28 rt	4 27 rm	5 26 RT	6 24 md	7 24 mg	9	8 22 MF	9 21 MR	10 21 MF	11 20 MR	12 19 ef	1 18 er
2 28 tr	3 29 TW	4 28 TH	5 27 rt	6 25 RM	7 25 RT	10	8 23 md	9 22 mg	10 22 md	11 21 mg	12 20 MF	1 19 MR
3 1 FR	3 30 tf	4 29 tr	5 28 TW	6 26 rm	7 26 rt	11	8 24 RM	9 23 RT	10 23 RM	11 22 RT	12 21 md	1 20 mg
3 2 fg	3 31 FF	4 30 FR	5 29 tf	6 27 TH	7 27 TW	12	8 25 rm	9 24 rt	10 24 rm	11 23 rt	12 22 RM	1 21 RT
3 3 ET	4 1 fd	5 1 fg	5 30 FF	6 28 tr	7 28 tf	13	8 26 TH	9 25 TW	10 25 TH	11 24 TW	12 23 rm	1 22 rt
3 4 et	4 2 EM	5 2 ET	5 31 fd	6 29 FR	7 29 FF	14	8 27 tr	9 26 tf	10 26 tr	11 25 tf	12 24 TH	1 23 TW
3 5 MW	4 3 em	5 3 et	6 1 EM	6 30 fg	7 30 fd	15	8 28 FR	9 27 FF	10 27 FR	11 26 FF	12 25 tr	1 24 tf
3 6 mf	4 4 MH	5 4 MW	6 2 em	7 1 ET	7 31 EM	16	8 29 fg	9 28 fd	10 28 fg	11 27 fd	12 26 FR	1 25 FF
3 7 RF	4 5 mr	5 5 mf	6 3 MH	7 2 et	8 1 em	17	8 30 ET	9 29 EM	10 29 ET	11 28 EM	12 27 fg	1 26 fd
3 8 rd	4 6 RR	5 6 RF	6 4 mr	7 3 MW	8 2 MH	18	8 31 et	9 30 em	10 30 et	11 29 em	12 28 ET	1 27 EM
3 9 TM	4 7 rg	5 7 rd	6 5 RR	7 4 mf	8 3 mr	19	9 1 MW	10 1 MH	10 31 MW	11 30 MH	12 29 et	1 28 em
3 10 tm	4 8 TT	5 8 TM	6 6 rg	7 5 RF	8 4 RR	20	9 2 mf	10 2 mr	11 1 mf	12 1 mr	12 30 MW	1 29 MH
3 11 FH	4 9 tt	5 9 tm	6 7 TT	7 6 rd	8 5 rg	21	9 3 RF	10 3 RR	11 2 RF	12 2 RR	12 31 mf	1 30 mr
3 12 fr	4 10 FW	5 10 FH	6 8 tt	7 7 TM	8 6 TT	22	9 4 rd	10 4 rg	11 3 rd	12 3 rg	1 1 RF	1 31 RR
3 13 ER	4 11 ff	5 11 fr	6 9 FW	7 8 tm	8 7 tt	23	9 5 TM	10 5 TT	11 4 TM	12 4 TT	1 2 rd	2 1 rg
3 14 eg	4 12 EF	5 12 ER	6 10 ff	7 9 FH	8 8 FW	24	9 6 tm	10 6 tt	11 5 tm	12 5 tt	1 3 TM	2 2 TT
3 15 MT	4 13 ed	5 13 eg	6 11 EF	7 10 fr	8 9 ff	25	9 7 FH	10 7 FW	11 6 FH	12 6 FW	1 4 tm	2 3 tt
3 16 mt	4 14 MM	5 14 MT	6 12 ed	7 11 ER	8 10 EF	26	9 8 fr	10 8 ff	11 7 fr	12 7 ff	1 5 FH	2 4 FW
3 17 RW	4 15 mm	5 15 mt	6 13 MM	7 12 eg	8 11 ed	27	9 9 ER	10 9 EF	11 8 ER	12 8 EF	1 6 fr	2 5 ff
3 18 rf	4 16 RH	5 16 RW	6 14 mm	7 13 MT	8 12 MM	28	9 10 eg	10 10 ed	11 9 eg	12 9 ed	1 7 ER	2 6 EF
3 19 TF	4 17 rr	5 17 rf	6 15 RH	7 14 mt	8 13 mm	29	9 11 MT	10 11 MM	11 10 MT	12 10 MM	1 8 eg	2 7 ed
	4 18 TR			7 15 RW		30	9 12 mt	10 12 mm	11 11 mt		1 9 MT	

2016 FM MONKEY

JAN MT	FEB mt	MAR RW	APR rf	MAY TF	JUN td	DAY OF MON	JUL FM	AUG fm	SEP EH	OCT er	NOV MR	DEC mg
27 WARM	27 CLEAR	29 SUMMER		1 GRAIN	4 HEAT		5 FALL	7 DEW	8 C DEW	8 WINTER	9 SNOW	8 CHILL
11:46	16:32	9:54		14:09	0:33		10:39	13:48	5:59	9:14	1:54	12:36
2 8 MM	3 9 MT	4 7 ed	5 7 eg	6 5 EF	7 4 fr	1	8 3 ff	9 1 FH	10 1 FW	10 31 FH	11 29 tt	12 29 tm
2 9 mm	3 10 mt	4 8 MM	5 8 MT	6 6 ed	7 5 ER	2	8 4 EF	9 2 fr	10 2 ff	11 1 fr	11 30 FW	12 30 FH
2 10 RH	3 11 RW	4 9 mm	5 9 mt	6 7 MM	7 6 eg	3	8 5 ed	9 3 ER	10 3 EF	11 2 ER	12 1 ff	12 31 fr
2 11 rr	3 12 rf	4 10 RH	5 10 RW	6 8 mm	7 7 MT	4	8 6 MM	9 4 eg	10 4 ed	11 3 eg	12 2 EF	1 1 ER
2 12 TR	3 13 TF	4 11 rr	5 11 rf	6 9 RH	7 8 mt	5	8 7 mm	9 5 MT	10 5 MM	11 4 MT	12 3 ed	1 2 eg
2 13 tg	3 14 td	4 12 TR	5 12 TF	6 10 rr	7 9 RW	6	8 8 RH	9 6 mt	10 6 mm	11 5 mt	12 4 MM	1 3 MT
2 14 FT	3 15 FM	4 13 tg	5 13 td	6 11 TR	7 10 rf	7	8 9 rr	9 7 RW	10 7 RH	11 6 RW	12 5 mm	1 4 mt
2 15 ft	3 16 fm	4 14 FT	5 14 FM	6 12 tg	7 11 TF	8	8 10 TR	9 8 rf	10 8 rr	11 7 rf	12 6 RH	1 5 RW
2 16 EW	3 17 EH	4 15 ft	5 15 fm	6 13 FT	7 12 td	9	8 11 tg	9 9 TF	10 9 TR	11 8 TF	12 7 rr	1 6 rf
2 17 ef	3 18 er	4 16 EW	5 16 EH	6 14 ft	7 13 FM	10	8 12 FT	9 10 td	10 10 tg	11 9 td	12 8 TR	1 7 TF
2 18 MF	3 19 MR	4 17 ef	5 17 er	6 15 EW	7 14 fm	11	8 13 ft	9 11 FM	10 11 FT	11 10 FM	12 9 tg	1 8 td
2 19 md	3 20 mg	4 18 MF	5 18 MR	6 16 ef	7 15 EH	12	8 14 EW	9 12 fm	10 12 ft	11 11 fm	12 10 FT	1 9 FM
2 20 RM	3 21 RT	4 19 md	5 19 mg	6 17 MF	7 16 er	13	8 15 ef	9 13 EH	10 13 EW	11 12 EH	12 11 ft	1 10 fm
2 21 rm	3 22 rt	4 20 RM	5 20 RT	6 18 md	7 17 MR	14	8 16 MF	9 14 er	10 14 ef	11 13 er	12 12 EW	1 11 EH
2 22 TH	3 23 TW	4 21 rm	5 21 rt	6 19 RM	7 18 mg	15	8 17 md	9 15 MR	10 15 MF	11 14 MR	12 13 ef	1 12 er
2 23 tr	3 24 tf	4 22 TH	5 22 TW	6 20 rm	7 19 RT	16	8 18 RM	9 16 mg	10 16 md	11 15 mg	12 14 MF	1 13 MR
2 24 FR	3 25 FF	4 23 tr	5 23 tf	6 21 TH	7 20 rt	17	8 19 rm	9 17 RT	10 17 RM	11 16 RT	12 15 md	1 14 mg
2 25 fg	3 26 fd	4 24 FR	5 24 FF	6 22 tr	7 21 TW	18	8 20 TH	9 18 rt	10 18 rm	11 17 rt	12 16 RM	1 15 RT
2 26 ET	3 27 EM	4 25 fg	5 25 fd	6 23 FR	7 22 tf	19	8 21 tr	9 19 TW	10 19 TH	11 18 TW	12 17 rm	1 16 rt
2 27 et	3 28 em	4 26 ET	5 26 EM	6 24 fg	7 23 FF	20	8 22 FR	9 20 tf	10 20 tr	11 19 tf	12 18 TH	1 17 TW
2 28 MW	3 29 MH	4 27 et	5 27 em	6 25 ET	7 24 fd	21	8 23 fg	9 21 FF	10 21 FR	11 20 FF	12 19 tr	1 18 tf
2 29 mf	3 30 mr	4 28 MW	5 28 MH	6 26 et	7 25 EM	22	8 24 ET	9 22 fd	10 22 fg	11 21 fd	12 20 FR	1 19 FF
3 1 RF	3 31 RR	4 29 mf	5 29 mr	6 27 MW	7 26 em	23	8 25 et	9 23 EM	10 23 ET	11 22 EM	12 21 fg	1 20 fd
3 2 rd	4 1 rg	4 30 RF	5 30 RR	6 28 mf	7 27 MH	24	8 26 MW	9 24 em	10 24 et	11 23 em	12 22 ET	1 21 EM
3 3 TM	4 2 TT	5 1 rd	5 31 rg	6 29 RF	7 28 mr	25	8 27 mf	9 25 MH	10 25 MW	11 24 MH	12 23 et	1 22 em
3 4 tm	4 3 tt	5 2 TM	6 1 TT	6 30 rd	7 29 RR	26	8 28 RF	9 26 mr	10 26 mf	11 25 mr	12 24 MW	1 23 MH
3 5 FH	4 4 FW	5 3 tm	6 2 tt	7 1 TM	7 30 rg	27	8 29 rd	9 27 RR	10 27 RF	11 26 RR	12 25 mf	1 24 mr
3 6 fr	4 5 ff	5 4 FH	6 3 FW	7 2 tm	7 31 TT	28	8 30 TM	9 28 rg	10 28 rd	11 27 rg	12 26 RF	1 25 RR
3 7 ER	4 6 EF	5 5 fr	6 4 ff	7 3 FH	8 1 tt	29	8 31 tm	9 29 TT	10 29 TM	11 28 TT	12 27 rd	1 26 rg
3 8 eg		5 6 ER			8 2 FW	30		9 30 tt	10 30 tm		12 28 TM	1 27 TT

2017 fm ROOSTER

JAN RT	FEB rt	MAR TW	APR ff	MAY FF	JUN fd	DAY OF	JUN fd	JUL EM	AUG em	SEP MH	OCT mr	NOV RR	DEC rg
7 SPRING	8 WARM	8 CLEAR	10 SUMMER	11 GRAIN	14 HEAT	MON	16 FALL	17 DEW	19 C DEW	19 WINTER	20 SNOW	19 CHILL	19 SPRING
23:49	17:36	22:20	15:42	19:46	6:21		16:27	19:46	11:47	15:03	7:40	18:26	5:38
1 28 tt	2 26 TM	3 28 TT	4 26 rd	5 26 rg	6 24 RF	1	7 23 mr	8 22 mf	9 20 MH	10 20 MW	11 18 em	12 18 et	1 17 em
1 29 FW	2 27 tm	3 29 tt	4 27 TM	5 27 TT	6 25 rd	2	7 24 RR	8 23 RF	9 21 mr	10 21 mf	11 19 MH	12 19 MW	1 18 MH
1 30 ff	2 28 FH	3 30 FW	4 28 tm	5 28 tt	6 26 TM	3	7 25 rg	8 24 rd	9 22 RR	10 22 RF	11 20 mr	12 20 mf	1 19 mr
1 31 EF	3 1 fr	3 31 ff	4 29 FH	5 29 FW	6 27 tm	4	7 26 TT	8 25 TM	9 23 rg	10 23 rd	11 21 RR	12 21 RF	1 20 RR
2 1 ed	3 2 ER	4 1 EF	4 30 fr	5 30 ff	6 28 FH	5	7 27 tt	8 26 tm	9 24 TT	10 24 TM	11 22 rg	12 22 rd	1 21 rg
2 2 MM	3 3 eg	4 2 ed	5 1 ER	5 31 EF	6 29 fr	6	7 28 FW	8 27 FH	9 25 tt	10 25 tm	11 23 TT	12 23 TM	1 22 TT
2 3 mm	3 4 MT	4 3 MM	5 2 eg	6 1 ed	6 30 ER	7	7 29 ff	8 28 fr	9 26 FW	10 26 FH	11 24 tt	12 24 tm	1 23 tt
2 4 RH	3 5 mt	4 4 mm	5 3 MT	6 2 MM	7 1 eg	8	7 30 EF	8 29 ER	9 27 ff	10 27 fr	11 25 FW	12 25 FH	1 24 FW
2 5 rr	3 6 RW	4 5 RH	5 4 mt	6 3 mm	7 2 MT	9	7 31 ed	8 30 eg	9 28 EF	10 28 ER	11 26 ff	12 26 fr	1 25 ff
2 6 TR	3 7 rf	4 6 rr	5 5 RW	6 4 RH	7 3 mt	10	8 1 MM	8 31 MT	9 29 ed	10 29 eg	11 27 EF	12 27 ER	1 26 EF
2 7 tg	3 8 TF	4 7 TR	5 6 rf	6 5 rr	7 4 RW	11	8 2 mm	9 1 mt	9 30 MM	10 30 MT	11 28 ed	12 28 eg	1 27 ed
2 8 FT	3 9 td	4 8 tg	5 7 TF	6 6 TR	7 5 rf	12	8 3 RH	9 2 RW	10 1 mm	10 31 mt	11 29 MM	12 29 MT	1 28 MM
2 9 ft	3 10 FM	4 9 FT	5 8 td	6 7 tg	7 6 TF	13	8 4 rr	9 3 rf	10 2 RH	11 1 RW	11 30 mm	12 30 mt	1 29 mm
2 10 EW	3 11 fm	4 10 ft	5 9 FM	6 8 FT	7 7 td	14	8 5 TR	9 4 TF	10 3 rr	11 2 rf	12 1 RH	12 31 RW	1 30 RH
2 11 ef	3 12 EH	4 11 EW	5 10 fm	6 9 ft	7 8 FM	15	8 6 tg	9 5 td	10 4 TR	11 3 TF	12 2 rr	1 1 rf	1 31 rr
2 12 MF	3 13 er	4 12 ef	5 11 EH	6 10 EW	7 9 fm	16	8 7 FT	9 6 FM	10 5 tg	11 4 td	12 3 TR	1 2 TF	2 1 TR
2 13 md	3 14 MR	4 13 MF	5 12 er	6 11 ef	7 10 EH	17	8 8 ft	9 7 fm	10 6 FT	11 5 FM	12 4 tg	1 3 td	2 2 tg
2 14 RM	3 15 mg	4 14 md	5 13 MR	6 12 MF	7 11 er	18	8 9 EW	9 8 EH	10 7 ft	11 6 fm	12 5 FT	1 4 FM	2 3 FT
2 15 rm	3 16 RT	4 15 RM	5 14 mg	6 13 md	7 12 MR	19	8 10 ef	9 9 er	10 8 EW	11 7 EH	12 6 ft	1 5 fm	2 4 ft
2 16 TH	3 17 rt	4 16 rm	5 15 RT	6 14 RM	7 13 mg	20	8 11 MF	9 10 MR	10 9 ef	11 8 er	12 7 EW	1 6 EH	2 5 EW
2 17 tr	3 18 TW	4 17 TH	5 16 rt	6 15 rm	7 14 RT	21	8 12 md	9 11 mg	10 10 MF	11 9 MR	12 8 ef	1 7 er	2 6 ef
2 18 FR	3 19 tf	4 18 tr	5 17 TW	6 16 TH	7 15 rt	22	8 13 RM	9 12 RT	10 11 md	11 10 mg	12 9 MF	1 8 MR	2 7 MF
2 19 fg	3 20 FF	4 19 FR	5 18 tf	6 17 tr	7 16 TW	23	8 14 rm	9 13 rt	10 12 RM	11 11 RT	12 10 md	1 9 mg	2 8 md
2 20 ET	3 21 fd	4 20 fg	5 19 FF	6 18 FR	7 17 tf	24	8 15 TH	9 14 TW	10 13 rm	11 12 rt	12 11 RM	1 10 RT	2 9 RM
2 21 et	3 22 EM	4 21 ET	5 20 fd	6 19 fg	7 18 FF	25	8 16 tr	9 15 tf	10 14 TH	11 13 TW	12 12 rm	1 11 rt	2 10 rm
2 22 MW	3 23 em	4 22 et	5 21 EM	6 20 ET	7 19 fd	26	8 17 FR	9 16 FF	10 15 tr	11 14 tf	12 13 TH	1 12 TW	2 11 TH
2 23 mf	3 24 MH	4 23 MW	5 22 em	6 21 et	7 20 EM	27	8 18 fg	9 17 fd	10 16 FR	11 15 FF	12 14 tr	1 13 tf	2 12 tr
2 24 RF	3 25 mr	4 24 mf	5 23 MH	6 22 MW	7 21 em	28	8 19 ET	9 18 EM	10 17 fg	11 16 fd	12 15 FR	1 14 FF	2 13 FR
2 25 rd	3 26 RR	4 25 RF	5 24 mr	6 23 mf	7 22 MH	29	8 20 et	9 19 em	10 18 ET	11 17 EM	12 16 fg	1 15 fd	2 14 fg
	3 27 rg		5 25 RR			30	8 21 MW		10 19 et		12 17 ET	1 16 EM	2 15 ET

2018 EH DOG

JAN TT	FEB tt	MAR FW	APR ff	MAY EF	JUN ed	DAY	JUL MM	AUG mm	SEP RH	OCT rr	NOV TR	DEC tg
18 WARM	21 CLEAR	20 SUMMER	23 GRAIN	24 HEAT	26 FALL	OF	29 DEW	29 C DEW	30 WINTER		1 SNOW	1 CHILL
						MON						0:16
23:25	4:20	21:31	1:29	12:09	22:15		1:35	17:36	20:54		13:30	30 SPRING
												11:28
2 16 et	3 17 EM	4 16 ET	5 15 fd	6 14 fg	7 13 FF	1	8 11 tr	9 10 tf	10 9 TH	11 8 TW	12 7 rm	1 6 rt
2 17 MW	3 18 em	4 17 et	5 16 EM	6 15 ET	7 14 fd	2	8 12 FR	9 11 FF	10 10 tr	11 9 tf	12 8 TH	1 7 TW
2 18 mf	3 19 MH	4 18 MW	5 17 em	6 16 et	7 15 EM	3	8 13 fg	9 12 fd	10 11 FR	11 10 FF	12 9 tr	1 8 tf
2 19 RF	3 20 mr	4 19 mf	5 18 MH	6 17 MW	7 16 em	4	8 14 ET	9 13 EM	10 12 fg	11 11 fd	12 10 FR	1 9 FF
2 20 rd	3 21 RR	4 20 RF	5 19 mr	6 18 mf	7 17 MH	5	8 15 et	9 14 em	10 13 ET	11 12 EM	12 11 fg	1 10 fd
2 21 TM	3 22 rg	4 21 rd	5 20 RR	6 19 RF	7 18 mr	6	8 16 MW	9 15 MH	10 14 et	11 13 em	12 12 ET	1 11 EM
2 22 tm	3 23 TT	4 22 TM	5 21 rg	6 20 rd	7 19 RR	7	8 17 mf	9 16 mr	10 15 MW	11 14 MH	12 13 et	1 12 em
2 23 FH	3 24 tt	4 23 tm	5 22 TT	6 21 TM	7 20 rg	8	8 18 RF	9 17 RR	10 16 mf	11 15 mr	12 14 MW	1 13 MH
2 24 fr	3 25 FW	4 24 FH	5 23 tt	6 22 tm	7 21 TT	9	8 19 rd	9 18 rg	10 17 RF	11 16 RR	12 15 mf	1 14 mr
2 25 ER	3 26 ff	4 25 fr	5 24 FW	6 23 FH	7 22 tt	10	8 20 TM	9 19 TT	10 18 rd	11 17 rg	12 16 RF	1 15 RR
2 26 eg	3 27 EF	4 26 ER	5 25 ff	6 24 fr	7 23 FW	11	8 21 tm	9 20 tt	10 19 TM	11 18 TT	12 17 rd	1 16 rg
2 27 MT	3 28 ed	4 27 eg	5 26 EF	6 25 ER	7 24 ff	12	8 22 FH	9 21 FW	10 20 tm	11 19 tt	12 18 TM	1 17 TT
2 28 mt	3 29 MM	4 28 MT	5 27 ed	6 26 eg	7 25 EF	13	8 23 fr	9 22 ff	10 21 FH	11 20 FW	12 19 tm	1 18 tt
3 1 RW	3 30 mm	4 29 mt	5 28 MM	6 27 MT	7 26 ed	14	8 24 ER	9 23 EF	10 22 fr	11 21 ff	12 20 FH	1 19 FW
3 2 rf	3 31 RH	4 30 RW	5 29 mm	6 28 mt	7 27 MM	15	8 25 eg	9 24 ed	10 23 ER	11 22 EF	12 21 fr	1 20 ff
3 3 TF	4 1 rr	5 1 rf	5 30 RH	6 29 RW	7 28 mm	16	8 26 MT	9 25 MM	10 24 eg	11 23 ed	12 22 ER	1 21 EF
3 4 td	4 2 TR	5 2 TF	5 31 rr	6 30 rf	7 29 RH	17	8 27 mt	9 26 mm	10 25 MT	11 24 MM	12 23 eg	1 22 ed
3 5 FM	4 3 tg	5 3 td	6 1 TR	7 1 TF	7 30 rr	18	8 28 RW	9 27 RH	10 26 mt	11 25 mm	12 24 MT	1 23 MM
3 6 fm	4 4 FT	5 4 FM	6 2 tg	7 2 td	7 31 TR	19	8 29 rf	9 28 rr	10 27 RW	11 26 RH	12 25 mt	1 24 mm
3 7 EH	4 5 ft	5 5 fm	6 3 FT	7 3 FM	8 1 tg	20	8 30 TF	9 29 TR	10 28 rf	11 27 rr	12 26 RW	1 25 RH
3 8 er	4 6 EW	5 6 EH	6 4 ft	7 4 fm	8 2 FT	21	8 31 td	9 30 tg	10 29 TF	11 28 TR	12 27 rf	1 26 rr
3 9 MR	4 7 ef	5 7 er	6 5 EW	7 5 EH	8 3 ft	22	9 1 FM	10 1 FT	10 30 td	11 29 tg	12 28 TF	1 27 TR
3 10 mg	4 8 MF	5 8 MR	6 6 ef	7 6 er	8 4 EW	23	9 2 fm	10 2 ft	10 31 FM	11 30 FT	12 29 td	1 28 tg
3 11 RT	4 9 md	5 9 mg	6 7 MF	7 7 MR	8 5 ef	24	9 3 EH	10 3 EW	11 1 fm	12 1 ft	12 30 FM	1 29 FT
3 12 rt	4 10 RM	5 10 RT	6 8 md	7 8 mg	8 6 MF	25	9 4 er	10 4 ef	11 2 EH	12 2 EW	12 31 fm	1 30 ft
3 13 TW	4 11 rm	5 11 rt	6 9 RM	7 9 RT	8 7 md	26	9 5 MR	10 5 MF	11 3 er	12 3 ef	1 1 EH	1 31 EW
3 14 tf	4 12 TH	5 12 TW	6 10 rm	7 10 rt	8 8 RM	27	9 6 mg	10 6 md	11 4 MR	12 4 MF	1 2 er	2 1 ef
3 15 FF	4 13 tr	5 13 tf	6 11 TH	7 11 TW	8 9 rm	28	9 7 RT	10 7 RM	11 5 mg	12 5 md	1 3 MR	2 2 MF
3 16 fd	4 14 FR	5 14 FF	6 12 tr	7 12 tf	8 10 TH	29	9 8 rt	10 8 rm	11 6 RT	12 6 RM	1 4 mg	2 3 md
	4 15 fg		6 13 FR			30	9 9 TW		11 7 rt		1 5 RT	2 4 RM

2019 er BOAR

JAN FT			FEB ft			MAR EW			APR ef			MAY MF			JUN md			DAY OF MON	JUL RM			AUG rm			SEP TH			OCT tr			NOV FR			DEC fg		
			1 WARM			1 CLEAR			2 SUMMER			4 GRAIN			5 HEAT				8 FALL			10 DEW			10 C DEW			12 WINTER			12 SNOW			12 CHILL		
			5:14			9:59			3:20			7:33			17:57				4:03			7:24			23:25			2:42			19:20			6:06		
2	5	rm	3	6	RT	4	5	RM	5	5	RT	6	3	md	7	3	mg	1	8	1	MF	8	30	er	9	29	ef	10	28	EH	11	26	ft	12	26	fm
2	6	TH	3	7	rt	4	6	rm	5	6	rt	6	4	RM	7	4	RT	2	8	2	md	8	31	MR	9	30	MF	10	29	er	11	27	EW	12	27	EH
2	7	tr	3	8	TW	4	7	TH	5	7	TW	6	5	rm	7	5	rt	3	8	3	RM	9	1	mg	10	1	md	10	30	MR	11	28	ef	12	28	er
2	8	FR	3	9	tf	4	8	tr	5	8	tf	6	6	TH	7	6	TW	4	8	4	rm	9	2	RT	10	2	RM	10	31	mg	11	29	MF	12	29	MR
2	9	fg	3	10	FF	4	9	FR	5	9	FF	6	7	tr	7	7	tf	5	8	5	TH	9	3	rt	10	3	rm	11	1	RT	11	30	md	12	30	mg
2	10	ET	3	11	fd	4	10	fg	5	10	fd	6	8	FR	7	8	FF	6	8	6	tr	9	4	TW	10	4	TH	11	2	rt	12	1	RM	12	31	RT
2	11	et	3	12	EM	4	11	ET	5	11	EM	6	9	fg	7	9	fd	7	8	7	FR	9	5	tf	10	5	tr	11	3	TW	12	2	rm	1	1	rt
2	12	MW	3	13	em	4	12	et	5	12	em	6	10	ET	7	10	EM	8	8	8	fg	9	6	FF	10	6	FR	11	4	tf	12	3	TH	1	2	TW
2	13	mf	3	14	MH	4	13	MW	5	13	MH	6	11	et	7	11	em	9	8	9	ET	9	7	fd	10	7	fg	11	5	FF	12	4	tr	1	3	tf
2	14	RF	3	15	mr	4	14	mf	5	14	mr	6	12	MW	7	12	MH	10	8	10	et	9	8	EM	10	8	ET	11	6	fd	12	5	FR	1	4	FF
2	15	rd	3	16	RR	4	15	RF	5	15	RR	6	13	mf	7	13	mr	11	8	11	MW	9	9	em	10	9	et	11	7	EM	12	6	fg	1	5	fd
2	16	TM	3	17	rg	4	16	rd	5	16	rg	6	14	RF	7	14	RR	12	8	12	mf	9	10	MH	10	10	MW	11	8	em	12	7	ET	1	6	EM
2	17	tm	3	18	TT	4	17	TM	5	17	TT	6	15	rd	7	15	rg	13	8	13	RF	9	11	mr	10	11	mf	11	9	MH	12	8	et	1	7	em
2	18	FH	3	19	tt	4	18	tm	5	18	tt	6	16	TM	7	16	TT	14	8	14	rd	9	12	RR	10	12	RF	11	10	mr	12	9	MW	1	8	MH
2	19	fr	3	20	FW	4	19	FH	5	19	FW	6	17	tm	7	17	tt	15	8	15	TM	9	13	rg	10	13	rd	11	11	RR	12	10	mf	1	9	mr
2	20	ER	3	21	ff	4	20	fr	5	20	ff	6	18	FH	7	18	FW	16	8	16	tm	9	14	TT	10	14	TM	11	12	rg	12	11	RF	1	10	RR
2	21	eg	3	22	EF	4	21	ER	5	21	EF	6	19	fr	7	19	ff	17	8	17	FH	9	15	tt	10	15	tm	11	13	TT	12	12	rd	1	11	rg
2	22	MT	3	23	ed	4	22	eg	5	22	ed	6	20	ER	7	20	EF	18	8	18	fr	9	16	FW	10	16	FH	11	14	tt	12	13	TM	1	12	TT
2	23	mt	3	24	MM	4	23	MT	5	23	MM	6	21	eg	7	21	ed	19	8	19	ER	9	17	ff	10	17	fr	11	15	FW	12	14	tm	1	13	tt
2	24	RW	3	25	mm	4	24	mt	5	24	mm	6	22	MT	7	22	MM	20	8	20	eg	9	18	EF	10	18	ER	11	16	ff	12	15	FH	1	14	FW
2	25	rf	3	26	RH	4	25	RW	5	25	RH	6	23	mt	7	23	mm	21	8	21	MT	9	19	ed	10	19	eg	11	17	EF	12	16	fr	1	15	ff
2	26	TF	3	27	rr	4	26	rf	5	26	rr	6	24	RW	7	24	RH	22	8	22	mt	9	20	MM	10	20	MT	11	18	ed	12	17	ER	1	16	EF
2	27	td	3	28	TR	4	27	TF	5	27	TR	6	25	rf	7	25	rr	23	8	23	RW	9	21	mm	10	21	mt	11	19	MM	12	18	eg	1	17	ed
2	28	FM	3	29	tg	4	28	td	5	28	tg	6	26	TF	7	26	TR	24	8	24	rf	9	22	RH	10	22	RW	11	20	mm	12	19	MT	1	18	MM
3	1	fm	3	30	FT	4	29	FM	5	29	FT	6	27	td	7	27	tg	25	8	25	TF	9	23	rr	10	23	rf	11	21	RH	12	20	mt	1	19	mm
3	2	EH	3	31	ft	4	30	fm	5	30	ft	6	28	FM	7	28	FT	26	8	26	td	9	24	TR	10	24	TF	11	22	rr	12	21	RW	1	20	RH
3	3	er	4	1	EW	5	1	EH	5	31	EW	6	29	fm	7	29	ft	27	8	27	FM	9	25	tg	10	25	td	11	23	TR	12	22	rf	1	21	rr
3	4	MR	4	2	ef	5	2	er	6	1	ef	6	30	EH	7	30	EW	28	8	28	fm	9	26	FT	10	26	FM	11	24	tg	12	23	TF	1	22	TR
3	5	mg	4	3	MF	5	3	MR	6	2	MF	7	1	er	7	31	ef	29	8	29	EH	9	27	ft	10	27	fm	11	25	FT	12	24	td	1	23	tg
			4	4	md	5	4	mg				7	2	MR				30				9	28	EW							12	25	FM	1	24	FT

2020 MR RAT

JAN ET	FEB et	MAR MW	APR mf	APR mf	MAY RF	DAY OF MON	JUN rd	JUL TM	AUG tm	SEP FH	OCT fr	NOV ER	DEC eg
11 SPRING	12 WARM	12 CLEAR	13 SUMMER	14 GRAIN	16 HEAT		18 FALL	20 DEW	22 C DEW	22 WINTER	23 SNOW	22 CHILL	22 SPRING
17:18	11:03	15:48	9:48	13:22	23:46		9:51	13:12	5:15	8:31	1:09	11:55	23:08
1 25 ft	2 23 FM	3 24 FT	4 23 FM	5 23 FT	6 21 td	1	7 21 tg	8 19 TF	9 17 rr	10 17 rf	11 15 RH	12 15 RW	1 13 mm
1 26 EW	2 24 fm	3 25 ft	4 24 fm	5 24 ft	6 22 FM	2	7 22 FT	8 20 td	9 18 TR	10 18 TF	11 16 rr	12 16 rf	1 14 RH
1 27 ef	2 25 EH	3 26 EW	4 25 EH	5 25 EW	6 23 fm	3	7 23 ft	8 21 FM	9 19 tg	10 19 td	11 17 TR	12 17 TF	1 15 rr
1 28 MF	2 26 er	3 27 ef	4 26 er	5 26 ef	6 24 EH	4	7 24 EW	8 22 fm	9 20 FT	10 20 FM	11 18 tg	12 18 td	1 16 TR
1 29 md	2 27 MR	3 28 MF	4 27 MR	5 27 MF	6 25 er	5	7 25 ef	8 23 EH	9 21 ft	10 21 fm	11 19 FT	12 19 FM	1 17 tg
1 30 RM	2 28 mg	3 29 md	4 28 mg	5 28 md	6 26 MR	6	7 26 MF	8 24 er	9 22 EW	10 22 EH	11 20 ft	12 20 fm	1 18 FT
1 31 rm	2 29 RT	3 30 RM	4 29 RT	5 29 RM	6 27 mg	7	7 27 md	8 25 MR	9 23 ef	10 23 er	11 21 EW	12 21 EH	1 19 ft
2 1 TH	3 1 rt	3 31 rm	4 30 rt	5 30 rm	6 28 RT	8	7 28 RM	8 26 mg	9 24 MF	10 24 MR	11 22 ef	12 22 er	1 20 EW
2 2 tr	3 2 TW	4 1 TH	5 1 TW	5 31 TH	6 29 rt	9	7 29 rm	8 27 RT	9 25 md	10 25 mg	11 23 MF	12 23 MR	1 21 ef
2 3 FR	3 3 tf	4 2 tr	5 2 tf	6 1 tr	6 30 TW	10	7 30 TH	8 28 rt	9 26 RM	10 26 RT	11 24 md	12 24 mg	1 22 MF
2 4 fg	3 4 FF	4 3 FR	5 3 FF	6 2 FR	7 1 tf	11	7 31 tr	8 29 TW	9 27 rm	10 27 rt	11 25 RM	12 25 RT	1 23 md
2 5 ET	3 5 fd	4 4 fg	5 4 fd	6 3 fg	7 2 FF	12	8 1 FR	8 30 tf	9 28 TH	10 28 TW	11 26 rm	12 26 rt	1 24 RM
2 6 et	3 6 EM	4 5 ET	5 5 EM	6 4 ET	7 3 fd	13	8 2 fg	8 31 FF	9 29 tr	10 29 tf	11 27 TH	12 27 TW	1 25 rm
2 7 MW	3 7 em	4 6 et	5 6 em	6 5 et	7 4 EM	14	8 3 ET	9 1 fd	9 30 FR	10 30 FF	11 28 tr	12 28 tf	1 26 TH
2 8 mf	3 8 MH	4 7 MW	5 7 MH	6 6 MW	7 5 em	15	8 4 et	9 2 EM	10 1 fg	10 31 fd	11 29 FR	12 29 FF	1 27 tr
2 9 RF	3 9 mr	4 8 mf	5 8 mr	6 7 mf	7 6 MH	16	8 5 MW	9 3 em	10 2 ET	11 1 EM	11 30 fg	12 30 fd	1 28 FR
2 10 rd	3 10 RR	4 9 RF	5 9 RR	6 8 RF	7 7 mr	17	8 6 mf	9 4 MH	10 3 et	11 2 em	12 1 ET	12 31 EM	1 29 fg
2 11 TM	3 11 rg	4 10 rd	5 10 rg	6 9 rd	7 8 RR	18	8 7 RF	9 5 mr	10 4 MW	11 3 MH	12 2 et	1 1 em	1 30 ET
2 12 tm	3 12 TT	4 11 TM	5 11 TT	6 10 TM	7 9 rg	19	8 8 rd	9 6 RR	10 5 mf	11 4 mr	12 3 MW	1 2 MH	1 31 et
2 13 FH	3 13 tt	4 12 tm	5 12 tt	6 11 tm	7 10 TT	20	8 9 TM	9 7 rg	10 6 RF	11 5 RR	12 4 mf	1 3 mr	2 1 MW
2 14 fr	3 14 FW	4 13 FH	5 13 FW	6 12 FH	7 11 tt	21	8 10 tm	9 8 TT	10 7 rd	11 6 rg	12 5 RF	1 4 RR	2 2 mf
2 15 ER	3 15 ff	4 14 fr	5 14 ff	6 13 fr	7 12 FW	22	8 11 FH	9 9 tt	10 8 TM	11 7 TT	12 6 rd	1 5 rg	2 3 RF
2 16 eg	3 16 EF	4 15 ER	5 15 EF	6 14 ER	7 13 ff	23	8 12 fr	9 10 FW	10 9 tm	11 8 tt	12 7 TM	1 6 TT	2 4 rd
2 17 MT	3 17 ed	4 16 eg	5 16 ed	6 15 eg	7 14 EF	24	8 13 ER	9 11 ff	10 10 FH	11 9 FW	12 8 tm	1 7 tt	2 5 TM
2 18 mt	3 18 MM	4 17 MT	5 17 MM	6 16 MT	7 15 ed	25	8 14 eg	9 12 EF	10 11 fr	11 10 ff	12 9 FH	1 8 FW	2 6 tm
2 19 RW	3 19 mm	4 18 mt	5 18 mm	6 17 mt	7 16 MM	26	8 15 MT	9 13 ed	10 12 ER	11 11 EF	12 10 fr	1 9 ff	2 7 FH
2 20 rf	3 20 RH	4 19 RW	5 19 RH	6 18 RW	7 17 mm	27	8 16 mt	9 14 MM	10 13 eg	11 12 ed	12 11 ER	1 10 EF	2 8 fr
2 21 TF	3 21 rr	4 20 rf	5 20 rr	6 19 rf	7 18 RH	28	8 17 RW	9 15 mm	10 14 MT	11 13 MM	12 12 eg	1 11 ed	2 9 ER
2 22 td	3 22 TR	4 21 TF	5 21 TR	6 20 TF	7 19 rr	29	8 18 rf	9 16 RH	10 15 mt	11 14 mm	12 13 MT	1 12 MM	2 10 eg
	3 23 tg	4 22 td	5 22 tg		7 20 TR	30			10 16 RW		12 14 mt		2 11 MT

2021 mg OX

JAN MT	FEB mt	MAR RW	APR rf	MAY TF	JUN td	DAY OF MON	JUL FM	AUG fm	SEP EH	OCT er	NOV MR	DEC mg
22 WARM	23 CLEAR	24 SUMMER	25 GRAIN	28 HEAT	29 FALL			1 DEW	3 C DEW	3 WINTER	4 SNOW	3 CHILL
16:54	21:37	14:57	19:09	5:33	15:40			19:01	11:04	14:21	7:00	17:46
2 12 mt	3 13 MM	4 12 MT	5 12 MM	6 10 eg	7 10 ed	1	8 8 ER	9 7 EF	10 6 fr	11 5 ff	12 4 FH	1 3 FW
2 13 RW	3 14 mm	4 13 mt	5 13 mm	6 11 MT	7 11 MM	2	8 9 eg	9 8 ed	10 7 ER	11 6 EF	12 5 fr	1 4 ff
2 14 rf	3 15 RH	4 14 RW	5 14 RH	6 12 mt	7 12 mm	3	8 10 MT	9 9 MM	10 8 eg	11 7 ed	12 6 ER	1 5 EF
2 15 TF	3 16 rr	4 15 rf	5 15 rr	6 13 RW	7 13 RH	4	8 11 mt	9 10 mm	10 9 MT	11 8 MM	12 7 eg	1 6 ed
2 16 td	3 17 TR	4 16 TF	5 16 TR	6 14 rf	7 14 rr	5	8 12 RW	9 11 RH	10 10 mt	11 9 mm	12 8 MT	1 7 MM
2 17 FM	3 18 tg	4 17 td	5 17 tg	6 15 TF	7 15 TR	6	8 13 rf	9 12 rr	10 11 RW	11 10 RH	12 9 mt	1 8 mm
2 18 fm	3 19 FT	4 18 FM	5 18 FT	6 16 td	7 16 tg	7	8 14 TF	9 13 TR	10 12 rf	11 11 rr	12 10 RW	1 9 RH
2 19 EH	3 20 ft	4 19 fm	5 19 ft	6 17 FM	7 17 FT	8	8 15 td	9 14 tg	10 13 TF	11 12 TR	12 11 rf	1 10 rr
2 20 er	3 21 EW	4 20 EH	5 20 EW	6 18 fm	7 18 ft	9	8 16 FM	9 15 FT	10 14 td	11 13 tg	12 12 TF	1 11 TR
2 21 MR	3 22 ef	4 21 er	5 21 ef	6 19 EH	7 19 EW	10	8 17 fm	9 16 ft	10 15 FM	11 14 FT	12 13 td	1 12 tg
2 22 mg	3 23 MF	4 22 MR	5 22 MF	6 20 er	7 20 ef	11	8 18 EH	9 17 EW	10 16 fm	11 15 ft	12 14 FM	1 13 FT
2 23 RT	3 24 md	4 23 mg	5 23 md	6 21 MR	7 21 MF	12	8 19 er	9 18 ef	10 17 EH	11 16 EW	12 15 fm	1 14 ft
2 24 rt	3 25 RM	4 24 RT	5 24 RM	6 22 mg	7 22 md	13	8 20 MR	9 19 MF	10 18 er	11 17 ef	12 16 EH	1 15 EW
2 25 TW	3 26 rm	4 25 rt	5 25 rm	6 23 RT	7 23 RM	14	8 21 mg	9 20 md	10 19 MR	11 18 MF	12 17 er	1 16 ef
2 26 tf	3 27 TH	4 26 TW	5 26 TH	6 24 rt	7 24 rm	15	8 22 RT	9 21 RM	10 20 mg	11 19 md	12 18 MR	1 17 MF
2 27 FF	3 28 tr	4 27 tf	5 27 tr	6 25 TW	7 25 TH	16	8 23 rt	9 22 rm	10 21 RT	11 20 RM	12 19 mg	1 18 md
2 28 fd	3 29 FR	4 28 FF	5 28 FR	6 26 tf	7 26 tr	17	8 24 TW	9 23 TH	10 22 rt	11 21 rm	12 20 RT	1 19 RM
3 1 EM	3 30 fg	4 29 fd	5 29 fg	6 27 FF	7 27 FR	18	8 25 tf	9 24 tr	10 23 TW	11 22 TH	12 21 rt	1 20 rm
3 2 em	3 31 ET	4 30 EM	5 30 ET	6 28 fd	7 28 fg	19	8 26 FF	9 25 FR	10 24 tf	11 23 tr	12 22 TW	1 21 TH
3 3 MH	4 1 et	5 1 em	5 31 et	6 29 EM	7 29 ET	20	8 27 fd	9 26 fg	10 25 FF	11 24 FR	12 23 tf	1 22 tr
3 4 mr	4 2 MW	5 2 MH	6 1 MW	6 30 em	7 30 et	21	8 28 EM	9 27 ET	10 26 fd	11 25 fg	12 24 FF	1 23 FR
3 5 RR	4 3 mf	5 3 mr	6 2 mf	7 1 MH	7 31 MW	22	8 29 em	9 28 et	10 27 EM	11 26 ET	12 25 fd	1 24 fg
3 6 rg	4 4 RF	5 4 RR	6 3 RF	7 2 mr	8 1 mf	23	8 30 MH	9 29 MW	10 28 em	11 27 et	12 26 EM	1 25 ET
3 7 TT	4 5 rd	5 5 rg	6 4 rd	7 3 RR	8 2 RF	24	8 31 mr	9 30 mf	10 29 MH	11 28 MW	12 27 em	1 26 et
3 8 tt	4 6 TM	5 6 TT	6 5 TM	7 4 rg	8 3 rd	25	9 1 RR	10 1 RF	10 30 mr	11 29 mf	12 28 MH	1 27 MW
3 9 FW	4 7 tm	5 7 tt	6 6 tm	7 5 TT	8 4 TM	26	9 2 rg	10 2 rd	10 31 RR	11 30 RF	12 29 mr	1 28 mf
3 10 ff	4 8 FH	5 8 FW	6 7 FH	7 6 tt	8 5 tm	27	9 3 TT	10 3 TM	11 1 rg	12 1 rd	12 30 RR	1 29 RF
3 11 EF	4 9 fr	5 9 ff	6 8 fr	7 7 FW	8 6 FH	28	9 4 tt	10 4 tm	11 2 TT	12 2 TM	12 31 rg	1 30 rd
3 12 ed	4 10 ER	5 10 EF	6 9 ER	7 8 ff	8 7 fr	29	9 5 FW	10 5 FH	11 3 tt	12 3 tm	1 1 TT	1 31 TM
	4 11 eg	5 11 ed		7 9 EF		30	9 6 ff		11 4 FW		1 2 tt	

2022 RT TIGER

JAN RT	FEB rt	MAR TW	APR tf	MAY FF	JUN fd	DAY OF MON	JUL EM	AUG em	SEP MH	OCT mr	NOV RR	DEC rg
4 SPRING	3 WARM	5 CLEAR	5 SUMMER	8 GRAIN	9 HEAT		10 FALL	13 DEW	13 C DEW	14 WINTER	14 SNOW	14 CHILL
4:58	22:42	3:22	20:45	0:58	11:52		21:28	0:50	16:53	20:11	12:49	23:35
2 1 tm	3 3 tt	4 1 TM	5 1 TT	5 30 rd	6 29 rg	1	7 29 rd	8 27 RR	9 26 RF	10 25 mr	11 24 mf	12 23 MH
2 2 FH	3 4 FW	4 2 tm	5 2 tt	5 31 TM	6 30 TT	2	7 30 TM	8 28 rg	9 27 rd	10 26 RR	11 25 RF	12 24 mr
2 3 fr	3 5 ff	4 3 FH	5 3 FW	6 1 tm	7 1 tt	3	7 31 tm	8 29 TT	9 28 TM	10 27 rg	11 26 rd	12 25 RR
2 4 ER	3 6 EF	4 4 fr	5 4 ff	6 2 FH	7 2 FW	4	8 1 FH	8 30 tt	9 29 tm	10 28 TT	11 27 TM	12 26 rg
2 5 eg	3 7 ed	4 5 ER	5 5 EF	6 3 fr	7 3 ff	5	8 2 fr	8 31 FW	9 30 FH	10 29 tt	11 28 tm	12 27 TT
2 6 MT	3 8 MM	4 6 eg	5 6 ed	6 4 ER	7 4 EF	6	8 3 ER	9 1 ff	10 1 fr	10 30 FW	11 29 FH	12 28 tt
2 7 mt	3 9 mm	4 7 MT	5 7 MM	6 5 eg	7 5 ed	7	8 4 eg	9 2 EF	10 2 ER	10 31 ff	11 30 fr	12 29 FW
2 8 RW	3 10 RH	4 8 mt	5 8 mm	6 6 MT	7 6 MM	8	8 5 MT	9 3 ed	10 3 eg	11 1 EF	12 1 ER	12 30 ff
2 9 rf	3 11 rr	4 9 RW	5 9 RH	6 7 mt	7 7 mm	9	8 6 mt	9 4 MM	10 4 MT	11 2 ed	12 2 eg	12 31 EF
2 10 TF	3 12 TR	4 10 rf	5 10 rr	6 8 RW	7 8 RH	10	8 7 RW	9 5 mm	10 5 mt	11 3 MM	12 3 MT	1 1 ed
2 11 td	3 13 tg	4 11 TF	5 11 TR	6 9 rf	7 9 rr	11	8 8 rf	9 6 RH	10 6 RW	11 4 mm	12 4 mt	1 2 MM
2 12 FM	3 14 FT	4 12 td	5 12 tg	6 10 TF	7 10 TR	12	8 9 TF	9 7 rr	10 7 rf	11 5 RH	12 5 RW	1 3 mm
2 13 fm	3 15 ft	4 13 FM	5 13 FT	6 11 td	7 11 tg	13	8 10 td	9 8 TR	10 8 TF	11 6 rr	12 6 rf	1 4 RH
2 14 EH	3 16 EW	4 14 fm	5 14 ft	6 12 FM	7 12 FT	14	8 11 FM	9 9 tg	10 9 td	11 7 TR	12 7 TF	1 5 rr
2 15 er	3 17 ef	4 15 EH	5 15 EW	6 13 fm	7 13 ft	15	8 12 fm	9 10 FT	10 10 FM	11 8 tg	12 8 td	1 6 TR
2 16 MR	3 18 MF	4 16 er	5 16 ef	6 14 EH	7 14 EW	16	8 13 EH	9 11 ft	10 11 fm	11 9 FT	12 9 FM	1 7 tg
2 17 mg	3 19 md	4 17 MR	5 17 MF	6 15 er	7 15 ef	17	8 14 er	9 12 EW	10 12 EH	11 10 ft	12 10 fm	1 8 FT
2 18 RT	3 20 RM	4 18 mg	5 18 md	6 16 MR	7 16 MF	18	8 15 MR	9 13 ef	10 13 er	11 11 EW	12 11 EH	1 9 ft
2 19 rt	3 21 rm	4 19 RT	5 19 RM	6 17 mg	7 17 md	19	8 16 mg	9 14 MF	10 14 MR	11 12 ef	12 12 er	1 10 EW
2 20 TW	3 22 TH	4 20 rt	5 20 rm	6 18 RT	7 18 RM	20	8 17 RT	9 15 md	10 15 mg	11 13 MF	12 13 MR	1 11 ef
2 21 tf	3 23 tr	4 21 TW	5 21 TH	6 19 rt	7 19 rm	21	8 18 rt	9 16 RM	10 16 RT	11 14 md	12 14 mg	1 12 MF
2 22 FF	3 24 FR	4 22 tf	5 22 tr	6 20 TW	7 20 TH	22	8 19 TW	9 17 rm	10 17 rt	11 15 RM	12 15 RT	1 13 md
2 23 fd	3 25 fg	4 23 FF	5 23 FR	6 21 tf	7 21 tr	23	8 20 tf	9 18 TH	10 18 TW	11 16 rm	12 16 rt	1 14 RM
2 24 EM	3 26 ET	4 24 fd	5 24 fg	6 22 FF	7 22 FR	24	8 21 FF	9 19 tr	10 19 tf	11 17 TH	12 17 TW	1 15 rm
2 25 em	3 27 et	4 25 EM	5 25 ET	6 23 fd	7 23 fg	25	8 22 fd	9 20 FR	10 20 FF	11 18 tr	12 18 tf	1 16 TH
2 26 MH	3 28 MW	4 26 em	5 26 et	6 24 EM	7 24 ET	26	8 23 EM	9 21 fg	10 21 fd	11 19 FR	12 19 FF	1 17 tr
2 27 mr	3 29 mf	4 27 MH	5 27 MW	6 25 em	7 25 et	27	8 24 em	9 22 ET	10 22 EM	11 20 fg	12 20 fd	1 18 FR
2 28 RR	3 30 RF	4 28 mr	5 28 mf	6 26 MH	7 26 MW	28	8 25 MH	9 23 et	10 23 em	11 21 ET	12 21 EM	1 19 fg
3 1 rg	3 31 rd	4 29 RR	5 29 RF	6 27 mr	7 27 mf	29	8 26 mr	9 24 MW	10 24 MH	11 22 et	12 22 em	1 20 ET
3 2 TT		4 30 rg		6 28 RR	7 28 RF	30		9 25 mf		11 23 MW		1 21 et

2023 rt RABBIT

JAN TT	FEB tt	FEB tt	MAR FW	APR ff	MAY EF	DAY OF MON	JUN ed	JUL MM	AUG mm	SEP RH	OCT rr	NOV TR	DEC tg
14 SPRING	15 WARM	15 CLEAR	17 SUMMER	18 GRAIN	20 HEAT		22 FALL	24 DEW	24 C DEW	25 WINTER	25 SNOW	25 CHILL	25 SPRING
10:47	4:31	9:14	2:33	6:46	18:10		3:16	6:38	22:41	2:00	18:38	5:25	16:37
1 22 MW	2 20 em	3 22 et	4 20 EM	5 20 ET	6 18 fd	1	7 18 fg	8 16 FF	9 15 FR	10 15 FF	11 13 tr	12 13 tf	1 11 TH
1 23 mf	2 21 MH	3 23 MW	4 21 em	5 21 et	6 19 EM	2	7 19 ET	8 17 fd	9 16 fg	10 16 fd	11 14 FR	12 14 FF	1 12 tr
1 24 RF	2 22 mr	3 24 mf	4 22 MH	5 22 MW	6 20 em	3	7 20 et	8 18 EM	9 17 ET	10 17 EM	11 15 fg	12 15 fd	1 13 FR
1 25 rd	2 23 RR	3 25 RF	4 23 mr	5 23 mf	6 21 MH	4	7 21 MW	8 19 em	9 18 et	10 18 em	11 16 ET	12 16 EM	1 14 fg
1 26 TM	2 24 rg	3 26 rd	4 24 RR	5 24 RF	6 22 mr	5	7 22 mf	8 20 MH	9 19 MW	10 19 MH	11 17 et	12 17 em	1 15 ET
1 27 tm	2 25 TT	3 27 TM	4 25 rg	5 25 rd	6 23 RR	6	7 23 RF	8 21 mr	9 20 mf	10 20 mr	11 18 MW	12 18 MH	1 16 et
1 28 FH	2 26 tt	3 28 tm	4 26 TT	5 26 TM	6 24 rg	7	7 24 rd	8 22 RR	9 21 RF	10 21 RR	11 19 mf	12 19 mr	1 17 MW
1 29 fr	2 27 FW	3 29 FH	4 27 tt	5 27 tm	6 25 TT	8	7 25 TM	8 23 rg	9 22 rd	10 22 rg	11 20 RF	12 20 RR	1 18 mf
1 30 ER	2 28 ff	3 30 fr	4 28 FW	5 28 FH	6 26 tt	9	7 26 tm	8 24 TT	9 23 TM	10 23 TT	11 21 rd	12 21 rg	1 19 RF
1 31 eg	3 1 EF	3 31 ER	4 29 ff	5 29 fr	6 27 FW	10	7 27 FH	8 25 tt	9 24 tm	10 24 tt	11 22 TM	12 22 TT	1 20 rd
2 1 MT	3 2 ed	4 1 eg	4 30 EF	5 30 ER	6 28 ff	11	7 28 fr	8 26 FW	9 25 FH	10 25 FW	11 23 tm	12 23 tt	1 21 TM
2 2 mt	3 3 MM	4 2 MT	5 1 ed	5 31 eg	6 29 EF	12	7 29 ER	8 27 ff	9 26 fr	10 26 ff	11 24 FH	12 24 FW	1 22 tm
2 3 RW	3 4 mm	4 3 mt	5 2 MM	6 1 MT	6 30 ed	13	7 30 eg	8 28 EF	9 27 ER	10 27 EF	11 25 fr	12 25 ff	1 23 FH
2 4 rf	3 5 RH	4 4 RW	5 3 mm	6 2 mt	7 1 MM	14	7 31 MT	8 29 ed	9 28 eg	10 28 ed	11 26 ER	12 26 EF	1 24 fr
2 5 TF	3 6 rr	4 5 rf	5 4 RH	6 3 RW	7 2 mm	15	8 1 mt	8 30 MM	9 29 MT	10 29 MM	11 27 eg	12 27 ed	1 25 ER
2 6 td	3 7 TR	4 6 TF	5 5 rr	6 4 rf	7 3 RH	16	8 2 RW	8 31 mm	9 30 mt	10 30 mm	11 28 MT	12 28 MM	1 26 eg
2 7 FM	3 8 tg	4 7 td	5 6 TR	6 5 TF	7 4 rr	17	8 3 rf	9 1 RH	10 1 RW	10 31 RH	11 29 mt	12 29 mm	1 27 MT
2 8 fm	3 9 FT	4 8 FM	5 7 tg	6 6 td	7 5 TR	18	8 4 TF	9 2 rr	10 2 rf	11 1 rr	11 30 RW	12 30 RH	1 28 mt
2 9 EH	3 10 ft	4 9 fm	5 8 FT	6 7 FM	7 6 tg	19	8 5 td	9 3 TR	10 3 TF	11 2 TR	12 1 rf	12 31 rr	1 29 RW
2 10 er	3 11 EW	4 10 EH	5 9 ft	6 8 fm	7 7 FT	20	8 6 FM	9 4 tg	10 4 td	11 3 tg	12 2 TF	1 1 TR	1 30 rf
2 11 MR	3 12 ef	4 11 er	5 10 EW	6 9 EH	7 8 ft	21	8 7 fm	9 5 FT	10 5 FM	11 4 FT	12 3 td	1 2 tg	1 31 TF
2 12 mg	3 13 MF	4 12 MR	5 11 ef	6 10 er	7 9 EW	22	8 8 EH	9 6 ft	10 6 fm	11 5 ft	12 4 FM	1 3 FT	2 1 td
2 13 RT	3 14 md	4 13 mg	5 12 MF	6 11 MR	7 10 ef	23	8 9 er	9 7 EW	10 7 EH	11 6 EW	12 5 fm	1 4 ft	2 2 FM
2 14 rt	3 15 RM	4 14 RT	5 13 md	6 12 mg	7 11 MF	24	8 10 MR	9 8 ef	10 8 er	11 7 ef	12 6 EH	1 5 EW	2 3 fm
2 15 TW	3 16 rm	4 15 rt	5 14 RM	6 13 RT	7 12 md	25	8 11 mg	9 9 MF	10 9 MR	11 8 MF	12 7 er	1 6 ef	2 4 EH
2 16 tf	3 17 TH	4 16 TW	5 15 rm	6 14 rt	7 13 RM	26	8 12 RT	9 10 md	10 10 mg	11 9 md	12 8 MR	1 7 MF	2 5 er
2 17 FF	3 18 tr	4 17 tf	5 16 TH	6 15 TW	7 14 rm	27	8 13 rt	9 11 RM	10 11 RT	11 10 RM	12 9 mg	1 8 md	2 6 MR
2 18 fd	3 19 FR	4 18 FF	5 17 tr	6 16 tf	7 15 TH	28	8 14 TW	9 12 rm	10 12 rt	11 11 rm	12 10 RT	1 9 RM	2 7 mg
2 19 EM	3 20 fg	4 19 fd	5 18 FR	6 17 FF	7 16 tr	29	8 15 tf	9 13 TH	10 13 TW	11 12 TH	12 11 rt	1 10 rm	2 8 RT
	3 21 ET		5 19 fg		7 17 FR	30		9 14 tr	10 14 tf		12 12 TW		2 9 rt

2024 TW DRAGON

JAN FT	FEB ft	MAR EW	APR ef	MAY MF	JUN md	DAY OF MON	JUL RM	AUG rm	SEP TH	OCT tr	NOV FR	DEC fg
25 WARM	26 CLEAR	27 SUMMER	29 GRAIN		1 HEAT		4 FALL	5 DEW	6 C DEW	7 WINTER	7 SNOW	6 CHILL
10:21	15:03	8:22	12:34		22:58		9:05	12:27	4:31	7:49	0:29	11:15
2 10 TW	3 10 rm	4 9 rt	5 8 MM	6 6 mg	7 6 md	1	8 4 MR	9 3 MF	10 3 MR	11 1 ef	12 1 er	12 31 ef
2 11 tf	3 11 TH	4 10 TW	5 9 rm	6 7 RT	7 7 MM	2	8 5 mg	9 4 md	10 4 mg	11 2 MF	12 2 MR	1 1 MF
2 12 FF	3 12 tr	4 11 tf	5 10 TH	6 8 rt	7 8 rm	3	8 6 RT	9 5 MM	10 5 RT	11 3 md	12 3 mg	1 2 md
2 13 fd	3 13 FR	4 12 FF	5 11 tr	6 9 TW	7 9 TH	4	8 7 rt	9 6 rm	10 6 rt	11 4 MM	12 4 RT	1 3 MM
2 14 EM	3 14 fg	4 13 fd	5 12 FR	6 10 tf	7 10 tr	5	8 8 TW	9 7 TH	10 7 TW	11 5 rm	12 5 rt	1 4 rm
2 15 em	3 15 ET	4 14 EM	5 13 fg	6 11 FF	7 11 FR	6	8 9 tf	9 8 tr	10 8 tf	11 6 TH	12 6 TW	1 5 TH
2 16 MH	3 16 et	4 15 em	5 14 ET	6 12 fd	7 12 fg	7	8 10 FF	9 9 FR	10 9 FF	11 7 tr	12 7 tf	1 6 tr
2 17 mr	3 17 MW	4 16 MH	5 15 et	6 13 EM	7 13 ET	8	8 11 fd	9 10 fg	10 10 fd	11 8 FR	12 8 FF	1 7 FR
2 18 RR	3 18 mf	4 17 mr	5 16 MW	6 14 em	7 14 et	9	8 12 EM	9 11 ET	10 11 EM	11 9 fg	12 9 fd	1 8 fg
2 19 rg	3 19 RF	4 18 RR	5 17 mf	6 15 MH	7 15 MW	10	8 13 em	9 12 et	10 12 em	11 10 ET	12 10 EM	1 9 ET
2 20 TT	3 20 rd	4 19 rg	5 18 RF	6 16 mr	7 16 mf	11	8 14 MH	9 13 MW	10 13 MH	11 11 et	12 11 em	1 10 et
2 21 tt	3 21 TM	4 20 TT	5 19 rd	6 17 RR	7 17 RF	12	8 15 mr	9 14 mf	10 14 mr	11 12 MW	12 12 MH	1 11 MW
2 22 FW	3 22 tm	4 21 tt	5 20 TM	6 18 rg	7 18 rd	13	8 16 RR	9 15 RF	10 15 RR	11 13 mf	12 13 mr	1 12 mf
2 23 ff	3 23 FH	4 22 FW	5 21 tm	6 19 TT	7 19 TM	14	8 17 rg	9 16 rd	10 16 rg	11 14 RF	12 14 RR	1 13 RF
2 24 EF	3 24 fr	4 23 ff	5 22 FH	6 20 tt	7 20 tm	15	8 18 TT	9 17 TM	10 17 TT	11 15 rd	12 15 rg	1 14 rd
2 25 ed	3 25 ER	4 24 EF	5 23 fr	6 21 FW	7 21 FH	16	8 19 tt	9 18 tm	10 18 tt	11 16 TM	12 16 TT	1 15 TM
2 26 MM	3 26 eg	4 25 ed	5 24 ER	6 22 ff	7 22 fr	17	8 20 FW	9 19 FH	10 19 FW	11 17 tm	12 17 tt	1 16 tm
2 27 mm	3 27 MT	4 26 MM	5 25 eg	6 23 EF	7 23 ER	18	8 21 ff	9 20 fr	10 20 ff	11 18 FH	12 18 FW	1 17 FH
2 28 RH	3 28 mt	4 27 mm	5 26 MT	6 24 ed	7 24 eg	19	8 22 EF	9 21 ER	10 21 EF	11 19 fr	12 19 ff	1 18 fr
2 29 rr	3 29 RW	4 28 RH	5 27 mt	6 25 MM	7 25 MT	20	8 23 ed	9 22 eg	10 22 ed	11 20 ER	12 20 EF	1 19 ER
3 1 TR	3 30 rf	4 29 rr	5 28 RW	6 26 mm	7 26 mt	21	8 24 MM	9 23 MT	10 23 MM	11 21 eg	12 21 ed	1 20 eg
3 2 tg	3 31 TF	4 30 TR	5 29 rf	6 27 RH	7 27 RW	22	8 25 mm	9 24 mt	10 24 mm	11 22 MT	12 22 MM	1 21 MT
3 3 FT	4 1 td	5 1 tg	5 30 TF	6 28 rr	7 28 rf	23	8 26 RH	9 25 RW	10 25 RH	11 23 mt	12 23 mm	1 22 mt
3 4 ft	4 2 FM	5 2 FT	5 31 td	6 29 TR	7 29 TF	24	8 27 rr	9 26 rf	10 26 rr	11 24 RW	12 24 RH	1 23 RW
3 5 EW	4 3 fm	5 3 ft	6 1 FM	6 30 tg	7 30 td	25	8 28 TR	9 27 TF	10 27 TR	11 25 rf	12 25 rr	1 24 rf
3 6 ef	4 4 EH	5 4 EW	6 2 fm	7 1 FT	7 31 FM	26	8 29 tg	9 28 td	10 28 tg	11 26 TF	12 26 TR	1 25 TF
3 7 MF	4 5 er	5 5 ef	6 3 EH	7 2 ft	8 1 fm	27	8 30 FT	9 29 FM	10 29 FT	11 27 td	12 27 tg	1 26 td
3 8 md	4 6 MR	5 6 MF	6 4 er	7 3 EW	8 2 EH	28	8 31 ft	9 30 fm	10 30 ft	11 28 FM	12 28 FT	1 27 FM
3 9 RM	4 7 mg	5 7 md	6 5 MR	7 4 ef	8 3 er	29	9 1 EW	10 1 EH	10 31 EW	11 29 fm	12 29 ft	1 28 fm
	4 8 RT			7 5 MF		30	9 2 ef	10 2 er		11 30 EH	12 30 EW	

2025 tf SNAKE

JAN ET	FEB et	MAR MW	APR mf	MAY RF	JUN rd	DAY OF MON	JUN rd	JUL TM	AUG tm	SEP FH	OCT fr	NOV ER	DEC eg
6 SPRING	6 WARM	7 CLEAR	8 SUMMER	10 GRAIN	13 HEAT		14 FALL	16 DEW	17 C DEW	18 WINTER	18 SNOW	17 CHILL	17 SPRING
22:27	16:11	20:52	14:11	18:22	4:46		14:53	18:15	10:19	13:40	6:18	17:05	4:16
1 29 EH	2 28 EW	3 29 fm	4 28 ft	5 27 FM	6 25 tg	1	7 25 td	8 23 TR	9 22 TF	10 21 rr	11 20 rf	12 20 rr	1 19 rf
1 30 er	3 1 ef	3 30 EH	4 29 EW	5 28 fm	6 26 FT	2	7 26 FM	8 24 tg	9 23 td	10 22 TR	11 21 TF	12 21 TR	1 20 TF
1 31 MR	3 2 MF	3 31 er	4 30 ef	5 29 EH	6 27 ft	3	7 27 fm	8 25 FT	9 24 FM	10 23 tg	11 22 td	12 22 tg	1 21 td
2 1 mg	3 3 md	4 1 MR	5 1 MF	5 30 er	6 28 EW	4	7 28 EH	8 26 ft	9 25 fm	10 24 FT	11 23 FM	12 23 FT	1 22 FM
2 2 RT	3 4 RM	4 2 mg	5 2 md	5 31 MR	6 29 ef	5	7 29 er	8 27 EW	9 26 EH	10 25 ft	11 24 fm	12 24 ft	1 23 fm
2 3 rt	3 5 rm	4 3 RT	5 3 RM	6 1 mg	6 30 MF	6	7 30 MR	8 28 ef	9 27 er	10 26 EW	11 25 EH	12 25 EW	1 24 EH
2 4 TW	3 6 TH	4 4 rt	5 4 rm	6 2 RT	7 1 md	7	7 31 mg	8 29 MF	9 28 MR	10 27 ef	11 26 er	12 26 ef	1 25 er
2 5 tf	3 7 tr	4 5 TW	5 5 TH	6 3 rt	7 2 RM	8	8 1 RT	8 30 md	9 29 mg	10 28 MF	11 27 MR	12 27 MF	1 26 MR
2 6 FF	3 8 FR	4 6 tf	5 6 tr	6 4 TW	7 3 rm	9	8 2 rt	8 31 RM	9 30 RT	10 29 md	11 28 mg	12 28 md	1 27 mg
2 7 fd	3 9 fg	4 7 FF	5 7 FR	6 5 tf	7 4 TH	10	8 3 TW	9 1 rm	10 1 rt	10 30 RM	11 29 RT	12 29 RM	1 28 RT
2 8 EM	3 10 ET	4 8 fd	5 8 fg	6 6 FF	7 5 tr	11	8 4 tf	9 2 TH	10 2 TW	10 31 rm	11 30 rt	12 30 rm	1 29 rt
2 9 em	3 11 et	4 9 EM	5 9 ET	6 7 fd	7 6 FR	12	8 5 FF	9 3 tr	10 3 tf	11 1 TH	12 1 TW	12 31 TH	1 30 TW
2 10 MH	3 12 MW	4 10 em	5 10 et	6 8 EM	7 7 fg	13	8 6 fd	9 4 FR	10 4 FF	11 2 tr	12 2 tf	1 1 tr	1 31 tf
2 11 mr	3 13 mf	4 11 MH	5 11 MW	6 9 em	7 8 ET	14	8 7 EM	9 5 fg	10 5 fd	11 3 FR	12 3 FF	1 2 FR	2 1 FF
2 12 RR	3 14 RF	4 12 mr	5 12 mf	6 10 MH	7 9 et	15	8 8 em	9 6 ET	10 6 EM	11 4 fg	12 4 fd	1 3 fg	2 2 fd
2 13 rg	3 15 rd	4 13 RR	5 13 RF	6 11 mr	7 10 MW	16	8 9 MH	9 7 et	10 7 em	11 5 ET	12 5 EM	1 4 ET	2 3 EM
2 14 TT	3 16 TM	4 14 rg	5 14 rd	6 12 RR	7 11 mf	17	8 10 mr	9 8 MW	10 8 MH	11 6 et	12 6 em	1 5 et	2 4 em
2 15 tt	3 17 tm	4 15 TT	5 15 TM	6 13 rg	7 12 RF	18	8 11 RR	9 9 mf	10 9 mr	11 7 MW	12 7 MH	1 6 MW	2 5 MH
2 16 FW	3 18 FH	4 16 tt	5 16 tm	6 14 TT	7 13 rd	19	8 12 rg	9 10 RF	10 10 RR	11 8 mf	12 8 mr	1 7 mf	2 6 mr
2 17 ff	3 19 fr	4 17 FW	5 17 FH	6 15 tt	7 14 TM	20	8 13 TT	9 11 rd	10 11 rg	11 9 RF	12 9 RR	1 8 RF	2 7 RR
2 18 EF	3 20 ER	4 18 ff	5 18 fr	6 16 FW	7 15 tm	21	8 14 tt	9 12 TM	10 12 TT	11 10 rd	12 10 rg	1 9 rd	2 8 rg
2 19 ed	3 21 eg	4 19 EF	5 19 ER	6 17 ff	7 16 FH	22	8 15 FW	9 13 tm	10 13 tt	11 11 TM	12 11 TT	1 10 TM	2 9 TT
2 20 MM	3 22 MT	4 20 ed	5 20 eg	6 18 EF	7 17 fr	23	8 16 ff	9 14 FH	10 14 FW	11 12 tm	12 12 tt	1 11 tm	2 10 tt
2 21 mm	3 23 mt	4 21 MM	5 21 MT	6 19 ed	7 18 ER	24	8 17 EF	9 15 fr	10 15 ff	11 13 FH	12 13 FW	1 12 FH	2 11 FW
2 22 RH	3 24 RW	4 22 mm	5 22 mt	6 20 MM	7 19 eg	25	8 18 ed	9 16 ER	10 16 EF	11 14 fr	12 14 ff	1 13 fr	2 12 ff
2 23 rr	3 25 rf	4 23 RH	5 23 RW	6 21 mm	7 20 MT	26	8 19 MM	9 17 eg	10 17 ed	11 15 ER	12 15 EF	1 14 ER	2 13 EF
2 24 TR	3 26 TF	4 24 rr	5 24 rf	6 22 RH	7 21 mt	27	8 20 mm	9 18 MT	10 18 MM	11 16 eg	12 16 ed	1 15 eg	2 14 ed
2 25 tg	3 27 td	4 25 TR	5 25 TF	6 23 rr	7 22 RW	28	8 21 RH	9 19 mt	10 19 mm	11 17 MT	12 17 MM	1 16 MT	2 15 MM
2 26 FT	3 28 FM	4 26 tg	5 26 td	6 24 TR	7 23 rf	29	8 22 rr	9 20 RW	10 20 RH	11 18 mt	12 18 mm	1 17 mt	2 16 mm
2 27 ft		4 27 FT			7 24 TF	30		9 21 rf		11 19 RW	12 19 RH	1 18 RW	

2026 FT HORSE

JAN MT	FEB mt	MAR RW	APR rf	MAY TF	JUN td	DAY OF MON	JUL FM	AUG fm	SEP EH	OCT er	NOV MR	DEC mg
17 WARM	18 CLEAR	19 SUMMER	21 GRAIN	23 HEAT	25 FALL		27 DEW	28 C DEW	29 WINTER	29 SNOW	28 CHILL	28 SPRING
22:00	2:41		0:11	10:34	20:41		0:04	16:08	19:29	12:08	22:55	10:06
2 17 RH	3 19 RW	4 17 mm	5 17 mt	6 15 MM	7 14 eg	1	8 13 ed	9 11 ER	10 10 ff	11 9 fr	12 9 ff	1 8 fr
2 18 rr	3 20 rf	4 18 RH	5 18 RW	6 16 mm	7 15 MT	2	8 14 MM	9 12 eg	10 11 EF	11 10 ER	12 10 EF	1 9 ER
2 19 TR	3 21 TF	4 19 rr	5 19 rf	6 17 RH	7 16 mt	3	8 15 mm	9 13 MT	10 12 ed	11 11 eg	12 11 ed	1 10 eg
2 20 tg	3 22 td	4 20 TR	5 20 TF	6 18 rr	7 17 RW	4	8 16 RH	9 14 mt	10 13 MM	11 12 MT	12 12 MM	1 11 MT
2 21 FT	3 23 FM	4 21 tg	5 21 td	6 19 TR	7 18 rf	5	8 17 rr	9 15 RW	10 14 mm	11 13 mt	12 13 mm	1 12 mt
2 22 ft	3 24 fm	4 22 FT	5 22 FM	6 20 tg	7 19 TF	6	8 18 TR	9 16 rf	10 15 RH	11 14 RW	12 14 RH	1 13 RW
2 23 EW	3 25 EH	4 23 ft	5 23 fm	6 21 FT	7 20 td	7	8 19 tg	9 17 TF	10 16 rr	11 15 rf	12 15 rr	1 14 rf
2 24 ef	3 26 er	4 24 EW	5 24 EH	6 22 ft	7 21 FM	8	8 20 FT	9 18 td	10 17 TR	11 16 TF	12 16 TR	1 15 TF
2 25 MF	3 27 MR	4 25 ef	5 25 er	6 23 EW	7 22 fm	9	8 21 ft	9 19 FM	10 18 tg	11 17 td	12 17 tg	1 16 td
2 26 md	3 28 mg	4 26 MF	5 26 MR	6 24 ef	7 23 EH	10	8 22 EW	9 20 fm	10 19 FT	11 18 FM	12 18 FT	1 17 FM
2 27 RM	3 29 RT	4 27 md	5 27 mg	6 25 MF	7 24 er	11	8 23 ef	9 21 EH	10 20 ft	11 19 fm	12 19 ft	1 18 fm
2 28 rm	3 30 rt	4 28 RM	5 28 RT	6 26 md	7 25 MR	12	8 24 MF	9 22 er	10 21 EW	11 20 EH	12 20 EW	1 19 EH
3 1 TH	3 31 TW	4 29 rm	5 29 rt	6 27 RM	7 26 mg	13	8 25 md	9 23 MR	10 22 ef	11 21 er	12 21 ef	1 20 er
3 2 tr	4 1 tf	4 30 TH	5 30 TW	6 28 rm	7 27 RT	14	8 26 RM	9 24 mg	10 23 MF	11 22 MR	12 22 MF	1 21 MR
3 3 FR	4 2 FF	5 1 tr	5 31 tf	6 29 TH	7 28 rt	15	8 27 rm	9 25 RT	10 24 md	11 23 mg	12 23 md	1 22 mg
3 4 fg	4 3 fd	5 2 FR	6 1 FF	6 30 tr	7 29 TW	16	8 28 TH	9 26 rt	10 25 RM	11 24 RT	12 24 RM	1 23 RT
3 5 ET	4 4 EM	5 3 fg	6 2 fd	7 1 FR	7 30 tf	17	8 29 tr	9 27 TW	10 26 rm	11 25 rt	12 25 rm	1 24 rt
3 6 et	4 5 em	5 4 ET	6 3 EM	7 2 fg	7 31 FF	18	8 30 FR	9 28 tf	10 27 TH	11 26 TW	12 26 TH	1 25 TW
3 7 MW	4 6 MH	5 5 et	6 4 em	7 3 ET	8 1 fd	19	8 31 fg	9 29 FF	10 28 tr	11 27 tf	12 27 tr	1 26 tf
3 8 mf	4 7 mr	5 6 MW	6 5 MH	7 4 et	8 2 EM	20	9 1 ET	9 30 fd	10 29 FR	11 28 FF	12 28 FR	1 27 FF
3 9 RF	4 8 RR	5 7 mf	6 6 mr	7 5 MW	8 3 em	21	9 2 et	10 1 EM	10 30 fg	11 29 fd	12 29 fg	1 28 fd
3 10 rd	4 9 rg	5 8 RF	6 7 RR	7 6 mf	8 4 MH	22	9 3 MW	10 2 em	10 31 ET	11 30 EM	12 30 ET	1 29 EM
3 11 TM	4 10 TT	5 9 rd	6 8 rg	7 7 RF	8 5 mr	23	9 4 mf	10 3 MH	11 1 et	12 1 em	12 31 et	1 30 em
3 12 tm	4 11 tt	5 10 TM	6 9 TT	7 8 rd	8 6 RR	24	9 5 RF	10 4 mr	11 2 MW	12 2 MH	1 1 MW	1 31 MH
3 13 FH	4 12 FW	5 11 tm	6 10 tt	7 9 TM	8 7 rg	25	9 6 rd	10 5 RR	11 3 mf	12 3 mr	1 2 mf	2 1 mr
3 14 fr	4 13 ff	5 12 FH	6 11 FW	7 10 tm	8 8 TT	26	9 7 TM	10 6 rg	11 4 RF	12 4 RR	1 3 RF	2 2 RR
3 15 ER	4 14 EF	5 13 fr	6 12 ff	7 11 FH	8 9 tt	27	9 8 tm	10 7 TT	11 5 rd	12 5 rg	1 4 rd	2 3 rg
3 16 eg	4 15 ed	5 14 ER	6 13 EF	7 12 fr	8 10 FW	28	9 9 FH	10 8 tt	11 6 TM	12 6 TT	1 5 TM	2 4 TT
3 17 MT	4 16 MM	5 15 eg	6 14 ed	7 13 ER	8 11 ff	29	9 10 fr	10 9 FW	11 7 tm	12 7 tt	1 6 tm	2 5 tt
3 18 mt		5 16 MT			8 12 EF	30			11 8 FH	12 8 FW	1 7 FH	

2027 fd RAM

JAN RT	FEB rt	MAR TW	APR tf	MAY FF	JUN fd	DAY OF MON	JUL EM	AUG em	SEP MH	OCT mr	NOV RR	DEC rg
29 WARM	29 CLEAR		1 SUMMER	2 GRAIN	4 HEAT		7 FALL	8 DEW	9 C DEW	1 WINTER	10 SNOW	10 CHILL
3:49	8:31		1:46	5:58	16:22		2:30	5:52	21:56	1:18	17:58	4:44
2 6 FW	3 8 FH	4 7 FW	5 6 tm	6 5 tt	7 4 TM	1	8 2 rg	9 1 rd	9 30 RR	10 29 mf	11 28 mr	12 28 mf
2 7 ff	3 9 fr	4 8 ff	5 7 FH	6 6 FW	7 5 tm	2	8 3 TT	9 2 TM	10 1 rg	10 30 RF	11 29 RR	12 29 RF
2 8 EF	3 10 ER	4 9 EF	5 8 fr	6 7 ff	7 6 FH	3	8 4 tt	9 3 tm	10 2 TT	10 31 rd	11 30 rg	12 30 rd
2 9 ed	3 11 eg	4 10 ed	5 9 ER	6 8 EF	7 7 fr	4	8 5 FW	9 4 FH	10 3 tt	11 1 TM	12 1 TT	12 31 TM
2 10 MM	3 12 MT	4 11 MM	5 10 eg	6 9 ed	7 8 ER	5	8 6 ff	9 5 fr	10 4 FW	11 2 tm	12 2 tt	1 1 tm
2 11 mm	3 13 mt	4 12 mm	5 11 MT	6 10 MM	7 9 eg	6	8 7 EF	9 6 ER	10 5 ff	11 3 FH	12 3 FW	1 2 FH
2 12 RH	3 14 RW	4 13 RH	5 12 mt	6 11 mm	7 10 MT	7	8 8 ed	9 7 eg	10 6 EF	11 4 fr	12 4 ff	1 3 fr
2 13 rr	3 15 rf	4 14 rr	5 13 RW	6 12 RH	7 11 mt	8	8 9 MM	9 8 MT	10 7 ed	11 5 ER	12 5 EF	1 4 ER
2 14 TR	3 16 TF	4 15 TR	5 14 rf	6 13 rr	7 12 RW	9	8 10 mm	9 9 mt	10 8 MM	11 6 eg	12 6 ed	1 5 eg
2 15 tg	3 17 td	4 16 tg	5 15 TF	6 14 TR	7 13 rf	10	8 11 RH	9 10 RW	10 9 mm	11 7 MT	12 7 MM	1 6 MT
2 16 FT	3 18 FM	4 17 FT	5 16 td	6 15 tg	7 14 TF	11	8 12 rr	9 11 rf	10 10 RH	11 8 mt	12 8 mm	1 7 mt
2 17 ft	3 19 fm	4 18 ft	5 17 FM	6 16 FT	7 15 td	12	8 13 TR	9 12 TF	10 11 rr	11 9 RW	12 9 RH	1 8 RW
2 18 EW	3 20 EH	4 19 EW	5 18 fm	6 17 ft	7 16 FM	13	8 14 tg	9 13 td	10 12 TR	11 10 rf	12 10 rr	1 9 rf
2 19 ef	3 21 er	4 20 ef	5 19 EH	6 18 EW	7 17 fm	14	8 15 FT	9 14 FM	10 13 tg	11 11 TF	12 11 TR	1 10 TF
2 20 MF	3 22 MR	4 21 MF	5 20 er	6 19 ef	7 18 EH	15	8 16 ft	9 15 fm	10 14 FT	11 12 td	12 12 tg	1 11 td
2 21 md	3 23 mg	4 22 md	5 21 MR	6 20 MF	7 19 er	16	8 17 EW	9 16 EH	10 15 ft	11 13 FM	12 13 FT	1 12 FM
2 22 RM	3 24 RT	4 23 RM	5 22 mg	6 21 md	7 20 MR	17	8 18 ef	9 17 er	10 16 EW	11 14 fm	12 14 ft	1 13 fm
2 23 rm	3 25 rt	4 24 rm	5 23 RT	6 22 RM	7 21 mg	18	8 19 MF	9 18 MR	10 17 ef	11 15 EH	12 15 EW	1 14 EH
2 24 TH	3 26 TW	4 25 TH	5 24 rt	6 23 rm	7 22 RT	19	8 20 md	9 19 mg	10 18 MF	11 16 er	12 16 ef	1 15 er
2 25 tr	3 27 tf	4 26 tr	5 25 TW	6 24 TH	7 23 rt	20	8 21 RM	9 20 RT	10 19 md	11 17 MR	12 17 MF	1 16 MR
2 26 FR	3 28 FF	4 27 FR	5 26 tf	6 25 tr	7 24 TW	21	8 22 rm	9 21 rt	10 20 RM	11 18 mg	12 18 md	1 17 mg
2 27 fg	3 29 fd	4 28 fg	5 27 FF	6 26 FR	7 25 tf	22	8 23 TH	9 22 TW	10 21 rm	11 19 RT	12 19 RM	1 18 RT
2 28 ET	3 30 EM	4 29 ET	5 28 fd	6 27 fg	7 26 FF	23	8 24 tr	9 23 tf	10 22 TH	11 20 rt	12 20 rm	1 19 rt
3 1 et	3 31 em	4 30 et	5 29 EM	6 28 ET	7 27 fd	24	8 25 FR	9 24 FF	10 23 tr	11 21 TW	12 21 TH	1 20 TW
3 2 MW	4 1 MH	5 1 MW	5 30 em	6 29 et	7 28 EM	25	8 26 fg	9 25 fd	10 24 FR	11 22 tf	12 22 tr	1 21 tf
3 3 mf	4 2 mr	5 2 mf	5 31 MH	6 30 MW	7 29 em	26	8 27 ET	9 26 EM	10 25 fg	11 23 FF	12 23 FR	1 22 FF
3 4 RF	4 3 RR	5 3 RF	6 1 mr	7 1 mf	7 30 MH	27	8 28 et	9 27 em	10 26 ET	11 24 fd	12 24 fg	1 23 fd
3 5 rd	4 4 rg	5 4 rd	6 2 RR	7 2 RF	7 31 mr	28	8 29 MW	9 28 MH	10 27 et	11 25 EM	12 25 ET	1 24 EM
3 6 TM	4 5 TT	5 5 TM	6 3 rg	7 3 rd	8 1 RR	29	8 30 mf	9 29 mr	10 28 MW	11 26 em	12 26 et	1 25 em
3 7 tm	4 6 tt		6 4 TT			30	8 31 RF			11 27 MH	12 27 MW	

2028 EM MONKEY

JAN TT			FEB tt			MAR FW			APR ff			MAY EF			MAY EF			DAY OF MON	JUN ed			JUL MM			AUG mm			SEP RH			OCT rr			NOV TT			DEC tg		
10 SPRING			10 WARM			10 CLEAR			11 SUMMER			13 GRAIN			14 HEAT				17 FALL			19 DEW			20 C DEW			21 WINTER			21 SNOW			21 CHILL			20 SPRING		
15:56			9:38			14:19			7:36			11:47							8:17			11:41			3:46			7:07			23:47			10:34			21:45		
1	26	MH	2	25	MW	3	26	MH	4	25	MW	5	24	em	6	23	et	1	7	22	EM	8	20	fg	9	19	fd	10	18	FR	11	16	tf	12	16	tr	1	15	tf
1	27	mr	2	26	mf	3	27	mr	4	26	mf	5	25	MH	6	24	MW	2	7	23	em	8	21	ET	9	20	EM	10	19	fg	11	17	FF	12	17	FR	1	16	FF
1	28	RR	2	27	RF	3	28	RR	4	27	RF	5	26	mr	6	25	mf	3	7	24	MH	8	22	et	9	21	em	10	20	ET	11	18	fd	12	18	fg	1	17	fd
1	29	rg	2	28	rd	3	29	rg	4	28	rd	5	27	RR	6	26	RF	4	7	25	mr	8	23	MW	9	22	MH	10	21	et	11	19	EM	12	19	ET	1	18	EM
1	30	TT	2	29	TM	3	30	TT	4	29	TM	5	28	rg	6	27	rd	5	7	26	RR	8	24	mf	9	23	mr	10	22	MW	11	20	em	12	20	et	1	19	em
1	31	tt	3	1	tm	3	31	tt	4	30	tm	5	29	TT	6	28	TM	6	7	27	rg	8	25	RF	9	24	RR	10	23	mf	11	21	MH	12	21	MW	1	20	MH
2	1	FW	3	2	FH	4	1	FW	5	1	FH	5	30	tt	6	29	tm	7	7	28	TT	8	26	rd	9	25	rg	10	24	RF	11	22	mr	12	22	mf	1	21	mr
2	2	ff	3	3	fr	4	2	ff	5	2	fr	5	31	FW	6	30	FH	8	7	29	tt	8	27	TM	9	26	TT	10	25	rd	11	23	RR	12	23	RF	1	22	RR
2	3	EF	3	4	ER	4	3	EF	5	3	ER	6	1	ff	7	1	fr	9	7	30	FW	8	28	tm	9	27	tt	10	26	TM	11	24	rg	12	24	rd	1	23	rg
2	4	ed	3	5	eg	4	4	ed	5	4	eg	6	2	EF	7	2	ER	10	7	31	ff	8	29	FH	9	28	FW	10	27	tm	11	25	TT	12	25	TM	1	24	TT
2	5	MM	3	6	MT	4	5	MM	5	5	MT	6	3	ed	7	3	eg	11	8	1	EF	8	30	fr	9	29	ff	10	28	FH	11	26	tt	12	26	tm	1	25	tt
2	6	mm	3	7	mt	4	6	mm	5	6	mt	6	4	MM	7	4	MT	12	8	2	ed	8	31	ER	9	30	EF	10	29	fr	11	27	FW	12	27	FH	1	26	FW
2	7	RH	3	8	RW	4	7	RH	5	7	RW	6	5	mm	7	5	mt	13	8	3	MM	9	1	eg	10	1	ed	10	30	ER	11	28	ff	12	28	fr	1	27	ff
2	8	rr	3	9	rf	4	8	rr	5	8	rf	6	6	RH	7	6	RW	14	8	4	mm	9	2	MT	10	2	MM	10	31	eg	11	29	EF	12	29	ER	1	28	EF
2	9	TR	3	10	TF	4	9	TR	5	9	TF	6	7	rr	7	7	rf	15	8	5	RH	9	3	mt	10	3	mm	11	1	MT	11	30	ed	12	30	eg	1	29	ed
2	10	tg	3	11	td	4	10	tg	5	10	td	6	8	TR	7	8	TF	16	8	6	rr	9	4	RW	10	4	RH	11	2	mt	12	1	MM	12	31	MT	1	30	MM
2	11	FT	3	12	FM	4	11	FT	5	11	FM	6	9	tg	7	9	td	17	8	7	TR	9	5	rf	10	5	rr	11	3	RW	12	2	mm	1	1	mt	1	31	mm
2	12	ft	3	13	fm	4	12	ft	5	12	fm	6	10	FT	7	10	FM	18	8	8	tg	9	6	TF	10	6	TR	11	4	rf	12	3	RH	1	2	RW	2	1	RH
2	13	EW	3	14	EH	4	13	EW	5	13	EH	6	11	ft	7	11	fm	19	8	9	FT	9	7	td	10	7	tg	11	5	TF	12	4	rr	1	3	rf	2	2	rr
2	14	ef	3	15	er	4	14	ef	5	14	er	6	12	EW	7	12	EH	20	8	10	ft	9	8	FM	10	8	FT	11	6	td	12	5	TR	1	4	TF	2	3	TR
2	15	MF	3	16	MR	4	15	MF	5	15	MR	6	13	ef	7	13	er	21	8	11	EW	9	9	fm	10	9	ft	11	7	FM	12	6	tg	1	5	td	2	4	tg
2	16	md	3	17	mg	4	16	md	5	16	mg	6	14	MF	7	14	MR	22	8	12	ef	9	10	EH	10	10	EW	11	8	fm	12	7	FT	1	6	FM	2	5	FT
2	17	RM	3	18	RT	4	17	RM	5	17	RT	6	15	md	7	15	mg	23	8	13	MF	9	11	er	10	11	ef	11	9	EH	12	8	ft	1	7	fm	2	6	ft
2	18	rm	3	19	rt	4	18	rm	5	18	rt	6	16	RM	7	16	RT	24	8	14	md	9	12	MR	10	12	MF	11	10	er	12	9	EW	1	8	EH	2	7	EW
2	19	TH	3	20	TW	4	19	TH	5	19	TW	6	17	rm	7	17	rt	25	8	15	RM	9	13	mg	10	13	md	11	11	MR	12	10	ef	1	9	er	2	8	ef
2	20	tr	3	21	tf	4	20	tr	5	20	tf	6	18	TH	7	18	TW	26	8	16	rm	9	14	RT	10	14	RM	11	12	mg	12	11	MF	1	10	MR	2	9	MF
2	21	FR	3	22	FF	4	21	FR	5	21	FF	6	19	tr	7	19	tf	27	8	17	TH	9	15	rt	10	15	rm	11	13	RT	12	12	md	1	11	mg	2	10	md
2	22	fg	3	23	fd	4	22	fg	5	22	fd	6	20	FR	7	20	FF	28	8	18	tr	9	16	TW	10	16	TH	11	14	rt	12	13	RM	1	12	RT	2	11	RM
2	23	ET	3	24	EM	4	23	ET	5	23	EM	6	21	fg	7	21	fd	29	8	19	FR	9	17	tf	10	17	tr	11	15	TW	12	14	rm	1	13	rt	2	12	rm
2	24	et	3	25	em	4	24	et				6	22	ET				30				9	18	FF							12	15	TH	1	14	TW			

2029 em ROOSTER

JAN FT	FEB ft	MAR EW	APR ef	MAY MF	JUN md	DAY OF MON	JUL RM	AUG rm	SEP TH	OCT tr	NOV FR	DEC fg
21 WARM	21 CLEAR	22 SUMMER	24 GRAIN	26 HEAT	28 FALL		29 DEW		1 C DEW	2 WINTER	3 SNOW	2 CHILL
15:29	20:08	13:26	17:35	3:58	14:06		17:29		9:35	12:57	5:37	16:24
2 13 TH	3 15 TW	4 14 TH	5 13 rt	6 12 rm	7 11 RT	1	8 10 RM	9 8 mg	10 8 md	11 6 MR	12 5 ef	1 4 er
2 14 tr	3 16 tf	4 15 tr	5 14 TW	6 13 TH	7 12 rt	2	8 11 rm	9 9 RT	10 9 RM	11 7 mg	12 6 MF	1 5 MR
2 15 FR	3 17 FF	4 16 FR	5 15 tf	6 14 tr	7 13 TW	3	8 12 TH	9 10 rt	10 10 rm	11 8 RT	12 7 md	1 6 mg
2 16 fg	3 18 fd	4 17 fg	5 16 FF	6 15 FR	7 14 tf	4	8 13 tr	9 11 TW	10 11 TH	11 9 rt	12 8 RM	1 7 RT
2 17 ET	3 19 EM	4 18 ET	5 17 fd	6 16 fg	7 15 FF	5	8 14 FR	9 12 tf	10 12 tr	11 10 TW	12 9 rm	1 8 rt
2 18 et	3 20 em	4 19 et	5 18 EM	6 17 ET	7 16 fd	6	8 15 fg	9 13 FF	10 13 FR	11 11 tf	12 10 TH	1 9 TW
2 19 MW	3 21 MH	4 20 MW	5 19 em	6 18 et	7 17 EM	7	8 16 ET	9 14 fd	10 14 fg	11 12 FF	12 11 tr	1 10 tf
2 20 mf	3 22 mr	4 21 mf	5 20 MH	6 19 MW	7 18 em	8	8 17 et	9 15 EM	10 15 ET	11 13 fd	12 12 FR	1 11 FF
2 21 RF	3 23 RR	4 22 RF	5 21 mr	6 20 mf	7 19 MH	9	8 18 MW	9 16 em	10 16 et	11 14 EM	12 13 fg	1 12 fd
2 22 rd	3 24 rg	4 23 rd	5 22 RR	6 21 RF	7 20 mr	10	8 19 mf	9 17 MH	10 17 MW	11 15 em	12 14 ET	1 13 EM
2 23 TM	3 25 TT	4 24 TM	5 23 rg	6 22 rd	7 21 RR	11	8 20 RF	9 18 mr	10 18 mf	11 16 MH	12 15 et	1 14 em
2 24 tm	3 26 tt	4 25 tm	5 24 TT	6 23 TM	7 22 rg	12	8 21 rd	9 19 RR	10 19 RF	11 17 mr	12 16 MW	1 15 MH
2 25 FH	3 27 FW	4 26 FH	5 25 tt	6 24 tm	7 23 TT	13	8 22 TM	9 20 rg	10 20 rd	11 18 RR	12 17 mf	1 16 mr
2 26 fr	3 28 ff	4 27 fr	5 26 FW	6 25 FH	7 24 tt	14	8 23 tm	9 21 TT	10 21 TM	11 19 rg	12 18 RF	1 17 RR
2 27 ER	3 29 EF	4 28 ER	5 27 ff	6 26 fr	7 25 FW	15	8 24 FH	9 22 tt	10 22 tm	11 20 TT	12 19 rd	1 18 rg
2 28 eg	3 30 ed	4 29 eg	5 28 EF	6 27 ER	7 26 ff	16	8 25 fr	9 23 FW	10 23 FH	11 21 tt	12 20 TM	1 19 TT
3 1 MT	3 31 MM	4 30 MT	5 29 ed	6 28 eg	7 27 EF	17	8 26 ER	9 24 ff	10 24 fr	11 22 FW	12 21 tm	1 20 tt
3 2 mt	4 1 mm	5 1 mt	5 30 MM	6 29 MT	7 28 ed	18	8 27 eg	9 25 EF	10 25 ER	11 23 ff	12 22 FH	1 21 FW
3 3 RW	4 2 RH	5 2 RW	5 31 mm	6 30 mt	7 29 MM	19	8 28 MT	9 26 ed	10 26 eg	11 24 EF	12 23 fr	1 22 ff
3 4 rf	4 3 rr	5 3 rf	6 1 RH	7 1 RW	7 30 mm	20	8 29 mt	9 27 MM	10 27 MT	11 25 ed	12 24 ER	1 23 EF
3 5 TF	4 4 TR	5 4 TF	6 2 rr	7 2 rf	7 31 RH	21	8 30 RW	9 28 mm	10 28 mt	11 26 MM	12 25 eg	1 24 ed
3 6 td	4 5 tg	5 5 td	6 3 TR	7 3 TF	8 1 rr	22	8 31 rf	9 29 RH	10 29 RW	11 27 mm	12 26 MT	1 25 MM
3 7 FM	4 6 FT	5 6 FM	6 4 tg	7 4 td	8 2 TR	23	9 1 TF	9 30 rr	10 30 rf	11 28 RH	12 27 mt	1 26 mm
3 8 fm	4 7 ft	5 7 fm	6 5 FT	7 5 FM	8 3 tg	24	9 2 td	10 1 TR	10 31 TF	11 29 rr	12 28 RW	1 27 RH
3 9 EH	4 8 EW	5 8 EH	6 6 ft	7 6 fm	8 4 FT	25	9 3 FM	10 2 tg	11 1 td	11 30 TR	12 29 rf	1 28 rr
3 10 er	4 9 ef	5 9 er	6 7 EW	7 7 EH	8 5 ft	26	9 4 fm	10 3 FT	11 2 FM	12 1 tg	12 30 TF	1 29 TR
3 11 MR	4 10 MF	5 10 MR	6 8 ef	7 8 er	8 6 EW	27	9 5 EH	10 4 ft	11 3 fm	12 2 FT	12 31 td	1 30 tg
3 12 mg	4 11 md	5 11 mg	6 9 MF	7 9 MR	8 7 ef	28	9 6 er	10 5 EW	11 4 EH	12 3 ft	1 1 FM	1 31 FT
3 13 RT	4 12 RM	5 12 RT	6 10 md	7 10 mg	8 8 MF	29	9 7 MR	10 6 ef	11 5 er	12 4 EW	1 2 fm	2 1 ft
3 14 rt	4 13 rm		6 11 RM		8 9 md	30		10 7 MF			1 3 EH	

2030 MH DOG

JAN ET	FEB et	MAR MW	APR mf	MAY RF	JUN rd	DAY OF MON	JUL TM	AUG tm	SEP FH	OCT fr	NOV ER	DEC eg
3 SPRING	2 WARM	3 CLEAR	4 SUMMER	5 GRAIN	7 HEAT		9 FALL	10 DEW	12 C DEW	12 WINTER	13 SNOW	12 CHILL
3:35	21:18	1:57	19:13	23:23	9:46		19:54	23:18	15:24	18:47	11:27	22:14
2 2 EW	3 4 EH	4 3 EW	5 2 fm	6 1 ft	7 1 fm	1	7 30 FT	8 29 FM	9 27 tg	10 27 td	11 25 TR	12 25 TF
2 3 ef	3 5 er	4 4 ef	5 3 EH	6 2 EW	7 2 EH	2	7 31 ft	8 30 fm	9 28 FT	10 28 FM	11 26 tg	12 26 td
2 4 MF	3 6 MR	4 5 MF	5 4 er	6 3 ef	7 3 er	3	8 1 EW	8 31 EH	9 29 ft	10 29 fm	11 27 FT	12 27 FM
2 5 md	3 7 mg	4 6 md	5 5 MR	6 4 MF	7 4 MR	4	8 2 ef	9 1 er	9 30 EW	10 30 EH	11 28 ft	12 28 fm
2 6 RM	3 8 RT	4 7 RM	5 6 mg	6 5 md	7 5 mg	5	8 3 MF	9 2 MR	10 1 ef	10 31 er	11 29 EW	12 29 EH
2 7 rm	3 9 rt	4 8 rm	5 7 RT	6 6 RM	7 6 RT	6	8 4 md	9 3 mg	10 2 MF	11 1 MR	11 30 ef	12 30 er
2 8 TH	3 10 TW	4 9 TH	5 8 rt	6 7 rm	7 7 rt	7	8 5 RM	9 4 RT	10 3 md	11 2 mg	12 1 MF	12 31 MR
2 9 tr	3 11 tf	4 10 tr	5 9 TW	6 8 TH	7 8 TW	8	8 6 rm	9 5 rt	10 4 RM	11 3 RT	12 2 md	1 1 mg
2 10 FR	3 12 FF	4 11 FR	5 10 tf	6 9 tr	7 9 tf	9	8 7 TH	9 6 TW	10 5 rm	11 4 rt	12 3 RM	1 2 RT
2 11 fg	3 13 fd	4 12 fg	5 11 FF	6 10 FR	7 10 FF	10	8 8 tr	9 7 tf	10 6 TH	11 5 TW	12 4 rm	1 3 rt
2 12 ET	3 14 EM	4 13 ET	5 12 fd	6 11 fg	7 11 fd	11	8 9 FR	9 8 FF	10 7 tr	11 6 tf	12 5 TH	1 4 TW
2 13 et	3 15 em	4 14 et	5 13 EM	6 12 ET	7 12 EM	12	8 10 fg	9 9 fd	10 8 FR	11 7 FF	12 6 tr	1 5 tf
2 14 MW	3 16 MH	4 15 MW	5 14 em	6 13 et	7 13 em	13	8 11 ET	9 10 EM	10 9 fg	11 8 fd	12 7 FR	1 6 FF
2 15 mf	3 17 mr	4 16 mf	5 15 MH	6 14 MW	7 14 MH	14	8 12 et	9 11 em	10 10 ET	11 9 EM	12 8 fg	1 7 fd
2 16 RF	3 18 RR	4 17 RF	5 16 mr	6 15 mf	7 15 mr	15	8 13 MW	9 12 MH	10 11 et	11 10 em	12 9 ET	1 8 EM
2 17 rd	3 19 rg	4 18 rd	5 17 RR	6 16 RF	7 16 RR	16	8 14 mf	9 13 mr	10 12 MW	11 11 MH	12 10 et	1 9 em
2 18 TM	3 20 TT	4 19 TM	5 18 rg	6 17 rd	7 17 rg	17	8 15 RF	9 14 RR	10 13 mf	11 12 mr	12 11 MW	1 10 MH
2 19 tm	3 21 tt	4 20 tm	5 19 TT	6 18 TM	7 18 TT	18	8 16 rd	9 15 rg	10 14 RF	11 13 RR	12 12 mf	1 11 mr
2 20 FH	3 22 FW	4 21 FH	5 20 tt	6 19 tm	7 19 tt	19	8 17 TM	9 16 TT	10 15 rd	11 14 rg	12 13 RF	1 12 RR
2 21 fr	3 23 ff	4 22 fr	5 21 FW	6 20 FH	7 20 FW	20	8 18 tm	9 17 tt	10 16 TM	11 15 TT	12 14 rd	1 13 rg
2 22 ER	3 24 EF	4 23 ER	5 22 ff	6 21 fr	7 21 ff	21	8 19 FH	9 18 FW	10 17 tm	11 16 tt	12 15 TM	1 14 TT
2 23 eg	3 25 ed	4 24 eg	5 23 EF	6 22 ER	7 22 EF	22	8 20 fr	9 19 ff	10 18 FH	11 17 FW	12 16 tm	1 15 tt
2 24 MT	3 26 MM	4 25 MT	5 24 ed	6 23 eg	7 23 ed	23	8 21 ER	9 20 EF	10 19 fr	11 18 ff	12 17 FH	1 16 FW
2 25 mt	3 27 mm	4 26 mt	5 25 MM	6 24 MT	7 24 MM	24	8 22 eg	9 21 ed	10 20 ER	11 19 EF	12 18 fr	1 17 ff
2 26 RW	3 28 RH	4 27 RW	5 26 mm	6 25 mt	7 25 mm	25	8 23 MT	9 22 MM	10 21 eg	11 20 ed	12 19 ER	1 18 EF
2 27 rf	3 29 rr	4 28 rf	5 27 RH	6 26 RW	7 26 RH	26	8 24 mt	9 23 mm	10 22 MT	11 21 MM	12 20 eg	1 19 ed
2 28 TF	3 30 TR	4 29 TF	5 28 rr	6 27 rf	7 27 rr	27	8 25 RW	9 24 RH	10 23 mt	11 22 mm	12 21 MT	1 20 MM
3 1 td	3 31 tg	4 30 td	5 29 TR	6 28 TF	7 28 TR	28	8 26 rf	9 25 rr	10 24 RW	11 23 RH	12 22 mt	1 21 mm
3 2 FM	4 1 FT	5 1 FM	5 30 tg	6 29 td	7 29 tg	29	8 27 TF	9 26 TR	10 25 rf	11 24 rr	12 23 RW	1 22 RH
3 3 fm	4 2 ft		5 31 FT	6 30 FM		30	8 28 td		10 26 TF		12 24 rf	

Printed by BoD™ in Norderstedt, Ge

9 781609 111045